T0178439

Lecture Notes in Computer Science

Lecture Notes in Artificial Intelligence   14141

Founding Editor

Jörg Siekmann

Series Editors

Randy Goebel, *University of Alberta, Edmonton, Canada*
Wolfgang Wahlster, *DFKI, Berlin, Germany*
Zhi-Hua Zhou, *Nanjing University, Nanjing, China*

The series Lecture Notes in Artificial Intelligence (LNAI) was established in 1988 as a topical subseries of LNCS devoted to artificial intelligence.

The series publishes state-of-the-art research results at a high level. As with the LNCS mother series, the mission of the series is to serve the international R & D community by providing an invaluable service, mainly focused on the publication of conference and workshop proceedings and postproceedings.

Stewart Massie · Sutanu Chakraborti

Editors

Case-Based Reasoning Research and Development

31st International Conference, ICCBR 2023
Aberdeen, UK, July 17–20, 2023
Proceedings

Springer

Editors
Stewart Massie ⓘ
Robert Gordon University
Aberdeen, UK

Sutanu Chakraborti
Indian Institute of Technology Madras
Chennai, Tamil Nadu, India

ISSN 0302-9743   ISSN 1611-3349 (electronic)
Lecture Notes in Artificial Intelligence
ISBN 978-3-031-40176-3   ISBN 978-3-031-40177-0 (eBook)
https://doi.org/10.1007/978-3-031-40177-0

LNCS Sublibrary: SL7 – Artificial Intelligence

This Springer imprint is published by the registered company Springer Nature Switzerland AG
The registered company address is: Gewerbestrasse 11, 6330 Cham, Switzerland

Preface

This volume contains the papers presented at the 31st International Conference on Case-Based Reasoning (ICCBR 2023), which was held on July 17–20, 2023, at Robert Gordon University in Aberdeen, Scotland, UK. ICCBR is the premier annual meeting of the Case-Based Reasoning (CBR) research community. The theme of ICCBR 2023 was "CBR in a Data-Driven World", with the aim of considering the question "What is the role of CBR in the modern data-driven world?" The conference encouraged submissions from our invited speakers, researchers, policy makers, and practitioners in the CBR community that consider the current challenges and opportunities for CBR.

Previous ICCBRs, including the merged European Workshops and Conferences on CBR, were as follows: Otzenhausen, Germany (1993); Chantilly, France (1994); Sesimbra, Portugal (1995); Lausanne, Switzerland (1996); Providence, USA (1997); Dublin, Ireland (1998); Seeon Monastery, Germany (1999); Trento, Italy (2000); Vancouver, Canada (2001); Aberdeen, UK (2002); Trondheim, Norway (2003); Madrid, Spain (2004); Chicago, USA (2005); Fethiye, Turkey (2006); Belfast, UK (2007); Trier, Germany (2008); Seattle, USA (2009); Alessandria, Italy (2010); Greenwich, UK (2011); Lyon, France (2012); Saratoga Springs, USA (2013); Cork, Ireland (2014); Frankfurt, Germany (2015); Atlanta, USA (2016); Trondheim, Norway (2017); Stockholm, Sweden (2018); Otzenhausen, Germany (2019); Salamanca, Spain (2020); Salamanca, Spain (2021); and Nancy, France (2022).

Recent years have been very challenging for conference organisation generally and it is a credit to the strength of the CBR community that the conferences have continued over this period. The conferences in 2020 and 2021 were held virtually and it was disappointing that we did not get to meet in Spain as planned. It was down to the excellent organisation of last year's program chairs (Mark Keane and Nirmalie Wiratunga) and local organisers (Emmanuel Nauer and Nicolas Lasolle) that the conference in Nancy, France returned to a face-to-face format although still delivered as a hybrid event. And while this year's conference was also available online the transition back to a face-to-face format continued and it was fantastic to see the return to in-person conferences continuing with the vast majority of participants attending the sessions in person.

ICCBR 2023 received 72 submissions from authors in 15 countries, spanning Europe, North America, and Asia. Each submission was single-blind reviewed by at least two reviewers and most papers were reviewed by three Program Committee members, with tied decisions being resolved by additional reviewing. Of the 72 submissions, the committee decided to accept 26 papers in total with 18 (25%) selected for oral presentations, and a further 8 (11%) being accepted as posters. The program also included three invited talks and a panel discussion session.

The pre-conference events for ICCBR 2023 began on Sunday, July 16 with a visit to Royal Deeside and Lochnagar distillery. After this visit, there was the first meeting for participants in the Doctoral Consortium (DC), who met their mentors face-to-face for the first time, and prepared for their upcoming presentations. The DC is designed to provide opportunities for PhD students to present their work to senior CBR researchers and their peers, as well as obtain feedback on their research and career objectives. Pre-conference events continued Monday, July 17 and the morning of the 18th with the Doctoral Consortium presentations, four Workshops covering breaking topics in CBR, and two hands-on tutorials. These events gave rise to lively presentations and discussions on current advances in CBR.

The conference itself kicked off on Tuesday, July 18, 2023, with an invited talk from Ben Horsburgh, a Principal ML Engineer at the AI consultancy group QuantumBlack based in London (UK). The talk on emerging trends in real-world AI addressed the conference theme on the role of CBR. This invited talk was followed by two technical sessions on "CBR and Deep Learning" and "Representation & Similarity". Day 1 ended with a welcome drinks reception to formally open the conference.

The second day started with a keynote invited talk from Ruth Byrne, a Cognitive Scientist from Trinity College Dublin, and 2021 recipient of the Gold Medal for Social Sciences from the Royal Irish Academy. The invited talk on "How people reason with counterfactual explanations for AI decisions" was followed by the first poster session, which began with a Poster Gong Show of rapid two-minute presentations which in turn was followed by poster-board discussions involving all the attendees. Six papers were then presented during two technical sessions on "CBR and Explainable AI" and "Case Base Maintenance". The second day concluded with a sight-seeing trip of historic Aberdeen and the Gala Dinner.

The final day of the conference began with the last invited talk on the use of Knowledge Graphs in Recommendation and CBR from Derek Bridge, a senior lecturer at University College Cork. This was followed by a panel discussion and the final two technical sessions on "Adaptation: Techniques and Application" and "Case-Based Applications". The conference concluded with the community meeting, where the Local Chairs (Anjana Wijekoon and Kyle Martin) were thanked for their efforts in staging the conference, as were the Chair of the Doctoral Consortium (Kerstin Bach), and Workshop Chairs (Lukas Malburg and Deepika Verma).

As Program Chairs, our thanks go out to the Advisory Committee who we relied on for advice as an experienced sounding board for many of the key decisions we had to make. Our thanks also to the Program Committee and additional reviewers for handling the large reviewing load at short notice, and for their thoughtful assessments of the submissions and willingness to help. Finally, many thanks to all the participants and sponsors who helped make the conference a successful event.

July 2023   Stewart Massie
                                                                                Sutanu Chakraborti

Organization

Program Chairs

Stewart Massie   Robert Gordon University, UK
Sutanu Chakraborti   Indian Institute of Technology Madras, India

Local Chairs

Anjana Wijekoon   Robert Gordon University, UK
Kyle Martin   Robert Gordon University, UK

Workshop Chairs

Deepika Verma   Norwegian University of Science and Technology, Norway
Lukas Malburg   University of Trier/DFKI, Germany

Doctoral Consortium Chair

Kerstin Bach   Norwegian University of Science and Technology, Norway

Advisory Committee

Barry Smyth   University College Dublin, Ireland
Belén Díaz Agudo   Universidad Complutense de Madrid, Spain
David Aha   Naval Research Laboratory, USA
David Leake   Indiana University, USA
Isabelle Bichindaritz   State University of New York at Oswego, USA
Mirjam Minor   Goethe University Frankfurt, Germany
Nirmalie Wiratunga   Robert Gordon University, UK
Rosina Weber   Drexel University, USA

Program Committee

Alexandra Coman	Capital One, USA
Antonio A. Sánchez-Ruiz	Universidad Complutense de Madrid, Spain
Ashok Goel	Georgia Institute of Technology, USA
David Wilson	University of North Carolina at Charlotte, USA
Derek Bridge	University College Cork, Ireland
Emmanuel Nauer	Université de Lorraine, LORIA, France
Enric Plaza	Artificial Intelligence Research Institute (IIIA-CSIC), Spain
Frode Sørmo	Amazon, UK
Hayley Borck	SIFT, USA
Jakob Michael Schoenborn	University of Hildesheim/DFKI, Germany
Jean Lieber	Université de Lorraine, LORIA, France
Joseph Kendall-Morwick	Washburn University, USA
Juan A. Recio-Garcia	Universidad Complutense de Madrid, Spain
Klaus-Dieter Althoff	University of Hildesheim/DFKI, Germany
Luc Lamontagne	Laval University, Canada
Luigi Portinale	Università del Piemonte Orientale, Italy
Mark T. Keane	University College Dublin, Ireland
Michael Floyd	Knexus Research, USA
Odd Erik Gundersen	Norwegian University of Science and Technology, Norway
Pascal Reuss	Universität Hildesheim, Germany
Ralph Bergmann	University of Trier, Germany
Sarah Jane Delany	Technological University Dublin, Ireland
Stefania Montani	University of Piemonte Orientale, Italy
Stelios Kapetanakis	University of Brighton, UK
Viktor Eisenstadt	University of Hildesheim/DFKI, Germany

Additional Reviewers

Adwait Parsodkar
Christian Zeyen
Deepak P.
Lena Jedamski
Lisa Grumbach
Maximilian Hoffmann
Mirko Lenz
Premtim Sahitaj
Stuart Ottersen

Contents

CBR and Explainable AI

Case Base Maintenance

Adaptation: Techniques and Application

Case-Based Applications

CBR and Deep Learning

Examining the Impact of Network Architecture on Extracted Feature Quality for CBR

David Leake, Zachary Wilkerson$^{(\boxtimes)}$, Vibhas Vats, Karan Acharya, and David Crandall

Luddy School of Informatics, Computing, and Engineering, Indiana University, Bloomington, IN 47408, USA
{leake,zachwilk,vkvats,karachar,djcran}@indiana.edu

Abstract. Classification accuracy for case-based classifiers depends critically on the features used for case retrieval. Feature extraction from deep learning classifier models has proven a useful method for generating case-based classifier features, especially for domains in which manual feature engineering is costly or difficult. Previous work has explored how the quality of extracted features is influenced by structural choices such as the number of features extracted and the location/depth of extraction. This paper investigates how feature quality is influenced by another factor: the choice of the network model itself. We consider a selection of deep learning models for a computer vision classification task and test the accuracy of a case-based classifier using features extracted from them, both as the sole feature source and in combination with a supplementary set of knowledge-engineered features. Results suggest that feature quality reflects a trade-off between model complexity and training data requirements and provide lessons for the selection of deep learning architectures for feature extraction to support case-based classification.

Keywords: Case-Based Reasoning · Deep Learning · Feature Learning · Hybrid Systems · Indexing · Integrated Systems · Retrieval

1 Introduction

The accuracy of case-based classification depends on retrieving useful cases from the system's case base. In turn, retrieval efficacy depends on the quality of indices used. Traditionally, indices have been generated based on knowledge-engineered features supplied by domain experts, with feature values determined based on a combination of problem input and a situation assessment process performed by the case-based reasoning (CBR) system [9,16,27]. Indices based on knowledge-engineered features may capture key domain properties and are inherently interpretable, facilitating explanation of retrieval. However, knowledge engineering can be expensive, and there exist numerous domains for which hand-coded features are difficult to identify or only partially capture the domain. For example,

S. Massie and S. Chakraborti (Eds.): ICCBR 2023, LNAI 14141, pp. 3–18, 2023.
https://doi.org/10.1007/978-3-031-40177-0_1

in image processing domains, it is difficult to formulate effective feature vocabularies by hand.

Classifiers using deep learning (DL) have achieved impressive accuracy in hard-to-characterize domains such as computer vision (e.g., [6]) and their ability to learn effectively from raw data makes them promising for a wide variety of domains. However, DL models require considerable training data to achieve such accuracy, limiting their applicability for data-sparse domains. Furthermore, DL systems are "black-box" models without natural human-understandable justifications for their reasoning, limiting their application for domains in which high system trust is imperative. Considerable research seeks to mitigate this shortcoming through post-hoc explanation [11], but Rudin illustrates the limitations of post-hoc methods and shows that critical tasks may demand inherently interpretable methods [25].

CBR systems can learn from single examples and can leverage retrieval and case adaptation knowledge to operate effectively in data-sparse domains, and they can explain their decisions by presenting cases [17]. Consequently, methods that blend the complimentary strengths offered by DL and CBR approaches are appealing and are receiving much attention in CBR. Some methods integrate CBR concepts directly into DL models [3,7,20], some pair networks with CBR to explain DL-based decisions [13], and others apply network learning for tasks such as similarity assessment [23] and adaptation learning [21,34] or coordinate network learning for both [19].

This paper begins with an overview of our DL-CBR hybrid approach applying DL systems as feature extractors for CBR retrieval. The results of such feature extractors still depend on the availability of sufficient training data for network learning. However, the ability of CBR to exploit additional knowledge containers [24] in concert with the DL features, including knowledge in the case base, case representation vocabulary, knowledge-engineered indices, and similarity and adaptation knowledge, reduces this dependence for the system as a whole and can result in superior performance [32]. Previous CBR research on extracting features from deep neural networks has taken the network to use as a given, exploring methods for extraction from that architecture. However, DL research studies multiple alternative architectures and parameterizations and has shown them to have strong impact on performance [14]. This raises two important questions for extracting features from DL networks to use for CBR: (1) which network architectures are most suitable as substrates for generating CBR features, and (2) how network parameters and training strategies may be fine-tuned to best support the CBR system. This paper presents, to our knowledge, the first attempt to address these questions.

Specifically, we outline an experimental approach for exploring the impact of DL architecture of the feature extraction model on feature quality for a selection of DL models. Experimental results show that more complex or recently developed DL models (e.g., that have higher task performance than previous models used to study CBR feature extraction) do not necessarily generate more useful features. The model architecture and parameters do have a significant impact on feature quality, but performance also depends on the balance between model complexity and the number of training examples. In this context, the paper identifies some DL architectures that were better able to maintain performance with less data. In addition, it highlights the benefit of combining learned and knowledge-engineered features for overcoming some limitations of DL features learned from small data sets, and we have explored avenues for optimizing DL-based feature extraction for use in conjunction with knowledge-engineered features to increase transparency of the retrieval process [18,32]. We begin by discussing related work, then present our general approach followed by the candidate network architectures, and close with evaluation, next steps, and conclusions.

2   Related Work

CBR retrieval performance depends significantly on indexing quality, which in turn depends on the feature vocabulary used for similarity assessment. Traditionally, features are generated through knowledge engineering, reflecting domain expertise [9,16,27]. However, manually developing features in this way can be expensive, and feature sets may incompletely or inaccurately capture domain properties when the domain is poorly understood. Initially, this issue was addressed through symbolic learning methods (e.g., [2,4,5,8,10]). However, the ability of DL systems to learn features makes integrating DL and CBR systems appealing to address this problem. Previous research has investigated integration approaches such as injecting CBR knowledge into the DL model directly using prototypes to facilitate more interpretable feature generation [3,7,20], twinning CBR systems with DL systems to retrieve explanatory cases [13], using a series of networks to classify problems hierarchically into subclasses until a single case is found [22], and using DL-extracted features for similarity calculations for retrieval [26,30,31].

2.1   Extracting DL Features for CBR

Previous studies have combined DL index extraction with CBR systems to develop hybrid systems, sometimes even enabling performance superior to end-to-end DL classification (e.g., [26,31]). In such implementations, feature vectors are extracted prior to the output layer of a convolutional neural network (CNN) for use in the CBR similarity calculation for retrieval. Turner et al. apply this process for classification of novel images [30,31]. Their approach trains and uses a CNN image classifier for end-to-end classification, while simultaneously associating each image with its corresponding extracted feature vector in a separate case base. Based on clusters that arise in the case base, the system can assign a relative classification for images for which the CNN has a low classification confidence and for classes it has not seen before. Sani et al. take this approach a step further, extracting features in the same way but using the CBR system as the classifier [26]; this facilitates a degree of explanation via presentation of the nearest-neighbor case that is not present in the end-to-end CNN model.

Both approaches assume that the CNN is the only source of similarity knowledge via feature extraction. In contrast, our previous work [32] uses knowledge-engineered features in concert with extracted features for similarity calculations, resulting in an increase in retrieval accuracy when knowledge-engineered features accurately–but incompletely–capture the domain. We have also explored relationships between both feature extraction location/depth in the CNN and number of features extracted and feature quality [18]. Results of that work suggested that extraction of features before the output layer of the network may result in the highest quality features. That work also introduced a novel multi-net architecture to minimize the number of extracted features required for strong performance.

3 A General Architecture for DL-CBR Integration

3.1 The Structure of Convolutional Neural Networks

Because our work explores DL-CBR performance for computer vision, we illustrate our feature extraction model in the context of CNNs, which are well-suited to vision tasks. CNNs process raw input data into refined features that can be used to classify the original image. At a high level, a CNN begins with a set of convolution and pooling steps designed to condense the multi-dimensional pixel data into numeric features. Each convolution layer consists of filters that are applied iteratively across regions of the input image; this process can be represented by:

$$O_{xy} = \sum_{i=-k}^{k} \sum_{j=-l}^{l} F_{ij}(I_{(x-i)(y-j)}) \tag{1}$$

In this equation, O_{xy} is a single value in the output feature map, I is the input image (and so indexing into I references a single pixel), and F is the convolution filter of size $(2k+1) \times (2l+1)$. The filter may be conceptualized as a matrix of weights that are applied to pixels based on their location in the image, with the results for all filter weights then summed to create the output value. Following the convolution layers are pooling layers, which further reduce the resolution of the post-convolution feature maps by selecting representative regional values.

After the last pooling layer, the remaining features are flattened into a linear feature vector. This vector passes through multiple densely-connected layers (that together resemble a multilayer perceptron network), with the final outputs being used as inputs to the output layer for classification. We note that not all DL computer vision models conform to all aspects of this outline, but the models discussed in this paper each apply this methodology to varying degrees; for each one we will discuss deviations. Additionally, while we present a proof-of-concept implementation for CNN-based feature extraction for classification, we believe that other DL models from which linear feature vectors may be extracted could leverage our approach, and that it could apply for regression as well.

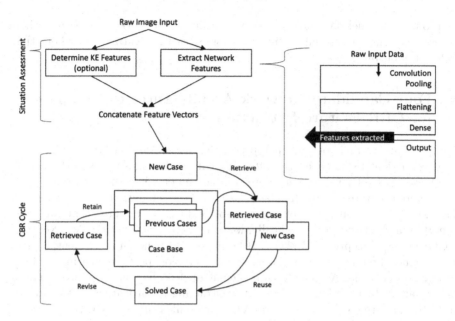

Fig. 1. Feature extraction dataflow between the CBR cycle (after Aamodt and Plaza [1]; bottom left) and the DL process (right). The figure illustrates a CNN structure for feature extraction but may be generalized to other DL models.

3.2   Extracting CBR Features from DL Models

CBR systems using nearest-neighbor similarity calculations for retrieval commonly characterize cases with linear feature vectors. This conveniently parallels the flattened feature vectors that are generated later in the CNN's data flow, and could also generalize well for other architectures such as artificial neural networks and multilayer perceptron models that employ linear layers for processed features. We have developed methods for extracting features for CBR retrieval from a CNN by removing the CNN's output layer from consideration post-training, and then extracting the outputs of the preceding layer for a target image (Fig. 1) [18,32]. These features may be augmented by concatenating them with a vector of knowledge-engineered features if available [32], with the final feature vector being associated with the image's ground truth class, as the solution part, to create a case.

It is possible to extract features from elsewhere in the CNN model, such as immediately after flattening (in which case all subsequent layers are removed from consideration), providing different feature information [18]. However, our previous work suggests that extracting after the densely-connected layers leads to the highest feature quality. This appears to apply especially for the more complex DL models for computer vision to be described in the following section. Such models follow a less linear conceptualization of data flow than typical CNN models (described in detail in Sect. 4). Because their layers may be interconnected or promote parallel data flow pathways within the network architecture, there is less clear-cut conceptual justification for extracting features elsewhere than before the output layer.

4   Four Candidate Network Architectures to Compare for CBR Feature Extraction

Our previous research focused on applying the classic AlexNet model [15] for feature extraction [18,32], because of its simplicity and compatibility with nearest-neighbor CBR retrieval. Other, more complex models have been shown to produce more accurate end-to-end classifications. Here we investigate whether basing extraction on such models may enable extracting features that are more useful for a CBR system. Specifically, we compare extraction from AlexNet with VGGNet [28], Inception V3 [29], and DenseNet [12], chosen as influential models designed to improve upon AlexNet classification performance in DL literature. For example, AlexNet's arrangement of densely-connected layers in the latter half of the model is convenient for extracting linear feature vectors for use in CBR similarity calculations, and VGGNet builds upon this with additional parameters/structural optimizations for training and feature refinement [28].

Inception V3 addresses a key shortcoming of CNNs like AlexNet and VGGNet, for which the size of the features to which they are sensitive is dependent on the size of the convolution filters used, which must be chosen as a parameter in advance. Inception takes a different approach by using modules that contain differently-sized convolution filters in parallel [29]. This enables features of varying granularity to be captured and concatenated together to be processed by the rest of the model. Furthermore, Inception is used as a feature extractor model for CBR by Turner et al. [31], giving particular interest to assessment of its properties compared to alternatives.

DenseNet addresses the possibility that—because fine-grained feature generation depends on a combination of atomic features from earlier in the network—training steps for earlier layers should be dependent on the outputs from later layers [12]. DenseNet compartmentalizes the typical CNN architecture in a series of "blocks" repeated throughout the model; each block connects to each other block, resulting in both a sequential flow of information reminiscent of AlexNet and VGGNet and an interconnected behavior through which various blocks influence one another during training.

As Inception and DenseNet have a less obvious layered structure than AlexNet and VGGNet, they are less naturally suited for feature extraction anywhere but at the end of the network. Consequently, for them our feature extraction approach extracts features from after the global average pooling (GAP) layer, which is positioned similarly to the densely-connected layers in AlexNet and VGGNet models. In addition, based on promising preliminary results from using VGGNet (potentially due to the presence of densely-connected layers), we investigate using a flattened layer followed by densely-connected layers instead of GAP for feature extraction for Inception and DenseNet (Fig. 2).

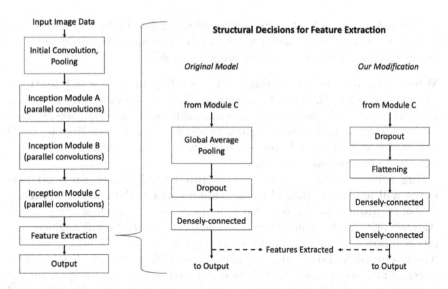

Fig. 2. High-level organization of Inception V3 [29] (left), and comparison of original layer organization post-convolution with our modification, applying densely-connected layers more directly rather than using GAP (right). All features are extracted immediately before the output layer.

Once the neural model is trained for end-to-end classification, features are extracted by removing the output layer from consideration post-training—for AlexNet and VGGNet—or by removing the final few layers from the network from consideration to expose the GAP layer outputs—for Inception V3 and DenseNet—and then extracting the outputs of the preceding layer (Fig. 1). These features are provided for use by the CBR classifier.

5   Evaluation

We test how using each of the four DL models for feature extraction affects feature quality (and by extension, CBR classification accuracy) for various potential scenarios. The aim of the evaluation is twofold: (1) to better understand the characteristics of feature extraction from each model, and (2) to provide information to help CBR practitioners to select suitable DL architectures for feature extraction for their tasks. For all tests, we use CBR classification accuracy as a proxy for feature quality.

One scenario concerns the use of DL features in concert with knowledge-engineered features. Our previous research found that using extracted features from AlexNet with knowledge-engineered features could produce a net increase in classification accuracy compared to either alone [32]. When performing feature extraction in domains with existing retrieval knowledge, it would be desirable to select DL models supporting this property. Additionally, it may be useful to identify models whose extracted feature quality suffers minimally from overfitting for comparatively small-data domains to which CBR systems may be applied.

Specifically, we investigate the following hypotheses:

1. **When training on small data sets, quality of extracted features may reflect the DL model overfitting.** To test the suitability of feature extraction for the sizes of data sets commonly used in CBR, we evaluate the models after training on comparatively small training sets. Because small data sets may result in DL models overfitting, we expect that the quality of extracted features will reflect that.
2. **Using a combination of extracted and knowledge-engineered features will lead to higher classification accuracy than with extracted features alone.** We expect that—similarly to our previous study using AlexNet [32]—high-quality knowledge-engineered features will augment the retrieval power of the extracted feature vectors.
3. **More complex DL feature extractors will generate better features.** More recent models with superior end-to-end classification performance (exemplified in our study by VGGNet, Inception, and DenseNet) will generate higher-quality features than older/simpler models (e.g., AlexNet).
4. **Models with densely-connected layers will generate higher-quality extracted features.** DL models that employ densely-connected layers prior to feature extraction (e.g., VGGNet and modified Inception and DenseNet structures) will generate higher-quality features (e.g., than post-GAP extraction), reflecting the hypothesis that densely-connected layers combine atomic features into more complex indices. This could apply to AlexNet as well, though we expect it will still generate lower-quality features due to a reduced number of available parameters.

5.1 Testbed Case-Based Classifier

We explore the performance of case-based classifiers using either extracted features alone or in concert with knowledge-engineered features. As this research focuses only on feature quality for CBR retrieval, we use a simple case-based classifier with no adaptation component. It performs 1-NN classification. Similarity calculations use unweighted Euclidean distance, with numeric analogs for nominal feature values provided in the data set (see Sect. 5.2).

5.2 Data Set Considerations and Model Training

Model training and evaluation use the Animals with Attributes 2 (AwA2) data set [33]. In particular, network models are trained, and the full system is tested, on image data in the AwA2 data set, and knowledge-engineered features are simulated by perturbing the per-class supplementary features from AwA2 as in Wilkerson et al. [32]. The training data set for each experimental iteration (30 iterations total) is defined from scratch, containing 500 images randomly selected from and evenly distributed among AwA2's 50 classes. Each DL model is trained for 50 epochs, and the case base is instantiated by extracting features for each training image to create cases as in Sect. 3.2, and then storing each result.

For hybrid models, determining how to divide data into training and testing sets involves additional issues because of having to accommodate differences between the normal evaluation processes for CBR and DL. CBR evaluation is traditionally performed using leave-one-out testing, and so the differentiation between training and testing cases is temporary and implicit, rather than permanent and explicit, as it is for DL models. Leave-one-out testing can be seen as testing a CBR system on its training data using k-fold cross-validation where k is the number of cases/training examples. This raises the question of whether it is most appropriate to evaluate a DL-CBR hybrid classifier on its own training data or an independent test set. For evaluation on the training data, the CBR system will still classify "novel" examples via leave-one-out testing, but any example during testing will correspond to a training example from the DL model's perspective [18,32]. This assumption could be desirable in applications where CBR system performance with extracted features is the principal focus. That is, especially for domains for which novel training examples occur infrequently, and/or for which the DL model may be easily retrained to consider novel examples, evaluating the DL-CBR model on training data approximates "ideal" or "upper bound" feature extraction performance for the DL feature extractor, moving evaluation focus to how the CBR system leverages extracted features.

By contrast, testing on an independent test set provides a stricter criterion for the DL system, assuming that DL overfitting may limit the applicability of a hybrid system evaluated only on training data. In the independent approach, evaluation occurs on a set of novel images, and the CBR classifier is evaluated based on classification accuracy for dynamically-generated cases for these images. We present results for both evaluation approaches in this paper.

6   Results and Discussion

Results presented in this section concern experiments both with and without supplementary knowledge-engineered features, as well as evaluated both on the training data and on an independent testing set of 500 images selected in the same way as the training data (Figs. 3, 4, and 5).

These data suggest several broad trends. At the outset, we see ample evidence of DL model overfitting on the small training sets used, though some do still generalize relatively well. Using knowledge-engineered features in concert with extracted features generally can increase overall system accuracy, though the phenomenon is actually quite nuanced, as we discuss in Sect. 6.2. Whether including knowledge-engineered features or not, there appears to be no one "best" model; instead classification accuracy appears to fluctuate based on the conditions of case base instantiation and which of the two evaluation criteria is considered more important. Finally, replacing GAP with densely-connected structures does not appear to improve the quality of extracted features; in fact, the opposite appears to be true with a few exceptions. We explore these conclusions in greater detail in the sections below.

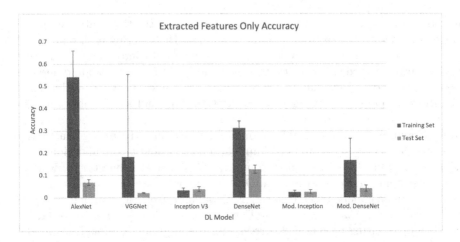

Fig. 3. CBR classification accuracy values when using extracted features alone, evaluated using leave-one-out testing on the training set or on an independently-selected testing set. All error bars represent one standard deviation.

6.1   Using Extracted Features only and Model Overfitting

When performing CBR retrieval using extracted features only (Fig. 3), we note significant differences in performance, both between feature extraction models and between evaluation approaches. Notably, the Inception model posts accuracy values on par with random guessing; VGGNet has a higher average accuracy value on the training set, but its significant standard deviation suggests inconsistency in model learning that often results in poor performance similar to that of Inception. In these instances, it seems that VGGNet and Inception are not learning well, likely due to an unsuitable ratio of trainable parameters to training examples. By contrast, AlexNet and DenseNet appear to generate features that facilitate higher classification accuracy values. One caveat of this observation is that given DenseNet's architecture, if the same number of features were extracted as for other models (2048), then the necessary structural change could have influenced the entire architecture through the interdependence of DenseNet's blocks; so, only 1024 features were extracted. As shown in Leake et al. [18], the number of features extracted can significantly impact CBR classification accuracy, so it is possible that the unmodified DenseNet accuracy values are slightly inflated.

In addition, it appears that each model overfits on the relatively small training data sets used. In particular, AlexNet generates features that appear to characterize the training data well but generalize poorly on novel data; by contrast, DenseNet appears to suffer least from overfitting. This supports our hypothesis that small training set size does lead to overfitting that is reflected in extracted feature quality, and we conclude that DenseNet–while far from an ideal performer–is the most resilient model given minimal training data, as well

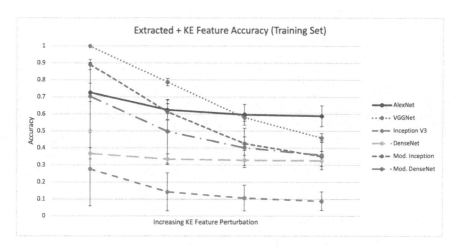

Fig. 4. CBR classification accuracy values when using extracted features and simulated knowledge-engineered (KE) features in concert, evaluated using leave-one-out testing on the training set. All error bars represent one standard deviation.

as that having more training data would lead to improvements in feature quality and generalization across the board.

6.2 Potentially Inflated Accuracy Values with Knowledge-Engineered Features

At first glance, it appears that when knowledge-engineered features are concatenated onto the extracted feature vectors for retrieval (Figs. 4 and 5), VGGNet and the modified Inception model are highly accurate, especially for minimally perturbed knowledge-engineered feature values. However, these methods have pronounced accuracy loss for higher degrees of perturbation. For evaluation on the training set, AlexNet outperforms either of these models as a feature extractor for higher perturbation values. Additionally, the accuracy values for both models are very similar when comparing accuracy on the independent test set versus on the training set, despite being dramatically lower for other models.

We hypothesize that these phenomena further point to VGGNet and Inception learning poorly from training based on the limited training set size. Specifically, in the absence of effective learning, randomly-initialized feature values in the network remain essentially random; when they are extracted and concatenated with knowledge-engineered feature values, the resulting feature sets have large subsets that are essentially equidistant from the corresponding feature subsets for all other cases due to their mutual near-randomness. In that instance, only the distances that correspond to knowledge-engineered features are significant. This explains both the consistency between the two testing strategies and–as in Wilkerson et al. [32]–high accuracy values for smaller perturbations.

Concerning the other models, there is not a clear front-runner in terms of performance; the modified DenseNet appears to generate features that facili-

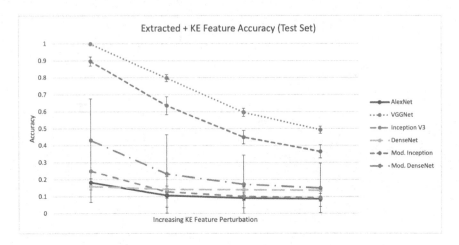

Fig. 5. CBR classification accuracy values when using extracted features and simulated knowledge-engineered (KE) features in concert, evaluated on an independently-selected testing set. All error bars represent one standard deviation.

tate reasonably high-accuracy classification, but high standard deviation values make the significance unclear. That said, it appears that including knowledge-engineered features with extracted features results in accuracy increases for all models, supporting our corresponding hypothesis and our earlier work [32].

6.3 Best Approaches Overall for Feature Quality

These results suggest that there may be no "catchall" model for generating high-quality features for CBR retrieval. Our hypothesis that more advanced DL models generate higher-quality features is generally not supported for small training set sizes that we have used for our research to date; models that have large numbers of trainable parameters actually perform poorly because of large training data requirements. It may be the case that complex DL generates better CBR features given large training sets, but because of practical data limitations for many CBR domains, this might not be actionable.

Encouraging preliminary results shaped our hypothesis that densely-connected layers help generate useful features and led to the inclusion of modified Inception and DenseNet models that incorporated densely-connected layers during experimentation. However, it appears that densely-connected layers do not improve feature quality unilaterally. It is possible that the appended densely-connected layers do provide some benefit for DenseNet in the form of increased compatibility with knowledge-engineered features (Figs. 4 and 5), but this is somewhat unclear due to the different numbers of features extracted as discussed previously, as well as the high accuracy variability illustrated in the large standard deviation values. This leaves open the possibility that DL models may be modified/parameterized to align with CBR needs, but such modifications likely will need to be made on a per-model basis.

In sum, some models (e.g., VGGNet and Inception) clearly do not facilitate useful feature extraction under the tested circumstances, and models such as AlexNet and DenseNet show some promise–though they are prone to overfitting given minimal training data, as evidenced by their lower accuracy on the test set. The inclusion/appending of densely-connected layers is not an indicator of useful feature generation in general; careful parameterization considerations and interplay between the DL and CBR models still appear to be the dominant factor for architecture selection and modification. That said, using both knowledge-engineered and extracted features in concert still appears to improve CBR classification accuracy in general, with the caveat that when comparing results, the accuracy effects of high-quality knowledge-engineered features can mask deficiencies in model learning.

7 Next Steps: Other Models, Transfer Learning, and Integrated Training

This research explores a necessarily incomplete subset of DL models. With the speed of new discoveries and development of new implementations, novel DL architectures will continue to be available for further testing. Models such as MLP mixer and transformer architectures appear especially promising for feature extraction. They represent additional approaches for feature extraction for computer vision, and they are also useful in other broad domains (e.g., transformers for natural language processing); they are also promising candidates for linear feature vector extraction from similarly-shaped layers, potentially facilitating application of our DL-CBR methodology to other domains.

It may be rewarding to focus on addressing the relationship between model complexity/modeling power and larger training data requirements. This may manifest as evaluation of DL-CBR feature quality given different training set sizes (e.g., to quantify how CBR classification may reduce training data needs for the hybrid system); alternatively, using pretrained models appears promising for minimizing training data requirements. That is, a pretrained DL model may be specialized to the data set in question via transfer learning and then leveraged for feature extraction for CBR retrieval. In this way, the model may generate more useful features for the CBR system without having to significantly increase the size of the training set. Indeed, we are beginning to address this, and preliminary results in this direction appear extremely promising, even using the VGGNet and Inception architectures, which this study finds to be difficult to train in data-light scenarios (Table 1).

Finally, a tighter coupling of DL and CBR systems during model training may increase extracted feature quality as well. Specifically, rather than training the DL model end-to-end independently before evaluating the CBR classifier using features extracted from it, it might be more appropriate to use the CBR system's classification loss to supplement or replace the end-to-end DL loss. As a result, weight updates in the DL system are sensitized to the needs of the CBR system, ideally resulting in higher-quality extracted features for CBR retrieval.

Table 1. Preliminary accuracy values using pretrained models for feature extraction, evaluating CBR classification accuracy on the training set (500 training examples– 10 for each of the 50 classes) using extracted features only. Models are trained for 25 epochs, and ten trials are conducted for each model to determine standard deviation values. Accuracy values illustrate the potential for pretraining to increase system accuracy.

Extractor Model	Accuracy	St. Dev.
VGGNet	0.890	0.021
Inception	0.713	0.026

8   Conclusions

We presented a comparative analysis of feature quality for case retrieval features extracted from several DL models with the goal of maximizing classification accuracy, aimed at illuminating which DL models are most suitable to use as a basis for feature extraction in different scenarios. It is clear that this is a complex issue for which no all-purpose solution exists; model selection is highly dependent on the balance between DL model complexity and available training data, and the novelty of potential test data versus training data is important as well. This study supports prior observations about the effectiveness of using knowledge-engineered and network-extracted features in concert [32], and about the influence of DL structure on feature quality [18].

In addition to the avenues for future work discussed in Sect. 7, it would be useful to investigate additional domains involving image classification and supplementary knowledge-engineered features, feature weighting methods applied to extracted features (building on Wilkerson et al. [32]), and applications for DL-based feature extraction in CBR adaptation.

Acknowledgments. This work was funded by the US Department of Defense (Contract W52P1J2093009), and by the Department of the Navy, Office of Naval Research (Award N00014-19-1-2655).

References

1. Aamodt, A., Plaza, E.: Case-based reasoning: foundational issues, methodological variations, and system approaches. AI Commun. **7**(1), 39–52 (1994)
2. Barletta, R., Mark, W.: Explanation-based indexing of cases. In: Kolodner, J. (ed.) Proceedings of a Workshop on Case-Based Reasoning, pp. 50–60. DARPA, Morgan Kaufmann, Palo Alto (1988)
3. Barnett, A.J., et al.: Interpretable mammographic image classification using case-based reasoning and deep learning. In: IJCAI Workshops 2021 (2021)
4. Bhatta, S., Goel, A.: Model-based learning of structural indices to design cases. In: Proceedings of the IJCAI-93 Workshop on Reuse of Design, pp. A1–A13. IJCAI, Chambery (1993)

5. Bonzano, A., Cunningham, P., Smyth, B.: Using introspective learning to improve retrieval in CBR: a case study in air traffic control. In: Leake, D.B., Plaza, E. (eds.) ICCBR 1997. LNCS, vol. 1266, pp. 291–302. Springer, Heidelberg (1997). https://doi.org/10.1007/3-540-63233-6_500

6. Chai, J., Zeng, H., Li, A., Ngai, E.W.: Deep learning in computer vision: a critical review of emerging techniques and application scenarios. Mach. Learn. Appl. **6**, 100134 (2021)

7. Chen, C., Li, O., Tao, D., Barnett, A., Rudin, C., Su, J.K.: This looks like that: deep learning for interpretable image recognition. In: Advances in Neural Information Processing Systems, vol. 32, pp. 8930–8941. Curran (2019)

8. Cox, M., Ram, A.: Introspective multistrategy learning: on the construction of learning strategies. Artif. Intell. **112**(1–2), 1–55 (1999)

9. Domeshek, E.: Indexing stories as social advice. In: Proceedings of the Ninth National Conference on Artificial Intelligence, pp. 16–21. AAAI Press, Menlo Park (1991)

10. Fox, S., Leake, D.: Introspective reasoning for index refinement in case-based reasoning. J. Exp. Theor. Artif. Intell. **13**(1), 63–88 (2001)

11. Guidotti, R., Monreale, A., Ruggieri, S., Turini, F., Giannotti, F., Pedreschi, D.: A survey of methods for explaining black box models. ACM Comput. Surv. **51**(5), 1–42 (2018)

12. Huang, G., Liu, Z., van der Maaten, L., Weinberger, K.Q.: Densely connected convolutional networks (2016). arXiv:1608.06993

13. Kenny, E.M., Keane, M.T.: Twin-systems to explain artificial neural networks using case-based reasoning: comparative tests of feature-weighting methods in ANN-CBR twins for XAI. In: Proceedings of the Twenty-Eighth International Joint Conference on Artificial Intelligence (2019)

14. Khan, A., Sohail, A., Zahoora, U., Qureshi, A.S.: A survey of the recent architectures of deep convolutional neural networks. Artif. Intell. Rev. **53**, 5455–5516 (2019)

15. Krizhevsky, A., Sutskever, I., Hinton, G.E.: ImageNet classification with deep convolutional neural networks. In: Proceedings of the 25th International Conference on Neural Information Processing Systems, vol. 1, pp. 1097–1105 (2012)

16. Leake, D.: An indexing vocabulary for case-based explanation. In: Proceedings of the Ninth National Conference on Artificial Intelligence, pp. 10–15. AAAI Press, Menlo Park (1991)

17. Leake, D.: CBR in context: the present and future. In: Leake, D. (ed.) Case-Based Reasoning: Experiences, Lessons, and Future Directions, pp. 3–30. AAAI Press, Menlo Park (1996). http://www.cs.indiana.edu/~leake/papers/a-96-01.html

18. Leake, D., Wilkerson, Z., Crandall, D.: Extracting case indices from convolutional neural networks: a comparative study. In: Keane, M.T., Wiratunga, N. (eds.) ICCBR 2022. LNCS, vol. 13405, pp. 81–95. Springer, Cham (2022). https://doi.org/10.1007/978-3-031-14923-8_6

19. Leake, D., Ye, X.: Harmonizing case retrieval and adaptation with alternating optimization. In: Sánchez-Ruiz, A.A., Floyd, M.W. (eds.) ICCBR 2021. LNCS (LNAI), vol. 12877, pp. 125–139. Springer, Cham (2021). https://doi.org/10.1007/978-3-030-86957-1_9

20. Li, O., Liu, H., Chen, C., Rudin, C.: Deep learning for case-based reasoning through prototypes: a neural network that explains its predictions. In: Proceedings of the Thirty-Second AAAI Conference on Artificial Intelligence (2017)

21. Liao, C., Liu, A., Chao, Y.: A machine learning approach to case adaptation. In: 2018 IEEE First International Conference on Artificial Intelligence and Knowledge Engineering (AIKE), pp. 106–109 (2018)

22. Main, J., Dillon, T.S.: A hybrid case-based reasoner for footwear design. In: Althoff, K.-D., Bergmann, R., Branting, L.K. (eds.) ICCBR 1999. LNCS, vol. 1650, pp. 497–509. Springer, Heidelberg (1999). https://doi.org/10.1007/3-540-48508-2_36

23. Mathisen, B.M., Aamodt, A., Bach, K., Langseth, H.: Learning similarity measures from data. Progr. Artif. Intell. **9**, 129–143 (2019)

24. Richter, M.: Introduction. In: Lenz, M., Bartsch-Spörl, B., Burkhard, H.D., Wess, S. (eds.) CBR Technology: From Foundations to Applications, chap. 1, pp. 1–15. Springer, Berlin (1998)

25. Rudin, C.: Please stop explaining black box models for high stakes decisions. Nature Mach. Intell. **1**, 206–215 (2019)

26. Sani, S., Wiratunga, N., Massie, S.: Learning deep features for kNN-based human activity recognition. In: Proceedings of ICCBR 2017 Workshops (CAW, CBRDL, PO-CBR), Doctoral Consortium, and Competitions co-located with the 25th International Conference on Case-Based Reasoning (ICCBR 2017), Trondheim, Norway, 26–28 June 2017. CEUR Workshop Proceedings, vol. 2028, pp. 95–103. CEUR-WS.org (2017)

27. Schank, R., et al.: Towards a general content theory of indices. In: Proceedings of the 1990 AAAI Spring Symposium on Case-Based Reasoning. AAAI Press, Menlo Park (1990)

28. Simonyan, K., Zisserman, A.: Very deep convolutional networks for large-scale image recognition (2014). https://doi.org/10.48550/ARXIV.1409.1556, arXiv:1409.1556

29. Szegedy, C., Vanhoucke, V., Ioffe, S., Shlens, J., Wojna, Z.: Rethinking the inception architecture for computer vision (2015). arXiv:1512.00567

30. Turner, J.T., Floyd, M.W., Gupta, K.M., Aha, D.W.: Novel object discovery using case-based reasoning and convolutional neural networks. In: Cox, M.T., Funk, P., Begum, S. (eds.) ICCBR 2018. LNCS (LNAI), vol. 11156, pp. 399–414. Springer, Cham (2018). https://doi.org/10.1007/978-3-030-01081-2_27

31. Turner, J.T., Floyd, M.W., Gupta, K., Oates, T.: NOD-CC: a hybrid CBR-CNN architecture for novel object discovery. In: Bach, K., Marling, C. (eds.) ICCBR 2019. LNCS (LNAI), vol. 11680, pp. 373–387. Springer, Cham (2019). https://doi.org/10.1007/978-3-030-29249-2_25

32. Wilkerson, Z., Leake, D., Crandall, D.J.: On combining knowledge-engineered and network-extracted features for retrieval. In: Sánchez-Ruiz, A.A., Floyd, M.W. (eds.) ICCBR 2021. LNCS (LNAI), vol. 12877, pp. 248–262. Springer, Cham (2021). https://doi.org/10.1007/978-3-030-86957-1_17

33. Xian, Y., Lampert, C.H., Schiele, B., Akata, Z.: Zero-shot learning - a comprehensive evaluation of the good, the bad and the ugly. IEEE Trans. Pattern Anal. Mach. Intell. (T-PAMI) **40**(8), 1–14 (2018)

34. Ye, X., Leake, D., Crandall, D.: Case adaptation with neural networks: capabilities and limitations. In: Keane, M.T., Wiratunga, N. (eds.) ICCBR 2022. LNCS, vol. 13405, pp. 143–158. Springer, Cham (2022). https://doi.org/10.1007/978-3-031-14923-8_10

Synergies Between Case-Based Reasoning and Deep Learning for Survival Analysis in Oncology

Isabelle Bichindaritz$^{(\boxtimes)}$ ⓘ and Guanghui Liu ⓘ

Department of Computer Science, State University of New York, Oswego, NY, USA
{ibichind,guanghui.liu}@oswego.edu

Abstract. Survival analysis is a field of statistics specialized in making predictions about the survival length of patients, even though it can be applied to the prediction of any future event. It is routinely used in medical research to stratify patients in groups based on risk, such as high-risk groups and low-risk groups, and has paramount important in patient stratification and treatment. Recently, deep neural networks (DNNs) have raised considerable attention for survival analysis because of their non-linear nature and their excellent ability to predict survival, in comparison to statistical methods. In this domain, case-based survival methods have started to by applied as well, with some success. It is therefore interesting to study how to synergistically combine the two for improved performance for several reasons. From the case-based reasoning standpoint, the deep neural network can detect deep similarity between cases with a time-to-event structure and from the DNN standpoint, case-based reasoning can provide the glass-box approach that remedies the "black box" label attached to them. In this study, we propose a synergy between case-based reasoning and Long Short-Term Memory (LSTM) model for survival prediction in oncology. In this deep survival model network, the total loss function combines four different factors and uses an adaptive weights approach to combine the four loss terms. The network learns a prototype layer during training which naturally comes with an explanation for each prediction. This study employs cross-validation and the concordance index for assessing the survival prediction performance and demonstrate on two cancer methylation data sets that the developed approach is effective.

Keywords: Survival Analysis · Deep Network · Case-based Reasoning · Objective Loss · Explainable Model

1 Introduction

Cancer is the most common disease in the world. Because genetic factors have been associated with this disease with a preponderance of evidence, genomic data are key to understand the complex biological mechanisms of cancer patient survival. This approach could lead to the development of new treatments for patients and improved survival predictions. An easily measurable genomic factor is the DNA methylation process. DNA

S. Massie and S. Chakraborti (Eds.): ICCBR 2023, LNAI 14141, pp. 19–33, 2023.
https://doi.org/10.1007/978-3-031-40177-0_2

methylation levels exhibit differential expressions in a variety of tissues [27]. One goal of cancer studies refers to gaining the ability to identify prediction-related elements to determine the survival length of a patient, thereby allowing clinical personnel to perform early treatment decision-making. Prediction-related disease signatures are critical to split cases between risk groups for personalized cancer management, which could avoid either overtreatment or under treatment. For instance, cases classified into the high-risk group may benefit from closer follow-up, more aggressive therapies, and advanced care planning [30]. Consequently, to explore the utility of DNA methylation data for cancer diagnosis, it is very useful to analyze DNA methylation of tumors from cases with cancers to identify potential cancer-specific survival risk.

In case-based reasoning (CBR), similarity assessment can be complex, in particular in domains involving temporal or sequential data. In bioinformatics in particular, most biological data are high dimensional and with low-sample size. To overcome the high-dimensional feature space and low-sample size problem in bioinformatics, dimensionality reduction techniques are often used to reduce the dimension of the input data. In particular, deep feature selection was developed to identify discriminative features in deep learning models [7]. This problem has been well studied in deep learning, where model overfitting often occurs because gradients tend to have high variance in backpropagation.

In domains involving temporal or sequential data, deep learning models can be advantageous to perform similarity assessment. As a matter of fact, deep Learning techniques can be used directly in survival analysis to learn the hazard function and create deep models [1]. However, if the input and output are understood, the processing that occurs in-between is obscure, so that a black- box effect in DNNs is alluded to. The large number of parameters and the typical non-linearity of the activation functions are the main reasons why this task is practically impossible. Nevertheless, interpretable approaches are necessary in medicine because users are ultimately responsible for their clinical decisions and therefore need to make informed decisions [19, 20]. In survival analysis, the model interpretability is more of a concern than simply predicting patient survival with high accuracy. Therefore, the ability to provide explicit model interpretation in deep neural networks remains highly desirable in survival analysis.

In this study, we create a synergistic system between case-based reasoning and deep learning for survival analysis. The contribution of deep learning is two-fold. Firstly, an autoencoder reduces the dimensionality of the input space. Our purpose for using the encoder layers is to reduce the dimensionality of the original input features. Secondly, a Long-Short Term Memory (LSTM) learns the similarity between input cases and test cases. The survival prediction architecture is capable of explaining its own reasoning process. The learned model naturally provides explanations for each prediction, and these explanations are faithful to what the network is actually computing. An architecture is used to encode its own explanation in contrast to creating an explanation for a previously trained black-box model. We create a prototype layer, where each prototype corresponds to a case, to store the weight vector following the encoded input, and to receive the output from the encoder layers. The prototype layer, inspired by case-based reasoning, utilizes the strategy of the nearest distance retrieval in case-based reasoning (CBR) to provide a useful insight into the inner workings of the deep network. We can use this prototype layer to explain the input data features.

The contributions of this paper are the following:

1) The synergy between case-based reasoning and deep learning is explored in the context of survival analysis, which is a very different machine learning task from classification or prediction. Very few CBR systems have tackled this task.
2) The deep learning architecture used, LSTM, has not been used in synergy with CBR, to the best of our knowledge. LSTM belongs to the recurrent neural networks family and excels in sequence and temporal data analysis.
3) The application to methylation data in oncology has been rarely studied from a CBR standpoint. However, it is of growing importance in bioinformatics, in which this type of data has been shown to better classify and predict many diseases than gene expression alone.
4) Unlike many approaches to the synergy between CBR and deep learning, the proposed system adopts a balanced approach between the two, since the deep learning model mostly performs deep similarity learning, taking temporal data into account. CBR is not used in the system solely for explainability.

2 Research Background

DNA methylation has recently become more prevalent in genetic research in oncology. This paper proposes to apply these findings to the study of DNA methylation signatures for cancer prognostic survival analysis. Cancer cases can be divided into two categories i.e., censored cases and non-censored cases [2]. For censored cases, the death events were not observed during the follow-up period, and thus their genuine survival times are longer than the recorded data, while for non-censored cases their recorded survival times are the exact time from initial diagnosis to event – very often the event is death.

Several survival analysis approaches have been proposed in the literature. LASSO method [18, 25] applies the lasso feature selection method for selecting the parts associated with cancer prediction. Random Survival Forests (RSF) [10] calculates a random forest with the log-rank test as the splitting standard. Though much progress has been made using above approaches, Yet the predicting performance of the previously proposed approaches remains far from satisfying, and room remains for subsequent advancement.

The deep learning models overcome many of the restrictions of Cox-based models like the proportionality assumption. DeepSurv [13] was developed with a cutting-edge deep neural network. It is based on the Cox proportional hazards method associated with a deep neural network to perform a prediction of time-to-event and facilitate risk stratification with the goal of enabling treatment efficacy by providing individual treatment suggestions [14]. However, DeepSurv lacked interpretability. It was urgent to propose interpretable nonlinear models for survival prediction.

3 Related Work

3.1 Case-Based Reasoning

Case-based reasoning (CBR) is a method of reasoning based on analogy. Its fundamental idea is to reuse similar previous experiences in order to solve new problems. The CBR methods have in common the following processes: retrieve, reuse, revise, and retain. The most used case retrieval strategy is the nearest neighbor strategy or k-nearest neighbors algorithm (kNN). kNN is one of the most explainable algorithms and belongs to instance-based learners, for which decisions are made by similarity between a new case and solved retrieved cases, which can serve as explanations for a system recommendation. CBR within the domain of microarray analysis is mostly unexplored, especially for epigenetic data. The primary foundation for CBR is its ability to consistently update from new cases, and to adapt prior solutions to a new problem. Within microarray analysis, however, problems exist that render updating and adaptation particularly difficult. The first problem is the high dimensionality with few samples. There are thousands of features for a small subset of samples (specifically tens of thousands for the standard chipset used in DNA methylation), and these samples are often imbalanced between cases and controls. Therefore, little work has been done so far in genetic survival analysis with case-based reasoning, We can cite Karmen et al., who calculate similarity based on survival functions [12]. Bartlett et al. (2021) consider clinical covariates when retrieving genetic cases for case-based survival prediction [2].

3.2 Synergies Between Deep Learning and CBR

A number of approaches have been proposed to combine case-based reasoning and deep learning. Approaches range from resorting to deep learning in subtasks, to resorting to CBR to make deep learning more explainable. In the former approach, for example, several systems use deep learning for some tasks within a case-based reasoning architecture. Eisenstadt et al. classify design cases from labels to select most relevant cases during retrieval [8]. In the latter approach, deep learning systems mostly resort to CBR to provide explanations of their reasoning processes (XAI) [5, 22, 23]. Li et al. construct a prototype layer by adding an autoencoder to deep convolutional networks [17]. Their application processed image data, for which convolutional neural networks are particularly adapted. By contrast, our approach fits clinical and multi-omics data, using LSTM as the main deep learning method, and performs survival prediction tasks. Our approach can also tackle classical classification and regression tasks since LSTM can be adjusted for that purpose as well, even though they excel particularly on data having a serial form, such as time series and other forms of sequences. Several deep learning systems learn prototypes for grouping input cases and explaining deep learning results [11, 15, 16]. Our system uses deep learning methods to encode each case in a prototype, not for grouping several cases into a prototype. The prototype provides a representation of a case after encoding features. Although our system could learn prototypes for grouping, we prefer to keep each case separate in the current system.

3.3 Survival Analysis

Survival analysis is considered as a specific machine learning task predicting a time to event based on incomplete data, which refers to a mix of censored and uncensored data. Although it performs a prediction into the future, it is quite different from forecasting as well as from classification or prediction. Very specific machine learning models, mostly from statistics, have been applied to this task with the goal of evaluating the risk of patients into risk categories to reach an event in the future. Cox proportional hazard model [18] is one of the most popular survival prediction models. Recently, based on the Cox model, several regularization approaches have been proposed in the literature. The Least Absolute Shrinkage and Selection Operator COX model (LASSO-COX) [24, 25, 28] applies the lasso feature selection method for selecting parts associated with carcinoma prediction. Random survival forests (RSF) [10] calculates a random forest with the log-rank test as the splitting standard. It determines the cumulative hazards of the leaf nodes while averaging them over the totality of elements. Cox regression with neural networks by a one hidden layer multilayer perceptron (MLP) [29] was proposed to replace the linear predictor of the Cox model. Some novel networks were suggested to be capable of outperforming typical Cox models [26]. DeepSurv [13, 14] refers to a deep Cox proportional hazards neural network as well as a survival approach to model interacting processes of a case's covariates and treatment modalities for providing individual treatment suggestions. DeepSurv is developed upon Cox proportional assumption with a cutting-edge deep neural network. MTLSA [17] is a recently proposed model which regards survival analysis to be a multi-task learning issue. Following in this trend, Bichindaritz et al. [4] proposed an adaptive multi-task learning method, which combines the Cox loss task with the ordinal loss task, for survival prediction of breast cancer patients using multi-modal learning to integrate gene expression and methylation data instead of performing survival analysis on each feature data set. However, these models lacked interpretability.

4 Methods

In survival analysis, prediction of the time duration until a certain event occurs is the goal and the death of a cancer case is the event of interest in this study. We propose a synergy between CBR and deep learning to achieve this goal. The model learning process, highlighted in its architecture (see Fig. 1), comprises three stages: prototype learning to encode each case into a compact representation, similarity learning through LSTM model training, and survival prediction. The trained model then can be applied to new input cases, also referred to as test cases, for survival prediction (see Fig. 2).

4.1 Autoencoder

We use an autoencoder (an encoder and a decoder) with the leaky ReLU activation function in all autoencoder layers.

The autoencoder is used to reduce the dimensionality of the input and to learn useful features for prediction; then the encoded input is used to produce a deep Cox model through the prototype layer. The prototype layer receives the output from the encoder. Because the prototype layer output vectors live in the same space as the encoded inputs, we can feed these vectors into the decoder and visualize the learned custom network throughout the training process. In case-based reasoning, to determine the solution of new problems, the process of case retrieval uses a similarity function to find some similar problems and their solutions from the historical case base. Similarity functions are generally obtained by calculating their distances in the feature space. In this system, we minimize the distance between the output and input of the prototype layer during the model iteration training. The output of the prototype layer can then be used to interpret the input data features. This property can interpret how the network reaches its predictions and visualize the learning process.

In fact, the purpose of creating the prototype layer is to obtain a dimensionality reduction vector of the original input by autonomously training a model to represent and explain the original input. For each training sample, the linear expression of each feature was calculated and used to construct one prototypical case. Each prototype case would then represent typical DNA methylation patterns present in different samples. The Euclidean distance between each encoder from the case base and its respective proto-type is used to determine how similar the prototype is to its own. This will appropriately determine how well the case fits a collection of unsolved cases during the prediction.

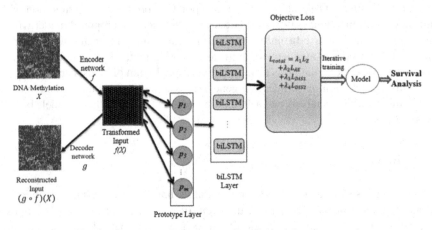

Fig. 1. Illustration of the proposed model training framework

4.2 BiLSTM

A bidirectional Long Short-Term Memory (biLSTM) [9] is then trained as the last output layer.

In this deep survival model network, the total loss function consists of four terms: the negative log partial likelihood function of the Cox model, the autoencoder loss, and two required distances. These distances ensure that every feature vector in the original input looks like at least one of the prototype layer feature vectors and that every prototype layer feature vector looks like at least one of the feature vectors in the original input. We use an adaptive weights approach to combine the four loss terms. The network that the prototype layer learns during training naturally comes with an explanation for each prediction.

The negative log partial likelihood function of the Cox hazard model is defined as follows by Sy and Taylor [5]:

$$L_Z(\theta) = -\sum_{i=1}^{n} \delta_i \left(\theta^T x_i - log \sum_{j \in R(t_i)} exp(\theta^T x_j) \right) \tag{1}$$

where $x = (x_1, x_2, \cdots, x_n)$ corresponds to the covariate variable of dimensionality n, δ_i is a binary value indicating whether the event happened or not, and $R(t_i)$ denotes the set of all individuals at risk at time t_i, which represents the set of cases that are still at risk before time t_i. $\theta^T x_i$ is called the risk (or survival) function, in which θ can be estimated by minimizing its corresponding negative log partial likelihood function; n denotes the number of patients.

The autoencoder loss uses the squared L2 distance between the original and reconstructed input for penalizing the autoencoder's reconstruction error. We denote this loss as:

$$L_{AE} = \frac{1}{n} \sum_{i=1}^{n} \|(g \circ f)(x_i) - x_i\|_2^2 \tag{2}$$

where $(g \circ f)(x_i)$ is the decoder network reconstructed input.

The two required distances loss, which are two interpretability regularization terms, are formulated as follows:

$$L_{DIS1} = \frac{1}{m} \sum_{j=1}^{m} \min_{i \in [1,n]} \|p_j - f(x_i)\|_2^2 \tag{3}$$

$$L_{DIS2} = \frac{1}{n} \sum_{i=1}^{n} \min_{j \in [1,m]} \|f(x_i) - p_j\|_2^2 \tag{4}$$

where $f(x_i)$ is the encoded input vector, p_i is the vector learned from the prototype layer. The prototype layer p computes the squared L_2 distance between the encoded input $f(x_i)$ and each of the prototype layer vectors. Minimization of L_{DIS1} will make each prototype vector as close as possible to at least one training case. The minimization of L_{DIS2} will make each encoded training example as close as possible to some prototype vector. It is worth noting that the purpose of minimizing the distances L_{DIS2} is to find the most similar case to the test case in the prototype outputs of the training set. This implements the nearest neighbor strategy method from case-based reasoning in the deep network. We use the two terms L_{DIS1} and L_{DIS2} in our cost function to illustrate the interpretability. The network chooses prototypes that fully represent the input space, and some of the prototypes tend to be similar to each other. Intuitively, L_{DIS1} approximates each prototype to a potential training example, making the decoded prototype realistic, while L_{DIS2} forces each training example to find a close prototype in the latent space, thus encouraging the prototypes to spread out over the entire latent space and to be distinct from each other. In the latent space, they are different from each other.

By combining the above 4 loss terms, the objective loss function can be formulated as follows:

$$L_{total} = \lambda_1 L_Z + \lambda_2 L_{AE} + \lambda_3 L_{DIS1} + \lambda_4 L_{DIS2} \qquad (5)$$

where $\lambda_i (i = 1, 2, 3, 4)$ is the regularization weight for the regularization terms respectively. Instead of fixing the weights, we use these weights as trainable parameters in the deep network for adaptive optimization [3].

This network architecture, unlike traditional case-based learning methods, automatically learns useful features. For methylated feature data, those methods (e.g., k-nearest neighbors) tend to perform poorly if we use the raw input space or use a hand-crafted feature space for predictions. We feed the sequence vectors into the decoder and train them throughout learned variables during the process. This approach will enable the system to explain how the network reaches its predictions and will show the learning process of the input variables without post-hoc analysis.

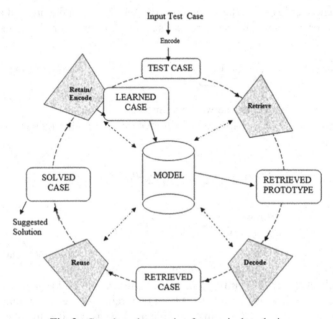

Fig. 2. Case-based reasoning for survival analysis

4.3 Survival Prediction

The survival prediction of the system can then be provided for any test case, associated with one input case corresponding to the nearest prototype activated by the biLSTM layer (see Fig. 2). Since the output of the prototype layer is generated during the iterative optimization of the model, it represents the characteristics of the training set. Minimizing the distance between the encoder output and prototype output means finding the nearest neighbor to this test case in the training set. If the minimum prototype distance is found, it means that one prototype case can represent the encoder output of this test case. This method exactly utilizes the strategy of the nearest distance retrieval in case-based reasoning.. For each training sample, the linear expression of each feature was calculated and used to construct one prototypical case. Each prototype case would then represent typical DNA methylation patterns present in a sample. The Euclidean distance between each encoder from the case base and its respective prototype is used to determine how similar the prototype is to its own. This will appropriately determine how well the case fits a collection of unsolved cases during the prediction. The ability to trace the nearest neighbor, according to the deep similarity calculated by the model, adds to the transparency and explainability of the system.

5   Results and Discussions

5.1   Benchmark Datasets

In this section, we assess the performance of the proposed method and carry out experiments on two cancer DNA methylation datasets through ten-fold cross validation. We selected Glioma cohort (GBMLGG) cancer and Pan-kidney cohort (KIPAN) cancer, two datasets from Firehose [6]. The GBMLGG datasets include 1129 samples for clinical data and 20116 gene-level features for DNA methylation data. The KIPAN datasets contain 973 samples and 20533 DNA methylation features. In our case, we will also use the clinical data. Two clinical variables are used: survival status and survival time. In survival status, 'Deceased' represents the patient deceased, 'Living' means that he/she is living at the time of the last follow-up. The survival time represents the number of days between diagnosis and date of death or last follow-up. This study removes cases with survival days that were not recorded or negative. For these reasons, this study extracts 650 samples for GBMLGG data and 654 samples for KIPAN data that have both DNA methylation data and clinical data respectively after merging and filtering.

Table 1. Gene and clinical characteristics in two cancers.

Characteristics	GBMLGG	KIPAN
Patient no.	650	654
Gene no.		
DNA Methylation	20116	20533
Selected features	586	749
Survival status		
Living	434	500
Deceased	216	154
Follow up (days)	1–481	3–5925

The high-dimension and low-sample size methylation data posed a challenge for obtaining sufficient statistical power. To accurately describe local features and all the levels (high & low) in feature representation of cancer samples, we use a multivariate Cox regression preprocess to extract the biomarkers. We calculate the log rank of each gene feature and select the gene features whose p-value are less than 0.01. Thus, we can get the preliminarily reduced features. For GBMLGG data, by using this method, we extract 586 methylation features. Similarly, we can obtain 749 methylation features for KIPAN data. Table 1 shows the Gene and clinical characteristics for the selected cases.

As is classical in survival analysis, we use Concordance index (C-index) [21] to assess the performance of the developed approach and other comparable methods. C-index is the probability that the predicted survival time of a random pair of individuals is in the same order as their actual survival time. It is very useful for evaluating proportional hazard models.

5.2 Convergence Analysis

To investigate the convergence of the proposed method, we calculate the corresponding loss curves of Eq. 5 on two datasets. Figure 3 shows the training loss curves of the five different loss functions we used concerning the GBMLGG and KIPAN datasets respectively. As shown in Fig. 3, the values of the training objective function loss decrease with respect to iterations on both datasets. The four loss terms (L_Z, L_{AE}, L_{DIS1}, and L_{DIS2}) and the total loss value (L_{total}) combined from them all converge to some stable values after a few iterations. Therefore, our proposed optimization algorithm is reliable and convergent.

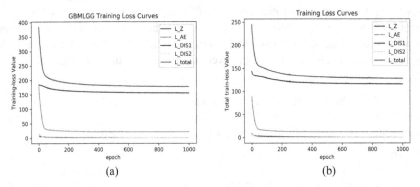

Fig. 3. The training loss curves using the proposed methods on two datasets. (a) the curves of training losses on GBMLGG dataset; (b) the curves of training losses on KIPAN dataset.

Let us investigate the autoencoder loss and the two interpretability prototype distance terms for a test case. We randomly select a test case from the GBMLGG and KIPAN datasets respectively for the experiments. Figure 3 shows the curves of three distance terms (L_{AE}, L_{DIS1}, and L_{DIS2}) during the prediction iterations for one test case of each of the two datasets. In Fig. 3(a), the values (L_{AE}, L_{DIS1}, and L_{DIS2}) are changed to

(0.01671, 2.82664, and 0.02032) when 1000 epochs are completed. As also can be seen from Fig. 3(b), the three values will converge to (0.005529, 2.0152, and 0.07098).

Obviously, by searching for the smallest distance L_{DIS2}, for GBMLGG, we can find the most similar case No. 356 in the training set to the test case No. 62. This means that we can use the characteristics of the known cases in the case base to explain the unsolved cases. Similarly, for KIPAN, we can find the most similar case No. 266 in the training set to match the test case No. 319.

From Fig. 4, we can find that the curve of L_{AE} (purple) and the curve of L_{DIS2} (pink) both converge to almost the same value when the model converges after 1000 epochs. The results of the two different datasets are consistent. The autoencoder loss L_{AE} is the distance between the original and reconstructed input. We use the autoencoder to create a latent low-dimensional space. The smaller the distance between the decoder and the original input, the more the encoder output can represent the original input. The interpretability prototype distance L_{DIS2} means the minimum distance between the encoder output and prototype output. When the two distances (L_{AE} and L_{DIS2}) tend to be the same, the prototype features will explain the original input data.

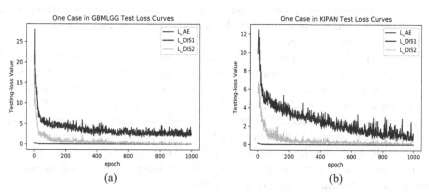

Fig. 4. Three curves of distance terms on two test cases from two datasets. (a) the curves of distance terms on one test case in GBMLGG dataset; (b) the curves of distance terms on one test case in KIPAN dataset

As also can be seen from Fig. 4, for the values of L_{DIS1} and L_{DIS2}, although their equations (Eq. 3 and Eq. 4) look similar, they are actually different. Actually, L_{DIS1} helps make the prototypes meaningful, and L_{DIS2} keeps the explanations faithful in forcing the network to use nearby prototypes.

Table 2. Performance comparison between two models by C-index (higher is better) on two datasets (with standard deviations)

Models	GBMLGG	KIPAN
Prototype	0.7132 (0.0166)	0.7246 (0.0149)
Without prototype	**0.7157 (0.0234)**	**0.7313 (0.0188)**

5.3 Survival Prediction Performance and Interpretability

We compared our model to a network without the explainable parts, in which we removed the autoencoder layers and the prototype layer. We replaced the prototype output vectors with original input vectors (without prototype) as the input for the last output layer directly. Table 2 shows the performance comparison between these two models by the measurements of C-index on GBMLGG and KIPAN datasets. As demonstrated in Table 2, compared with no prototype model performance, the C-index of the prototype model is only 0.25% and 0.67% lower on GBMLGG and KIPAN datasets respectively. From Table 2, the result illustrates that we do not sacrifice much C-index when including the interpretability elements into the network.

5.4 Comparison with Different Survival Prediction Methods

To explore the effectiveness of the proposed method, we compare the developed method with three existing machine learning survival prediction approaches: LASSO, RSF, and DeepSurv. For the sake of fairness, this part of the study runs the same input feature set in all cross-validation tests. Table 4 presents the performance comparison between the proposed method and the three stated methods by the measurements of the C-index on GBMLGG and KIPAN datasets.

As shown in Table 3, it can be found that our proposed method outperforms all the other three methods. Compared with the approaches: LASSO, RSF, and DeepSurv, the C-index of the proposed method is improved by 10.97 percent, 12.96 percent, and 5.85 percent on GBMLGG data; and by 11%, 11.13%, and 3.88% on KIPAN data, respectively. As also can be seen from Table 3, the prognosis power of the deep cox model (i.e., DeepSurv) is superior to the other traditional regularized Cox model methods (i.e., LASSO and RSF). It is worth mentioning that DeepSurv method uses a linear network, but our method outperforms DeepSurv. So, it demonstrates the advantage in survival prediction and the efficacy of the proposed method.

Table 3. Performance comparison among a range of survival prediction approaches by C-index (higher is better) on two datasets (with standard deviations)

Methods	GBMLGG	KIPAN
LASSO	0.6035 (0.0141)	0.6146 (0.0246)
RSF	0.5836 (0.0238)	0.6133 (0.0233)
DeepSurv	0.6547 (0.0216)	0.6858 (0.0173)
Proposed Method	**0.7132 (0.0166)**	**0.7246 (0.0149)**

6   Discussion

In this study, we developed a synergistic machine learning combining CBR, an autoencoder, and a LSTM prediction model for survival analysis. In comparison with state-of-the-art survival analysis models, the proposed model performs better in predicting survival, while providing transparency and explainability through a prototype layer where each prototype can be traced back to a training case. This approach provides same transparency as case-based reasoning by tracing which training inputs have influenced the model behavior.

In a previous study, Bartlett et al. [2] used solely case-based reasoning, without the synergy with deep learning used in this paper for autoencoding and similarity assessment. The results of this study are not comparable with the current study because the datasets were not the same: breast cancer in [2] and glioma and pan-kidney in the current study.

We plan in the future to compare the two systems on the same three datasets, both on the entire feature set and with same feature selection methods.

7   Conclusions

In this study, we developed a synergistic system between CBR, autoencoding, and LSTM for survival analysis in oncology. This system provides an explainable survival analysis framework of cancer patients, which uses an autoencoder network to reconstruct features of the training input and uses a prototype layer to store the weight vector following the encoded input. This deep survival prediction architecture can explain its own reasoning process and can provide explanations for each prediction, based on retrieved cases. We performed ten-fold cross-validation experiments on the DNA methylation data from two cancer types (GBMLGG and KIPAN). We have compared the performance of the proposed method with that of three other state-of-the-art existing methods (i.e., LASSO, RSF, and DeepSurv) through the performance measurement of C-index. The test results demonstrate that the survival prediction ability of the proposed method is better than that of the other three reported methods. We also investigate the convergence of the proposed method. The prototype layer can provide useful insight into the inner workings of the network. This method can partially trace the path of survival time prediction for a new observation to a previous case. This approach can partially trace the path of changes of the original input data in the deep network for survival prediction. Future plans include a comparison with CBR for survival analysis without LSTM, an evaluation of the interpretability of this model, and the addition of adaptation to the system's capability. The current approach has broader applications in the entire field of survival analysis as well as time series and sequence prediction in any domain.

References

1. Amiri, Z., Mohammad, K., Mahmoudi, M., Zeraati, H., Fotouhi, A.: Assessment of gastric cancer survival: using an artificial hierarchical neural network. Pak. J. Biol. Sci. **11**, 1076–1084 (2008)

2. Bichindaritz, I., Bartlett, C., Liu, G.: Predicting with confidence: a case-based reasoning framework for predicting survival in breast cancer. In: The International FLAIRS Conference Proceedings, vol. 34 (2021)

3. Bichindaritz, I., Liu, G., Bartlett, C.: Survival prediction of breast cancer patient from gene methylation data with deep LSTM network and ordinal cox model. In: The Thirty-Third International Flairs Conference (2020)

4. Bichindaritz, I., Liu, G., Bartlett, C.: Integrative survival analysis of breast cancer with gene expression and DNA methylation data. Bioinformatics **37**, 2601–2608 (2021)

5. Caruana, R., Kangarloo, H., Dionisio, J.D., Sinha, U., Johnson, D.: Case-based explanationof non-case-based learning methods. In: Proceedings of the AMIA Symposium, p. 212. American Medical Informatics Association (1999)

6. Deng, M., Brägelmann, J., Kryukov, I., Saraiva-Agostinho, N., Perner, S.: FirebrowseR: an R client to the broad institute's Firehose Pipeline. Database **2017** (2017)

7. Farzindar, A.A., Kashi, A.: Multi-task survival analysis of liver transplantation using deep learning. In: The Thirty-Second International Flairs Conference (2019)

8. Eisenstadt, V., Langenhan, C., Althoff, K.-D., Dengel, A.: Improved and visually enhanced case-based retrieval of room configurations for assistance in architectural design education. In: Watson, I., Weber, R. (eds.) ICCBR 2020. LNCS (LNAI), vol. 12311, pp. 213–228. Springer, Cham (2020). https://doi.org/10.1007/978-3-030-58342-2_14

9. Hochreiter, S., Schmidhuber, J.: Long short-term memory. Neural Comput. **9**, 1735–1780 (1997)

10. Ishwaran, H., Kogalur, U.B., Blackstone, E.H., Lauer, M.S.: Random survival forests. Ann. Appl. Stat. **2**, 841–860 (2008)

11. Joshi, S., Koyejo, O., Vijitbenjaronk, W., Kim, B., Ghosh, J.: Towards realistic individual recourse and actionable explanations in black-box decision making systems. arXiv preprint arXiv:1907.09615. (2019)

12. Karmen, C., Gietzelt, M., Knaup-Gregori, P., Ganzinger, M.: Methods for a similarity measure for clinical attributes based on survival data analysis. BMC Med. Inform. Decis. Mak. **19**, 1–14 (2019)

13. Katzman, J.L., Shaham, U., Cloninger, A., Bates, J., Jiang, T., Kluger, Y.: Deep survival: a deep cox proportional hazards network. Stat **1050**, 2 (2016)

14. Katzman, J.L., Shaham, U., Cloninger, A., Bates, J., Jiang, T., Kluger, Y.: DeepSurv: personalized treatment recommender system using a Cox proportional hazards deep neural network. BMC Med. Res. Methodol. **18**, 24 (2018)

15. Kim, B., Khanna, R., Koyejo, O.O.: Examples are not enough, learn to criticize! criticism for interpretability. In: Advances in Neural Information Processing Systems, pp. 2280–2288 (2016)

16. Kim, B., Rudin, C., Shah, J.A.: The Bayesian case model: a generative approach for case-based reasoning and prototype classification. In: Advances in Neural Information Processing Systems, vol. 27 (2014)

17. Li, O., Liu, H., Chen, C., Rudin, C.: Deep learning for case-based reasoning through prototypes: a neural network that explains its predictions. In: Thirty-Second AAAI Conference on Artificial Intelligence (2018)

18. Lin, D.Y., Wei, L.-J., Ying, Z.: Checking the Cox model with cumulative sums of martingale-based residuals. Biometrika **80**, 557–572 (1993)

19. Lundberg, S.M., Lee, S.-I.: A unified approach to interpreting model predictions. In: Advances in Neural Information Processing Systems, vol. 30 (2017)

20. Lundberg, S.M., Nair, B., Vavilala, M.S., Horibe, M., Eisses, M.J., Adams, T., et al.: Explainable machine-learning predictions for the prevention of hypoxaemia during surgery. Nat. Biomed. Eng. **2**, 749–760 (2018)

21. Mayr, A., Schmid, M.: Boosting the concordance index for survival data. Ulmer Inform.-Berichte **26** (2014)

22. Ramos, B., Pereira, T., Moranguinho, J., Morgado, J., Costa, J.L., Oliveira, H.P.: An interpretable approach for lung cancer prediction and subtype classification using gene expression. In: 2021 43rd Annual International Conference of the IEEE Engineering in Medicine & Biology Society (EMBC), pp. 1707–1710. IEEE (2021)

23. Ramon, Y., Martens, D., Provost, F., Evgeniou, T.: A comparison of instance-level counterfactual explanation algorithms for behavioral and textual data: SEDC, LIME-C and SHAP-C. Adv. Data Anal. Classif. **14**(4), 801–819 (2020)

24. Ryall, S., Tabori, U., Hawkins, C.: A comprehensive review of paediatric low-grade diffuse glioma: pathology, molecular genetics and treatment. Brain Tumor Pathol. **34**(2), 51–61 (2017). https://doi.org/10.1007/s10014-017-0282-z

25. Shao, W., et al.: Ordinal multi-modal feature selection for survival analysis of early-stage renal cancer. In: Frangi, A., Schnabel, J., Davatzikos, C., Alberola-López, C., Fichtinger, G. (eds.) MICCAI 2018. LNCS, vol. 11071, pp. 648–656. Springer, Cham (2018). https://doi.org/10.1007/978-3-030-00934-2_72

26. Sy, J.P., Taylor, J.M.G.: Estimation in a Cox proportional hazards cure model. Biometrics **56**(1), 227–236 (2020)

27. Suzuki, H., Maruyama, R., Yamamoto, E., Kai, M.: DNA methylation and microRNA dysregulation in cancer. Mol. Oncol. **6**, 567–578 (2012)

28. Tibshirani, R.: The lasso method for variable selection in the Cox model. Stat. Med. **16**, 385–395 (1997)

29. Xiang, A., et al.: Comparison of the performance of neural network methods and Cox regression for censored survival data. Comput. Stat. Data Anal. **34**, 243–257 (2000)

30. Yu, K.-H., et al.: Predicting non-small cell lung cancer prognosis by fully automated microscopic pathology image features. Nat. Commun. **7**, 12474 (2016)

CBR Assisted Context-Aware Surface Realisation for Data-to-Text Generation

Ashish Upadhyay[1,2(✉)] and Stewart Massie[1]

[1] Robert Gordon University, Aberdeen, UK
{a.upadhyay,s.massie}@rgu.ac.uk
[2] J.P. Morgan Chase & Co., Glasgow, UK

Abstract. Current state-of-the-art neural systems for Data-to-Text Generation (D2T) struggle to generate content from past events with interesting insights. This is because these systems have limited access to historic data and can also hallucinate inaccurate facts in their generations. In this paper, we propose a CBR-assisted context-aware methodology for surface realisation in D2T that carefully selects important contextual data from past events and utilises a hybrid CBR and neural text generator to generate the final event summary. Through extensive experimentation on a sports domain dataset, we empirically demonstrate that our proposed method is able to accurately generate contextual content closer to human-authored summaries when compared to other state-of-the-art systems.

Keywords: Textual Case-Based Reasoning · Data-to-Text Generation · Content Selection · Surface Realisation

1 Introduction

Data-to-Text Generation (D2T) summarises complex insights extracted from non-linguistic structured data into textual format [3,10]. D2T systems address two main problems: content planning, to outline the summary plan; and surface realisation, using the plan to generate the final textual summary [7,17]. D2T problems consist of a series time-stamped events where a textual summary is written for each event. The summaries can be rich and may also contain contextual information derived from past events in the time-series [14]. For example, the excerpt of a basketball summary shown in Fig. 1, shows the contextual content derived from past event's data (bold-faced).

Current state-of-the-art neural systems despite being able to generate fluent and human-looking texts often hallucinate with inaccurate generations. They struggle to generate contextual content from past events which is often included in human generated summaries. In this paper, we present a CBR-assisted methodology for including context-aware content in the surface realisation stage.

Work done during time at Robert Gordon University, Aberdeen.

S. Massie and S. Chakraborti (Eds.): ICCBR 2023, LNAI 14141, pp. 34–49, 2023.
https://doi.org/10.1007/978-3-031-40177-0_3

TEAM	WIN	LOSS	PTS	FG_PCT	REB	AST	...
Pacers	4	6	99	42	40	17	⋯
Celtics	5	4	105	44	47	22	⋯

PLAYER	H/V	AST	REB	PTS	FG	CITY
Myles Turner	H	1	8	17	6	Indian
Thaddeus Young	H	3	8	10	5	Indian
Isaiah Thomas	V	5	0	23	4	Bosto
Kelly Olynyk	V	4	6	16	6	Bosto
...						

The Boston Celtics defeated the host Indiana Pacers 105-99 at Bankers Life Fieldhouse on Saturday. **It was the second victory over Pacers for the Celtics this season after emerging victorious in Boston 91-84 on Nov. 16**. ... Isaiah Thomas led the team in scoring, totaling 23 points and five assists on 4-of-13 shooting. Kelly Olynyk got a rare start and finished second on the team with his 16 points, six rebounds and four assists. ... Boston will return to action on Monday against the New Orleans Pelicans.

Fig. 1. Input table and output summary from a basketball game [12].

Context aware content is generated in a two stage process. First, machine learning is used to select potential context-aware content on selected themes from previously occurring events. Then a case-based approach is used to select the specific content that gets merged with a textual summary generated by a state-of-the-art neural system.

In this work, we develop full summaries including both the content planning and surface realisation stages. For content planning, we employ a previously developed approach in [13]. But have developed novel approach for surface realisation. The key contributions are:

- developing machine learning approach for selecting potential context-aware content for the selected themes;
- employing a case-based approach to identify relevant templates that are used to select the specific content examples for an event summary; and
- a human-based evaluation of our approach to measure the accuracy of the generated summaries;

The rest of the paper is organised as follows. We first present some literature that considers different approaches to D2T in the related works, and then discuss some background information. We continue to discuss our methodology in two sections: first, content selection, to outline the CBR process of selecting important and relevant historic content; and then surface realisation, the process of utilising the CBR method in generating the textual summary. The experiment setting and results are discussed next, before finally finishing with conclusions and future directions.

2   Related Works

Data-to-Text Generation is the process of summarising non-linguistic structured data into a textual summary as compared to Text-to-Text Generation that aims to generate textual summaries from linguistic input [3]. Traditional approaches to D2T have solved the task in modular fashion with multiple modules solving different sub-tasks [9]. Recent advancements in neural systems have approached D2T as an end-to-end system as well as in a modular manner but with evidence backing in favour of latter [2,7,17].

Traditional rule-based D2T systems use domain-specific engineered rules and templates in different modules while recent neural systems use data-driven learning based approach for text generation. Rule-based systems produce high quality texts in terms of accuracy but are often monotonous and lack diversity. In contrast, neural systems are able to generate fluent and human-like texts but hallucinate with inaccurate generations. On the other hand, CBR systems are able to complement both types of systems by employing a data-driven dynamic template approach that is able to generate accurate as well as fluent and diverse texts [13,15].

There has been some work that consider the historic aspects of time-stamped event summaries in D2T domains. Authors in [14] propose a typology of content type in human authored D2T summaries and empirically demonstrate the struggle of neural systems in generating content of historic type. Few earlier works, both in neural as well as traditional systems, have tried to include some form of historic content in final event summary with different methods [4,11]. However, these still struggle with the fundamental problems of accuracy vs diversity trade-off.

In our work, we propose a method of content selection for selecting important historic events that can be utilised by any neural system. We then propose a CBR-inspired surface realisation method that uses both neural and CBR systems in a collaborative manner to improve the accuracy of the generations without harming the fluency.

3   Background

The content of the event summaries generated from D2T problems can typically be broken down and classified into three categories: **Intra-Event Basic (B)**, facts directly copied from the current event's input data; **Intra-Event Complex (C)**, facts derived from the current event's input data; **Inter-Event (I)**, facts copied or derived from other events' data (see Fig. 3) [14].

The process of generating an event summary consists of multiple stages: content planning, planning the layout of summary's content; content selection, selecting important content from the input data to display in the summary according to the plan; surface realisation, taking the selected important content in accordance with the content plan and generating textual summary.

The content plan is a list of placeholders denoting the organisation of the summary, while the content selection selects a subset of data (either verbatim or derived) from the input data. These steps have been usually performed separately, however recent neural models have also combined: either all three in a single step [6,8,17]; or content planning and selection into one step and surface realisation into another [5,7].

Authors in [13] proposed a CBR approach to content planning in D2T where the plan (the case solution) is a sequence of concepts represented by the sentence

Sentence	Entities	Content Types	Concept
<u>Sixers</u> came out in domination mode in the third and outscored <u>Bulls</u>, 37-18, to take a 102-76 lead heading into the fourth.	Team, Team	Complex	$T\&T - C$
<u>Bulls</u> put up a fight in the fourth but the <u>Sixers</u> were able to cruise to their first win of the season without a problem.	Team, Team	Complex, Inter	$T\&T - C\&I$
<u>Joel Embiid</u> led the <u>Sixers</u> with 30 points on 9-of-14 shooting, in 33 minutes of action.	Player, Team	Basic, Complex	$P\&T - B\&C$
⋮	⋮	⋮	⋮
<u>Bobby Portis</u> is averaging 20 points and 10 rebounds on the season.	Player	Inter	$P - I$

Content-Plan: { $T\&T - C$, $T\&T - C\&I$, $P\&T - B\&C$, $\cdots$, $P - I$ }

Fig. 2. Content-plan of a summary taken from SportSett dataset.

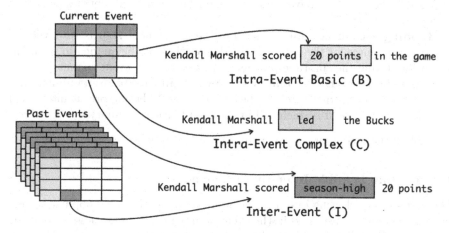

Fig. 3. Content Types in a human written D2T summary.

structure of the summary. Figure 2 shows the content plan extracted from a basketball summary using this approach. The content plan is a list of concepts, each denoting a sentence structure conveying the entity and content type to describe in that sentence. As denoted, the first sentence in the summary should describe two team entities with intra-event complex type content.

In this paper, we take the content plan generated from this approach and propose a method to generate the final event summary according to the plan. The method works in two stages: first, content selection, where we use a novel technique to select important historical data in order to generate inter-event type content; and second, surface realisation, where we use a hybrid method of neural and CBR systems for text generation.

4   Content Selection

Content Selection is an important stage in the data-to-text generation process. It is the process of selecting a subset of input data, either verbatim or derived, to include in the final summary. To generate any inter-event content in the final summary, a D2T system needs to process data from all previous events in the event time-series where any entity from the current event was involved. This massively increases the amount of data that needs to be processed by the system during run-time.

In this section, we describe our methodology to organise and generate all possible inter-event (historic) content from the historic events and then select the important ones to be included in the summary. This method of content-selection involves the following steps:

- **Finding Possible Inter-Event Themes**: The first step is to identify the possible themes that convey inter-event information about entities present in the event.
- **Building Resources for these Themes**: The next step is to develop a parallel resource for these inter-event themes that can be queried to get information during the run-time processing to generate an event summary.
- **Select the Inter-Event Themes to include in the summary**: Finally, for each summary, during run-time processing, select the important inter-event features that should be included in the final textual summary.

Each of these content selection steps are now discussed in more detail.

4.1   Finding Possible Inter-Event Themes

The first step in selecting inter-event content is to identify some popular themes that are commonly discussed in the event summaries. To find these we perform some analysis on the data by applying the following steps:

- break the summaries into sentences and then classify the sentences into their content-types (as in Fig. 3);
- take the sentences classified as containing 'inter-event' and divide them into different entity types (in sports domains: players and teams)
- apply topic modelling on sentences from each entity type and select the top topics;

By this process, we select a dominant topic from each of the entity type (player and team), which are:

1. **Players' Average Stats**: player A is averaging X points in last Y games;
2. **Teams' Win/Loss Streak**: this was team B's j^{th} straight loss/win;

In our topic modelling, we also found some other common themes such as: player's total double-double scores[1] of the season; or, team's standing in the

---

[1] https://en.wikipedia.org/wiki/Double-double.

league/conference. However, we decide to experiment with only two themes selected above to keep the problem complexity simple and evaluate the idea properly.

4.2 Building Resources for These Themes

Once the inter-event themes have been identified, the next step is to build some parallel resources that can be used during run-time to query and get the information about a theme for an entity in an event. This parallel resource will store the inter-event information relating to the theme for each entity in the event.

We first identify a few inter-event features that will be used to represent the entities along with their existing intra-event features. For the player average theme, the features chosen are: *average/total X in last Y games*, where $X \in$ (points, rebounds, assists, blocks, steals) and $Y \in (2, 10)$. For the team streak theme, the features selected are: streak count, and streak type, where streak count $\in (0, 82)$ and streak type can be win or loss.

After identifying these features, for each entity from every event in the dataset, we generate the values for these identified inter-event features and store them into a separate parallel resource for each theme (currently json, but a better choice could be a relational database). The process of generating the values for these features is as follows:

- **Filter**: filter all the events from time-series containing a given entity and happening before the current event;
- **Sort**: sort these events based on the timestamp in ascending order of time delta, where the most recent event is the closest; and
- **Aggregate**: aggregate all the relevant values of the entity feature into the identified inter-event feature;

As an example, consider an event which is the 25th match for player Kevin Durant. To calculate his average points in last 5 games: we first filter all the matches from this season in which Durant played and the match happened before this one; we then sort these matches based on their date and then average the number of points made by Durant in the most recent 5 games.

4.3 Selecting Important Attributes

After building the parallel resource, the next step is to select the inter-event features from each theme that could be included in the final summary. This is done by training a binary classifier for each theme whose task is: given an inter-event feature for an inter-event theme, classify if it should be added to the final summary or not.

To build a theme classifier, an important step is to identify attributes needed to train these classifiers. Through our domain knowledge, we identify the following attributes for the two themes:

- Player average theme

- **player name** - converted into a number using label encoding;
- **player popularity** - calculated as the ratio of number of game summaries mentioning the player to the number of games the player has played;
- **record type** - label encoded value for point, rebound, assist, steal or block;
- **last Y games** - number of games totalling or averaging for (2 to 10)
- **value** - actual value of the inter-event feature
- **average or total** - a binary attribute denoting if this average score or total score over last Y games

– Team streak theme

- **team name** - converted into a number using label encoding;
- **team popularity** - ratio of the number of sentences mentioning the team to the number of sentences in the summary averaged over toal number of games in the season;
- **streak count** - count of the streak;
- **streak type** - a binary value denoting if this is a win or loss;
- **broken streak count** - denoting if the team has been on a different streak than current result (if there has been a winning streak before if the current one was the lost game)
- **broken streak type** - type of the broken streak

We build the train and test set for these theme classifiers using the train and validation set of D2T dataset respectively.

5   Surface Realisation

Now with the important inter-event content selected, we move on to using this content in accordance to the plan derived from [13] to generate the final summary. This stage of text generation in D2T is known as surface realisation. Earlier studies have shown that neural networks are capable of producing good content for intra-event types (both basic and complex), however struggle in producing content of inter-event type [14]. Thus in this work, we propose two alternative methods to improve the inter-event content of summaries generated by neural systems.

– **Input Augmentation**: the first approach is to augment the input of neural system by adding the content plan and selected inter-event content to its input and train the model to generate summaries with better coverage; and
– **Post-Editing**: the second approach is to further post-edit the output of neural system by identifying the sentences with inter-event content and replacing those with sentences generated using the CBR-D2T dynamic template method from [15];

These two approaches to providing inter-event content are now discussed in more detail.

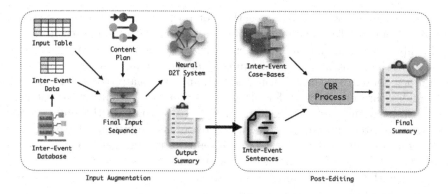

Fig. 4. Surface Realisation process with post-editing.

5.1 Problem Representation Augmentation

In the first stage, we augment the problem representation from the current event with the data associated with the machine learning identified potential context-aware content for the selected themes from previously occurring events. This augmented problem representation is the input to the neural D2T system employed in our approach.

The current state-of-the-art in neural D2T uses a pipeline approach with separate planning and realisation phases [7]. The planning module outputs a sequence of paragraph plans, known as a macro plan, which is similar to the concepts described in Sect. 3 except they only contain the entity information and not the content type information. These paragraph plans also only contain the intra-event data for the entities. This macro plan is then fed to the surface realiser, which is a sequence-to-sequence model, to produce the final neural summary.

In our approach, we generate a similar macro-plan but which follows the content plan created by [13]. For each concept in the plan with intra-event type content, we keep the paragraph plan the same as before, i.e., only contain the current event data of the entity. However, for each inter-event concept in the plan, we append the inter-event features with their values in the paragraph sequence which were classified as 'yes' in the content selection process described in Sect. 4. Finally, this input sequence of paragraph plans is fed into the neural surface realiser to produce the textual summary.

The intuition here is that this process of augmenting the problem representation will provide the neural D2T system with the opportunity to generate context-aware content derived from previously occurring events. A pictorial representation of the process is shown in Fig. 4.

5.2 Post-Editing

Even with the input augmentation, it is difficult to control the learning of neural systems and it is possible to still have inaccuracies in the generated summary.

Thus, to this end, we propose a method of post-editing the neural system's summary using a CBR-D2T method of dynamic templating proposed in [15].

In this post-editing method, the neural network summary is broken into sentences and then sentences identified in content plan as inter-event are replaced with a new sentence generated using the dynamic template CBR-D2T method. We build separate case-bases for player inter-event and team inter-event concepts. Cases in the case-base contain inter-event features on the problem-side and an associated inter-event content template as a solution. The process of building a case-base and generating a new sentence for a target problem is same as in [15]. The post-editing process is described pictorially in Fig. 4. The idea here is that the output summaries should have similar distribution of content types as found in human written summaries.

6   Experiment Setup

We now define the experiment setup used to evaluate our proposed method.

6.1   Dataset

The SportSett dataset [12] of NBA matches is used to evaluate the proposed content selection and surface realisation algorithms[2]. Each match from the dataset contains a textual summary as the output and the associated match statistics, with the box- and line-scores, as the problem input. There is a temporal aspect involved here, as future matches should not be available to the learner. Hence the training set contains the earlier matches from the 2014, 2015 and 2016 seasons (total of 4775, some matches from the 2016 season have more than one summary) while the validation and test sets contain matches from the 2017 and 2018 seasons (1230 matches each) respectively.

The data for training the theme classifier for content selection, is build using the train and validation sets of SportSett. For each theme, if its inter-event features are included in a summary for an entity of the event, then its label is given as 1 otherwise 0. We use samples from the training set of SportSett for building the train set of the theme classifier while the validation set is used for building the test set for the classifiers (see the statistics of dataset used for building inter-event theme classifiers in Table 1).

6.2   Content Selection Models

We experiment with several binary classifiers for building the theme classifiers for content selection: Logisitic Regression (**LR**), k-Nearest Neighbours (**kNN**), Support Vector Machines (**SVM**), Multi-Layer Perceptron (**MLP**), and Random Forest (**RF**)[3].

---

[2] we use the GEM version of the dataset from https://huggingface.co/datasets/GEM/sportsett_basketball.

[3] these models are trained with https://scikit-learn.org/stable/.

Table 1. Dataset stats for building theme classifiers.

Label	Player Average		Team Streak	
	Train Size	Test Size	Train Size	Test Size
Positive	3790	65	1707	488
Negative	73850	1470	5673	1972
Total	77640	1535	7380	2460

6.3 Surface Realisation Systems

For surface realisation, we select the current state-of-the-art macro-plan model (MP) [7] as the benchmark to compare our methods. We use the same macro-plan model for input augmentation and the post-editing methodologies. This is a pipeline-based neural network model with two components: a content planner, which combines planning and selection and is based on [16] that takes the event input data and generates a content plan (also referred to as a macro-plan); and a surface realiser, which is a sequence-to-sequence neural model with a Bi-LSTM encoder and an LSTM decoder that takes the macro-plan as input and generates the textual summary as output.

Thus, in our experiments we have three model's outputs to compare against each other:

– MP_{base}: the base MP model of [7] with the authors input and training configuration. We also use the original content planning method proposed by their authors;
– MP_{aug}: this model is the surface realiser from MP_{base} that takes the augmented input as described in Sect. 5. The augmented input is derived from taking the content plan from [13] and adding the inter-event content selected (using Sect. 4 method) to other intra-event content generated from the current event's data; and
– MP_{pe}: this is the post-editing model which utilises the CBR-D2T method from [15] to post edit the output of the MP_{aug} model.

6.4 Evaluation Metrics

For content selection, basic classification metrics such as: Precision, Recall, and F1 score are used. Since the dataset is imbalanced, we report the marco-average of these metrics and use them for model selection.

For surface realisation, the following automated metrics are used:

– **Extractive Evaluation**: Inspired by information extraction evaluations from [17], we use a set of regular expressions to extract inter-event tuples from the system generations. These extracted tuples are then matched with the input data to evaluate the performance of text generation model;

Table 2. Performance of Theme Classifiers for inter-event content selection.

Model	Player Average				Team Streak			
	Accuracy	F1	Precision	Recall	Accuracy	F1	Precision	Recall
LR	**95.77**	48.92	47.85	50	80.69	54.19	69.08	54.72
kNN	94.79	53.20	56.68	52.43	75.41	55.07	56.72	54.74
SVM	**95.77**	48.92	47.88	50	80.20	44.71	90.1	50.1
MLP	94.20	**60.49**	**61.74**	**59.48**	**80.85**	51.72	**72.61**	53.44
RF	94.85	57.09	61.44	55.41	79.07	**58.06**	63.42	**57.18**

– **Content Type Distribution and Concept Selection**: we also check the content type distribution of summaries generated from these models using the method proposed in [14]. The concept selection abilities of these models is also evaluated in accordance with the content selection process described in [13]. Here we check the precision, recall, f1, and DLD [1] scores of concepts selected in each summary against the human written gold summaries. A concept denotes the sentences structure identifying the type of entity and content described in the sentence.

We also used human evaluation to measure the accuracy of inter-event content in the system generated summaries. We utilise the human evaluation method used in previous research in the field [5,7,8,17]. In this evaluation, the human annotators are given some sentences from a summary along with the input data given to the system and asked to report the number of supporting and contradicting claims made in those sentences.

7   Results

The results are discussed in two parts: first, we briefly discuss the results of content selection, where we identify the best learning algorithm for building a theme classifier; and second, we discuss the results of surface realisation experiments, where we compare the effectiveness of the different methods proposed for adding inter-event content to the summaries.

7.1   Content Selection

The performance of theme classifiers built using different learning algorithms is shown in Table 2. We report the macro averaged scores of precision, recall and F1 metrics along-with accuracy of the classifiers. It can be observed that despite a higher accuracy, the other metrics have lower scores. This is expected as the dataset for these theme classifiers is imbalanced towards the negative class. Still we can see learners, such as MLP and RF, achieve around 60% for F1 scores. Since there will be another training with the neural network to generate the final summary by using the human written summaries, these results can be accepted we select MLP as the Player Average Theme classifier and RF as the Team Streak Theme classifier.

Table 3. RegEx evaluation results.

Systems	Player Average			Team Streak		
	%Correct	#Supp.	#Contr.	%Correct	#Supp.	#Contr.
MP_{base}	20	4	16	0	0	0
MP_{aug}	42.65	29	39	0	0	1
MP_{pe}	63.41	1813	1046	38.04	35	57

7.2 Surface Realisation

Extractive Evaluations: We start with discussing the results from regular expression evaluation of the surface realisation outputs. The evaluation consists of a few regular expressions per theme that count the mention of inter-event content in the generated summaries. These expressions extract a tuple of information in the form of (*entity_name, value, inter_event_feature_name*) and match these with the input to count the number of supporting and contradicting claims. For example, for the given sentence - *"Kevin Durant is averaging 14 points over his last 5 outings"*; the extracted tuple would be - (*Kevin_Durant, 14, AVG_PTS_LAST_5_GAMES*). This would then be matched to the input data to identify if this is supporting or contradicting claim. The results from this experiment for both themes is shown in Table 3. The column name '#Supp.' shows the number of supporting claims, '#Contr.' shows the number of contradicting claims, while '%Correct' is the percentage of correct/supporting claims out of total extracted claims.

The results clearly demonstrate the benefit of including inter-event content to the input data in order to include better inter-event content in the summaries. We see that MP_{base} only generates 20 inter-event examples for the player average theme with only 4 of those being correct. It also doesn't generate any inter-event content for team streak theme at all. Next, we see a good performance gain with MP_{aug} when the input of model is augmented with the selected inter-event content. This model generates 68 player average theme claims out of which 42% are correct. However, it still doesn't generate any supporting team streak theme claims. This suggests that it is difficult to make neural models generate a specific type of content if there aren't sufficient examples of it in the training set. Finally, we observe the MP_{pe} model's performance and immediately notice massive improvements across both themes. This model is able to generate around 2.9k player average theme claims, out of which 63% are also correct. For team streak theme as well, the model is generating 90+ claims with 38% of them being correct.

Content Type Distribution and Concept Selection: Next we investigate the content type distribution of summaries generated from these different systems. Figure 5 shows the percentage of sentences with different content types in summaries generated from the three systems and the human written gold

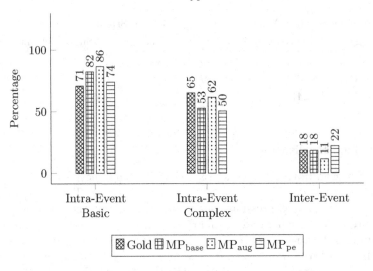

Content Type Distribution

Fig. 5. Content-Type distribution of summaries from different systems.

Table 4. Concept selection ability of different systems.

CBR-Plan$_{euc}$	CS			CO	Length
	F1	Precision	Recall	DLD	Avg
Gold	-	-	-	-	12.76
MP$_{base}$	28.63	33.13	25.2	8.8	9.71
MP$_{aug}$	46.18	33.82	39.04	13.03	9.35
MP$_{pe}$	40.71	29.88	34.47	9.49	9.37

summaries[4]. MP$_{pe}$ produces most amount of inter-event content, even higher than Gold. However, MP$_{base}$ is also able to generate equal amount of inter-event content as Gold but most of which is incorrect as identified in extractive evaluation results. We see that MP$_{aug}$ has the lowest amount of inter-event sentences despite having more content relating to inter-event themes as described in Table 3. This suggests that the MP$_{base}$ also generates some sentences with inter-event content that are not identified by regex evaluations. A quick look to the generated summaries will show that sentences such as: 'this was player X's first game after missing Y games due to injury'. These sentences, even though classified as inter-event, do not contain any information to be easily verified via automated metrics or even quick human evaluation.

---

[4] It is to note that a sentence can have multiple types of content, thus adding the percentage of different content types will not be equal to 100.

Table 5. Human evaluation results along with BLEU scores of different systems.

Systems	#Support (↑)	#Contra (↓)	BLEU (↑)
MP$_{\text{base}}$	0	3.75	17.6
MP$_{\text{aug}}$	0.42	1.57	15.76
MP$_{\text{pe}}$	1.22	0	15.08

We also investigate the content planning ability of the three systems using their generated summaries as evaluation method described in [13]. This method extracts a concept list (as shown in Fig. 2) from a system generated summary and then compares it with the concept list from the gold summary. In Table 4, we show the F1, Precision, and Recall scores to compare the concepts selected in system generations, while DLD (edit-distance) scores to compare the ordering of these concept lists. We can see that both the MP$_{\text{aug}}$ and MP$_{\text{pe}}$ systems are able to improve all four scores when compared to MP$_{\text{base}}$. This suggests that adding inter-event content to the input data helps in improving the organisation of a generated summary that is more similar to the human written one.

7.3 Human Evaluation of Surface Realisation

Although automated evaluations are quick and easy to obtain, they may fail sometimes, particularly on new or edge-cases. Due to the richness of vocabulary of sports domain summaries, it is helpful to have some human judgement to support the automated evaluations. We randomly select 20 summaries generated from each system and then select at-most three sentences classified as across event.

We ask the annotators to count the number of supporting vs contradicting predictions, for which the results are shown in Table 5. We observe that MP_{pe} has the highest number of supporting facts, 1.22, with no contradicting facts in its generated summaries. Next we see that MP_{aug} has higher number of supporting facts as compared to MP_{base}, 0.42 against 0, while also having lower number of contradicting facts, 1.57 against 3.75, respectively. This can be expected as the MP_{pe} is using a CBR based dynamic template system to produce accurate texts. On the other hand, MP_{base} and MP_{aug} are relying on the generation process of neural systems which can be prone to hallucinations. The systems with contextual information also maintain similar fluency in their generations compared to their counterparts, as demonstrated in the BLEU scores.

These results prove that providing contextual information from past events to neural systems improve the quality of their generated summaries. The generations are much closer to the human written summaries in terms of content type and content plan, and are also more accurate without sacrificing fluency.

8   Conclusion

Current state-of-the-art D2T systems, despite achieving good performance, struggle to generate accurate context-aware content derived from past events. In this paper, we propose a CBR-assisted methodology for editing the summaries produced by neural D2T systems in order to produce summaries with both accurate inter-event content and content distributions similar to that found in human generated solutions.

A two-staged approach requires first content selection and then surface realisation. For content selection, machine learning is used to identify potential inter-event content whose associated data augments the current event's problem representation. For surface realisation, the output summary of a neural D2T system is edited with inter-event content identified using a CBR-D2T approach to produce the final event summary.

Extensive experimentation with both automated and human evaluation is performed on a sports domain dataset. Results demonstrate that our method is able to produce summaries that are more accurate than other neural systems. On average more than twice as many supporting facts and no contradicting errors in an inter-event sentence. The summaries generated from our system are also closer to human written summaries in terms of their content plan and content type distribution.

References

1. Brill, E., Moore, R.C.: An improved error model for noisy channel spelling correction. In: Proceedings of the 38th Annual Meeting of the Association for Computational Linguistics, pp. 286–293 (2000)
2. Ferreira, T.C., van der Lee, C., van Miltenburg, E., Krahmer, E.: Neural data-to-text generation: a comparison between pipeline and end-to-end architectures. In: Proceedings of the 2019 Conference on Empirical Methods in Natural Language Processing and the 9th International Joint Conference on Natural Language Processing (EMNLP-IJCNLP), pp. 552–562 (2019)
3. Gatt, A., Krahmer, E.: Survey of the state of the art in natural language generation: core tasks, applications and evaluation. J. Artif. Intell. Res. **61**, 65–170 (2018)
4. Gong, H., Feng, X., Qin, B., Liu, T.: Table-to-text generation with effective hierarchical encoder on three dimensions (row, column and time). In: Proceedings of the 2019 Conference on Empirical Methods in Natural Language Processing and the 9th International Joint Conference on Natural Language Processing (EMNLP-IJCNLP), pp. 3143–3152. Association for Computational Linguistics, Hong Kong, China (2019). https://aclanthology.org/D19-1310
5. Puduppully, R., Dong, L., Lapata, M.: Data-to-text generation with content selection and planning. In: The Thirty-Third AAAI Conference on Artificial Intelligence, AAAI 2019, pp. 6908–6915 (2019)
6. Puduppully, R., Dong, L., Lapata, M.: Data-to-text generation with entity modeling. In: Proceedings of the 57th Annual Meeting of the Association for Computational Linguistics, pp. 2023–2035 (2019)
7. Puduppully, R., Lapata, M.: Data-to-text generation with macro planning. Trans. Assoc. Comput. Linguist. **9**, 510–527 (2021)

8. Rebuffel, C., Soulier, L., Scoutheeten, G., Gallinari, P.: A hierarchical model for data-to-text generation. In: Jose, J.M., et al. (eds.) ECIR 2020. LNCS, vol. 12035, pp. 65–80. Springer, Cham (2020). https://doi.org/10.1007/978-3-030-45439-5_5

9. Reiter, E.: An architecture for data-to-text systems. In: Proceedings of the 11th European Workshop on Natural Language Generation, pp. 97–104 (2007)

10. Reiter, E., Dale, R.: Building Natural Language Generation Systems. Cambridge University Press, Cambridge (2000)

11. Robin, J., McKeown, K.: Empirically designing and evaluating a new revision-based model for summary generation. Artif. Intell. **85**(1), 135–179 (1996). https://www.sciencedirect.com/science/article/pii/0004370295001255

12. Thomson, C., Reiter, E., Sripada, S.: SportSett: basketball - a robust and maintainable data-set for natural language generation. In: Proceedings of the Workshop on Intelligent Information Processing and Natural Language Generation (2020)

13. Upadhyay, A., Massie, S.: A case-based approach for content planning in data-to-text generation. In: Case-Based Reasoning Research and Development: 30th International Conference, ICCBR 2022, Nancy, France, 12–15 September 2022, Proceedings, pp. 380–394. Springer, Cham (2022). https://doi.org/10.1007/978-3-031-14923-8_25

14. Upadhyay, A., Massie, S.: Content type profiling of data-to-text generation datasets. In: Proceedings of the 29th International Conference on Computational Linguistics, pp. 5770–5782. International Committee on Computational Linguistics, Gyeongju, Republic of Korea (2022). https://aclanthology.org/2022.coling-1.507

15. Upadhyay, A., Massie, S., Singh, R.K., Gupta, G., Ojha, M.: A case-based approach to data-to-text generation. In: Sánchez-Ruiz, A.A., Floyd, M.W. (eds.) ICCBR 2021. LNCS (LNAI), vol. 12877, pp. 232–247. Springer, Cham (2021). https://doi.org/10.1007/978-3-030-86957-1_16

16. Vinyals, O., Fortunato, M., Jaitly, N.: Pointer networks. In: Cortes, C., Lawrence, N., Lee, D., Sugiyama, M., Garnett, R. (eds.) Advances in Neural Information Processing Systems, vol. 28 (2015)

17. Wiseman, S., Shieber, S., Rush, A.: Challenges in data-to-document generation. In: Proceedings of the 2017 Conference on Empirical Methods in Natural Language Processing, pp. 2253–2263 (2017)

Representation and Similarity

Explanation of Similarities in Process-Oriented Case-Based Reasoning by Visualization

Alexander Schultheis[1]([✉]) [iD], Maximilian Hoffmann[1,2] [iD], Lukas Malburg[1,2] [iD], and Ralph Bergmann[1,2] [iD]

[1] German Research Center for Artificial Intelligence (DFKI), Branch University of Trier, Behringstraße 21, 54296 Trier, Germany
{alexander.schultheis,maximilian.hoffmann,lukas.malburg,
ralph.bergmann}@dfki.de
[2] Artificial Intelligence and Intelligent Information Systems, University of Trier, 54296 Trier, Germany
{hoffmannm,malburgl,bergmann}@uni-trier.de
http://www.wi2.uni-trier.de

Abstract. Modeling similarity measures in Case-Based Reasoning is a knowledge-intensive, demanding, and error-prone task even for domain experts. Visualizations offer support for users, but are currently only available for certain subdomains and case representations. Currently, there are only visualizations that can be used for local attributes or specific case representations. However, there is no possibility to visualize similarities between complete processes accordingly so far, although complex domains may be present. Therefore, an extension of existing approaches or the design of new suitable concepts for this application domain is necessary. The contribution of this work is to enable a more profound understanding of similarity for knowledge engineers who create a similarity model and support them in this task by using visualization methods in *Process-Oriented Case-Based Reasoning* (POCBR). For this purpose, we present related approaches and evaluate them against derived requirements for visualizations in POCBR. On this basis, suitable visualizations are further developed as well as new approaches designed. Three such visualizations are created: (1) a graph mapping approach, (2) a merge graph, and (3) a visualization based on heatmaps. An evaluation of these approaches has been performed based on the requirements in which the domain experts determine the graph-mapping visualization as best-suited for engineering of similarity models.

Keywords: Visualization · Explanation · Similarity · Process-Orien-ted Case-Based Reasoning · Explainable Case-Based Reasoning

1 Introduction

In *Case-Based Reasoning* (CBR) [1], cases are retrieved by approximating the a-posteriori utility of a case with mostly knowledge-intensive a-priori similarity

S. Massie and S. Chakraborti (Eds.): ICCBR 2023, LNAI 14141, pp. 53–68, 2023.
https://doi.org/10.1007/978-3-031-40177-0_4

measures [5,37]. Developing such similarity measures can be performed manually by a domain expert or learned automatically, e. g., with machine learning methods [18,29]. Whereas automatically generated similarity measures limit the knowledge acquisition and modeling effort, the entire required knowledge cannot always be learned and, thus, integrated into the similarity measure. For this reason, similarity measures are mainly created manually by a knowledge engineer, based on information from domain experts. However, this knowledge-intensive acquisition process is a demanding and error-prone task, since the knowledge from the domain expert must be acquired, transferred, and, finally, encoded by the knowledge engineer during similarity measure development. This especially holds for complex and deeply nested measures based on the local-global principle. For instance, a global similarity measure usually aggregates individual local similarities between several attributes, which, in turn, use further similarity measures for different data types [5], so that this nested structure can be cluttered for a knowledge engineer. In this context, a profound understanding of the similarity and its aggregation results in a better explainability that increases trust and transparency of the Case-Based Reasoning (CBR) system [12]. Although similarity-based retrieval is one of the most important phases in CBR, and, thus, similarity measures should be well-defined, the development process is only weakly supported by current research (e. g., [3]). Therefore, the knowledge engineer should be supported in manual modeling of complex and knowledge-intensive similarity measures. An understanding of the similarity is necessary for this, including both the value of the similarity itself and its calculation.

One approach for making similarities more accessible and providing confidence in CBR applications is *visualization* [3]. Visualizations map discrete data to a visual representation and support users in problem-solving [26]. In the context of *Explainable Case-Based Reasoning* (XCBR), they are successfully used in CBR domains to investigate similarities between simple case representations [39]. Of particular interest is to make complex similarities, e. g., based on nested similarity measures, accessible using visualizations. Another application area is *Process-Oriented Case-Based Reasoning* (POCBR) [31] in which CBR methods are applied to procedural experiential knowledge. Cases in Case-Based Reasoning (POCBR) are expressed as complex graph representations, and similarity assessment is mainly performed by aggregating several local similarities on a global level. Especially these complex case representations are currently not supported by any visualization method. For this purpose, this paper presents how visualizations can be used in POCBR and, in general, for more complex case representations that go beyond attribute-value-based cases. To determine the eligibility of a visualization for this purpose, we survey fundamental requirements from CBR developers. We present three visualization methods for complex cases in POCBR based on these requirements, namely a *Graph Mapping*, a *Merge Graph*, and a *Heatmap* approach. We compare them regarding the requirements in an experimental evaluation to validate their suitability. The key question for CBR developers in this evaluation is how well which requirement is being fulfilled by the corresponding visualization method and, whether, the approaches provide a better explainability of similarities for knowledge engineers.

The paper is structured as follows: First, an overview of the necessary foundations of POCBR is provided, and related work is discussed (see Sect. 2). Then requirements for visualizations in POCBR are established by interviews with experts and from literature (see Sect. 3). Based on these requirements, applicable approaches from the literature are examined and adapted for the use in POCBR (see Sect. 4). The suitability of the approaches is determined based on a user evaluation (see Sect. 5). Finally, the paper is concluded and areas for future work are discussed (see Sect. 6).

2   Foundations and Related Work

In this section, the semantic workflow graph representation as well as the similarity assessment between such workflow graphs is introduced (see Sect. 2.1). Afterward, the research topic of this work is differentiated to other works, presenting approaches that are thematically relevant or not applicable w. r. t. this question (see Sect. 2.2 and Sect. 2.3).

2.1   Semantic Workflow Representation and Similarity Assessment

The proposed visualizations address process-oriented cases. In the research area of POCBR, various types of graphs exist [20] as well as multiple applicable similarity measures for these [9,34]. To be able to perform the requirements analysis and design the visualizations, a concrete form of case representation must be addressed. So, this paper uses semantic workflow graphs represented as *NEST* graphs [7] for this purpose and aims at similarity measures based on graph matching.

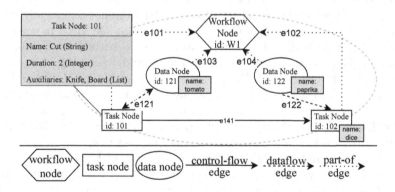

Fig. 1. An Exemplary Cooking Recipe represented as *NEST* Graph.

A NEST graph is a semantically labeled directed graph [7] represented as a quadruple $W = (N, E, S, T)$, whereby N is a set of nodes and $E \subseteq N \times N$ a set of edges. $T : N \cup E \rightarrow \Omega$ assigns a type from Ω to each node and each edge. Furthermore, $S : N \cup E \rightarrow \Sigma$ allocates a semantic description from a semantic metadata language Σ to each node and edge and annotates the graph structure with semantic knowledge. Each NEST graph is part of a case base, which is denoted as $W \in CB$. In Fig. 1, an exemplary NEST graph is shown that represents a simple cooking recipe with different node and edge types and an exemplary semantic description.

For the similarity computation between two such NEST graphs, suitable similarity measures for this case representation are required. Bergmann and Gil [7] have developed a similarity measure that computes this similarity based on the local-global principle [5,10]. Here, the global similarity is composed of the local similarities computed between the individual graph elements, based on corresponding similarity measures [7]. The local similarity is always 0.0 if the types of the graph elements to be compared are not identical. If the types are equal, a similarity calculation is initiated, which calculates a similarity value based on the semantic descriptions. When computing the global similarity, several possible mappings of the query and case graphs to each other exist. To determine the suitability of a case, the highest possible global similarity value must be calculated, which is based on the mapping that leads to the highest local similarities. This mapping is found by conducting an A* search in the solution space, for which various heuristics are used. An optimized form of this search procedure is presented by Zeyen and Bergmann [44]. The described similarity assessment based on the local-global principle and the large search space of possible mappings of graph items make it difficult for a knowledge engineer to understand the composition of a similarity value on a conceptual level.

2.2 Distinction from Related Explanation Approaches

This contribution uses visualizations as a method to explain similarities in CBR applications. Thereby, the proposed approach differs from thematically related work in the area of Explainable Case-Based Reasoning (XCBR). In some publications of this research field, CBR is utilized as a method to explain other artificial intelligence approaches, such as Kenny and Keane [21], Nugent and Cunningham [33], Gates et al. [15] or Recio-García et al. [36]. In other XCBR work, visualizations are used to explain similarity measures, as in Batyrshin et al. [4]. This work differs in that it is not the measure itself that is to be visualized, but the individual similarity value. Furthermore, visualizations for similarity distributions are used, for example, in case bases, as in Rostami et al. [38] or Namee and Delany [32]. Other works deal with visualizing retrieval results, such as Lamy et al. [23] or Paola and Bach [27]. These approaches visualize the similarity distribution in a case base or from a query to the best retrieval results, but they do not offer an explanation for the respective similarities, which are considered in this work.

2.3   Approaches for Visualizing Similarities

The following methods visualize similarities in CBR or between graphs and are, thus, identified as thematically relevant approaches. Bach and Mork [3] examine visualizations of similarities in CBR. The focus of their work is the visualization of similarity measures during the retrieval phase. In the underlying similarity computation, the local-global principle is applied, to which this approach is restricted. Massie et al. [28] address explanations in CBR by visualization. They aim to extend the explanation provided by the CBR system in the form of a single case with a similarity value to make the knowledge more accessible to users. For this purpose, they visualize the similarities of cases representing lists of numerical values in coordinate diagrams. The merge graph designed by Andrews et al. [2] stems from the field of Business Process Visualization. A merged graph is computed from two input graphs and the corresponding similarities between the graph nodes, allowing a visual comparison of the two graphs. For the merging procedure, it is required that the two graphs are pretty similar to have useful overlaps in the merged graph. The authors also mention that this approach is not infinitely scalable and that the computation of the graph layout results in a high computational complexity. Ivanov et al. [19] deal with an automatic comparison of business processes in the field of Business Process Management. They present a tool that can be used to detect and visualize discrepancies in two processes to check them for conformance. It can also help to find duplicates or to classify a new process. When mapping two processes onto each other, the similarity can be computed as a label match, a structural similarity or a graph edit distance. Also related is the general approach of heatmaps [42], which is a data visualization technique that uses colors and their intensity to visually indicate clusters in a two-dimensional table. These are used in CBR to show how the similarity values of one case relate to all other cases in the case base [30]. The use of such heatmaps can also be adapted to other domains. The approaches presented in this section are evaluated in Sect. 4.1 based on the elicited requirements.

3   Requirements for Visualization

To review the related approaches presented in Sect. 2.3 regarding their suitability to be used in POCBR, a list of requirements is needed. These requirements can also be used to derive necessary extensions for the existing approaches or to provide a guideline for the creation of a new visualization technique. Initially, established requirements are identified by a literature research and adapted for the application area of this contribution. Due to the small number of publications in this area, we derived further requirements from researchers, who are involved in this area, through a focus group interview [35]. We conducted this method of elicitation with a group of five people. First, they were confronted with the requirements that are collected based on the literature. Then, two visualization approaches from the literature according to Bach and Mork [3] and Andrews et al. [2] (see Sect. 2.3) were presented, whereupon the researchers had to justify why they found the approach suitable or not suitable in detail. In the interview, the participants discussed their answers, but overall agreed on the desired requirements.

Based on the literature review and the focus group interview, the following seven requirements are derived:

Req. 1 Explanation for Resulting Similarity: The visualization should comprehensibly justify the calculated similarity value and its composition. This is inspired by the goal of justification according to Sørmo et al. [41] as well as by the requirements for XCBR systems of Hall et al. [16].

Req. 2 Representation of Process Data: The visualization must support a case representation of processes, in the context of this contribution, as semantic graphs [7]. In addition to representing processes, the visualization approach must be able to show the similarities between them. So, the similarity measure used at the global level for process-oriented cases must be included in the visualization.

Req. 3 Representation of Similarities Between Graph Components: The visualization should include the local similarities by explaining their values and the measures used for their calculation. This is analogous to the requirement of Hall et al. [16] that explanations in XAI systems should be provided on the local level. If no local information contributes to the similarity computation, then no similarities need to be visualized there.

Req. 4 Visualization From the Query's Perspective: The explanation of the visualization should be from the query's perspective. For example, if a case contains an element that is not considered in the global similarity calculation, it is irrelevant knowledge in this context. This should be visually marked accordingly.

Req. 5 Representation of All Features Involved in the Similarity and of their Influence on the Similarity: The visualization should represent all features involved in the composition of the similarity. This is inspired by the prioritization of decision information by Hall et al. [16], according to which appropriately relevant features and feature relationships are selected for representation in the explanation. In the context of POCBR, this refers to the influence of these elements on the overall similarity, which can also be explored interactively. This requirement is specified in four sub-requirements, which were identified in the focus group interview.

Req. 5a Marking All Similarities With a Desired Value: The visualization should mark all similarities with a defined value, so these local similarities can be considered in detail. For example, the origin of similarities that values are very high like 1.0 or very low like 0.0 can be investigated.

Req. 5b Flexible Changes of Similarity Measures: To be able to estimate the influence of used similarity measures on the overall similarity value, the visualization should provide an interactive element that allows a flexible adjustment of these measures. This allows changes to the similarity model to be tracked. These adjustments should be possible on both, the global and the local level.

Req. 5c Filter Functions for Graph Elements: The visualization shall provide a function to hide selected types of graph items. This should make it possible to better assess the influence of certain graph item types on the overall similarity.

Req. 5d Pre-definition of Mappings: In the visualization, it should be possible to manually specify mappings based on which a new similarity calculation is performed. This is a functional requirement where the developer can manually check the influence of mapping pairs. It should only be possible to set valid mappings according to the definition of the semantic graphs [7].

Req. 6 Pairwise Visualization of Similarities: The similarity to be visualized always consists of a pair of query and case to ensure its traceability. For example, this would not occur, if the similarity of a query to an entire case base is visualized. The elements of the tuple are restricted to the query and case only.

Req. 7 Relation to Other Cases: The visualization should classify the similarity within the case base as well as in comparison with specific other cases. This requirement comes entirely from the focus group interview and is specified in two sub-requirements.

Req. 7a Classification Within Similarities of the Case Base: The similarity value should be ranked within the similarity distribution of the case base and visually represented. This allows to detect if all similarity values are close together or widely distributed, thus, identifying necessary adjustments to the similarity model for higher discriminatory power.

Req. 7b Comparison With Other Cases: The visualization shall include multiple pairwise visualizations to provide comparison to other similarity calculations. For this purpose, it should be possible to compare several visualizations in parallel. This should be used to identify possible adjustments in the similarity model that would not be noticeable when inspected individually.

4   Techniques for Similarity Visualization

Based on the presented requirements, the identified publications from the related work (see Sect. 2.3) are examined for their suitability, and new visualization forms are considered (see Sect. 4.1). The graph mapping approach is then presented (see Sect. 4.2), followed by the merge graph approach (see Sect. 4.3) and the heatmap approach (see Sect. 4.4)[1].

4.1   Suitable Visualization Approaches

Based on the presented requirements, the approaches introduced in Sect. 2.3 are reviewed for their suitability for use as visualizations for POCBR. The

---

[1] A detailed description of all visualization approaches, including various mock-ups, is available at https://git.opendfki.de/easy/explanation-of-similarities-in-pocbr-by-visualization/-/blob/main/Detailed_Description_of_Visualization_Approaches.pdf.

approaches of Bach and Mork [3] and Massie et al. [28] are identified as not suitable because they could not fulfill Req. 2 of representing the process data. Both approaches are constructed too restrictively for the respective form of case representation, and it is not possible to convert the cases into a suitable form of representation. For the visualization of local similarities demanded in Req. 3, these approaches are suitable under the condition that an appropriate data structure is available there. The approach of Ivanov et al. [19] does not meet Req. 3 of representing the similarities between graph components, as it only supports similarity measures such as a graph edit distance that does not consider local similarities in its pure form. Since in this contribution only similarities based on a mapping of graphs to each other are considered, this requirement is not fulfilled. The merge graph approach according to Andrews et al. [2] and an extended heatmap approach, which represents the graph elements in the tables, can generally fulfill all requirements. Some requirements need further extensions to be fulfilled, like Req. 5b, Req. 5c and Req. 7. Thus, based on the requirements' analysis, the merge graph and heatmap approaches are identified as suitable for visualization in POCBR.

Due to the lack of suitable related work, attempts are made to design further visualization approaches from scratch. Thereby, one visualization is designed fundamentally new: the graph mapping approach. There are no comparable approaches to this visualization form in the literature. Some existing ones follow a similar basic idea, for example in psychology by Xuu [43] or for the visualization of similarity graphs by Rostami et al. [38]. But their adaptation for the application field in POCBR would be so extensive that it would also become a new approach.

These three visualization approaches are considered according to the requirements and appropriate adjustments are made to satisfy them. All three methods are designed according to Shneiderman's Visual Information-Seeking Mantra [40] which is a common method in the field of information visualization [11]. It specifies that a visualization should first give an overview of all the available information [40]. Then, it should be possible to zoom and filter, so that ultimately details are provided on demand. The visualizations are illustrated using various static mock-ups to present their design and indicate the functionalities. A simple comparison between two short recipes is used as an example.

4.2   Approach of Graph Mapping

A mock-up for the graph mapping approach can be found in Fig. 2, where the display of multiple visualization instances described in Req. 7b is omitted for a clearer overview. This is given by a configurable number of instances that are displayed below each other. In the graph mapping visualization, the similarities are represented as directed edges starting from the query. These contain the information about the local similarities and their composition. The thickness of the edges provides additional information about the similarity, which is a common method in information visualization techniques [14]. When displaying edges, a distinction is made according to whether they are mappings between

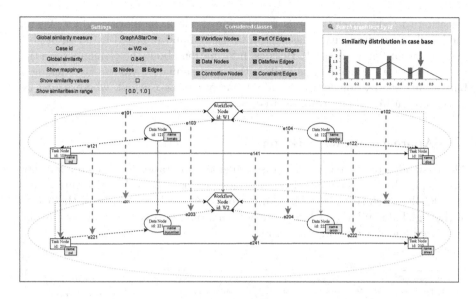

Fig. 2. Overview of the Graph Mapping Approach.

nodes or edges. The mapping edges between nodes are solid, the edges between edges are dashed.

The visualization has a header that contains a menu with general information about the case and the similarity calculation, where the global similarity measure can also be adjusted, according to Req. 5b. In addition, there is the possibility to hide nodes or edges, to display similarity values on the edges, as well as to display only similarities whose values are within a given interval according to Req. 5a. A second menu contains the filter functions for the different graph element types according to Req. 5c. Next to it, a histogram illustrates the similarity distribution in the case base according to Req. 7a. Above this, a search function is provided that can be used to find elements from the query and case, for example based on their ID or a textual attribute expression.

In the graph mapping approach, the query graph as well as the case graph are each aligned according to the longest path algorithm [13]. The mapping edges always run between the elements mapped onto each other and are represented with sufficient spacing. The example in Fig. 2 is the optimal case, where all edges are parallel, which is not true for most examples. If 50% or more edges run in the opposite direction, the case graph is mirrored to provide a better overview. If the case graph contains unmapped elements, these are displayed transparent and in a light shade of gray. They are irrelevant for the similarity calculation and, thus, Req. 4 is also considered. As defined in Req. 5d, mappings can be set by drawing a line from an element of the query to an element of the case, whereby only valid mappings are possible. Afterward, a new similarity calculation is started with this mandatory mapping, whereupon all similarity values in the visualization change. After such a change, the function for annotating the similarity values, which are displayed at the edges, is also selected there.

Selecting the edge opens a menu for viewing the local similarity values. There, the locally used similarity measure can be viewed and replaced by a compatible measure according to Req. 5b. Besides, information about the elements from the query and case is included, as well as the local similarity values. By clicking a button, a visualization for the local similarity can be opened, where it can be traced and adjusted according to Req. 3.

4.3   Approach of Merge Graph

The basic idea of the merge graph is to merge two graphs to be compared into one graph, thereby showing the similarities between them. For the application in POCBR, similarities between graphs are displayed independent of the height of their global similarity value. Moreover, mapping between edges must also be visualized and not only between nodes.

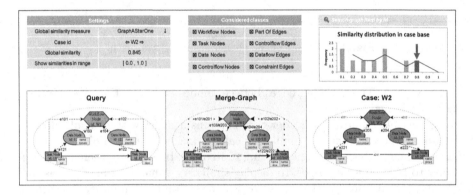

Fig. 3. Overview of the Merge Graph Approach.

Figure 3 shows a mock-up of the adapted merge graph, where Req. 7b is integrated as in the graph mapping and omitted here. The header is identical to that of the graph mapping approach, except that the entries for displaying specific mappings and annotating the similarity values are omitted. The query and case graphs are again based on the longest common path algorithm [13], and both are color-coded. The merge graph always adopts the layout of the query graph to ensure comparability with other similarity calculations, according to Req. 4 and Req. 7b. The nodes in the merge graph contain a gradient of both colors if they are mapping nodes. Unmapped elements of the query are taken over unchanged, while unmapped elements of the case are weakly transparent. The mapped nodes can always be mapped to the nodes of the query in the merge graph. This is not always the case for edges. If a mapped edge runs between two nodes to which their corresponding nodes have also been mapped, then this mapping edge is displayed in the merge graph. However, if this is not the case, the edge is hidden from the case and can only be identified by looking at the local similarities. The representation of similarities is done analogously to the graph mapping approach, using different thicknesses of the nodes' frames as well as of the edges. Selecting an element of the merge graph opens the menu for displaying local similarities, which is analogous to graph mapping. To set mappings as required by Req. 5d, a connection is drawn from an element in the query to an element in the case graph. With this preset, the other mappings are recalculated and visualized, whereby the old mapping cannot be marked.

4.4 Approach of Heatmaps

Instead of using heatmaps to visualize similarity distributions in the case base as in the literature [30, 42], heatmaps are used in this contribution to compare elements of two different cases. Each entry in the heatmap thereby symbolizes a mapping of an element of the query to an element of the case. An analogous idea exists in the original merge graph approach to represent metadata [2]. In addition to the color representation, where a bright red represents high similarity and a dark red low similarity, the numerical similarity values are also included in the tables. The heatmap requires the calculation of the individual similarity values if they have not already been determined and cached as part of the original similarity calculation.

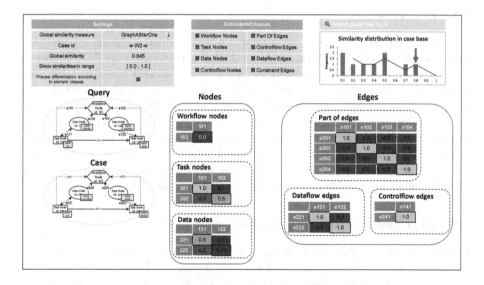

Fig. 4. Overview of the Heatmap Approach.

Figure 4 shows a mock-up of such an extended merge graph, where Req. 7b is considered as in the other two approaches and omitted here. Basically, two heatmaps are shown, one for the nodes and one for the edges. They contain several non-selectable fields, since no mapping is allowed at these points. These can be split as shown in the mock-up into several individual tables for the different graph element types, omitting the invalid fields by a function provided in the header. This header is similar to the one in the graph mapping approach, except that the entries for displaying specific mappings and annotating the similarity values are not contained. Selecting a field opens the menu for displaying local similarities, which is analogous to graph mapping and merge graph. The fields that represent the current mappings are outlined and thus made recognizable. In addition to the heatmaps, the query and the case graphs are shown, again using the longest path algorithm [13]. Both are displayed independently and serve to clarify the graph elements in the heatmaps. When a field is selected, the elements in the graphs are marked accordingly. Mappings according to Req. 5d can be set by selecting other fields. The originally selected mappings are marked by dashed borders.

5   Experimental Evaluation

The evaluation examines the hypothesis that the designed visualizations of similarities enable domain experts and knowledge engineers to acquire a more profound understanding of the similarity model and make targeted adjustments to it. First, the setup of the evaluation is presented (see Sect. 5.1). It is followed by a presentation of the results and their discussion (see Sect. 5.2).

5.1   Experimental Setup

The evaluation of the developed approaches was performed based on the presented requirements (see Sect. 3). A total of ten researchers in POCBR were recruited, who have been involved in this area for several years, so they are familiar with the subject, and have built similarity models themselves in the role of knowledge engineers. They were presented with the requirements and the three developed approaches, which were shown by mock-ups. With this background, they rated the three visualization approaches using five-point, ordinal, and interval-scaled Likert scales [25] and school grades. The participants were asked to select which approach best met the respective requirements compared with the other approaches, and to select their overall favorite approach.

5.2   Experimental Results and Discussion

In the individual evaluation for Req. 1 of the explanation of similarity, all three approaches are rated positively, with graph mapping and heatmaps both scoring best. To compare the individual evaluations, the Likert items are evaluated in the interval $[0, 4]$ and the mean value per requirement is calculated. This mean value based on each requirement is shown in Fig. 5. Overall, the average value indicates the graph mapping approach as the most suitable, with an absolute score of 3.12. The other two approaches are not rated significantly lower in total, with heatmap second scoring 2.76 and merge graph third scoring 2.75. The grading of the approaches also suggests this order when looking at the mean, with merge graph and heatmap again having a minimal difference. Looking at the median, confirms graph mapping in first place, with the other two approaches tied.

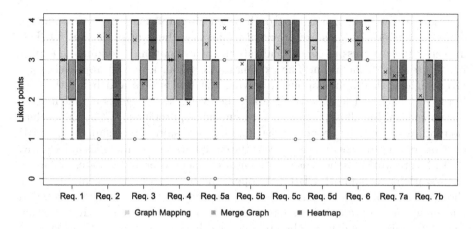

Fig. 5. Scored Likert Values for the Visualization Approaches Visualized as Boxplots.

In the selection of the favored approach for each requirement, graph mapping clearly dominates. Overall, the graph mapping approach is rated best for five requirements and tied with others for one requirement. In the other five requirements, participants could not decide on a favorite. When asked for the overall best approach, seven experts rated the graph mapping approach best. In this question, the margin is the clearest, with merge graph second and heatmap third.

The working hypothesis of this contribution is to achieve better explainability of similarities in POCBR for knowledge engineers by using visualization techniques. Based on the experts' assessment of requirements fulfillment, the evaluation suggests that this goal is achieved for all approaches created. Both, based on the Req. 1 of explainability and generally recognizable from the requirement evaluation, the approach of graph mapping stands out as the best approach to increase explainability. Based on the evaluation results, the graph mapping approach has been prototypically implemented in the ProCAKE framework [8] to be reused by the research community[2].

6 Conclusion and Future Work

In this paper, we present novel visualization approaches for complex case representations, enabling a better explainability of similarity for knowledge engineers in POCBR. For this purpose, first, we conduct a literature study and, second, we build a catalog of requirements for visualization approaches. Based on these requirements, the merge graph approach [2] and a heatmap approach are further investigated as they promise good support for developers. However, the approaches need to be tailored and extended for the application in POCBR. In

---

[2] The implementation is available at https://git.opendfki.de/easy/explanation-of-similarities-in-pocbr-by-visualization.

addition, a new visualization approach based on graph mapping is introduced. Thus, three visualizations are provided to increase the explanation in POCBR. To verify their successful conceptualization, the evaluation is conducted, explicitly addressing explanation. The explanation capabilities of all approaches are rated high, with graph mapping receiving the best scores and being the preferred approach of the experts. Overall, the evaluation suggests a contribution to explanation for all approaches based on the requirements. Thus, the evaluation indicates that the proposed visualizations are suitable for supporting CBR developers in their task and to increase the explanation of similarities in POCBR.

In future work, further case representations should be investigated for using visualizations to support CBR developers in their work. As recent literature shows [3,28], only rather simple case representations are currently investigated and many case representations have not even been considered, such as textual cases. Visualizations can also be created for other case representations, such as the simple ones, which have not been covered in the literature so far, or more complex structures. On a global level, an extension to represent dependencies between processes [22] or an adaptation for usage with other similarity measures are conceivable. Another research possibility is the application to other domains, such as argument graphs [6], in which a similarity visualization can be used to explain argumentation processes [24]. To support the knowledge engineer in the pre-definitions of mappings as stated in the requirements, a procedure must also be designed to search for a configuration of the similarity model that actually achieves the specified mapping during the similarity calculation. Currently, this is only possible by a manual configuration. For this purpose, methods from the field of intelligent search [17] can be applied, for example. In this work, we focus on supporting CBR system developers for their work. In future work, we want to examine what changes need to be performed on the visualization approaches to support end users. In this context, other aspects of the similarity calculation are probably more important, e.g., the differences between multiple query-case pairs and their similarities.

Acknowledgments. This work is funded by the Federal Ministry for Economic Affairs and Climate Action under grant No. 01MD22002C *EASY*.

References

1. Aamodt, A., Plaza, E.: Case-based reasoning: foundational issues, methodological variations, and system approaches. AI Commun. **7**(1), 39–59 (1994)
2. Andrews, K., Wohlfahrt, M., Wurzinger, G.: Visual graph comparison. In: 13th IV, pp. 62–67. IEEE (2009)
3. Bach, K., Mork, P.J.: On the explanation of similarity for developing and deploying CBR systems. In: 33rd FLAIRS, pp. 413–416. AAAI Press (2020)
4. Batyrshin, I.Z., Kubysheva, N., Solovyev, V., Villa-Vargas, L.A.: Visualization of similarity measures for binary data and 2x2 tables. CyS **20**(3), 345–353 (2016)
5. Bergmann, R.: Experience Management: Foundations, Development Methodology, and Internet-Based Applications, LNCS, vol. 2432. Springer, Cham (2003). https://doi.org/10.1007/3-540-45759-3_4

6. Bergmann, R., et al.: The ReCAP Project. Datenbank-Spektrum **20**(2), 93–98 (2020)

7. Bergmann, R., Gil, Y.: Similarity assessment and efficient retrieval of semantic workflows. Inf. Syst. **40**, 115–127 (2014)

8. Bergmann, R., Grumbach, L., Malburg, L., Zeyen, C.: ProCAKE: a process-oriented case-based reasoning framework. In: Proceedings of the 27th ICCBR Workshop (2019)

9. Bunke, H., Messmer, B.T.: Similarity measures for structured representations. In: Wess, S., Althoff, K.-D., Richter, M.M. (eds.) EWCBR 1993. LNCS, vol. 837, pp. 106–118. Springer, Heidelberg (1994). https://doi.org/10.1007/3-540-58330-0_80

10. Burkhard, H., Richter, M.M.: On the Notion of Similarity in Case Based Reasoning and Fuzzy Theory. In: Pal, S.K., Dillon, T.S., Yeung, D.S. (eds.) Soft Computing in CBR, pp. 29–45. Springer, London (2001). https://doi.org/10.1007/978-1-4471-0687-6_2

11. Card, S.K., Mackinlay, J.D., Shneiderman, B.: Readings in Information Visualization: Using Vision to Think. Academic Press, Cambridge (1999)

12. Das, A., Rad, P.: Opportunities and Challenges in Explainable Artificial Intelligence (XAI): A Survey. CRR 2006.11371 (2020)

13. Eades, P., Xuemin, L.: How to draw a directed graph. In: IEEE Workshop on Visual Languages, pp. 13–14. IEEE Computer Society (1989)

14. Epskamp, S., Cramer, A.O., Waldorp, L.J., Schmittmann, V.D., Borsboom, D.: qgraph: network visualizations of relationships in psychometric data. J. Stat. Softw. **48**, 1–18 (2012)

15. Gates, L., Kisby, C., Leake, D.: CBR confidence as a basis for confidence in black box systems. In: Bach, K., Marling, C. (eds.) ICCBR 2019. LNCS (LNAI), vol. 11680, pp. 95–109. Springer, Cham (2019). https://doi.org/10.1007/978-3-030-29249-2_7

16. Hall, M., et al.: A Systematic Method to Understand Requirements for Explainable AI (XAI) Systems. In: Proceedings of the 28th IJCAI Workshop, vol. 11 (2019)

17. Hart, P.E., Nilsson, N.J., Raphael, B.: A formal basis for the heuristic determination of minimum cost paths. IEEE Trans. Syst. Sci. Cybern. **4**(2), 100–107 (1968)

18. Hoffmann, M., Bergmann, R.: Informed Machine Learning for Improved Similarity Assessment in Process-Oriented Case-Based Reasoning. CoRR abs/2106.15931 (2021)

19. Ivanov, S., Kalenkova, A.A., van der Aalst, W.M.P.: BPMNDiffViz: a tool for BPMN Models Comparison. In: Procedings of the 13th BPM, CEUR Workshop, vol. 1418, pp. 35–39. CEUR-WS.org (2015)

20. Kendall-Morwick, J., Leake, D.: A study of two-phase retrieval for process-oriented case-based reasoning. In: Montani, S., Jain, L. (eds.) Successful Case-based Reasoning Applications-2. Studies in Computational Intelligence, pp. 7–27. Springer, Berlin (2014). https://doi.org/10.1007/978-3-642-38736-4_2

21. Kenny, E.M., Keane, M.T.: Twin-systems to explain artificial neural networks using case-based reasoning: comparative tests of feature-weighting methods in ANN-CBR twins for XAI. In: 28th IJCAI, pp. 2708–2715 (2019)

22. Kumar, R., Schultheis, A., Malburg, L., Hoffmann, M., Bergmann, R.: Considering inter-case dependencies during similarity-based retrieval in process-oriented case-based reasoning. In: 35th FLAIRS. FloridaOJ (2022)

23. Lamy, J.B., Sekar, B., Guezennec, G., Bouaud, J., Séroussi, B.: Explainable artificial intelligence for breast cancer: a visual case-based reasoning approach. Artif. Intell. Med. **94**, 42–53 (2019)

24. Lenz, M., et al.: Towards an argument mining pipeline transforming texts to argument graphs. In: 8th COMMA. FAIA, vol. 326, pp. 263–270. IOS Press (2020)
25. Likert, R.: A technique for the measurement of attitudes. Arch. Psychol. (1932)
26. Manovich, L.: What is visualization. paj: J. Initiative Digital Hum. Media Cult. **2**(1) (2010)
27. Marín-Veites, P., Bach, K.: Explaining CBR systems through retrieval and similarity measure visualizations: a case study. In: Keane, M.T., Wiratunga, N. (eds.) ICCBR 2022. Lecture Notes in Computer Science, vol. 13405, pp. 111–124. Springer, Cham (2022)
28. Massie, S., Craw, S., Wiratunga, N.: Visualisation of case-base reasoning for explanation. In: Proceedings of the 7th ECCBR, pp. 135–144 (2004)
29. Mathisen, B.M., Aamodt, A., Bach, K., Langseth, H.: Learning similarity measures from data. Prog. Artif. Intell. **9**(2), 129–143 (2020)
30. McArdle, G., Wilson, D.C.: Visualising Case-Base Usage. In: Proceedings of the 5th ICCBR Workshop, pp. 105–114 (2003)
31. Minor, M., Montani, S., Recio-García, J.A.: Process-oriented case-based reasoning. Inf. Syst. **40**, 103–105 (2014)
32. Namee, B.M., Delany, S.J.: CBTV: visualising case bases for similarity measure design and selection. In: Bichindaritz, I., Montani, S. (eds.) ICCBR 2010. LNCS (LNAI), vol. 6176, pp. 213–227. Springer, Heidelberg (2010). https://doi.org/10.1007/978-3-642-14274-1_17
33. Nugent, C., Cunningham, P.: A case-based explanation system for black-box systems. Artif. Intell. Rev. **24**(2), 163–178 (2005)
34. Ontañón, S.: An overview of distance and similarity functions for structured data. Artif. Intell. Rev. **53**(7), 5309–5351 (2020)
35. Rabiee, F.: Focus-group interview and data analysis. PNS **63**(4), 655–660 (2004)
36. Recio-García, J.A., Parejas-Llanovarced, H., Orozco-del-Castillo, M.G., Brito-Borges, E.E.: A case-based approach for the selection of explanation algorithms in image classification. In: Sánchez-Ruiz, A.A., Floyd, M.W. (eds.) ICCBR 2021. LNCS (LNAI), vol. 12877, pp. 186–200. Springer, Cham (2021). https://doi.org/10.1007/978-3-030-86957-1_13
37. Richter, M.M.: Knowledge containers. In: Readings in CBR. MKP (2003)
38. Rostami, M.A., Saeedi, A., Peukert, E., Rahm, E.: Interactive visualization of large similarity graphs and entity resolution clusters. In: 21th EDBT, pp. 690–693. OpenProceedings.org (2018)
39. Schoenborn, J.M., Weber, R.O., Aha, D.W., Cassens, J., Althoff, K.D.: Explainable case-based reasoning: a survey. In: AAAI-21 Workshop Proceedings (2021)
40. Shneiderman, B.: The eyes have it: a task by data type taxonomy for information visualizations. In: Proceedings of IEEE Symposium on Visual Languages, pp. 336–343. IEEE Computer Society (1996)
41. Sørmo, F., Cassens, J., Aamodt, A.: Explanation in case-based reasoning-perspectives and goals. Artif. Intell. Rev. **24**(2), 109–143 (2005)
42. Wilkinson, L., Friendly, M.: The history of the cluster heat map. Am. Stat. **63**(2), 179–184 (2009)
43. Xuu, A.B.: Structure mapping in the comparison process. AJP **113**(4), 501–538 (2000)
44. Zeyen, C., Bergmann, R.: A*-based similarity assessment of semantic graphs. In: Watson, I., Weber, R. (eds.) ICCBR 2020. LNCS (LNAI), vol. 12311, pp. 17–32. Springer, Cham (2020). https://doi.org/10.1007/978-3-030-58342-2_2

On-Demand and Model-Driven Case Building Based on Distributed Data Sources

Mark van der Pas[1,2]([✉]) [ID], Remco Dijkman[1] [ID], Alp Akçay[1] [ID], Ivo Adan[1] [ID], and John Walker[2]

[1] Department of Industrial Engineering and Innovation Sciences,
Eindhoven University of Technology, 5600MB Eindhoven, The Netherlands
`m.c.a.v.d.pas@tue.nl`
[2] Semaku B.V., 5617BC Eindhoven, The Netherlands

Abstract. The successful application of Case-Based Reasoning (CBR) depends on the availability of data. In most manufacturing companies these data are present, but distributed over many different systems. The distribution of the data makes it difficult to apply CBR in real-time, as data have to be collected from the different systems. In this work we propose a framework and algorithm to efficiently build a case representation on-demand and solve the challenge of distributed data in CBR. The main contribution of this work is a framework using an index for objects and the sources where data about those objects can be found. Next to the framework, we present an algorithm that operates on the framework and can be used to build case representations and construct a case base on-demand, using data from distributed sources. There are several parameters that influence the performance of the framework. Accordingly, we show in a conceptual and experimental evaluation that in highly-distributed and segregated environments the proposed approach reduces the time complexity from polynomial to linear order.

Keywords: CBR frameworks · Case representation · Case base building · Distributed systems · Industry 4.0 · Semantic Web

1 Introduction

One of the challenges identified for Case-Based Reasoning (CBR) research is the acquisition of cases from raw data [11]. In complex manufacturing settings numerous different systems are used, that typically operate independently, in which these raw data are stored. Especially in Industry 4.0 with the digitization of individual assets, for example using the Asset Administration Shell (AAS) [20], data will be highly distributed. On top of that data from multiple companies along the supply chain might be required. This distribution poses a challenge of collecting the data from the relevant sources. One solution to make these distributed data available for CBR is to push all data to the CBR system at

S. Massie and S. Chakraborti (Eds.): ICCBR 2023, LNAI 14141, pp. 69–84, 2023.
https://doi.org/10.1007/978-3-031-40177-0_5

the moment they are generated. However, this means duplicating large amounts of data, the majority of which might not be relevant. Duplicating data can be avoided by only storing the data in the source systems and collecting the data on-demand, i.e. during case retrieval. The challenge in on-demand data collection is to minimize the time it takes to collect the data and construct the case base. A good example where those problems are seen is the handling of manufacturing quality incidents [4]. Those incidents are related to a small fraction of produced objects and data from many different systems is required to analyze them. Generating a case representation in such scenarios often requires significant manual effort and is based on a fixed structure, see for example [8].

To solve the challenge of distributed data, we propose a framework in which only information about what sources contain data about what objects is stored centrally. Specifically, all relevant objects are indexed with pointers to the sources where data about those objects can be found. The case model (also referred to as case structure or vocabulary), which defines the object classes as well as the properties (relations and attributes) required to describe a case, can be used to select the relevant objects. We identify multiple dimensions that impact the time complexity of the problem. In both a conceptual and experimental evaluation we show how the proposed algorithm performs compared to an approach with no index, taking into account the identified dimensions. Finally, we demonstrate that the proposed framework and algorithm reduce the time complexity significantly and enable real-time building of case representations.

The remainder of this work is structured as follows. First, we will introduce the related work in Sect. 2. Subsequently, Sect. 3 describes the proposed method in more detail, followed by a conceptual evaluation in Sect. 4. Section 5 presents our implementation based on Semantic Web Technologies and Industry 4.0 concepts, including an experimental evaluation of its performance. The last sections contain a discussion, a conclusion with a summary of the findings and ideas for future work.

2   Related Work

In this section we look into related research on distributed systems in CBR and approaches for collecting data from distributed sources.

One of the architectural patterns in CBR is distributed case-based reasoning [21]. In distributed CBR systems the cases are stored in multiple distributed sources (knowledge bases). Distributed CBR systems are applied to several domains. Pla et al. [19] propose a CBR system for medical diagnosis, whereas Tran et al. [27] for fault management in communication networks. On the other hand Clood CBR [18], SEASALT [1,2], jcolibri2 [23] and F-CBR [16] are domain independent frameworks for sharing and retrieving knowledge. The frameworks use a modular and agent- or microservices-based design, where the cases are distributed over multiple case bases and the main challenge is to retrieve similar cases from those distributed bases. In contrast, we consider a situation where the data for one case is split over multiple sources and the main challenge is to collect the data from the distributed sources, build the case representation(s) and construct the case base in an efficient way.

Most work on collecting data from distributed sources is about the development of efficient federated query engines. The main challenge here is to efficiently query multiple (distributed) data sources. The engines operate over distributed servers that expose data. The main engines developed are FedX [25], SPLENDID [12], and SemaGrow [9]. All of them use information and metadata about the federated data sources to optimize the query plan. The generation of the query plan introduces quite some overhead, which limits the performance of the engines. The federated query engines are often optimized to execute analytic style queries that operate over large parts of the data set. However, in CBR we are often interested in only a small fraction of the data set for describing cases.

Verborgh et al. [28] propose a framework for more efficient querying of distributed sources, that aims to balance the costs between the client and server. Different link-based traversal algorithms are proposed for querying those sources [26,28]. The main idea is to iterate through the sources to discover the data matching query patterns. The query engine does not know beforehand what objects are present in what sources, therefore all sources have to be requested, which will limit the performance when there are many sources. In comparison to our approach, federated query engines support more complex queries, but this comes at the cost of more complex and less efficient data collection.

An alternative to the federated query engines is Linked Data crawling [10]. Those crawling approaches assume that every source contains pointers to the other sources where data about certain objects can be found, such that software agents can autonomously query and discover the data sources. In large manufacturing organizations there are often many different legacy and siloed systems, that do not have the required pointers to other systems.

3   On-Demand and Model-Driven Case Building

In Sect. 3.1 the conceptual framework that supports on-demand case building is described along with the notation that is used throughout the paper. This is followed by a description of the algorithm in Sect. 3.2.

3.1   The Framework

Figure 1 gives an overview of the framework and notation we use to refer to parts of the framework, which is further elaborated in Table 1. The framework consists of three parts: a set of data sources, a case data model and an index. We will discuss the parts one by one. The data sources are the distributed systems where data about objects is stored that are relevant for a case. These sources can be large databases that contain data about many objects, or systems that serve data for a small set of objects. In a manufacturing setting an object can be a specific machine and data about this machine can be stored on some local server. The case representation model or vocabulary defines what type of data

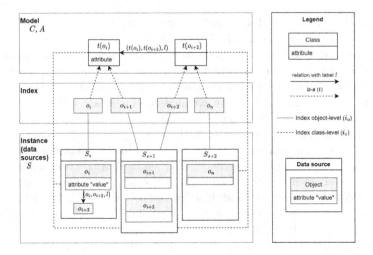

Fig. 1. Framework and notation.

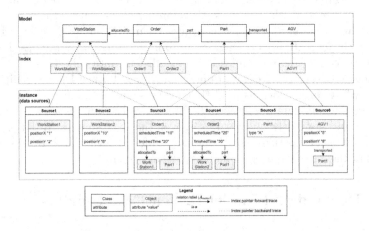

Fig. 2. Illustration of the framework based on an example.

(classes, relations and attributes) should be used to describe a case and defines the structure of the case base. In this work we consider an object-oriented case representation [5,6] that consists of a collection of objects that belong to a certain class, are described by a set of attribute-value pairs, and are related to each other by a set of relations. Note that relations are a special case of attribute-value pairs with a value referring to another object. Because the relations play an important role in the framework, we distinguish the relations from the simple attribute-value pairs (that have a literal value). For example, in a manufacturing setting with quality incidents the case model might consist of the classes 'product' and 'machine', with relation 'produced on'. In the remainder of this work we will ignore the simple attributes. We assume that every object together with its simple attribute-value pairs can be retrieved in one request and therefore do not impact the complexity of the problem. The last component of the framework is the index that relates the data model to the data sources and can be used for efficient on-demand building of the case base according to the case model with data from the distributed sources. For that purpose the index will contain pointers to the data sources, where we consider indexing the sources on object- or class-level. The object-level index contains pointers for every object, while the class-level index only contains pointers for every class in the model. An example of the framework applied to a typical manufacturing setting can be found in Fig. 2. Generating and updating the index is implementation specific. In Sect. 5.1 we describe the Industry 4.0 and Semantic Web [7] technologies that are used in our implementation.

Table 1. Overview of notation.

Model	
C	set of classes
L	set of relation labels
$A \subseteq C \times C \times L$	set of (directed) relations between classes (C) with label (L)
Instance	
O	set of objects
$t : O \rightarrow C$	type of object (assignment to a class)
$E \subseteq O \times O \times L$	set of relations between objects (O) with label (L) if $(o, m, l) \in E$, then $(t(o), t(m), l) \in A$
$S = \{S_1, ..., S_s\}$, where $S_i \subseteq E$	set of data sources with relations stored in every source
Index	
$i_c : C \rightarrow \mathcal{P}(S)$[a]	pointer from class to source(s) where data about objects of that class can be found
$i_o : O \rightarrow \mathcal{P}(S)$[a]	pointer from object to source(s) where data about that object can be found

[a] $\mathcal{P}(S)$ denotes the power set of S

3.2 Algorithm

The next step is the definition of the algorithm to construct a case base with data from distributed sources. The index is used to target the relevant data sources to collect data from, which will reduce the number of requests required for the construction. Algorithm 1 takes as arguments the set of objects of interest to build a case representation for (O_{query}) and the case model, consisting of classes $(C_{case} \subseteq C)$ and relations $(A_{case} \subseteq A)$. Starting from the objects of interest, the algorithm iterates over the objects it encounters until no new objects of interest

Algorithm 1 Model-driven case building

1: **Input**
2: O_{query} ▷ set of objects of interest
3: C_{case} ▷ set of classes in the case model
4: A_{case} ▷ set of relations in the case model
5: $O_{base} \leftarrow \emptyset$
6: $O_{next} \leftarrow O_{query}$
7: **while** $|O_{next}| \neq \emptyset$ **do**
8:     $O_{selected} \leftarrow O_{next} - O_{base}$
9:     $O_{next} \leftarrow \emptyset$
10:    **for all** $o \in O_{selected}$ **do**
11:        **for all** $S_k \in i_o(o)$ **do**
12:            $O_{forward} \leftarrow \{m | (o, m, l) \in S_k \wedge t(m) \in C_{case} \wedge (t(o), t(m), l) \in A_{case}\}$
13:            $O_{backward} \leftarrow \{m | (m, o, l) \in S_k \wedge t(m) \in C_{case} \wedge (t(m), t(o), l) \in A_{case}\}$
14:            $O_{next} \leftarrow O_{next} \cup O_{forward} \cup O_{backward}$
15:        **end for**
16:        $O_{base} \leftarrow O_{base} \cup \{o\}$
17:    **end for**
18: **end while**
19: **return** O_{base}

for the case base are found (line 7). For each object it encounters (line 10), all sources where data about those objects are stored (line 11) have to be checked. The relevant sources can be retrieved from the index, in Algorithm 1 the object-level index is used, so it checks what sources are in the index for an object o ($i_o(o)$). Alternatively, the class-level index can be used, in that case the sources are selected by checking the sources for the class that an object belongs to ($i_c(t(o))$). For a given source, the next objects to explore are retrieved by checking the relations to other objects that are stored in the source. For forward trace the relations are selected where o is the origin (line 12), thus following the direction of the relations. Following the relations in the opposite direction, with o as the target (line 13), we refer to as backward trace. Furthermore, only relations that are present in the case model (A_{case}) and objects that belong to a class in the case model ($t(m) \in C_{case}$) are of interest. Both the objects retrieved in forward and backward trace are selected for the next iteration. The last step is to add the object (and its attribute-value pairs) to the case base on line 16. Once the algorithm terminates it returns the constructed case base (O_{base}), which is a union of the case representation for the objects of interest: $O_{base} = \bigcup_{o \in O_{query}} c_o$, where c_o is the set containing the representation of one case for an object o.

For example, suppose there was some incident with Order1 from Fig. 2 and we need to build a case representation for it. The representation should contain the workstation, the order it was assigned to and the part worked on by that order. Algorithm 1 is then initiated with $O_{query} = \{\text{Order1}\}$, $C_{case} = \{\text{Order}\}$, and $A_{case} = \{(\text{Order}, \text{Workstation}, \text{allocatedTo}), (\text{Order}, \text{Part}, \text{part})\}$. In the first iteration of the algorithm there will be a request to Source3, resulting in $O_{next} = \{\text{WorkStation1}, \text{Part1}\}$ and $O_{base} = \{\text{Order1}\}$. The next iteration will request `Source1` and `Source5`, with result $O_{next} = \emptyset$ and $O_{base} = \{$`Order1`, `WorkStation1`, `Part1`$\}$. After this iteration the algorithm terminates.

4   Conceptual Evaluation

In this section we present a conceptual evaluation of the framework and algorithm defined in the previous section. For the evaluation of the performance in terms of time complexity, we compare the proposed method to a naïve approach. The naïve approach assumes that there is no index and thus all sources have to be checked. The other extreme is to duplicate all data to the case base independent of the case model and the objects of interest for case representation (O_{query}). In this work, we assume that duplicating all data is not feasible and it is required to construct the case base on-demand. Therefore, we will focus on the computational costs of case building in terms of the number of requests to the distributed sources. In the evaluation the following dimensions are considered:

- Total number of objects ($n = |O|$);
- Fraction of objects of interest for the case base ($p = \frac{|O_{base}|}{|O|}$);
- Number of sources ($s = |S|$);
- Degree, which we define as the average fraction of sources an element in the index has pointers to ($d = \sum_{o \in O} \left(\frac{|\{S_k | S_k \in S \land ((o,m,l) \in S_k \lor (m,o,l) \in S_k)\}|}{|S|} \right) / |O|$);
- Number of classes in the model ($|C|$).

Note that in practice there can be many other factors that impact the actual time it takes to construct the case base, for example the network bandwidth. However, we assume that in general those costs grow proportionally to the number of requests, and therefore a lower number of requests means lower costs and better performance.

Given the dimensions above, we will evaluate the costs, expressed in the number of requests to sources (R), for three different protocols:

- naïve: no pointers, check all sources for a given object;
- object-level index: pointers for every object to sources for that object;
- class-level index: pointers for every class to sources for objects from that class.

Note that for the conceptual evaluation we assume that there is no overlap between case representations ($\bigcap_{o \in O_{query}} c_o = \emptyset$). However, in the experimental evaluation in Sect. 5 we will show that the amount of overlap between case representations will have an impact on the number of requests.

First, let us consider the naïve approach. Using this approach there has to be a request to every source (s) for every object that has to end up in the case base (np), such that:

$$R_{naïve} = nps. \tag{1}$$

Alternatively, if we use the proposed framework and Algorithm 1, only sd sources have to be requested. Thus,

$$R_{index} = npsd. \tag{2}$$

Note that if every object or class is present in every source, $d = 1$ and $R_{index} = R_{naïve}$.

In the evaluation we consider a highly distributed environment, where data about each object is stored in a separate source, such that $s = n$. For this scenario we will investigate three relations. The first one is shown in Fig. 3a where the number of sources and objects is fixed, such that if p increases, the difference in costs between the naïve ($R_{naïve}$) and index-based approach (R_{index}) will decrease linearly. Secondly, we can see in Fig. 3a that the difference in costs is higher, when the data are more segregated between sources, thus if d increases the difference in costs between the two approaches decreases. Finally, when all objects can be reached using only forward trace, then $d = 1/s$ and the difference in costs between the two approaches will decrease polynomial in n (for a fixed p). This is shown in Fig. 3b.

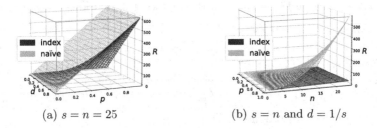

(a) $s = n = 25$ (b) $s = n$ and $d = 1/s$

Fig. 3. Costs of building a case base in terms of the number of requests to sources (R).

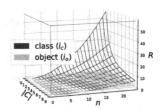

Fig. 4. Costs of building a case base in terms of the number of requests to sources (R), comparing class- and object-level index ($s = n$ and $p = 0.1$).

Next, we would like to quantify the difference between using the object- and class-level index. If we consider only forward trace, the average degree for the object-level index is $d_o = \frac{1}{s} = \frac{1}{n}$. Furthermore, if we assume that every object belongs to one class, then this degree for class-level index is $d_c = \frac{n/|C|}{n} = \frac{1}{|C|}$. This results in the following expressions for the costs using i_c and i_o, respectively:
$R_{i_c} = n^2 p \frac{1}{|C|} = \frac{n^2 p}{|C|}$ and $R_{i_o} = n^2 p \frac{1}{n} = np$. From those expressions, we can derive that the difference between the costs using the class-level index (R_{i_c}) and

the object-level index (R_{i_o}) will increase if the number of classes $(|C|)$ decreases. More specifically, it is beneficial to use the object-level index, unless $n < |C|$. This is also visualized in Fig. 4.

5 Experimental Evaluation

In this section our implementation of the framework, the experimental setup, and results are presented. The experiments are conducted using our implementation of the framework that adopts the Industry 4.0 (semantic) AAS [3,13] and Semantic Web [7] technologies as foundations. Therefore, also the data set is inspired by a Industry 4.0 modular production use case. The first goal of the experimental evaluation is to validate the implementation against the conceptual results and vice-versa. Subsequently, we will look at different scenarios with overlapping case representations.

5.1 Setup

Implementation of the Framework. In terms of the levels used in Fig. 1, 'Instance (data sources)' are implemented as AAS server(s), so the data are exposed according to the AAS model enriched with semantic identifiers accessible on a server[1]. The 'Model' is defined in SHACL [17], which is a more recent addition to the Semantic Web stack that it is used more regularly to define models and constraints in the manufacturing domain [15]. For the implementation of the algorithm we use an agent-based system implemented in Python, where every agent represents a specific source and maintains the 'Index' for that source. For the experiments only the forward trace pointers are included. The index is generated based on AAS metadata, consisting of the path where the data can be retrieved and the semantic identifier, which corresponds to a relation label (L) in the case model [24]. The index is updated based on events published by the AASs.

The agent-based approach makes the system modular and scalable, as data from different sources can be collected in parallel. Next to the AAS server and the agent-based system that implements the algorithm, there is a graph database (RDF [22] store) where all data collected by the agents is stored, and as such forms a case base. Using a graph structured case representation fits naturally with the structure of the AAS. However, for the implementation we made some assumptions to limit the scope and complexity of the data integration. First, we define the data set and sources, such that there is a straightforward mapping from the data elements in the AASs to unique identifiers. Next to that, we only consider 'simple' data types that can be one on one mapped to RDF literals.

---

[1] https://wiki.eclipse.org/BaSyx_/_Documentation_/_Components_/_AAS_Server.

Hypotheses. The first goal is to validate the implementation against the conceptual results from Sect. 4 and vice-versa. The validation should ensure that we did not miss an important dimension or interaction in the conceptual evaluation, which might occur in a practical setting. For this purpose we defined four hypotheses that are formulated based on the conceptual evaluation. The first three compare the costs for using no index (naïve approach) and the object-level index, while the last hypothesis is designed to show the difference between using the class- and object-level index.

H1 If p increases, the difference between $R_{naïve}$ and R_{index} will decrease.

H2 If d increases, the difference between $R_{naïve}$ and R_{index} will decrease.

H3 If $s = n$, the difference between $R_{naïve}$ and R_{index} will increase polynomial in n.

H4 If $|C|$ decreases, while n stays constant and there are multiple sources per class, the difference between R_{i_c} and R_{i_o} will increase.

For the conceptual evaluation, we assumed that there is no overlap between case representations. In the last experiments we will relax this assumption and show the impact of having overlapping case representations ($\bigcap_{o \in O_{query}} c_o \neq \emptyset$) when using the object-level index. More specifically, we look into how the system behaves when there is overlap between the case representations for increasing number of objects to build a case representation for. It is expected that more overlap between case representations will reduce the number of requests. For example, when multiple orders in the case base are related to the same workstation, then data about that workstation will only have to be collected once. To test this hypothesis the average overlap between representations can be altered, by varying the average number of relations per object in the data set ($\frac{|E|}{|O|}$). In general, we can state that if the average number of relations per object is higher, the probability that this object occurs in two distinct case representations is also higher, as it is related to more other objects. For example, if a workstation is related to all orders, it will occur in the case representation of each order and the number of relations of that workstation is higher compared to when it is related to only one order. The expected behaviour is captured in the last two hypotheses:

H5 If there is overlap between case representations, R will increase sub-linear in $|O_{query}|$.

H6 If $\frac{|E|}{|O|}$ is higher, the reduction in R due to overlapping case representations will be lower.

Data Set. For the evaluation of our methodology we use a simulated data set describing a set of manufacturing assets, similar to the example in Fig. 2. The data set is based on an actual use case using an Industry 4.0 modular production environment. In such an environment the objects are treated as independent entities and have their own AAS. The complete data set consists of 272 **Orders**, 14 **Workstations**, 17 **Parts**, and 20 **AGVs**. Every order is related to one workstation with relation `allocatedTo` and one part with relation `part`. Furthermore, every AGV is related to one or multiple parts (`transported`). All objects have their own AAS, with multiple elements representing the relations to other objects. The case model consists of all classes and relations, except `AGV` and `transported`. The objects of interest for case representation are from the class `Order`.

For testing the different hypotheses we use different subsets of the data set described above:

1. For the first hypothesis only orders are included (excluding the relations to other objects), we can then vary the fraction selected for the case base (p), by increasing the number of orders to build a case representation for.
2. For the second hypothesis, orders and their relation to workstations and parts are stored in different elements of the AAS. The fraction of sources each object is connected to (d) can then be altered by varying the connected AAS elements.
3. For the third hypothesis again only orders are included, but now the number of sources is altered by varying the number of orders that is included.
4. For the fourth hypothesis, different subsets of the data set are used to vary the number of classes ($|C|$). The number of objects is constant, but they are split over different classes.

Hypotheses 5 and 6 (overlapping case representations) require a slightly different setup. For testing those hypotheses we generated distinct data sets, while utilizing the same underlying data model. In each data set a different number of workstations and parts is included, but again each order is related to one workstation and one part. This means that the number of relations remains constant, but the average number of relations per object differs. An overview of the four generated data sets can be found in Table 2.

Table 2. Description of the generated data sets for testing Hypotheses 5 and 6.

Scenario	# Orders	# Workstations	# Parts	Average # relations ($\frac{|E|}{|O|}$)
1	272	272	272	1.19
2	272	94	10	1.85
3	272	92	10	2.53
4	272	1	1	3.97

5.2   Results

Hypothesis 1. The results of the experiments for Hypothesis 1 can be found in Fig. 5a. In accordance with the conceptual results, the number of requests, R, grows linearly in p for both the index-based and the naïve approach. However, there is a difference in the slope, which is equal to nds ($= 272 \times 1/272 \times 272 = 272$) for the index-based approach, compared to ns ($= 272 \times 272 = 73984$) for the naïve approach.

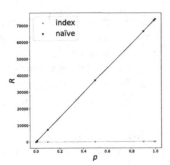

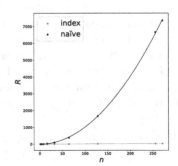

(a) Number of requests for different fraction of objects for case base.

(b) Number of requests for different number of objects in the sources.

Fig. 5. Results of experiments testing hypothesis 1 and 3, including regression lines.

Hypothesis 2. Based on the results in Table 3 we can accept Hypothesis 2: the number of requests for the naïve approach is constant if only d is varied, while the requests increase linear in d when the index-based approach is used. Therefore, the benefit of using the index will decrease if objects or classes are present in an increasing fraction of all sources.

Table 3. Results for testing Hypothesis 2.

d	0.0037	0.0074	0.011	0.015
$R_{naïve}$	29376	29376	29376	29376
R_{index}	27	54	81	108

Hypothesis 3. We can accept this hypothesis based on the results in Fig. 5b. The number of requests is linear in n for the index-based approach, but (second order) polynomial for the naïve approach, which corresponds to the conceptual results in Sect. 4 in a scenario with $s = n$.

Hypothesis 4. As can be seen in Fig. 6, the number of requests when using the object-level index is independent of the number of classes the objects are distributed over, while the number of requests when using the class-level index decreases when more classes are considered. These results correspond with the findings in Sect. 4, and therefore we can also accept Hypothesis 4.

Hypotheses 5 and 6. The results are summarized in Fig. 7. In Scenario 1, where there is no overlap in case representation, similar behaviour is observed

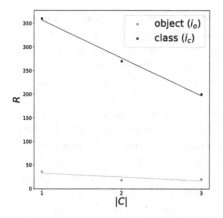

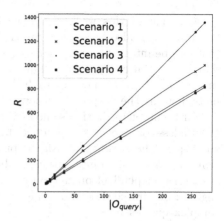

Fig. 6. Results of experiments testing hypothesis 4, including regression lines.

Fig. 7. Results for the scenarios in Table 2 (including regression lines).

as in Fig. 5a). Similarly, in Scenario 4 the number of requests increases linearly for increasing number of cases, this can be explained by the fact that the same workstation and part occur in all case representations, so the workstation and part will be collected once the first case representation is built. The sub-linear behaviour is especially clear for Scenario 2 with overlap between every two to four case representations. In summary, the effect of overlapping case representations increases with increasing number of cases and increasing average number of relations per object.

6 Discussion

We found that the experimental results follow the conceptual results for the computational complexity, which means the relatively straightforward expressions can be used to extrapolate theoretical complexity from smaller instances of the problem. The extrapolation can be used to evaluate bigger instances of the problem without the effort to develop complex simulations. The worst-case performance was observed for a highly distributed environment where every object has its own data source. In this scenario the performance for the naïve approach behaves polynomial versus linear if the proposed index-based approach is used. Polynomial behaviour of order two is not by definition unacceptable, but on industry scale the performance will rapidly decrease if every request takes a couple of milliseconds. Note that in the evaluations of the framework, the time and effort to build and maintain the index itself are not considered. Both can be achieved in different ways, but in general push-based (or event-driven) mechanisms are especially efficient for such tasks [29], and we argue that those costs are negligible in comparison to the cost savings that we found in our evaluation.

Although in this work the focus is on manufacturing environments, the framework can also be applied in other domains with distributed data sources that can be integrated using some (semantic) model. One example is the Web, that is distributed by nature. Furthermore, many web pages embed semantic (meta)data [14], which can be useful to include in a case representation that can be built using the proposed framework.

For the implementation some assumptions were made to make the data integration less complex, but in practice there might be heterogeneity in data sources and types. The advantage with the proposed framework and implementation is that most of the data integration can be done client-side, which makes the CBR system less dependent on the source systems. In comparison to federated query engines, our framework and implementation does not support executing more complex queries directly on the data sources. Instead, this could be an additional post-processing step, for example by executing a SPARQL query on the constructed RDF case base.

7   Conclusion and Future Work

In this work we proposed a framework that enables efficient construction of a case base from distributed sources. The main contributions are the model-based index and the algorithm to construct the case base. We demonstrated both conceptually and experimentally that the benefit of using the proposed index-based approach is most significant for highly distributed environments, where the complexity is reduced from polynomial to linear. Distributed environments are seen in multi-national (manufacturing) companies and supply chains that deal with big data volumes distributed over different locations and systems. Therefore, we showed the benefits of applying the framework to a manufacturing use case.

More research is required on integration of the framework in a complete CBR system, especially the retrieval step. There are multiple approaches to this integration, one option is to keep the representations of the cases in a central case base once they are built, then only the data for a new case presented to the system have to be collected from the distributed sources. An alternative is to only store the main case object identifiers centrally and construct the complete case base on demand, by collecting data describing the cases from the distributed sources. Also a combination of both is possible.

The framework presented in this work only supports retrieving data from the distributed sources, in contrast to distributed CBR frameworks which mainly focus on case retrieval and case base maintenance. An interesting direction to explore is how the framework proposed in this work can be combined with for example the SEASALT framework [1]. Another opportunity is to integrate the similarity computation in the framework. The algorithm can be adapted to stop retrieving data when it concludes that certain cases will not be among the most similar cases.

Acknowledgements. This project is supported by the European Union's Horizon 2020 research and innovation programme under grant agreement No. 957204, the project MAS4AI (Multi-Agent Systems for Pervasive Artificial Intelligence for assisting Humans in Modular Production). In special we would like to thank the project partners for providing insights in their use cases and the reviewers for providing valuable comments and suggestions.

References

1. Bach, K.: Knowledge engineering for distributed case-based reasoning systems. Synergies Between Knowledge Engineering and Software Engineering **626**, 129–147 (2018). https://doi.org/10.1007/978-3-319-64161-4_7
2. Bach, K., Reichle, M., Althoff, K.D.: A Domain Independent System Architecture for Sharing Experience. In: LWA. pp. 296–303. Halle (9 2007)
3. Bader, S.R., Maleshkova, M.: The semantic asset administration shell. In: International Conference on Semantic Systems. pp. 159–174. Springer, Cham (2019). https://doi.org/10.1007/978-3-030-33220-4_12
4. Bergmann, R., Althoff, K., Breen, S., Göker, M., Manago, M.: Developing industrial case-based reasoning applications: The INRECA methodology. Springer Science & Business Media, Berlin (2003)
5. Bergmann, R.: Experience Management. Lecture Notes in Computer Science, vol. 2432. Springer, Berlin Heidelberg, Berlin, Heidelberg (2002)
6. Bergmann, R., Kolodner, J., Plaza, E.: Representation in case-based reasoning. The Knowledge Engineering Review **20**(3), 209–213 (2005). https://doi.org/10.1017/S0269888906000555
7. Berners-Lee, T., Hendler, J., Lassila, O.: The semantic web. Scientific American **284**(9), 34–43 (2001)
8. Camarillo, A., Ríos, J., Althoff, K.D.: Knowledge-based multi-agent system for manufacturing problem solving process in production plants. Journal of Manufacturing Systems **47**, 115–127 (2018). https://doi.org/10.1016/j.jmsy.2018.04.002
9. Charalambidis, A., Troumpoukis, A., Konstantopoulos, S.: SemaGrow: Optimizing Federated SPARQL queries. In: Proceedings of the 11th International Conference on Semantic Systems. pp. 121–128. ACM, New York, NY, USA (2015). https://doi.org/10.1145/2814864
10. Charpenay, V.: Semantics for the Web of Things, Modeling the Physical World as a Collection of Things and Reasoning with their Descriptions. Ph.D. thesis, Universität Passau (2019)
11. Goel, A.K., Diaz-Agudo, B.: What's Hot in Case-Based Reasoning. In: Proceedings of the Thirty-First AAAI Conference on Artificial Intelligence. pp. 5067–5069 (2017). https://doi.org/10.1609/aaai.v31i1.10643
12. Görlitz, O., Staab, S.: SPLENDID: SPARQL Endpoint Federation Exploiting VOID Descriptions. In: Proceedings of the Second International Workshop on Consuming Linked Data (2011)
13. Grangel-González, I., Halilaj, L., Auer, S., Lohmann, S., Lange, C., Collarana, D.: An RDF-based approach for implementing industry 4.0 components with Administration Shells. In: 2016 IEEE 21st International Conference on Emerging Technologies and Factory Automation (ETFA). pp. 1–8. IEEE (2016). https://doi.org/10.1109/ETFA.2016.7733503

14. Guha, R.V., Brickley, D., Macbeth, S.: Schemaorg: Evolution of structured data on the web. Communications of the ACM 59(2), 44–51 (2 2016). https://doi.org/10.1145/2844544

15. Hooshmand, Y., Resch, J., Wischnewski, P., Patil, P.: From a Monolithic PLM Landscape to a Federated Domain and Data Mesh. Proceedings of the Design Society 2, 713–722 (5 2022). https://doi.org/10.1017/PDS.2022.73

16. Jaiswal, A., Yigzaw, K.Y., Ozturk, P.: F-CBR: An Architecture for Federated Case-Based Reasoning. IEEE Access **10**, 75458–75471 (2022). https://doi.org/10.1109/ACCESS.2022.3188808

17. Knublauch, H., Kontokostas, D.: Shapes Constraint Language (SHACL) (2017). https://www.w3.org/TR/2017/REC-shacl-20170720/

18. Nkisi-Orji, I., Wiratunga, N., Palihawadana, C., Recio-García, J.A., Corsar, D.: Clood CBR: Towards Microservices Oriented Case-Based Reasoning. In: ICCBR 2020: Case-Based Reasoning Research and Development. vol. 12311 LNAI, pp. 129–143. Springer Science and Business Media Deutschland GmbH (2020). https://doi.org/10.1007/978-3-030-58342-2_9/FIGURES/6

19. Pla, A., López, B., Gay, P., Pous, C.: eXiT*CBR.v2: Distributed case-based reasoning tool for medical prognosis. Decision Support Systems 54(3), 1499–1510 (2 2013). https://doi.org/10.1016/J.DSS.2012.12.033

20. Plattform Industrie 4.0: Plattform Industrie 4.0 - Asset Administration Shell - Reading Guide (2 2022), https://www.plattform-i40.de/IP/Redaktion/EN/Downloads/Publikation/AAS-ReadingGuide202201.html

21. Plaza, E., McGinty, L.: Distributed case-based reasoning. The Knowledge Engineering Review **20**, 261–265 (2006). https://doi.org/10.1017/S0269888906000683

22. RDF Working Group: Resource Description Framework (RDF) (2014). https://www.w3.org/2001/sw/wiki/RDF

23. Recio-García, J.A., González-Calero, P.A., Díaz-Agudo, B.: jcolibri2: a framework for building case-based reasoning systems. Sci. Comput. Program. **79**, 126–145 (2014). https://doi.org/10.1016/j.scico.2012.04.002

24. Rongen, S., Nikolova, N., van der Pas, M.: Modelling with AAS and RDF in Industry 4.0. Comput. Ind. **148**, 103910 (2023). https://doi.org/10.1016/J.COMPIND.2023.103910

25. Schwarte, A., Haase, P., Hose, K., Schenkel, R., Schmidt, M.: FedX: a federation layer for distributed query processing on linked open data. In: Antoniou, G., et al. (eds.) ESWC 2011. LNCS, vol. 6644, pp. 481–486. Springer, Heidelberg (2011). https://doi.org/10.1007/978-3-642-21064-8_39

26. Taelman, R., Van Herwegen, J., Vander Sande, M., Verborgh, R.: Comunica: a modular SPARQL query engine for the web. In: Vrandečić, D., et al. (eds.) ISWC 2018. LNCS, vol. 11137, pp. 239–255. Springer, Cham (2018). https://doi.org/10.1007/978-3-030-00668-6_15

27. Tran, H.M., Schönwälder, J.: DisCaRia - distributed case-based reasoning system for fault management. IEEE Trans. Netw. Serv. Manage. **12**(4), 540–553 (2015). https://doi.org/10.1109/TNSM.2015.2496224

28. Verborgh, R.: Triple pattern fragments: a low-cost knowledge graph interface for the web. J. Web Seman. **37**, 184–206 (2016). https://doi.org/10.1016/j.websem.2016.03.003

29. Wingerath, W., Ritter, N., Gessert, F.: Real-Time & Stream Data Management. SpringerBriefs in Computer Science, Springer, Cham (2019). https://doi.org/10.1007/978-3-030-10555-6

The Case for Circularities in Case-Based Reasoning

Adwait P. Parsodkar[1]([⊠]), Deepak P.[1,2], and Sutanu Chakraborti[1]

[1] Indian Institute of Technology, Madras, Chennai, India
{cs20d404,sutanuc}@cse.iitm.ac.in, deepaksp@acm.org
[2] Queen's University Belfast, Belfast, UK

Abstract. In this paper, we demonstrate that diverse CBR research contexts share a common thread, in that their origin can be traced to the problem of *circularity*. An example is where the knowledge of property A requires us to know property B, but B, in turn, is not known unless A is determined. We examine the root cause of such circularities and present fundamental impossibility results in this context. We show how a systematic study of circularity can motivate the quest for novel CBR paradigms and lead to novel approaches that address circularities in traditional CBR retrieval, adaptation, and maintenance tasks. Furthermore, such an analysis can help in extending the solution of one problem to solve an apparently unrelated problem, once we discover the commonality they share deep down in terms of the circularities they address.

Keywords: Circularity · Truth Discovery · Knowledge Containers

1 Introduction

Case-Based Reasoning (CBR) is an inherently cyclical problem-solving paradigm where problem-solving and learning go hand in hand [1]. Given a target problem to solve, relevant past cases are retrieved, and their solutions are adapted to propose a solution. If the solution works, a new case comprising the target problem and the verified solution is stored in the case base. With each new case being added, the system gets more competent, and this constitutes learning. If the system is good at problem-solving, the cases fetched using retrieval and the solutions proposed using adaptation stand a better chance of being useful - such successful episodes of problem solving help in growing the case base and making it more competent. However, it is also that true problem solving cannot be effective unless the case base is competent. Such circularities abound more generally in the broader context of knowledge representation and reasoning: the effectiveness of the reasoning mechanism critically depends on the knowledge representation, but then, the knowledge itself is acquired by way of reasoning.

The circular dependence of problem solving and learning in CBR is just an instance of circularities that manifest in diverse research sub-themes of CBR.

S. Massie and S. Chakraborti (Eds.): ICCBR 2023, LNAI 14141, pp. 85–101, 2023.
https://doi.org/10.1007/978-3-031-40177-0_6

This paper is intended to be an exploratory one, where we attempt to examine the genesis, the nature, and implications of such circularities. In particular, we attempt to substantiate our central claim: whenever we run into a circularity, it makes sense not to sweep it under the carpet. A critical examination can help us gain foundational insights on the nature of a problem, and spawn interesting research themes that can mitigate, if not resolve, the underlying circularity. At the very least, we emerge more well-informed of the unwritten assumptions behind existing approaches.

The structure of the paper is as follows. Section 2 presents the big picture, where we position the circularities observed in CBR in the context of a wider class of circularities that arise in the context of knowledge representation, and demonstrate how they share common origins. We introduce the notion of "representation gap", a term we use to denote the disparity between the knowledge as represented in a CBR system, and the actual experiences they attempt to encode. Our central thesis is that representation gap is the single most fundamental source of circularities. In Sect. 3, we show how an in-depth appreciation of the knowledge representation gap can lead to questioning the fundamental assumptions of traditional CBR, which are often taken to be granted, and thereby motivate research into non-conventional paradigms in CBR. Section 4 is about the more commonplace ways of dealing with circularity, where we operate within the framework of traditional CBR and address circularities as and where they surface. One auxiliary goal of our paper is to pave the way for a unifying framework, where apparently unrelated research problems in diverse areas of CBR are found to share commonalities in terms of the underlying circularities that they set out to resolve. Such revelations can open up opportunities for transplanting or adapting the solution of one problem to another. We present some examples to illustrate this in Sect. 5. Finally, Sect. 6 concludes the work and reflects on potential research directions that it can open up.

2   Circularities: The Big Picture

An interesting case of circularities is one of loops and self-reference in dictionary definitions [21]. For example, the definition of the word "green" makes use of the word "leaf" (to give examples of objects that are green), but "leaf", in turn, is defined using the word "green". Such circularities arise because of limits of language: the perception of the colour "green" cannot be communicated to a visually challenged person using language alone. This is an instance of a wider class of circularities that originate because of the "representation gap": the fact that the perceptual grounding of symbols [14] is not contained in the language itself. In the context of CBR, we can show that irrespective of the richness of knowledge contained in vocabulary, case base, similarity, and adaptation [32], the representation is, at best, a surrogate for the experiences that give birth to the cases and the underlying design choices are in the mind of the designer, not in the system itself. This places a natural upper bound on the effectiveness of the system when viewed as an autonomous agent. In Sects. 3 and 4, we deliberate on ways of mitigating the effects of circularities whose genesis can be traced back to the representation gap.

Let us examine more closely the nature of the representation gap, its theoretical implications, and how it manifests as circularities in the context of CBR. Formal arguments that demonstrate the limits of language were advanced by the noted philosopher of language Ludwig Wittgenstein. In Wittgenstein's words [39]:

> *"In order that you should have a language which can express or say everything that can be said, this language must have certain properties; and when this is the case, that it has them can no longer be said in that language or any language."*

While this is cryptic on the surface, the essence can be distilled using a simple example. The coupling of the word "green" to the perceptual experience of the colour "green" in language L_1 (say English) is not contained in L_1 - so one would require a second language L_2 to establish that association. But any symbol that constitutes the alphabet of L_2 suffers from the same limitation, in that it requires a third language L_3 to establish the grounding of its symbols. L_3 similarly calls for yet another language L_4, and so on, giving rise to an infinite regress. This is an intuitive sketch of the argument used to show that no language is self-contained.

Closely related to the unsurmountable limits of language are problems originating from an (unwritten) assumption in science that an observer can study nature as an objective reality outside him. When the mind studies itself, however, the observer becomes identical to the observed, leading to a fundamental circularity. For an engaging account of the implications of such circularities see [2]. Even in physics which studies matter and shies itself away from studying mind, and where the traditional view has been that the observer is distinct from the observed, the advent of quantum mechanics has dealt a heavy blow, questioning its foundations. In particular, we have impossibility results like the Heisenberg's uncertainty principle. Interestingly, Heisenberg is categorical in attributing aspects of his results to fundamental limits of languages as revealed by Wittgenstein [39]. In the words of Heisenberg:

> *"Words have no well-defined meaning. We can sometimes by axioms give a precise meaning to words, but still we never know how these precise words correspond to reality, whether they fit reality or not. We cannot help the fundamental situation - that words are meant as a connection between reality and ourselves - but we can never know how well these words or concepts fit reality. This can be seen in Wittgenstein's later work."*

Interestingly, a recent paper by Bender and Koller [4] has argued that despite the impressive achievements in the field of Large Language Models (LLMs), since the latter only use form as training data, it can never lead to learning of meaning, where meaning is the relation between linguistic form and communicative intent. This is in strong agreement with our observations on the representation gap.

The implications in the context of CBR follow naturally. The knowledge of a CBR system can never be self-contained. Irrespective of how rich its knowledge containers [32], i.e., the case base, vocabulary, similarity, and adaptation are, a CBR system will always fall short of what we would ideally expect of it. The case base and the vocabulary used to express and index the same can never capture the totality of experiences of problem-solving in any domain, nor can the similarity and adaptation knowledge capture all the diverse settings in which such experiences can and cannot be applied.

This representation gap manifests itself in various kinds of circularities in the context of CBR. One potent example is related to the inherent challenge in defining the utility of a case with respect to a target problem [5]. In particular, the statement of circularity is *Given a target problem, a case should be retrieved only if it is useful in solving the target problem. However, we cannot ascertain the utility of a case with respect to the target problem unless it is retrieved in the first place.*

Since it is impossible to resolve this circularity, we often bypass it by using similarity as a surrogate for utility. Unlike utility which is an "a posteriori" criterion in that we can know the utility only after we have solved the target problem, similarity is "a priori" in nature: we can estimate similarity and use it as the basis for retrieving cases while acknowledging that the cases thus retrieved are not necessarily the ones most useful in the "a posteriori" sense (for details, see Sect. 4.1 in [5]).

A second example is in the context of purely introspective learning, where similarity knowledge is acquired (inductively) in a purely bottom-up fashion from the cases, and there is no external knowledge separate from the case repository that provides that knowledge. Let us consider the case where cases are represented in terms of attribute values. We encounter a circularity of the kind - *Two cases are regarded as similar when they have similar attribute values. However, two attribute values are regarded as similar when they occur in similar cases.* It is interesting to note that there is no such circularity in settings that are not purely introspective, such as those in which domain experts explicitly provide local similarity functions.

As would be expected, such circularities are commonly encountered in several contexts in machine learning, which is largely based on inducing hypotheses introspectively from data. For example, in learning distributional measures of word similarity (or more appropriately, word relatedness) from a given document corpus, we exploit underlying word co-occurrence patterns. In particular, we observe: *Two words are similar if they occur in similar documents*[1]. *However, two documents are similar if they have similar words.* The circularity inherent here is isomorphic to the circularity we observed in the context of cases and attribute values. In text mining literature, several approaches have been proposed for estimating the relatedness of words and documents by addressing such circularities. Examples are: (a) factor-analytic approaches like Latent Semantic

---

[1] Instead of documents we can choose to consider paragraphs, or some other unit of discourse.

Analysis (LSA) [8] (b) the use of Expectation Maximization for parameter estimation as in Probabilistic LSA, (c) distributional representations which explicitly model homophily [25], and (d) the SimRank algorithm [19], which can be viewed as an extension of the PageRank algorithm [29]. Interestingly, we find that the use of such approaches for addressing the problem of circularity is not surprising: PageRank, which is designed to identify web page importance based on the hyperlink structure of the web, for instance, already solves a circularity: *A web-page is important if it is pointed to by several important web-pages.* Similarly, the E and M steps in the EM algorithm are known to handle circularities inherent in parameter estimation from incomplete data. In particular, we can only estimate parameters when the data is completed; but the data cannot be completed unless we know the parameters [24]. The discussion above points to the fact that if we handle circularity effectively in one context, the solution can be reused in addressing circularities in other contexts as well. We will have more to comment on this, especially in the context of CBR, in Sect. 5. When knowledge is acquired externally, circularities of the kind shown above do not appear. For example, if relatedness between two words is externally provided by a source like WordNet [26], word similarities are no longer circularly dependent of document similarities. However, even while using WordNet, there would still be issues in grounding meanings of words. In the context of Word Sense Disambiguation, which is used to identify which of the several senses of a polysemous word (like "bank") must be chosen given some context words, we encounter a fresh kind of circularity: *the correct sense of a word W_1 can only be known if we know the correct sense of a context word W_2, but the disambiguation of W_2 needs W_1 to be disambiguated in the first place.* Thus the circularity takes a different form, but does not completely disappear. This is not surprising, given our central argument that the representation gap can, at best, be minimized; it can never be done away with.

A concept very closely related to the representation gap is that of "structure function correspondence" [35]. In structural CBR (as with relational databases), the structure of a case is strongly representative of the functions that it can carry out, so the structure-function correspondence is strong. On the other hand, we have relatively weak structure function correspondence in textual CBR - this is because words in text interact with each other non-linearly to give rise to emergent "meaning" that may not be carried by any of the words in isolation. Poetry, satire or humour are at the extreme end of the spectrum, where structure function correspondence is very weak. The weaker the structure function correspondence, the larger the representation gap.

There is yet another perspective that is relevant: one that posits that circularity originates from the dichotomy of the whole versus parts. St. Augustine theorized that children learn the meanings of words by the following simple process: an adult points his finger to an object and says "chair", the child associates her visual perception of that object with the word "chair". This theory has glaring loopholes, however. Based on such a limited interaction with the adult, it is virtually impossible for the child to tell whether "chair" refers to "anything made of wood", "any object on which we can sit", or "any object with a flat surface", "the particular object being pointed to alone", or any of other such possibilities. Thanks to Ferdinand de Saussure and his theory of structuralism [10], we now know that this is not how word meanings are acquired. Words refer to concepts are abstract entities that can only be defined by means of their relationship to other concepts. For example, the word "chair" does not refer to any specific instance of a chair or to the collection of all chairs in the universe - rather, it is an abstract concept that can only be defined in terms of associations with other concepts that define its function ("sit"), constituents ("wood" or "steel"), the super-category or hypernym ("furniture"), subcategories ("easy chair" or "office chair"), and concepts that have similar functions ("stool" or "bench"), for example (refer [3] for a relevant discussion on the Protos system in the context of CBR). *An entity A cannot be ontologically defined without reference to a related entity B; the definition of B, in turn, requires A to be defined.* This reminds us of the mutual dependence of the words "leaf" and "green" in dictionary definitions and hence the circularity originating from structuralist assumptions, at its core, is closely related to circularity that stems from the representation gap.

3   Taking Circularity Head On: Alternate Paradigms

The first way to address circularities emanating from the representation gap is to come up with novel paradigms that challenge the foundational assumptions behind traditional CBR systems. In this section, we present two illustrations of such paradigm-level changes.

The first is the existing holographic CBR paradigm [11,37]. The Holographic CBR paradigm was first proposed by Devi et al. [11] with the goal of making CBR more cognitively appealing. It was subsequently extended by Renganathan et al. [37]. In traditional CBR systems, cases can be added or deleted without affecting the rest of the case base. Human memories, in contrast, are far from passive - we tend to actively reorganize our experiences. To cite an example by Roger Schank [34], whose early work on the role of memory structures played an important role in shaping up the field of CBR, we tend to forget details of individual visits to restaurants (unless something very different from the norm happens) - instead the specifics gets "mushed up" to create more general structures that are effective in raising expectations about future trips, and seeking explanations in case the event of expectation failures. The departures from conventional models are not just at the level of high-level cognition; there are interesting findings from neuroscience as well. In particular, we now know that when portions of the brain are damaged or surgically removed, it is not that memories are wiped out completely. Instead, what we have is a hazy reconstruction of what was stored previously. This can be attributed to non-localized or holographic memories, where each component carries an imprint of the whole.

Holographic CBR draws inspiration from these ideas. We have seen in the last section that the part-whole dichotomy leads naturally to the representation gap which manifests itself in the form of circularities. Holographic CBR attempts to address the sharp divide between the whole and parts by making sure that each case is no longer a passive record of problem solving, but they house similarity and adaptation knowledge locally, proactively interact with each other in the course of problem solving in a distributed way, and offer resilience in the face of case deletion and the ability to generalize when cases come in. This is in sharp contrast to traditional CBR system, where cases are passive and the reasoner, which has access to similarity and adaptation knowledge, has centralized control of how cases are used for problem solving. A conventional CBR system is analogous to an organization where the manager runs the show himself, and each of his subordinates passively execute the job given to them, while being agnostic to the overall objective, or the competencies of their co-workers. In contrast, a holographic CBR system is analogous to an organization where the employees are aware of the overall goals and competencies of their colleagues, actively collaborate with each other in problem solving, possess the ability to take over responsibilities from their co-workers in case any of them leave the organization (case deletion) and can also hire new workers if needed (case addition). In the context of CBR, the central insight from this analogy, the closer the case representations are, to the intent for which they have been created in the first place, the lower the representation gap.

A second example of a paradigm level shift can potentially be made by use of quantum models. In the context of quantum mechanics, Heisenberg's uncertainty principle declares fundamental limits to the precision with which certain pairs of physical properties of a particle, such as position and momentum, can be known. Interestingly, Heisenberg attributes aspects of his results to Wittgenstein's work on limits on languages [31], which directly relates to the representation gap and consequently the problem of circularity as we have seen earlier. The mathematical framework of quantum physics has been exploited by Busemeyer [6] in the context of quantum models of cognition. The seminal work of Rijsbergen [33] in the area of quantum information retrieval is also a case in point. In future, we may see extensions of the quantum models pave way for novel paradigms that can effectively contain representation gap in CBR.

4   Addressing Circularity as and Where it Appears

Our discussion in the last section illustrated how a study of circularities at a fundamental level can motivate research into non-conventional paradigms in CBR. It should be noted, however, that occurrences of circularities are also observed to manifest within the current framework of CBR. In this section, we show how a few of these have been addressed in the literature.

4.1   Addressing The Problem of Modelling Case Utility

The issue of defining the utility of a case with respect to a target problem has been highlighted in Sect. 2 with emphasis on the fact that the similarity is only a proxy to its utility. The CBR literature recognizes the limitations of the use of similarity as a surrogate for utility and has proposed measures such as those based on diversity, adaptability, and compromise to complement similarity.

A diversity-conscious retrieval will allow the recommendation (of, say, houses) of heterogeneous characteristics that are relevant to the query. Such a strategy allows the system to learn about the user's preferences in situations of uncertainty (for instance, whether or not the user wants a house with an open layout). Compromise-driven retrieval, yet another approach to expose the users to a diversity of products, operates by providing the user with recommendations that make compromises across different attributes (price of the house, for instance). Rounds of interactions with a system employing a compromise-driven retrieval can reveal the attributes on which the user is willing to make compromises and allow navigation to products with, say, the minimum number of compromises.

An adaptation-guided retrieval takes into account the adaptability of cases to suit the query and retrieves cases that are not only close to the query but are also highly adaptable. As an illustrative example, while a laptop may not have on-paper specifications that closely resemble the user's requirements, if it can be customized to meet the user's needs precisely, it should ideally be retrieved.

It is critical to note that these measures, much like similarity, are "a priori" in nature thereby fundamentally limiting them from being good estimates of utility that is "a posteriori" in nature. This aligns with the impossibility result in Sect. 2 where we argue as to why the representation gap can never be bridged completely. However, a variety of "a priori" measures can be used to arrive at a better estimate of the utility of a case to a query, and hence serves as means to narrow the representation gap.

4.2   Reducing Representation Gap with Better Interfaces

An attribute-value style description of cases in CBR is fundamentally bound by the amount of details that can be captured about the corresponding entity. The same applies in the context of Information Retrieval where the query is not adequately expressive of the underlying intent of the user, and similarly, the document indices also fail to capture all the different ways in which it may potentially be found useful.

Attempts have been made in the CBR community to reduce this representational gap by exploiting user feedback to compensate for the lack of richness in the utility function. The provision of allowing user feedback of varying characteristics over the set of candidates can allow the system to learn the user's implicit preferences. In particular, feedback that highlights a user's preference for one product over another can provide valuable insights into the features favored by the user. This type of feedback can also be memoized to identify broader product preference trends among users with similar preferences [38]. The user may also *critique* a recommendation (a camera for instance), by requesting a product with better characteristics (higher resolution or lower price, for instance) [7]. Furthermore, a *more like this* [12] feedback mechanism allows the system to recommend options that are still similar to the selected product in aspects previously expressed by the user while offering a diverse range of options across other features. For instance, a user expressing a *more like this* feedback for a budget laptop can be further exposed to options from diverse brands in order to understand her brand preference.

In the light of the discussions in Sect. 2, these approaches improve structure-function correspondence and hence reduce the representation gap.

4.3 Narrowing Representation Gap By a Way of Novel Retrieval Formalisms

Case Retrieval Networks [20] is a spreading activation model that facilitates flexible and efficient retrieval in CBR. The network involves a set of information entities (the set of all attribute values), denoted by IE, and a set of case nodes. In order to reflect the non-orthogonality of the IEs, weighted connections, referred to as the *similarity arcs*, between IEs are introduced. The association between each pair comprising of an IE and a case is expressed via *relevance arcs*. Upon encountering a query that is viewed as a subset of all the IEs, activation is first spread within the IEs via the similarity arc. This is followed by the propagation of values to the cases by means of the relevance arcs. The cases are then sorted based on the aggregated values.

It is to be noted that the retrieval in CRN is dependent only on the input query (feature values, in the CBR context) and is based on (a rather optimistic) assumption that all the information in a case is captured by the totality of the information contained in the IEs. While this might be the case in situations with strong structure-function correspondence (such as a task involving the prediction of house prices), it often remains inapplicable in those with poor structure-function correspondence which is often characterized by a large representational gap. A book recommender system, one of the several settings where attribute-value representations fall short, is associated with the representation strategy exhibiting poor structure-function correspondence in that the attributes of a book are not necessarily indicative of its contents.

Collaborative filtering style approach [18] serves as a viable option to handle this issue that estimates relatedness between books, in our example, based on the relatedness of the users who rate them. This allows the incorporation of user preference knowledge into the system that is manifested in the CRN architecture via arcs between cases [35]. Notice that the integration of arcs between cases facilitates retrieval that is not solely committed to the features but takes into account knowledge from a host of users, thereby allowing the narrowing of the representation gap.

4.4 Case Reliability

In large-scale CBR applications, the knowledge contained in the case base in the form of cases can be sourced from an array of external sources such as datasets, websites, etc. Since these sources might cater to different quality standards, the resulting case base need not necessarily be composed of homogeneous quality cases. A case exhibiting poor quality in a classification setup might correspond to what is often referred to as noisy, in machine learning literature (e.g., noisy labels [27]). The presence of such cases in the case base can significantly impact the prediction performance of the system. While it is theoretically possible for a domain expert to manually assess these cases for quality, it is apparently infeasible in practice. Arriving at approaches that arrive at estimates of the quality of the cases, in the absence of labeled data, appears promising with regards to improving the efficacy of the reasoner.

Although measures have been proposed to identify cases of substandard quality ([23], for instance), they often rely on the underlying definition that a case is unreliable if it disagrees with its neighbors. Such approaches implicitly assign a homogeneous quality to all the neighbors - something that might rarely be true in several settings with unvalidated cases. We would, however, like to take into account the contribution of neighbors of a case in proportion to their quality while estimating the quality of a case. This leads to an immediate circularity - inferring the quality of a case requires the knowledge of the quality of the individuals in its neighborhood. RelCBR [30] proposes the following definition for the *reliability* of cases based on the following circular definition.

Definition 1. A case is reliable if it can be solved by its reliable neighbors.

The circularity resolution approach involves translating this statement into an objective function that is optimized for reliability scores using the projected gradient descent approach [30]. Empirical results demonstrate that this definition facilitates appropriate assignment of reliability to cases even if they appear in a neighborhood of noisy cases, a situation where the baseline methods arrive at misleading conclusions.

4.5   Case Acquisition in Textual CBR

In this section, we highlight a previously established approach, called Correlation and Cohesion Driven Segmentation (CCS) [28], which attempts to segment a set of textual incident reports into a case base. Specifically, each report is to be split into two components, namely, a problem component and a solution component. The basis for this approach is founded upon a circular theme expressed in the following statement.

Definition 2. Good segmentation of each of the documents can serve as a valuable means to understand the behavior of the problem and solution segments. Well-learned solution and problem segment behavior can facilitate the derivation of good segmentation.

Here, the *behavior* of the problem and solution segment is modeled using language and translation models, details of which can be found in [28].

This circularity, much like most others, appears like the "chicken egg" problem [9]. In the situation at hand, if one were to arrive at a good understanding of how the problem and solution components corresponding to documents look like, a good segmentation strategy would be required; however, a good segmentation strategy can only be arrived at when the system has a good understanding of the problem and solution components. The EM algorithm is employed to resolve this circularity. In that, the E-step estimates the posterior probabilities associated with each potential segmentation, given the language and translation models, while the M-step reconstructs these models based on the probabilities.

4.6 Enriching Case Descriptions

Traditionally, the similarity function in CBR often only takes into account the query input to the system alongside the problem parts of the cases, disregarding the useful information gathered by the reasoner over interactions with its users. The system should ideally minimize the number of interactions with the customer and should therefore place *better* products at the top of the recommendation list. Notably, customers tend to favor products with positive collective reviews, such as bestsellers, over products with favorable on-paper features alone.

Since the case representation often falls short of such information, enriching the representation strategy based on knowledge drawn from user interactions holds promise for better recommendations [38]. In particular, we want criterion (such as *extent of violence* in a movie domain) to reflect as attributes in the case representation. Given the information about the preference of a product over another based on multiple users in the context of the criterion, useful insights can be drawn about the involved products. It is important to note that merely tallying the number of times a product has been preferred over other products is not a reliable measure of its overall *preferability*. This is attributed to the fact that a preference over a highly sought-after product is worth much more than that over a moderately preferred one. The following definition can be used to quantify the preferability of a product given a context.

Definition 3. A case is preferable in a given context if it is preferred over other preferable cases by multiple users in the same context.

This circularity resembles the PageRank style of rank-ordering pages. The knowledge of the preferability of the products, the analog of the importance scores in PageRank, can now be incorporated in the case representation by treating the preferability score as a value to the criterion considered as a feature.

5 Transplanting Solutions of One Kind of Circularity to Solve Another

Following on from Sect. 4 that presents a range of circularities in CBR and approaches employed to resolve them, we now highlight approaches that have conventionally been used in diverse CBR tasks like retrieval, adaptation, and maintenance and have been agnostic to the circularities latent in the problem definitions. Highlighting the underlying statements of circularity can open up fresh research directions towards improving the efficacy of the reasoner. By taking into account the underlying circularity, we can arrive at improved variants of these approaches. Based on the discussion presented in this section, it may be noted that circularities associated with seemingly unrelated problems may have analogous resolution strategies.

5.1   Ensemble of Knowledge Containers

Consider a setting that requires assigning reliability to the reviewers of a conference, wherein each reviewer is tasked with rating the work they review over a maximum score of, say, 5. In the absence of a higher authority that assesses the reviewer, reviewers whose rating is close to the inferred *trustworthy score* of, say, 4 for a paper are deemed *reliable*. However, the score 4 is determined based on the reliability of the reviewers in the first place, leading to a circular dependence. Truth Discovery [22] deals with the task of assigning reliability scores to a set of potentially conflicting sources (reviewers, in our example) that provide values (scores out of 5) to objects (research papers) in the absence of any form of supervision. The fundamental principle of circularity is captured in the statement: *A source is reliable if it provides trustworthy solutions. A solution is trustworthy if it is supported by reliable sources.* We now highlight how ideas inspired by the Truth Discovery literature can be leveraged in the context of CBR, where an ensemble of knowledge containers of the same kind is available.

5.1.1   Ensemble of Similarity Functions

Literature in CBR has proposed multiple ways of arriving at a similarity function in situations where top-down expert knowledge is not accessible (see [15] for instance). However, no single method is consistently shown to outperform others across multiple datasets, so the varied knowledge captured in a variety of similarity functions can be leveraged to result in improved performance. A rudimentary approach for aggregating these can involve taking a weighted combination of the different similarity values. This, however, requires similar distribution to be associated with the similarity functions in order to prevent a similarity function that is liberal in the assignment of similarity scores from overpowering another that usually assigns low similarity scores.

It is, therefore, advantageous to aggregate the rankings generated by these similarity functions instead, in addition to assigning them reliability scores that are learned in a bottom-up fashion. Notably, the statement of circularity in Truth Discovery, is analogous to the situation at hand, wherein a ranker (similarity function) corresponds to a knowledge source that generates rankings of cases as a solution to an input query. The following definition can be used to arrive at the reliability of the similarity functions.

Definition 4. A ranker is reliable if it produces trustworthy rankings for several queries. A ranking is trustworthy if it is supported by reliable rankers.

5.1.2   Ensemble of Adaptation Strategies

A bottom-up approach for learning adaptation rules, particularly in numerical prediction tasks, is to use the *case difference heuristic* [13]. In particular, for a pair of neighboring cases (c_i, c_j), an adaptation rule can be generated that states *'A difference of $p_i - p_j$ on the problem side results in a solution side difference of $s_i - s_j$'* where p_i and s_i indicate the problem and solution part of the case c_i.

Apparently, methodologies that use this strategy as a basis for acquiring adaptation knowledge are susceptible to two primary setbacks. The first of these pertains to the possibility of a drastic increase in the number of adaptation rules. Further, while existing approaches tend to assign uniform reliability to each adaptation rule in the ensemble [17], we envisage that several adaptation rules learned from the data might be incorrect owing to their derivation from poor-quality cases. Thus, assigning reliability scores to these rules hold potential for improved efficacy of the system.

The method outlined in [16] involves quantifying the reliability of an adaptation strategy by evaluating the goodness of the modified solution it generates for several queries, possibly in a leave-one-out style strategy. Although this methodology yields good reliability estimates when the cases in the case base are accurately labeled, it could lead to erroneous conclusions when dealing with noisy cases. In particular, a rule may be deemed unreliable due to its inability to accommodate poor-quality cases. Consequently, a more appropriate approach would be to verify if other reliable adaptation strategies concur with the rule under evaluation, in which case, the rule can be rightfully considered reliable. Much like our discussion in Sect. 5.1.1, we foresee the applicability of the Truth Discovery style of circularity to gauge the reliability of the adaptation rules using the following definition.

Definition 5. An adaptation strategy is reliable if it produces trustworthy solutions for several queries. The solution corresponding to each of these queries is trustworthy if it is agreed upon by several reliable adaptation strategies.

5.2   Robust Estimates of Case Competence

In the context of lazy learners such as Case-Based Reasoners, the query response time is typically found to increase with an increase in the number of instances (cases in CBR) [36]. The underlying reason being the increase in time required for the computation of similarity (or equivalently, distance) between the query and (potentially) every case in the case base. The Footprint Algorithm [36] returns a subset of the entire case base, referred to as the footprint set, while preserving the problem-solving ability, but eliminating redundant cases, thereby improving the efficiency of the system.

The set of cases that constitute the footprint set is critically determined by scores assigned to them that indicate their problem-solving abilities. Notice that approaches that indicate the goodness of the case (reliability, for instance) are not indicative of the redundant nature of the cases. Instead, the Relative

Coverage [36] measure is often employed to assess the competence of a case, assigning it a high value if it solves cases that are not solved by many cases.

Consider a sample example where a case c_1 solves a case c_2 that is also solved by c_3. The Relative Coverage of c_1 is only dependent on the number of cases it solves (such as c_2) and the count of cases with which its coverage sets intersect (like with c_3). Apparently, the Relative Coverage score of c_1 is independent of that of c_3. However, the competence of c_1 should ideally be high if c_3 has a low competence (heuristically speaking, is likely to be dropped, thus making c_1 likely the only one that may be able to solve c_2 in a compacted case base such as the footprint). In effect, the competence of c_1 can be known only when that of c_3 is known, while the determination of competence of c_3 requires the knowledge of competence of c_1, leading to a circular dependence. To capture this, we propose a measure of competence of a case grounded upon the following definition.

Definition 6. A case is highly competent if it solves several cases that are solved by cases of low competence.

6   Conclusion

In this paper, we outlined how circularities manifest in diverse contexts in CBR, and how such circularities are organically grounded within understandings of knowledge representations and insights from cognitive and neurological sciences. We illustrated how a systematic study of such circularities can help us in three distinct ways. Firstly, it can spawn research on novel paradigms. Secondly, when we question the assumptions behind approaches in traditional CBR that are used for specific tasks, such as those involved in retrieval, adaptation, and maintenance, we often find that there are underlying circularities, which, when resolved effectively, can potentially lead us to improved variants of these algorithms. Thus a study of this kind has the potential to spawn fresh research across a wide range of themes within CBR. Finally, we have also seen how such a unified perspective helps in reusing solutions to circularity in one setting to other areas that, on the surface, appear unrelated.

References

1. Aamodt, A., Plaza, E.: Case-based reasoning: foundational issues, methodological variations, and system approaches. AI Commun. **7**(1), 39–59 (1994)
2. Aharoni, R.: Circularity. WORLD SCIENTIFIC, September 2015. https://doi.org/10.1142/9805
3. Bareiss, E.R., Porter, B.W., Wier, C.C.: Protos: an exemplar-based learning apprentice. Int. J. Man-Mach. Stud. **29**(5), 549–561 (1988). https://doi.org/10.1016/S0020-7373(88)80012-9
4. Bender, E.M., Koller, A.: Climbing towards NLU: on meaning, form, and understanding in the age of data. In: Proceedings of the 58th Annual Meeting of the Association for Computational Linguistics, pp. 5185–5198. Association for Computational Linguistics, Online, July 2020. https://doi.org/10.18653/v1/2020.acl-main.463

5. Bergmann, R. (ed.): Experience Management. Springer, Berlin Heidelberg (2002). https://doi.org/10.1007/3-540-45759-3
6. Busemeyer, J.R., Bruza, P.D.: Quantum Models of Cognition and Decision. Cambridge University Press, Cambridge, July 2012. https://doi.org/10.1017/cbo9780511997716
7. Chen, L., Pu, P.: Critiquing-based recommenders: survey and emerging trends. User Model. User-Adap. Interact. **22**(1–2), 125–150 (2011). https://doi.org/10.1007/s11257-011-9108-6
8. Deerwester, S., Dumais, S.T., Furnas, G.W., Landauer, T.K., Harshman, R.: Indexing by latent semantic analysis. J. Am. Soc. Inf. Sci. **41**(6), 391–407 (1990). https://doi.org/10.1002/(SICI)1097-4571(199009)41:6⟨391::AID-ASI1⟩3.0.CO;2-9
9. Domingos, P.: The Master Algorithm: How the Quest for the Ultimate Learning Machine Will Remake Our World. Basic Books, New York (2015)
10. Elffers, E.: Saussurean structuralism and cognitive linguistics. Hist. Épistémol. Lang. **34**(1), 19–40 (2012). https://doi.org/10.3406/hel.2012.3235
11. Ganesan, D., Chakraborti, S.: Holographic case-based reasoning. In: Watson, I., Weber, R. (eds.) ICCBR 2020. LNCS (LNAI), vol. 12311, pp. 144–159. Springer, Cham (2020). https://doi.org/10.1007/978-3-030-58342-2_10
12. Ginty, L.M., Smyth, B.: Comparison-based recommendation. In: Craw, S., Preece, A. (eds.) ECCBR 2002. LNCS (LNAI), vol. 2416, pp. 575–589. Springer, Heidelberg (2002). https://doi.org/10.1007/3-540-46119-1_42
13. Hanney, K., Keane, M.T.: Learning adaptation rules from a case-base. In: Smith, I., Faltings, B. (eds.) EWCBR 1996. LNCS, vol. 1168, pp. 179–192. Springer, Heidelberg (1996). https://doi.org/10.1007/BFb0020610
14. Harnad, S.: Categorical Perception. In: Nadel, L. (ed.) Encyclopedia of Cognitive Science, pp. 67–4. Nature Publishing Group (2003)
15. Jaiswal, A., Bach, K.: A data-driven approach for determining weights in global similarity functions. In: Bach, K., Marling, C. (eds.) ICCBR 2019. LNCS (LNAI), vol. 11680, pp. 125–139. Springer, Cham (2019). https://doi.org/10.1007/978-3-030-29249-2_9
16. Jalali, V., Leake, D.: On retention of adaptation rules. In: Lamontagne, L., Plaza, E. (eds.) ICCBR 2014. LNCS (LNAI), vol. 8765, pp. 200–214. Springer, Cham (2014). https://doi.org/10.1007/978-3-319-11209-1_15
17. Jalali, V., Leake, D., Forouzandehmehr, N.: Ensemble of adaptations for classification: learning adaptation rules for categorical features. In: Goel, A., Díaz-Agudo, M.B., Roth-Berghofer, T. (eds.) ICCBR 2016. LNCS (LNAI), vol. 9969, pp. 186–202. Springer, Cham (2016). https://doi.org/10.1007/978-3-319-47096-2_13
18. Jannach, D., Zanker, M., Felfernig, A., Friedrich, G.: Recommender Systems: An Introduction. Cambridge University Press, Cambridge (2010)
19. Jeh, G., Widom, J.: Simrank: a measure of structural-context similarity. In: Proceedings of the Eighth ACM SIGKDD International Conference on Knowledge Discovery and Data Mining, pp. 538–543 (2002). https://doi.org/10.1145/775047.775126
20. Lenz, M., Burkhard, H.-D.: Case retrieval nets: basic ideas and extensions. In: Görz, G., Hölldobler, S. (eds.) KI 1996. LNCS, vol. 1137, pp. 227–239. Springer, Heidelberg (1996). https://doi.org/10.1007/3-540-61708-6_63
21. Levary, D., Eckmann, J.P., Moses, E., Tlusty, T.: Loops and self-reference in the construction of dictionaries. Phys. Rev. X **2**, 031018 (2012). https://doi.org/10.1103/PhysRevX.2.031018
22. Li, Y., et al.: A survey on truth discovery. ACM SIGKDD Explorations Newsl. **17**(2), 1–16 (2016)

23. Massie, S., Craw, S., Wiratunga, N.: Complexity profiling for informed case-base editing. In: Roth-Berghofer, T.R., Göker, M.H., Güvenir, H.A. (eds.) ECCBR 2006. LNCS (LNAI), vol. 4106, pp. 325–339. Springer, Heidelberg (2006). https://doi.org/10.1007/11805816_25

24. Meng, X.L., Van Dyk, D.: The EM algorithm—an old folk-song sung to a fast new tune. J. R. Stat. Soc. Ser. B Stat. Methodol. **59**(3), 511–567 (1997)

25. Mikolov, T., Chen, K., Corrado, G., Dean, J.: Efficient estimation of word representations in vector space. arXiv preprint arXiv:1301.3781 (2013)

26. Miller, G.A.: WordNet. Commun. ACM **38**(11), 39–41 (1995). https://doi.org/10.1145/219717.219748

27. Natarajan, N., Dhillon, I.S., Ravikumar, P., Tewari, A.: Learning with noisy labels. In: Burges, C.J.C., Bottou, L., Welling, M., Ghahramani, Z., Weinberger, K.Q. (eds.) Advances in Neural Information Processing Systems 26: 27th Annual Conference on Neural Information Processing Systems 2013. Proceedings of a Meeting Held, Lake Tahoe, Nevada, United States, 5–8 December 2013, pp. 1196–1204 (2013). https://proceedings.neurips.cc/paper/2013/hash/3871bd64012152bfb53fdf04b401193f-Abstract.html

28. P., D., Visweswariah, K., Wiratunga, N., Sani, S.: Two-part segmentation of text documents, October 2012. https://doi.org/10.1145/2396761.2396862

29. Page, L., Brin, S., Motwani, R., Winograd, T.: The PageRank Citation Ranking: Bringing Order to the Web. Technical report, Stanford Digital Library Technologies Project (1998)

30. Parsodkar, A.P., P., D., Chakraborti, S. Never judge a case by its (unreliable) neighbors: estimating case reliability for CBR. In: Keane, M.T., Wiratunga, N. (eds.) Case-Based Reasoning Research and Development. ICCBR 2022. LNCS, vol. 13405, pp. 256–270. Springer, Cham (2022). https://doi.org/10.1007/978-3-031-14923-8_17

31. Peat, P.F.D.B.: Glimpsing Reality: Ideas in Physics and the Link to Biology. Routledge, Abingdon (2008)

32. Richter, M.M.: The knowledge contained in similarity measures. Invited Talk at the First International Conference on Case-Based Reasoning, ICCBR'95, Sesimbra, Portugal (1995)

33. van Rijsbergen, C.J.: The Geometry of Information Retrieval. Cambridge University Press, Cambridge, August 2004. https://doi.org/10.1017/cbo9780511543333

34. Schank, R.C.: Dynamic Memory: A Theory of Reminding and Learning in Computers and People. Cambridge University Press, USA (1983)

35. Shekhar, S., Chakraborti, S., Khemani, D.: Linking cases up: an extension to the case retrieval network. In: Lamontagne, L., Plaza, E. (eds.) ICCBR 2014. LNCS (LNAI), vol. 8765, pp. 450–464. Springer, Cham (2014). https://doi.org/10.1007/978-3-319-11209-1_32

36. Smyt, B., McKenna, E.: Footprint-based retrieval. In: Althoff, K.-D., Bergmann, R., Branting, L.K. (eds.) ICCBR 1999. LNCS, vol. 1650, pp. 343–357. Springer, Heidelberg (1999). https://doi.org/10.1007/3-540-48508-2_25

37. Subramanian, R., Ganesan, D., P, D., Chakraborti, S.: Towards richer realizations of holographic CBR. In: Sánchez-Ruiz, A.A., Floyd, M.W. (eds.) ICCBR 2021. LNCS (LNAI), vol. 12877, pp. 201–215. Springer, Cham (2021). https://doi.org/10.1007/978-3-030-86957-1_14

38. Vasudevan, S.R., Chakraborti, S.: Enriching case descriptions using trails in conversational recommenders. In: Lamontagne, L., Plaza, E. (eds.) ICCBR 2014. LNCS (LNAI), vol. 8765, pp. 480–494. Springer, Cham (2014). https://doi.org/10.1007/978-3-319-11209-1_34
39. Wittgenstein, L., von Wright, G.H., Anscombe, G.E.M.: Notebooks, 1914–1916. Mind **73**(289), 132–141 (1964)

A Contextual Information-Augmented Probabilistic Case-Based Reasoning Model for Knowledge Graph Reasoning

Yuejia Wu[1,2,3,4,5,6,7] and Jian-tao Zhou[1,2,3,4,5,6,7](✉)

[1] College of Computer Science, Inner Mongolia University, Hohhot, China
wuyuejia@imudges.com, cszjtao@imu.edu.cn
[2] National & Local Joint Engineering Research Center of Intelligent Information Processing Technology for Mongolian, Hohhot, China
[3] Engineering Research Center of Ecological Big Data, Ministry of Education, Hohhot, China
[4] Inner Mongolia Engineering Laboratory for Cloud Computing and Service Software, Hohhot, China
[5] Inner Mongolia Key Laboratory of Social Computing and Data Processing, Hohhot, China
[6] Inner Mongolia Key Laboratory of Discipline Inspection and Supervision Big Data, Hohhot, China
[7] Inner Mongolia Engineering Laboratory for Big Data Analysis Technology, Hohhot, China

Abstract. Knowledge Graph Reasoning (KGR) is one effective method to improve incompleteness and sparsity problems, which infers new knowledge based on existing knowledge. Although the probabilistic case-based reasoning (CBR) model can predict attributes for an entity and outperform other rule-based and embedding-based methods by gathering reasoning paths from similar entities in KG, it still suffers from some problems such as insufficient graph feature acquisition and omission of contextual relation information. This paper proposes a contextual information-augmented probabilistic CBR model for KGR, namely CICBR. The proposed model frame the reasoning task as the query answering and evaluates the likelihood that a path is valuable at answering a query about the given entity and relation by designing a joint contextual information-obtaining algorithm with entity and relation features. What's more, to obtain a more fine-grained representation of entity features and relation features, the CICBR introduces Graph Transformer for KG's representation and learning. Extensive experimental results on various benchmarks prominently demonstrate that the proposed CICBR model can obtain the state-of-the-art results of current CBR-based methods.

Keywords: Knowledge Graph Reasoning · Case-based Reasoning · Graph Neural Network · Graph Transformer · Query Answering

© The Author(s), under exclusive license to Springer Nature Switzerland AG 2023
S. Massie and S. Chakraborti (Eds.): ICCBR 2023, LNAI 14141, pp. 102–117, 2023.
https://doi.org/10.1007/978-3-031-40177-0_7

1   Introduction

A Knowledge Graph (KG) is essentially a semantic network that reveals the relations between entities. Existing KGs such as NELL [1], Freebase [2], and WordNet [3] have been widely used for Knowledge-Based Question Answering [4], Recommendation System [5], Anomaly Detection [6], etc. However, the KG is usually incomplete and sparse, which still suffers from some limitations in the above applications.

Knowledge Graph Reasoning (KGR) is one of the main methods to improve those problems by inferring new knowledge based on the existing knowledge in the KG. Recent studies on KGR have shown that case-based reasoning approaches [7–10] solve a new problem by retrieving "cases" that are similar to the given problem, which can achieve advanced results more than rule-based and embedding-based reasoning models. Although the approach proposed in literature [10] can outperform state-of-the-art (SOTA) methods and nearly match the best offline method, there are still two kinds of problems that influence its performance. Firstly, the learning of graph features is inadequate, which makes the model insensitive to finer-grained differences between entities and relations. Secondly, the effects of relations between entities are ignored when obtaining and inferring paths, which leads to a lack of effective reasoning paths and may affect the accuracy of prediction.

In this paper, we present a KGR model based on the contextual information-augmented probabilistic CBR algorithm, referred to as CICBR. Our approach first introduces Graph Transformer [11] architecture, which is a generalization of transformer neural network architecture for arbitrary graphs, to obtain more finer-grained entity and relation characteristics to reasoning, and then joint finds similar entities and relations through feature representations and generate contextual information to augment the probabilistic case-based reasoning model. The main contributions of this paper are as follows:

- We utilize the Graph Transformer architecture for learning and acquiring more detailed entity and relation feature representations. To the best of our current knowledge, this is the first approach that introduces the Graph Transformer architecture into the field of CBR-based KGR.
- We present a joint contextual information-obtaining algorithm with entity and relation features, namely J_{ER}-CIO. Compared to the previous contextual information acquiring algorithm, J_{ER}-CIO is the first method that considers the contextual relations between entities, which can obtain more effective inference paths by combining with contextual entity extraction to enhance inference performance.
- We conduct extensive experiments on three benchmark datasets and the results demonstrate that the proposed KGR model CICBR can effectively outperform existing CBR-based models and obtain optimal experimental results.

2   Related Work

In this section, we mainly state KG's incompleteness and sparsity [12] and briefly summarize the solution to these problems based on KGR technology. As shown in Fig. 1, we give the ubiquitous manifestations of incompleteness and sparsity in KG: (i) incompleteness of entities and relationships: entity incompleteness is represented by missing knowledge about people related to "Lionel Messi" and others; relationship incompleteness is instantiated in the absence of the "father & son" relationship of "Lionel Messi" and "Ciro Messi". (ii) Sparsity of entities and relations: it can be intuitionistically found from Fig. 1 that the ratio of entities' kind (7) and relations' kind (3) to the number of facts (13) is relatively small.

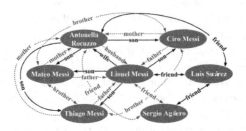

Fig. 1. An example of KG. The solid black line is existing relations, and the dashed red line is relations obtained by KGR.

KGR is one of the main methods to improve the above problems and recent studies have shown that CBR-based methods can obtain the most advanced reasoning results than rule-based and embedding-based models. In detail, the solutions in these methods [9,10] first regard the reasoning task as a query answering, i.e. answering questions of the form ("*Antonella Rocuzzo*", "*husband*", ?). Then retrieve k similar entities (cases) to the query entity and find multiple KG paths, which are the solution to retrieved cases, to the entity they are connected by the query relation.

Although the advanced CBR-based KGR approach proposed in the literature [10] can gather reasoning paths from entities that are similar to the query entity and estimate parameters of the model efficiently using simple count statistics, there are still two problems. Firstly, the lack of learning ability of entity features and relation features in knowledge graphs leads to the insufficient perception of fine-grained differences between entities and relations when calculating the similarity of contextual information. Secondly, only entities that are similar to the query entity are considered when obtaining the contextual information, while the contextual information of the relations that are similar to the query relation is ignored, resulting in the loss of a large number of useful paths affecting the prediction results. This paper focuses on those problems and proposes a contextual information-augmented probabilistic CBR model CICBR that jointly obtains contextual entities and relations information from KG's entities and relations feature representations, which are learned and generated from Graph Transformer architecture.

3 Methodology

In this section, we first introduce the preliminaries used in this paper, and then establish our proposed model in detail.

3.1 Preliminaries

In order to facilitate the understanding of the subsequent formulae, the general definition of KG is defined as follows:

Definition 1 (Knowledge Graph). A Knowledge Graph $\mathcal{G} = (V, E, \mathcal{R})$, where V represents the set of entities, $\mathcal{R}$ represents the set of binary relations, $E \subseteq V \times \mathcal{R} \times V$ represents the edges of the KG, and a KG is a collection of facts stored as triplets (e_1, r, e_2) where $e_1, e_2 \in V, r \in \mathcal{R}$. Also, following previous approaches [10], we add the inverse relation of every fact, i.e., for a fact $(e_1, r, e_2) \in E$, we add the fact (e_2, r^{-1}, e_1) to the KG. (If the set of binary relations $\mathcal{R}$ does not contain the inverse relation r^{-1}, it is added to $\mathcal{R}$ as well.)

This paper frames the reasoning as a query answering task on KG, i.e., answering questions of the form $(e_{1q}, r_q, ?)$, where the answer is an entity in the KG. Its definition is as follows:

Definition 2 (Query Answering Task). Given an input query of the form $(e_{1q}, r_q, ?)$, starting from vertex corresponding to e_{1q} in $\mathcal{G}$, the query answering model follows a path in the graph stopping at a node that it predicts as the answer.

The paths used in the query answering task in the KG are defined as follows [10]:

Definition 3 (KG Paths). A path $p = (e_1, r_1, e_2, r_2, ..., r_n, e_{n+1})$ with $st(p) = e_1$, $en(p) = e_{n+1}$, $len(p) = n$, and $type(p) = (r_1, r_2, ..., r_n)$ in a KG between two entities e_1 and e_{n+1} is defined as a sequence of alternating entities and relations that connect them. Let $\mathcal{P}$ represents the set of all paths in $\mathcal{G}$ and $\mathcal{P}_n \subseteq \mathcal{P} = \{p \mid len(p) \leq n\}$ be the set of all paths of length up to n. Let $P_n = \{type(p) \mid p \in \mathcal{P}_n\}$ denotes the set of all path types with length up to n and $P_n(e_1, r) \subseteq P_n$ represents all path types of length up to n that originate at e_1 by a direct edge of type r, i.e., if $S_{e_1 r} = \{e_2 \mid (e_1, r, e_2) \in \mathcal{G}\}$ is the set of entities that are connected to e_1 via a direct edge r, then $P_n(e_1, r)$ denotes the set of all path types of length up to n that start from e_1 and end at entities in $S_{e_1 r}$. Also, $\mathcal{P}_n(e_1, r)$ is defined to represent paths instead of path types.

3.2 The Proposed Model ICCBR

In this section, we first present the overall architecture of the model, and then elaborate on the architecture in the next two subsections.

Overview

To improve the problems mentioned above, we propose the CICBR model to approach KGR. As shown in Fig. 2, the proposed CICBR architecture can be equipped with two stages: (a) joint contextual entities and relations information obtaining and (b) augmented probabilistic cased-based reasoning. Specifically, given an input KG and a query, CICBR's first stage, which will be presented in the next subsection, is to learn the graph feature representations from the Graph Transformer architecture and then utilize them to jointly acquire contextual entities and relations information by finding the entities and relations that are similar to the query entity and relation respectively. Next, CICBR's second stage, which will be described in the next subsection, aims to generate reasoning paths from contextual information, compute the score of each answer candidate and weigh paths with an estimate of their frequency and precision.

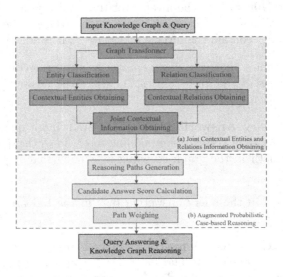

Fig. 2. Overview of the Proposed CICBR model.

Joint Contextual Entities and Relations Information Obtaining

In the previous CBR-based KGR model [10], each entity is represented as a sparse vector of its outgoing edge types, which is an extremely simple way of representing entities. However, this setting leads to a lack of ability to perceive entity characteristics and to gain fine-grained differences between entities, especially when clustering the entity and acquiring contextual entities information. To improve this problem, we present to utilize the Graph Transformer architecture [11] into the CBR field for better utilization of rich feature information available in the knowledge graph in the form of entity and relation attributes.

In addition, the previous work only considered the contextual entity information in the knowledge graph and ignored the importance of the relationship between entities, i.e. the contextual relations information, which may lead to the loss of a large number of valid inference paths and the failure to obtain the correct answer. To improve this problem, we propose a joint contextual information-obtaining algorithm named J_{ER}-CIO, which can effectively obtain the contextual entities and contextual relations information, and contribute to the generation of candidate paths in the next stage.

Specifically, following previous approaches [11], we pre-compute the Laplacian eigenvectors of knowledge graphs, which are defined as follows:

$$\Delta = I - D^{-\frac{1}{2}}AD^{-\frac{1}{2}} = U^T \Lambda U \tag{1}$$

where A is a $n \times n$ adjacency matrix, D is a degree matrix, and Λ, U correspond to the eigenvalues and eigenvectors respectively.

After pre-computing the Laplacian eigenvectors of KGs, we prepare the input entity and relation embeddings passed to the Graph Transformer. For a Graph $\mathcal{G}$ with entity features $\alpha_i \in \mathbb{R}^{d_n \times 1}$ for each entity i and relation features $\beta_{ij} \in \mathbb{R}^{d_e \times 1}$ for each relation between entities i and j, the input entity features α_i and relation features β_{ij} are passed through a linear projection to embed those to d-dimensional hidden features h_i^0 and e_{ij}^0.

$$\begin{aligned}
\hat{h}_i^0 &= A^0 \alpha_i + a^0 \\
e_{ij}^0 &= B^0 \beta_{ij} + b^0
\end{aligned} \tag{2}$$

where $A^0 \in \mathbb{R}^{d \times k}$, $B^0 \in \mathbb{R}^{d \times d_e}$ and a^0, $b^0 \in \mathbb{R}^d$ are the parameters of the linear projection layers. Then, we embed the pre-computed entity positional encoding of dim k via a linear projection and add to the entity features $\hat{h}_i^0$.

$$\begin{aligned}
\lambda_i^0 &= C^0 \lambda_i + c^0 \\
h_i^0 &= \hat{h}_i^0 + \lambda_i^0
\end{aligned} \tag{3}$$

where $C^0 \in \mathbb{R}^{d \times k}$ and $c^0 \in \mathbb{R}^d$.

Then, as shown in Fig. 3, we define the layer update equations for a layer ℓ as follows:

$$\hat{h}_i^{\ell+1} = O_h^\ell \overset{H}{\underset{k=1}{\|}} \left(\sum_{j \in \mathcal{N}_i} w_{ij}^{k,\ell} V^{k,\ell} h_j^\ell \right) \tag{4}$$

$$\hat{e}_{ij}^{\ell+1} = O_e^\ell \overset{H}{\underset{k=1}{\|}} (\hat{w}_{ij}^{k,\ell}) \tag{5}$$

$$w_{ij}^{k,\ell} = Softmax_j(\hat{w}_{ij}^{k,\ell}) \tag{6}$$

$$\hat{w}_{ij}^{k,\ell} = \left(\frac{Q^{k,\ell} h_i^\ell \cdot K^{k,\ell} h_j^\ell}{\sqrt{d_k}} \right) \cdot E^{k,\ell} e_{ij}^\ell \tag{7}$$

where $Q^{k,\ell}$, $K^{k,\ell}$, $V^{k,\ell}$, $E^{k,\ell} \in \mathbb{R}^{d_k \times d}$, O_h^ℓ, $O_e^\ell \in \mathbb{R}^{d \times d}$, $k = 1$ to H represents the number of attention heads, and $\|$ denotes a concatenation operation.

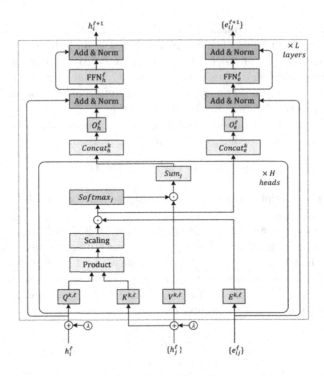

Fig. 3. Overview of the Graph Transformer architecture.

The attention outputs $\hat{h}_i^{\ell+1}$ and $\hat{e}_{ij}^{\ell+1}$ are then passed to separate Feed Forward Network (FFN) preceded and succeeded by residual connections and normalization layers as follows:

$$\hat{\hat{h}}_i^{\ell+1} = Norm(h_i^\ell + \hat{h}_i^{\ell+1}) \tag{8}$$

$$\hat{\hat{\hat{h}}}_i^{\ell+1} = W_{h,2}^\ell ReLU(W_{h,1}^\ell \hat{\hat{h}}_i^{\ell+1}) \tag{9}$$

$$h_i^{\ell+1} = Norm(\hat{\hat{h}}_i^{\ell+1} + \hat{\hat{\hat{h}}}_i^{\ell+1}) \tag{10}$$

$$\hat{\hat{e}}_{ij}^{\ell+1} = Norm(e_{i,j}^\ell + \hat{e}_{ij}^{\ell+1}) \tag{11}$$

$$\hat{\hat{\hat{e}}}_{ij}^{\ell+1} = W_{e,2}^\ell ReLU(W_{e,1}^\ell \hat{\hat{e}}_{ij}^{\ell+1}) \tag{12}$$

$$e_{ij}^{\ell+1} = Norm(\hat{\hat{e}}_{ij}^{\ell+1} + \hat{\hat{\hat{e}}}_{ij}^{\ell+1}) \tag{13}$$

where $W_{h,1}^\ell \in \mathbb{R}^{2d \times d}$, $W_{h,2}^\ell \in \mathbb{R}^{d \times 2d}$, $\hat{\hat{h}}_i^{\ell+1}$, $\hat{\hat{\hat{h}}}_i^{\ell+1}$, $W_{e,1}^\ell \in \mathbb{R}^{2d \times d}$, $W_{e,2}^\ell \in \mathbb{R}^{d \times 2d}$, $\hat{\hat{e}}_{ij}^{\ell+1}$, $\hat{\hat{\hat{e}}}_{ij}^{\ell+1}$ represent intermediate representations.

After obtaining entity and relation features representation, we first find similar entities to the query entity that has at least a relation r_q, i.e., for a query (*"Lionel Messi"*, *"works_for_country"*,?), if there is (*"Emiliano Martínez"*,*"works_for_country"*, *"Argentina"*), the *"Emiliano Martínez"* may be considered and those entities are regarded as 'contextual entities'.

Different from previous approaches, then we added additional 'contextual relations' to get more useful reasoning paths by finding similar relations linked to the query entity e_{1_q}, i.e., we would consider *"lives_in_country"* if we obverse (*"Lionel Messi"*, *"lives_in_country"*, *"Argentina"*). Therefore, we let $E_{c_e,q}$ and $E_{c_r,q}$ denote the set of contextual entities and contextual relations for the query q respectively.

To compute $E_{c_e,q}$ and $E_{c_r,q}$, we propose a joint contextual information-obtaining algorithm with entity and relation features namely J_{ER}-CIO, which is shown in Algorithm 1. Lines 3–18 are to acquire the input knowledge graph representation with entity features and relation features for contextual information obtaining in the next step. Lines 19–26 sort entities with respect to their cosine distance with respect to query entity and select the K_1 entities with the least distance and which have the query relation r_q. For each contextual entity e_c, we gather the path types that connect e_c to the entities it is connected by the relation r_q. Lines 27–34 sort relations with respect to their cosine distance with respect to query relation and select the K_2 relations with the least distance and which connect the query entity e_{1_q}. For each contextual relation r_c, we aggregate the path types starting from e_{1_q} and containing similarity relation r_c. These extracted path will be used to reason about the query entity.

Augmented Probabilistic Case-Based Reasoning

After jointly obtaining the contextual entities and relations, we give the representation of the entity retrieved according to the context information as follows:

$$P_n(E_{c_e,q}, r_q) = \bigcup_{e_c \in E_{c_e,q}} P_n(e_c, r_q) \tag{14}$$

$$P_n(e_{1_q}, E_{c_r,q}) = \bigcup_{r_c \in E_{c_r,q}} P_n(e_{1_q}, r_c) \tag{15}$$

Then, the probability of finding the answer entity e_2 given the query is given by:

$$P(e_2 \mid e_{1_q}, r_q) = \sum_{p \in P_n(E_{c_e,q},r_q) \cup P_n(e_{1_q}, E_{c_r,q})} P(e_2, p \mid e_{1_q}, r_q)$$
$$= \sum_p P(p \mid e_{1_q}, r_q) P(e_2 \mid p, e_{1_q}, r_q) \tag{16}$$

Next, we marginalize the random variable representing the path types obtained from $E_{c_e,q}$ and $E_{c_r,q}$. $P(p \mid e_{1_q}, r_q)$ denotes the probability of finding a path type given the query, which captures how frequently each path type

---

Algorithm 1 Joint contextual information-obtaining algorithm with entity and relation features (J_{ER}-CIO)

Input: Knowledge Graph $\mathcal{G} = (V, E, \mathcal{R})$ with entity features α_i for each entity i, positional encoding λ_i for each entity i, and relation features β_{ij} for each relation between entities i and j, query q with entity feature $h_{e_{1_q}}$ and relation feature e_{r_q}, and hyper-parameters K_1 and K_2.

Output: A set of contextual entities $E_{c_e,q}$ of query q and a set of contextual relations $E_{c_r,q}$ of query q.

1: $E_{c_e,q} \leftarrow []$
2: $E_{c_r,q} \leftarrow []$
3: % Graph feature acquiring
4: **for** i in V **do**
5: $\quad h_i^0 \leftarrow A^0 \alpha_i + C^0 \lambda_i + a^0 + c^0$
6: $\quad$ **for** $j.isNeighbor(i)$ **do**
7: $\quad\quad e_{ij}^0 \leftarrow B^0 \beta_{ij} + b^0$
8: $\quad$ **end for**
9: $\quad$ **for** ℓ in L **do**
10: $\quad\quad \hat{h}_i^{\ell+1} \leftarrow O_h^\ell \overset{H}{\underset{k=1}{\|}} (\sum_{j \in \mathcal{N}_i} Softmax_j((\frac{Q^{k,\ell} h_i^\ell \cdot K^{k,\ell} h_j^\ell}{\sqrt{d_k}}) \cdot E^{k,\ell} e_{ij}^\ell) V^{k,\ell} h_j^\ell)$
11: $\quad\quad \hat{e}_{ij}^{\ell+1} \leftarrow O_e^\ell \overset{H}{\underset{k=1}{\|}} ((\frac{Q^{k,\ell} h_i^\ell \cdot K^{k,\ell} h_j^\ell}{\sqrt{d_k}}) \cdot E^{k,\ell} e_{ij}^\ell)$
12: $\quad\quad h_i^{\ell+1} \leftarrow Norm(Norm(h_i^\ell + \hat{h}_i^{\ell+1}) + W_{h,2}^\ell ReLU(W_{h,1}^\ell \hat{h}_i^{\ell+1}))$
13: $\quad\quad e_{ij}^{\ell+1} \leftarrow Norm(Norm(e_{i,j}^\ell + \hat{e}_{ij}^{\ell+1}) + W_{e,2}^\ell ReLU(W_{e,1}^\ell \hat{e}_{ij}^{\ell+1}))$
14: $\quad$ **end for**
15: $\quad$ **if** $i.equal(e_{1_q})$ **then**
16: $\quad\quad h_{e_{1_q}} \leftarrow h_i^L$
17: $\quad$ **end if**
18: **end for**
19: % Contextual entities obtaining
20: $similarity_e \leftarrow []$
21: **for** i in V **do**
22: $\quad similarity_e.add(\frac{h_i^L \cdot h_{e_{1_q}}}{|h_i^L||h_{e_{1_q}}|})$
23: **end for**
24: **for** k in K_1 **do**
25: $\quad E_{c_e,q}.add(reverseSort(similarity_e)[k])$
26: **end for**
27: % Contextual relations obtaining
28: $similarity_r \leftarrow []$
29: **for** r in $\mathcal{R}$ **do**
30: $\quad similarity_r.add(\frac{e_r^L \cdot e_{r_q}}{|e_r^L||e_{r_q}|})$
31: **end for**
32: **for** k in K_2 **do**
33: $\quad E_{c_r,q}.add(reverseSort(similarity_r)[k])$
34: **end for**
35: **return** $E_{c_e,q}, E_{c_r,q}$

---

co-occurs with a query and represents the prior probability for a path type. $P(e_2 \mid p, e_{1q}, r_q)$ captures the proportion of times, when a path type p is traversed starting from the query entity, we reach the correct answer instead of some other entity, which can be understood as capturing the likelihood of reaching the right answer or the "precision" of a reasoning path type.

Follow the settings in the previous approaches, we let c be a random variable representing the cluster assignment of the query entity. Then for the path-prior term, we have

$$P(p \mid e_{1q}, r_q) = \sum_c P(c \mid e_{1q}, r_q) P(p \mid c, e_{1q}, r_q) \tag{17}$$

where $P(c \mid e_{1q}, r_q)$ is zero for all clusters except the cluster in which the query entity belongs to. And if $c_{e_{1q}}$ is the cluster in which the e_{1q} has been assigned, then $P(p \mid c_{e_{1q}}, e_{1q}, r_q) = P(p \mid c_{e_{1q}}, r_q)$. Instead of per-entity parameters, we now aggregate statistics over entities in the same cluster and have per-cluster parameters. To perform clustering, we use hierarchical agglomerative clustering with average linkage mentioned in the literature [10] with the entity-entity similarity defined in the previous subsection.

Then, we estimate parameters by simple count statistics from the KG. i.e., the path prior $P(p \mid c, r_q)$ is estimated as follows:

$$\frac{\sum_{e_c \in c} \sum_{p' \in \mathcal{P}_n(e_c, r_q) \cup \mathcal{P}_n(e_{1q}, r_c)} \mathbb{1}[type(p') = p]}{\sum_{e_c \in c} \sum_{p' \in \mathcal{P}_n(e_c, r_q) \cup \mathcal{P}_n(e_{1q}, r_c)} \mathbb{1}} \tag{18}$$

For each entity in cluster c, we consider the paths that connect e_c to entities it is directly connected to via edge type r_q and its contextual relations E_{c_r}. The path prior for a path type p is calculated as the proportion of times the type of paths in $\mathcal{P}_n(e_c, r_q)$ is equal to p. Note that in Eq. 18, if a path type occurs multiple times, all instances are counted. Similarly, the path-precision probability ($P(e_2 \mid p, c, r_q)$) can be estimated as follows:

$$\frac{\sum_{e_c \in c} \sum_{p' \in \mathcal{P}_n(e_c)} \mathbb{1}[type(p') = p] \cdot \mathbb{1}[en(p') \in S_{e_c r_q}]}{\sum_{e_c \in c} \sum_{p' \in \mathcal{P}_n(e_c)} \mathbb{1}[type(p') = p]} \tag{19}$$

where $\mathcal{P}_n(e_c)$ represents the paths of up to length n starting from the entity e_c, $en(p)$ represents the end entity for a path p and $S_{e_c r_q}$ represents the set of entities that are connected to e_c through a direct relation of type r_q. Then, given r_q, the Eq. 19 estimates the proportion of times the path p successfully ends at one of the answer entities when starting from e_c.

In general, given a query (e_{1q}, r_q), our proposed CBR-based KGR model CICBR first learns the representations of entities and relations features through Graph Transformer architecture and then proposes a joint contextual information obtaining algorithm to gather reasoning paths from K_1 similar entities to e_{1q} and K_2 similar relations to r_q and then traverse those generated reasoning paths in the KG starting from e_{1q}, which can obtain a set of candidate answer entities.

Then, the score of each answer entity candidate is computed as a weighted sum of the reasoning paths, which is weighed with an estimate of its frequency and precision given the query relation.

4   Experiments and Results

In this section, we conduct extensive comparison experiments to verify the performance of the proposed CICBR model.

4.1   Experimental Datasets

To sufficiently verify the effectiveness of the proposed CBR-based KGR model CICBR, we use three different knowledge graph reasoning standard datasets: NELL-995 [13], FB122 [14], and WN18RR [15] in the experiment, which as shown in Table 1. Among them, NELL-995 is a subset of the NELL derived from the 995th iteration of the system. FB122 is a subset of the dataset derived from Freebase, FB15K, which contains 122 relations regarding people, locations, and sports. WN18RR is created from WN18 by removing inverse relation test-leakage.

Table 1. Overview of the experimental datasets.

Dataset	#Ent	#Rel	#Train	#Valid	#Test-I	#Test-II	#Test-ALL
NELL-995	75,492	200	149,678	543	–	–	3,992
FB122	9,738	122	91,638	9,595	5,057	6,186	11,243
WN18RR	40,943	11	86,835	3,034	–	–	3,134

4.2   Baselines and Evaluation Metrics

The experiment represents the rule-based, embedding-based, and case-based reasoning methods as baselines comparing our proposed model CICBR to prove the model's validity thoroughly. The rule-based baselines include KALE [14], ASR [16], and KG$_{LR}$ [17]. The embedding-based baselines contain TransE [18], DistMult [19], ComplEx [20], ConvE [15], RotatE [21], GNTP [22], and MINERVA [23]. The CBR-based baselines consist of CBR [9] and PCBR [10]. Notability, because the research of combining CBR into the field of KGR is still in the development stage, there are few baselines for comparison.

In the link prediction task, two kinds of standard metrics were used to evaluate the experimental performance, including Mean Reciprocal Ranking (MRR) and Hits@K. For each metric, a higher score indicates a better effect. The MRR is calculated as follows:

$$MRR = \frac{1}{|N|} \sum_{i=1}^{|N|} \frac{1}{rank_i} = \frac{1}{|N|} \left(\frac{1}{rank_1} + \frac{1}{rank_2} + ... + \frac{1}{rank_{|N|}} \right) \quad (20)$$

N is the set of triples and $rank_i$ is the link prediction ranking (which is a triple ranks by its score in the overall link prediction task results) of the i-th triple.

In addition, $Hits@K (K = 1, 3, 5, 10)$ is described as follows:

$$Hits@K = \frac{1}{|N|} \sum_{i=1}^{|N|} \mathbb{I}(rank_i \leq K) \quad (21)$$

where $\mathbb{I}(\cdot)$ is an indicator function that the value sets to 1 if the condition is true, otherwise it sets to 0.

4.3   Results and Analysis

The link prediction overall results for the three standard datasets are shown in Table 2, Table 3, and Table 4, where "†" indicates the results taken from literature [10]. It can be seen that the proposed CICBR model is explicitly improved compared with CBR-based KGR approaches that the CICBR model can improve the {Hits@3, Hits@5, Hits@10, MRR} average prediction accuracy compared with CBR-based baselines by {17.604%, 14.989%, 12.866%, 20.392%} under the FB122 dataset and improve the {Hits@1, Hits@3, Hits@10, MRR} average prediction accuracy compared with CBR-based baselines under the NELL-995 and WN18RR datasets by {9.091%, 4.777%, 1.149%, 7.664%} and {14.015%, 5.368%, 11.480%, 12.427%} respectively.

Table 2. Overall results of link prediction task on FB122 datasets (Part 1).

Models	Test-I				Test-II			
	Hits@K			MRR	Hits@K			MRR
	3	5	10		3	5	10	
KALE-Pre (Guo et al., 2016)†	0.358	0.419	0.498	0.291	0.829	0.861	0.899	0.713
KALE-Joint (Guo et al., 2016)†	**0.384**	**0.447**	**0.522**	0.325	0.797	0.841	0.896	0.684
ASR-DistMult (Minervini et al., 2017)†	0.363	0.403	0.449	0.330	0.980	0.990	0.992	0.948
ASR-ComplEx (Minervini et al., 2017)†	0.373	0.410	0.459	**0.338**	**0.992**	**0.993**	**0.994**	**0.984**
TransE (Bordes et al., 2013)†	0.360	0.415	0.481	0.296	0.775	0.828	0.884	0.630
DistMult (Yang et al., 2015)†	0.360	0.403	0.453	0.313	0.923	0.938	0.947	0.874
ComplEx (Trouillon et al., 2016)†	0.370	0.413	0.462	0.329	0.914	0.919	0.924	0.887
RotatE (Sun et al., 2019)†	**0.511**	**0.551**	**0.603**	**0.471**	0.868	0.886	0.907	0.846
GNTPs (Minervini et al., 2020)†	0.337	0.369	0.412	0.313	**0.982**	**0.990**	**0.993**	**0.977**
CBR (Das et al., 2020)†	0.400	0.445	0.488	0.359	0.678	0.718	0.759	0.636
PCBR (Das et al., 2020)†	0.490	0.527	0.571	0.457	0.948	0.950	0.953	0.948
CICBR (Ours)	**0.508**	**0.543**	**0.592**	**0.465**	**0.959**	**0.971**	**0.975**	**0.956**

Table 3. Overall results of link prediction task on FB122 datasets (Part 2).

Models	Test-ALL			MRR
	Hits@K			
	3	5	10	
KALE-Pre (Guo et al., 2016)[†]	0.617	0.662	0.718	0.523
KALE-Joint (Guo et al., 2016)[†]	0.612	0.664	0.728	0.523
ASR-DistMult (Minervini et al., 2017)[†]	0.707	0.731	0.752	0.675
ASR-ComplEx (Minervini et al., 2017)[†]	0.717	0.736	0.757	0.698
KG$_{LR}$ (Garcia-Duran and Niepert, 2017)[†]	**0.740**	**0.770**	**0.797**	**0.702**
TransE (Bordes et al., 2013)[†]	0.589	0.642	0.702	0.480
DistMult (Yang et al., 2015)[†]	0.674	0.702	0.729	0.628
ComplEx (Trouillon et al., 2016)[†]	0.673	0.695	0.719	0.641
RotatE (Sun et al., 2019)[†]	0.708	**0.736**	**0.770**	**0.678**
GNTPs (Minervini et al., 2020)[†]	**0.692**	0.711	0.732	**0.678**
CBR (Das et al., 2020)[†]	0.570	0.612	0.653	0.527
PCBR (Das et al., 2020)[†]	0.742	0.760	0.782	0.727
CICBR (Ours)	**0.749**	**0.771**	**0.788**	**0.733**

Table 4. Overall results of link prediction task on NELL-995 and WN18RR datasets.

Models	NELL-995				WN18RR			
	Hits@K			MRR	Hits@K			MRR
	1	3	10		1	3	10	
TransE (Bordes et al., 2013)[†]	0.53	0.79	**0.87**	0.67	–	–	0.50	0.23
DistMult (Yang et al., 2015)[†]	0.61	0.73	0.79	0.68	0.39	0.44	0.49	0.43
ComplEx (Trouillon et al., 2016)[†]	0.61	0.76	0.83	0.69	0.41	0.46	0.51	0.44
ConvE (Dettmers et al., 2018)[†]	**0.67**	0.81	0.86	**0.75**	0.40	0.44	0.52	0.43
RotatE (Sun et al., 2019)[†]	0.65	**0.82**	**0.87**	0.74	**0.43**	**0.49**	**0.57**	**0.48**
GNTP (Minervini et al., 2020)[†]	–	–	–	–	0.41	0.44	0.48	0.43
MINERVA (Das et al., 2017)[†]	0.66	0.77	0.83	0.72	0.40	0.43	0.49	0.43
CBR (Das et al., 2020)[†]	0.70	0.83	0.87	0.77	0.38	0.46	0.51	0.43
PCBR (Das et al., 2020)[†]	0.77	0.85	**0.89**	0.81	0.43	0.49	0.55	0.48
CICBR (Ours)	**0.80**	**0.88**	**0.89**	**0.85**	**0.46**	**0.50**	**0.59**	**0.51**

Compared with CBR-based baselines, the link prediction results of our proposed CICBR model on all experimental datasets are obviously improved. What's more, under the FB122 (Test-ALL), NELL-995 and WN18RR datasets, our CICBR model also can obtain the SOTA results against the rule-based and embedding-based methods. This is because: (i) by utlizing the Graph Transformer architecture for earning and representing entities and relations in the

KG, richer feature information can be obtained to enhance inference and the ability of perceptual feature difference between entities and relations; (ii) the joint contextual entities and contextual relations information obtaining algorithm J_{ER}-CIO is proposed to acquire more effective and roundly contextual information for generating candidate paths in the reasoning stage, which can as fully as possible generate and calculate candidate entities so as to improving the accuracy of model's resoning precision.

In conclusion, based on the above comparative experiments, it is indicated that by using the CICBR model proposed in this paper, more plentiful graph features can be acquired, especially the relations information, and more effective contextual information can be obtained to generate more paths conducive to the reasoning for improving model's reasoning accuracy and gain SOTA results on all experimental datasets.

5   Conclusion

In this paper, we proposed a contextual information-augmented probabilistic case-based reasoning model for KGR named CICBR. First, CICBR enhanced the ability to extract and learn graph features, especially the easily neglected relation features, by utilizing the Graph Transformer architecture. Secondly, CICBR proposed a contextual information acquisition algorithm combining contextual entities and contextual relations, which can obtain candidate paths through similarity calculation and processing of the obtained entity and relation features for further reasoning. Third, the probabilistic case-based reasoning method is adopted to reason from the augmented acquired contextual information, which can not only enhance the sensitivity to entity correlation but also provide more attention to the relations between entities. Finally, extensive comparison experiments on three benchmarks demonstrated that our proposed CICBR model can achieve the SOTA reasoning performance against current CBR-based baselines.

Although our work can make improvements to current CBR-based approaches, there still exists the problem of how to obtain more effective contextual information. In the future, we are interested in presenting CBR methods that are more in line with the KGR to improve the reasoning ability of the model.

Acknowledgments. This work is supported by the National Natural Science Foundation of China under Grant No. 62162046, the Inner Mongolia Science and Technology Project under Grant No. 2021GG0155, the Natural Science Foundation of Major Research Plan of Inner Mongolia under Grant No. 2019ZD15, and the Inner Mongolia Natural Science Foundation under Grant No. 2019GG372.

References

1. Carlson, A., Betteridge, J., Kisiel, B., Settles, B., Hruschka, E., Mitchell, T.: Toward an architecture for never-ending language learning. In: Proceedings of the AAAI Conference on Artificial Intelligence, vol. 24, no. 1, pp. 1306–1313, July 2010
2. Bollacker, K., Evans, C., Paritosh, P., Sturge, T., Taylor, J.: Freebase: a collaboratively created graph database for structuring human knowledge. In: Proceedings of the 2008 ACM SIGMOD International Conference on Management of Data, pp. 1247–1250, June 2008
3. Miller, G.A.: WordNet: a lexical database for English. Commun. ACM **38**(11), 39–41 (1995)
4. Behmanesh, S., Talebpour, A., Shamsfard, M., Jafari, M.M.: Improved relation span detection in question answering systems over extracted knowledge bases. Expert Syst. Appl. **224**, 119973 (2023)
5. Lin, R., Tang, F., He, C., Wu, Z., Yuan, C., Tang, Y.: DIRS-KG: a KG-enhanced interactive recommender system based on deep reinforcement learning. World Wide Web, pp. 1–23 (2023)
6. Tailhardat, L., Chabot, Y., Troncy, R.: Designing NORIA: a knowledge graph-based platform for anomaly detection and incident management in ICT systems (2023)
7. Dubitzky, W., Büchner, A.G., Azuaje, F.J.: Viewing knowledge management as a case-based reasoning application. In: AAAI Workshop Technical Report WS-99-10, pp. 23–27 (1999)
8. Bartlmae, K., Riemenschneider, M.: Case based reasoning for knowledge management in KDD projects. In: PAKM, October 2000
9. Das, R., Godbole, A., Dhuliawala, S., Zaheer, M., McCallum, A.: A simple approach to case-based reasoning in knowledge bases (2020). arXiv preprint arXiv:2006.14198
10. Das, R., Godbole, A., Monath, N., Zaheer, M., McCallum, A.: Probabilistic case-based reasoning for open-world knowledge graph completion (2020). arXiv preprint arXiv:2010.03548
11. Dwivedi, V.P., Bresson, X.: A generalization of transformer networks to graphs (2020). arXiv preprint arXiv:2012.09699
12. Pujara, J., Augustine, E., Getoor, L.: Sparsity and noise: where knowledge graph embeddings fall short. In: Proceedings of the 2017 Conference on Empirical Methods in Natural Language Processing, pp. 1751–1756, September 2017
13. Xiong, W., Hoang, T., Wang, W.Y.: Deeppath: a reinforcement learning method for knowledge graph reasoning (2017). arXiv preprint arXiv:1707.06690
14. Guo, S., Wang, Q., Wang, L., Wang, B., Guo, L.: Jointly embedding knowledge graphs and logical rules. In: Proceedings of the 2016 Conference on Empirical Methods in Natural Language Processing, pp. 192–202, November 2016
15. Dettmers, T., Minervini, P., Stenetorp, P., Riedel, S.: Convolutional 2D knowledge graph embeddings. In: Proceedings of the AAAI Conference on Artificial Intelligence, vol. 32, no. 1, April 2018
16. Minervini, P., Demeester, T., Rocktäschel, T., Riedel, S.: Adversarial sets for regularising neural link predictors (2017). arXiv preprint arXiv:1707.07596
17. García-Durán, A., Niepert, M.: KBLRN: end-to-end learning of knowledge base representations with latent, relational, and numerical features (2017). arXiv preprint arXiv:1709.04676

18. Bordes, A., Usunier, N., Garcia-Duran, A., Weston, J., Yakhnenko, O.: Translating embeddings for modeling multi-relational data. Adv. Neural Inf. Process. Syst. **26** (2013)

19. Yang, B., Yih, W.T., He, X., Gao, J., Deng, L.: Embedding entities and relations for learning and inference in knowledge bases. In: ICLR (2015)

20. Trouillon, T., Welbl, J., Riedel, S., Gaussier, É., Bouchard, G.: Complex embeddings for simple link prediction. In: International Conference on Machine Learning, pp. 2071–2080. PMLR, June 2016

21. Sun, Z., Deng, Z.H., Nie, J.Y., Tang, J.: Rotate: knowledge graph embedding by relational rotation in complex space (2019). arXiv preprint arXiv:1902.10197

22. Minervini, P., Bošnjak, M., Rocktäschel, T., Riedel, S., Grefenstette, E.: Differentiable reasoning on large knowledge bases and natural language. In: Proceedings of the AAAI Conference on Artificial Intelligence, vol. 34, no. 04, pp. 5182–5190, April 2020

23. Das, R., et al.: Go for a walk and arrive at the answer: reasoning over paths in knowledge bases using reinforcement learning (2017). arXiv preprint arXiv:1711.05851

Case-Based Sample Generation Using Multi-Armed Bandits

Andreas Korger and Joachim Baumeister[(✉)]

University of Würzburg, Am Hubland, 97074 Würzburg, Germany
a.korger@informatik.uni-wuerzburg.de, joba@uni-wuerzburg.de

Abstract. A central problem in knowledge-based tasks is to provide a collection of reusable knowledge samples extracted from a textual corpus. Often, such corpora are structured into different documents or topics, respectively. The samples need to be proven for usability and adapted by a domain expert requiring a certain processing time for each sample taken. The goal is to achieve an optimal retrieval and adaptation success meeting the time budget of the domain expert. In this work, we formulate this task as a constrained multi-armed bandit model. We combine it with the model of a configurable data-driven case-based learning agent. A case study evaluates the theoretical considerations in a scenario of regulatory knowledge acquisition. Therefore, a data set is constructed out of a corpus of nuclear safety documents. We use the model to optimize the evaluation process of sample generation of adaptational knowledge. The corresponding knowledge graph has been created in an information extraction step by automatically identifying semantic concepts and their relations.

Keywords: Case-Based Reasoning · Multi-Armed Bandits · Agent-Based Modeling · Semantics · Knowledge Management · Sampling

1 Introduction

Let us consider the following situation: a domain expert needs to write a new safety document. He has a corpus available with a collection of documents similar to a safety domain. So he may reuse knowledge contained in the corpus and collect new safety knowledge by searching the existent corpus. He adapts promising textual passages to his needs and drops others. In complex domains an unknown document is like a black box which has to be understood, even for domain experts. Therefore, he has to analyze and interpret passages of the documents in the corpus, assess their quality, and adapt them to his specific domain. In the end, if the expert finds the knowledge he is looking for, he is satisfied with the selection of documents he made. This simple process is complicated by various factors.

The expert has special characteristics. He has some prior knowledge and he has limited time. Subsequently, he expects to find the knowledge in the corpus

S. Massie and S. Chakraborti (Eds.): ICCBR 2023, LNAI 14141, pp. 118–133, 2023.
https://doi.org/10.1007/978-3-031-40177-0_8

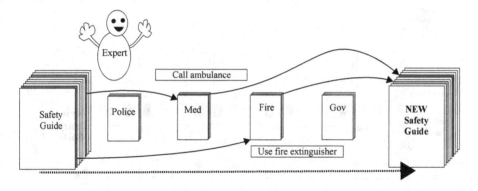

Fig. 1. Retrieval and adaptation of existent textual samples to support an expert in the creation of a new safety document.

he is searching for, within the time budget he has available. Additionally to the time budget the expert is characterized by a certain preference. He is interested in certain topics. Despite that, the expert hopes to find new helpful knowledge he does not yet know. A fact, that leverages his task, is that the corpus is structured by domain experts into documents representing a self-contained knowledge scheme as illustrated in Fig. 1. In summary, every document of the corpus has a certain quality which is initially unknown to the reader and comes up step by step with every textual sample processed. The following exemplary textual sample is taken from a document for nuclear safety which is part of the evaluating case study presented in Sect. 4.

(1)   **Example:** The *staff assigned* the *responsibility* for carrying out such *reviews* for issues of *fire safety* should be suitably *qualified* to *evaluate* the potential effect of any *modification* on *fire safety* and should have sufficient *authority* to *prevent* or *suspend* modification work, if necessary, until any *issues* identified have been satisfactorily *resolved.*

The task of retrieving good new adaptation candidates inherits two competing goals. On the one hand, the expert needs to distribute his search in the corpus to find the documents that fit his expectations (*explore corpus*). On the other hand, when he found a good document, he does not want to waste time (*exploit good document*) searching for other documents, that may fit his expectations better. A well accepted strategy to model the before described scenario of sequential resource (*time*) distribution amongst competing alternatives (*documents*) is the bandit model [21]. The case-based paradigm, that similar problems (*retrieved textual passage*) have similar solutions (*adapted textual passage*), aids to connect the bandit model with the characterization of the expert [7]. The expert is modeled as a data-based agent [22]. The character of the agent regarding his prior knowledge, preferences, and learning goal are modeled as a case base together with a configurable similarity model.

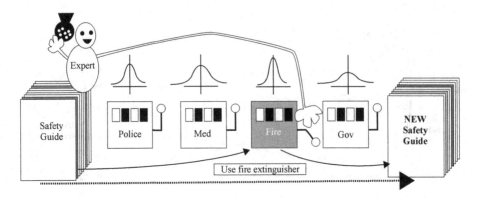

Fig. 2. Representation of the textual sampling process as a bandit model. Every document is represented as one bandit arm having a certain mean and variance of quality distribution for the contained information units (cases).

1.1   Problem Description

The described scenario is connected with the solving or mitigating of the following problems. The *exploration-exploitation dilemma* of using already visited "good" documents for sample generation rather than sampling completely unknown or allegedly "bad" documents. How can a sequential reward model be constructed that bases solely on the existent data. Can the model be used to calculate the quality of a retrieved sample depending on the characteristics of the agent and thus defining "good" and "bad" quality of documents.

1.2   Solution Approach

We facilitate and formulate the scenario as a constrained multi-armed bandit model which offers strategies to mitigate the *exploration-exploitation dilemma* in a configurable way. We use case-based reasoning (CBR) strategies incorporating an initial agent setup (*initial case base*) together with a learning goal (*optimum case solutions*) to construct a configurable reward model on the base of *similarity assessment*. We use statistical language models to calculate similarity components of the retrieved information for *sample adaptation*.

1.3   Contribution and Research Question

With the presented approach we aim to answer the following research question. Is it possible to formulate the sampling process of a textual corpus as a multi-armed bandit problem in combination with a data-driven agent characterization. Can the phrases (*samples*), documents (*bandit arms*), and corpus (*agent environment*) thereby be considered as discrete semantic unities even though they are interrelated. Do the documents have a mean quality and variance of quality regarding the sampling process of contained phrases as depicted in Fig. 2.

2   Related Work

There exist several works describing document retrieval or ranking using the strategy of multi-armed bandits. Perotto et al. [18] use bandits for document retrieval in the juridical domain. They incorporate the searching characteristics coded in queries done by previous users to leverage the performance for the current query. While this work has interesting ideas to use past user behavior, it differs in its structure in that way that it bases on single queries and lacks the integration of an agent based user characterization. Losada et al. [17] propose a bandit-based pooling strategy for document adjudication. A combination of active learning and multi-armed bandits is proposed by Rahman et al. [20] with the intent of selecting the best document for a testing collection for evaluation purposes. Most approaches focus on document selection or ranking wheres we focus on sample selection and just exploit the documental clustering.

Related work that supports the construction of a convenient agent model treated the following topics. A resource oriented variation of the multi-armed bandit problem is presented by Bengs and Hüllermeier [6]. It aims to minimize the resource limit and the risk of exceeding resources. The idea of introducing a learning goal is also picked up by Brändle et al. [8]. Racharak et al. [19] present a concept-based similarity measure that incorporates the preferences of an agent in description logic. Insight into the relation between human psychology and the multi-armed bandid strategy was given by Schulz et al. [23]. Their work investigates how a latent structure in the bandit task is connected to the natural learning behavior of a searching agent.

Concerning variants of multi-armed bandit modeling an outstanding approach is the hierarchical structuring of the action space of the agent. As documents are most often structured into a hierarchy of topics this can yield significant improvements in the overall performance. Especially, as the here presented case study relies on hierarchical structuring of semantic concepts synergies should not be neglected. Hong et al. [12] present fundamental considerations in this direction. Kumar et al. [15] use a hierarchical bandit model in combination with decision tree algorithms for the identification of users in social networks having special attributes. This problem setting shows similar characteristics as the hierarchical structuring of attributes is similar to the hierarchical structuring of semantic concepts. Carlsson et al. [9] show how a clustered structure of bandit arms can be exploited to improve the Thompson sampling strategy. Important aspects of linked data in connection to non stochastical bandit modeling are addressed in the work of Alon et al. [2]. Basic considerations about non-stochastical bandit models have been presented by Auer et al. [4]. A different hierarchical modeling approach is presented by Sen et al. [24]. They chose to represent the problem with hierarchically structured arms.

We will address, integrate, and extend different aspects of these related approaches into a new combination of agent-bandit model which is explained in the following.

3 Setting

In the following we will formalize the introduced problem description. We start
with assumptions that are made to facilitate the scenario. We present and explain
the ideas behind formal definitions of the learning agent and the reward model.
We outline solution strategies using the presented setting.

3.1 Assumptions

The textual corpus is analyzed in a natural language processing step. The documents are chunked into *uniform informational pieces* of a certain meaningful
size. Such units can be retrieved as samples, for instance, a paragraph or sentence. The textual corpus is enriched by *semantic meta knowledge* identifying
and annotating safety related semantic concepts and their relations. We assume
a closed world, namely, the textual corpus together with its semantic representation. This means that the learning agent is provided with some *prior knowledge*
that is part of the textual corpus and its semantic representation. We assume a
given *learning goal* which is also part of the textual corpus but is hidden to the
agent. The *preferences* of the agent are provided by a set of semantic concepts
defined on base of the semantically annotated textual corpus saved in a knowledge graph $\mathcal{O}$. It is unknown what would be an ideal learning goal. Therefore,
we assume a subset of the corpus as learning goal. The agent is informed about
the fulfillment of the goal by similarity information given to him by a hypothetic
teacher. There are some flaws in this modeling: The prior knowledge increases
with every sample processed by the agent and the learning goal decreases if
partially met. This would lead to a non stationary reward model which changes
over time. For simplification we assume a stationary model with the same reward
configuration over the whole sampling process.

3.2 Formal Representation

We consider a corpus $\mathcal{C} = \{D_1, ..., D_m\}$ divided into m documents each consisting
of $I_n, n \in \{1, .., m\}$ information units with $i_i \cap i_j = \emptyset \ \forall i \neq j$. Let $\mathcal{I}_\mathcal{C} = \{I_1, .., I_m\}$
be the set of all information units contained in the corpus. This corpus is represented as a K-armed bandit $\mathcal{K} = \{1, ..., K\}, K = |\mathcal{C}|$ with a set of K arms where
each arm stands for one document. The agent is willing to read a number of
b retrieved passages of text. By the action a_i of pulling the arm k at time t a
sample piece of the document k is provided which is denoted as A_t. The quality
of the sample piece generated by this action is the reward $R_k \in \{0, 1\}$ (with
$R_k = 0$ meaning sample rejected and $R_k = 1$ meaning sample accepted). With
ongoing time steps a sequence of actions $(A_1, A_2, .., A_b)$ with according rewards
$(R_1, R_2, .., R_b)$ is produced. The (discrete) time goes on until the budget of the
expert is consumed and he is not willing to take more sampling actions. What
we are searching for is the optimal combination of actions to make the best out
of the experts budget. The "expert" is formalized as an agent with the following
characteristics.

Definition 1 (Learning Agent Scenario). *Let $\mathcal{E} = \langle \mathcal{P}, \mathcal{G}, \mathcal{L}, b \rangle$ be an agent that is modeling an expert with a prior knowledge $\mathcal{P} \subset \mathcal{I}_{\mathcal{C}}$, with the preferences $\mathcal{L} \subset \mathcal{O}$ regarding topics he is interested in. We define a learning goal aligned to the agent as a subset $\mathcal{G} \subset \mathcal{I}_{\mathcal{C}}$. The agent has a budget of b samples that he is willing to take, meaning the bandit game goes T rounds ($T = b$). The environment of the agent is the textual corpus. The agent has the actions of pulling a bandit arm, accepting a sample, and rejecting a sample.*

Altogether, the information units that define the agent are considered as the initial case base. Each sample is considered as a new case, potentially representing a (partial) solution for the agent's task. If samples are indeed adaptable, is decided by comparing the new solutions to the existing case base. Finally, the agent is capable of solving his problem of creating the new document.

(2) **Example:** An exemplary corpus consists of four different safety documents. With the topics "fire safety", "police guidelines", "medical guidelines", and "governmental security" as depicted in the Figs. 1 and 2. Each document consists of 1,000 relevant phrases and the expert has a budget of 100 samples, which he is capable of reading and analyzing. His preferences are "transportation" and "mobile fire safety" and he wants to create a document for the safety of utility vehicles in factories. He is a governmental fire safety expert and his prior knowledge is a subset of 50 phrases each of the fire safety and the governmental document. How does he distribute his 100 samples over the 4,000 existing phrases providing the best sampling success to him.

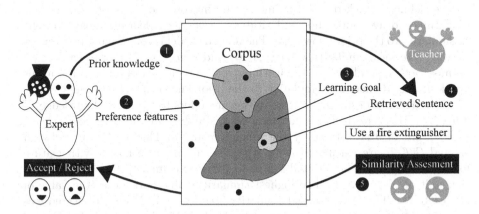

Fig. 3. Case-based cycle of corpus sample retrieval with joined agent-teacher similarity assessment. The expert has some prior knowledge (1) and preference features (2). The teacher defines a learning goal (3) which is hidden to the expert but gives him feedback about the quality of retrieved samples (4). Via a similarity assessment (5) the expert accepts or rejects the sample, then adapts it to his needs and retains it in the new corpus as a new case.

3.3 Reward Model

For every sampling action the agent is rewarded. To create a model for this reward we exploit the case-based paradigm that similar problems have similar solutions [7]. We therefore construct a similarity model that calculates the similarity between the retrieved sample (new case) and the characteristics of the agent defined by the agent model (case base). The higher the similarity the better the sample quality. If this numerical quality lies above a certain threshold the agent accepts the sample for adaptation, otherwise it is rejected. An illustration of this process is depicted in Fig. 3.

Definition 2 (Reward Function). *Let $sim(A_t, \mathcal{G})$ be the similarity of the retrieved sample as action A_t with the learning goal, $sim(A_t, \mathcal{L})$ the similarity between the retrieved sample and the preferences of the agent, and $sim(A_t, \mathcal{P})$ the similarity between the sample and the prior knowledge. Then the reward function $R(A_t) \in \{0, 1\}$ with $\alpha, \beta, \gamma \geq 0$ is defined as:*

$$sim_R(A_t) = \frac{\alpha sim_X(A_t, \mathcal{G}) + \beta sim_X(A_t, \mathcal{L}) + \gamma(1 - sim_X(A_t, \mathcal{P}))}{\alpha + \beta + \gamma} \tag{1}$$

$$R(A_t) = \begin{cases} 1 & for\ sim_R(A_t) \geq \delta \\ 0 & for\ sim_R(A_t) < \delta \end{cases} \tag{2}$$

$$sim_X(A_t, X) = \max(Sim_{SLMF}(A_t, I) \forall I \in X) \tag{3}$$

$$sim_{SLMF}(A_t, I) = sim_{SLM}\left(\frac{\sum_{k=1}^{m} f_j}{m} \forall f \in A_t, \frac{\sum_{l=1}^{n} g_l}{n} \forall g \in I\right) \tag{4}$$

We define a stacked reward function basing on the similarity assessment weighting and averaging the similarities to preferences, learning goal, and the dissimilarity to the prior knowledge. The reward model is constructed in a heuristic way. The local similarities $sim_X(A_t, \mathcal{G})$ and $sim_X(A_t, \mathcal{L})$ add to each other because both a similarity to the learning goal and the preferences of the agent are desirable. If there is a similarity to the prior knowledge of the agent this is considered as not desirable because the agent prefers to learn new knowledge. If $sim_X(A_t, \mathcal{P})$ is zero then R is not influenced, a high similarity of A_t and P leads to a reward of 0 adjustable by the weights γ and δ. The similarities between A_t and $\mathcal{G}, \mathcal{L}, \mathcal{P}$ are calculated using a statistical language model with feature focus (SLMF) [27]. The selected sample is pairwise compared to every information unit of $X \in \mathcal{G}, \mathcal{L}, \mathcal{P}$. The highest similarity value is taken as the value of $sim_X(A_t, X)$. The feature-based similarity $sim_{SLMF}(A_t, I)$ for all selected features $f, g \in A_t, I$ is calculated by taking the average of the embedded feature vectors [27]. Which features are selected is left as a hyper-parameter of the sampling process. Selected features could be for instance only nouns, relevant safety features, only verbs, specific relations, etc [13].

3.4 Solution Strategies

Solution strategies for bandit models use different approaches to find a balance of exploiting good bandit arms already visited and exploring unknown bandit arms. We present and evaluate three approaches to the presented setting. The naive strategy of selecting randomly will be used as a baseline for the evaluation of the heuristic strategies. Let $\mu_k \in [0, 1]$ be the mean reward of pulling an arm k at time step t $-$ 1. This is the expected reward for the next time step t for this arm which is denoted as $Q_t(a_k) = \mathbb{E}[R_t \mid A_t = a_k]$. In a "real" stochastic setting, if an arm was pulled infinite times the true mean value would be known. If $Q(a_k)$ is calculated for the discrete number of all information units contained in a document then the expected mean reward of the document is known. If the agent would know this hidden quality of all documents he could choose an optimal sequence of actions $a_* = \text{argmax}_a \mathbb{E}[R_t \mid A_t = a_k]$. Which will later be used to evaluate the performance of solution strategies.

Epsilon-Greedy Strategy. A baseline strategy to address the exploration-exploitation dilemma is the epsilon-greedy strategy (EG) [25]. The parameter epsilon (ε) defines how eager the agent is for exploration. The higher the value of ε the more unknown documents will be visited. At each time step an unknown document out of $\mathcal{D}$ is chosen with a probability of ε for sample retrieval. At a probability of $1 - \varepsilon$ the document is selected for the next retrieval out of which the sample with the maximum reward so far was generated: $A_t = \text{argmax}_a Q_t(a)$ which is the "greedy" or exploiting component of the algorithm.

Upper Confidence Bound Strategy. The epsilon-greedy strategy takes samples from random documents at a constant percentage. This neglects that in the later time steps there is already knowledge about the environment available. The Upper Confidence Bound strategy (UCB) makes use of this knowledge and changes the ratio of exploration and exploitation [3]. This is achieved with a bias added to the actually expected mean value of an action which decreases with increasing number of pulls of the according bandit arm. The greedy step changes to: $A_t = \text{argmax}_a[Q_t(a) + c\sqrt{\frac{\log t}{N-t(a)}}]$ where $N_t(a)$ denotes the number a document has been already selected for sampling and c is a parameter which controls the ratio of exploration, the bigger c the more exploration is done.

Thompson Sampling Strategy. The Thompson sampling strategy (TS) [26] differs from the previous approaches. From the received rewards a probability model is calculated for each bandit arm and refined with every sample received. These probability models are then used to decide which action to take best. In the present setting actions are considered to have only two outcomes, sample accepted or sample not accepted. This binary reward scenario can be described by a Beta distribution which approximates the behavior of each bandit arm [26]. The so far made theoretical considerations are used in practical application in the following case study.

4   Case Study

The spark for this work developed out of the task of evaluating the quality of an automatically populated ontology. The available time budget allowed for a maximum analyzation capacity of some hundred annotated textual samples. Compared to a dataset size of more than 200,000 samples a better strategy than random sampling was necessary. Additionally, a configurable sampling setup was desired depending on the task and user profile.

For the present experimental evaluation we use a dataset created from a textual corpus published in the domain of nuclear safety. This corpus was previously annotated and transformed into an according dataset of about 222,000 sentences. The corpus consists of publicly available 143 documents containing in total about 14,000 pages of English text. These documents were published by the IAEA (International Atomic Energy Association), which is a sub organization of the United Nations [1]. The IAEA aims to regulate the domain of nuclear safety on an international level and gives advise and support to national authorities. Table 1 gives an insight into selected subjects the documents of the corpus are aiming to regulate.

Table 1. Selected documents of the corpus.

Number	Document Title
(1091)	"Fire Safety in the Operation of Nuclear Power Plants"
(1159)	"External Events Excluding Earthquakes in Nuclear Power Plants"
(1191)	"Protection against Internal Hazards other than Fires"
(1798)	"Regulations for the Safe Transport of Radioactive Material ..."
(1368)	"Predisposal Management of Radioactive Waste"
(1546)	"Nuclear Security Systems and Measures for Major Public Events"

4.1   Semantic Fundamentals

Additionally to the plain documents, a terminology is published and maintained by the IAEA covering about 1,500 semantic concepts of the domain using the RDF data model [29] and the SKOS standard for knowledge organization [28]. The terminology is structured into several hierarchical layers and contains concepts like :fire, :manualFireFighting, and :fireProtection together with definitions and explanations. Out of these concepts, *incidents* and *safety measures* where identified using lexico-syntactic patterns and an open information extraction approach [5,11]. The retrieved information was annotated using the RDF-star data model [10] and saved in a knowledge graph [13,14].

Example 3 shows a phrase extracted from the Document 1191 listed in Table 1. Because of the concepts "vessel" and "fuel" this phrase is similar to the "utility vehicle" scenario described in Example 2. This example points out the time-consuming and pseudo-stochastic nature of the adaptational process. The success of having retrieved a good passage is not guaranteed. For instance, "vessel" is here used in the sense of a "container" and not a vehicle-like object. Nevertheless, concepts seem similar and the phrase might be promising. To proof and adapt this phrase the expert needs to research, what should be done in this context for the incident of a "missile", what is meant by "special design features", then proof whether this would be a good strategy for his own scenario, maybe consult other experts, and finally rewrite the phrase.

(3) **Example:** For reactors equipped with vessel closure plugs to retain the fuel in position, special design features should be provided to ensure that the probability of *ejection of the closure plug* is low. In the absence of such special features, the consequences of the *failure or the ejection of a single closure plug* should be evaluated as for a *missile*.

Beyond that, the semantic knowledge can be used for the purpose of document filtering. It is not necessary to use all information units in a document. In a filter step only those units relevant for a certain task can be pre-selected. For instance, only sentences that contain a certain type of relation, that fall under a certain topic, and show other distinct characteristics. A second benefit is the availability of meta-knowledge about features to calculate similarity functions and adapt retrieved information units to different scenarios [7]. Furthermore, it is not obligatory to stay in the document-based clustering of information units. The bandits can also be setup using other arbitrary clustering approaches. For instance, by creating one bandit arm for each class of relations available, for a selection of topics, specific case attribute oriented clusters, and algorithmic provenance of annotation. In this manner the approach generalizes to a variety of possible application scenarios.

4.2   Experiments

In the following we present a collection of experiments that describe determination of hyper-parameters, individual characteristics of each solution policy, and comparable aspects of the bandit problem solution strategies. We compare the experiments against a baseline of random sampling and use the concept of *regret* for performance evaluation. The dataset was divided into an experimental data environment with training, validation, and test splits, leaving 10% of all sentences for each; validation and testing. We initially tested the algorithms with a small selection of 3 documents, that where known in terms of document content to investigate the behavior with human insight. We then scaled the algorithms to a number of 10 and 100 documents. We used two different agent configurations A_1 and A_2 as described in Fig. 4.

Initialization, Hyper-parameters and Optimal Strategy. For the EG and the UCB algorithms we initialize all arms with a mean reward of 1. This ensures

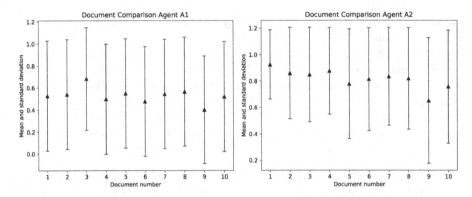

Fig. 4. The figure shows the mean of the reward for each document together with the standard deviation for a fixed reward configuration for ten documents of the corpus amongst which the documents mentioned in Table 1. With $\alpha = 1$, $\beta = 0$, $\gamma = 0$, $\delta = 0.8$ for Configuration A_1 where just the learning goal was defined as a fixed single sentence with $\mathcal{G} = 1$, $\mathcal{P} = 0$ sentences and $\mathcal{L} = []$. For Configuration A_2 and $\alpha = 1$, $\beta = 1$, $\gamma = 1$, $\delta = 0.5$, a fixed set of $\mathcal{G} = 17$ random sentences sampled from three documents, $\mathcal{P} = 1$ fixed sentence, and $\mathcal{L}$ the preferred semantic concepts :fire, :transportation, and :leakage.

that each arm is visited at least once. For the same reason for the TS policy the distribution of each arm is initialized with a count of positives $= 1$ and negatives $= 1$. These starting values determine a wide spread initial distribution. To determine a reasonable range of time steps a human expert would accept, we considered the following. We estimated about five minutes of time to manually execute the adaptational steps needed in case of Example 3. The documents in the corpus consist of about 500 to 1,500 phrases. According to this, 1,000

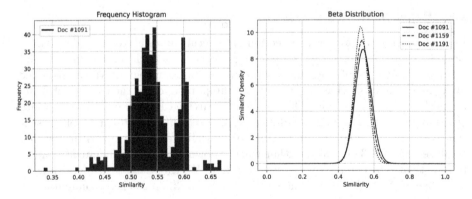

Fig. 5. The left shows the frequency histogram of continuous similarity values for one document. The right displays the beta distribution for three different documents constrained to binary values with δ and configuration A_2.

time steps would meet the mean of the document length in the present corpus. Furthermore, this would lead to a net time budget of about 10 working days of eight hours. Which seems a reasonable effort for the research to create a sophisticated document.

The fully informed scenario calculated as explained in Sect. 3.4 is shown in Fig. 4. It visualizes which strategy would be statistically optimal. The agent would then only use a selection of the best ranked documents with the highest mean. Figure 5 shows how the threshold turns the documents at random retrieval into a stochastic unit with a beta distribution of positive and negative action rewards. This distribution we interpret as the characteristic of the according bandit arms.

Epsilon Greedy. Before applying complicated strategies we wanted to investigate how a simple mixture of greedy and random ratio would behave. We therefore let the epsilon greedy algorithm run with epsilon values from 0 to 1 in steps of 0.1. With $\varepsilon = 0$ having a complete greedy approach and $\varepsilon = 1$ having a fully random algorithm. We then compared the average reward of 10 epochs of 1000 simulations for the agent configurations A_1 and A_2. The graphical representation for a selection of epsilon values is shown in Fig. 6.

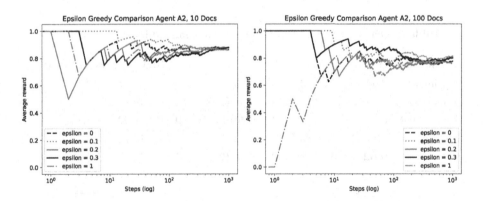

Fig. 6. Epsilon variation for 10 and 100 documents for agent configuration A_2.

Upper Confidence Bound. The UCB approach was optimized but even so showed the worse performance of all algorithms. We see the reason for this in the high variance of the document similarity distribution. Additionally, the configuration of the hyper-parameters to determine the confidence interval and bias model requires efforts if applied to new corpora [3]. In a fixed scenario this might be reasonable and then the strategy could outperform simple EG. But in the present volatile scenario, UCB is not a policy to recommend.

Thompson Sampling. The Thompson Sampling strategy incorporates the nature of the binary reward scenario. It models as well mean and variance of each document. It showed good results throughout the whole evaluation process and all configurations. It lacks in this basic version the possibility to adjust the ratio of exploration and exploitation.

Comparative Evaluation. It turned out that the way of using a textual similarity to create a data-driven bandit model leads to a scenario of high variance. Combined with a constrained number of time steps this has significant influence on the solution policies. The EG approach has the advantage of being easily understandable and configurable. Additionally, the volatile scenario mitigates the shortcoming of revisiting "bad" arms. The high variance might also be the reason for the in total worst performance of the UCB approach as shown in Table 2. The Thompson algorithm showed good results and achieved in most experiments a higher reward in less time steps compared to the other algorithms. All algorithms are capable of approximately recreating the fully informed ranking of documents induced by each mean calculated in Fig. 4. To pay respect to the aspects of configurability we suggest a combined approach of EG and TS. For instance, to randomly explore all arms for some steps and then start to use the Thompson Sampling approach (Fig. 7).

Table 2. Overall performance of optimal, random, and bandit strategies.

Agent/Docs	$A_1/10$	$A_2/10$	$A_1/100$	$A_2/100$	Mean Regret
Optimal	0.68	0.93	0.69	0.89	0%
Random	0.53 (28%)	0.81 (19%)	0.54 (28%)	0.77 (16%)	22%
EG $\varepsilon = 0.2$	0.61 (11%)	**0.90 (3%)**	**0.59 (17%)**	**0.80 (11%)**	11%
UCB c = 2	0.54 (26%)	0.83 (12%)	0.56 (23%)	0.78 (14%)	19%
TS	**0.62 (9%)**	0.88 (5%)	0.56 (23%)	0.79 (12%)	13%

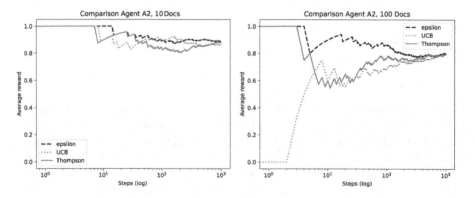

Fig. 7. Performance for 10 and 100 documents for agent configuration A_2.

5 Conclusion and Future Work

This work addressed the problem of distributing a limited budget of textual sampling over a corpus of documents. The lack of real life experts is mitigated by a data-driven agent model with special characteristics to estimate the quality of the samples for adaptational purposes. Therefore, we presented an approach to consider the documents of a corpus as bandit arms in a (constrained) multi-armed bandit setting. A case-based agent model was presented that can be configured together with a reward model to adjust the approach to different application scenarios. Hyper-parameters have been partially optimized in a learning phase. An evaluation was presented on a corpus of nuclear safety documents.

The evaluation showed that documents can be indeed considered as a kind of stochastically distributed entities with a mean reward under variation regarding a similarity-based reward model. The experiments showed that the characteristics of sample retrieval out of documents varies from a "real" stochastic bandit environment in severals aspects which leaves space for the following future work.

Several variations of the setting seem promising and other application domains are worth to investigate. This would give insight to the needs of other user groups with different requirements and possibly improve the performance of the present setting. The following aspects became obvious in the stage of development but eventually exceeded this work.

The underlying data has an inherent structure which can be exploited to create a more distinct bandit architecture. Even though the documents are discrete semantic objects, most likely, there will be a strong correlation amongst them if they belong to the same corpus. On the base of the correlation the reward could be adjusted for every bandit arm. The agent-teacher relationship could have an adversarial character. The teacher wants to challenge the agent. This could be implemented by reducing the reward of certain bandit arms.

An improvement of the agent model would be to switch from a stationary reward to a non-stationary setting that adapts the agent step by step to the character of the data. This could be used to learn agent models from the data. A further benefit would be to set up a contextual bandit model basing on this scenario to find correlations between the agent model and the data [16]. A distant perspective would be a full reinforcement learning model.

The calculation of textual similarities can be quite resource consuming. This might be an issue for complex similarity configurations of the agents, larger corpora, and applications with time pressure. In that case the complexity of algorithms will surely contain potential for improvement.

Finally, a case study with real life experts would help to refine the model. On the one hand it would be good to observe how real experts would choose an agent configuration according to their preferences and task characterization. A survey to determine hyper-parameters should yield insight into human behavior. For instance, taken the parameter δ which determines the threshold when to drop and when to keep a sample. At which similarity threshold does a real life expert tend to drop a sample?

References

1. International Atomic Energy Association. https://www.iaea.org
2. Alon, N., Cesa-Bianchi, N., Gentile, C., Mannor, S., Mansour, Y., Shamir, O.: Non-stochastic multi-armed bandits with graph-structured feedback. SIAM J. Comput. **46**, 1785–1826 (2014)
3. Auer, P.: Using confidence bounds for exploitation-exploration trade-offs. J. Mach. Learn. Res. **3**, 397–422 (2002)
4. Auer, P., Cesa-Bianchi, N., Freund, Y., Schapire, R.: The nonstochastic multiarmed bandit problem. SIAM J. Comput. **32**, 48–77 (2003)
5. Banko, M., Cafarella, M.J., Soderland, S., Broadhead, M., Etzioni, O.: Open information extraction from the web. In: Proceedings of the 20th International Joint Conference on Artificial Intelligence, IJCAI 2007, pp. 2670–2676. Morgan Kaufmann Publishers Inc., San Francisco (2007)
6. Bengs, V., Hüllermeier, E.: Multi-armed bandits with censored consumption of resources. Mach. Learn. **112**(1), 217–240 (2023). https://doi.org/10.1007/s10994-022-06271-z
7. Bergmann, R.: Experience Management. Springer, Heidelberg (2002). https://doi.org/10.1007/3-540-45759-3
8. Brändle, F., Binz, M., Schulz, E.: Exploration beyond bandits, pp. 147–168. Cambridge University Press, Cambridge (2022)
9. Carlsson, E., Dubhashi, D.P., Johansson, F.D.: Thompson sampling for bandits with clustered arms. In: IJCAI International Joint Conference on Artificial Intelligence (2021)
10. Hartig, O.: Foundations of RDF* and SPARQL*: (an alternative approach to statement-level metadata in RDF). In: Alberto Mendelzon Workshop on Foundations of Data Management (2017)
11. Hearst, M.A.: Automatic acquisition of hyponyms from large text corpora. In: COLING 1992 Volume 2: The 15th International Conference on Computational Linguistics, pp. 539–545 (1992)
12. Hong, J., Kveton, B., Katariya, S., Zaheer, M., Ghavamzade, M.: Deep hierarchy in bandits. In: ICML International Conference on Machine Learning (2022)
13. Korger, A., Baumeister, J.: The SECCO ontology for the retrieval and generation of security concepts. In: Cox, M.T., Funk, P., Begum, S. (eds.) ICCBR 2018. LNCS (LNAI), vol. 11156, pp. 186–201. Springer, Cham (2018). https://doi.org/10.1007/978-3-030-01081-2_13
14. Korger, A., Baumeister, J.: Case-based generation of regulatory documents and their semantic relatedness. In: Arai, K., Kapoor, S., Bhatia, R. (eds.) FICC 2020. AISC, vol. 1130, pp. 91–110. Springer, Cham (2020). https://doi.org/10.1007/978-3-030-39442-4_9
15. Kumar, S., Gao, H., Wang, C., Chang, K., Sundaram, H.: Hierarchical multi-armed bandits for discovering hidden populations. In: ASONAM 2019: International Conference on Advances in Social Networks Analysis and Mining, pp. 145–153, August 2019
16. Langford, J., Zhang, T.: The epoch-greedy algorithm for contextual multi-armed bandits. In: Proceedings of the 20th International Conference on Neural Information Processing Systems, NIPS 2007, pp. 817–824. Curran Associates Inc., Red Hook (2007)
17. Losada, D.E., Parapar, J., Barreiro, Á.: Multi-armed bandits for adjudicating documents in pooling-based evaluation of information retrieval systems. Inf. Process. Manag. **53**, 1005–1025 (2017)

18. Perotto, F.S., Verstaevel, N., Trabelsi, I., Vercouter, L.: Combining bandits and lexical analysis for document retrieval in a juridical corpora. In: Bramer, M., Ellis, R. (eds.) SGAI 2020. LNCS (LNAI), vol. 12498, pp. 317–330. Springer, Cham (2020). https://doi.org/10.1007/978-3-030-63799-6_24
19. Racharak, T., Suntisrivaraporn, B., Tojo, S.: sim$^\pi$: a concept similarity measure under an agent's preferences in description logic ELH. In: 8th International Conference on Agents and Artificial Intelligence, pp. 480–487, January 2016
20. Rahman, M.M., Kutlu, M., Lease, M.: Constructing test collections using multi-armed bandits and active learning. In: The Web Conference, San Francisco, May 2019
21. Robbins, H.E.: Some aspects of the sequential design of experiments. Bull. Am. Math. Soc. **58**, 527–535 (1952)
22. Schelling, T.C.: Dynamic models of segregation. J. Math. Sociol. **1**(2), 143–186 (1971)
23. Schulz, E., Franklin, N., Gershman, S.: Finding structure in multi-armed bandits. Cogn. Psychol. **119**, 101261 (2020)
24. Sen, R., et al.: Top-k extreme contextual bandits with arm hierarchy, February 2021
25. Sutton, R.S., Barto, A.G.: Reinforcement Learning: An Introduction, 2nd edn. The MIT Press, Cambridge (2018)
26. Thompson, W.R.: On the likelihood that one unknown probability exceeds another in view of the evidence of two samples. Biometrika **25**, 285–94 (1933)
27. Vaswani, A., et al.: Attention is all you need. In: Guyon, I., et al. (eds.) Advances in Neural Information Processing Systems, vol. 30. Curran Associates, Inc. (2017)
28. W3C: SKOS Simple Knowledge Organization System Reference, August 2009. http://www.w3.org/TR/skos-reference
29. Wood, D., Lanthaler, M., Cyganiak, R.: RDF 1.1 concepts and abstract syntax, February 2014. http://www.w3.org/TR/2014/REC-rdf11-concepts-20140225/

Hybrid Event Memory as a Case Base for State Estimation in Cognitive Agents

David H. Ménager[1(✉)] and Dongkyu Choi[2]

[1] Parallax Advanced Research, Beavercreek, OH 45431, USA
`david.menager@parallaxresearch.org`
[2] Institute of High Performance Computing (IHPC), Agency for Science, Technology and Research (A*STAR), 1 Fusionopolis Way, #16-16 Connexis, Singapore 138632, Republic of Singapore
`Choi_Dongkyu@ihpc.a-star.edu.sg`

Abstract. State estimation is a fundamental problem in artificial intelligence that involves inferring the state of a system based on available measurements. We investigate the role an integrated event memory can play in tackling state estimation of complex domains. Our approach uses the hybrid event memory developed in our previous work as a case base within a cognitive architecture, which enables agents to incrementally learn and represent large joint probability distributions over states as Bayesian networks. To facilitate near real-time execution of this process for agents, we extended the event memory system with a rule-based representation for encoding large probability distributions in its networks. After a review of our cognitive architecture and its event memory, we describe the representational extension before presenting experimental results demonstrating our system's ability to scale to large state estimation problems under various partial observability conditions in the Minecraft domain.

Keywords: hybrid event memory · cognitive architecture · Bayesian networks · state estimation

1 Introduction

State estimation is one of the fundamental problems in artificial intelligence that involves inferring the underlying state of a system from a set of available observations. It is essential in many applications, such as robotics [3], machine learning [12,39], and decision-making [15]. The state estimation problem has been widely studied in the literature [10,26,34–36], and various methods have been proposed to address it. However, this problem still poses significant challenges in complex domains as the number of states and observations can be prohibitively large. One promising approach for solving this is to use Bayesian networks [31], which provide a powerful framework for modeling complex systems and incorporating uncertainty into the estimation process [17,27].

We believe Bayesian networks provide a powerful and flexible framework suitable for representing *cases*, but their usage in this manner have been sparse in the case-based reasoning (CBR) literature [32], despite the growing interests in integrating data-driven techniques with CBR methodologies [21]. Instead, Bayesian networks have typically been used to enhance inference engines supporting existing CBR systems by capturing general background knowledge about a problem. In [1,29], for example, Bayesian networks are used to improve similarity assessment by encoding general domain knowledge like relationships about cooking processes. In [16], the authors present a Bayesian clustering algorithm that uses prototype exemplars in salient feature subspaces to describe clusters. Clustering is done in batch using a Bayesian technique, but the clustered objects are the data samples, from which the prototypes are sourced. Additionally, in [7], the authors report a context-aware Bayesian CBR system for constructing dynamic checklists. To form a case, the system augments observed data with the outputs of naïve Bayes inference for estimating answer probabilities.

In contrast, our present work represents cases themselves as Bayesian networks in our event memory that acts as a case base. Furthermore, we explore ways to integrate such CBR systems within a unified theory of cognition, which is an understudied area of research. Our work makes progress along both of these fronts by extending our hybrid event memory system introduced in prior work [24,25], which is integrated into a cognitive architecture, ICARUS [4]. As we will show later in this paper, the current extension gives our event memory-enabled agent the near real-time capability to learn probability distributions of the state space as Bayesian networks, making it possible to estimate the states continuously during execution.

In Sect. 2 below, we will briefly review the ICARUS cognitive architecture and its hybrid event memory. We will start by discussing the architecture's knowledge structures that support conceptual inference and skill execution. We will then describe how its long-term event memory represents cases and operates over the stored cases for state estimation. After that, in Sect. 3, we will describe two extensions to our event memory system that enable faster and more efficient storage and retrieval of cases, which is essential for near real-time state estimation in agent settings. In Sect. 4, we introduce a popular video game, Minecraft, as our evaluation domain and present experimental results demonstrating the effectiveness of our approach for state estimation. Finally, we will review related literature in Sect. 5 before closing the paper with discussions of our plans for future work and drawing conclusions in Sect. 6.

2   Review of ICARUS and Its Hybrid Event Memory

Cognitive architectures provide computational infrastructure for modeling general intelligence. One such architecture, ICARUS, makes specific commitments to the representation of knowledge, their organization of memories, and various processes that work over these memories. ICARUS shares some of these with other architectures like ACT-R [2], SOAR [19,20], and CLARION [37]. The common features include the distinction between long-term and short-term memories, its use of relational pattern matching to access long-term contents, and the cognitive processes that occur through recognize-act cycles, to name a few. But ICARUS also makes more distinctive assumptions like the hierarchical organization of long-term knowledge, its grounding of cognition on perception and action, and the structural distinction of categories and procedures. Some of these appeared elsewhere in the cognitive systems literature over time, but only the ICARUS architecture makes a continuous commitment to this set of features and integrates them in a unified manner.

2.1   Conceptual and Procedural Memories

ICARUS distinguishes between long-term knowledge and short-term contents, and between categorical and procedural knowledge. The architecture organizes these using distinct representations and stores them in separate memories. Its long-term conceptual memory houses definitions of categories, or *concepts*, that are similar to Horn clauses [11] and describe different relational situations, while a long-term skill memory stores definitions of procedures, or *skills*, that can be considered as hierarchical versions of STRIPS operators [5] and specify ways to achieve certain situations.[1]

Table 1 shows some sample concepts for the Minecraft domain. The first concept, `carrying`, describes a situation where the agent has a non-zero amount of an object type in its possession. This concept refers to a perceived object, `hotbar`, and its attributes, but it does not rely on any other concept, making it a *primitive* concept. The second concept, however, is a *non-primitive* one, which refers to other concept instances like `resource`, `right_of`, `left_of`, and `carrying` in addition to a perceived object, `self`. This concept depicts a situation where the agent and a resource object is vertically aligned and the agent is not in possession of the object.

Similarly, Table 2 shows two sample skills. The first skill, `make_torch`, describes the procedure of making a torch out of a `stick` and a `coal`, simply by executing a direct action `*make` in the world. This primitive definition includes conditions for its execution, the action to take, and its effects, but it does not involve any other skill instances. But the second skill, `craft_torch`, defines a complex procedure that involves gathering necessary resource before attempting to make a torch using the first skill, making it non-primitive.

ICARUS places the instances of its concepts and skills in respective short-term memories. Its belief memory stores inferred concept instances, or *beliefs*, that the agent believes to be true at any given time. A short-term goal memory houses instantiated top-level goals and subgoals, along with the corresponding skill instances, or *intentions* of the agent for the goals.

---

[1] In addition, there is another storage, a long-term goal memory, for the ICARUS agent's top-level goals and their relevance conditions, which are described using generalized concepts. But this memory and the goal reasoning process that works over it is not relevant to the current discussion.

Table 1. Sample ICARUS concepts for the Minecraft domain.

```
((carrying ?o1 ^type ?type ^location ?loc ^size ?size)
 :elements ((hotbar ?o1 type ?type location ?loc size ?size))
 :tests ((> ?size 0)))

((on_vertical_axis ?o1 ?self)
 :elements ((self ?self))
 :conditions ((resource ?o1)
              (not (right_of ?o1 ?self))
              (not (left_of ?o1 ?self))
              (not (carrying ?o1))))
```

Table 2. Sample ICARUS skills for the Minecraft domain.

```
((make_torch)
 :conditions ((carrying ?o1 ^type ?t1)
              (carrying ?o2 ^type ?t2))
 :tests ((eq ?t1 'stick)
         (eq ?t2 'coal))
 :actions ((*make "torch"))
 :effects ((carrying ?torch ^type torch ^location ?l ^size ?s)))

((craft_torch)
 :conditions ((resource ?o2 ^type coal)
              (resource ?o3 ^type stick))
 :subskills ((gather_resource ?o3 stick)
             (gather_resource ?o2 coal)
             (make_torch))
 :effects ((carrying ?torch ^type torch ^location ?l ^size ?s)))
```

2.2 Inference and Execution

The ICARUS architecture operates in recognize-act cycles. As shown in Fig. 1, the system first receives sensory data from its environment in its perceptual buffer and subsequently infers concepts that are true in the current situation. This inference process applies to primitive concepts first, finding all instances of these concepts that hold based on perceived objects and their attributes. Then the system infers non-primitive concept instances that refer to objects and other concept instances.

Once the architecture finishes inferring all beliefs for the current situation, it retrieves skills with matched conditions that are known to achieve its goals.

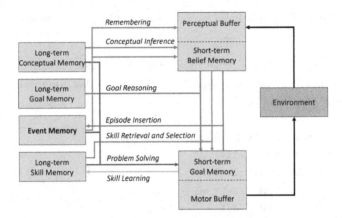

Fig. 1. Block diagram of the extended ICARUS architecture featuring an integrated long-term event memory. The memory system forms episodes by combining the agent's perceptions, beliefs, and actions and supports cue-based retrieval into working memory.

Upon selecting one of the relevant skill instances as its current intention, the agent executes this skill instance in the world, thus changing the environment and its subsequent perceptions. This cyclic operation continues until the agent achieves all its goals.

2.3 Hybrid Event Memory

The ICARUS architecture includes a long-term event memory [24]. This memory serves as a case base for the agent's experiences, storing propositional representation of states that occurred during execution as *episodic* cases. But the memory system also adds generalized *schematic* cases over those at the same time, which serve as propositional templates that aggregates cases in a probabilistic manner.

This memory system is a hybrid, because it represents a middle ground between the two predominant philosophical perspectives on event memory: the causal theory [23] and the simulation theory [28]. The causal theory supports memory systems that represent and maintain discrete, or episodic, events, and thus act like an archive of specific cases. Conversely, the simulationist perspective relies principally on a generalized schema to generate recollections through a reconstructive process. Similarly, our hybrid event memory system stores both episodic and schematic cases in a hierarchy, unifying causal and simulationist views into an elegant theory that exhibits the advantages of both while avoiding their shortcomings.

The long-term event memory forms cases by translating perceived objects and inferred beliefs from a relational description to a propositional one. Figure 2 shows how the architecture encodes a state where the agent is holding a stick and a piece of coal and a feather are visible in the scene. The current state includes some perceived objects like self, hotbar, feather, and coal, as well as some beliefs, shown in capital letters, that the agent inferred from the observed objects

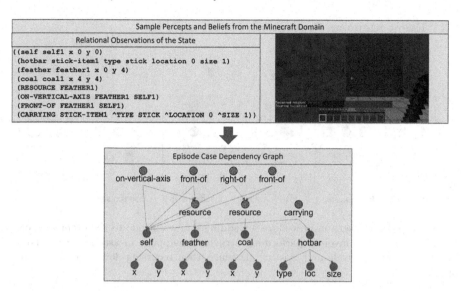

Fig. 2. Representing a relational observations as a dependency graph. For expositional simplicity, this figure does not show existing edges from the belief nodes to perceptual attributes. (Color figure online)

and their attributes. This state is then represented in a *dependency graph* shown below, which depicts the contents of the episodic case. Relational predicates are shown in grey, while perceived objects and their attributes are shown in blue. Each episodic case is a directed acyclic dependency graph where the nodes in the graph contain their observed values from the environment. This graph structure is an episode in the system that represents a single observed state of affairs.

In contrast, schemas are *contextually scoped* cases that aggregate multiple episodes and other schemas together in a probabilistic manner. They encode Bayesian networks that specify the joint probability distribution of a set of correlated variables, X. This joint distribution can be written as:

$$p(x_1, x_2, ..., x_m) = p(x_1|x_2, x_3, ..., x_m)p(x_2|x_3, x_4, ..., x_m)...p(x_m)$$
$$= p(x_m) \prod_{t=1}^{m-1} p(x_t|Pa_{x_t}), \tag{1}$$

where Pa_{x_t} are the parent nodes of x_t. The advantage of using Bayesian networks to encode schematic cases comes from their systematic reliance on conditional independence assumptions. They are the key to compactly representing complex joint distributions since they reduce the number of parameters necessary to encode the full joint probability distribution.

2.4   Event Memory Processes

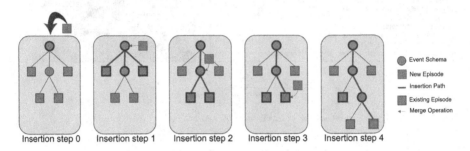

Insertion step 0   Insertion step 1   Insertion step 2   Insertion step 3   Insertion step 4

● Event Schema
■ New Episode
— Insertion Path
■ Existing Episode
◄ Merge Operation

Fig. 3. Top-down insertion procedure for adding a new episode to the event memory. Each insertion step involves performing structure mapping to assess the similarity between the new episode and existing elements, then recursing down the lowest cost branch.

As shown above, ICARUS' long-term event memory stores and maintains episodic and schematic cases in a probabilistic taxonomic hierarchy such that similar elements are grouped together separate from dissimilar ones. Episodic cases exist at the leaf nodes in the hierarchy. On top of these are progressively more general schematic cases that summarize their children in a probabilistic manner. The top-level case in the hierarchy encompasses all the agent's experiences and is the most diffuse. In this way, the event memory system maintains a general-to-specific taxonomy. This taxonomy, however, not only serves to index episodes, but also to store a full-fledged probabilistic model in each intermediate schema that supports Bayesian inference. Unlike other CBR systems that use Bayesian networks, schematic cases in our system have a locally defined context via descendant paths in the hierarchy and therefore are not an amalgamation of general domain knowledge.

Within cases stored in the memory system, the boundary between problem and solution is not defined a priori, and this instead depends on the inputs passed to event memory processes for episodic insertion and cue-based retrieval. The former, depicted in Fig. 3, occurs in an incremental manner, incorporating new episodes as they are encountered. On each cycle, the ICARUS agent generates an episode including its perceptions and beliefs. The system then uses the best-first search to insert the episode top-down through the event hierarchy. At each insertion step, ICARUS assesses similarity between the new episode and the existing event memory elements. By doing this for each element along the insertion path of the new episodic case, the system makes analogical comparisons between the new case and existing event memory elements.

Once the system identifies the best-matching event memory element at one level, it merges the new episodic case into the element, according to the correspondences found during the similarity computation, and updates the probability distribution in the matched element. Then, insertion continues down the subtree.

The insertion procedure completes whenever the new episode becomes a child of the current case at the root of the subtree, or if the new episode merges with a pre-existing case in the hierarchy. The end result of this insertion process is an updated event memory hierarchy with the new example incorporated.

The retrieval process sorts a retrieval cue through the hierarchy employing the same best-first search mechanism as insertion. Instead of adding the retrieval cue to the memory at the end of the search, however, it returns the case that matches best to the cue. Once the system obtains the best-matching event memory element (typically a schematic case), it can use that to perform state estimation through probabilistic inference.

Given the retrieved case, the event memory system takes the observed values from the retrieval cue and sets them as observed variables in the corresponding schema. This creates a problem-solution pair suitable for state estimation such that the problem part corresponds to the observed variables, and the solution part corresponds to the remaining hidden variables, which have not been observed, whose values must be inferred based on the given observations. The probabilistic inference engine in the agent's long-term event memory system is a sum-product message passing algorithm that operates over an approximation of the network, known as a Bethe cluster graph [18]. The system outputs the posterior marginal distribution of each variable given the supplied evidence.

3   Extended Event Memory for State Estimation

In prior work, our event memory system used table-based representations for encoding conditional probability distributions (CPDs) contained in the cases. This was done to ensure efficient retrieval of information by providing random access to the data. This look-up time efficiency, however, came with the disadvantage of imposing high costs on the space requirements of the system. As the dimensionality of the tables increased linearly, the space requirements to encode their distributions grew *exponentially*. Additionally, the large number of parameters in table CPDs burdened the probabilistic inference steps required for performing state estimation. In this section, we describe our latest extensions to the memory system that address these problems.

3.1   Rule-Based Conditional Probability Distributions

The need to have both space- and time-efficient event memory processing for storage and estimation motivated a switch from table-based representations to rule-based ones. Intuitively, a rule in a rule-based conditional probability distribution is a tuple whose left hand side is an assignment to some of the variables in the distribution, denoted as $Scope[\rho]$, while the right hand side specifies the probability for that variable assignment. Rules may be understood as slices of the conditional probability distribution having equal probability. Two rules are *compatible* if the intersection of their left-hand side variables share the same assignments. From this notion of rules, we can formally define rule-based conditional probability distributions below.

Definition 1. A *rule-based* CPD $P(X|Pa_X)$ is a set of rules $\mathcal{R}$ such that:

- For each $\rho \in \mathcal{R}$, we have that $Scope[\rho] \subseteq \{X\} \cup Pa_X$.
- For each assignment $(x, \mathbf{u})$ to $\{X\} \cup Pa_X$, we have one rule $\langle \mathbf{c}; p, i \rangle$ such that $\mathbf{c}$ is compatible with $(x, \mathbf{u})$. In this case we say that $P(X = x|Pa_x = \mathbf{u}) = p$ and has occurred i times.
- The resulting CPD $P(X|\mathbf{U})$ is a legal CPD in that

$$\sum_x P(x|\mathbf{u}) = 1.$$

Definition 1 is taken from [18] with the modification that we add count information to the rule. When interpreting the assertions from Definition 1, it is useful to imagine rules serving as *local coverings* of the table-based CPD. The first item from the definition states that rules must be defined over a subset of variables in the CPD. Next, the second item asserts that each rule represents a slice of the distribution, defined by variables in the left-hand side of the rule, such that each slice covers a region in the table-based CPD. Then, the third statement claims that the sum of each row in the CPD must equal to 1.

With this in mind, it becomes clear that the rule-based representation is a powerful abstraction for achieving *lossless* compression of table-based CPDs by exploiting their local structure. To illustrate this point, consider the example shown in Table 3 depicting the notional conditional probability distribution $P(A|B, C, D)$. Table 3a shows the table CPD for this distribution contains $2^4 = 16$ parameters. By encoding this distribution as a set of rules, as shown in Table 3b, we reduce the space requirements to store the table in half, generating only eight rules. Key to this improvement lies in the fact that one rule can cover multiple slots in the table. For example, for Rule 0, the value of D is ignored allowing it to cover the cases when $D = 0$ and $D = 1$. Additionally, the rule set also contains rules whose counts equal zero. Because these are rules for which outcomes were never observed, we can safely drop them from the rule set to obtain the minimal number of rules, as shown in Table 3c. If there is a query about one of the dropped rules, we can recover the appropriate value from the default distribution, $[1, 0]^2$.

The ability to only store rules for which outcomes have been observed is a boon for building Bayesian networks, captured inside cases, in incremental fashion. As examples are encountered, the architecture can efficiently flesh out the CPDs. In contrast, a table-based representation must reserve space even for outcomes which have not, and may never occur during an agent's operation. This, in combination with exponential growth of table CPDs makes it apparent that they are not appropriate for supporting agents in complex structured environments, and instead rules should be preferred.

---

[2] In Table 3a, rows with distribution $[1, 0]$ have not been observed. For the purpose of exposition, such rows were chosen arbitrarily.

Table 3. Encoding table and rule-based CPDs.

(a) Table CPD

$P(A|B,C,D)$

D	C	B	a^0	a^1
d^0	c^0	b^0	1	0
d^0	c^0	b^1	1	0
d^0	c^1	b^0	1/3	2/3
d^0	c^1	b^1	1	0
d^1	c^0	b^0	1	0
d^1	c^0	b^1	1	0
d^1	c^1	b^0	1/3	2/3
d^1	c^1	b^1	0	1

(b) Rule-based CPD

$P(A|B,C,D)$

0 $\langle a^1 b^0 c^1; 2/3, 3 \rangle$
1 $\langle a^0 b^0 c^1; 1/3, 3 \rangle$
2 $\langle a^1 b^1 c^1 d^1; 1, 1 \rangle$
3 $\langle a^0 b^1 c^1 d^1; 0, 1 \rangle$
4 $\langle a^1 b^1 c^1 d^0; 0, 0 \rangle$
5 $\langle a^0 b^1 c^1 d^0; 1, 0 \rangle$
6 $\langle a^1 c^0; 0, 0 \rangle$
7 $\langle a^0 c^0; 1, 0 \rangle$

(c) Minimal Rules

$P(A|B,C,D)$

0 $\langle a^1 b^0 c^1; 2/3, 3 \rangle$
1 $\langle a^0 b^0 c^1; 1/3, 3 \rangle$
2 $\langle a^1 b^1 c^1 d^1; 1, 1 \rangle$
3 $\langle a^0 b^1 c^1 d^1; 0, 1 \rangle$

3.2 Similarity via Analogical Reasoning for Insertion and Retrieval

The insertion and retrieval processes rely on structure mapping [9] to guide search through the event memory hierarchy. To efficiently solve this problem, ICARUS converts it to a local optimization problem and applies simulated annealing to obtain matches in polynomial time. Simulated annealing returns a solution by iteratively making random matches between nodes in the new episode and existing memory element nodes. On each iteration, the event memory generates a partial solution and scores it using the Bayesian Information Criterion [33].

Additionally, the architecture also places extra constraints on the structure mapping process to enable it to quickly find solutions. These are:

1. Structure mapping is performed in top-down manner;
2. Matched nodes must share the same type; and
3. Candidate match pairs must have the same matched parents.

The structure mapping procedure terminates whenever the simulated annealing temperature arrives at zero. At that point, the architecture returns the best solution to the upstream process, which is either insertion or retrieval.

4 Empirical Evaluations

To evaluate our system's ability to build its case base from experience and use it for state estimation, we programmed an ICARUS agent for Minecraft, a popular sandbox-style video game developed by Mojang Studios[3]. This game presents a unique and challenging environment for artificial intelligence research. It allows players to explore an expansive world and manipulate their surroundings through the use of blocks. The game's open-world environment, coupled with its complexity, requires artificial agents to possess high-level decision-making skills and faculties for handling partial observability to navigate and accomplish goals.

---

[3] We use Minecraft (https://www.minecraft.net/) with its agent interface, Malmo [13].

To facilitate the agent's efficient operation, we assumed a flat world where the agent only perceives objects on the floor and limited the agent's inventory slots to three. Nonetheless, the agent could infer spatial relations such as (left_of ?a ?b) and (right_of ?a ?b) based on these simplified perceptions, maintaining the generality of our experiments. In addition, we simplified the programming of our agent by having it issue only discrete movement commands through the interface. Our agent can choose to move forward, backward, and strafe by one step, as well as turn left or right by 90°.

In our experiment, the agent operated in a 7 × 5 room with the objective of making a torch from component resources found in the room. A different resource existed at each corner in the room, and the agent had to walk to the appropriate ones to fashion the item that satisfied its goal. The recipe for making a torch required one item each of stick and coal. We generated 24 different maps by permuting the locations of the resources in the room. We also gave the agent two skills each for making a torch, resulting in 48 different possible scenarios. In each scenario, the agent followed a recipe for crafting a torch. During the course of execution, we recorded the agent's observations and beliefs about the world, thus generating an execution trace. This enabled us to create a rich dataset of examples from which to build the agent's event memory.

Given this dataset, we split it into training and testing partitions, and performed 10-fold cross validation to build the agent's event memory by inserting the execution traces sequentially. Then in test, we compared our agent's ability to perform state estimation under various partial observability conditions. Under these conditions, the agent received a subset of the perceptual information sensed from the environment, then had to elaborate all missing perceptions, if any, and infer all beliefs since these were never directly perceived.

In Fig. 4a, we present the average cycle duration across 10 folds as the ICARUS agent inserts the observation traces through its event memory. The figure shows that time it took to insert the examples moved from around three to five seconds initially and progresses down to less then one second at the end of the trace. We believe that because the initial state is similar across the observation traces, inserting them into the event hierarchy progressively expanded the same subtree. As a result, the insertion time for these early observations was comparatively higher than the later observations because the event memory system needed to complete more insertion steps. In contrast, later observations which had more distinguishing features, consequently, wound up in more shallow, less developed parts of the hierarchy resulting in faster insertion times.

Figure 4b compares the number of parameters needed to encode the case distributions at the top-level of the hierarchy by table- and rule-based CPDs. In the figure, the y-axis is the log transform of the number of parameters, while the x-axis shows the percentage of traces observed in the fold. The trends show an order of magnitude savings for rule-based CPDs meaning that this representation scales nicely to highly structured domains.

Next, we present training performance results for state estimation in Fig. 5. Figure 5a measures the *local* likelihood of the model, meaning we measure the

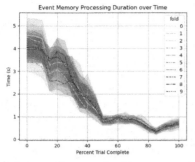 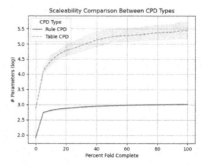

(a) Average time required to process state in ICARUS cognitive cycle.

(b) Comparing space requirements of rule-based CPDs with table-based CPDs.

Fig. 4. Insertion performance results of the long-term event memory.

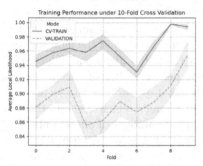 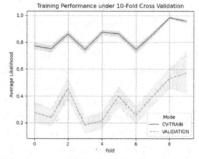

(a) Average *local* likelihood of reconstructing the ground truth from the retrieved model.

(b) Average likelihood of reconstructing the ground truth from the retrieved model.

Fig. 5. Training performance results.

likelihood of each individual state variable in the model, then report the average. By comparison, Fig. 5b measures the average likelihood of the *joint assignment* of the state variables in the model. During training, the system obtained high marks, but differences in performance arose under the validation set. The local likelihood measure remained high, but a significant drop in performance is observed for the likelihood. This difference in performance occurred because the likelihood measure is conjunctive. This means that if the model assigned low probability to one of the ground truth state variables, it significantly decrease the likelihood score of the model because the low probability value is multiplied to the other probability assignments in the network. Despite this, the likelihood of recovering the ground truth state using the retrieved case significantly exceeds random chance because the space over which the Bayesian network is defined covers, on average, 3.07×10^{29} number of outcomes (Fig. 6).

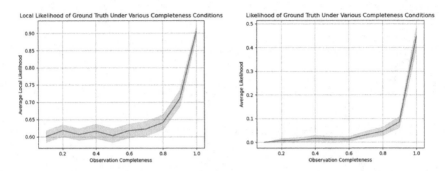

Fig. 6. Likelihood measures under various partial observability conditions.

During test, the ICARUS agent performed state estimation under various partial observability conditions. When the agent had complete observations of the perceived objects both likelihood measures obtained their maximum results, with the local measure achieving greater than 90% performance and the joint measure recovering the ground truth state with greater than 40% likelihood. The performance fell sharply when the agent could not perceive 10% of the perceptual environment, but gracefully degraded beyond that point. For the local likelihood, performance did not drop below 60% on average, which suggests that the state estimation was largely correct with a moderate amount of uncertainty. This uncertainty, however, proved costly for the joint likelihood because it reduced the likelihood of the model generating the ground truth state down to 0% by the time the agent could only observe 10% of the perceptual environment.

5   Related Work

In addition to the previous work from the case-based reasoning literature that we discussed earlier in Sect. 1, there are other groups of work that our system shares insights with. Most importantly, our event memory system descends intellectually from incremental concept formation systems like COBWEB, TRESTLE and LABYRINTH [6,8,22,38]. Such systems gradually acquire knowledge about a problem domain by clustering examples, as they are encountered, into probabilistic hierarchies. Incremental concept formation emphasizes the compositional nature of knowledge, continual learning, and improvement in predictive performance over time. The event memory system in ICARUS differs from these mainly in that nodes in the hierarchy are Bayesian networks, and it is capable of scaling to a broader range of inference tasks.

Event memory has been modeled as declarative episodic memory in another cognitive architecture, SOAR [19]. SOAR's episodic memory stores contents of the agent's working memory in a flat storage container. It supports insertion and cue-based retrieval of content to aid in other cognitive tasks such as problem solving [30] and anticipatory thinking [14]. Unlike ICARUS, episodes in SOAR's episodic memory cannot serve as predictive models of the world. ACT-R and CLARION have declarative memories, but do not make clear distinctions between semantic and episodic content.

6 Future Work and Conclusions

Future research extending this work could include inference over continuous- and discrete-valued variables, insertion strategies that efficiently assess the similarity between related event memory elements, and learning approaches for acquiring conceptual knowledge that enable the agent to describe and categorize states. Pushing the research in these directions can significantly enhance the efficiency and accuracy of state estimation in event memory-enabled agents across a wide array of domains, and we hope to report our results in a near future.

State estimation is a crucial problem in various fields of AI, and the extended ICARUS cognitive architecture offers a powerful approach to it, which relies on its event memory system storing and maintaining Bayesian network representations. Studies have shown the benefits and utility of Bayesian networks, but challenges still remain when dealing with complex structured domains. Our work represents a step towards addressing these challenges by integrating our Hybrid Event Memory System into the ICARUS cognitive architecture to create an event memory-enabled agent capable of learning probability distributions of the state space as Bayesian networks in an online manner. This research opens up new avenues for exploring the integration of data-driven techniques with Case-Based Reasoning and for unifying theories of cognition.

Acknowledgments. This research is supported in part by Agency for Science, Technology and Research (A*STAR) under its Human-Robot Collaborative AI for Advanced Manufacturing and Engineering (Award A18A2b0046). Any opinions, findings and conclusions, or recommendations expressed in this material are those of the authors and may not necessarily reflect the views of the agency. No official endorsement should be inferred.

References

1. Aamodt, A., Langseth, H.: Integrating Bayesian networks into knowledge-intensive CBR. In: AAAI Workshop on Case-Based Reasoning Integrations, pp. 1–6 (1998)
2. Anderson, J.R., Matessa, M., Lebiere, C.: ACT-R: a theory of higher level cognition and its relation to visual attention. Hum.-Comput. Interact. **12**(4), 439–462 (1997)
3. Barfoot, T.D.: State Estimation for Robotics. Cambridge University Press, Cambridge (2017)
4. Choi, D., Langley, P.: Evolution of the ICARUS cognitive architecture. Cogn. Syst. Res. **48**, 25–38 (2018)
5. Fikes, R., Nilsson, N.: STRIPS: a new approach to the application of theorem proving to problem solving. Artif. Intell. **2**, 189–208 (1971)
6. Fisher, D.H.: Knowledge acquisition via incremental conceptual clustering. Mach. Learn. **2**(2), 139–172 (1987). https://doi.org/10.1007/BF00114265
7. Flogard, E.L., Mengshoel, O.J., Bach, K.: Creating dynamic checklists via Bayesian case-based reasoning: towards decent working conditions for all (2022)

8. Gennari, J.H., Langley, P., Fisher, D.: Models of incremental concept formation. Artif. Intell. **40**(1–3), 11–61 (1989)
9. Gentner, D.: Structure-mapping: a theoretical framework for analogy. Cogn. Sci. **7**(2), 155–170 (1983)
10. Hausknecht, M., Stone, P.: Deep recurrent Q-learning for partially observable MDPs. In: 2015 AAAI Fall Symposium Series (2015)
11. Horn, A.: On sentences which are true of direct unions of algebras. J. Symb. Log. **16**(1), 14–21 (1951)
12. Hu, X., Li, S.E., Yang, Y.: Advanced machine learning approach for lithium-ion battery state estimation in electric vehicles. IEEE Trans. Transp. Electrification **2**(2), 140–149 (2015)
13. Johnson, M., Hofmann, K., Hutton, T., Bignell, D.: The Malmo platform for artificial intelligence experimentation. In: Proceedings of the Twenty-Fifth International Joint Conference on Artificial Intelligence, pp. 4246–4247 (2016)
14. Jones, S., Laird, J.: Anticipatory thinking in cognitive architectures with event cognition mechanisms. In: Cognitive Systems for Anticipatory Thinking at the AAAI Fall Symposium (2021)
15. Kebriaei, H., Rahimi-Kian, A., Ahmadabadi, M.N.: Model-based and learning-based decision making in incomplete information cournot games: a state estimation approach. IEEE Trans. Syst. Man Cybern. Part A Syst. Hum. **45**(4), 713–718 (2014)
16. Kim, B., Rudin, C., Shah, J.A.: The Bayesian case model: a generative approach for case-based reasoning and prototype classification. In: Advances in Neural Information Processing Systems, vol. 27 (2014)
17. Kim, D., Park, M., Park, Y.L.: Probabilistic modeling and Bayesian filtering for improved state estimation for soft robots. IEEE Trans. Robot. **37**(5), 1728–1741 (2021)
18. Koller, D., Friedman, N.: Probabilistic Graphical Models: Principles and Techniques. MIT Press, Cambridge (2009)
19. Laird, J.E.: The Soar Cognitive Architecture. MIT Press, Cambridge (2012)
20. Laird, J.E., Newell, A., Rosenbloom, P.S.: SOAR: an architecture for general intelligence. Artif. Intell. **33**(1), 1–64 (1987)
21. Leake, D., Crandall, D.: On bringing case-based reasoning methodology to deep learning. In: Watson, I., Weber, R. (eds.) ICCBR 2020. LNCS (LNAI), vol. 12311, pp. 343–348. Springer, Cham (2020). https://doi.org/10.1007/978-3-030-58342-2_22
22. MacLellan, C.J., Harpstead, E., Aleven, V., Koedinger, K.R.: TRESTLE: incremental learning in structured domains using partial matching and categorization. In: Proceedings of the Third Annual Conference on Advances in Cognitive Systems (2015)
23. Martin, C.B., Deutscher, M.: Remembering. Philos. Rev. **75**(2), 161–196 (1966)
24. Ménager, D.H., Choi, D., Robins, S.K.: A hybrid theory of event memory. Minds Mach. **32**, 365–394 (2022). https://doi.org/10.1007/s11023-021-09578-3
25. Ménager, D.H., Choi, D., Robins, S.K.: Modeling human memory phenomena in a hybrid event memory system. Cogn. Syst. Res. **75**, 25–35 (2022)
26. Ménager, D.H., Choi, D., Floyd, M.W., Task, C., Aha, D.W.: Dynamic goal recognition using windowed action sequences. In: Workshops at the Thirty-First AAAI Conference on Artificial Intelligence (2017)
27. Mengshoel, O.J., Darwiche, A., Uckun, S.: Sensor validation using Bayesian networks. In: International Symposium on Artificial Intelligence Robotics, and Automation in Space (2008)

28. Michaelian, K.: Mental Time Travel: Episodic Memory and Our Knowledge of the Personal Past. MIT Press, Cambridge (2016)
29. Nikpour, H., Aamodt, A.: Inference and reasoning in a Bayesian knowledge-intensive CBR system. Prog. Artif. Intell. **10**, 49–63 (2021). https://doi.org/10.1007/s13748-020-00223-1
30. Nuxoll, A.M., Laird, J.E.: Extending cognitive architecture with episodic memory. In: Proceedings of the Twenty-Second National Conference on Artificial Intelligence, pp. 1560–1565 (2007)
31. Pearl, J.: Fusion, propagation, and structuring in belief networks. Artif. Intell. **29**(3), 241–288 (1986)
32. Richter, M.M., Weber, R.O.: Case-Based Reasoning. Springer, Heidelberg (2016)
33. Schwarz, G., et al.: Estimating the dimension of a model. Ann. Stat. **6**(2), 461–464 (1978)
34. Seo, T., Bayen, A.M., Kusakabe, T., Asakura, Y.: Traffic state estimation on highway: a comprehensive survey. Annu. Rev. Control. **43**, 128–151 (2017)
35. Shivakumar, N., Jain, A.: A review of power system dynamic state estimation techniques. In: 2008 Joint International Conference on Power System Technology and IEEE Power India Conference, pp. 1–6. IEEE (2008)
36. Sukthankar, G., Geib, C., Bui, H.H., Pynadath, D., Goldman, R.P.: Plan, Activity, and Intent Recognition: Theory and Practice. Newnes (2014)
37. Sun, R.: Anatomy of the Mind: Exploring Psychological Mechanisms and Processes with the Clarion Cognitive Architecture. Oxford University Press, Oxford (2016)
38. Thompson, K., Langley, P.: Concept formation in structured domains. In: Concept Formation, pp. 127–161. Elsevier (1991)
39. Zamzam, A.S., Sidiropoulos, N.D.: Physics-aware neural networks for distribution system state estimation. IEEE Trans. Power Syst. **35**(6), 4347–4356 (2020)

CBR and Explainable AI

Cases Are King: A User Study of Case Presentation to Explain CBR Decisions

Lawrence Gates, David Leake$^{(\boxtimes)}$, and Kaitlynne Wilkerson

Luddy School, Indiana University, Bloomington, IN 47408, USA
{gatesla,leake,kwilker}@indiana.edu

Abstract. From the early days of case-based reasoning research, the ability of CBR systems to explain their decisions in terms of past cases has been seen as an important advantage. However, there have been few studies on the factors affecting the effectiveness of explaining CBR decisions by cases. This paper presents results from a human subjects study that examined how alternative retrieval processes (one-shot or conversational) and case presentation approaches affect the perceived goodness of case-based explanations for explaining system behavior, their convincingness, and the trust they engender. The study corroborates that cases are well received as explanations, with some benefit for providing information to support similarity comparison, and suggests that elucidating the retrieval process has little effect on explanatory effectiveness.

Keywords: Case-based reasoning · conversational case-based reasoning · counterfactuals · explanation · interfaces · XAI · human subjects study

1 Introduction

The growing deployment of AI systems for high-impact tasks, coupled with governmental policies such as the EU GDPR regulations providing the right to "meaningful information" about AI system decisions, often called "right to explanation" [31], have spurred much interest into eXplainable AI (XAI) [9]. Case-based reasoning (CBR) has long been seen as well-suited to explanation because it is intrinsically interpretable, in that a CBR system can account for its decisions by presenting the cases on which its solutions are based [20]. Much research has studied methods to explain the CBR process and to leverage CBR to facilitate explanation of other AI methods, leading to an active CBR explanation community and a series of workshops on XCBR (e.g., [27]).

In both XAI and XCBR, much of the research focus has been technical, aimed at the development of methods to provide AI systems with new explanatory capabilities. However, human subjects studiesto assess the response of users to those capabilities have been less widespread. Keane and Kenny's [14] survey of research on twinning CBR with neural networks for explanation described the "embarrassment of user testing," noting that only "a handfull" of the works that they surveyed on twinning included user tests; a survey of other aspects of explanation using CBR by Gates and Leake [8] found similarly sparse coverage.

S. Massie and S. Chakraborti (Eds.): ICCBR 2023, LNAI 14141, pp. 153–168, 2023.
https://doi.org/10.1007/978-3-031-40177-0_10

In seminal work, Cunningham et al. [3] performed a human subjects study that supported the convincingness of cases as explanations, compared to rules. However, despite the importance of that work, important questions remain for knowing how cases can be used most effectively as explanations. One question is how best to present explanatory cases to users. Explanatory cases may be presented to users in different ways, including different types of contextualizing information; this raises the question of what forms of case presentation and contextual information may enhance the explanatory value of cases. If certain forms are more effective, knowledge of which to apply can provide "low-hanging fruit" for enhancing the explanatory benefit of CBR systems: system designers can adapt the case presentation interface accordingly.

A second question concerns the effect of different modes of interaction with a CBR system. Interactions between CBR systems and their users are commonly managed in one of two ways. In traditional "one-shot" CBR systems, a problem is presented to the system, which then presents its solution. In conversational case-based reasoning (CCBR), users provide information incrementally, guided by questions the system provides, with questions aimed at identifying the most similar case in the case base rapidly [1]. The conversational interaction can be seen as making the case retrieval process transparent, which might be seen as an additional implicit explanation of case relevance, which might increase the user's sense of understanding of the system process. If either interaction type affects user perception of explanation quality, designers could use that information to guide decisions of which interaction to select when both are applicable.[1]

A third question concerns the effects of case presentation on user perceptions of different measures of explanation quality. Cunningham et al. [3] focused on convincingness, the ability of the explanation to convince users that the decision was correct. In addition to convincingness, this paper considers effects on the *goodness* of the explanations for explaining current system decision-making and the *trust* they engender for future system decisions.

Our human subjects study tests the effects of three types of CBR system interactions—standard CBR, CCBR with question retrieval based on information gain, and CCBR retrieval based on individual feature importance—and of four explanation presentation designs. For each, we measure impact on the convincingness, goodness for understanding system behavior, and future trust of the system. We also test whether successive exposures to each explanation design affect the reported scores. Finally, we test whether scores are affected when incorrect solutions provided to users and by the level of similarity between the problem case and solution case presented to the user.

Analysis of our results suggests that the form of CBR interaction, one-shot or CCBR, was not important—only explanation type played a role in the observed goodness of, convincingness of, and trust in explanations. It also supported that the similarity of the prior case to the new situation had an impact on convincingness and trust. This suggests that the key aspect determining the usefulness of

---

[1] When the user does not have a full description of the problem, using CCBR may be necessary to guide problem elaboration.

explanations by cases is the case provided to explain the system decision. This provides support for the common CBR intuition that case presentation carries the primary burden for explaining CBR decisions. Our results also suggest that simply presenting the current problem and most similar case is an effective explanation approach, and that presentation of supplementary information about similarity in tabular form is helpful for all three criteria. Supplementing the nearest neighbor with the counterexample of the nearest unlike neighbor (NUN) was expected to improve explanations by helping users assess scope, but surprisingly was found to be detrimental for goodness, convincingness, and trust compared to the most similar case alone. However, no presentation variants were ranked negatively.

2 Related Work

Metrics for Assessing Explanations: XAI research has used a variety of metrics to assess the explanations generated by AI systems. Two of the most common metrics are trust and goodness, where goodness takes various forms [28]. It has been defined based on a wide variety of aspects of the explanation and the context in which it is presented, as well as in relationship to the explainer's purpose (e.g. [19,32]), and its presentation. A central point is how the information and format of an explanation are received by a human [11], which has been assessed by criteria such as whether the explanation was easy to understand, and satisfying and useful towards understanding the domain and/or the AI system's reasoning [11,28]. Another metric, convincingness, can be linked to discussions of goodness and trust. Previous studies examining the convincingness of explanations have relied on subjects assessing its common parlance meaning [3,29], and we follow that approach.

Another common evaluation criterion is trust. Trust can be conceptualized in terms of user vulnerability and the extent to which the user accepts the risk present in an interaction [12,23,28]. In our study, we again rely on the user understanding the common parlance meaning of trust. The task domain we will use in our study, blood alcohol content estimation—which is used for breathalyzer tests of whether it is safe to drive—is one for which in principle risks could result from wrong predictions, which gives implicit stakes for the trust assessment.

Human Subjects Studies on Explaining by Cases: In a landmark human subjects study, Cunnningham et al. [3] compared case-based and rule-based explanations of whether the blood alcohol levels of drinkers was over or under the limit, given information about pub visits such as visit duration and number of drinks consumed. Subjects were presented with predictions in three conditions, with a case as explanation, with a rule-based explanation, or with no explanation, and asked the convincingness of the prediction. In their results case-based explanation decisively outperformed rule-based explanation.

A later study by Doyle et al. [6] considered explanation by cases for three domains, hospital admission and discharge decisions for bronchiolitis, an e-clinic domain, and the blood alcohol domain. Subjects were provided with a system decision (e.g., a recommendation about admission or discharge), an explanation case (not necessarily the nearest neighbor but selected by a hand-coded utility function to be closer to the decision boundary [5]), justification text, and a confidence value. The justification text presented pros and the cons for the recommendation. Cases as explanations were useful for all domains, but with a split in the cases found most useful: cases selected by utility-based criteria were favored for bronchiolitis but not for the blood alcohol or e-clinic domains. Doyle et al. hypothesized that the difference was due to the increased complexity of the bronchiolitis domain, which made the directional effects less apparent.

Presentation of counterexamples enables a "compare and contrast" process to determine case applicability [2,17,21]. Doyle at al. also assessed the effects of presenting nearest unlike neighbors. Including this counterexample was found to be useful when subjects considered recommendations incorrect but overall had little effect.

Lamy et al. [18] performed a small scale (N=11) human subjects study of cases as explanation for a breast cancer domain, with primary focus on the benefit of visualization of similarity to explain case relevance; they reported a very positive response. Massie, Craw, and Wiratunga [24] studied the benefit of a visualization interface for explaining problem and solution similarities in a tablet formulation domain. A small-scale human subjects study (N=2) supported the usefulness of the visualizations of similarity and a preference for visualizations over text. McSherry [26] notes the subtlety that for prediction tasks, similarity between features that mitigate against the outcome may not strengthen the conclusion, and proposes an evidential approach that presents supporting and opposing features.

Kenny and Keane [15] conducted large-scale user studies (N=184) of the effects of post-hoc case-based explanations of black box systems. In their results, the primary impact of explanations was on mental models of misclassifications.

Warren et al. [33] conducted a human subjects study that compared counterfactual and causal explanations in a blood alcohol domain. It showed that counterfactuals were slightly more effective than causal explanations in improving user knowledge of the operation of an AI system (in terms of predictive accuracy), and which also raised concerns for a possible human tendency to overestimate their own causal understanding.

3   Methods

The study protocol was approved by Indiana University's ethics review board (Indiana University IRB: 16546).

3.1   Participants

We recruited 110 participants via flyers, mailing lists, and word-of-mouth. They were paid $8 for participation in the 20–30 min study. 89 participants correctly completed all 12 trials. We discarded the data of participants who did not correctly complete all trials. Each participant was randomly assigned to one of the system design groups, corresponding to one-shot CBR (26 participants) and to either of two CCBR groups, one with question order guided by information gain (30 participants) and the other with an alternative question ordering (33 participants). Section 3.2 provides more details on the CCBR systems.

Participants were generally young and well educated. Approximately 50% were born between 1994 and 2003, approximately 70% held a Bachelor's degree or higher. 90% had background in STEM. Concerning depth of understanding of AI mechanisms, 37% reported that they could write AI code, 29% could program but could not write AI code, 15% worked with AI-powered systems, and 19% had only heard about AI. Participants generally reported being interested in (70%) and excited (60%) about the progress being made in AI, while also being concerned about the prevalence of AI (53%) and how AI systems arrive at conclusions (97%). The majority of participants reported being neutral (41%) to open (40%) to trusting the information provided by AI systems. Given the homogeneity of our respondents backgrounds, our results may not be representative of individuals outside of these demographics.

3.2   Materials

Case Data Set. Case data was a Blood Alcohol Content (BAC) data set of 85 cases collected from people leaving a pub [4], available online with documentation[2]. Cases included the categorical features Gender, Frame Size, Amount Consumed, Meal Consumed, and Duration, which were used to predict BAC. Approximately 52% of the cases were over the limit (0.8).

Each participant was presented with scenarios based on the same 12 cases[3]. The 12 were chosen to obtain a representative distribution of feature values and an even distribution of similarity levels between the problem case and the nearest neighbor that would be used in the explanation, to be able to assess whether similarity level affected goodness, convincingness, and trust. Features were weighted equally for similarity calculations. The set of selected cases included approximately 50% for which leave-one-out testing would generate an incorrect prediction, to assess whether system error affected participant judgments of goodness, convincingness, and trust. The user was not informed when predictions were incorrect. Ideally, explanation methods would tend to reveal likely errors and support higher ratings for correct solutions than for erroneous ones.

Participants interacted with one of the three CBR system variants whose results were presented in four explanation design templates. The systems performed a Blood Alcohol Content (BAC) prediction task to predict whether an individual's BAC level would be over or under the legal limit for driving.

---

[2] GitHub Link: https://github.com/gateslm/Blood-Alcohol-Domain.

[3] The cases were presented in the following order (based on the case number in the dataset): 2, 8, 9, 12, 19, 33, 45, 48, 58, 82, 4, 54.

System Types. The study tested response to one of three CBR systems to assess how the interaction type and system process may effect observed levels of goodness, convincingness, and trust. The systems are a traditional CBR system and two versions of CCBR system, differing in question ordering:

- **CBR:** Traditional CBR; This system provides data fields to enter information; when all information is entered the system provides a prediction.
- **CCBR-IG:** CCBR - Information Gain (IG); Question ordering was determined by generating a prediction decision tree and ordering questions based on their first appearance in the tree, with the question process terminating when a unique best-match case is identified. (There were no ties in the examples used in the study.)
- **CCBR-CF:** CCBR - Combined Features (CF); The first questions asked concern the two features most predictive individually for the case base: amount of alcohol consumed and meal consumed. The other features were asked in the arbitrary order gender, frame size, and duration.

Explanation Designs. For each of the three systems, four types of explanations were tested for system predictions: Nearest Neighbor (NN), Nearest Neighbor+Similarity in two variants, one presenting similarity in tabular form and the other in textual form (NN+Sim:tab and NN+Sim:txt), and nearest neighbor with NUN as counterexample (NN+CE):

- **NN**: Nearest Neighbor (Fig. 1a); This presents the most similar case and its solution without any other information.
- **NN+Sim:tab**: Nearest Neighbor + Similarity Tabular Form (Fig. 1b); This augments the NN information with a brief tabular summary of similarities and differences between the nearest neighbor and the current problem.
- **NN+CE**: Nearest Neighbor + Counterexample (Fig. 1c); This presents two cases for comparison: the most similar case over the limit and the most similar case under the limit. This relates to the counterexample presentation studied by Doyle et al. [6] but differs in presenting the nearest unlike neighbor rather than selecting by their utility function. It parallels the "bracketing case" approach of Leake et al. [22].
- **NN+Sim:txt**: Nearest Neighbor + Similarity Textual Form (Fig. 1d); This presents information about the most similar case and its similarity to the current problem in textual form. Text passages were generated using a simple template-based generator.

Experimental Data Collection Process. Data collection was online. The need to provide the interactive experience of a CCBR dialogue precluded using survey tools that simply present questionnaires. We used psiTurk, an interactive tool that can handle data collection while running Python code [7,10].

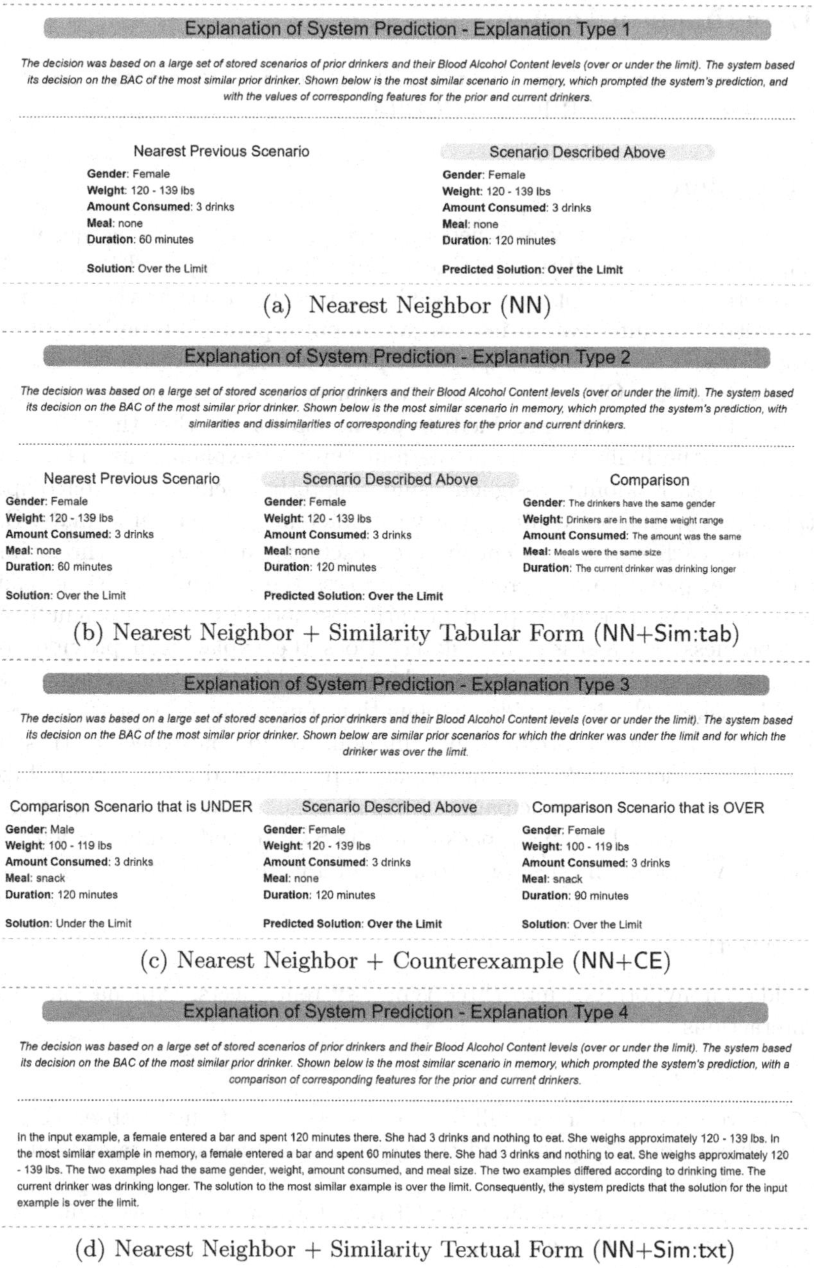

Explanation of System Prediction - Explanation Type 1

The decision was based on a large set of stored scenarios of prior drinkers and their Blood Alcohol Content levels (over or under the limit). The system based its decision on the BAC of the most similar prior drinker. Shown below is the most similar scenario in memory, which prompted the system's prediction, and with the values of corresponding features for the prior and current drinkers.

Nearest Previous Scenario

Gender: Female
Weight: 120 - 139 lbs
Amount Consumed: 3 drinks
Meal: none
Duration: 60 minutes

Solution: Over the Limit

Scenario Described Above

Gender: Female
Weight: 120 - 139 lbs
Amount Consumed: 3 drinks
Meal: none
Duration: 120 minutes

Predicted Solution: Over the Limit

(a) Nearest Neighbor (NN)

Explanation of System Prediction - Explanation Type 2

The decision was based on a large set of stored scenarios of prior drinkers and their Blood Alcohol Content levels (over or under the limit). The system based its decision on the BAC of the most similar prior drinker. Shown below is the most similar scenario in memory, which prompted the system's prediction, with similarities and dissimilarities of corresponding features for the prior and current drinkers.

Nearest Previous Scenario	Scenario Described Above	Comparison
Gender: Female	**Gender**: Female	**Gender**: The drinkers have the same gender
Weight: 120 - 139 lbs	**Weight**: 120 - 139 lbs	**Weight**: Drinkers are in the same weight range
Amount Consumed: 3 drinks	**Amount Consumed**: 3 drinks	**Amount Consumed**: The amount was the same
Meal: none	**Meal**: none	**Meal**: Meals were the same size
Duration: 60 minutes	**Duration**: 120 minutes	**Duration**: The current drinker was drinking longer
Solution: Over the Limit	**Predicted Solution: Over the Limit**	

(b) Nearest Neighbor + Similarity Tabular Form (NN+Sim:tab)

Explanation of System Prediction - Explanation Type 3

The decision was based on a large set of stored scenarios of prior drinkers and their Blood Alcohol Content levels (over or under the limit). The system based its decision on the BAC of the most similar prior drinker. Shown below are similar prior scenarios for which the drinker was under the limit and for which the drinker was over the limit.

Comparison Scenario that is UNDER	Scenario Described Above	Comparison Scenario that is OVER
Gender: Male	**Gender**: Female	**Gender**: Female
Weight: 100 - 119 lbs	**Weight**: 120 - 139 lbs	**Weight**: 100 - 119 lbs
Amount Consumed: 3 drinks	**Amount Consumed**: 3 drinks	**Amount Consumed**: 3 drinks
Meal: snack	**Meal**: none	**Meal**: snack
Duration: 120 minutes	**Duration**: 120 minutes	**Duration**: 90 minutes
Solution: Under the Limit	**Predicted Solution: Over the Limit**	**Solution**: Over the Limit

(c) Nearest Neighbor + Counterexample (NN+CE)

Explanation of System Prediction - Explanation Type 4

The decision was based on a large set of stored scenarios of prior drinkers and their Blood Alcohol Content levels (over or under the limit). The system based its decision on the BAC of the most similar prior drinker. Shown below is the most similar scenario in memory, which prompted the system's prediction, with a comparison of corresponding features for the prior and current drinkers.

In the input example, a female entered a bar and spent 120 minutes there. She had 3 drinks and nothing to eat. She weighs approximately 120 - 139 lbs. In the most similar example in memory, a female entered a bar and spent 60 minutes there. She had 3 drinks and nothing to eat. She weighs approximately 120 - 139 lbs. The two examples had the same gender, weight, amount consumed, and meal size. The two examples differed according to drinking time. The current drinker was drinking longer. The solution to the most similar example is over the limit. Consequently, the system predicts that the solution for the input example is over the limit.

(d) Nearest Neighbor + Similarity Textual Form (NN+Sim:txt)

Fig. 1. Sample screen images for the four presentation types tested.

4   Experimental Design

Our experiments compare the four types of explanation presentation and three system types: CBR, CCBR-IG and CCBR-CF.

4.1   Procedure

Participants were randomly assigned to three groups, each interacting with a different system for the entire experiment. Participants completed 12 trials. The entire experiment lasted approximately 30 min. During each trial, the participant was provided with information from a case about a person's time in a bar and was asked, based on system group, either to fill in the features of the bar visit description (one-shot CBR) or to answer a sequence of system-selected questions (CCBR). The system then provided its prediction for whether the visitor was over or under the limit and one of the four types of explanations. The explanation type was randomly assigned using counterbalancing. Each participant saw the same explanation content, but with different explanation formats. Over the 12 trials, each participant encountered each explanation type three times. For each case, participants were asked to assess the system's decision-making and explanation along three dependent variables: goodness, convincingness, and trust. Goodness was assessed by asking "Does the explanation provide good information for assessing the system's decision making?". Convincingness was assessed by asking "Is the provided explanation convincing?" Trust was assessed by asking "Based on the provided information, would you expect to trust the system's future decisions?" The questions were answered on a 5-point Likert scale. After the 12 trials participants provided demographic data (year of birth, highest education level attained, background in STEM, and familiarity with and opinions of AI) based on questions from the literature [13,16,30].

4.2   Hypotheses

We divide our hypotheses into three types: system effects, explanation effects and interactions.

System Effects

- **S1:** Conversational systems will have a positive impact on the observed levels of goodness, convincingness and trust, due to the increased transparency on the system retrieval process.
- **S2:** The average scores of the two CCBR systems will differ according to the question selection strategy used.

Explanation Effects

- **E1:** NN+Sim:tab, NN+Sim:txt, and NN+CE designs will have more positive levels of goodness, convincingness and trust than NN because NN+CE provides more information to the user, while NN+Sim:tab and NN+Sim:txt make explicit similarity comparisons between solution and problem.

Interactions

- **I1:** CCBR systems using the NN+Sim:tab, NN+Sim:txt, and NN+CE designs will score better on each measure compared to the non-conversational system using the same designs due to increased system process transparency.
- **I2:** Correctness of solutions will have an effect on scores.
- **I3:** The level of similarity between the problem case and the cases used in explanation will have an impact on the scores.

We also analyzed whether perceptions changed with increasing exposure to a given explanation type. However, we generated no hypotheses for this.

4.3 Analysis

To assess the hypotheses stated above (excluding I2 and I3), we used three mixed model, repeated measures ANOVAs with one between-subjects factor (System Type) and two within-subjects factors (Explanation Type and Exposure) for goodness, convincingness, and trust. As discussed in Sect. 4.1, our study considered three system types and four explanation types. Each explanation type was seen by participants 3 times, enabling consideration of effects of exposure. A mixed model, repeated measures ANOVA was used to assess whether significant differences exist in average scores for system type, explanation type, exposure or some combination of the three. We used a pairwise comparison of means to parse any significant results and determine which values of each were particularly influential. Significance was set at 0.05.

To assess hypotheses I2 and I3, we used three mixed model, repeated measures ANCOVAs with two time-varying covariates: similarity level and incorrect responses. Each test was structured like the ANOVAs with the exception of the addition of the covariate variables. The ANCOVAs allow controlling for certain factors that may have influenced the results, and illuminate whether the listed covariates had an influence in the results obtained from the ANOVA. A pairwise comparison of means was also used on the significant results obtained by this test. The comparison provides corrected average scores for each factor value along with mean differences between factor values. Significance was set at 0.05.

5   Results

5.1 ANOVA Results

As discussed in the previous section, a mixed model, repeated measures ANOVA was run to assess whether system, explanation, exposure, or some combination of these factors had an impact on assessments of goodness, convincingness, and trust. The test showed statistically significant results for explanation type for goodness (F $= 6.937, \mathrm{p} < 0.001, \eta^2 = 0.071$), convincingness (F $= 5.02$, p $= 0.002, \eta^2 = 0.055$) and trust (F $= 4.749, \mathrm{p} = 0.004, \eta^2 = 0.052$). No other statistically significant main effects or interactions were found.

Table 1. For pairs of explanation types with statistically significant differences, percentages of participants who preferred each type over the other. Not shown are the percentages for "draws" between the pair (for each pair, wins and draws add up to 100%).

	NN	NN+CE	NN+Sim:tab	NN+CE	NN+Sim:txt	NN+CE
Goodness						
CBR	42%	23%	54%	23%	46%	27%
CCBR-IG	45%	24%	58%	24%	55%	27%
CCBR-CF	50%	20%	57%	23%	57%	23%
Convincingness						
CBR	58%	15%	50%	27%	46%	19%
CCBR-IG	61%	18%	58%	24%	55%	21%
CCBR-CF	50%	30%	57%	27%	43%	43%
Trust						
CBR	46%	31%	46%	23%	38%	35%
CCBR-IG	61%	12%	52%	27%	55%	21%
CCBR-CF	43%	27%	60%	27%	47%	27%

Explanation was found to be a significant factor for all three measurements, but the ANOVA results do not tell us how individual explanation types contributed to this result. To find out, we ran a pairwise comparison of means and found a statistically significant difference in the average scores between NN+Sim:tab and NN+CE for goodness ($p = 0.002$, 95% C.I. $= [0.115, 0.681]$), convincingness ($p = 0.004$, 95% C.I. $= [0.088, 0.659]$) and trust ($p = 0.004$, 95% C.I. $= [0.073, 0.559]$). NN+Sim:txt and NN+CE had statistically significant differences for goodness ($p = 0.002$, 95% C.I. $= [0.106, 0.624]$) and trust ($p = 0.018$, 95% C.I. $= [0.030, 0.474]$). NN and NN+CE for convincingness ($p = 0.026$, 95% C.I. $= [0.024, 0.579]$) and trust ($p = 0.032$, 95% C.I. $= [0.015, 0.509]$). Figure 2 shows confidence intervals for each of these significantly different pairs.

To illuminate how pairwise differences corresponded to explanation type preferences, we calculated the percentage of times that each explanation type "won" over the other in our data (Table 1). This was assessed by averaging all of the explanation type scores for one participant, grouping the scores by system type and comparing which had a higher score. Identical scores were counted as a "draw." To obtain the percentages, the number of raw win values was divided by the total number of participants for that system group. Generally, the type in each pair with a significantly greater average score also had a higher percentage of wins than their pairwise counterpart, which is to be expected. However, these wins percentages were not always above 50%, such as NN+Sim:txt when paired with CBR and measured with goodness. This may suggest that certain type, system, and measurement pairs are less effective, but as no interaction was found we draw no conclusion.

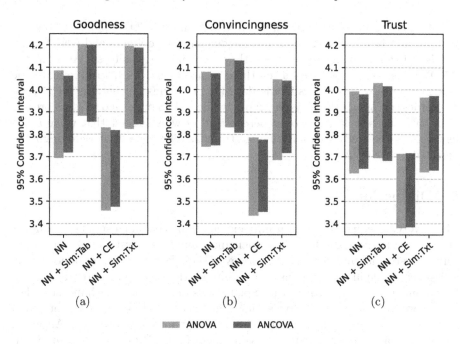

Fig. 2. 95% Confidence Intervals for Explanation Type Average Scores.

5.2   ANCOVA Results

When considering both similarity level and incorrect response as time-varying covariates, a mixed model, repeated measures ANCOVA showed significant results for both covariates and explanation type for convincingness (explanation: (F = 5.981, p < 0.001), similarity level: (F = 9.586, p = 0.002), incorrectness: (F = 19.980, p < 0.001)) and trust (explanation: (F = 5.646, p < 0.001), similarity level: (F = 8.223, p = 0.004), incorrectness: (F = 10.511, p = 0.001)). Only explanation type and incorrectness were significant for goodness (explanation: (F = 9.571, p < 0.001), incorrectness: (F = 18.762, p < 0.001)).

Because incorrectness, and under certain conditions similarity level, were found to be influential in the responses participants had to the explanations. We ran a pairwise comparison of means to assess whether and what differences between explanation types existed when these factors were controlled for. We found significantly greater average scores for NN & NN+CE (goodness: (p = 0.023, 95% C.I. = [0.022, 0.471]), convincingness: (p = 0.01, 95% C.I. = [0.049, 0.547]), trust: (p = 0.012, 95% C.I. = [0.039, 0.487])), NN+Sim:tab & NN+CE (goodness: (p < 0.001, 95% C.I. = [0.159, 0.603]), convincingness: (p = 0.001, 95% C.I. = [0.106, 0.605]), trust: (p = 0.003, 95% C.I. = [0.075, 0.523])), and NN+Sim:txt & NN+CE (goodness: (p < 0.001, 95% C.I. = [0.148, 0.592]), convincingness: (p = 0.031, 95% C.I. = [0.015, 0.514]), trust: (p = 0.016, 95% C.I. = [0.031, 0.48])) for all three dependent variables.

The major difference between the ANOVA and ANCOVA pairwise comparisons is that NN & NN+CE was now significant for goodness and NN+Sim:txt & NN+CE for convincingness when they were not originally so. As with the ANOVA results, the wins data for these comparisons can help illuminate the magnitude of the differences in the data (1). The wins percentages for NN are 50% or less across all three system types, while NN+Sim:txt had wins no greater than 55%. These relatively lower percentages of wins suggest that while a difference was detected, it may not be as strong as differences that were originally detected by ANOVA.

6 Discussion

The ANOVA results showed that only explanation type had a significant impact on observed levels of goodness, convincingness and trust. System type and exposure, as well as an interaction between any of these factors, was not found to play a significant role in user responses. This implies that these have little impact on how a human user experiences the explanations in relation to each measure. For hypotheses S1 and S2, both concerning differences in CCBR systems compared to the other systems tested, both failed to be supported by the data. Although this result was surprising, it may be convenient for CBR practice: system developers need only apply CCBR when the domain requires it (e.g., for diagnosis), without consideration of whether to include it for explanation purposes.

Likewise, the result suggests that only the retrieved case, rather than details of the CCBR retrieval process, is likely to be important for explanation. CCBR retrieval often focuses on distinguishing the target case rapidly from other cases, which might have raised concerns that its question sequence could be unintuitive to a user who unaware of details of the process and case base contents. The primacy of case and similarity suggest that CCBR question order is unlikely to reduce goodness, convincingness, or trust assessments.

Hypothesis I1, regarding CCBR systems scoring better than CBR systems when using NN+Sim:tab, NN+Sim:txt and NN+CE, was also not supported. This again suggests that the case itself and its presentation are the primary concern for explanation, rather than how it was found.

Concerning how to present explanations to a user, no explanation type was consistently worse than all others, but pairwise comparison of means showed clear preferences between certain pairs according to the quality criterion of greatest interest, as described below.

NN+Sim:tab Surpassed NN+CE for all Three Measures: NN+Sim:tab had statistically greater average scores than NN+CE for all measures. This suggests that for this scenario, the most similar supporting case was most compelling, and that presentation of the closest conflicting case did not have the expected effect of increasing explanation quality by helping to delineate the applicability of the current case. Thus in this context, the NN+Sim:tab was a more appropriate explanation type than NN+CE for maximizing observed levels of goodness, convincingness, and trust. However, we note that in a domain that requires more expertise, the observed measurements for NN+CE might have differed. It is possible that in such a domain experts would make more use of the counterexample case to determine the decision boundary and consider that in their assessment, as has been hypothesized in Doyle et al. [5] and Leake et al. [21].

NN+Sim:txt and NN Surpassed NN+CE for Some Measures: NN+Sim:txt and NN types produced consistently statistically greater average scores than NN+CE for goodness and trust and convincingness and trust, respectively. These results are somewhat consistent with hypothesis E1. We believed we would see NN+Sim:tab, NN+Sim:txt and NN+CE score better than NN. NN+Sim:tab and NN+Sim:txt performed better than NN+CE, which performed worse than all other presentations. No statistically significant differences existed between scores for NN+Sim:tab, NN+Sim:txt, and NN.

Similarity Level and Incorrect Responses Influence Participant Assessments: Based on the ANCOVA results, explanation type had an impact across the board and the similarity level of the nearest neighbor used in the explanation affected convincingness and trust. Whether the system was providing an incorrect answer affected the goodness of, convincingness of, and trust in the same explanations. These results support hypotheses I2 and I3, both stating that similarity level and incorrect solutions would have an impact on scores. These results appear suggestive of low similarity between problem and solution cases and incorrect solutions resulting in lower scores on each of the relevant measurements. However, we cannot definitively state this and leave it for further study.

Interestingly, controlling for these factors generalized the relations (i.e., made all three significantly different pairs significant for each measure) between NN & NN+CE and NN+Sim:txt & NN+CE to all three dependent variables, where originally NN & NN+CE were only significantly different when considering convincingness and trust and NN+Sim:txt & NN+CE were only significantly different when considering goodness and trust. This essentially extends the options available for choosing certain explanation types over others in certain contexts.

7   Ramifications: Cases Are King

Explanation type alone is only part of the equation for good, convincing, and trustworthy explanations. The results show that aspects of the explanation case are important as well. Whether the system presents a decision supported by an incorrect solution case, and in certain circumstances, the level of similarity between the problem case and the retrieved case, have an impact on observed levels of goodness, convincingness, and trust.

Furthermore, the results did not suggest a significant difference in subjects' perceptions of the quality of case-based explanations when they knew how cases had been retrieved (comparing case presentation alone with both of the CCBR conditions). This suggests that, at least in this commonsense domain, the result case presented to the user is a key factor. That cases had primary importance is encouraging for the use of CBR-Neural Network hybrid systems that use learned similarity judgments (e.g., [25, 34]): Having an opaque similarity process may not decrease user perceptions that the decision of a CBR system is well explained.

Similarly, the absence of significant difference when similarity was highlighted suggests that in this commonsense domain, subjects are comfortable doing their own similarity judgments and do not need component explanation. For complex domains in which similarity may be hard to assess without support we still expect that explanations of similarity would generally be useful, as supported by Massie, Craw and Wiratunga [24]. This remains a topic for further study. However, that explanations of similarity do not affect perceived explanation quality in this domain is consistent with early intuitions that CBR decisions are well explained simply by presenting the cases on which they are based (e.g., [20]).

8   Conclusions

A human subjects study was run to assess the impact of system type, explanation type, and exposure to explanation types on goodness and convincingness of and trust, when presenting explanations based on cases to the user. It was found that only explanation type played a significant role in the observed scores of each measurement, which suggests that users are less influenced by system interactions during case retrieval and that exposure to a given explanation type over the course of the study not change perceptions. Furthermore, all other explanation types were found to be preferred over explaining with an example and counterexample (NN+CE). When controlling for correct vs. incorrect solutions presented to users and the similarity between the problem and solution cases, explanation type was still significant, but similarity and incorrectness played a role in the scores obtained. This underlines the importance of case base competence and having sufficiently similar cases. It also suggests that the benefit of cases as explanations is fairly robust to potential presentation variants for the tested scenarios.

As in results by Doyle et al. [6], our study did not find benefit for presenting counterexamples. An interesting future research path would be to compare user preferences for the four explanation types for more complex domains, exploring Doyle et al.'s hypothesis that explanations involving counterexamples may be preferred in that context. Given the high proportion of participants with STEM backgrounds, it would also be interesting to examine whether these results hold among highly skeptical, low trust individuals and among those with other backgrounds. The effects of the explanation types on user models, as explored in some other work [15], would be another interesting subject for future study.

Acknowledgments. This work was funded by the US Department of Defense (Contract W52P1J2093009), and by the Department of the Navy, Office of Naval Research (Award N00014-19-1-2655).

References

1. Aha, D., Munoz, H.: Interactive Case-Based Reasoning, vol. 14. Kluwer (2001). Special Issue of Applied Intelligence

2. Ashley, K.: Modeling Legal Argument: Reasoning with Cases and Hypotheticals. MIT Press, Cambridge (1990)
3. Cunningham, P., Doyle, D., Loughrey, J.: An evaluation of the usefulness of case-based explanation. In: Ashley, K.D., Bridge, D.G. (eds.) ICCBR 2003. LNCS (LNAI), vol. 2689, pp. 122–130. Springer, Heidelberg (2003). https://doi.org/10.1007/3-540-45006-8_12
4. Doyle, D.: A knowledge-light mechanism for explanation in case-based reasoning. Ph.D. thesis, University of Dublin, Trinity College. Department of Computer Science (2005). http://www.tara.tcd.ie/handle/2262/847
5. Doyle, D., Cunningham, P., Bridge, D., Rahman, Y.: Explanation oriented retrieval. In: Funk, P., González Calero, P.A. (eds.) ECCBR 2004. LNCS (LNAI), vol. 3155, pp. 157–168. Springer, Heidelberg (2004). https://doi.org/10.1007/978-3-540-28631-8_13
6. Doyle, D., Cunningham, P., Walsh, P.: An evaluation of the usefulness of explanation in a case-based reasoning system for decision support in bronchiolitis treatment. Comput. Intell. **22**(3–4), 269–281 (2006)
7. Eargle, D., Gureckis, T., Rich, A.S., McDonnell, J., Martin, J.B.: psiTurk: an open platform for science on Amazon Mechanical Turk (2020). https://doi.org/10.5281/zenodo.3598652
8. Gates, L., Leake, D.: Evaluating CBR explanation capabilities: survey and next steps. In: ICCBR Workshops, pp. 40–51 (2021)
9. Gunning, D., Aha, D.W.: DARPA's explainable artificial intelligence program. AI Mag. **40**(2), 44–58 (2019)
10. Gureckis, T.M., et al.: psiTurk: an open-source framework for conducting replicable behavioral experiments online. Behav. Res. Methods **48**, 829–842 (2016)
11. Hoffman, R.R., Mueller, S.T., Klein, G., Litman, J.: Metrics for explainable AI: challenges and prospects. arXiv preprint arXiv:1812.04608 (2018)
12. Jacovi, A., Marasović, A., Miller, T., Goldberg, Y.: Formalizing trust in artificial intelligence: prerequisites, causes and goals of human trust in AI. In: Proceedings of the 2021 ACM Conference on Fairness, Accountability, and Transparency, FAccT 2021, pp. 624–635. Association for Computing Machinery, New York (2021)
13. Jin, W., Fan, J., Gromala, D., Pasquier, P., Hamarneh, G.: EUCA: the end-user-centered explainable AI framework. arXiv preprint arXiv:2102.02437 (2021)
14. Keane, M.T., Kenny, E.M.: How case-based reasoning explains neural networks: a theoretical analysis of XAI using *Post-Hoc* explanation-by-example from a survey of ANN-CBR twin-systems. In: Bach, K., Marling, C. (eds.) ICCBR 2019. LNCS (LNAI), vol. 11680, pp. 155–171. Springer, Cham (2019). https://doi.org/10.1007/978-3-030-29249-2_11
15. Kenny, E.M., Ford, C., Quinn, M., Keane, M.T.: Explaining black-box classifiers using post-hoc explanations-by-example: the effect of explanations and error-rates in XAI user studies. Artif. Intell. **294**, 103459 (2021)
16. Knapič, S., Malhi, A., Saluja, R., Främling, K.: Explainable artificial intelligence for human decision support system in the medical domain. Mach. Learn. Knowl. Extraction **3**(3), 740–770 (2021)
17. Kolodner, J., Leake, D.: A tutorial introduction to case-based reasoning. In: Leake, D. (ed.) Case-Based Reasoning: Experiences, Lessons, and Future Directions, pp. 31–65. AAAI Press, Menlo Park (1996)
18. Lamy, J.B., Sekar, B., Guezennec, G., Bouaud, J., Séroussi, B.: Explainable artificial intelligence for breast cancer: a visual case-based reasoning approach. Artif. Intell. Med. **94**, 42–53 (2019)

19. Leake, D.: Goal-based explanation evaluation. Cogn. Sci. **15**(4), 509–545 (1991)
20. Leake, D.: CBR in context: the present and future. In: Leake, D. (ed.) Case-Based Reasoning: Experiences, Lessons, and Future Directions, pp. 3–30. AAAI Press, Menlo Park (1996)
21. Leake, D.B., Birnbaum, L., Hammond, K., Marlow, C., Yang, H.: Integrating information resources: a case study of engineering design support. In: Althoff, K.-D., Bergmann, R., Branting, L.K. (eds.) ICCBR 1999. LNCS, vol. 1650, pp. 482–496. Springer, Heidelberg (1999). https://doi.org/10.1007/3-540-48508-2_35
22. Leake, D., Birnbaum, L., Hammond, K., Marlow, C., Yang, H.: An integrated interface for proactive, experience-based design support. In: Proceedings of the 2001 International Conference on Intelligent User Interfaces, pp. 101–108 (2001)
23. Lee, M.K.: Understanding perception of algorithmic decisions: fairness, trust, and emotion in response to algorithmic management. Big Data Soc. **5**(1), 2053951718756684 (2018)
24. Massie, S., Craw, S., Wiratunga, N.: A visualisation tool to explain case-base reasoning solutions for tablet formulation. In: Macintosh, A., Ellis, R., Allen, T. (eds.) SGAI 2004, pp. 222–234. Springer, London (2005). https://doi.org/10.1007/1-84628-103-2_16
25. Mathisen, B.M., Aamodt, A., Bach, K., Langseth, H.: Learning similarity measures from data. Prog. Artif. Intell. **9**(2), 129–143 (2019). https://doi.org/10.1007/s13748-019-00201-2
26. McSherry, D.: Explaining the pros and cons of conclusions in CBR. In: Funk, P., González Calero, P.A. (eds.) ECCBR 2004. LNCS (LNAI), vol. 3155, pp. 317–330. Springer, Heidelberg (2004). https://doi.org/10.1007/978-3-540-28631-8_24
27. Minor, M. (ed.): Proceedings of XCBR: Case-Based Reasoning for the Explanation of Intelligent Systems, Workshop at the 26th International Conference on Case-Based Reasoning. Stockholm, Sweden (2018). https://iccbr18.com/wp-content/uploads/ICCBR-2018-V3.pdf
28. Mueller, S.T., et al.: Principles of explanation in human-AI systems. arXiv preprint arXiv:2102.04972 (2021)
29. Nugent, C., Cunningham, P.: A case-based recommender for black-box systems. Artif. Intell. Rev. **24**(2), 163–178 (2005)
30. Sarwar, S., et al.: Physician perspectives on integration of artificial intelligence into diagnostic pathology. Digit. Med. **2**(1), 28 (2019)
31. Selbst, A., Powles, J.: Meaningful information and the right to explanation. In: Proceedings of the 1st Conference on Fairness, Accountability and Transparency. Proceedings of Machine Learning Research, vol. 81, p. 48. PMLR (2018). https://proceedings.mlr.press/v81/selbst18a.html
32. Sormo, F., Cassens, J., Aamodt, A.: Explanation in case-based reasoning–perspectives and goals. Artif. Intell. Rev. **24**(2), 109–143 (2005)
33. Warren, G., Byrne, R.M.J., Keane, M.T.: Categorical and continuous features in counterfactual explanations of AI systems. In: Proceedings of the 28th International Conference on Intelligent User Interfaces (IUI-23), pp. 171–187. ACM, New York (2023)
34. Ye, X., Leake, D., Crandall, D.: Case adaptation with neural networks: capabilities and limitations. In: Keane, M.T., Wiratunga, N. (eds.) ICCBR 2022. LNCS, vol. 13405, pp. 143–158. Springer, Cham (2022). https://doi.org/10.1007/978-3-031-14923-8_10

CBR Driven Interactive Explainable AI

Anjana Wijekoon[1]([✉]), Nirmalie Wiratunga[1], Kyle Martin[1], David Corsar[1],
Ikechukwu Nkisi-Orji[1], Chamath Palihawadana[1], Derek Bridge[2],
Preeja Pradeep[2], Belen Diaz Agudo[3], and Marta Caro-Martínez[3]

[1] Robert Gordon University, Aberdeen, UK
{a.wijekoon1,n.wiratunga,k.martin3,
d.corsar1,i.nkisi-orji,c.palihawadana}@rgu.ac.uk
[2] University College Cork, Cork, Ireland
{derek.bridge,preeja.pradeep}@insight.org
[3] Universidad Complutense de Madrid, Madrid, Spain
{belend,martcaro}@ucm.es

Abstract. Explainable AI (XAI) can greatly enhance user trust and satisfaction in AI-assisted decision-making processes. Numerous explanation techniques (explainers) exist in the literature, and recent findings suggest that addressing multiple user needs requires employing a combination of these explainers. We refer to such combinations as explanation strategies. This paper introduces iSee - Intelligent Sharing of Explanation Experience, an interactive platform that facilitates the reuse of explanation strategies and promotes best practices in XAI by employing the Case-based Reasoning (CBR) paradigm. iSee uses an ontology-guided approach to effectively capture explanation requirements, while a behaviour tree-driven conversational chatbot captures user experiences of interacting with the explanations and provides feedback. In a case study, we illustrate the iSee CBR system capabilities by formalising a real-world radiograph fracture detection system and demonstrating how each interactive tools facilitate the CBR processes.

Keywords: Interactive XAI · Ontology-based CBR · Conversational AI

1 Introduction

Explainable AI (XAI) is needed to guide users in understanding AI systems and their decisions. XAI systems must be able to address a range of user explanation needs (such as transparency, scrutability, and fairness) and must do so in a manner that is relevant to a range of stakeholders. Moreover, a successful adaptation of XAI should generate personalised explanations that better align with

This research is funded by the iSee project. iSee is an EU CHIST-ERA project which received funding for the UK from EPSRC under grant number EP/V061755/1, for Ireland from the Irish Research Council under grant number CHIST-ERA-2019-iSee and for Spain from the MCIN/AEI and European Union "NextGenerationEU/PRTR" under grant number PCI2020-120720-2.

S. Massie and S. Chakraborti (Eds.): ICCBR 2023, LNAI 14141, pp. 169–184, 2023.
https://doi.org/10.1007/978-3-031-40177-0_11

end-user mental models and cater to their specific needs. An interactive XAI system naturally creates a convenient feedback loop between the user and the XAI system, which is valuable for gathering user feedback to inform the system about their satisfaction regarding their needs. This feedback can refine the AI system and its explanation capabilities, improving its performance, reliability, and trustworthiness.

It is evident that developing meaningful XAI systems with positive user experiences is a multi-faceted endeavour. Consequently, it is essential for an AI system that is looking to adapt XAI practices to learn from past experiences of successful XAI adaptations. Case-based Reasoning (CBR) caters to the need to learn from past experiences. Accordingly, this paper presents the tools and processes that create a CBR recommender for reusing explanation experiences.

iSee is a consortium of researchers who proposed the use of the CBR paradigm to capture the knowledge and experience of successful adaptation of explainability within AI systems. iSee reuses these experiences with AI systems that are looking for the expertise to build explainability in their AI systems in line with regulations such as a right to obtain an explanation in the EU [5]. This paper presents the interactive tools in the iSee[1] platform that facilitate the explanation experience creation and reuse. The primary contributions lie in introducing three essential tools to enable CBR processes:

- requirements capture tool, to formalise explanation requirements modelled using the iSee Ontology;
- explanation strategy recommendation tool, to find similar past explanation experiences using case representation and retrieval; and
- feedback generation for revision and retention, by creating conversational explanation experiences modelled using a behaviour tree-driven dialogue model.

We demonstrate the effectiveness of the above-mentioned tools in the iSee system by presenting a case study that involves a radiograph fracture detection system. The outline of this paper is as follows. Section 2 provides the background and related work and Sect. 3 presents the overall CBR paradigm for interactive XAI. We describe the interactive components of the iSee platform in Sects. 4, 5 and 6 respectively. Section 7 demonstrates the case study. Finally, Sect. 8 offers some conclusions and future directions.

2   Related Work

The CBR paradigm has played a key role in the development of methods and tools for reusing experiential knowledge. The flexibility of CBR lends well to capturing expert knowledge, modelling generalisable solutions and subsequent adaptation for bespoke scenarios. A key advantage of this is the ability to model solutions as plans; a sequence of steps to achieve a specific goal given a list of

---

[1] https://isee4xai.com/.

resources and constraints. Plans offer a rich representation whereby knowledge of conditions of success and failure can be stored [10]. For example, CHEF [9] maintains knowledge of case outcomes to prevent the repetition of erroneous recipe adaptations. Business processes [27], production systems [19] and treatment strategies [17] are further examples of experience-driven domains that are satisfied by planning solutions. Similarly, we leverage CBR principles in reusing XAI experiences. We formalise and capture explanation experiences knowledge within the CBR cycle in the form of explanation requirements and strategies that satisfy them. It allows AI systems to reuse past experiences in validating the AI decisions, identifying potential issues, and improving trust [12].

2.1 Interaction Modelling of XAI

Conceptual models have attempted to capture multiple facets of XAI with the common theme that stakeholders have variable needs that are addressed by explainability techniques [2,14,16]. Two key components of such models focused on in this paper are the explanation techniques (i.e. strategies) and interactive interfaces to address stakeholder needs [24,25]. The authors of [25] and [2] designed generalised strategies consisting of multiple explainers that addressed the needs of several application domains. In contrast, the authors of [24] derived XAI strategies specific to the healthcare domain from expert users. The process included studies to learn explanation needs, the results of which were used by the researchers to curate XAI strategies. There are both data-driven and expert knowledge-driven methods that exist to curate XAI strategies, but the challenge remains with their reusability across domains.

The usability of these strategies is linked to interfaces that interact with the users to extract knowledge, understand explanation needs, present explanations using different modalities, and generate feedback. Conversation is a medium for implementing interactive XAI, offering an alternative to graphical or text-based user interfaces [6,18,25]. Conventionally, conversational interactions are formalised as dialogue models using Argumentation Frameworks such as AAF [3] or ADF [20]. Alternatively, dialogue models are graphically represented using State Transition Models (STM) [11,18] or Finite State Machines (FSM) [15].

The lack of shared conceptual modelling across XAI strategies and interactions discourages interoperability and reusability. This paper proposes the use of a unified conceptual modelling technique to model both XAI strategies and interactions using Behaviour Trees (BT). BTs are a less frequent choice for XAI dialogue modelling, although they have often been used to model robot interactions [4,13,26]. The design of an interactive model using BTs is either knowledge-driven by domain-experts [4,13] or data-driven [26]. In this paper, we take a knowledge-driven approach using interaction requirements extracted from domain knowledge and previous work [11,18].

3 CBR Driven Explanation Experiences

In iSee, the Case-Based Reasoning (CBR) cycle [1], retrieves, reuses, revises, and retains explanation experiences as cases (Fig. 1-left). We describe an explanation

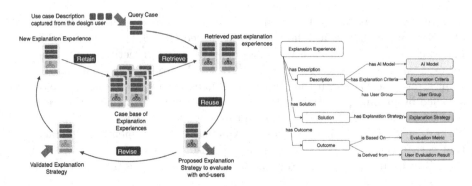

Fig. 1. iSee CBR System (left) and the high-level case structure (right).

experience as a snapshot that captures the adaptation of XAI within an AI system. Accordingly, it is multi-dimensional, describing: the attributes of the AI system; user groups and their explanation needs; the explanation strategy; and user experience feedback. We formalise explanation experience cases using the iSee Ontology (iSeeOnto) as shown in Fig. 1-right.

This paper focuses on three processes within the CBR cycle: 1) knowledge capture to form the case description; 2) case retrieval to recommend candidate explanation solutions from past experiences; and 3) conversational feedback gathering for collaborative case revision and retention. During the knowledge capture stage, we use iSeeOnto to understand and formalise the requirements for building an explanation experience. As a first point of interaction, we capture these requirements through a user interface from a design user of the AI system who has a working knowledge of the system's development and stakeholders. These requirements form the query to our case base of past experiences, facilitating retrieval of the most suitable explanation strategies. A selected strategy is then provided to end-users for feedback in the collaborative revision stage. The following sections describe the tools and their underlying interaction models developed within the iSee platform to facilitate each process.

4   Explanation Experience Requirements Capture

To create meaningful user experiences, we structure interactions to manage the acquisition of explanation requirements. iSeeOnto bears the burden of information provisioning by dictating permissible features and values for each attribute such that the knowledge extracted from the design user conforms to a formal structure. These attributes describe the explanation needs of stakeholders associated with the AI system and provide information used to recommend an executable explanation strategy that best satisfies those needs.

An interactive interface is designed to capture knowledge from the design user and its driven by four ontologies: *AI Model, Explanation Criteria, User Group,* and *Evaluation Metric*. High-level classes and relationships in these ontologies are depicted in Fig. 2. Each class is further expressed by a taxonomy of classes or individuals. For instance, *AI Task* from the *AI Model* ontology is extended as a taxonomy with 50 hierarchical concepts, and *Intent* from the *User Group* ontology has 14 individuals identified from the literature. More detailed versions of each ontology can be found here[2].

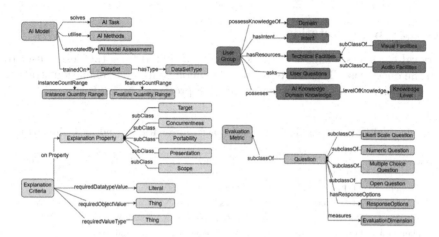

Fig. 2. Ontologies associated with the explanation requirements capture (best viewed digitally in colour). (Color figure online)

From a design user perspective, these ontologies formalise information to be displayed and acquired through the structured user interface called the iSee Dashboard. We propose that information requested by the dashboard should be provisioned by an individual familiar with an AI system and its stakeholders. We call this individual a design user and envision that they act on behalf of end-user stakeholders who will make routine use of, or have an interest in, the operations of the AI system. Inputs within the dashboard are divided into relevant sections to ease the design user's cognitive burden and guide their provision of knowledge as explanation requirements. User input is also validated against the ontologies to ensure that only permissible values are captured, with support for users in the form of tooltips. As a result, once we capture these requirements from a design user, we build the description of a new explanation experience case. The design and implementation process of the dashboard is influenced by co-creation feedback from industry use case partners in the iSee project.

---

[2] https://w3id.org/iSeeOnto/explanationexperience.

5   Explanation Strategy Recommendation

The next stage of the CBR process is case retrieval. Specifically, in iSee, this uses explanation requirements to find similar past cases that can recommend a candidate explanation strategy. Accordingly, this section describes the case representation, initial case base, and the interactive retrieval process.

5.1   Case Representation

Retrieval considers a subset of the knowledge acquired from the design user to form the query case. The attributes selected, along with an explanation strategy as the solution, forms the case representation presented in Table 1.

Table 1. Explanation Experience retrieval case representation and local similarities.

Ontology	Case Attribute	Ontology Component	Similarity Metric	Solution
AI Model	AI Task	Class	Wu&Palmer [22]	–
	AI Method	Class	Wu&Palmer [22]	–
	Dataset Type	Individual	Exact Match	–
Explanation Criteria	Portability	Individual	Exact Match	–
	Scope	Individual	Exact Match	–
	Target	Individual	Exact Match	–
	Presentation	Class	Exact Match	–
	Concurrentness	Individual	Exact Match	–
User Group	Intent	Individual	Exact Match	–
	TechnicalFacilities	Individual Set	Query Intersection	–
	AIKnowledgeLevel	Individual	Exact Match	–
	DomainKnowledgeLevel	Individual	Exact Match	–
	User Questions	Individual Set	Query Intersection	–
Behaviour Tree	Explanation Strategy	N/A	N/A	✓

Case Description consists of 13 attributes. We select AI Task, AI Method, and Dataset Type classes from the AI Model ontology as attributes. AI Task and AI Method classes are expressed using their own taxonomies in iSee. The Dataset Type class consists of 5 individuals. Five Explanation Properties (Portability, Scope, Target, Presentation, and Concurrentness) were selected as case attributes. These case attribute values are inferred based on a set of rules (instead of asking the design-user) to ensure that the retrieved explanation strategy is compatible (for both implementation and execution) with the query case. AI and Domain Knowledge Levels and Intent attributes are selected from the User Group ontology, where the attribute values are individuals of the respective classes. Finally, we consider Technical Facilities and User Questions classes where the case attribute value is a set of class individuals. For example, Technical Facilities are expressed using two sub-classes Audio Facilities and Visual Facilities and individuals such as *Speaker, Microphone, Touch Screen, Mouse,* and so on. Accordingly, a case can have multiple technical facilities; similarly, multiple user questions can express an explanation needs.

Case Solution is an explanation strategy composed of one or more explainers that address an explanation need. In iSee, an explanation strategy is modelled using Behaviour Trees (BT) and formalised using the Behaviour Tree ontology (high-level classes and relationships depicted in Fig. 3).

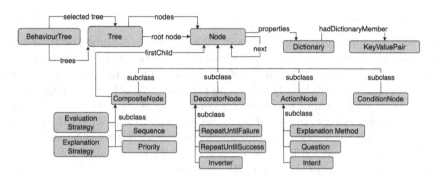

Fig. 3. Behaviour Tree ontology in iSee.

A BT is a conceptual model that formalises the behaviours of an actor in a given environment [7]. In addition to standard nodes and navigations (detailed in Sect. 6), we define and implement several specialised nodes to model explanation strategy behaviours. These include Composite Nodes *Variant, Supplement, Replacement* and *Complement* that model the relationships between multiple explainers or multiple presentations of an explanation. These are defined and formalised in the iSeeOnto. An example explanation strategy that satisfies two intents using three explainers is depicted in Fig. 4. This explanation strategy can be interpreted as follows:

- If the user indicates *Transparency* as their intent,
  1. execute the Integrated Gradients explainer and show the explanation;
  2. afterwards, if the user indicates that they would like to *verify* (i.e. Variant Node) the explanation using a different explainer, execute the Nearest Neighbour explainer and show the explanation.
- If the user indicates *Performance* is their intent, execute the AI Model performance explainer and show the explanation.

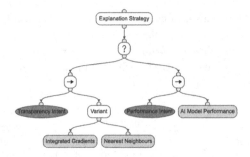

Fig. 4. Example explanation strategy modelled using Behaviour Trees.

5.2 Case Base

The iSee case-base currently consists of 12 *seed-cases*, captured from the literature; each describes the experience of adapting XAI within AI systems with user evaluation. This is a filtered list of cases from a literature review of 50 peer-reviewed papers to include only those who proposed reusable explanation strategies. All seed case explanation strategies consist of a single explainer addressing an explanation need (i.e. intent) of one or more stakeholders. We continue to add seed cases from the literature. In addition, we expect with time, the case base will grow by retaining new explanation experiences with more complex explanation strategies created within the iSee CBR platform.

5.3 Case Retrieval

Given a case with query attributes populated by iSee ontology classes or individuals, the retrieval task is to find explanation strategies from its nearest neighbours. We assign a local similarity metric for each attribute, as shown in Table 1. The details of those local similarity metrics are as follows.

Wu & Palmer (WP) is a taxonomy path-based similarity metric originally implemented for calculating word similarities. For AI Task and AI Method case attributes, we use the CloodCBR implementation [22] where, given a taxonomy, it calculates the similarity between two classes by considering the depths of each class from their least common subsummer.

Query Intersection (QI) is applicable for attributes where the data type is a set of ontology individuals like in Technical Facilities and User questions. Given a set of individuals from the query, s^q, and a case, s^c, it calculates the similarity as the intersection between two sets normalised by the length of the query set as $\frac{|s^q \cap s^c|}{|s^q|}$ where $|.|$ indicates the size.

Exact Match (EM) similarity indicates a string match. This is applied both for case attributes that are ontology individuals and classes.

We formalise a case c as a list of N query attributes (a_i) and a solution (s) as in Eq. 1. A query case q is a case where the solution s is empty $(s = \emptyset)$.

$$c = [a_1, ..., a_N, s] \tag{1}$$

$$global\_sim(q, c) = \frac{1}{N} \sum_{i=1}^{N} local\_sim(a_i^q, a_i^c)$$

$$local\_sim = \begin{cases} WP & \text{if } a_i \in [\text{AI Task, AI Method}] \\ QI & \text{if } a_i \in [\text{Technical Facilities, User Questions}] \\ EM & \text{otherwise} \end{cases} \tag{2}$$

The similarity between the query case q, and a case c from the case base is calculated as the aggregation of local similarities as in Eq. 2. Note for iSee retrieval case structure, $N = 13$ as in Table 1. iSee case retrieval is implemented using the CloodCBR framework [22]. It is integrated with the iSee Dashboard, where the design user interacts with it by retrieving top k (configurable) cases, exploring the design of recommended explanation strategies, and making manual revisions to a selected explanation strategy. Aggregation of local similarities is currently unweighted, but CloodCBR allows for a weighted aggregation should that prove more useful, when the platform matures.

6 Conversational Feedback for Revision and Retention

As discussed in Sect. 5.3, we use Behaviour Trees (BT) to represent explanation strategies, these being the solution parts of our cases. But, additionally, we use BTs to model explanation experience interactions. We use them for this purpose because of their many desirable properties [7,8] and also to give compatibility with the way we model explanation strategies. The tree structure is made of different types of nodes that implement behaviours and navigation. Each node has a state that indicates if the execution of the node was a success or failure. Composite nodes control navigation and the leaf nodes implement specific behaviour (Action Nodes). There are also decorator nodes and condition nodes to control access and repetition of a sub-tree. The types of nodes in the iSee dialogue model and their functionalities are briefly discussed as follows.

Sequence Node can have one or more child nodes and child nodes are executed from left to right until one fails.

Priority Node can have one or more child nodes and child nodes are executed from left to right until one succeeds.

Condition Node performs a Boolean check, often used as the first child node of a composite node with multiple child action nodes. The Boolean check helps to control the access to all its siblings to the right. For example, Figs. 5 and 6 show two scenarios where setting the $value = True$ lets us control the access to the sibling nodes. In iSee conversations, this will help to avoid repetition and improve execution efficiency.

Explanation Strategy Node is a custom composite node introduced for iSee that can dynamically plug and play explanation strategies as the conversation progresses. It can be seen as a placeholder to be *replaced* when the specific explanation strategy is made available through the retrieval process (see Sect. 5.3).

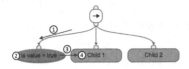 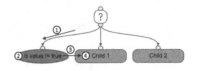

Fig. 5. Condition node in a sequence sub-tree.

Fig. 6. Condition node in a priority sub-tree.

Evaluation Strategy Node is a custom composite node introduced for iSee that is a placeholder to *append* evaluation metrics (i.e. lists of questions) as the conversation progresses to multiple intents.

Action Node implements a specific behaviour. For example, in the iSee dialogue model, it will be behaviours of a chatbot in the format of *the chatbot prompting the user with an utterance, waiting for a response* and *analysing the response*. Based on the response, the business logic will determine its status as failure or success which helps the parent composite node to decide which node to navigate and execute next. iSee interactions are implemented in three custom Action Nodes: Question-Answer Node, AI-Model Node and Explainer Node. A Question-Answer Node will pose a question to the user and wait for a response which decides the node status. It is utilised to implement Start, Persona and Evaluation sub-trees. The AI-Model Node encapsulates the business logic related to the AI Model execution and is used in the Explanation Target sub-tree. Finally, the Explainer Node executes an explainer algorithm to generate explanations for the user and is utilised in the Explanation Strategy sub-tree.

6.1   iSee Dialogue Model

An abstract BT of the iSee dialogue model is presented in Fig. 7. Each child is an abstraction of a sub-tree that handles a specific conversational behaviour.

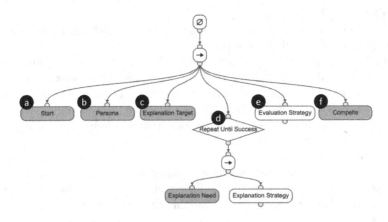

Fig. 7. Explanation Experience Dialogue Model.

The most high-level navigation control is a sequence node, which means each child node should be executed successfully to complete an explanation experience. How each child (i.e. sub-tree) defines success is left to the business logic of the sub-tree. A simple execution of the conversation would be from left to right with the following steps: **a)** start the interaction by greeting the user and receiving consent to proceed; **b)** establish the persona, based on knowledge levels; **c)** establish the explanation target, i.e. the data instance and its AI system outcome; **d)** establish the user's explanation need by asking questions, and present explanations to answer those questions by executing the suitable explainers of the explanation strategy; this is repeated until the user has no other questions or the XAI system is unable to answer any more questions; **e)** evaluate the experience using the evaluation questionnaire; and **f)** complete the explanation experience conversation. A fine-grained BT of the iSee dialogue model is included here[3] where each action node is expanded to its sub-tree.

At the end of a conversation, feedback for the Evaluation Metric of the case (questionnaire) is gathered and formalised as an individual of the User Evaluation Result (see Fig. 8) to complete the case. Once there are multiple end-user experiences completed, we envision that those *User Evaluation Result* individuals will be analysed by the design user. If the feedback indicates failing to address explanation needs or disagreement with the explanations provided, the design user can iteratively revise the explanation strategy using the retrieval interaction. Otherwise, if the feedback indicates user satisfaction, the case is retained in the case base as a successful explanation experience for future reuse.

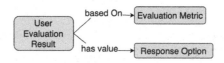

Fig. 8. User Evaluation Result ontology in iSee.

7   Case Study: Radiology Fracture Detection (RFD)

AI-assisted fracture detection through radiograph analysis accelerates diagnosis and treatment, which is particularly crucial in emergencies or high-volume cases [21]. However, achieving performance beyond established benchmarks requires Machine Learning algorithms, such as Convolutional Neural Networks (CNNs), which are black boxes whose outcomes are difficult to explain. Explanations help healthcare professionals understand the rationale behind the detection, offering insights to support their decision-making. In a recent survey of 411 UK radiographers, the most popular trust-building features of AI systems were *indication of overall performance* and *visual explanation* [23]. Based on

---

[3] https://isee4xai.com/bt-2/.

such evidence and co-creation with industry partners we demonstrate how iSee utilises the interactive tools to create explanation experiences for the RFD system stakeholders. We capture the explanation requirements of stakeholders using the iSee Dashboard and utilise it to find suitable explanation strategies from past cases using retrieval tools. Finally, iSee dialogue model is instantiated to create interactive explanation experiences and collect feedback from stakeholders and complete the RFD case.

7.1   Explanation Experience Requirements Capture

Figure 9 presents part of the explanation experience requirements capture process with a design user of the RFD system. In AI model settings (left screenshot) the design user is using the iSee ontology concepts to describe their CNN model that performs Binary Classification which has been trained using an Image dataset. Also, they describe the performance of the AI model using two metrics F1-score and accuracy. RFD system has two main stakeholders who are interested in explanations, Clinicians and Managers. Clinicians can have explanation needs that are related to *transparency* or *performance* of the AI system. Managers mainly inquire about the *performance* of the AI system. The right screenshot demonstrates how the requirements of the *Clinician* user group are being captured in the iSee Dashboard.

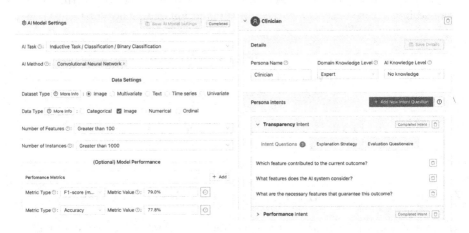

Fig. 9. Explanation experience requirements captured in the iSee Dashboard with a design user of the RFD system (best viewed digitally).

7.2   Explanation Strategy Recommendation

Figure 10 demonstrates the case retrieval tool. The design user has retrieved top k (k = 3 in the example) cases where each card component refers to a recommended explanation strategy. A strategy card provides additional information on how well the case description matches the query (global similarity) and what explainers are in the strategy. The design user can use this information to *select* an explanation strategy (the second strategy from Fig. 4 is selected) and there are tools linked to *view* and *edit* the selected strategy.

Fig. 10. Case retrieval: case solutions from the top-3 neighbours for the *Transparency* intent of the *Clinician* user group (best viewed digitally).

7.3 Conversational Feedback for Revision and Retention

Figure 11 presents an instantiation of the iSee dialogue model by a clinician of the RFD system. First, the clinician is greeted and they select the user group they identify with. Next, they are presented with a test instance and its AI system prediction (Explanation Target sub-tree) which can lead to different explanation needs. The clinician selects a question that indicates transparency intent, accordingly, the explanation strategy selected by the design user for the transparency intent is executed. First, they are presented with an Integrated Gradients explanation, and upon requesting verification with a different explainer they receive a Nearest Neighbour explanation. At this point, the explanation strategy recommended for the transparency intent is completely executed. Now the clinician indicates they want to know about the AI performance (i.e. performance intent). Accordingly, the chatbot executes the explanation strategy recommended to answer performance-related questions. When the XAI system cannot answer any more questions (or if the clinician indicates they have no other questions), the BT exits the *Repeat Until Success* loop to the evaluation strategy sub-tree. It presents the clinician with evaluation metrics linked to both transparency and performance intents and collects their feedback. At this stage, the conversation is concluded and creates an explanation experience instance.

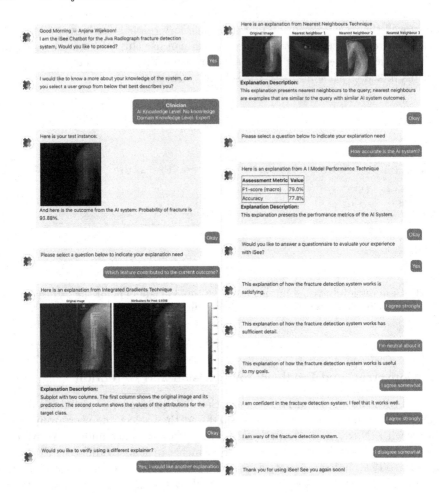

Fig. 11. Explanation Experience of a clinician (best viewed digitally).

8   Conclusions

This paper presented the interactive tools that drive the iSee CBR cycle to reuse explanation experiences. The iSee ontology-driven Dashboard captures explanation requirements from the *design users* of an AI system, which is then used by the interactive case retrieval tool to find explanation strategies from past similar experiences. The iSee dialogue model facilitates *end users* of the AI system to create explanation experiences and provide feedback which then can be used in revision and retention. These interactive tools were co-created with industry partners and we demonstrated the tools on one such use case for detecting fractures in radiographs. In the next steps, user studies are planned to evaluate generalisability and user acceptance. This will also expand the range of explanation experiences to build a stronger case base.

References

1. Aamodt, A., Plaza, E.: Case-based reasoning: foundational issues, methodological variations, and system approaches. AI Commun. **7**(1), 39–59 (1994)
2. Arya, V., et al.: One explanation does not fit all: a toolkit and taxonomy of AI explainability techniques. arXiv preprint arXiv:1909.03012 (2019)
3. Baumann, R., Ulbricht, M.: Choices and their consequences-explaining acceptable sets in abstract argumentation frameworks. In: KR, pp. 110–119 (2021)
4. Bouchard, B., Gaboury, S., Bouchard, K., Francillette, Y.: Modeling human activities using behaviour trees in smart homes. In: Proceedings of the 11th PErvasive Technologies Related to Assistive Environments Conference, pp. 67–74 (2018)
5. Cath, C., Wachter, S., Mittelstadt, B., Taddeo, M., Floridi, L.: Artificial intelligence and the 'good society': the US, EU, and UK approach. Sci. Eng. Ethics **24**, 505–528 (2018)
6. Chromik, M., Butz, A.: Human-XAI interaction: a review and design principles for explanation user interfaces. In: Ardito, C., et al. (eds.) INTERACT 2021. LNCS, vol. 12933, pp. 619–640. Springer, Cham (2021). https://doi.org/10.1007/978-3-030-85616-8_36
7. Colledanchise, M., Ögren, P.: Behavior Trees in Robotics and AI: An Introduction. CRC Press (2018)
8. Flórez-Puga, G., Gomez-Martin, M., Diaz-Agudo, B., Gonzalez-Calero, P.: Dynamic expansion of behaviour trees. In: Proceedings of the AAAI Conference on Artificial Intelligence and Interactive Digital Entertainment, vol. 4, pp. 36–41 (2008)
9. Hammond, K.J.: Chef: a model of case-based planning. In: AAAI, vol. 86, pp. 267–271 (1986)
10. Hammond, K.J.: Case-based planning: a framework for planning from experience. Cogn. Sci. **14**(3), 385–443 (1990)
11. Hernandez-Bocanegra, D.C., Ziegler, J.: Conversational review-based explanations for recommender systems: Exploring users' query behavior. In: 3rd Conference on Conversational User Interfaces, CUI 2021, pp. 1–11 (2021)
12. Hoffman, R.R., Mueller, S.T., Klein, G., Litman, J.: Metrics for explainable AI: challenges and prospects. arXiv preprint arXiv:1812.04608 (2018)
13. Iovino, M., Scukins, E., Styrud, J., Ögren, P., Smith, C.: A survey of behavior trees in robotics and AI. Robot. Auton. Syst. **154**, 104096 (2022)
14. Langer, M., et al.: What do we want from explainable artificial intelligence (XAI)?– a stakeholder perspective on XAI and a conceptual model guiding interdisciplinary XAI research. Artif. Intell. **296**, 103473 (2021)
15. Le, N.T., Wartschinski, L.: A cognitive assistant for improving human reasoning skills. Int. J. Hum. Comput. Stud. **117**, 45–54 (2018)
16. Liao, Q.V., Zhang, Y., Luss, R., Doshi-Velez, F., Dhurandhar, A.: Connecting algorithmic research and usage contexts: a perspective of contextualized evaluation for explainable AI. In: Proceedings of the AAAI Conference on Human Computation and Crowdsourcing, vol. 10, pp. 147–159 (2022)
17. Lopez, B., Plaza, E.: Case-based learning of strategic knowledge. In: Kodratoff, Y. (ed.) EWSL 1991. LNCS, vol. 482, pp. 398–411. Springer, Heidelberg (1991). https://doi.org/10.1007/BFb0017033
18. Madumal, P., Miller, T., Sonenberg, L., Vetere, F.: A grounded interaction protocol for explainable artificial intelligence. In: Proceedings of the 18th International Conference on Autonomous Agents and MultiAgent Systems, pp. 1033–1041 (2019)

19. Malburg, L., Brand, F., Bergmann, R.: Adaptive management of cyber-physical workflows by means of case-based reasoning and automated planning. In: Sales, T.P., Proper, H.A., Guizzardi, G., Montali, M., Maggi, F.M., Fonseca, C.M. (eds.) EDOC 2022. LNBIP, vol. 466, pp. 79–95. Springer, Cham (2023). https://doi.org/10.1007/978-3-031-26886-1_5
20. McBurney, P., Parsons, S.: Games that agents play: a formal framework for dialogues between autonomous agents. J. Logic Lang. Inform. **11**(3), 315–334 (2002)
21. Moreno-Garcia, C., et al.: Assessing the clinicians' pathway to embed artificial intelligence for assisted diagnostics of fracture detection. In: CEUR Workshop Proceedings (2020)
22. Nkisi-Orji, I., Palihawadana, C., Wiratunga, N., Corsar, D., Wijekoon, A.: Adapting semantic similarity methods for case-based reasoning in the cloud. In: Keane, M.T., Wiratunga, N. (eds.) ICCBR 2022. LNAI, vol. 13405, pp. 125–139. Springer, Cham (2022). https://doi.org/10.1007/978-3-031-14923-8_9
23. Rainey, C., et al.: UK reporting radiographers' perceptions of AI in radiographic image interpretation-current perspectives and future developments. Radiography **28**(4), 881–888 (2022)
24. Schoonderwoerd, T.A., Jorritsma, W., Neerincx, M.A., Van Den Bosch, K.: Human-centered XAI: developing design patterns for explanations of clinical decision support systems. Int. J. Hum. Comput. Stud. **154**, 102684 (2021)
25. Sokol, K., Flach, P.: One explanation does not fit all. KI-Künstliche Intelligenz **34**(2), 235–250 (2020)
26. Suddrey, G., Talbot, B., Maire, F.: Learning and executing re-usable behaviour trees from natural language instruction. IEEE Robot. Autom. Lett. **7**(4), 10643–10650 (2022)
27. Weber, B., Wild, W., Breu, R.: CBRFlow: enabling adaptive workflow management through conversational case-based reasoning. In: Funk, P., González Calero, P.A. (eds.) ECCBR 2004. LNCS (LNAI), vol. 3155, pp. 434–448. Springer, Heidelberg (2004). https://doi.org/10.1007/978-3-540-28631-8_32

Selecting Explanation Methods for Intelligent IoT Systems: A Case-Based Reasoning Approach

Humberto Parejas-Llanovarced, Jesus M. Darias, Marta Caro-Martínez(✉)⬤,
and Juan A. Recio-Garcia⬤

Department of Software Engineering and Artificial Intelligence,
Instituto de Tecnologías del Conocimiento, Universidad Complutense de Madrid,
Madrid, Spain
{hparejas,jdarias,martcaro,jareciog}@ucm.es

Abstract. The increasing complexity of intelligent systems in the Internet of Things (IoT) domain makes it essential to explain their behavior and decision-making processes to users. However, selecting an appropriate explanation method for a particular intelligent system in this domain can be challenging, given the diverse range of available XAI (eXplainable Artificial Intelligence) methods and the heterogeneity of IoT applications. This paper first presents a novel case base generated from an exhaustive literature review on existing explanation solutions for AIoT (Artificial Intelligence of the Things) systems. Then, a Case-Based Reasoning (CBR) approach is proposed to address the challenge of selecting the most suitable XAI method for a given IoT domain, AI task, and model. Both the case base and the CBR process are evaluated, showing their effectiveness in selecting appropriate explanation methods for different AIoT systems. The paper concludes by discussing the potential benefits and limitations of the proposed approach and suggesting avenues for future research.

Keywords: eXplainable Artificial Intelligence · Artificial Intelligence of the Things · Internet of Things · Case-Based Reasoning

1 Introduction

Recently, eXplainable Artificial Intelligence (XAI) has appeared intending to make users understand Artificial Intelligence (AI) models. The need to include explanations in AI models is crucial nowadays due to the application of AI in many domains, like medicine or security [4,20,27]. However, XAI is not only important in those domains, but in every domain where we are using black-box AI models, i.e. AI models not interpretable and understandable by their users, and, in consequence, not trustworthy [16]. Then XAI is an AI subfield whose main goal is to explain the underlying behavior of black-box AI systems to the final users, especially in critical domains [10]. The Internet of Things (IoT)

S. Massie and S. Chakraborti (Eds.): ICCBR 2023, LNAI 14141, pp. 185–199, 2023.
https://doi.org/10.1007/978-3-031-40177-0_12

encompasses some of these domains. IoT appeared recently with the objective of exploiting the potential of connected devices. Moreover, these devices can complete intelligent tasks by integrating AI models. Like any other AI system, these AIoT (Artificial Intelligence of the Things) [21] systems must also include explanations to improve the users' trust, especially when the results obtained with this kind of system are crucial in decisive situations. This way, we can coin the term XAIoT to refer eXplainable IA models applied to IoT solutions.

XAI is a field in continuous change, and consequently, there is a wide range of explainers (XAI methods) that can be applied to explain AI models [5]. However, the amount of XAI methods available is so huge that it is often difficult to know which method best applies to a concrete intelligent system. Every XAI method has its own features and can be more suitable for different explanation needs [5]. Therefore, picking the XAI method for a given AIoT system is a very complex and challenging decision-making task.

The *iSee project*[1] aims to build a platform based on a complex Case-Based Reasoning (CBR) system, where users could reuse explanation experiences for their intelligent systems. Previous results of this project [8] proposed a CBR approach that reuses knowledge about specific explanation needs and decides which XAI method is most appropriate. By extending this work to the IoT domain, in this paper we aim to build a CBR system that helps to decide which XAI method is the most suitable to explain an AIoT system. The contribution of this paper is two-fold: first, we have generated a novel case base of explanation solutions for the AIoT domain, and second, a CBR system able to identify the best explanation method for a given XAIoT need.

The paper is structured as follows. In Sect. 2, we study the related work about XAIoT and CBR systems. Section 3 describes the case base, its elicitation process, and formalization. We detail the CBR process in Sect. 4. Finally, we explain the evaluation performed (Sect. 5) and present the conclusions in Sect. 6.

2   Literature Review

To understand the existing works in XAI for case-based reasoning systems in the IoT domain, we have conducted an exhaustive literature review[2] creating and employing different search queries in a systematic way, which is described below. First, we focused our search on the existing works on Case-Based Reasoning and Explainability during the last five years. As a result, we got 143[3] articles, 76% of them published in the last two years. This publication increment shows the CBR community's interest in the XAI field. Then, we extended our search to publications concerning CBR and XAI applied to IoT systems. The outcome

---

[1] http://isee4xai.com.

[2] The database used for the review is Google Scholar https://scholar.google.com/.

[3] Terms used in the query: *"Explainability"*, *"Case-Based Reasoning"*. We delimited the search retrieving papers dated between: *2018 -2023*. We also filtered the search using only *review articles*.

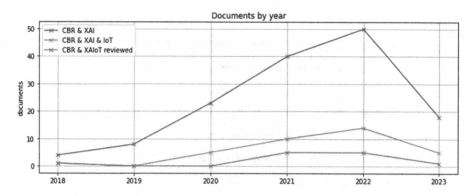

Fig. 1. Quantitative analysis of the review on explainable CBR, XAI, and IoT.

was 35[4] documents, 83% of which have been published since 2021. In Fig. 1, we depict this quantitative information.

To understand the impact of XAI applied to IoT, we analyzed eighty-two (82) publications[5] obtaining a total number of one-hundred (100) different XAIoT approaches. In Fig. 2, we can observe the distribution of XAI solutions according to the AI task and the IoT domain. The most prevalent task in the XAIoT literature is *Decision Support* with a prevalence of 42%, the next is *Image Processing* with 11%, and *Predictive maintenance* with 9%. Concerning the XAI methods applied to each IoT domain, most existing works are in the *Healthcare* domain. The three most applied XAI methods are *SHAP* with 18%, *LIME* with 13%, and *Grad-CAM* with 9%.

After the quantitative analysis of the existing works in XAIoT, we describe next the most relevant works and their association with CBR. Abioye et al. [1] examined several AI techniques identifying opportunities and challenges for AI applications in the construction industry. CBR systems were depicted as part of knowledge-based systems as a branch of AI. Atakishiyev et al. [6] in their study sheds comprehensive light on the development of explainable artificial intelligence (XAI) approaches for autonomous vehicles, pointing out potential applications of CBR. Islam et al. [12] consider CBR as a model for pattern recognition, validation, and contextualization. They highlight Weber et al.'s work [28], who proposed textual CBR (TCBR) utilizing patterns of input-to-output relations in order to recommend citations for academic researchers through textual explanations (mainly generated at the local scope, i.e., for an individual decision). Caruana et al. [7] demonstrated how case-based reasoning could be used to generate explanations for a neural network by using the latter to compute the distance metric for case retrieval. Sado et al. [25] review approaches on explainable goal-

---

[4] Terms used in the query: *"Explainability"*, *"Case-Based Reasoning"*, *"Internet of Things"*. We delimited the search retrieving papers dated between: *2018 -2023*. Again, filtered the search using only *review articles*.

[5] Forty-six works proposed by [12], twenty-eight papers recommended by [15], two articles presented by [2], and six recently published researches [3,9,11,14,18,22].

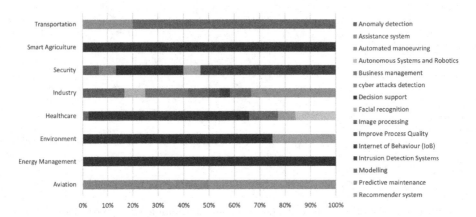

Fig. 2. Quantitative analysis of the distribution of papers on eXplainable Artificial Intelligence according to the IoT domain and AI task.

driven intelligent agents and robots, focusing on techniques for explaining and communicating agents' perceptual functions and cognitive reasoning. CBR is presented as a technique in eXplainable Goal-driven artificial intelligence (XGDAI) that enable continual learning of explanatory knowledge, domain knowledge, domain models, or policies (e.g., sets of environment states) for explanation generation. Senevirathna et al. [26] explore the potential of Explainable AI (XAI) methods, which would allow the next generation beyond 5G (B5G) stakeholders to inspect intelligent black-box systems used to secure B5G networks. Vilone and Longo [27] present a systematic review aimed at organizing XAI methods into a hierarchical classification system that builds upon and extends existing taxonomies by adding a significant dimension-the output formats. Among the XAI methods, a combination of a Neural Network and Case Base Reasoning (CBR) Twin-systems [13] maps the features' weights from the Deep Neural Network (DNN) to the CBR system to find similar cases from a training dataset that explains the prediction of the network of a new instance. Finally, we can cite *CBR-LIME* [24] as an XAI method where a CBR approach is used to find the optimal setup of the LIME explanation method. Regarding similar approaches for selecting the most suitable explanation method using CBR, in Darias et al. [8], the authors proposed capturing the user preferences about explanation results into a case base. Then, they defined the corresponding CBR process to help retrieve a suitable explainer from a catalog of existing XAI libraries.

3   The XAIoT Case Base

From the previous literature review, we can conclude that there is a wide variety of XAI methods for explaining intelligent systems in the IoT domain. All these experiences can be compiled into a case base to guide the selection of the proper explanation method for a new AIoT scenario. This is the first contribution of this paper: the elicitation of a case base of explanation solutions for the AIoT domain[6].

In this section, we describe how we formalize these cases and analyze the resulting case base.

3.1 Case Formalization

The formalization of this case base is rooted in the previous analysis of existing literature on XAI solutions in the IoT domain. From this analysis, we have inferred the different features required to describe a XAIoT experience. In our formalization, the case description defines the XAIoT problem, while the solution determines the method applied to explain that situation. In the description D of a XAIoT case C, we have defined the following attributes:

- **Domain (DO).** The domain is the area of expertise or application to which the problem described in this case belongs to. The domains we find in the IoT field are *Aviation, Energy Management, Environment, Healthcare, Industry, Security, Smart Agriculture*, and *Transportation*.
- **AI model (AIM).** The AI model is the algorithm or technique applied to solve the problem. It is the model to be explained to the user. In the IoT field, we can find the following AI models: *Case-Based Reasoning, Ensemble Model, Fuzzy Model, Neuro-Fuzzy Model, Neural Network, Nearest Neighbors Model, Tree-Based Model*, and *Unsorted Model*.
- **AI task (AIT).** The AI task is the challenge that the AI model aims to solve. We can identify the following AI tasks in the IoT domains: *Anomaly detection, Assistance, Automated maneuvering, Autonomous processes and robotics, Business Management, Cyber attacks detection, Decision support, Facial recognition, Image processing, Process quality improvement., Internet of Behaviour, Intrusion detection, Modelling, Predictive maintenance, Recommendation*, and *Risk prediction*.
- **AI problem (AIP).** This is the problem that the AI task implements. We can have *classification* or *regression* problems in a XAIoT case. We have considered other AI problems, but they do not apply to the IoT field.
- **XAI method input format (IF).** The input format is the type of data the XAI method can accept and process to produce the explanations. Allowed values are: *images, time series, text*, or *tabular data*.
- **XAI method Concurrentness (CO).** Determines if the XAI method is independent (or not) of the AI model that is explaining. If the user needs an explanation method that depends on some knowledge from the AI model, then this model is *ante-hoc*. On the contrary, if the user needs an explainable method fully independent of the AI model, then she needs a *post-hoc* XAI method.
- **XAI method Scope (SC).** The scope can be *local* if the XAI method only explains a prediction or an instance of data, whereas it is *global* if the method explains the whole AI model or dataset.

---

[6] Available at: https://dx.doi.org/10.21227/4nb2-q910 [23].

- **XAI method Portability (P).** This is another property of the XAI methods that is very well-known in the literature and that we consider in the description of each case. The portability feature points out if the XAI method is only applicable to explain a specific AI model (then the portability is *model-specific*) or applicable to explain any AI model (*model-agnostic*).

Finally, the solution S in each case denotes the XAI method to be applied to explain the XAIoT problem represented by the description D. We can use many XAI methods as a solution for a XAIoT problem. Some are very well-known in the literature, like *LIME, XRAI, Integrated Gradients*, or *SHAP*, but others are less common, like *FFT, LORE*, or *SIDU*. The solution also includes the explanation technique that the XAI method belongs to. It will enable the reuse of alternative methods from other similar cases. This way, the solution is defined by the following features:

- **XAI method (XM).** The XAI method to explain a XAIoT system. We have collected 47 different explainers from the literature review.
- **Explanation technique (ET).** We can classify each XAI method regarding the explanation technique that the method belongs to. We have extracted this classification from the work by [8]: *Activation Clusters, Architecture Modification, Composite, Data-drive, Feature Relevance, Filter, Knowledge Extraction, Optimisation Based, Probabilistic, Simplification*, and *Statistics*.

Consequently, we can formalize the case base as follows:

$$case = \langle D, S \rangle$$
where
$$D = \langle DO, AIT, AIM, AIP, IF, CO, SC, P \rangle$$
$$S = \langle XM, ET \rangle. \tag{1}$$

3.2 Case Base Analysis

The resulting case base includes a total of 513 cases from the literature review of 100 papers of XAIoT solutions described in Sect. 2.

Figure 3, shows the distribution of the XAI Methods regarding the IoT domains. As we can observe the 45% of the cases are applied to the *Healthcare* domain, the 26% to the *Industry* domain, 11% to de *Security* domain, 9% to the *Aviation* domain, and 2% to each of the *Energy Management, Environment Smart Agriculture*, and *Transportation* domains. Regarding the distribution of the XAI Methods according to the AI Models, Fig. 4 illustrates that the AI model with more cases is *Neuronal Network* with 43%, followed by *Agnostic Models* with 18%, *Ensemble Models* with 12% and *Tree-Based Models* with 9%. Figure 5 shows the distribution of the XAI Methods w.r.t. Concurrentness. As we can note, 86% of the cases refer to *Post-hoc* and the remaining ones to *Ante-hoc* methods. The distribution of XAI Methods according to Scope is shown in Fig. 6, wherein 60% of the cases are *Local* and 40% *Global*. Figure 7 represents the distribution of the XAI Methods according to the Input Format, in which the 53%

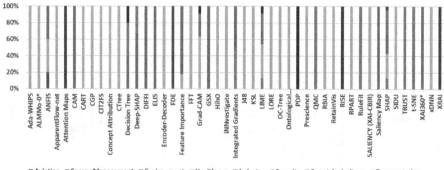

Fig. 3. Case base analysis: explanation methods per domain.

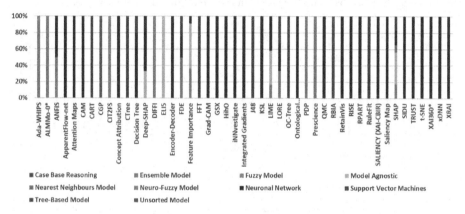

Fig. 4. Case base analysis: explanation methods per models.

of the cases are *Numeric*, 24% *Text*, 22% *Visual* and 1% Rule. Finally, in Fig. 8 we can see the distribution of the XAI Methods according to the Portability, where 56% of the cases are *Model Specific* and 44% *Model Agnostic*.

Once we have defined and analyzed the structure of the case base, the following section describes the proposed CBR system for selecting the most suitable explanation method for a XAIoT system.

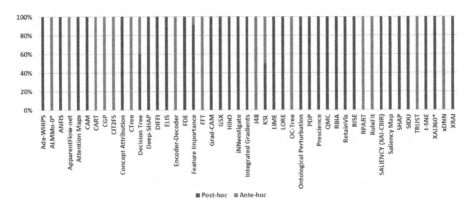

Fig. 5. Case base analysis: explanation methods per concurrentness.

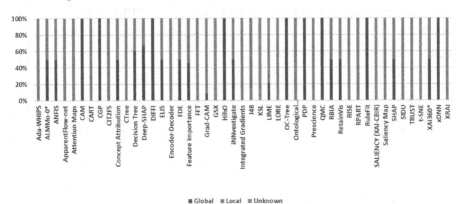

Fig. 6. Case base analysis: explanation methods per scope.

4   CBR Process

The second contribution of this paper is the definition of a CBR system able to identify the best explanation method for a given XAIoT problem[7]. Next, we present both the retrieval and reuse stages of the proposed CBR system.

4.1   Retrieval

We propose a CBR retrieval process following the MAC/FAC (many-are-called, few-are-chosen) schema [19].

The *filtering step* (MAC) is necessary to discard the XAI methods unsuitable for a query q and to guarantee that all the retrieved explainers are valid solutions. Therefore, this step filters the compatible XAI methods according to hard restrictions such as the input format, target AI model, or type of AI problem.

---

[7] Available at https://github.com/UCM-GAIA/XAIoT.

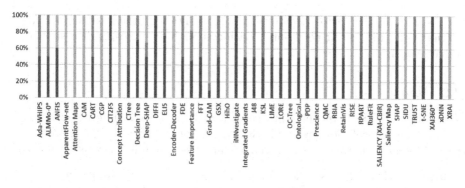

Fig. 7. Case base analysis: explanation methods per input format.

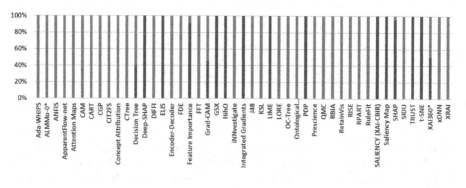

Fig. 8. Case base analysis: explanation methods per portability.

These filtering attributes are $\mathcal{FA} = \{IF, AIM, AIP\}$, and the corresponding MAC function is defined as:

$$filter(q, C) = \{c \in C : q.a \neq null \land q.a = c.a, \forall a \in \mathcal{FA}\} \tag{2}$$

The *sorting step* (FAC) obtains the most similar cases to q using a similarity metric that compares the remaining attributes in the description, denoted as $\mathcal{SA}$. We have defined the following similarity metric:

$$sim(q, c) = \frac{1}{W} \sum_{a \in \mathcal{SA}} w_a \cdot equal(q.a, c.a) \tag{3}$$

where c is a case within the case base and $\mathcal{SA} = \{DO, AIT, CO, SP, P\}$ is the set of attributes from D that we consider to obtain the most similar cases to q (domain, AI task, concurrentness, scope, and portability). The values w_a are the weights assigned to each property, so $w_a \in [0..1]$ and $W = \sum w_a$. We calculated these values using a greedy optimization method to minimize the error.

As a result, the *sorting step* returns a list containing the most similar cases to the query (its nearest neighbors). Each case with its corresponding similarity value $sim(c)$.

4.2 Reuse

After the MAC/FAC retrieval process, the CBR process includes a *reuse step*. In this step, the solution and similarity values of the nearest neighbors are used to build a final solution for the query. We propose two different reuse strategies:

Simple voting. The simple voting strategy returns the majoritarian XAI method in the nearest neighbors. We can define it as the explanation method xm with maximal multiplicity $M(xm)$ in the multiset S that aggregates all the explanation methods in the retrieved solutions:

$$sv(s_1, \ldots, s_k) = \arg\max_{xm} M(xm)$$

where

$$M(xm) = \sum_{m \in S} 1_{\{xm=m\}}$$

$$S = \bigcup_{i \in \{1,\ldots,k\}} s_i.xm \tag{4}$$

Weighted voting. The weighted voting strategy calculates the solution for q as a weighted addition of our nearest neighbor solutions. This method returns the explanation method xm with maximal weighted multiplicity $WM(xm)$ that takes into account the similarity of the case $sim(c)$.

$$wv(s_1, \ldots, s_k) = \arg\max_{xm} WM(xm)$$

where

$$WM(xm) = \sum_{m \in S} sim(c)_{\{c.xm=m\}}$$

$$S = \bigcup_{i \in \{1,\ldots,k\}} s_i.xm \tag{5}$$

5 Evaluation

To demonstrate the benefits of our case-based approach to finding the most suitable explanation method for a given XAIoT problem, we performed an evaluation using cross-validation. The main goal is to evaluate and compare the accuracy of the reuse strategies presented in the previous section.

Results, using a 20-times leave-one-out evaluation, are summarized in Fig. 9. We can observe the accuracy of the prediction of the two variables in the solution of the cases: *XAI method* and *Explanation Technique*. The accuracy of *XAI Method* and *Explanation Technique* obtain the highest values of 0.74 and 0.9, for

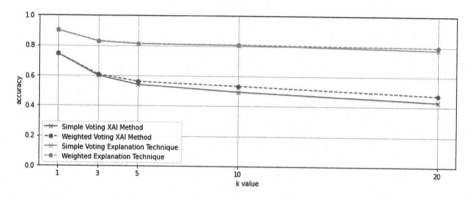

Fig. 9. Evaluation result for several values of k using the Simple Voting and Weighted Voting reuse strategies.

$k = 1$ in *simple* and *weighted* voting, respectively. From a baseline of a random choice between 47 XAI methods (2% random probability) and 11 explanation techniques (9% random probability), these are very significant results. Thus, we can conclude that the CBR process is able to achieve a remarkable performance when predicting the best explanation technique and concrete explanation method for a given XAIoT problem. Here, it is worth noting that this performance is based on the quality of the cases elicited from the literature review.

Regarding the comparison of the reuse strategies, the accuracy of *weighted voting* is almost similar to the accuracy reached by the *simple voting* strategy for different values of k. The analysis of the k parameter shows that, independently of the reuse strategy, the second-best accuracy is obtained when the number of nearest neighbors is $k = 3$. When increasing this value, most of the configurations of the CBR system achieve an accuracy close to 0.83 for *the Explanation technique* and 0.60 for the *XAI Method*.

We have also studied the impact of the case base size on the performance. Being CBR a lazy-learning process where cases are incrementally included in the case base, it is necessary to analyze its behavior to find the required minimum number of cases. This analysis is presented in Fig. 10, where the number of cases in the case base increases from 5% to 100% of the total dataset. This Figure shows that performance stabilizes approximately when 85% of the cases have been included in the case base. This tendency led us to conclude that the proposed CBR system will increase its performance as other new cases are included in the case base.

Finally, we have analyzed the competence of the case base. Competence is the ability of a system's case base to support the solution of potential target problems [17]. It is usually estimated as the coverage of the cases that can be computed as all the possible combinations of attribute values in the case description. To illustrate this analysis, we have generated scatter plots for the most relevant pairs of attributes. Figure 11 shows the coverage for all the possible combinations of AI Tasks and XAI Methods. Although there are empty areas

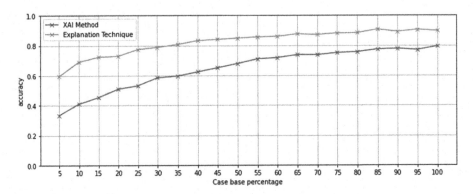

Fig. 10. Learning process of the CBR system showing performance as the case base grows.

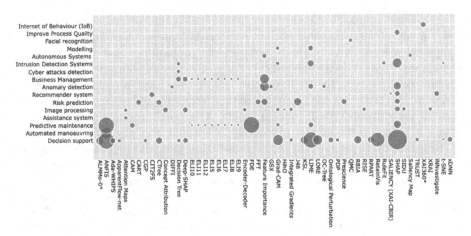

Fig. 11. Case base coverage. Scatter plot showing the number of cases (bubble size) available in the case base, w.r.t AI Task (y-axis) and XIA Method (x-axis).

in this plot, it is essential to note that many XAI methods are not applicable to solve several tasks. Therefore, we can conclude that the case base provides quite good coverage. A complementary view is provided by Fig. 12. This figure contains two scatter plots illustrating the case base coverage regarding the AI Movel Vs. Domain and AI Task Vs. Explanation Technique. Here we can also observe a satisfactory coverage of all the potential problems with respect to these attributes.

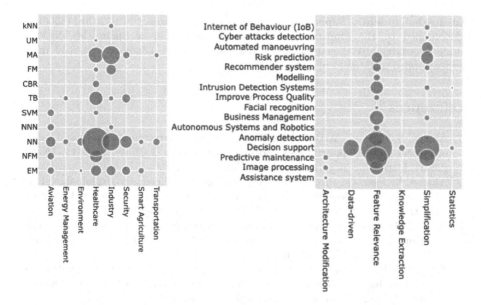

Fig. 12. Case base coverage. Scatter plot showing the number of cases (bubble size) available in the case base. (LEFT) AI Model (y-axis) and Domain (x-axis). (RIGHT) AI Task (y-axis) and Explanation Technique (x-axis).

6   Conclusions

The great amount of different XAI methods that we can find in the literature and the novelty of the AIoT systems make it necessary to support the task of deciding which XAI method is the most adequate for their explanation to users. However, the choice is challenging since designers of XAIoT systems should consider many facets to make the best decision. To address this problem, we present a CBR solution that uses a wide case base of 513 cases extracted from an exhaustive literature review [23]. We propose a formalization of such cases together with a retrieval process and two different reuse strategies.

From the experimental cross-validation evaluation, we can conclude that our approach achieves a significant performance in determining which XAI method or explainability technique is more suitable for a given XAIoT problem.

As future work, we could evaluate our approach with users, since users' opinions are fundamental to evaluating users' satisfaction and trust in the explanations. Consequently, we would also need to incorporate knowledge about the target users in the case description, like their goals or knowledge. Finally, another line of future work could be to apply this approach and our previous approach [8] to other AI fields. The case description could be adapted to the specific field where we are going to apply our approach, but mainly our proposed approach could be used like it is now because our case description is general and could be transferred to other problems and tasks.

Acknowledgements. Supported by the PERXAI project PID2020-114596RB-C21, funded by the Ministry of Science and Innovation of Spain (MCIN/AEI/10.13039/501100011033) and the BOSCH-UCM Honorary Chair on Artificial Intelligence applied to Internet of Things.

References

1. Abioye, S.O., et al.: Artificial intelligence in the construction industry: a review of present status, opportunities and future challenges. J. Build. Eng. **44**, 103299 (2021). https://doi.org/10.1016/J.JOBE.2021.103299

2. Ahmed, I., Jeon, G., Piccialli, F.: From artificial intelligence to explainable artificial intelligence in industry 4.0: a survey on what, how, and where. IEEE Trans. Industr. Inf. **18**(8), 5031–5042 (2022). https://doi.org/10.1109/TII.2022.3146552

3. Alani, M.M.: BotStop: packet-based efficient and explainable IoT botnet detection using machine learning. Comput. Commun. **193**, 53–62 (2022). https://doi.org/10.1016/J.COMCOM.2022.06.039

4. Angelov, P.P., Soares, E.A., Jiang, R., Arnold, N.I., Atkinson, P.M.: Explainable artificial intelligence: an analytical review. Wiley Interdisc. Rev.: Data Min. Knowl. Discov. **11**(5) (2021). https://doi.org/10.1002/widm.1424

5. Arrieta, A.B., et al.: Explainable artificial intelligence (XAI): concepts, taxonomies, opportunities and challenges toward responsible ai. Inf. fusion **58**, 82–115 (2020)

6. Atakishiyev, S., Salameh, M., Yao, H., Goebel, R.: Explainable artificial intelligence for autonomous driving: a comprehensive overview and field guide for future research directions (2021). https://doi.org/10.48550/arxiv.2112.11561

7. Caruana, R., Kangarloo, H., Dionisio, J.D., Sinha, U., Johnson, D.: Case-based explanation of non-case-based learning methods. In: Proceedings of the AMIA Symposium, p. 212 (1999). https://www.ncbi.nlm.nih.gov/pmc/articles/PMC2232607/

8. Darias, J.M., Caro-Martínez, M., Díaz-Agudo, B., Recio-Garcia, J.A.: Using case-based reasoning for capturing expert knowledge on explanation methods. In: Keane, M.T., Wiratunga, N. (eds.) ICCBR 2022. LNCS, vol. 13405, pp. 3–17. Springer, Cham (2022). https://doi.org/10.1007/978-3-031-14923-8_1

9. Elayan, H., Aloqaily, M., Karray, F., Guizani, M.: Internet of behavior (IoB) and explainable AI systems for influencing IoT behavior. IEEE Netw. (2022). https://doi.org/10.1109/MNET.009.2100500

10. Gunning, D., Stefik, M., Choi, J., Miller, T., Stumpf, S., Yang, G.Z.: XAI-explainable artificial intelligence. Sci. Robot. **4**(37), eaay7120 (2019)

11. Houda, Z.A.E., Brik, B., Khoukhi, L.: 'Why should i trust your IDS?': an explainable deep learning framework for intrusion detection systems in internet of things networks. IEEE Open J. Commun. Soc. **3**, 1164–1176 (2022). https://doi.org/10.1109/OJCOMS.2022.3188750

12. Islam, M.R., Ahmed, M.U., Barua, S., Begum, S.: A systematic review of explainable artificial intelligence in terms of different application domains and tasks. Appl. Sci. **12**(3), 1353 (2022). https://doi.org/10.3390/APP12031353

13. Kenny, E.M., Keane, M.T.: Twin-systems to explain artificial neural networks using case-based reasoning: comparative tests of feature-weighting methods in ANN-CBR twins for XAI. In: IJCAI International Joint Conference on Artificial Intelligence, pp. 2708–2715 (2019). https://doi.org/10.24963/IJCAI.2019/376

14. Khan, I.A., et al.: XSRU-IoMT: explainable simple recurrent units for threat detection in internet of medical things networks. Futur. Gener. Comput. Syst. **127**, 181–193 (2022). https://doi.org/10.1016/j.future.2021.09.010

15. Kok, I., Okay, F.Y., Muyanli, O., Ozdemir, S.: Explainable artificial intelligence (XAI) for internet of things: a survey (2022). https://doi.org/10.48550/arxiv.2206.04800

16. Lakkaraju, H., Arsov, N., Bastani, O.: Robust and stable black box explanations. In: International Conference on Machine Learning, pp. 5628–5638. PMLR (2020)

17. Leake, D., Wilson, M.: How many cases do you need? Assessing and predicting case-base coverage. In: Ram, A., Wiratunga, N. (eds.) ICCBR 2011. LNCS (LNAI), vol. 6880, pp. 92–106. Springer, Heidelberg (2011). https://doi.org/10.1007/978-3-642-23291-6_9

18. Mansouri, T., Vadera, S.: A deep explainable model for fault prediction using IoT sensors. IEEE Access **10**, 66933–66942 (2022). https://doi.org/10.1109/ACCESS.2022.3184693

19. de Mántaras, R.L., et al.: Retrieval, reuse, revision and retention in case-based reasoning. Knowl. Eng. Rev. **20**(3), 215–240 (2005). https://doi.org/10.1017/S0269888906000646

20. McDermid, J.A., Jia, Y., Porter, Z., Habli, I.: Artificial intelligence explainability: the technical and ethical dimensions. Philos. Trans. R. Soc. A: Math. Phys. Eng. Sci. **379**(2207), 20200363 (2021). https://doi.org/10.1098/rsta.2020.0363, https://royalsocietypublishing.org/doi/10.1098/rsta.2020.0363

21. Mukhopadhyay, S.C., Tyagi, S.K.S., Suryadevara, N.K., Piuri, V., Scotti, F., Zeadally, S.: Artificial intelligence-based sensors for next generation IoT applications: a review. IEEE Sens. J. **21**(22), 24920–24932 (2021). https://doi.org/10.1109/JSEN.2021.3055618

22. Naeem, H., Alshammari, B.M., Ullah, F.: Explainable artificial intelligence-based IoT device malware detection mechanism using image visualization and fine-tuned CNN-based transfer learning model. Comput. Intell. Neurosci. **2022** (2022). https://doi.org/10.1155/2022/7671967

23. Parejas-Llanovarced, H., Darias, J., Caro-Martinez, M., Recio-Garcia, J.A.: A case base of explainable artificial intelligence of the things (XAIoT) systems (2023). https://doi.org/10.21227/4nb2-q910, https://dx.doi.org/10.21227/4nb2-q910

24. Recio-García, J.A., Díaz-Agudo, B., Pino-Castilla, V.: CBR-LIME: a case-based reasoning approach to provide specific local interpretable model-agnostic explanations. In: Watson, I., Weber, R. (eds.) ICCBR 2020. LNCS (LNAI), vol. 12311, pp. 179–194. Springer, Cham (2020). https://doi.org/10.1007/978-3-030-58342-2_12

25. Sado, F., et al.: Explainable goal-driven agents and robots - a comprehensive review. ACM Comput. Surv. **1**(211) (2023). https://doi.org/10.1145/3564240

26. Senevirathna, T et al.: A survey on XAI for beyond 5G security: technical aspects, use cases, challenges and research directions (2022)

27. Vilone, G., Longo, L.: Classification of explainable artificial intelligence methods through their output formats. Mach. Learn. Knowl. Extract. **3**(3), 615–661 (2021). https://doi.org/10.3390/MAKE3030032

28. Weber, R.O., Johs, A.J., Li, J., Huang, K.: Investigating textual case-based XAI. In: Cox, M.T., Funk, P., Begum, S. (eds.) ICCBR 2018. LNCS (LNAI), vol. 11156, pp. 431–447. Springer, Cham (2018). https://doi.org/10.1007/978-3-030-01081-2_29

CBR-fox: A Case-Based Explanation Method for Time Series Forecasting Models

Moisés F. Valdez-Ávila[1] , Carlos Bermejo-Sabbagh[1] , Belen Diaz-Agudo[2] ,
Mauricio G. Orozco-del-Castillo[1] , and Juan A. Recio-Garcia[2(✉)]

[1] Tecnológico Nacional de México/IT de Mérida,
Departamento de Sistemas y Computación, Mérida, Mexico
{e18081131,carlos.bs,mauricio.orozco}@itmerida.edu.mx
[2] Department of Software Engineering and Artificial Intelligence,
Instituto de Tecnologías del Conocimiento, Universidad Complutense de Madrid,
Madrid, Spain
{belend,jareciog}@ucm.es

Abstract. Explainable Artificial Intelligence refers to methods that help human experts understand solutions developed by Artificial Intelligence systems in the form of black-box models, making them transparent and understandable. This paper describes CBR-fox, a post-hoc model-agnostic case-based explanation method for forecasting models. This method generates a case base of explanation examples through a sliding-window technique applied over the time series. Then, these explanation cases can be retrieved using a wide range of well-established metrics for time series comparison. Moreover, we introduce and evaluate a novel similarity metric named Combined Correlation Index. The proposed retrieval approach considers as a signal the similarity series resulting from applying the comparison metrics. This way, the signal can be smoothed using noise removal filters, such as the Hodrick-Prescott and low-pass filters, to avoid maximally similar cases that may overlap or represent a local slice of the source time series.. The resulting signal allows then to foster diversity in the retrieved explanation cases presented to the user The proposed case-based explanation approach is evaluated in the weather forecasting domain using an artificial neural network as the black-box model to be explained.

Keywords: Explainable Artificial Intelligence · Time Series Forecasting · Case-based Explanation · Artificial Intelligence of the Things

1 Introduction

The current rise of the Internet of Things (IoT) technology has produced a wide range of sensing solutions that are progressively being integrated into our daily life devices such as mobile phones or wearables [11]. The combination of

S. Massie and S. Chakraborti (Eds.): ICCBR 2023, LNAI 14141, pp. 200–214, 2023.
https://doi.org/10.1007/978-3-031-40177-0_13

such sensing capabilities with Artificial Intelligence (AI) is producing Artificial Intelligence of Things (AIoT) and Internet of Everything (IoE) applications that provide an enhanced user experience [33].

Since IoT sensing devices obtain readings that vary in time, they have been subject to time series analysis and modeling. A time series is a sequence of observed values of a variable at equally spaced timestamps t, represented as a set of discrete values [22]. Time series forecasting is the prediction of future data values based on collected data and has been an area of great interest in science, engineering, and business. Traditional time series forecasting is usually approached by the analysis of its internal structure: autocorrelation, trend, seasonality, etc., to capture the pattern of the long-time behavior of the system [22]. These models predict future values of a target $y_i(t)$ for a given observed value i at a time t. In IoT, these observed values usually represent measurements from sensors. While this applies to univariate forecasting, the extension to multivariate models can be performed without loss of generality [27]. Machine Learning (ML) has, however, positioned as the next generation of time series forecasting models [1] due to increasing data availability and computing power. One of the main techniques in ML is artificial neural networks (ANNs), which have proven to be a reliable tool for time series analysis [3], and numerous ANNs design choices have emerged given the diversity of time series problems across multiple domains. Of these designs, the most commonly used one in time series forecasting is recurrent neural networks (RNNs) due to the natural interpretation of time series data as sequences of inputs and targets [17].

Although ML approaches have demonstrated very good prediction performance, they have significant limitations regarding their explainability. Neural network models are considered as "black boxes" because their internal processes are challenging to interpret with respect to the predictions they produce [10]. EXplainable AI (XAI) methods help human experts understand solutions developed by AI. Solving the black-box problem is a requirement for auditing the reasoning behind incorrect predictions taken by AIoT systems, and foreseeing the data patterns that may lead to a concrete prediction.

This paper describes CBR-fox (**CBR** - **fo**recasting e**x**planation), a post-hoc sliding-window explanation-by-example method that enables the explanation of black-box forecasting models using Case-Based Reasoning (CBR). This method follows the twin surrogate CBR explanation approach that enables making the forecasting process understandable [13]. Here, time series are split into different time-window cases that serve as explanation cases for the outcome of the prediction model. This paper exemplifies and evaluates the benefits of CBR-fox in the weather forecasting domain. The presented use case is based on the readings from an environmental sensor for mobile devices[1] capable of sensing several weather variables [20,30], with the potential of ANNs to compute climate predictions.

---

[1] BOSCH Sensortec BME680: https://www.bosch-sensortec.com/products/environmental-sensors/gas-sensors/bme680/.

The paper runs as follows. Section 2 presents the background of this work. Then, Sect. 3 describes our case-based explanation method. Section 4 presents the evaluation results and Sect. 5 concludes the paper and opens lines of future work.

2   Background

This paper proposes the use of CBR as an explanation method for black-box forecasting models. However, there are other approaches that have used CBR as a forecasting technique itself in various domains, such as finance, energy, and healthcare [9,16,24]. The benefits of generating predictions based on past cases are the inherent interpretability of the CBR process. However, its accuracy has been outperformed by other black-box models such as ANNs. This way, CBR is more valuable as a post-hoc explanation method than as a forecasting model. The work by [13] presents a systematic review of "ANN-CBR twins": post-hoc explanation-by-example approaches that rely on the twinning of ANNs with CBR systems. One example is the proposal by Li et al. [15] which combines the strength of deep learning and the interpretability of CBR to make an interpretable deep ANN. This approach modifies the ANN architecture to encode prototypes in the output layer that partially allows tracing the classification path for a new observation. Bebarta et al. [2] also present an intelligent stock trading system utilizing dynamic time windows with case-based reasoning, and a recurrent function link artificial neural network (FLANN).

However, there are few works on case-based explanations for time series forecasting. Some of them have focused on counterfactual explanations [8], but not many have aimed at time series. Corchado and Lees [7] presented a hybrid approach to forecasting the thermal structure of the water ahead of a moving vessel that combines CBR and ANNs. Nevertheless, this approach is not a post-hoc explanation method as it exploits the generalizing ability of the ANN to guide the adaptation stage of the CBR mechanism. The paper by Olsson et al. [21] presents a general method for explaining the predictions made by probabilistic ML algorithms using cases. The method comprises two main parts: 1) a measure of similarity between cases, which is defined with respect to a probability model, and 2) a case-based approach to explaining the probabilistic prediction by estimating the prediction error. The paper demonstrates the use of this method in explaining the predictions of the energy performance of households. Other related case-based explanation methods also use sliding-window approaches to generate cases. For example, in electric load forecasting [23] or speech emotion recognition [25]. However, Lorenzo and Arroyo [18] present an alternative approach where clustering is applied over time series to obtain prototypes that act as cases.

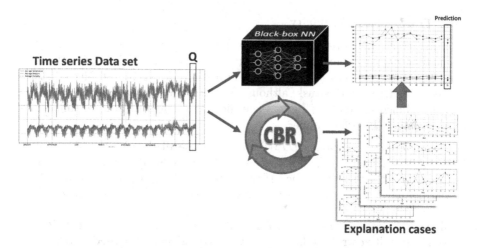

Fig. 1. Global schema of the ANN-CBR twin approach of CBR-fox.

3 Method

The main contribution of this paper is the use of CBR for the generation of explanations associated with the prediction of a certain black-box ANN model. However, it is important to note that the proposed explanation method—CBR-fox—is applicable to other forecasting black-box models. We propose a solution for the explanation of the outcomes of the ANN, where a black-box system is explained by an interpretable twin CBR system [13]. This approach is illustrated in Fig. 1, where the same dataset is used as the input of the ANN and to create the explanatory cases provided by the CBR system.

Explanatory cases are generated using a sliding-window method over the whole time series: $C_t = \langle [t - w, t], R_{t+1} \rangle$ for $t \in [w, L - 1]$ where w is the window size and R_{t+1} is the solution of the case, which corresponds to the following reading, and L is the length of the time series. This way, the case base is generated from the source time series ts and contains $len(ts) - w - 1$ cases that will be used to explain any forthcoming prediction of the ANN. It is important to note that, by using this sliding-window method, consecutive cases C_t and C_{t+1} overlap in $w - 1$ timestamps.

Once the case base is generated, the twin system works as follows. Given a query timestamp t_q, the ANN predicts the following time series values: $Pred(t_q)$. In parallel, the CBR explanation system receives the corresponding time window query $Q = [t_q - 1 - w, t_q - 1]$ and returns the most similar explanatory cases to explain the prediction $Pred(t_q)$. These explanatory cases can be directly presented to the user or combined into a single explanation case.

The critical elements of the CBR-fox explanation method are the similarity metrics, the retrieval and reuse processes, and the visualization of the explanation cases. These steps are explained next.

3.1   Time Series Similarity

The quality of the retrieved explanation cases highly depends on the similarity metrics used to compare them. Next, we present several metrics that are integrated into our case-based explanation method. Most are established state-of-the-art metrics for this task, although we introduce a novel metric—denoted CCI, Combined Correlation Index—specifically designed to retrieve time series that resembles the original query.

- *Dynamic Time Warping (DTW)* computes the distance between two time series by considering the pointwise (usually Euclidean) distance between all elements of the two-time series. It then uses dynamic programming to find the warping path that minimizes the total pointwise distance between realigned series [26].
- *Weighted Dynamic Time Warping (WDTW)* incorporates a multiplicative weight penalty corresponding to the warping distance (time series with lower phase differences have a smaller weight imposed) [12].
- *Derivate Dynamic Time Warping (DDTW)* considers the 'shape' of the time series represented by the first derivative of the sequence in an attempt to improve on DTW [14].
- *Weighted derivative dynamic time warping (WDDTW)* considers not only the shape, but also the phase, of the time series by adding a weight to the derivative [12].
- *Move-Split-Merge (MSM)* uses three fundamental operations: Move, Split, and Merge, which have an associated cost and can be applied in sequence to transform any time series into any other time series. The MSM distance is defined as the cost of the cheapest sequence of operations that transforms the first time series into the second one [29].
- *Edit Distance For Real Penalty (ERP)* proposes the idea of sequences of points that have no matches [4] and attempts to align time series by carefully considering how indexes are carried forward through the cost matrix.
- *Longest Common Subsequence (LCSS)* looks for the longest common sequence between two time series and returns the percentage of the longest common sequence [32].
- *Time Warp Edit (TWE)*, a measure for discrete time series matching with time 'elasticity', is well-suited for the processing of event data for which each data sample is associated with a timestamp [19].
- *Edit Distance for Real Sequences (EDR)* determines the percentage of elements that should be removed from the input signals x and y such that the sum of distances between the remaining elements is below a specified tolerance level [5].
- *Combined Correlation Index (CCI)* is a novel metric presented in this paper specifically designed from the point of view of explainability. It is aimed to optimize the similarity between to time series according to the shape and distance. It provides a way to measure how a given time window case $\mathbf{C}$ is related to a target query window $\mathbf{Q}$:

$$\text{CCI}(\mathbf{C}, \mathbf{Q}) = (\alpha_1 + \rho(\mathbf{C}, \mathbf{Q}) - \alpha_2 \|(\mathbf{C}, \mathbf{Q})\|) \cdot \alpha_3 \tag{1}$$

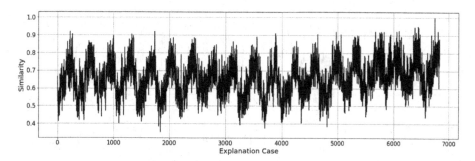

Fig. 2. Example of the similarity series (n = 6847). Maximally similarity peaks tend to focus on a local portion of the case base.

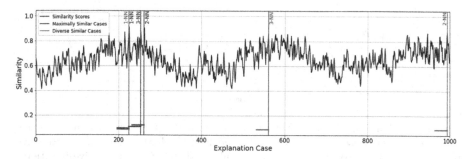

Fig. 3. Example of high-frequency components (maximally similarity peaks) in a sub-sample of the similarity series ($n = 1000$). Blue lines represent the maximally similar cases (that tend to overlap or focus on a concrete portion of the case base) whereas red lines represent similar but diverse cases.

where ρ is the function that calculates the Pearson correlation coefficient, and the double bars represent the normalized Euclidean distance between those vectors. The correlation component deals with the morphological similarity of the time windows, while the Euclidean distance component deals with the proximity between the time series in the given time windows. Remaining parameters are used to shift the correlation coefficient (α_1), normalize the Euclidean distance (α_2), and reshape the resulting values to the [0–1] range (α_3).

3.2 Retrieval Process

The retrieval process first computes the similarity between the query and each explanation case. It is computed using any of the metrics presented in the previous section, producing a *similarity signal* analogous to the one presented in Fig. 2, where values correspond to the similarity between the query and the cases generated for every timestamp.

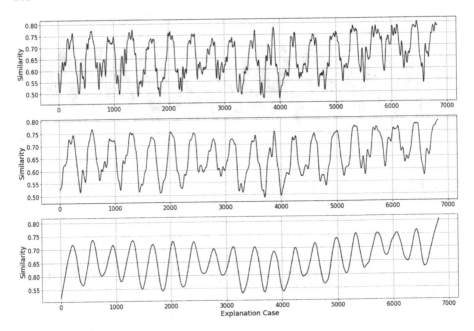

Fig. 4. Top chart: application of the Hodrick-Prescott filter to obtain the tendency series of the similarity signal. The middle and bottom charts represent the iterative application of the LOWESS filter to the resulting signal. After successive iterations, the similarity signal converges (bottom chart), allowing the identification of the most similar but diverse explanation cases.

As we can observe, the similarity values for overlapping consecutive cases yield undesirable high-frequency components. Figure 3 illustrates this problem with a limited portion of the case base. Overlapping time windows tend to obtain a very close similarity value, and therefore, if the retrieval process returns the maximally similar cases directly, they will overlap and focus on a concrete slice of the case. This is a well-known problem in the CBR field related to the retrieved cases' diversity [28]. In this figure, the indexes (timestamp t) of the maximally similar cases are identified by a vertical blue line, whereas the horizontal segment on the bottom represents the time window $[t - w, t]$ to be retrieved as the explanation case. We can clearly observe that these maximally similar cases overlap and only represent a concrete slice of the time series. In contrast, cases represented in red are the top similar but diverse cases, where the locality effect of maximal similarity is avoided by retrieving other suboptimal cases.

To address this problem, we apply the Hodrick-Prescott (HP) filter, a mathematical tool used in time series analysis for removing the cyclic component. The HP filter has become a benchmark for getting rid of cyclic movements in data and is broadly employed for macroeconomics research [31]. This filter returns the tendency component of the signals represented by the top chart in Fig. 4. Then, a low-pass filter can be applied over this tendency signal to smooth it progressively. Concretely, CBR-fox applies the Locally Weighted Scatterplot Smoothing (LOWESS) method, a non-parametric technique for fitting a smooth curve to data points [6]. After iteratively applying this filter until the resulting signal no longer changes, we obtain a smoothed similarity signal as presented in the bottom chart of Fig. 4.

This smoothed similarity signal allows us to identify the k most similar explanation cases to the query Q. To do so, its numerical derivative is obtained, helping in the identification of peaks and valleys, which will be used to segment the series into groups of convex and concave curves. Convex curves are then explored to find the timestamp with the highest similarity value. Only one timestamp is obtained for each convex curve. Once the maximal values for each convex curve have been collected, they are ranked and returned as the most similar explanation cases presented to the user to explain the prediction given by the black-box model.

3.3 Reuse

Once the k nearest neighbors have been retrieved, CBR-fox allows either to present them directly to the user or combine them to obtain a joint explanation case. In the latter case, we propose two different reuse strategies:

Simple Average. This strategy computes the average for each timestamp of the k nearest neighbors:

$$S(C_1, \ldots, C_k) = [S_0, \ldots, S_{w-1}],$$

where

$$S_t = \frac{1}{k} \sum_{i=1}^{k} C_i[t] \tag{2}$$

Weighted Average. Generates a combined solution through a weighted average according to the similarity of the k nearest neighbors:

$$W_t(C_1, \ldots, C_k) = [W_0, \ldots, W_{w-1}],$$

where

$$W_t = \frac{\sum_{i=1}^{k} C_i[t] \cdot sim(C_i, Q)}{\sum_{i=1}^{k} sim(C_i, Q)} \tag{3}$$

3.4 Visualization

The visualization of the explanation cases to the user is exemplified in Fig. 5. CBR-fox allows visualizing either all the k-NNs or the combined explanation case. Notice how it also includes the prediction of the ANN, $Pred(t_q)$, as well as the actual value stored in the solution of the case, R_{t+1}.

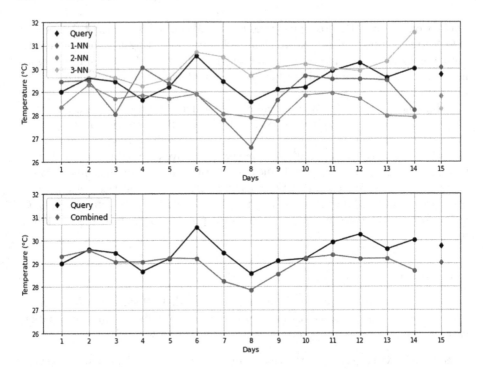

Fig. 5. Visualization of the explanation cases to the user. Best explanation cases (top) and combined explanation case (bottom). Window size: $w = 14$. The predictions from the ANN model, $Pred(t_q)$, and the case solutions, R_{t+1}, are also displayed to the user (day 15).

4   Evaluation

In this section, the evaluation of the CBR-fox system is addressed. First, we explain the dataset used to train the ML model, next, we discuss the validation and evaluation metrics and, finally, the results are presented.

4.1   Dataset and Model

The dataset used for the evaluation of CBR-fox consists of meteorological variables recorded by the Mexican National Water Council (*Comisión Nacional del Agua, CONAGUA*) ground station located at the city of Mérida; among the data provided, the following variables were found: temperature (T), vapor pressure (P), and relative humidity (H). Daily records were obtained from January 1, 2000, to September 30, 2018.

A recurrent neural network (RNN) using long short-term memory (LSTM) cells was trained over the dataset of time windows and weather labels. 70% of the dataset was used during training, while the remaining 30% was used for testing purposes. The dataset is then divided into cases (time windows) with $w = 14$, obtaining explanation cases with 14 days of weather evolution.

4.2   Methodology

The evaluation consists of leave-one-out cross-validation for each case (time window) where the k-nearest neighbors (explanation cases) are obtained using any of the similarity metrics presented in Sect. 3.1.

The quality of each explanation case is obtained by comparing the original query time series with the Euclidean distance. This distance is computed for all the timestamps in $[t-w, t]$ and then averaged to obtain the global distance to the query. This evaluation metric aims to resemble the perception of the user regarding the geometrical difference between the query and the explanation cases. In the case of several explanation cases ($k > 1$) the values for each timestamp within the time window are averaged, and this average is then compared to the query. This process is performed for the three time series (temperature, vapor pressure, and relative humidity) that compose the explanation case. The global quality of the explanation case is then computed as the root sum squared (RSS) of the three distances to the query.

Additionally, the diversity of the explanation cases is evaluated through a dispersion metric that estimates the distance between the timestamps of the retrieved explanation cases. Following the example in Fig. 3, diverse explanation cases will be scattered along the time series, whereas maximally similar cases without diversity will correspond to nearby timestamps. The dispersion metric used to measure the diversity is the average of the mutual differences between the timestamps of the k retrieved examples.

4.3   Results

Performance results are displayed in Fig. 6. This figure shows the quality of the explanation cases obtained through the similarity metrics available in CBR-fox for different values of k and both reuse strategies. The first conclusion is that there are no remarkable differences between the simple and weighted averages. This indicates that similarity values are very homogeneous without irregular differences between neighbors.

Globally, the best metric is *Edit Distance For Real Penalty (EDRP)* for an only explanation example. However, the most useful metric is the *Combined Correlation Index (CCI)* when presenting two or three explanation examples to the user. From more than five explanation cases, all the metrics perform similarly, except *Longest Common Subsequence (LCS)*, which always obtains unsatisfactory results. Further research is needed to gain insight about the deteriorating behavior of *CCI* as the value k increases.

The evaluation of the diversity of the retrieved explanation cases is presented in Fig. 7. Each plot in the figure corresponds to a similarity metric and compares the average of the mutual differences between the timestamps of the k retrieved examples between the smoothed similarity signal and the original one. As expected, diversity rises when the number of explanation cases presented to the user increases.

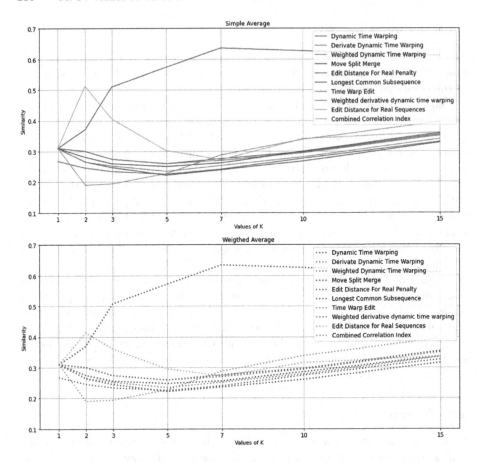

Fig. 6. Line plot showing the quality of the explanation cases obtained through the similarity metrics for different values of k and both reuse strategies: simple average (top), weighted average (bottom).

5   Conclusions

The rise of the IoT and its combination with AI (AIoT and IoE) has led to a wide range of systems based on analyzing time series corresponding to sensors' readings. These systems are primarily based on ML forecasting models such as ANNs due to their higher performance. However, these models lack enough transparency to let users understand the reasons for a given prediction. Here, CBR is a proven solution to twin the ML forecasting model and provide transparency by means of explanation cases.

In this paper, we present CBR-fox, a post-hoc sliding-window explanation-by-example method that enables the explanation of black-box forecasting models using CBR. The major novelty of this method is to consider the similarity values between the query and each explanation case as a signal. This signal results from

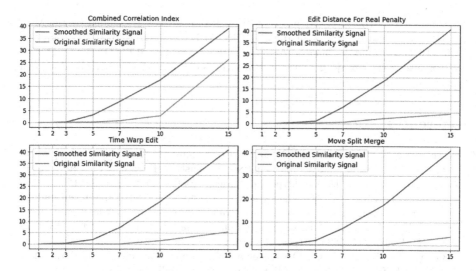

Fig. 7. Line plots comparing the diversity of the original and smoothed similarity signals for the most relevant metrics.

applying well-established similarity metrics to a case base generated by a sliding-window method that obtains a sequence of partially overlapping methods.

This way, the similarity signal can be processed to foster diversity in the explanation cases presented to the user. The application of noise removal filters, such as the HP and low-pass filters, avoids maximally similar cases that may overlap or represent a local slice of the source time series.

Additionally, we have presented a novel time series similarity metric – the Combined Correlation Index– designed explicitly for retrieving explanation examples as it is based on the comparison of shape and distance. This metric is experimentally compared to a wide range of established similarity metrics, achieving very high performance. This evaluation in the weather forecasting domain also highlights the impact of the proposed method regarding the diversity of the retrieved explanation examples.

This research opens many lines of future work. First, we will analyze the behavior of CBR-fox when reducing the overlapping of the generated cases by adding a step in the sliding window process. Additional evaluation metrics are also required to ensure the appropriateness of each similarity metric, which should be evaluated in further domains. This may lead to classifying the similarity metric according to their appropriateness to a concrete IoT domain.

The source code of CBR-fox and the dataset used for the evaluation presented in this paper are available at https://github.com/aaaimx/CBR-fox.

Acknowledgements. This research is a result of the Horizon 2020 Future and Emerging Technologies (FET) programme of the European Union through the iSee project (CHIST-ERA-19-XAI-008, PCI2020-120720-2).

Supported by the PERXAI project PID2020-114596RB-C21, funded by the Ministry of Science and Innovation of Spain (MCIN/AEI/10.13039/501100011033) and the BOSCH-UCM Honorary Chair on Artificial Intelligence applied to Internet of Things.
It is also part of projects 10428.21-P and 13933.22-P of the Tecnológico Nacional de México/IT de Mérida.

References

1. Ahmed, N.K., Atiya, A.F., El Gayar, N., El-Shishiny, H.: An empirical comparison of machine learning models for time series forecasting. Econom. Rev. **29**(5), 594–621 (2010). ISSN 07474938, https://doi.org/10.1080/07474938.2010.481556
2. Bebarta, D.K., Das, T.K., Chowdhary, C.L., Gao, X.Z.: An intelligent hybrid system for forecasting stock and forex trading signals using optimized recurrent FLANN and case-based reasoning. Int. J. Comput. Intell. Syst. **14**, 1763–1772 (2021). ISSN 1875–6883, https://doi.org/10.2991/ijcis.d.210601.001
3. Orozco-del Castillo, M.G., Ortiz-Alemán, J., Couder-Castañeda, C., Hernández-Gómez, J., Solís-Santomé, A.: High solar activity predictions through an artificial neural network. Int. J. Mod. Phys. C **28**(6) (2017). ISSN 01291831, https://doi.org/10.1142/S0129183117500759
4. Chen, L., Ng, R.: On the marriage of lp-norms and edit distance. In: Proceedings of the 2004 VLDB Conference, pp. 792–803, Morgan Kaufmann (2004). ISBN 978-0-12-088469-8, https://doi.org/10.1016/B978-012088469-8.50070-X
5. Chen, L., Özsu, M.T., Oria, V.: Robust and fast similarity search for moving object trajectories. In: Proceedings of the 2005 ACM SIGMOD International Conference on Management of Data, pp. 491–502, Association for Computing Machinery (2005). ISBN 1595930604, https://doi.org/10.1145/1066157.1066213
6. Cleveland, W.: LOWESS: a program for smoothing scatterplots by robust locally weighted regression. Am. Stat. **35**, 54 (1981)
7. Corchado, J.M., Lees, B.: A hybrid case-based model for forecasting. Appl. Artif. Intell. **15**(2), 105–127 (2001). https://doi.org/10.1080/088395101750065723
8. Delaney, E., Greene, D., Keane, M.T.: Instance-based counterfactual explanations for time series classification. In: Sánchez-Ruiz, A.A., Floyd, M.W. (eds.) ICCBR 2021. LNCS (LNAI), vol. 12877, pp. 32–47. Springer, Cham (2021). https://doi.org/10.1007/978-3-030-86957-1_3
9. Gogineni, V.R., Kondrakunta, S., Brown, D., Molineaux, M., Cox, M.T.: Probabilistic selection of case-based explanations in an underwater mine clearance domain. In: Bach, K., Marling, C. (eds.) ICCBR 2019. LNCS (LNAI), vol. 11680, pp. 110–124. Springer, Cham (2019). https://doi.org/10.1007/978-3-030-29249-2_8
10. Guidotti, R., Monreale, A., Ruggieri, S., Turini, F., Giannotti, F., Pedreschi, D.: A survey of methods for explaining black box models. ACM Comput. Surv. (CSUR) **51**(5), 1–42 (2018)
11. Jara, A.J.: Wearable internet: powering personal devices with the internet of things capabilities. In: 2014 International Conference on Identification, Information and Knowledge in the Internet of Things, p. 7 (2014). https://doi.org/10.1109/IIKI.2014.9
12. Jeong, Y.S., Jeong, M.K., Omitaomu, O.A.: Weighted dynamic time warping for time series classification. Pattern Recognit. **44**(9), 2231–2240 (2011). ISSN 0031-3203, https://doi.org/10.1016/j.patcog.2010.09.022

13. Keane, M.T., Kenny, E.M.: How case-based reasoning explains neural networks: a theoretical analysis of XAI using post-hoc explanation-by-example from a survey of ANN-CBR twin-systems. In: Bach, K., Marling, C. (eds.) Case-Based Reasoning Research and Development. ICCBR 2019. LNCS, vol. 11680, pp. 155–171. Springer, Cham (2019). ISBN 978-3-030-29249-2, https://doi.org/10.1007/978-3-030-29249-2_11

14. Keogh, E.J., Pazzani, M.J.: Derivative Dynamic Time Warping, pp. 1–11. SIAM (2001). https://doi.org/10.1137/1.9781611972719.1

15. Li, O., Liu, H., Chen, C., Rudin, C.: Deep learning for case-based reasoning through prototypes: a neural network that explains its predictions. In: Proceedings of the Thirty-Second AAAI Conference on Artificial Intelligence, AAAI'18, AAAI Press (2018). ISBN 978-1-57735-800-8

16. Li, W., Paraschiv, F., Sermpinis, G.: A data-driven explainable case-based reasoning approach for financial risk detection. Quant. Financ. **22**(12), 2257–2274 (2022)

17. Lim, B., Zohren, S., Roberts, S.: Recurrent neural filters: learning independent Bayesian filtering steps for time series prediction. In: Proceedings of the International Joint Conference on Neural Networks (2020). https://doi.org/10.1109/IJCNN48605.2020.9206906

18. Lorenzo, L., Arroyo, J.: Analysis of the cryptocurrency market using different prototype-based clustering techniques. Financ. Innov. **8**(1), 7 (2022). https://doi.org/10.1186/s40854-021-00310-9

19. Marteau, P.F.: Time warp edit distance with stiffness adjustment for time series matching. IEEE Trans. Pattern Anal. Mach. Intell. **31**(2), 306–318 (2009). https://doi.org/10.1109/TPAMI.2008.76

20. Newton, T., Meech, J.T., Stanley-Marbell, P.: Machine learning for sensor transducer conversion routines. IEEE Embed. Syst. Lett. **14**(2), 75–78 (2022). https://doi.org/10.1109/LES.2021.3129892

21. Olsson, T., Gillblad, D., Funk, P., Xiong, N.: Case-based reasoning for explaining probabilistic machine learning. Int. J. Comput. Sci. Inf. Technol. **6**, 87–101 (2014). https://doi.org/10.5121/ijcsit.2014.6206

22. Palit, A.K., Popovic, D.: Computational Intelligence in Time Series Forecasting, 1 edn. Advances in Industrial Control, Springer, London (2005). ISBN 1-85233-948-9, https://doi.org/10.1007/1-84628-184-9

23. Park, S., Jung, S., Jung, S., Rho, S., Hwang, E.: Sliding window-based lightgbm model for electric load forecasting using anomaly repair. J. Supercomput. **77**, 12857–12878 (2021)

24. Patel, A., Swathika, O.G.: Forecasting off-grid solar power generation using case-based reasoning algorithm for a small-scale system. In: Artificial Intelligence and Machine Learning in Smart City Planning, pp. 257–266. Elsevier (2023)

25. Pham, N.T., Nguyen, S.D., Nguyen, V.S.T., Pham, B.N.H., Dang, D.N.M.: Speech emotion recognition using overlapping sliding window and Shapley additive explainable deep neural network. J. Inf. Telecommun. 1–19 (2023)

26. Sakoe, H., Chiba, S.: Dynamic programming algorithm optimization for spoken word recognition. IEEE Trans. Acoust. Speech Signal Process. **26**(1), 43–49 (1978). https://doi.org/10.1109/TASSP.1978.1163055

27. Sen, R., Yu, H.F., Dhillon, I.: Think globally, act locally: a deep neural network approach to high-dimensional time series forecasting. Adv. Neural Inf. Process. Syst. **32**(NeurIPS), 1–10 (2019). ISSN 10495258

28. Smyth, B., McClave, P.: Similarity vs. diversity. In: Aha, D.W., Watson, I. (eds.) Case-Based Reasoning Research and Development. ICCBR 2001. LNCS, vol. 2080,

pp. 347–361. Springer, Berlin, Heidelberg (2001). ISBN 978-3-540-44593-7, https://doi.org/10.1007/3-540-44593-5_25

29. Stefan, A., Athitsos, V., Das, G.: The move-split-merge metric for time series. IEEE Trans. Knowl. Data Eng. **25**(6), 1425–1438 (2013). https://doi.org/10.1109/TKDE.2012.88

30. Vishnubhatla, A.: IoT based air pollution monitoring through Telit bravo kit. In: 2022 International Conference on Applied Artificial Intelligence and Computing (ICAAIC), pp. 1751–1755 (2022). https://doi.org/10.1109/ICAAIC53929.2022.9793252

31. Vishwas, B.V., Patel, A.: Time-Series Characteristics, pp. 1–21. Apress, Berkeley, CA (2020). ISBN 978-1-4842-5992-4, https://doi.org/10.1007/978-1-4842-5992-4_1

32. Vlachos, M., Kollios, G., Gunopulos, D.: Discovering similar multidimensional trajectories. In: Proceedings 18th International Conference on Data Engineering, pp. 673–684 (2002). https://doi.org/10.1109/ICDE.2002.994784

33. Zhang, J., Tao, D.: Empowering things with intelligence: a survey of the progress, challenges, and opportunities in artificial intelligence of things. IEEE Internet Things J. **8**(10), 7789–7817 (2021). https://doi.org/10.1109/JIOT.2020.3039359

Case Base Maintenance

Group Fairness in Case-Based Reasoning

Shania Mitra[1], Ditty Mathew[2], Deepak P.[1,3(✉)], and Sutanu Chakraborti[1]

[1] Indian Institute of Technology Madras, Chennai, India
shaniamitra9@gmail.com, deepaksp@acm.org, sutanuc@cse.iitm.ac.in
[2] University of Trier, Trier, Germany
[3] Queen's University Belfast, Belfast, UK
mathew@uni-trier.de

Abstract. There has been a significant recent interest in algorithmic fairness within data-driven systems. In this paper, we consider group fairness within Case-based Reasoning. Group fairness targets to ensure parity of outcomes across pre-specified sensitive groups, defined on the basis of extant entrenched discrimination. Addressing the context of binary decision choice scenarios over binary sensitive attributes, we develop three separate fairness interventions that operate at different stages of the CBR process. These techniques, called Label Flipping (LF), Case Weighting (CW) and Weighted Adaptation (WA), use distinct strategies to enhance group fairness in CBR decision making. Through an extensive empirical evaluation over several popular datasets and against natural baseline methods, we show that our methods are able to achieve significant enhancements in fairness at low detriment to accuracy, thus illustrating effectiveness of our methods at advancing fairness.

Keywords: Fairness · Group Fairness · Case-based Reasoning

1 Introduction

Algorithmic fairness [24] has attracted significant scholarly attention in recent times. While this has seen most interest in the case of machine learning (ML) [11], fairness has been explored within allied data-driven areas such as retrieval and recommenders [15] and natural language processing [10]. There has been emerging recent interest in fairness within Case-Based Reasoning (CBR) as well, with the first paper on algorithmic fairness in CBR appearing recently [8].

Fairness, as a concept with origins and a long legacy in the social sciences, is a deeply nuanced and contested construct. There are several different definitions of fairness [22], many of which are in conflict with one another. Two streams of fairness concepts, viz., individual and group fairness [14], have been subject to much study within data-driven learning. Individual fairness targets to ensure that all objects are treated uniformly, so that *similar* objects (similarity defined appropriate to the task) are accorded similar outcomes. In sharp contrast, group fairness is anchored on the notion of *sensitive attributes* (e.g., gender, race, nationality, religion), and seeks to ensure that outcomes are fairly

S. Massie and S. Chakraborti (Eds.): ICCBR 2023, LNAI 14141, pp. 217–232, 2023.
https://doi.org/10.1007/978-3-031-40177-0_14

distributed across groups defined on the basis of such sensitive attributes. Sensitive attributes are not defined at a technical level, but chosen on the basis of extant evidence of historical and contemporary discrimination. Group fairness, often referred to variously as outcome fairness and distributive justice, is thus focused on ensuring that the workings of the algorithms are not configured in a way that some sensitive groupings are advantaged more than others. Adherence to group fairness may thus require that individuals who are similar on a task-level basis be treated differently (leading to possible violations of individual fairness), so the outcomes along the sensitive groupings are uniform. In contemporary society, the workings of meritocracy could be thought of as close to the spirit of individual fairness, whereas affirmative action and policies targeted to level off gender and race gaps (in pay, education, or other forms of achievement) are aligned with the notion of group fairness. It is also useful to note that there are latent similarities in the structures of these notions [6].

CBR systems, in sharp contrast to mainstream ML, are non-parametric models in that they do not involve the construction of a statistical model of a fixed and predetermined capacity. This has significant ramifications in analyzing, assimilating and mitigating algorithmic unfairness within them. As a case in point, a recent fairness intervention in a non-parametric local neighborhood-based outlier detection mechanism [12] was based more on statistical corrections using local neighborhood properties, as opposed to the usage of fairness optimization objectives in conventional ML tasks (e.g., [3]). The only work on fair CBR [8] is also divergent from the additional objective approach in that it adopts a metric learning approach, which involves modifying the similarity knowledge container to achieve the desired fairness goal. Their model, FairRet [8], is focused on mitigating underestimation bias towards minority protected groups. This, while using sensitive groups, may be seen as using a restricted form of group fairness.

In this paper, for the first time to our best knowledge, we initiate research into group fairness - defined as parity of outcomes across sensitive groups - in case-based reasoning. Our focus is on CBR systems that assign binary outcomes and on enhancing uniformity of outcomes across two groups defined over a binary sensitive attribute (e.g., male/female, white/non-white). We develop separate fairness-targeted interventions at three stages viz., *pre-processing*, *weighting* and *retrieval*. While our pre-processing intervention targets changing the data labelling in a targeted manner, our weighting approach assigns weights to individual cases to enhance fairness in outcomes. The third approach is an adaptation-stage approach where the aggregation mechanism is modified towards the fairness goal. Through extensive empirical validation over several real-world datasets, we illustrate the effectiveness of our methods in reducing the disparity of outcomes across the sensitive attributes.

2   Related Work

While there has been much work on fairness within ML [11], there has been, as we mentioned earlier, just one prior work on fairness in CBR [8]. Fairness has also been explored within the context of information retrieval; this relates to CBR in that CBR also encompasses a retrieval step, though it goes much further than just presenting retrieval results. We briefly summarize related work within this section. We particularly focus on work relating to group fairness within this section, given the focus of this paper.

2.1 Fairness in Retrieval and Recommender Systems

Fairness considerations in retrieval and recommenders [15] have centred on ensuring diversity across sensitive attributes within the top-k retrieved results. This has often been termed as proportional fairness [30] given that the intent is to ensure that the top-k results reflect the proportions of sensitive attribute groups within the broader dataset. These are often realized using bespoke constraints such as diversity constraints [27]. Apart from demographic-sensitive groupings, fairness has also been explored over political bias [19] and popularity [31]. Another line of exploration has been to relax the query-level fairness proportionality constraint and ensure that there are no statistically significant deviations from proportionality across queries [29].

Apart from such generally applicable work on fairness in retrieval, fairness has been explored within specific contexts of retrieval, such as multi-stakeholder interactions within recommender systems viz., 2-sided fairness [23]. Work on group recommender systems [20, 26] has focused on delivering better recommendations to groups of people by aggregating individual preferences of group members, modelling social factors such as personality awareness and trust between them. These approaches, however, do not concern themselves with the disparity between different groups and thus, have limited applicability in group-fair CBR. Novel fairness constructs such as attention fairness have been devised to account for the case that human users tend to focus on the top results within an ordered result display paradigm [5]. While the above interventions are interesting and pertinent to the retrieval stage, fairness in CBR systems would need to be conceptualized across the different stages. For example, ensuring proportional representations in the results may do little to further fairness, unless the downstream aggregation/adaptation step is able to make use of it. Thus, such retrieval-focused work has limited applicability within the context of fair CBR.

2.2 Fair Local Outliers

Local neighborhood-based approaches have been quite popular within the task of outlier detection [9, 18]. While these have very limited relevance to CBR beyond the usage of local neighborhood-based retrieval, their meta structure of retrieval followed by bespoke processing of retrieved sets to arrive at a decision resonates with the spirit of CBR. The downstream processing is very specific to outlier detection and is thus highly divergent from the intent and structure of CBR systems.

A recent work [12] considers a fairness-oriented adaptation of arguably the most popular local neighborhood-based outlier detection algorithm, LOF [9].

The proposed method, FairLOF [2], does statistical 'corrections' for fairness at three levels, viz., the diversity of local neighborhood as measured over sensitive attributes, the overall representational skew between groups defined over sensitive attributes, and corrections for the extent to which the similarity knowledge container embeds sensitive attribute knowledge within itself. The corrections are focused on fairness insofar as they relate to the downstream statistical processing of the LOF method, and are, thus, again of limited applicability to the considerations of CBR.

There has been some work in detecting outlying cases for case base maintenance viz., the Repeated Edited Nearest Neighbour approach (RENN) [1]. Here, a case is considered noisy and is removed if its class label differs from the majority of its k nearest neighbors. While this case base maintenance paradigm aligns with the spirit of the CW approach that we present, RENN does not relate to sensitive attributes, and is thus orthogonal to group fairness.

2.3   FairRet: Algorithmic Fairness in CBR

We now briefly summarize a recent work [8], the only extant work on algorithmic fairness in CBR to our best knowledge. This work focuses on addressing an intricate notion of algorithmic discrimination called *underestimation bias*. We illustrate this by using a simplistic example. Consider a binary choice scenario such as those encountered in job application shortlisting, where each application is to be either shortlisted or rejected. Let us suppose that the shortlisting success rates for males and females are 50% and 40%, respectively, reflecting gender discrimination as often observed in society. However, the algorithmic decision-making process may further accentuate this skew and offer an even lower success rate, say 30%, to female applicants. This is an instance of *underestimation bias*, the focus of *FairRet*. The underestimation, in this case, may be quantified as 0.75 (i.e., 30/40, expressed as a percentage) ([8], Sec 2.1), and is sought to be remedied by modifying the similarity knowledge container using metric learning approaches realized using multi-objective particle swarm optimization.

It may be noted that rectifying underestimation bias would bring the success rates for females to 40%, which is still significantly lower than the success rates for males, which stands at 50%. Thus, *FairRet* is aligned with fairness conceptualizations such as *separation* [4] that seek to equalize deviations or error rates (cf. success rates) for different sensitive groups, thus implicitly considering the decision-profile embodied in the labelled data as the reference standard. In other words, addressing underestimation bias would not achieve group fairness which is often conceptualized as *independence*, the notion that seeks equalizing success rates across sensitive groupings. Independence, often referred to as statistical parity [16], requires that there be a parity in the distribution of outcomes across sensitive attribute groups. Thus, group fairness (or statistical parity or independence), as instantiated within our example scenario, would target that the success rates for females be enhanced to 50%, or otherwise equalized across the gender groups; for example, by equating the success rates in decision making for both groups at 45%.

Our work, in contrast to *FairRet*, considers achieving *independence* or *group fairness*, which is about equalizing success rates across demographic groups. To summarize, in contrast to *FairRet* that uses the decision profile within the labelled data as the target for fairness, our focus is on using uniformized success rates across sensitive groups as the fairness target. Yet, given the high-level similarity in that biased behavior is sought to be mitigated and given that *FairRet* is the only extant work on fairness in CBR, we use *FairRet* as a baseline.

3   Problem Definition

We first outline the CBR decision making context we address, followed by the targeted fairness requirement and the fairness metric which we consider.

3.1   CBR Decision Making Scenario

Consider a dataset $\mathcal{X} = \{\ldots, X, \ldots\}$, where each element X corresponds to a case. X, as is typical of cases in CBR, comprises two parts, the data d and the label l. Additionally, each X is also associated with a value for a sensitive attribute denoted as s. Thus, $X = [d, l, s]$; d, l and s will have overloaded interpretations for ease of ensuing narration, but the intended interpretation will be clear from the context. As a first work towards group fairness, we restrict our attention to binary decision choices (so, $l \in \{0, 1\}$) and binary sensitive attributes (so, $s \in \{0, 1\}$). In a concrete scenario within a job shortlisting context, each X could comprise a historical job application (as d), the decision accorded to it (as l), with s denoting a sensitive demographic of the applicant that is known to be a facet of social discrimination (e.g., male/non-male, or white/non-white).

We now consider a CBR system $\mathcal{C}$ which makes use of the case base $\mathcal{X}$ to make decisions over an incoming stream of data points (job applications), which we will denote as $\mathcal{Y} = \{\ldots, Y, \ldots\}$. Each data point is, much like the case of $\mathcal{X}$, associated with a value for the sensitive attribute too. Thus, $Y = [d, -, s]$. The task of the CBR system is to fill up the missing label for elements in $\mathcal{Y}$ with its predictions. We will denote the labelling choice offered by the CBR system as $l = \mathcal{C}(Y)$. In the interest of general applicability across diverse scenarios, we would like the CBR system to not explicitly refer to the sensitive attribute of Y in making its decision; thus, $\mathcal{C}(Y)$ does not depend on s. Within the job shortlisting scenario, this amounts to creating a CBR system that will make choices over applications without explicitly referring to gender/race membership.

3.2   Group Fairness

Having laid out the CBR decision-making scenario and pertinent notations, we are now ready to present our group fairness consideration in technical terms. Consider that $\mathcal{C}$ has been applied over all elements of $\mathcal{Y}$. We would be able to measure the success rates for the separate demographic subsets of $\mathcal{Y}$ under the decisions offered by $\mathcal{C}$.

$$SR_{\mathcal{C}}(\mathcal{Y}, s = 0) = \frac{\sum_{[d,-,s] \in \mathcal{Y}} \mathbb{I}(l = 1 \wedge s = 0)}{\sum_{[d,-,s] \in \mathcal{Y}} \mathbb{I}(s = 0)} \tag{1}$$

where $\mathbb{I}(.)$ is the identity function which evaluates to 1 when the inner condition is satisfied and 0 otherwise. Simply stated, $SR_{\mathcal{C}}(\mathcal{Y}, s = 0)$ is the success rates of the $s = 0$ subset of $\mathcal{Y}$ under $\mathcal{C}$. Analogously, $SR_{\mathcal{C}}(\mathcal{Y}, s = 1)$ is also defined. Our intent is to ensure that the success rates of the separate demographic groups are as similar as possible.

$$SR_{\mathcal{C}}(\mathcal{Y}, s = 0) \approx SR_{\mathcal{C}}(\mathcal{Y}, s = 1) \tag{2}$$

3.3   Disparity

Our focus is on ensuring that the design of $\mathcal{C}$ is such that the disparity between success rates of sensitive sub-groups is minimized as much as possible. Towards this, we use statistical disparity as the evaluation metric, defined as the following:

$$SDisp(\mathcal{C}, \mathcal{Y}) = |SR_{\mathcal{C}}(\mathcal{Y}, s = 0) - SR_{\mathcal{C}}(\mathcal{Y}, s = 1)| \tag{3}$$

This, or its variants, have been explored in various efforts in fair AI literature. For example, the above metric corresponds to the *violation of statistical parity* metric in [21] (Sec 2.3.1) and demographic (dis)parity in [25] (Sec 3.2). This will form our primary metric towards profiling the methods on group fairness in our empirical evaluation. As obvious lower values of $SDisp$ are more desirable.

4   GFCBR: Our Methods for Group Fair CBR

In this section, we now outline our suite of methods for group fairness within CBR, which we will denote as GFCBR. This comprises three approaches viz., *Label flipping* (LF) as a pre-processing method, *Case weighting* (CW) as a method to weigh cases based on their context, and *Weighted adaptation* (WA) as a method for aggregating/adapting retrieved results to form a labelling decision.

4.1   LF: Label Flipping

As outlined in Sect. 2.3, the target of group fairness may be misaligned with the labelling in the data within the case base $\mathcal{X}$. Even if the data labelling offers males and females success rates of 50% and 40% respectively, the intent of group fairness requires us to produce equalized success rates, one that cannot obviously be achieved by strict adherence to labelling patterns. In this backdrop, our label flipping technique targets to alter the ground truth labellings in the case base so that it becomes feasible for $\mathcal{C}$ to achieve group fairness.

CBR Model: To ensure generality of the label flipping-based pre-processing method, we assume a very simple design for a CBR decision maker which we outline upfront. Given a similarity function to judge similarities between cases, the CBR decision for an object is given as follows:

$$C_\mathcal{X}(d) = MajVote(top\text{-}k_\mathcal{X}(d)) \tag{4}$$

where $C_\mathcal{X}$ denotes the CBR system working over the case base $\mathcal{X}$, $top\text{-}k_\mathcal{X}(d)$ denotes the top-k most similar data objects to d from within $\mathcal{X}$, and $MajVote(.)$ simply computes the majority vote (recollect we are dealing with binary labellings) from across the objects. To avoid ties, k may be set to an odd number.

Leave-One-Out CBR: Towards ease of describing the label flipping approach, we introduce a leave-one-out instantiation of C which we denote as C^{L1O}. The leave-one-out CBR system operating over $\mathcal{X}$ takes each element of $\mathcal{X}$, $X = [d, l, s]$ and determines a label for it using the *other* objects in $\mathcal{X}$ as the case base. This determination may be different from the object's label l since the neighbors of the object may mostly have the other label. Once decisions are made for each element of $\mathcal{X}$ using the leave-one-out approach, we can compute the $SDisp(C^{L1O}, \mathcal{X})$ as the disparity between the success rates of the $s = 1$ and $s = 0$ subgroups within $\mathcal{X}$ when assessed using the decisions from the C^{L1O} model.

Label Flipping Approach: Having outlined the context and necessary background, we now describe our label flipping approach, which is outlined in Algorithm 1. The label flipping approach considers modifying the case base $\mathcal{X}$ by flipping some labels in its cases greedily, with an intent of choosing to flip the label of the object that reduces $SDisp(C^{L1O}, \mathcal{X})$ most, at each step. Once the $SDisp(.,.)$ stabilizes - i.e., further label flips cannot decrease the disparity any further - the flipping process is stopped. We also introduce an additional parameter called the budget b, which allows for stopping earlier as necessary. The budget is specified as a percentage of the case base (e.g., 1%) which restricts the label flipping approach to making at most $b\%$ label flips in the dataset, even if convergence is not achieved by then. The high-level intuition behind this label flipping approach is that a case base over which C^{L1O} is able to achieve low disparity would facilitate group fair decisions for new cases too.

Once the label flipping process is complete, we end up with a modified case base $\mathcal{X}'$ which differs from $\mathcal{X}$ in that some object labels have been flipped. The modified CBR system is simply $C_{\mathcal{X}'}$, which differs from $C_\mathcal{X}$ in that it works over the modified dataset. This modified CBR system $C_{\mathcal{X}'}$ is now ready to be applied over a new stream of cases - such as an unseen dataset $\mathcal{Y}$ - and that it works over a label-flipped dataset would aid it in achieving lower $SDisp$ over $\mathcal{Y}$. We note that this approach may be seen as creating an alternative case base which would be used for decision making. The original experiences in the case base may be maintained separately as a version of record.

4.2   CW: Case Weighting

Complementary to actually changing labellings in the data as the strategy in LF, CW adopts a different strategy towards the same goal of enhancing group

---

Algorithm 1: LABEL FLIPPING (LF)

Input: Case base $\mathcal{X}$, k, budget b
Output: A modified case base $\mathcal{X}'$
$\mathcal{X}' = \mathcal{X}$
while $SDisp(\mathcal{C}^{L1O}, \mathcal{X}')$ *has not converged and budget b has not been reached*
do

$\quad\Big|\quad X^* = \arg\min_{X \in \mathcal{X}'} SDisp(\mathcal{C}^{L1O}, \mathcal{X}' \cup \{labelflip(X)\} - \{X\})$
$\quad\Big|\quad \mathcal{X}' = \mathcal{X}' \cup \{labelflip(X^*)\} - \{X^*\})$

end
return $\mathcal{X}'$

---

fairness. The strategy within CW is to augment each case with a numeric weight within $[0, 1]$ in such a way that cases that are aligned with group fairness get a higher weighting than others. We use the leave-one-out mechanism introduced in Sect. 4.1 in determining case weights.

Advantaged Group: In our scenario of binary decision choices, the existence of disparity entails that one of the sensitive groups has a higher success rate than the other. In typical scenarios involving systemic discrimination, the advantaged group is often consistent. This could be *males* in the case of gender as the sensitive attribute or *white* in the case of ethnicity. Without loss of generality, we will assume that $s = 1$ is the advantaged group.

Neighborhood Misaligned Cases: Consider the leave-one-out mechanism, $\mathcal{C}^{L1O}$, applied over a case $X = [d, l, s] \in \mathcal{X}$. The decision by $\mathcal{C}^{L1O}$, denoted $l^{L1O} = \mathcal{C}^{L1O}(d)$, could be different from the actual label associated with X, i.e., l. These cases, where $l \neq l^{L1O}$, indicate that they are, to some extent, misaligned with their neighborhood. The decision preference of their neighboring cases, as reflected through $\mathcal{C}^{L1O}$, is different from their own label. Towards designing CW, we posit that such cases with neighborhood misalignment could be differentially weighted towards enhancing group fairness.

Differentiated Weighting: We now outline the differentiated weighting heuristic, which is at the core of the CW technique. Cases that are aligned with their neighborhood, i.e., with $l = l^{L1O}$, are assigned a weight of unity. For neighborhood misaligned cases, we set weights based on how well their neighborhood is aligned with the goal of group fairness. We will illustrate this briefly.

On considering the scenario of cases from the disadvantaged group, denoted as $s = 0$, if the neighborhood decision (l^{L1O}) indicates a positive outcome, but the actual label is negative, it implies that the case is in a neighborhood that supports group fairness, since the prediction favours the selection of disadvantaged cases. Group fairness means that cases from the disadvantaged group should be assigned positive outcomes more often than what the labels suggest. We assign a weight of $\lambda \in [0, 1]$ to such cases, since, the prediction albeit incorrect is one that promotes the selection of minorities. Second, if the neighborhood decision is in favour of a negative outcome, but the actual case label is positive, we judge this to be an outlier, and assign a weight of 0.

In other words, our case weight is dependent on how well the neighborhood, whose decision is reflected in l^{L1O}, is aligned with the notion of group fairness. The above logic is flipped in the case of the advantaged group, $s = 1$, since we would like them to be assigned positive decisions at a lower rate than that supported by the labels. This weighting scheme is summarized in Eq. 5. λ serves as a hyperparameter to this approach which would need to be pre-specified.

$$
w(X = [d, l, s]) = \begin{cases}
1 & l^{L1O} = l \\
\lambda & s = 0 \wedge l^{L1O} = 1 \wedge l = 0 \\
0 & s = 0 \wedge l^{L1O} = 0 \wedge l = 1 \\
0 & s = 1 \wedge l^{L1O} = 1 \wedge l = 0 \\
\lambda & s = 1 \wedge l^{L1O} = 0 \wedge l = 1
\end{cases}
\tag{5}
$$

Algorithm 2 is then a simple application of this weighting scheme in round-robin fashion across the cases in the case base.

Algorithm 2: CASE WEIGHTING (CW)

Input: Case base $\mathcal{X}$, k
Output: Weights for each case in $\mathcal{X}$, denoted $w(X), \forall X \in \mathcal{X}$
for $X = [d, l, s] \in \mathcal{X}$ **do**
$\quad | \quad l^{L1O} = \mathcal{C}_{\mathcal{X}}^{L1O}(X)$
$\quad | \quad$ Set $w(X)$ as in Eq. 5
end
return $\{w(X) | X \in \mathcal{X}\}$

CW-Weighted CBR: The weights assigned to cases would need to be exploited in decision making, should a CBR system working over a weighted case base is to provide enhanced group fairness. The natural way would be to aggregate the labels from the top-k neighbors for a new case using weighted aggregation, and choose the label associated with the highest aggregate weight. This is illustrated as below:

$$
\mathcal{C}_{\mathcal{X}}^{CW}(d) = \underset{label \in \{0,1\}}{\arg\max} \sum_{X=[d,l,s] \in top-k_{\mathcal{X}}(d)} w(X) \times \mathbb{I}(label = l)
\tag{6}
$$

In our empirical evaluation, we will consider such a CBR system while profiling the effectiveness of CW.

4.3   WA: Weighted Adaptation

Our third technique, WA, adopts a group-fairness oriented strategy that operates much more downstream than either LF or CW. In particular, the case base $\mathcal{X}$ is kept as such, without being subject to label modifications or apriori neighborhood-based weightings. However, cases that are retrieved as similar ones to a query case are accorded weights based solely on their (l, s) combination, while adapting their labels to make a decision on the query case.

Weight Formulation: The weight formulation in WA, unlike that in CW, is not dependent on the neighborhood of the case and is solely determined by the combination of (l, s) values associated with a case. Consider a particular (l, s) combination, such as $(l = 1, s = 0)$; this denotes a case where a positive outcome is assigned to a data object from the disadvantaged group. Similarly, $(l = 1, s = 1)$ denotes a case where a positive outcome is associated with a data object from the advantaged group. In the interest of ensuring group fairness, we would naturally like the former to have a higher influence in any decision-making process. Similarly, among $(l = 0, s = 0)$ and $(l = 0, s = 1)$, we may want the former to have a lower weighting in our interest to push up the success rate for the disadvantaged group. Additionally, we would like the differentiated weighting to reflect the quantum of the extant disparity in success rates across sensitive groups, as estimated using the leave-one-out mechanism. Our weighting scheme is outlined below:

$$w(l, s) = \frac{\frac{1}{|\mathcal{X}|} \times \sum_{X \in \mathcal{X}} \mathbb{I}(\mathcal{C}^{L1O}(X) = l)}{\frac{1}{\sum_{X \in \mathcal{X}} \mathbb{I}(X.s=s)} \times \sum_{X \in \mathcal{X}} \mathbb{I}(\mathcal{C}^{L1O}(X) = l \wedge X.s = s)} = \frac{p_{L1O}(l)}{p_{L1O}(l|s)} \quad (7)$$

The weighting for a case with $(l = 1, s = 0)$ would simply be the ratio of the rate of $l = 1$ decisions by the $\mathcal{C}^{L1O}$ system, to the rate of $l = 1$ decisions by the same system for $s = 0$ data objects. The shorthand representation at the right end of Eq. 7 illustrates the notion in more intuitive notation using probabilities and conditional probabilities. Suppose the overall success rate is 50%, with the disadvantaged group recording a success rate of 40% and the advantaged group recording 60%, the weight associated with positive-labelled data objects from the disadvantaged and advantaged group would respectively be 1.25 ($= \frac{0.5}{0.4}$) and 0.83 ($= \frac{0.5}{0.6}$). Thus, disadvantaged objects bearing a positive label get a higher say in the process, in alignment with the spirit of group fairness. If the overall success rate of 50% is borne out of a higher disparity - say, 70% and 30% for the advantaged and disadvantaged groups - the analogous weightings become more divergent, at 1.67 and 0.71. This illustrates how the quantum of extant disparity factors into the weightings.

Given that we address the binary decision choice scenario with binary sensitive attributes, there are only four distinct (l, s) combinations. Thus, each case would be associated with one of four weights, making WA an extremely simple weighting formulation.

WA-Weighted CBR: The WA weights, as introduced above, are incorporated into the decision-making process analogously to the case of CW weights.

$$\mathcal{C}_{\mathcal{X}}^{WA}(d) = \arg\max_{label \in \{0,1\}} \sum_{X=[d,l,s] \in top-k_{\mathcal{X}}(d)} w(l, s) \times \mathbb{I}(label = l) \quad (8)$$

As in the case of CW, we will use $\mathcal{C}^{WA}$ in our empirical evaluation to profile group fairness.

4.4 Discussion

All of the above three techniques involve the usage of the leave-one-out scheme, often multiple times. Given that all three techniques keep the similarity measure (i.e., the similarity knowledge container) consistent, one may pre-compute the nearest neighbor set for each object in the case base beforehand, and simply look-up nearest neighbors, rather than computing the top-k neighbors afresh. Such pre-computation would render the implementation of the techniques quite inexpensive in computational terms. Further, all our methods are best implemented as a pre-processing scheme, which may be performed once upfront at the CBR system deployment time, and do not have any further bearing on query response times. This allays computational cost considerations.

5 Experimental Evaluation

We now present an empirical analysis of our proposed approaches on several real-world datasets against the *FairRet* baseline.

5.1 Datasets, Setup and Evaluation Setting

We first start by describing our datasets and experimental/evaluation setup.

Datasets/Setup: We use four popular binary labelled datasets that have been popular in fairness-related studies viz., COMPAS violent recidivism [13], UCI Credit Card [28], Census [17], and Exemplar [7]. The COMPAS

Table 1. Dataset Summary.

Dataset	Number of Records	Protected Attribute	Percentage Disadvantaged
COMPAS	4743	Sex	19.8%
UCICC	30000	Gender	39.6%
Census	48842	Sex	33.2%
Exemplar	37607	Age	32.8%

dataset is used to predict violent recidivism, while the UCI Credit Card (UCICC) dataset predicts the risk of credit card default. The Census dataset, often called the Adult Income dataset, aims to predict income, and the Exemplar dataset predicts income brackets based on age (already binarized in the dataset, perhaps as *young* and *elderly*). In all of these datasets, gender/sex is a protected attribute, except for Exemplar, where age is used as the protected attribute. Table 1 summarizes the key statistics of each dataset, including the number of samples and the proportion of the minority group. Towards using these datasets in our empirical validation, we split each dataset into three parts: 70% as the case base (i.e., $\mathcal{X}$), 10% for validation, and 20% for evaluation (i.e., $\mathcal{Y}$). Unless mentioned otherwise, we consistently set $k = 5$ and $b = 2\%$ (LF), with λ tuned based on the validation set. Apart from comparing against *FairRet*, our main baseline, we also indicate the results achieved by a simple majority-voting based CBR system over the dataset; this will be denoted as *Base*.

Evaluation Metrics: Our primary evaluation metric, as introduced in Sect. 3.3, is the disparity in the outcome (measured as success or failure rate within the context of binary decision scenarios), which we would like to be as low as possible. We express disparity as the difference in percentage success rate and thus may be interpreted as a percentage. Typical fairness-agnostic algorithms target to achieve as high an accuracy as possible. In seeking to heed an additional constraint, that of fairness, it is natural to expect that the attention to accuracy, and thus, the accuracy achieved, will be affected. Yet, we can potentially claim some success as long as the fairness gains are significantly higher than the accuracy detriment. Thus, disparity and accuracy are the focus of our empirical evaluation.

5.2   Disparity Results

Table 2. Summary of Disparity Results.

Dataset	Label	Base	FairRet	LF	CW	WA
COMPAS	8.6%	6.3%	2.9%	**0.3%**	5.2%	0.6%
UCICC	3.4%	1.8%	1.7%	0.5%	1.1%	**0.2%**
Census	19.5%	17.8%	2.6%	7.9%	2.6%	**1.9%**
Exemplar	13.7%	8.1%	6.7%	6.3%	**0.5%**	2.2%

Our summary of disparity results appears in Table 2. The base system is seen to record a high disparity, even recording a high of ≈18% in the Census dataset. The disparity as assessed using the ground truth labels over the test set, is also shown for reference under the column *Label* in Table 2. *FairRet* is seen to bring down the disparity significantly from *Base* and *Label* in most cases. However, in each dataset, one of our methods ends up recording the lowest disparity, sometimes achieving levels as low as 0.2%. In particular, *WA* and *CW* beat the *FairRet* method in each dataset. This is quite expected, since the target of *Fair-Ret* is just to rectify underestimation bias, whereas our methods target to go further, and towards full parity of success (failure) rates.

The performance of the *LF* method deserves closer attention. The *LF* method is extremely effective for COMPAS and UCICC, whereas the effectiveness in the other datasets is not yet to desirable levels; in fact, it fares worse than *FairRet* on the Census dataset. *LF*, it may be recollected, is a post-processing method which makes use of the simple CBR system; thus, it is quite limited in its ability to address the fairness consideration, unless the extant unfairness may be attributed to a small number of labels. Its greedy choice of the label to flip is another limiting factor, as we will see in a later section.

In summary, our methods are able to achieve very low levels of disparity, and their effectiveness in advancing the group fairness consideration is very apparent from the results in Table 2. It is notable that the results are at <1% level in two datasets, indicating that the results are already very close to perfect group fairness.

5.3 Accuracy Results

Table 3 records the accuracy profile of our methods and the baselines. As expected, the *Base* CBR system achieves the best accuracy, with being truthful to labels being its sole focus. The key analysis point in this case is

Table 3. Summary of Accuracy Results.

Dataset	Base	FairRet	LF	CW	WA
COMPAS	**91.59%**	86.60%	84.31%	86.05%	84.27%
UCICC	**81.65%**	79.39%	78.92%	78.84%	78.24%
Census	**81.82%**	77.00%	79.78%	79.31%	79.10%
Exemplar	**86.46%**	79.62%	84.12%	79.56%	78.40%

that of the comparison between *FairRet* and our methods. While our methods record, for most cases, a significant improvement over *FairRet* and *Base* in terms of fairness, we would expect that there would be an analogous drop in accuracy for our methods. The effectiveness of our methods depends on how low that drop is, when measured against *FairRet*. We can see that the drop in accuracy for our methods against *FairRet* is limited to, in most cases in the ≈1% range, which contrasts favourably against the significant fairness gains analyzed earlier. This indicates that our methods are able to operate at an accuracy configuration similar to *FairRet*, while achieving moderate to significant fairness gains over it. In one case, that of Census, it is notable that our methods achieve an improvement in accuracy over *FairRet*, which is more than encouraging.

5.4 Parameter Sensitivity Analyses

Having established the effectiveness of our methods to improve fairness achievement at low costs to accuracy across a number of datasets, we now turn our attention to analyzing the sensitivity of our methods to their hyper-parameters. One may recollect that there are two hyper-parameters among our methods, the budget b which determines the number of label flips in LF, and the parameter λ within CW which determines the weights of some cases. This is in addition to the CBR neighborhood size parameter, i.e., k.

Table 4. Analysis of Flips by LF.

Dataset	#Flips	% of Dataset
COMPAS	41	0.86%
UCICC	37	0.12%
Census	78	0.16%
Exemplar	54	0.14%

Parameters Within Our Methods. We now analyze the two parameters within our methods viz., flipping budget b (LF) and weighting parameter λ (CW).

Label Flipping Budget: While we set $b = 2\%$ to allow for up to 2% label flips, the label flipping procedure stopped far earlier due to convergence in disparity (recall the stopping condition in Algorithm 1). As shown in Table 4, LF stopped after a few scores of flips even in our larger datasets. While it is promising to note that the fairness improvements achieved by LF are at the expense of just a few label flips, deepening the effectiveness of the LF technique may require devising a new non-greedy heuristic to continue label flips even when the disparity converges within the context of a single decision step.

Weighting Parameter in CW, λ: Another parameter within our methods is the weighting parameter in CW, denoted as λ. As indicated earlier, this was determined based on the validation set. Yet, across the widely varying datasets, a $\lambda \approx 0.1$ was found to be the most suitable value. This indicates that λ is not highly sensitive to changes in datasets, and a reasonably small value, one that has the ability to signal the direction of the intended change (wrt disparity), is what matters.

Neighborhood Size
The generic CBR parameter, that of the choice of neighborhood size, has been consistently set to $k = 5$ in our experiments. We did observe a small but consistent trend across variations in k, across datasets. Higher values of k led to improved fairness at the cost of reduced accuracy and vice versa. This is intuitively explained in that higher values of k lead to attention to wider neighborhoods, expanding the remit of the fairness interventions that are employed. These trends remained consistent across datasets; this could mean that k could work as a knob parameter to tune the attention to fairness.

6   Conclusions and Future Work

We considered the task of designing group fair CBR schemes, which seek to ensure that the disparity in outcomes across demographic groups is minimized. We developed three techniques, a pre-processing based label flipping scheme (LF), a contextual case weighting scheme (CW) and a weighted case-adaptation methodology (WA). We outlined how they would facilitate group fairness in CBR through various distinct ways. Further, in an empirical evaluation across multiple real-world datasets, we illustrated the empirical improvements in fairness that our methods achieve. Our experiments illustrate that improved fairness is achieved at low cost to accuracy, making them effective fairness-oriented CBR techniques.

Future Work. While our separate methods were designed for fairness interventions at different stages of the CBR process, it would be interesting to understand the complementarity between these methods and exploit them for application in scenarios where the user has control over all stages of the CBR process. We are considering extending this to cover multi-choice and structured decision scenarios and multi-valued sensitive attributes.

References

1. An experiment with the edited nearest-neighbor rule. IEEE Trans. Syst. Man Cybern. **SMC-6**(6), 448–452 (1976). https://doi.org/10.1109/TSMC.1976.4309523

2. Abraham, S.S.: FairLOF: fairness in outlier detection. Data Sci. Eng. **6**, 485–499 (2021)
3. Abraham, S.S., Sundaram, S.S., et al.: Fairness in clustering with multiple sensitive attributes. EDBT (2020)
4. Barocas, S., Hardt, M., Narayanan, A.: Fairness and Machine Learning: Limitations and Opportunities (2019). http://www.fairmlbook.org
5. Biega, A.J., Gummadi, K.P., Weikum, G.: Equity of attention: amortizing individual fairness in rankings. In: The 41st International ACM SIGIR Conference on Research & Development in Information Retrieval, pp. 405–414 (2018)
6. Binns, R.: On the apparent conflict between individual and group fairness. In: Proceedings of the 2020 Conference on Fairness, Accountability, and Transparency, pp. 514–524 (2020)
7. Blanzeisky, W., Cunningham, P., Kennedy, K.: Introducing a family of synthetic datasets for research on bias in machine learning (2021)
8. Blanzeisky, W., Smyth, B., Cunningham, P.: Algorithmic bias and fairness in case-based reasoning. In: Keane, M.T., Wiratunga, N. (eds.) ICCBR 2022. LNAI, vol. 13405, pp. 48–62. Springer, Cham (2022). https://doi.org/10.1007/978-3-031-14923-8_4
9. Breunig, M.M., Kriegel, H.P., Ng, R.T., Sander, J.: LOF: identifying density-based local outliers. In: Proceedings of the 2000 ACM SIGMOD International Conference on Management of Data, pp. 93–104 (2000)
10. Chang, K.W., Prabhakaran, V., Ordonez, V.: Bias and fairness in natural language processing. In: Proceedings of the 2019 Conference on Empirical Methods in Natural Language Processing and the 9th International Joint Conference on Natural Language Processing (EMNLP-IJCNLP): Tutorial Abstracts (2019)
11. Chouldechova, A., Roth, A.: A snapshot of the frontiers of fairness in machine learning. Commun. ACM **63**(5), 82–89 (2020)
12. Deepak, P., Abraham, S.S.: Fair outlier detection. In: 21th International Conference on Web Information Systems Engineering: WISE 2020, pp. 447–462 (2020)
13. Dressel, J., Farid, H.: The accuracy, fairness, and limits of predicting recidivism. Sci. Adv. **4**(1), eaao5580 (2018). https://doi.org/10.1126/sciadv.aao5580
14. Dwork, C., Hardt, M., Pitassi, T., Reingold, O., Zemel, R.: Fairness through awareness. In: Proceedings of the 3rd Innovations in Theoretical Computer Science Conference, pp. 214–226 (2012)
15. Ekstrand, M.D., Burke, R., Diaz, F.: Fairness and discrimination in retrieval and recommendation. In: Proceedings of the 42nd International ACM SIGIR Conference on Research and Development in Information Retrieval, pp. 1403–1404 (2019)
16. Hertweck, C., Heitz, C., Loi, M.: On the moral justification of statistical parity. In: Proceedings of the 2021 ACM Conference on Fairness, Accountability, and Transparency, pp. 747–757 (2021)
17. Kohavi, R.: Scaling up the accuracy of Naive-Bayes classifiers: a decision-tree hybrid. In: KDD (1997)
18. Kriegel, H.P., Kröger, P., Schubert, E., Zimek, A.: Loop: local outlier probabilities. In: Proceedings of the 18th ACM Conference on Information and Knowledge Management, pp. 1649–1652 (2009)
19. Kulshrestha, J., et al.: Search bias quantification: investigating political bias in social media and web search. Inf. Retrieval J. **22**, 188–227 (2019)
20. Kunaver, M., Porl, T.: Diversity in recommender systems a survey. Know.-Based Syst. **123**(C), 154–162 (2017). https://doi.org/10.1016/j.knosys.2017.02.009

21. Le Quy, T., Roy, A., Iosifidis, V., Zhang, W., Ntoutsi, E.: A survey on datasets for fairness-aware machine learning. Wiley Interdisc. Rev.: Data Min. Knowl. Discovery **12**(3), e1452 (2022)
22. Narayanan, A.: Translation tutorial: 21 fairness definitions and their politics. In: Proceedings of the Conference on Fairness Accountability and Transparency, New York, USA, vol. 1170, p. 3 (2018)
23. Patro, G.K., Biswas, A., Ganguly, N., Gummadi, K.P., Chakraborty, A.: FairRec: two-sided fairness for personalized recommendations in two-sided platforms. In: Proceedings of the Web Conference 2020, pp. 1194–1204 (2020)
24. Pessach, D., Shmueli, E.: Algorithmic fairness. arXiv preprint arXiv:2001.09784 (2020)
25. Pessach, D., Shmueli, E.: A review on fairness in machine learning. ACM Comput. Surv. (CSUR) **55**(3), 1–44 (2022)
26. Quijano-Sanchez, L., Recio-Garcia, J.A., Diaz-Agudo, B., Jimenez-Diaz, G.: Social factors in group recommender systems. ACM Trans. Intell. Syst. Technol. **4**(1) (2013). https://doi.org/10.1145/2414425.2414433
27. Yang, K., Gkatzelis, V., Stoyanovich, J.: Balanced ranking with diversity constraints. arXiv preprint arXiv:1906.01747 (2019)
28. Yeh, I.C., Lien, C.: The comparisons of data mining techniques for the predictive accuracy of probability of default of credit card clients. Expert Syst. Appl. **36**(2, Part 1), 2473–2480 (2009). https://doi.org/10.1016/j.eswa.2007.12.020
29. Zehlike, M., Bonchi, F., Castillo, C., Hajian, S., Megahed, M., Baeza-Yates, R.: Fa* ir: a fair top-k ranking algorithm. In: Proceedings of the 2017 ACM on Conference on Information and Knowledge Management, pp. 1569–1578 (2017)
30. Zehlike, M., Yang, K., Stoyanovich, J.: Fairness in ranking: a survey. arXiv preprint arXiv:2103.14000 (2021)
31. Zhang, Y., et al.: Causal intervention for leveraging popularity bias in recommendation. In: Proceedings of the 44th International ACM SIGIR Conference on Research and Development in Information Retrieval, pp. 11–20 (2021)

Addressing Underestimation Bias in CBR Through Case-Base Maintenance

William Blanzeisky[(✉)] and Pádraig Cunningham

School of Computer Science, University College Dublin, Dublin 4, Ireland
william.blanzeisky@ucdconnect.ie

Abstract. The knowledge containers perspective on CBR suggests that bias and fairness issues can be addressed in a number of different ways. In this paper we assess the use of case-base maintenance to ensure fairness. We present FairCBM, a strategy for removing cases that are causing biased classifications. We evaluate this strategy on five different datasets and show that it is effective for ensuring fairness with minimal impact on classification accuracy. FairCBM is also evaluated against an alternative metric learning strategy (similarity knowledge container); the evaluation shows that both strategies are equally effective. FairCBM has the benefit that it is quite transparent; by comparison the metric learning strategy is more opaque.

1 Introduction

Algorithmic bias and fairness has become a major concern in machine learning research in recent years and case-based reasoning (CBR) is not an exception in this regard. Recently Blanzeisky et al. [6] presented FairRet a metric learning strategy to help ensure fairness in CBR. From a knowledge containers perspective, this is just one way that bias and fairness can be addressed in CBR. Richter's knowledge container perspective on CBR includes four knowledge containers, vocabulary, case-base, similarity and adaptation [20]. Whereas metric learning addresses the similarity knowledge container, in this paper we consider tackling bias in the case-base itself.

Addressing fairness by removing cases causing bias rather than through tweaking the similarity metric has some advantages. There is merit in removing cases that are causing problems and this is quite transparent compared with adjustments to the similarity metric that can be quite opaque. CBR research on case-base maintenance (CBM) has a long history, the relevant aspects of which are reviewed in Sect. 2.2.

Our algorithm for removing cases causing bias is presented in Sect. 3. The basic idea is to identify the cases that cause biased predictions; these can be ranked by the number of biased predictions they cause. Then cases above a threshold count can be removed. This threshold is set through a cross-validation process on the training data.

© The Author(s), under exclusive license to Springer Nature Switzerland AG 2023
S. Massie and S. Chakraborti (Eds.): ICCBR 2023, LNAI 14141, pp. 233–243, 2023.
https://doi.org/10.1007/978-3-031-40177-0_15

An evaluation of this algorithm on five datasets is presented in Sect. 4. The relevant background research is reviewed in Sect. 2 and the paper finishes with some conclusions and discussion of future work in Sect. 5.

2   Related Research

This research is informed by other work relating to bias in machine learning (ML) and case-base manitenance in CBR. The relevant work in these areas is discussed in the following subsections.

2.1   Bias in ML

ML models play an increasingly important role in making decisions that impact people's lives, including those related to employment, credit, housing, and criminal justice. The issue of ensuring fairness in ML models is critical, as biased or unfair models can perpetuate existing inequalities and discrimination, with minority groups being particularly vulnerable. Several measures of unfairness have been proposed in recent years, each emphasizing different aspects of fairness [8]. In general, an ML model is considered 'fair' if it is not inclined to award desirable outcomes $Y = 1$ (e.g., loan approval/job offers) preferentially to one side of a protected category $S = 0$ (e.g. female/protected group). Disparate Impact (DI_S) is one of the accepted measures of unfairness [12]:

$$\text{DI}_S \leftarrow \frac{P[\hat{Y} = 1|S = 0]}{P[\hat{Y} = 1|S = 1]} < \tau \tag{1}$$

It is the ratio of desirable outcomes $\hat{Y}$ predicted for the protected minority $S = 0$ compared with that for the majority $S = 1$. However, this measure is independent of what is actually in the training data.

In this paper, we are particularly interested in the bias introduced by the algorithms themselves, usually referred to as *underestimation*. Underestimation bias arises when the distribution of predictions from an algorithm is not in line with the true underlying distribution of the data. This happens when the algorithm focuses on strong signals in the data thereby missing more subtle phenomena. Hence, the classifier accentuates bias that might be present in the data and underestimates the infrequent outcome for the minority group. An underestimation score (US_S) in line with DI_S (see Eq. 1) that compares predicted and actual outcomes for the protected minority would be [5]:

$$\text{US}_{S=0} \leftarrow \frac{P[\hat{Y} = 1|S = 0]}{P[Y = 1|S = 0]} \tag{2}$$

This is the ratio of desirable outcomes predicted by the classifier for the protected group compared with what is actually present in the data [5]. If $\text{US}_{S=0} < 1$ the classifier is under-predicting desirable outcomes for the minority. It is worth noting that when $US_{S=0} = 1$ the classifier may still be biased against the minority group; it is faithful to the data but there may still be a poor DI_S score.

An alternative underestimation score that considers divergences between overall actual and predicted distributions for all groups S is the underestimation index (UEI) based on the Hellinger distance [17]:

$$\text{UEI} = \sqrt{1 - \sum_{y,s \in D} \sqrt{P[\hat{Y} = y, S = s] \times P[Y = y, S = s]}} \qquad (3)$$

Here y and s are the possible values of Y and S respectively. This Hellinger distance is preferred to KL-divergence because it is bounded in the range [0,1] and KL-divergence has the potential to be infinite. UEI = 0 indicates that there is no difference between the probability distribution of the training samples and the prediction made by a classifier (no underestimation). [17] refer to underestimation as the state in which a learned model is not fully converged due to the finiteness of the size of a training dataset - i.e., the learned classifier may lead to more unfair determinations than that observed in the training sample distribution. Although this notion is useful when quantifying the extent to which a model's prediction deviates from the training samples, it does not directly tell us how the protected group is doing since it is an aggregate score across all protected attributes S and outcomes Y.

Bias mitigation strategies in machine learning (ML) can be broadly classified into three categories depending on the stage at which fairness measures are applied. These stages include the pre-processing, in-processing, and post-processing steps, each of which has its unique set of approaches towards ensuring fairness.

Pre-processing Techniques: In this category, the focus is on the data, which is often the root of bias issues. The strategies involve transforming the dataset to correct imbalances or unrepresentative aspects before feeding it into the ML model. A variety of methods have been proposed, including disparate impact repair strategies as proposed by Feldman et al. [12], and probabilistic mappings designed to maintain individual and group fairness, as suggested by Dwork et al [11]. Other techniques involve the re-labeling or perturbation of data to eliminate undesirable biases [16,24]. Our proposed strategy, FairCBM, falls under this category, addressing underestimation bias by removing cases from the training data that contribute to biased classifications.

In-processing Techniques: These approaches aim to reduce bias during the model-building process by adjusting the algorithm's objective function to account for fairness measures [17,22]. This is often achieved by enforcing a fairness constraint into the algorithm's optimization function, thereby transforming algorithmic bias into a multi-objective optimization problem (MOOP) [2,4,13,19,22]. Some strategies for handling the non-convex optimization problem that arises include leveraging recent advances in convex-concave programming or using a majorization-minimization procedure [23]. Other specific strategies include modifying decision trees' splitting criteria and pruning strategies [1] or adding a latent variable representing the unbiased label to the Bayesian model [7]. The FairRet method proposed by Blanzeisky et al. [6] also belongs to this category. It aims to correct underestimation in case-based reasoning (CBR) systems by including underestimation as an additional criterion in the ML optimization process.

Post-processing Techniques: The final category acknowledges that the ML model's output might be biased towards specific subgroups within the protected attribute. To mitigate this, transformations are applied to the model's output to ensure fairness, such as setting different thresholds for different subgroups [9].

Although pre- and post-processing techniques can effectively mitigate bias without explicitly modifying the ML optimization process, they may have legal implications and reduce the model's interpretability [8]. Despite the challenges, these approaches, along with in-processing methods, continue to play a crucial role in addressing algorithmic bias and fostering fairness in ML.

2.2   Case-Base Maintenance

As pointed out in the IJCAI 2018 review paper by Juarez *et al.* [15] Case-Base Maintenance has a long history dating back to the Condensed Nearest Neighbor paper by Hart in 1968 [14]. There can be two motivations for CBM, to improve the efficiency of the retrieval process by removing redundant cases [3] or to improve the *competence* of the system by removing noisy cases [10].

Juarez *et al.* point out that, when the objective is to improve system competence, the Smyth-Keane-McKenna competence model [18,21] has stood the test of time. This competence model is based on two key concepts, the Coverage Set and the Reachability Set. The Coverage Set (CS) of a case is the set of other cases that this case can be used to solve. In the same way, the Reachability Set (RS) of a case is the set of other cases that solve the case in question. In classification scenarios, *solves* simply means that one case is an appropriate retrieval for another, i.e. they are in the nearest neighbor set and have the same class. These can be expressed formally as follows:

$$CS(c, C) = \{c' \in C \mid c' \in NN(c, C) \wedge c \text{ solves } c'\} \qquad (4)$$

$$RS(c, C) = \{c' \in C \mid c \in NN(c', C) \wedge c' \text{ solves } c\} \qquad (5)$$

where C is the case-base and $NN(c, C)$ are the nearest neighbors of c. This model was extended by Delany and Cunningham [10] to include the concept of a Liability Set (LS), this is the set of cases that are misclassified by c.

$$LS(c, C) = \{c' \in C \mid c \text{ misclassifies } c'\} \qquad (6)$$

They present an algorithm for deleting cases that are causing misclassifications and are not required otherwise, i.e. the cases in their CS will be correctly classified even if they are deleted. Our algorithm for deleting cases that result in biased classifications is based on this idea - see Sect. 3.

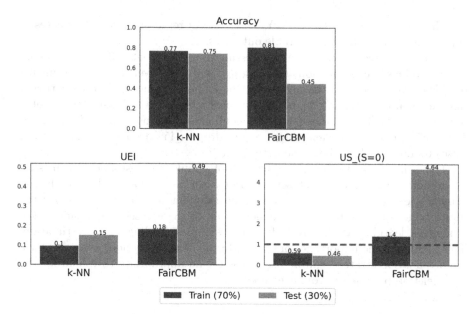

Fig. 1. These charts illustrates the performance of FairCBM with a naive policy of deleting all cases that contribute to biased classification ($|LS_{\text{FairCBM}}| > 0$) on Titanic dataset. The baseline k-NN is biased as we can see from the UEI and $US_{S=0}$ scores. The naive FairCBM policy removes 189 ($\sim$ 37%) samples from the training set. In terms of the $US_{S=0}$ score, this overshoots slightly on the training data and very significantly on unseen test data. The UEI scores are actually worse than the k-NN baseline on train and test data.

3   FairCBM: CBM Strategy to Ensure Fairness

This section introduces FairCBM, a Case-Base Maintenance strategy to address unfairness in CBR systems. Our focus is on situations where the model under-predicts desirable outcomes for minority groups (i.e., loan approvals for females), which can occur when the model prioritizes overall accuracy over fairness. To combat this, we propose FairCBM as a solution to maintain the case-base and reduce bias in the model.

FairCBM builds upon the Liability Set (LS) concept introduced by Delaney and Cunningham [10], but takes a novel approach to *tune* the amount of case deletion. Rather than removing cases that result in incorrect classifications, Fair-CBM identifies and removes cases that contribute to bias. This approach seeks to establish a case-base that is fair to all groups S while maintaining accuracy.

Focusing only on underestimation for the minority group, FairCBM first constructs a liability set LS_{FairCBM} to identify a set of cases that lead to biased classifications for the minority group:

$$LS_{\text{FairCBM}}(c, C) = \{c' \in Q \mid c \text{ misclassifies } c'\} \tag{7}$$

where $Q = \{q \in C \mid S_q = 0 \wedge Y_q = 1\}$, i.e. Q represents the set of cases in the minority group having desirable outcomes.

A naive strategy to mitigate underestimation is to delete all cases that contribute to biased classifications ($|LS_{\text{FairCBM}}| > 0$). However, initial experiments on this strategy showed worsened overall model performance and overshooting in underestimation ($US_{S=0} > 1$) on the test set. Figure 1 clearly illustrates this phenomenon on the Titanic dataset. Deleting all cases with non-empty LS removes 189 ($\sim$37%) cases. This causes accuracy to drop to 45% from 75% while $US_{S=0}$ raises to 4.64 which is above the target of 1.

This is likely due to the limited number of samples for desirable outcomes for the minority group in the dataset. In most cases, cases that lead to the biased classification ($|LS_{\text{FairCBM}}| > 0$) are samples for undesirable outcomes for the minority group ($S = 0|Y = 0$). Removing all of these cases may result in the model not learning as effectively for these samples, leading to overestimation. This highlights the importance of tuning. In the next subsection, we show how a cross-validation strategy can be used to select an appropriate threshold for the case deletion process to avoid overshooting.

3.1 Tuning

Given the importance of the case deletion process to the overall model performance, determining the appropriate deletion threshold τ is key. Cases causing at least τ biased classifications will be removed. In a hold-out-test scenario, we initially divide the initial training dataset into training and validation sets (as depicted in Fig. 2). Following this, we construct the liability set from the training set employing a leave-one-out method to identify biased classification. The validation set is then used to set the threshold τ for case deletion. We incrementally increase τ where $\tau \in Set(|LS_{\text{FairCBM}}(q, C)|)$ and select τ according to its performance on the validation set. Upon identifying the optimal τ, we construct

Table 1. The impact of different values of τ on the validation set.

τ	Accuracy	UEI	US_S=0	# of cases deleted
1	0.454	0.572	3.939	142 (46.4%)
2	0.605	0.232	2.576	112 (36.6%)
3	0.722	0.075	1.485	79 (25.8%)
4	0.722	0.067	1.273	45 (14.7%)
5	0.722	0.063	1.030	30 (9.8%)
6	0.702	0.075	0.970	26 (8.5%)
7	0.702	0.088	0.727	19 (6.2%)
8	0.707	0.099	0.636	16 (5.2%)
9	0.727	0.138	0.394	9 (2.9%)
10	0.732	0.154	0.333	10 (1.3%)

a new liability set, using the leave-one-out approach on the combined training and validation sets. Subsequently, we carry out the case deletion based on the optimized τ.

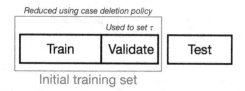

Reduced using case deletion policy

Used to set τ

| Train | Validate | | Test |

Initial training set

Fig. 2. The strategy for setting the deletion threshold τ. The initial training set is divided into Train and Validate sets and the validation set is used to find the optimal value for τ. Then this threshold is used when case deletion is applied in the initial training set.

An example of this method in operation on the Titanic dataset can be seen in Table 1. When $\tau = 1$ (all cases with non-empty LS are deleted) 142 cases are deleted. This reduces accuracy to 45% and we have almost 4-fold overestimation. By relaxing the threshold we can reduce this overshooting; we see that ($\tau = 5$) is enough to eliminate underestimation on the validation set so this is selected as the threshold.

Following the selection of the optimal value τ, we perform the case deletion process on the initial training data before assessing the models performance on the hold-out test set. Notably, the validation process for identifying the optimal value of τ uses only the training data.

Table 2. Summary details of all the datasets used in the experiments. The sensitive group is chosen to have a significant discrepancy between the majority and minority groups. For consistency, the positive class indicates the minority outcomes. In some cases, this may require some pre-processing.

Dataset	# of Instances	# of Attributes (cat./bin./num.)	Class ratio (+:-)	Sensitive group	Target class
Bike Sharing	731	5:3:2	1:3.55	working day	usage
Synthetic	5,000	0:1:2	1:1.48	gender	admit
red. Adult	48,842	0:1:6	1:3.03	gender	income
Titanic	891	4:1:2	1:1.61	sex	survived
Bank Marketing	45,211	6:4:7	1:21.64	age	subscription

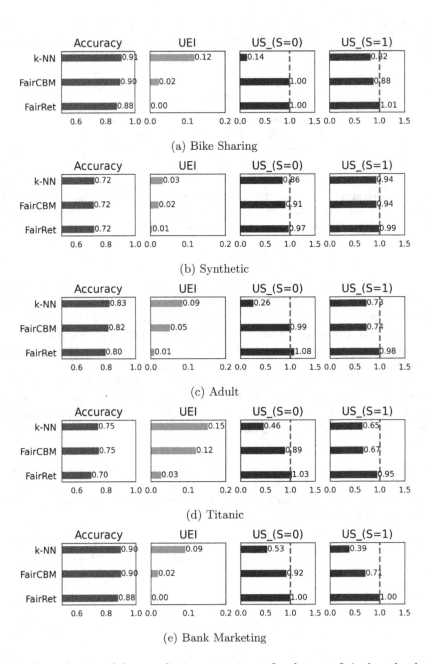

(a) Bike Sharing

(b) Synthetic

(c) Adult

(d) Titanic

(e) Bank Marketing

Fig. 3. An evaluation of the remediation strategies on five datasets. It is clear that both FairCBM and FairRet are effective in mitigating underestimation, but FairRet takes a bigger hit on the accuracy likely due to optimizing for UEI which is a broader criterion than $US_{S=0}$, whereas FairCBM focuses on $US_{S=0}$ only.

4   Evaluation

In this section, we evaluate FairCBM on one synthetic and four real-world datasets commonly used in the fairness literature. In each dataset, we choose a binary feature as the sensitive attribute S on which the model should be fair. Summary statistics for these datasets are provided in Table 2.

To illustrate the effectiveness of the proposed strategy, we compare FairCBM against standard k-NN and FairRet [6] the metric learning strategy to address underestimation mentioned in Sect. 2. The main results are plotted in Fig. 3:

- First it is clear that underestimation is an issue when standard k-NN is used. This is evident from the high UEI and low $US_{S=0}$ scores. This is not surprising since these models are optimized solely on accuracy, without consideration for how the inaccuracies distribute.
- Secondly, we can see that FairRet is effective in fixing underestimation, as measured by $US_{S=0}$ and UEI, compared to standard k-NN.
- This good performance on fairness by FairRet comes at a price in accuracy; for instance, for the Adult dataset, accuracy falls by 5%.
- Turning to FairCBM, we see that it is very effective in bringing $US_{S=0}$ close to 1. It is less effective in fixing UEI. Again, this is not surprising given that the FairCBM algorithm focuses on $US_{S=0}$ only and does not consider UEI which is a wider criterion.

In summary, when it comes to addressing underestimation, FairCBM performs equally well compared to FairRet specifically in relation to the minority group $US_{S=0}$. However, it falls short in terms of the broader UEI criterion. On the positive side, FairCBM excels at preserving accuracy, with a minimal decrease of only 1% observed across the five datasets.

5   Conclusions

In this paper, we introduce FairCBM, a case-base maintenance strategy designed to enhance fairness in Case-Based Reasoning (CBR) systems. This strategy works by eliminating cases that lead to underestimations of favorable outcomes for minority groups, such as loan approvals for females. Experimental results show that FairCBM performs on par with the metric learning strategy by Blanzeisky et al. [6] in terms of mitigating underestimation. An outstanding feature of FairCBM is its transparency, which stands in stark contrast to the relatively opaque nature of the metric learning approach. Looking forward, we aim to explore the possibility of integrating both strategies to enhance the effectiveness in rectifying bias.

Acknowledgements. This work was funded by Science Foundation Ireland through the SFI Centre for Research Training in Machine Learning (Grant No. 18/CRT/6183) with support from Microsoft Ireland. We wish to thank Sarah Jane Delany for comments on an earlier draft of this paper.

References

1. Discrimination aware decision tree learning, pp. 869–874 (2010). https://doi.org/10.1109/ICDM.2010.50
2. Agarwal, A., Beygelzimer, A., Dudík, M., Langford, J., Wallach, H.: A reductions approach to fair classification. In: 35th International Conference on Machine Learning, ICML 2018, vol. 1, pp. 102–119 (2018). arXiv:1803.02453
3. Aha, D.W., Kibler, D., Albert, M.K.: Instance-based learning algorithms. Mach. Learn. **6**, 37–66 (1991)
4. Bechavod, Y., Ligett, K.: Penalizing unfairness in binary classification (2017). arXiv:1707.00044
5. Blanzeisky, W., Cunningham, P.: Algorithmic factors influencing bias in machine learning. In: Kamp, M., et al. (eds.) Machine Learning and Principles and Practice of Knowledge Discovery in Databases, ECML PKDD 2021. Communications in Computer and Information Science, vol. 1524, pp. 559–574. Springer, Cham (2021). https://doi.org/10.1007/978-3-030-93736-2_41
6. Blanzeisky, W., Smyth, B., Cunningham, P.: Algorithmic bias and fairness in case-based reasoning. In: Keane, M.T., Wiratunga, N. (eds.) Case-Based Reasoning Research and Development: Proceedings 30th International Conference, ICCBR 2022, Nancy, France, 12–15 September 2022, vol. 13405, pp. 48–62. Springer, Cham (2022). https://doi.org/10.1007/978-3-031-14923-8_4
7. Calders, T., Verwer, S.: Three naive Bayes approaches for discrimination-free classification. Data. Min. Knowl. Disc. **21**, 277–292 (2010). https://doi.org/10.1007/s10618-010-0190-x
8. Caton, S., Haas, C.: Fairness in machine learning: a survey. arXiv preprint arXiv:2010.04053 (2020)
9. Corbett-Davies, S., Goel, S.: The measure and mismeasure of fairness: a critical review of fair machine learning (2018)
10. Delany, S.J., Cunningham, P.: An analysis of case-base editing in a spam filtering system. In: Funk, P., González Calero, P.A. (eds.) ECCBR 2004. LNCS (LNAI), vol. 3155, pp. 128–141. Springer, Heidelberg (2004). https://doi.org/10.1007/978-3-540-28631-8_11
11. Dwork, C., Hardt, M., Pitassi, T., Reingold, O., Zemel, R.: Fairness through awareness. In: Proceedings of the 3rd Innovations in Theoretical Computer Science Conference, pp. 214–226. ITCS '12, Association for Computing Machinery, New York, NY, USA (2012). https://doi.org/10.1145/2090236.2090255
12. Feldman, M., Friedler, S.A., Moeller, J., Scheidegger, C., Venkatasubramanian, S.: Certifying and removing disparate impact. In: proceedings of the 21th ACM SIGKDD International Conference on Knowledge Discovery and Data Mining, pp. 259–268 (2015)
13. Goh, G., Cotter, A., Gupta, M., Friedlander, M.: Satisfying Real-world Goals with Dataset Constraints. Technical report (2016)
14. Hart, P.: The condensed nearest neighbor rule (corresp.). IEEE Trans. Inf. Theory **14**(3), 515–516 (1968)
15. Juarez, J.M., Craw, S., Lopez-Delgado, J.R., Campos, M.: Maintenance of case bases: current algorithms after fifty years. In: Proceedings of the Twenty-Seventh International Joint Conference on Artificial Intelligence, IJCAI-18, pp. 5457–5463. International Joint Conferences on Artificial Intelligence Organization (2018)
16. Kamiran, F., Calders, T.: Data preprocessing techniques for classification without discrimination. Knowl. Inf. Syst. **33**(1), 1–33 (2012). https://doi.org/10.1007/s10115-011-0463-8

17. Kamishima, T., Akaho, S., Asoh, H., Sakuma, J.: Fairness-aware classifier with prejudice remover regularizer. In: Flach, P.A., De Bie, T., Cristianini, N. (eds.) ECML PKDD 2012. LNCS (LNAI), vol. 7524, pp. 35–50. Springer, Heidelberg (2012). https://doi.org/10.1007/978-3-642-33486-3_3

18. McKenna, E., Smyth, B.: Competence-guided case-base editing techniques. In: Blanzieri, E., Portinale, L. (eds.) EWCBR 2000. LNCS, vol. 1898, pp. 186–197. Springer, Heidelberg (2000). https://doi.org/10.1007/3-540-44527-7_17

19. Quadrianto, N., Sharmanska, V.: Recycling privileged learning and distribution matching for fairness. Technical report (2017)

20. Richter, M.: Introduction-the basic concepts of CBR. Case-Based Reasoning Technology: From Foundations to Applications, LNAI 1400 (1998)

21. Smyth, B., Keane, M.: Remembering to forget: a competence-preserving case deletion policy for case-based reasoning systems. In: Proceedings of the 14th International Joint Conference on Artificial Intelligence, pp. 377–382 (1995)

22. Woodworth, B., Gunasekar, S., Ohannessian, M.I., Srebro, N.: Learning non-discriminatory predictors. In: Conference on Learning Theory, pp. 1920–1953. PMLR (2017)

23. Zafar, M.B., Valera, I., Rodriguez, M.G., Gummadi, K.P.: Fairness constraints: mechanisms for fair classification. In: Proceedings of the 20th International Conference on Artificial Intelligence and Statistics, AISTATS 2017 (2015). arXiv:1507.05259

24. Zliobaite, I., Kamiran, F., Calders, T.: Handling conditional discrimination. In: Proceedings - IEEE International Conference on Data Mining, ICDM, pp. 992–1001 (2011). https://doi.org/10.1109/ICDM.2011.72

Towards Addressing Problem-Distribution Drift with Case Discovery

David Leake[(⊠)] and Brian Schack

Luddy School of Informatics, Computing, and Engineering, Indiana University, Bloomington, IN 47408, USA
{leake,schackb}@indiana.edu

Abstract. Case-based reasoning (CBR) is a problem-solving and learning methodology that applies records of past experiences, captured as cases, to solve new problems. The performance of CBR depends on retrieving cases relevant to each new problem that the reasoner encounters. In real-world applications, the distribution of problems can change over time, which can cause an issue for the competence and efficiency of CBR systems. This paper proposes addressing this issue through *predictive case discovery*, which involves predicting cases expected to be useful for future problems to acquire them in advance. It presents an overview of case discovery for problem-distribution drift, including the challenges involved, proposed strategies, and future research directions. It illustrates with a case study evaluating a clustering-based case discovery strategy in a path planning domain across four scenarios: no drift, non-cyclical drift, cyclical drift, and drift from obsolescence.

Keywords: adversarial drift · case-base maintenance · case discovery · data drift · problem-distribution drift · problem-distribution regularity · representativeness assumption

1 Introduction

Case-based reasoning (CBR) solves new problems by adapting solutions from similar past experiences to fit new circumstances (e.g. [16]). It is well known that the effectiveness of any CBR system depends on two types of regularity, which have been formalized as problem-solution regularity and problem-distribution regularity [14]. *Problem-solution regularity* can be informally characterized as, "Similar problems have similar solutions", and is needed in order for the adaptation of the solutions to retrieved cases to be useful in similar situations. *Problem-distribution regularity* can be informally be characterized as, "Future problems will resemble past problems". This property is necessary so that learned cases will tend to be useful in the future. In addition to these types of regularity, another regularity is required by machine learning systems more generally: the regularity that learned concepts tend to remain valid over time.

S. Massie and S. Chakraborti (Eds.): ICCBR 2023, LNAI 14141, pp. 244–259, 2023.
https://doi.org/10.1007/978-3-031-40177-0_16

The effectiveness of CBR applications suggests that a combination of careful system design and suitable problem environment can provide these properties in practical situations. However, they are not guaranteed. As CBR is used in long-lived systems, developments over time may diminish any of these regularities, presenting difficulties for those systems. When concepts change over time, the result is concept drift [32], which makes prior cases no longer apply and requires case base updating [3]. When similarity criteria no longer reflect similarity for system needs, for example due to changes in case adaptation knowledge, performance may degrade [12]. When the distribution of problems changes over time, the quality of case base coverage may degrade, contravening problem-distribution regularity and requiring maintenance to ensure that the system has the cases that it needs going into the future.

This paper first examines each of these types of regularity, and then focuses on problem-distribution regularity, which to the authors' knowledge, has received little prior attention in CBR. To mitigate problem-distribution regularity failures, it proposes *predictive case discovery:* developing methods that identify and anticipate problem-distribution drift to guide the selection of cases to request from an external source.

This paper identifies general requirements and classes of detection methods that may be used to guide case discovery. It then illustrates with a clustering-based method aimed at identifying "hot spots" in the problem space on which to focus discovery. It presents an evaluation of this sample method in a path planning domain across four scenarios: no drift, non-cyclical drift, cyclical drift, and drift from obsolescence. The results support the general effectiveness of the strategy and also illustrate its limitations. The paper concludes with future opportunities.

2   Regularities Underpinning CBR

Problem-Solution Regularity: The effectiveness of reuse of past cases depends on *problem-solution regularity*—the property that solutions to similar problems will provide a useful starting point for solving a new problem. Often in the CBR literature, the assumption is that adapting the solution to a similar problem should reduce solution generation cost compared to reasoning from scratch, for generating an acceptable solution. Systems achieving this type of problem-solution regularity have been demonstrated in multiple scenarios (e.g. [24,31]).

Problem-Distribution Regularity: The benefit to the CBR process of storing past cases depends on *problem-distribution regularity*—the property that the distribution of future problems will tend to reflect that of past problems, such that accumulated stored cases from past episodes tend to provide useful information for future problems.

Formalizing the Properties: Leake and Wilson [14] provide a formalization of these properties. They define problem-solution regularity as depending on:

1. The retrieval function the system uses to map problems to cases in the case base
2. A definition of the goals to be satisfied by retrieval – what would make a case a good starting point for solving a new problem.
3. The initial set of cases available to the system
4. The problems that the system is called upon to solve

Retrieval goals are often defined in terms of a predefined similarity measure, such as the semantic similarity between a target problem and the problem part of stored cases. However, they can be based on other criteria, e.g. that the solution to the retrieved case should be inexpensive to adapt to generate a correct solution to the new problem [24]. Another possible criterion is that the retrieved case should be adaptable to generate a result within a certain accuracy.

Items (3) and (4) reflect that problem-solution regularity must be measured in terms of the problems the system has to solve. Items (1), (2), and (3) are under the control of a system designer. For example, to further problem-solution regularity, a retrieval function aimed at retrieving adaptable cases could be hand-designed, or it could be learned (e.g. [15]). However, new cases received by the system, as referenced in (4), may cause changes in problem-solution regularity if the retrieval function is ill-suited to judging similarity for those cases.

Problem-distribution regularity reflects the correlation between the distribution of cases in the case base and the distribution of future problems. Even a case base evenly distributed across the problem space may have low problem-distribution regularity if upcoming problems are not evenly distributed.

Problem-distribution regularity has been formalized in terms of the long-term behavior of a CBR system: The probability that, at a given point in processing a stream of problems, the system will be able to retrieve a case sufficiently close to an input problem [14]. The assumption of problem-distribution regularity relates to the influential *representativeness assumption* of case-base maintenance, "The case base is a representative sample of the target problem space", [25]. This property is important for assessing case competence for the possible range of future problems. However, problem-distribution regularity only measures whether eventually the system will have a sufficient probability of containing the cases needed to cover new problems; it measures (after the fact) whether it was possible to cover most problems actually received by the system, rather than predicting whether the case base provides a good sample of possible future problems.

3   How Regularity May Degrade: Types of Drift

Even in suitable domains, regularities may not always hold. Existing cases may become obsolete [14], space or time requirements may necessitate deletion [26, 28] with corresponding competence loss [29], or the system may simply not have been provided with sufficient initial cases (or the experiences to acquire cases) to address current problems. The following subsections consider how drift may affect concept regularity and problem-distribution regularity.

3.1   Concept Drift

Concept drift, a widely explored phenomenon in machine learning [17], refers to the situation where the underlying concepts or relationships between the problem and solution change over time. For example, in a system for property valuation, inflation could cause prices to increase over time, providing a gradual transition, or a chemical spill could cause an abrupt decrease in valuations in a particular region. Or in a system for sentiment analysis, the evolution of slang could change the interpretation of the sentiment of online messages. By making cases inaccurate, concept drift can degrade the performance of a formerly accurate CBR system. When inaccuracy is associated with the time passed since acquiring the case, then this is characterized as *case obsolescence*.

3.2   Problem-Distribution Drift

Another issue arises in domains for which the problem distribution changes over time. For a disaster management system, climate change can lead to shifts in weather patterns, reducing the usefulness of a case base containing response plans for historical weather patterns. For a travel agency recommender system, certain areas may become "hot" destinations – resulting in a different range of necessary coverage. For a real estate appraisal system, developers may build newer properties with different characteristics from older properties and beyond the scope of reliable adaptation.

Problem-distribution drift refers to the change in the distribution of problems that the CBR system must solve. If a customer support system has cases for certain problems and the types of problems customers encounter change, the existing case base may become less useful, and the CBR system may need to acquire new cases that are relevant to the new problem distribution. Because problem-distribution regularity is defined in terms of the limit of case base growth, even when a domain satisfies problem-distribution regularity in the long term, practical issues can still arise in the short term.

Causes of Problem-Distribution Drift. Problem-distribution drift can be caused by various factors, including changes in the environment, changes in user preferences, changes in technology, or changes in the problem space itself.

Environmental changes The environment in which a CBR system operates can change over time, leading to changes in the distribution of problems that the system solves. For example, in a medical diagnosis system, changes in the prevalence of certain diseases can lead to changes in the distribution of medical problems that the system needs to diagnose and treat.

User preferences User desires or the problems that they wish to address may change. For example, a recommender system for clothing or travel packages needs to change seasonally as the problem distribution changes with user preferences. In some scenarios, changes in fashion may also render prior cases obsolete.

Technological changes As technology advances, new problems can arise that were not present before. For example, in a software support system, upgrades in the software can incorporate new features and associated bugs for which the system needs to provide support.

Changes in the problem space Changes in the underlying physics or changes in the social or economic context of a domain may affect problem distributions. For example, in a financial prediction system, changes in the market conditions or regulations can lead to changes in the distribution of financial problems that the system needs to predict.

3.3   Adversarial Drift

Adversarial drift refers to data drift in which a reasoner responds to cases presented by an adversary who presents characteristically different cases over time with the intention of degrading performance [10]. Adversarial drift could involve concept drift, problem-solution regularity drift, or problem-distribution regularity drift. Adversarial drift can be observed in imperfect information games such as poker, in which players benefit from associating their opponent's bets and "tells" to their strategic position or the strength thereof. In such games, the opponent may bluff their bets or fake their tells, intentionally breaking regularity to gain an advantage. Delany et al. [5] tracked and mitigated adversarial drift as spammers adapted their techniques to circumvent spam filters.

4   Addressing Problem-Distribution Drift with Guided Case Discovery

Problem-distribution drift may be addressed in a two-step process. First, the CBR system can detect and track drift. And second, it can extrapolate to anticipate the path of the drift and request cases in the path of the drift. For example, in a CBR system to recommend travel packages, if a new destination is published in a major magazine, then the number of requests for packages for that region may increase. If the trend of having more requests in that area can be detected, then the system could request additional cases in that area to better prepare for future requests.

4.1   Prior Work on Drift Detection

Drift detection algorithms generally fall into four categories: error rate-based drift detection, data distribution-based drift detection, multiple hypothesis-based drift detection, and competence-modeling strategies.

Error rate-based strategies compare the error rate of the model before and after a certain time period. These algorithms are commonly used in classification tasks, where the error rate can be calculated by comparing the predicted class labels to the true class labels. Increased error rate over time can indicate data drift. One common error rate-based algorithm is the ADWIN algorithm which adapts the window size based on observed changes in the error rate [2].

Data distribution-based strategies compare the data distribution before and after a certain time frame. These algorithms can detect gradual changes in the data distribution which may not be reflected in the error rate. One popular algorithm is the Kullback-Leibler (KL) divergence-based method which measures the difference between two probability distributions. If the divergence exceeds a threshold, then this can indicate data drift [4].

Multiple hypothesis-based strategies test multiple hypotheses simultaneously, making it possible to detect complex drift patterns. These algorithms are useful when the data drift is not well understood or cannot be modeled using a simple statistical model. One example of a multiple hypothesis-based algorithm is the Just-in-Time adaptive classifiers (JIT) algorithm which uses a sequence of hypotheses tests to detect changes in the data distribution [1].

Competence-modeling strategies, such as proposed by Lu et al. [18] detect drift based on changes in competence.

Depending on the strategy, the curse of dimensionality can also impact the detection of data drift. The *curse of dimensionality* refers to the problem of high dimensionality in a problem space leading to sparsity and high computational costs [11]. As the number of dimensions increases, cases can become widely dispersed in the high-dimensional space making changes in their distribution difficult to detect. One approach to addressing the curse of dimensionality is to reduce the dimensionality of the dataset by selecting relevant features before applying drift detection algorithms.

4.2   Case Discovery

When problem-distribution regularity decreases, a potential repair is to add cases to the case base. Case discovery can fill gaps in the distribution of the cases in the case base to cover upcoming problems that would otherwise fall into those gaps. In systems including a generative component capable of solving problems from scratch, discovery can be done by calling upon that component. In that situation, generating the solution in advance does not increase competence but provides speed-up learning by avoiding the need to generate a solution from scratch at run time (e.g., as in Prodigy/Analogy [31]). In other scenarios, discovery may be done by requesting cases beyond system competence from an external source such as a domain expert.

Which Cases to Discover: As the cost of case solicitation may be high, effectiveness of discovery depends on targeting [19–23]. For example, McKenna and Smyth [20] propose a case discovery strategy which identifies competence holes in a case base to fill by discovering spanning cases. Such approaches can be combined with problem prediction to further focus on the regions of the problem space likely to be relevant to incoming problems.

Additional methods could be brought to bear from outside CBR. For example, the SMOTE oversampling algorithm [6] mitigates class imbalance by

Let

- CB: the case base,
- *part*: a partition function,
- *active-part*: a function selecting one of the subsets of a partition,
- *rep*: a function generating a case to discover given a set of cases

Generate-target-case(CB, part, active-part, rep)

1. parts ← part(CB)
2. chosen-part ← active-part(parts)
3. target-case ← rep(chosen-part)
4. Return target-case

Fig. 1. General discovery procedure.

Let d be a distance metric, N the number of desired clusters, and CB the case base:

1. Divide the training cases into N clusters using the k-means algorithm for distance d.
2. Randomly choose a cluster CL of training cases.
3. Find cr = centroid case of CL.
4. Alter the value of a single feature of cr to yield a variation to request for discovery.

Fig. 2. K-means discovery algorithm.

generating synthetic instances by interpolating between neighboring minority instances. Extensions to SMOTE can handle concept drift on time series data [8]. Case discovery and oversampling can also be seen as similar in spirit to data augmentation for neural networks [9]. Applying a similar spirit to case-based reasoning, adaptation rules provide a knowledge-rich source of transformations that go beyond interpolation, yielding "ghost cases" that tend to preserve case cohesion [13]. Ghost cases generated by adaptation can improve efficiency but generally would not be expected to increase competence.

4.3 Clustering-Based Case Discovery

This paper proposes a general case discovery strategy of dividing the problem space into parts, predicting the most active part, selecting a point in that part, and then requesting discovery of that case. This is illustrated in Fig. 1. As an illustration and for empirical evaluation, the paper applies this strategy in a simple clustering-based approach that we call *k-means discovery*.

K-means discovery, shown in Fig. 2, uses k-means clustering to divide the problem space into N regions for a predefined value N. It then selects a random cluster from the N regions, meaning that N determines the balance between exploration (for large N, resulting in small regions) and exploitation (for small N, resulting in large regions). Alternative methods could, for example, favor "up and coming" clusters with recent activity.

After a cluster is selected, k-means discovery finds the case at the centroid of that cluster. Then it generates a variation on the centroid case by altering that case. In our simple demonstration, it does so by altering the value of a single feature. For example, in the path planning domain, the variation could be a path where one endpoint is the same as in the centroid path, and the other endpoint is randomly chosen from the entire graph. Richer methods could be used, such as adaptation strategies changing several features of the problem description in concert. (See Leake and Schack [13] for a discussion of adaptation of both problem and solution parts of cases to generate ghost cases.) The variation on the centroid case becomes the case to discover.

This paper uses clustering-based case discovery as an illustration because it is simple and requires minimal domain knowledge, making it suitable for domains where knowledge is scarce or costly to obtain. And because, by choosing the case at the centroid of the cluster, the strategy tends to discover a variant of a case representative of that cluster – which the authors hypothesized would reflect 'hot spots' because less representative cases would tend towards the edges. As needed, k-means could be replaced with other methods. For example, spherical k-means, using cosine similarity, could be used for textual cases, or affinity propagation could be used for clustering based on precomputed distances and without predetermining a number of clusters.

5   Managing Multiple Strategies

Drift detection and case discovery strategies may have different strengths and weaknesses depending on the characteristics of the problem domain and the data drift (if any). Additionally, each strategy may have parameters (such as window size or number of clusters) that need to be tuned to achieve optimal performance. Choosing the "right" strategies and parameters can impact the accuracy and efficiency of drift detection and case discovery.

A potential approach to dealing with this issue is to develop a library of strategies and select which to apply. Bandit meta-strategies provide a potential approach. If strategies are initially selected at random, and the choice between strategies is weighted based on the number of problems for which the strategies' cases were successfully used in the past, choices could be refined to favor successful strategies. However, for a rapidly-changing distribution, this information could quickly become obsolete. This is a subject for future study.

6   Evaluation

The experiments evaluate the proposed clustering-based case discovery strategy, examining the following question:

What effect does the k-means discovery strategy have on the adaptation cost of retrieved cases compared to random case discovery across four scenarios: no drift, non-cyclical drift, cyclical drift, and obsolescence?

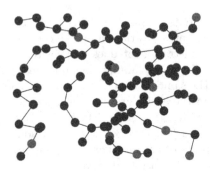

Fig. 3. An example of a graph modeling a randomly constructed transit network. Frequently visited nodes are red, and infrequently visited nodes are blue. (Color figure online)

6.1   Testing Scenario

The experiments are conducted in a simulated path planning domain. This is an established domain for evaluating CBR systems (e.g. PathFinder [27]), and it has practical applications such as for mobile robots [7] and autonomous underwater vehicles [30]. The intuitive motivation for the scenario is that an agent needs to travel from place to place. Cases are modeled with a problem part and a solution part. The problem part is the starting and ending points of the travel path, and the solution part is a list of nodes along the path from the starting point to the ending point.

Some routes and destinations will occur more frequently than others and the scenario can change over time due to moving homes, changing jobs, closing roads, and so on, providing problem distribution drift.

The experiments model the road and transit network as a graph in which each node is a destination. Variations on the scenario explore obsolescence of cases and cyclical and non-cyclical problem-distribution drift. Obsolescence is modeled by assigning an expiration age to cases; cases are no longer available after a certain number of problems have been solved. The following paragraphs in this section describe the details of the testing scenario, and code for replicating the evaluation is available in a public GitHub repository.[1]

Constructing the Graphs. Each iteration was done on a different graph generated with 100 nodes. Each node was positioned randomly in two-dimensional space. The edges were constructed with k-edge augmentation where $k = 1$. The edge augmentation ensures that the graph cannot be disconnected unless k or more edges are removed. Although the graphs were unweighted, the edge augmentation was weighted by the Euclidean distance between nodes. The number of edges varied from graph to graph.

The edge augmentation method served three purposes: First, some path should exist between any pair of nodes so that path planning is possible. Sec-

---

[1] https://github.com/schackbrian2012/ICCBR-2023.

ond, most paths should be longer than a single edge so that path planning is non-trivial. And third, edges should be more common between nearby pairs of nodes than between distant pairs of nodes, for a correlation between Euclidean distance (for retrieval) and graph distance (for adaptation). Figure 3 illustrates a graph constructed by this method.

Populating the Case Base. For each test, the case base was populated by first randomly choosing 10 distinct nodes from the graph, to serve as the frequently visited nodes. These were unequally weighted from most frequent (10) to least frequent (1). A node was randomly chosen from the frequently visited nodes, weighted by node weights. Another node was randomly chosen from the whole graph, giving each node an equal probability. Either a departing path (from a frequently visited node to a random node) or a returning path (from a random node to a frequently visited node) was constructed. The process was repeated to generate 1,000 paths.

This method of populating the case base served three purposes: First, because the nodes are randomly selected from the graph, the paths in the case base cover different parts of the graph. This diversity is important for evaluating the ability of the case discovery strategy to adapt to changes in the problem distribution. Second, by giving higher weights to frequently visited nodes, the method accounts for the fact that some parts of the graph may be more important than others, a realistic assumption for the path planning domain. Third, 1,000 paths is large enough to capture the variability in the problem distribution and the ability of the case discovery strategy to adapt to it.

Discovery Methods. The evaluation compared three discovery methods. The *No Discovery* method is a baseline that does not discover any cases. The *Random Discovery* and *Clustering-Based Discovery* methods discover one case at each time step. The Random Discovery method selects random values for each feature of the problem part of the case for discovery. In the path planning domain, the starting and ending points of the path for discovery are two nodes randomly chosen from the entire graph. The Clustering-Based Discovery method uses k-means discovery with eight clusters and a categorical distance metric. Exploratory analysis of different numbers of clusters showed that eight was effective for this task. The categorical distance metric treats each node as a category (instead of a two-dimensional coordinate) and compares nodes by exact match.

Distance Metric for Retrieval. The retrieval process yields the most similar training or discovery case to the testing problem measured according to the Euclidean distance between two four-dimensional vectors – the x- and y-coordinates of the source and target nodes of each path – resolving ties arbitrarily.

Performance Assessment Methods. The three discovery methods were compared using two performance assessment methods: Leave One Out and Time Series Cross-Validation. For both evaluation methods, at each time step, the reasoner is presented with the problem part of a different testing case – making the number of time steps equal to the number of folds. The order of testing is the same as the order of generation described in the previous "Populating the Case Base" subsection and Sect. 6.2. For the Leave One Out method, the training cases include all cases other than the testing case. For the Time Series Cross-Validation method, the training cases include all cases encountered prior to the testing case. The experiment ran for 10 iterations with different graphs and case bases in each iteration.

The Leave One Out method tests generalizability by iteratively training on all but one data point, and then testing on the left-out data point, to prevent over-fitting. The Time Series Cross-Validation method is suited for temporal data, as it evaluates the performance of the model on future time points based on the training data available up to that point, simulating a real-world scenario where the model has to predict future events based on past data.

Distance Metric for Evaluation. The distance metric for evaluating the adaptation cost of a solution sums of the number of edges in the shortest path to adapt the starting and ending points of a training case to the starting and ending points of the testing case. Unlike the distance metric for retrieval, the distance metric for evaluation ignores Euclidean distance. For an exact match, the distance metric returns zero.

6.2   Variations on the Testing Scenario

The experiments evaluated four variations on the testing scenario: No Drift, Non-Cyclical Drift, Cyclical Drift, and Obsolescence.

No Drift Scenario. The frequently visited nodes remain the same throughout the time series. The No Drift Scenario serves as a baseline for comparison with the other scenarios. It tests the ability of the case discovery strategy to handle a stable problem distribution where the frequently visited nodes remain the same throughout the time series.

Non-Cyclical Drift Scenario. Halfway through the time series, at time step 500, the frequently visited nodes are changed to a different set of frequently visited nodes constructed by the same random sampling of the nodes. This in turn abruptly changes the paths constructed from the frequently visited nodes. The Non-Cyclical Drift Scenario tests the ability of the case discovery strategy to handle abrupt changes in the problem distribution.

Cyclical Drift Scenario. This scenario alternates between two sets of frequently visited nodes for two equal-length phases of each set. It tests the ability of the case discovery strategy to handle cyclic changes in the problem distribution, which can occur due to seasonal changes or recurring patterns in the user behavior. Specifically, this scenario tests the ability of the case discovery strategy to adapt to two different sets of frequently visited nodes and construct paths that switch between the two sets.

Obsolescence Scenario. This scenario simulates case obsolescence by only reusing cases stored or discovered at less than 100 time steps before the testing problem that they solve (for the evaluation that allows use of all cases in the case stream, future cases are also only considered within 100 time steps). Evaluation penalizes the retrieval of an obsolete case by re-planning the entire path from the starting point to the ending point of the testing problem. The number of edges in the re-planned path is treated as the adaptation cost from the obsolete case to the testing problem. The distance metrics for retrieval and clustering do not consider obsolescence.

6.3   Experimental Results

Figure 4 shows the experimental results. The x-axis measures the time step of the testing case under evaluation. The y-axis measures the adaptation cost of the solution. Each graph presents the rolling average of adaptation cost over a window of 100 time steps.

The none_loo and none_tscv series use the No Discovery strategy. The random_loo and random_tscv series use the Random Discovery strategy. And the k-means_loo and k-means_tscv series use the Clustering-Based Discovery strategy. The none_loo, random_loo, and k-means_loo series use the Leave One Out evaluation method; the none_tscv, random_tscv, and k-means_tscv series use the Time Series Cross-Validation evaluation method.

No Drift Scenario – Figure 4a. The adaptation cost of Leave One Out evaluation remains steady over time because both past and future cases make up its training. The adaptation cost of Time Series Cross-Validation improves over time because the number of cases for training and discovery increase over time. The adaptation cost of each discovery method evaluated by Time Series Cross-Validation approaches the adaptation cost of the same discovery method evaluated by Leave One Out. Random Discovery outperforms No Discovery because discovery yields additional cases beyond the training cases. Clustering-Based Discovery outperforms Random Discovery because the cases discovered by the former tend to match the distribution of problems, and cases discovered by the latter tend towards an even distribution over the problem space.

Non-Cyclical Drift Scenario – Figure 4b. The earlier phase goes from time steps 0–500, and the later phase goes from time steps 500–1,000. The plot does not show time steps 0–100 because of the rolling window of 100 time steps. The earlier phase resembles the No Drift Scenario in Fig. 4a because no drift has yet occurred. Halfway through, at time step 500, adaptation cost increases for the Time Series Cross-Validation evaluation method because the problem distribution of training cases from the earlier phase does not match the problem distribution of testing cases from the later phase.

Adaptation cost increases more steeply for the none_tscv and k-means_tscv series than the random_tscv series because the latter discovers cases unbiased by the problem distribution of the earlier phase. The adaptation cost of k-means_loo also increases because it discovers the same cases as k-means_tscv which are

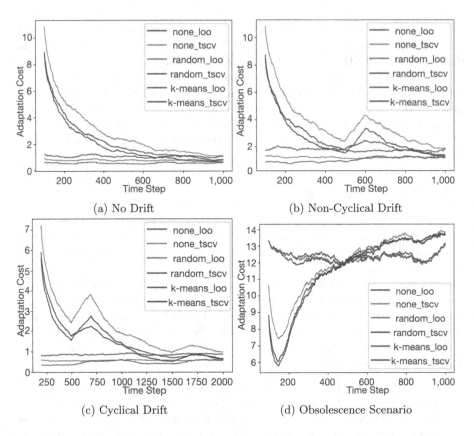

Fig. 4. Evaluation of clustering-based case discovery across four scenarios.

biased towards the problem distribution of the earlier phase. Around time step 600, adaptation cost for Time Series Cross-Validation begins to decrease again as training cases arrive from the later phase and the k-means clustering algorithm incorporates training cases from both phases. Like Fig. 4a, approaching the end at time step 1,000, the adaptation cost of each discovery method evaluated by Time Series Cross-Validation approaches the adaptation cost of the same discovery method evaluated by Leave One Out.

Cyclical Drift Scenario – Figure 4c. The first phase, from time steps 0–500, resembles the No Drift Scenario in Fig. 4a because no drift has occurred yet. The first two phases, from time steps 0–1,000, resemble the Non-Cyclical Drift Scenario in Fig. 4b because the drift has not yet repeated an earlier phase. The first drift (from the first phase to the second phase) and the third drift (from the third phase to the fourth phase) impact adaptation cost more than the second drift (from the second phase to the third phase) because the problem distribution of the training cases and the Guided Discovery cases in the first phase matches the third phase.

Obsolescence Scenario – Figure 4*d.* Adaptation cost drops for the Time Series Cross-Validation evaluation method before time step 200 as training and discovery cases arrive to solve testing problems. Then the ratio of obsolete to contemporary training and discovery cases increases – causing an increase in the number of obsolete cases retrieved and an increase in the adaptation cost. Adaptation cost increases for the Leave One Out evaluation method at the start and end of the time series. The window of contemporary cases is 100 time steps before and after the test problem, but the start (resp. end) of the time series has fewer cases before (resp. after) the test problem.

7 Conclusion

This paper discusses the regularities required for successful case-based reasoning and potential issues arising from various types of drift, including concept drift, problem-distribution drift, and adversarial drift. Then it discusses different strategies for detecting drift, such as error rate-based, data distribution-based, and multiple hypothesis-based strategies. It illustrates a case discovery strategy, k-means discovery, guided by k-means clustering, and evaluates its effectiveness on synthetic time series data in a path planning domain across four different scenarios. The evaluation demonstrates that it outperforms baselines. However, because the effectiveness of discovery strategies depends on characteristics of the drift itself, there is no universal strategy. An important next step is to explore additional strategies for drift prediction and identifying cases to discover, including drawing on methods from outside CBR, and investigating ways to select the right strategy for the domain.

Acknowledgments. This work was funded in part by the Department of the Navy, Office of Naval Research (Award N00014-19-1-2655).

References

1. Alippi, C., Roveri, M.: Just-in-time adaptive classifiers-part I: detecting nonstationary changes. IEEE Trans. Neural Netw. **19**(7), 1145–1153 (2008)
2. Bifet, A., Gavalda, R.: Learning from time-changing data with adaptive windowing. In: Proceedings of the 2007 SIAM International Conference on Data Mining, pp. 443–448. SIAM (2007)
3. Cunningham, P., Nowlan, N., Delany, S., Haahr, M.: A case-based approach to spam filtering that can track concept drift. Technicaal report TCD-CS-2003-16, Computer Science Department, Trinity College Dublin (2003)
4. Dasu, T., Krishnan, S., Venkatasubramanian, S., Yi, K.: An information-theoretic approach to detecting changes in multi-dimensional data streams. In: Proceedings of Symposium on the Interface of Statistics, Computing Science, and Applications (Interface) (2006)
5. Delany, S.J., Cunningham, P., Tsymbal, A., Coyle, L.: A case-based technique for tracking concept drift in spam filtering. In: Macintosh, A., Ellis, R., Allen, T. (eds.) SGAI 2004, pp. 3–16. Springer, London (2005). https://doi.org/10.1007/1-84628-103-2_1

6. Fernández, A., Garcia, S., Herrera, F., Chawla, N.V.: Smote for learning from imbalanced data: progress and challenges, marking the 15-year anniversary. J. Artif. Intell. Res. **61**, 863–905 (2018)
7. Hodál, J., Dvorák, J.: Using case-based reasoning for mobile robot path planning. Eng. Mech. **15**(3), 181–191 (2008)
8. Hoens, T.R., Polikar, R., Chawla, N.V.: Learning from streaming data with concept drift and imbalance: an overview. Progr. Artif. Intell. **1**(1), 89–101 (2012)
9. Iwana, B.K., Uchida, S.: An empirical survey of data augmentation for time series classification with neural networks. PLoS ONE **16**(7), e0254841 (2021)
10. Kantchelian, A., et al.: Approaches to adversarial drift. In: Proceedings of the 2013 ACM Workshop on Artificial Intelligence and Security, pp. 99–110 (2013)
11. Köppen, M.: The curse of dimensionality. In: 5th Online World Conference on Soft Computing in Industrial Applications (WSC5), vol. 1, pp. 4–8 (2000)
12. Leake, D., Kinley, A., Wilson, D.: Learning to integrate multiple knowledge sources for case-based reasoning. In: Proceedings of the Fourteenth International Joint Conference on Artificial Intelligence, pp. 246–251. Morgan Kaufmann (1997)
13. Leake, D., Schack, B.: Exploration vs. exploitation in case-base maintenance: leveraging competence-based deletion with ghost cases. In: Cox, M.T., Funk, P., Begum, S. (eds.) ICCBR 2018. LNCS (LNAI), vol. 11156, pp. 202–218. Springer, Cham (2018). https://doi.org/10.1007/978-3-030-01081-2_14
14. Leake, D.B., Wilson, D.C.: When experience is wrong: examining CBR for changing tasks and environments. In: Althoff, K.-D., Bergmann, R., Branting, L.K. (eds.) ICCBR 1999. LNCS, vol. 1650, pp. 218–232. Springer, Heidelberg (1999). https://doi.org/10.1007/3-540-48508-2_16
15. Leake, D., Ye, X.: Harmonizing case retrieval and adaptation with alternating optimization. In: Sánchez-Ruiz, A.A., Floyd, M.W. (eds.) ICCBR 2021. LNCS (LNAI), vol. 12877, pp. 125–139. Springer, Cham (2021). https://doi.org/10.1007/978-3-030-86957-1_9
16. López de Mántaras, R., et al.: Retrieval, reuse, revision, and retention in CBR. Knowl. Eng. Rev. **20**(3) (2005)
17. Lu, J., Liu, A., Dong, F., Gu, F., Gama, J., Zhang, G.: Learning under concept drift: a review. IEEE Trans. Knowl. Data Eng. **31**(12), 2346–2363 (2019)
18. Lu, N., Zhang, G., Lu, J.: Concept drift detection via competence models. Artif. Intell. **209**, 11–28 (2014)
19. Massie, S., Craw, S., Wiratunga, N.: Complexity-guided case discovery for case based reasoning. In: AAAI 2005: Proceedings of the 20th National Conference on Artificial Intelligence, pp. 216–221. AAAI Press (2005)
20. McKenna, E., Smyth, B.: Competence-guided case discovery. In: Bramer, M., Coenen, F., Preece, A. (eds.) Research and Development in Intelligent Systems XVIII, pp. 97–108. Springer, London (2002). https://doi.org/10.1007/978-1-4471-0119-2_8
21. McSherry, D.: Automating case selection in the construction of a case library. In: Bramer, M., Macintosh, A., Coenen, F. (eds.) Research and Development in Intelligent Systems XVI, pp. 163–177. Springer, London (2000). https://doi.org/10.1007/978-1-4471-0745-3_11
22. McSherry, D.: Intelligent case-authoring support in casemaker-2. Comput. Intell. **17**(2), 331–345 (2001)
23. Mehdi Owrang, O.M.: Case discovery in case-based reasoning systems. Inf. Syst. Manage. **15**(1), 74–78 (1998)
24. Smyth, B., Keane, M.: Adaptation-guided retrieval: questioning the similarity assumption in reasoning. Artif. Intell. **102**(2), 249–293 (1998)

25. Smyth, B., McKenna, E.: Competence models and the maintenance problem. Comput. Intell. **17**, 235–249 (2001)
26. Smyth, B.: Case-base maintenance. In: Pasqual del Pobil, A., Mira, J., Ali, M. (eds.) IEA/AIE 1998. LNCS, vol. 1416, pp. 507–516. Springer, Heidelberg (1998). https://doi.org/10.1007/3-540-64574-8_436
27. Smyth, B., Cunningham, P.: The utility problem analysed: a case-based reasoning perspective. In: Smith, I., Faltings, B. (eds.) EWCBR 1996. LNCS, vol. 1168, pp. 392–399. Springer, Heidelberg (1996). https://doi.org/10.1007/BFb0020625
28. Smyth, B., Keane, M.T.: Remembering to forget. In: Proceedings of the 14th International Joint Conference on Artificial Intelligence, pp. 377–382. Citeseer (1995)
29. Smyth, B., McKenna, E.: Competence models and the maintenance problem. Comput. Intell. **17**(2), 235–249 (2001)
30. Vasudevan, C., Ganesan, K.: Case-based path planning for autonomous underwater vehicles. Auton. Robot. **3**(2–3), 79–89 (1996)
31. Veloso, M.: Planning and Learning by Analogical Reasoning. Springer, Berlin (1994). https://doi.org/10.1007/3-540-58811-6
32. Widmer, G., Kubat, M.: Learning in the presence of concept drift and hidden contexts. Mach. Learn. **23**(1), 69–101 (1996)

Adaptation: Techniques and Application

Case-Based Adaptation of Argument Graphs with WordNet and Large Language Models

Mirko Lenz[1]([✉])[iD] and Ralph Bergmann[1,2][iD]

[1] Trier University, Universitätsring 15, 54296 Trier, Germany
info@mirko-lenz.de, bergmann@uni-trier.de,ralph.bergmann@dfki.de
[2] German Research Center for Artificial Intelligence (DFKI), Branch Trier
University, Behringstr. 21, 54296 Trier, Germany

Abstract. Finding information online is hard, even more so once you get into the domain of argumentation. There have been developments around the specialized argumentation machines that incorporate structural features of arguments, but all current approaches share one pitfall: They operate on a corpora of limited sizes. Consequently, it may happen that a user searches for a rather general term like cost increases, but the machine is only able to serve arguments concerned with rent increases. We aim to bridge this gap by introducing approaches to generalize/specialize a found argument using a combination of WordNet and Large Language Models. The techniques are evaluated on a new benchmark dataset with diverse queries using our fully featured implementation. Both the dataset and the code are publicly available on GitHub.

Keywords: argumentation · graphs · adaptation · background knowledge · natural language processing

1 Introduction

Due to the sheer amount on information available on the internet, is has become increasingly harder for users to find exactly what they are looking for. At the same time, traditional search engines like Google purely operate on the textual layer, neglecting any potentially relevant structural information. These issues led to the development of specialized systems optimized for certain tasks—for instance, finding relevant arguments as part of so-called *argumentation machines* [28]. However, one fundamental flaw remains: If a user wants to retrieve information that is not in the corpus indexed by the search engine, it will not be able to provide relevant results.

To better understand this issue, consider a user wanting arguments relevant to the following query:

Should we put a cap on cost increases of contracts when changing the payer?

© The Author(s), under exclusive license to Springer Nature Switzerland AG 2023
S. Massie and S. Chakraborti (Eds.): ICCBR 2023, LNAI 14141, pp. 263–278, 2023.
https://doi.org/10.1007/978-3-031-40177-0_17

Among others, the argumentation machine retrieved the following result from the microtexts corpus [25]:

> Rent prices are already regulated in favour of tenants due to existing laws and the rent index. In view of the high prices for buying flats with existing rent contracts, these are an unattractive investment.

This argument is already quite relevant, but while the query asked about "contract costs", the result is concerned with "rent costs". The relevance would be even higher if the machine was able to infer that "contract costs" is a generalized form of "rent costs" and automatically *adapts* the argument before presenting it to the user. Whereas the pure retrieval of arguments has been solved by multiple works [5,15,20,31,34], adaptation is rather difficult to solve and—to the best of our knowledge—has not yet been tackled in the literature.

Consequently, our work pursues the following research question: "Given a user-defined query together with arguments retrieved from a larger corpus, can we generalize or specialize the results to better match the user's query and provide a more relevant and useful set of results?" We tackle the *reuse* step that is performed after the *retrieval* in the context of a larger Case-Based Reasoning CBR [1] system. The main contributions of this paper are as follows: (i) An approach that extracts the most important keywords of an argument and adapts them using WordNet [17,22], (ii) multiple approaches leveraging state-of-the-art Large Language Models (LLMs), (iii) a hybrid approach where the identified keywords are adapted using a LLMs and validated with WordNet, (iv) a new benchmark dataset with diverse queries (including reference rankings for a retrieval system and possible adaptation results), and (v) a publicly available implementation[1] that powers an experimental evaluation assessing the impact of the proposed adaptation techniques on a retrieval system.

The presented techniques are in principle applicable to arbitrary types of texts. Some features of our heuristics—for instance, the identification of relevant keywords—use an argument's internal structure to make better informed decisions. We use an established graph-based representation—that is, *argument graphs* (see Sect. 2 for details)—with a large number of corpora available online. A major part of our efforts will be concerned with *explainability*: Since we alter the semantics of an argument, we argue that the user must have the ability to review any automatic change—otherwise the user's trust may be damaged.

To the best of our knowledge, this is the first paper to apply LLMs to the reuse phase of a CBR system. These models are particularly good at predicting the next word given a specific context which is exactly the kind of task we are trying to solve. We hope to pave the way for further developments in this area—especially Textual Case-Based Reasoning (TCBR) [35].

The remainder of this paper is structured as follows: Sect. 2 will introduce the most important foundations, followed by a review of related work in Sect. 3. In Sect. 4, we describe the three different adaptation approaches. Section 5 provides an experimental results and a discussion of our proposed approaches. Lastly, Sect. 6 concludes our findings.

---

[1] https://github.com/recap-utr/arguegen.

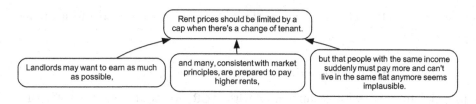

Fig. 1. Exemplary argument graph from the microtexts corpus.

2 Foundations

In this section, we briefly discuss the foundational concepts and techniques underpinning our proposed approach for argument generalization. To solve this rather difficult task, we combine multiple fields like Computational Argumentation (CA), CBR, and Natural Language Processing (NLP). We will start by introducing the type of data we are using: arguments.

2.1 Argumentation Theory

An *argument* consists of one *claim* together with one or several *premises* that are linked to the claim [24]. The debatable claim can be *attacked* or *supported* by its connected premises [32]. Claims and premises are the smallest self-contained units of argumentation and are also called Argumentative Discourse Units (ADUs). Using these building blocks it becomes possible to construct *argument graphs* to represent larger discourses. Such graphs make it possible for us to integrate structural information into the adaptation process. Consider the example shown in Fig. 1: The blue nodes represent the ADUs and as such store the argumentative content, whereas the arrows represent relationships between them. Most such graph have one *major claim* that defines the overall conclusion of an argument—in our example, this is the root node.

2.2 Automated Reasoning

As mentioned earlier, we follow the overall methodology of CBR to tackle the generalization of argument graphs. The basic assumption here is that similar problems (or *cases*) have similar solutions. By storing previous problems together with their solutions in a *case base*, it is possible to solve new problems with existing knowledge. CBR is a mere problem-solving methodology, meaning that it can be combined with various techniques—for instance, Machine Learning (ML). The branch of Textual Case-Based Reasoning (TCBR) [35] is concerned with cases stored as texts and as such utilizes NLP techniques. Čyras et al. propose Abstract Argumentation for CBR (AA-CBR) [12] and thus combine the Dung framework [16] with CBR. In this paper, we will utilize another reasoning approach—Analogy-Based Reasoning (ABR) [10,13]—to tackle the *reuse* step of CBR. ABR is based on the assumption that a is to b what c is to d (i.e.,

$a : b :: c : d$) [18]. Thus, by finding the triple (a, b, c), we are able to infer the missing value d [27].

2.3 Background Knowledge

In order to draw sensible inferences with ABR, we need some sort of background knowledge. Due to our focus on generalization/specialization, the lexical database WordNet is a fitting candidate. At its core, WordNet is composed of *lemmas* that are grouped together to so-called *synsets* when multiple lemmas share the same meaning (e.g., the lemmas "price" and "cost" could be grouped this way). Basically, a synset is an n-gram and thus can include compound words. In the following, we will also use the term "concept" when referring to a synset. These synsets are linked via six relationship types, out of which we will only consider *hypernyms* (i.e., generalizations) and *hyponyms* (i.e., specializations). A crucial component of all synsets and lemmas in WordNet is the accompanying Part of Speech (POS) tag, allowing to differentiate between the activity "shop" and the business "shop" [26]. For each synset, WordNet provides one definition along with multiple exemplary real-world uses of the underlying lemmas that may be used as additional contextual information for NLP operations like computing semantic similarities.

2.4 Natural Language Processing

Providing an introduction to all aspects of NLP is out of scope for this paper, we will instead focus on the advanced concept of LLMs here. They use the transformer architecture [33] which also powers models like Bidirectional Encoder Representations from Transformers (BERT) [14]. Compared to plain word embeddings like word2vec [21], transformers use an internal concept of *attention* that allows them to produce contextualized embeddings (i.e., the same word may have different vectors depending on its context). They may be *fine-tuned* on a new dataset, making it possible to apply them on specialized tasks—for instance, Sentence-Transformers (STRF) [29] have been fine-tuned to compute semantic similarities between sentences. Generative Pre-trained Transformer (GPT) models (a type of LLM) use a vastly higher number of internal parameters and are trained on larger corpora, enabling them to show state-of-the-art performance on a variety of tasks even without a fine-tuning step. Instead, they make use of *few-shot learning* (i.e., providing some examples with expected output) and *prompting* to instruct the model [8].

3 Related Work

In our literature research, we did not find prior works on generalizing or specializing argument graphs in a CBR context. Thus, the upcoming section will highlight a selection of contributions to (i) the case-based retrieval of argument graphs and (ii) the adaptation of arguments.

The retrieval of arguments has been covered by many works in recent past—for instance, by the search engines ARGS.ME [34] and ARGUMENTEXT [31]. These approaches however deal with simple argumentation structures—that is, they only consider individual ADUs and their stances (pro/con), not complete argument graphs. Bergmann and Lenz investigate the use of CBR methods for retrieving argument graphs based on a structural mapping between user queries and the stored cases [5,20]. For each node in the user query, a matching node in the case is determined by comparing the embeddings of the node's content. These local similarities are then aggregated to form a global measure incorporating both structural and semantic aspects.

Regarding the adaptation procedure itself, there are two perspectives on this task: (i) Change the structure of the graph or (ii) modify the textual content of the ADUs. A major issue for the former are so-called co-references—for instance, the word "he" might refer to a person described in another node. The latter perspective can be tackled using TCBR—which is concerned with textual adaptation and has its roots in the field of legal reasoning [2,30]. Bilu and Slonim propose a method to recycle claims for the use in a new domain with the help of Statistical Natural Language Generation (SNLG) [6]. CBR and ABR have been investigated in the area of mediation [3]. The underlying commonsense knowledge has also been applied to the area of argumentation in the past via manual annotation [4].

4   Case-Based Adaptation of Argument Graphs

Having provided the necessary foundations together with relevant works in the field, we will now present our proposed approach for adapting arguments. We will focus solely on *reusing* arguments, leaving the retrieval to the system introduced in [5] (see Sect. 3 for details). A total of 6 techniques divided in three broader categories will be introduced in this section: (i) two WordNet-based variants, (ii) three LLM-based ones, and (iii) one hybrid one. In addition to the reference implementation in Python used in Sect. 5, we present a high-level overview of all algorithms using flowcharts with exemplary content. Consistent with the research question (see Sect. 1), our overall goal is defined as follows: Show that it is possible to increase the relevance of a ranking produced by a retrieval system w.r.t. a given query by generalizing/adapting the found cases.

We consider both *non-interactive* (i.e., the adaptation happens automatically) and *interactive* (i.e., the user initiated the adaptation process) scenarios. In the former, the adaptation is performed automatically after the retrieval without any sort of interaction from the user. In the latter, a user initiates the adaptation process manually for a single case. To tailor the results to their needs, the user provides so-called *adaptation rules* (see Sect. 4.1) to the system that serve as a starting point for the process. All of our approaches therefore have the ability to honor certain wishes w.r.t. the adaptation.

4.1   Case Representation

Before proceedings with the algorithms, we will briefly establish some common notation: Each case $g \in$ CB of our case base CB is an argument graph and as such is composed of a set of ADUs $\text{adus}(g) := \{a_1, \ldots, a_n\}$. Concepts (i.e., the keywords of the graph's ADUs) $c_i \in C$ are mapped to a set of synsets $\{s_1, \ldots, s_n\} \in S$ with S being all nodes of WordNet. Each such concept c is an n-gram (typically $n \leq 3$) together with a POS tag. For each such concept c, we also store its POS tag. The user-provided query q is an argument graph (just like the stored cases), whereas the rules $\{(c_1, c_2), \ldots\} := R$ are source-target tuples of concepts that need to be replaced. The function $\text{vec}(x)$ denotes the vector/embedding of an arbitrary text x.

Based on this representation, we define the function $\text{score}(c)$ to assess the "relevance" of a concept c when (i) filtering relevant concepts to be extracted, (ii) comparing multiple adaptation candidates of a concept, and (iii) determining a sensible order when applying the adaptations. The score is an aggregation of multiple metrics that make use of so-called *related concepts* in the spirit of ABR $(a : b :: c : d)$. Let us give you a concrete example: We found out that the concept "landlord" (c) should be adapted know that the general topic of an argument shall be generalized from "rent" (a) to "cost" (b). We now try to find a generalization d of "landlord" that has a high similarity to both "cost" and "landlord". In our paper, such a *similarity function* shall produce a value in $[0, 1]$ when given two concepts c_1, c_2—for instance (i) the semantic similarity between the examples of connected synsets, (ii) the path-based distance of these synsets within WordNet, and (iii) the semantic similarity of the original ADUs. For a complete list, we refer the reader to our reference implementation. A concept's global score is finally defined as the arithmetic mean of all these local measures.

4.2   Adaptation with WordNet

With the case representation introduced, we will now proceed with presenting the first adaptation approach that is built on WordNet. In essence, we extract the most important keywords of an argument and follow their hypernym/hyponym relations to derive appropriate generalizations/specializations. This approach is explainable by default since the reasoning chain is completely known (something which is not the case for all other techniques that we propose). The procedure is depicted in Fig. 2 and discussed in the following paragraphs.

Generate Rules. In order to come up with adaptations for individual concepts, we first need to determine how the overall topic of the argument should be changed. In the context of ABR $(a : b :: c : d)$ that would mean finding the variables a and b. We generate them by extracting the keywords of the user's query and the argument's major claim with an established extraction algorithm like YAKE [9]. We then determine the shortest paths between the major claim's and the query's keywords and use those pairs having the smallest distance as our adaptation rules. For our previously used example, the resulting rule could

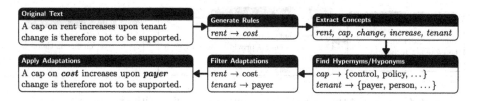

Fig. 2. Overview of the WordNet-based adaptation pipeline with exemplary values.

be "rent → cost". Note that we do not need our concept score in this stage. In case the adaptation is performed interactively (i.e., the user provided rules), the system skips this step.

Extract Concepts. Now that we know the left part of the ABR equation, we can move to the right part, starting with variable c. Since we determined both a and b through a keyword extraction algorithm like YAKE, we will do the same here to receive a set of *concept candidates*. When for example presented with the rule "rent → cost", one such candidate could be "landlord". We then compute the score of each candidate, enabling us to define a *threshold* that each candidate has to reach. The remaining ones are ordered by their score and optionally selected through a *cut-off*—that is, only the best x candidates are used. After this step, we have a list of *extracted concepts* which can be generalized.

Find Hypernyms/Hyponyms. The only variable missing in the ABR equation is d—that is, the generalized/specialized concept. We will first be concerned with finding potential *adaptation candidates* before filtering these based on their computed concept scores. Two variants for fetching those candidates are proposed: (i) Directly use the synsets connected to c (*taxonomy-based*) or (ii) replicate the WordNet paths between a, b with c as the new start node (*analogy-based*). The taxonomy-based one is faster to compute, but has the drawback of needing to compute the score for more concepts (since they are not filtered based on the paths between a and b). Another difference is that the analogy-based variant is much more strict on the potential adaptation targets.

Filter Adaptations. We now have multiple candidates for the variable d and are left with selecting the best one. The best synset is chosen based on the corresponding concept score, leaving the task of selecting the correct lemma for the given context. Again, we make use of ABR and select the lemma where the word embedding difference $\text{vec}(c) - \text{vec}(d)$ is closest to $\text{vec}(a) - \text{vec}(b)$.

Apply Adaptations. Now that all variables of the equation $a : b :: c : d$ are known, we can finally insert them into the Argument Graph (AG). In an effort to minimize the risk of applying "harmful" adaptations to the argument, we propose an *iterative* technique: Instead of applying all identified adaptations at once, we insert them one after each other and compute the similarity of the case to the query after each operation. As soon as the similarity score is identical or even

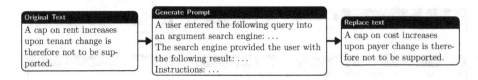

Fig. 3. Overview of the LLM-based adaptation pipeline with exemplary values.

reduced, we stop. The adapted lemmas are correctly inflected to minimize gram-matical errors. To minimize the runtime impact, we only consider the semantic similarity of the complete argument and skip the expensive structural matching. This optimization is consistent with the findings of Bergmann and Lenz [5,20] who report that the semantic retrieval alone produced almost the same ranking.

4.3 Adaptation with Large Language Models

We were mostly concerned with heuristics in the past section. Moving to LLMs, the focus now shifts towards *prompt engineering* as introduced in Sect. 2. These prompts have different requirements for different LLMs, so we will discuss two paradigms here: (i) edit-based models and (ii) chat-based models. The former ones are a perfect fit for the use-case of adapting arguments since they are specialized in editing texts based on an instruction. The latter family of models has seen an increasing interest by researchers lately and are equally relevant for our work as they are aware of previous responses—an ability that could be valuable for our task. Please note that due to space constraints, we are unable to present the complete prompts and instead show an excerpt of our prompt template in Fig. 3. We refer the interested reader to our implementation for more details.[2]

Edit-Based Models. The approach here is relatively simple: As an instruction, we present the model the query together with the case. For each ADU, the task is then to make it more relevant to the query by generalizing the presented snippet.

Chat-Based Models. These types of models allow greater degree of freedom. To account for that, we propose two different ways of approaching the adaptation of arguments with chat completions. We either try to (i) replicate the edit-based model and let the chat-based LLM rewrite an ADU's content or (ii) replicate the WordNet approach and let the model predict an adapted text together with the accompanying replacement rules. In other words, the LLM may rewrite the whole text in (i) whereas it should only substitute certain keywords in (ii). This is also why (i) is not explainable whereas (ii) is to a certain degree: There is no guarantee that the predicted texts and rules are consistent with each other, potentially causing user confusion if presented as is.

---

[2] https://github.com/recap-utr/arguegen.

For both techniques, we again present the query together with the retrieved argument as context to the model. Only for (ii) we add an instruction that edits should be limited and a list of adaptation rules has to be provided. We then iteratively let the model predict an output for each ADU and add those responses to the context presented to the LLM.

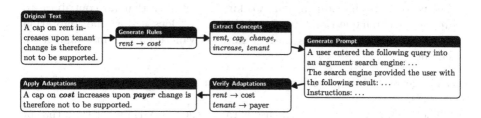

Fig. 4. Overview of the hybrid adaptation pipeline with exemplary values.

4.4 Hybrid Adaptation

While LLMs often generate text that on first glance seems correct, the results are not guaranteed to be valid in the real world or even consistent with previous responses within the same "conversation". We consequently propose a hybrid adaptation approach that tries to combine the best of both worlds: The word prediction capabilities of LLMs and the consistency checks possible with the taxonomy modeled in WordNet. The process is depicted in Fig. 4.

Compared to the WordNet-based approach seen in Fig. 2, the adaptation and filtering steps are replaced by prompt generation and validation steps. The remaining ones—that is, rule generation, keyword extraction, and application of adaptations—are used unchanged, so we refer to Sect. 4.2 for details. The new prompt is similar to the one used in Sect. 4.3: The LLM yet again receives the query and case as context, but this time we do not preset a single ADU to the model, but instead the output of our concept extraction step. In principle, we now have the same output as with the WordNet pipeline, but the predicted adaptations are not guaranteed to be correct. We argue that this attribute is a central aspect when dealing with arguments, so we add an additional *verification* step: For each adaptation rule, we check if it (i) is present in WordNet and (ii) does not exceed a (configurable) path distance threshold from the original concept. Finally, use the *iterative* replacement technique introduced in Sect. 4.2 to apply the generated adaptation rules. A side-effect of this technique is that it needs fewer predictions by the LLM (one per case here versus one per ADU for Sect. 4.3) and thus reduces the costs associated with the whole procedure.

5   Experimental Evaluation

The following section provides an experimental evaluation of our proposed approaches for the adaptation of argument graphs. We will define the hypotheses guiding our evaluation, present the experimental setup along with the metrics used, and provide a detailed analysis of the results. Since dealing with arguments often entails a subjective aspect, our evaluation will not solely rely on numbers and supplement the experiments with a detailed review of an exemplary adapted argument. Consequently, our quantitative evaluation in Sect. 5.2 will be accompanied by a case study in Sect. 5.3.

Let us start by introducing our working hypotheses that all contribute to answer our research question formulated in Sect. 1: "Does at least one adaptation approach for argument graphs lead to more relevant/useful results—and if so, which one?"

H1. The generated adaptation rules are a decent approximation the ones crafted by experts.

H2. The similarity of an adapted case w.r.t. to the query is higher than that of the original retrieved case.

H3. By combining the taxonomy of WordNet with the prediction capabilities of a LLM, the hybrid approach performs best.

H1 and H2 aim at making the rather vague notion of "better results" measurable and are complemented by H3 that checks whether the hybrid technique produces the best results w.r.t. those hypotheses. It is worth noting that in our evaluation, we focus solely on the *generalization* aspect of our proposed approach for argument retrieval. While specialization is an equally important task, this focus allows us to discuss the different techniques in more detail. Specialization can be seen as the opposite of generalization, meaning that these two directions may be swapped rather easily.

5.1 Experimental Setup

We wrote a fully working application in Python to enable running our experiments. In an effort to embrace reproducibility, both the software and our dataset (see below) are freely available under the permissive MIT license.[3] Our concept score relies partly on semantic similarity measures (i.e., embeddings). We run the experiments with plain fastText (FT) [7] as well as the contextualized Universal Sentence Encoder (USE) [11] and STRF. For the LLMs, we use the GPT family of models developed by OpenAI that have been popularized through ChatGPT.[4]

Corpus. As a data source containing AGs, we use the well-known microtexts corpus, containing a total of 110 graphs with a mean number of five ADUs per graph. It is composed of 23 distinct topics with relatively similar cases. Out of these, we selected nine topics based on their number of cases, leading to 62 graphs. Each of these has been annotated with a *query* for a retrieval system as

---

[3] https://github.com/recap-utr/arguegen.
[4] We used the following models: FT: `en_core_web_lg` from spaCy, USE: `v4`, STRF: `multi-qa-MiniLM-L6-cos-v1`, edit-based LLM: `text-davinci-edit-001`, chat-based LLM: `gpt-3.5-turbo`.

well as a list of *benchmark adaptations* independently by two experts, resulting in a total number cases of 124. The experts already had experience with AGs and were given detailed annotation guidelines. Both of them received the same cases—making it possible to determine the Inter-Annotator Agreement (IAA)—and were told not to talk about the task with each other. They were also told to order the generalizations based on their importance s.t. the adaptation having priority is at the top. For example, when presented with the argument shown in Fig. 1, one expert created the query "Why should we not put a cap on cost of contracts when changing contractual payer?" Based on the case and the query, they created the three generalizations (i) *rent* $\rightarrow$ *cost*, (ii) *tenant* $\rightarrow$ *payer*, and (iii) *flats* $\rightarrow$ *objects*.

Annotation Reliability. We will now determine the IAA between the annotations of the two experts to assess the reliability of the gathered data. Each expert assigned multiple rules to a case, thus we use Krippendorff's α [19] together with Measuring Agreement on Set-Valued Items (MASI) [23] as a weighting method for sets of values. Each rule is a tuple (source, target), meaning that we can differentiate between two *perspectives* of the IAA: (i) Treat identical sources as a perfect agreement (thus ignoring the specified target) or (ii) only treat rules as perfect agreement where both source and target match. Both perspectives yield quite poor agreement scores of (i) 0.20 and (ii) 0.03. Krippendorff recommends to discard all values <0.667 and as such tells us to not rely on the gathered data. Even if we only investigate the first rule (i.e., the one deemed to be the most important one by the experts), we only receive scores of (i) 0.44 and (ii) 0.08. The main conclusion we can draw from these annotations is the fact that argumentation in itself is highly subjective. As such, a generalization of the system might be sensible even though it does not perfectly resemble the ground truth—affirming the need for a case study.

5.2 Quantitative Results

With the setup explained, we may now proceed and conduct experiments to assess our hypotheses. We will use the standard Information Retrieval (IR) measures Precision P, recall R, and the ranking-aware nDCG. We have already seen in the last section that the IAA of correct sources *and* targets is almost zeros. Consequently, these IR metrics are computed by comparing the *sources* of the system and expert rules—consequently treating the latter as our ground truth. We will additionally report the metrics precision $P@1$ and recall $R@1$ for the first rule as well. Lastly, we measure the similarity improvement $sim_{\nearrow}$ which is defined as the similarity of the adapted case to the query divided by the similarity of the original case to the query—that is, sim_{adapt}/sim_{orig}—and indicates whether we succeeded in making the case more relevant to the user's query.

Before presenting our results, we need to discuss the edit-based LLM approaches. As mentioned in Sect. 4.3, these techniques directly alter the text and provide no trace of the changes which may be problematic for the domain of argumentation where factual correctness is crucial. As part of our experiments, we noticed that most ADU texts are changed completely and at the same time tend to be longer than their unmodified counterparts. We also faced issues when parsing the LLM responses—for instance, texts like the following were predicted: "This segment is not directly relevant to the presented query, but it could be adapted by changing . . . " Due to these inconsistencies and the fact that we cannot apply our metrics to them, we need to skip the evaluation of both edit-based models.

We will now proceed to discuss the findings based on the results depicted in Table 1. Among all methods, the chat-based LLM performs worst and even is the only one showing a decrease in semantic similarity. The WordNet approaches show different results depending on the underlying embedding model: FT already predicts a high similarity value between the case and the unmodified case, thus the improvement only changes slightly. It also shows that these plain embeddings are not as well suited as a heuristic to determine adaptation rules—all metrics are lower compared to the contextualized USE or STRF. The analogy-based heuristic delivers worse results than the taxonomy-based on across the board. Moving to the hybrid approach, you may have noticed that we tested two validation setups: *lenient* and *strict*. The lenient one accepts all adaptation rules that are part of WordNet, whereas the strict one only allows concepts in close vicinity to be used as rules. With lenient validation, we observe a higher recall paired with a lower precision. Strict validation leads to the exact opposite situation, meaning that both models are viable depending on the user's preference. The results w.r.t. the most suitable embedding models correlate with our findings of the WordNet approach: contextualized ones yield better metrics.

When analyzing the runtimes of the methods we get mixed results: On average, the WordNet techniques need 5 s with FT, 20 s with USE and 30 s with STRF per case. For the LLM based approaches, measuring the time is rather challenging due to rate limits imposed by OpenAI: once such a limit is reached, an exponential backoff has to be applied. With that in mind, we observed typical runtimes of 50 s for the chat-based LLM and 25 s for the hybrid technique. While the former performs one request for each ADU of an argument, the latter only requires one request per case, reducing the impact of the rate limits. Overall, the processing time is not optimal for interactive use—only WordNet wth FT could respond within a few seconds.

We will finish the quantitative evaluation by assessing our three hypotheses. To fully accept H1, our models would need to produce perfect precision/recall scores, which is not the case here. At the same time, we have seen that even two human annotators have no strong agreement, making it a difficult decision. Given the fact that the first adaptation rule is correct almost 80% of the time (see $P@1$) for the best performing models, we tend to cautiously accept H1. The situation is easier w.r.t. H2: Both WordNet and the hybrid technique yield more than 20% increase of the similarity score, leading to an acceptance of H2. Now we are only left with H3—is the hybrid approach the best one? The lenient variant has the best scores for $R, nDCG, sim_{\nearrow}$, whereas its strict counterpart boasts the highest values for P, meaning that we tend to accept H3. This is also confirmed

Table 1. Evaluation results the concept-based adaptation approaches.

Approach	P	R	$P@1$	$R@1$	nDCG	sim
WordNet (Analogy, FT)	.283	.433	.598	.155	.377	+1.03%
WordNet (Taxonomy, FT)	.304	.448	.620	.165	.400	+1.07%
WordNet (Analogy, USE)	.515	.412	.725	.193	.413	+16.3%
WordNet (Taxonomy, USE)	.517	.426	.717	.191	.420	+16.8%
WordNet (Analogy, STRF)	.519	.473	.770	.207	.450	+20.7%
WordNet (Taxonomy, STRF)	.525	.474	.777	.211	.450	+21.3%
LLM (Chat-based)	.049	.226	.050	.010	.088	−1.64%
Hybrid (Strict, FT)	.501	.357	.644	.170	.363	+0.54%
Hybrid (Lenient, FT)	.304	.437	.664	.178	.410	+0.86%
Hybrid (Strict, USE)	.587	.442	.714	.190	.432	+15.5%
Hybrid (Lenient, USE)	.361	**.544**	.738	.197	**.494**	+23.5%
Hybrid (Strict, STRF)	**.590**	.452	**.798**	**.218**	.445	+18.3%
Hybrid (Lenient, STRF)	.353	.528	.738	.200	.483	+23.5%

by our experience when running the experiments: The hybrid approach seems to be quite robust and in most cases comes up with adaptations that are sensible. The same is not true for the other approaches—they are more likely to predict generalizations that make it harder to understand the argument afterwards.

5.3 Case Study

We have now discussed how the approaches perform w.r.t. the evaluation metrics. To complement these numbers, we will in the following examine concrete adaptation outcomes based on the argument graph depicted in Fig. 1. An expert has created a query together with the corresponding adaptation rules—in fact, this example is part of our benchmark dataset used in the previous section. Please note that due to space constraints, we are unable to show full argument graphs and instead decided to present the beginning of each argument in plain text instead. The concepts changed from the original text are marked in italics.

Query: Should there be a cap on annuity increases for a change of remunerators?
Expert: *Annuity* prices should be limited by a cap when there's a change of *renumerator*. *Property owners* may want to earn as much as possible, and many, consistent with market principles, are prepared to pay higher *annuities,* ...
WordNet (Taxonomy, STRF): Rent prices should be limited by a cap when there's a change of *remunerator*. Landlords may want to earn as much as possible, and many, consistent with market principles, are prepared to pay higher rents, ...
LLM (chat-based): *Annuity increases* should be limited by a cap when there's a change of *remunerators*. *Annuity providers* may *be prepared to offer higher*

increases consistent with market principles, ... *Setting a cap on annuity increases in case of a change of remunerators is necessary since sudden changes in income and unaffordable annuity increases are unacceptable.*

Hybrid (Lenient, STRF): Rent costs should be limited by a cap when there's a change of *remunerator*. Landlords may want to earn as much as possible, and many, consistent with *economy* principles, are prepared to pay higher rents, ...

The conclusions one can draw from this example correspond to those of the previous section. The LLM reformulates large parts of the text and even adds new content at the end—an undesired behavior for our use case. The case adapted through WordNet only has one, but correct, adaptation: "tenant → remunerator". In addition to this one, the hybrid approach adapted "market → economy" which is equally sensible even though it is not part of the expert rules. When inspecting the generation process of the hybrid approach, we observed that many more rules were generated—for instance "rent → annuity". These were however not applied since they did not increase the similarity of the case to the query as much as other rule combinations. As such, it may not be the prime goal of an adaptation approach to maximize the similarity through generalization—an aspect that should be further investigated as part of future work.

6   Conclusion and Future Work

In this paper, we successfully designed and implemented an approach for generalizing argument graphs in the context of CBR. With the help of a new benchmark corpus, we demonstrated that the similarity between a retrieved case and a user's query can be increased by more than 20%. This is made possible by combining the taxonomic information obtained from WordNet with the generative powers of recent LLMs. Our tested approaches provide an easy-to-follow trace which changes have been made to an argument which is crucial to gain a user's trust. Revisiting the initial research question—can we increase the relevance of retrieved arguments through adaptation—it is now possible to answer it with a *cautious yes:* Despite needing more working in the future, our results are promising and show the potential even at this early stage. Given the low IAA of our benchmark corpus, using expert rules as a ground truth for this task should be questioned due to the inherent subjectivity involved in the annotation process.

In future work, one may use even more powerful LLMs to perform this task. Additionally, it may be worthwhile to fine-tune a LLM specific to generalizing/specializing argument graphs, the main obstacle here is the lack of adequate training data. Another useful aspect could be the introduction of a structural component to the adaptation—for instance, to remove nodes that are no longer relevant. Lastly, the runtime should be improved to enable the use of our approach in interactive scenarios.

Acknowledgements. This work has been funded by the DFG within the project *ReCAP-II* (No. 375342983) as part of the priority program RATIO (SPP-1999) as well as the *Studienstiftung*.

References

1. Aamodt, A., Plaza, E.: Case-based reasoning: foundational issues, methodological variations, and system approaches. AI Commun. **7**(1), 39–59 (1994)
2. Ashley, K.D.: Modelling legal argument: reasoning with cases and hypotheticals. Ph.D. thesis, University of Massachusetts, USA (1988)
3. Baydin, A.G., López de Mántaras, R., Simoff, S., Sierra, C.: CBR with common-sense reasoning and structure mapping: an application to mediation. In: Ram, A., Wiratunga, N. (eds.) ICCBR 2011. LNCS (LNAI), vol. 6880, pp. 378–392. Springer, Heidelberg (2011). https://doi.org/10.1007/978-3-642-23291-6_28
4. Becker, M., Staniek, M., Nastase, V., Frank, A.: Enriching argumentative texts with implicit knowledge. In: Frasincar, F., Ittoo, A., Nguyen, L.M., Métais, E. (eds.) NLDB 2017. LNCS, vol. 10260, pp. 84–96. Springer, Cham (2017). https://doi.org/10.1007/978-3-319-59569-6_9
5. Bergmann, R., Lenz, M., Ollinger, S., Pfister, M.: Similarity measures for case-based retrieval of natural language argument graphs in argumentation machines. In: The Thirty-Second International Flairs Conference, Florida, USA, pp. 329–334. AAAI Press (2019)
6. Bilu, Y., Slonim, N.: Claim synthesis via predicate recycling. In: 54th Annual Meeting of the ACL, Berlin, Germany, pp. 525–530 (2016)
7. Bojanowski, P., Grave, E., Joulin, A., Mikolov, T.: Enriching word vectors with subword information. arXiv (2016)
8. Brown, T.B., et al.: Language models are few-shot learners. arXiv (2020)
9. Campos, R., Mangaravite, V., Pasquali, A., Jorge, A.M., Nunes, C., Jatowt, A.: YAKE! collection-independent automatic keyword extractor. In: Pasi, G., Piwowarski, B., Azzopardi, L., Hanbury, A. (eds.) ECIR 2018. LNCS, vol. 10772, pp. 806–810. Springer, Cham (2018). https://doi.org/10.1007/978-3-319-76941-7_80
10. Carbonell, J.G.: Derivational analogy and its role in problem solving. In: Proceedings of the Third AAAI Conference on Artificial Intelligence, AAAI 1983, Washington, D.C., pp. 64–69. AAAI Press (1983)
11. Cer, D., et al.: Universal sentence encoder. arXiv (2018)
12. Cyras, K., Satoh, K., Toni, F.: Abstract argumentation for case-based reasoning. In: Baral, C., Delgrande, J.P., Wolter, F. (eds.) Principles of Knowledge Representation and Reasoning: Proceedings of the Fifteenth International Conference, KR 2016, Cape Town, South Africa, 25–29 April 2016, pp. 549–552. AAAI Press (2016). http://www.aaai.org/ocs/index.php/KR/KR16/paper/view/12879
13. Defourneaux, G., Peltier, N.: Analogy and abduction in automated deduction. In: Proceedings of the IJCAI 1997, pp. 216–221. Morgan Kaufmann (1997)
14. Devlin, J., Chang, M.W., Lee, K., Toutanova, K.: BERT: pre-training of deep bidirectional transformers for language understanding. arXiv (2018)
15. Dumani, L.: Good Premises Retrieval via a Two-Stage Argument Retrieval Model. Undefined (2019)
16. Dung, P.M.: On the acceptability of arguments and its fundamental role in non-monotonic reasoning, logic programming and n-person games. Artif. Intell. **77**(2), 321–357 (1995)

17. Fellbaum, C. (ed.): WordNet: An Electronic Lexical Database. Language, Speech and Communication. The MIT Press, Cambridge (1998)
18. Hesse, M.: On defining analogy. Proc. Aristotelian Soc. **60**, 79–100 (1959)
19. Krippendorff, K.: Reliability in content analysis: some common misconceptions and recommendations. Hum. Commun. Res. **30**(3), 411–433 (2004)
20. Lenz, M., Ollinger, S., Sahitaj, P., Bergmann, R.: Semantic textual similarity measures for case-based retrieval of argument graphs. In: Bach, K., Marling, C. (eds.) ICCBR 2019. LNCS (LNAI), vol. 11680, pp. 219–234. Springer, Cham (2019). https://doi.org/10.1007/978-3-030-29249-2_15
21. Mikolov, T., Chen, K., Corrado, G., Dean, J.: Efficient estimation of word representations in vector space. arXiv (2013)
22. Miller, G.A., Beckwith, R., Fellbaum, C., Gross, D., Miller, K.: WordNet: an on-line lexical database. Int. J. Lexicography (1990)
23. Passonneau, R.: Measuring agreement on set-valued items (MASI) for semantic and pragmatic annotation. In: Proceedings of LREC, Genoa, Italy. ELRA (2006)
24. Peldszus, A., Stede, M.: From argument diagrams to argumentation mining in texts: a survey. IJCINI **7**(1), 1–31 (2013)
25. Peldszus, A., Stede, M.: An annotated corpus of argumentative microtexts. In: Proceedings of the 1st European Conference on Argumentation, Lisbon, Portugal, vol. 2, pp. 801–815. College Publications (2015)
26. Petrov, S., Das, D., McDonald, R.: A universal part-of-speech tagset. In: Proceedings of LREC, Istanbul, Turkey, pp. 2089–2096. ELRA (2012)
27. Prade, H., Richard, G.: Analogical proportions and analogical reasoning - an introduction. In: Aha, D.W., Lieber, J. (eds.) ICCBR 2017. LNCS (LNAI), vol. 10339, pp. 16–32. Springer, Cham (2017). https://doi.org/10.1007/978-3-319-61030-6_2
28. Reed, C., Norman, T.J.: Argumentation Machines: New Frontiers in Argument and Computation, Argumentation Library, vol. 9. Springer, Dordrecht (2013)
29. Reimers, N., Gurevych, I.: Sentence-BERT: sentence embeddings using Siamese BERT-networks. In: Proceedings of EMNLP-IJCNLP, Hong Kong, China, pp. 3982–3992. ACL (2019)
30. Rissland, E.L., Ashley, K.D., Karl Branting, L.: Case-based reasoning and law. Knowl. Eng. Rev. **20**(3), 293–298 (2005)
31. Stab, C., et al.: ArgumenText: searching for arguments in heterogeneous sources. In: Proceedings of ACL, New Orleans, Louisiana, pp. 21–25. ACL (2018)
32. Stab, C., Gurevych, I.: Identifying argumentative discourse structures in persuasive essays. In: Proceedings EMNLP, Doha, Qatar, pp. 46–56. ACL (2014)
33. Vaswani, A., et al.: Attention is all you need. arXiv (2017)
34. Wachsmuth, H., et al.: Building an argument search engine for the web. In: Proceedings of the 4th Workshop on Argument Mining, Stroudsburg, PA, USA, pp. 49–59. ACL (2017)
35. Weber, R.O., Ashley, K.D., Brüninghaus, S.: Textual case-based reasoning. Knowl. Eng. Rev. **20**(3), 255–260 (2005)

Failure-Driven Transformational Case Reuse of Explanation Strategies in CloodCBR

Ikechukwu Nkisi-Orji[(✉)], Chamath Palihawadana, Nirmalie Wiratunga, Anjana Wijekoon, and David Corsar

School of Computing, Robert Gordon University, Aberdeen, UK
{i.nkisi-orji,c.palihawadana,n.wiratunga,a.wijekoon1,d.corsar1}@rgu.ac.uk

Abstract. In this paper, we propose a novel approach to improve problem-solving efficiency through the reuse of case solutions. Specifically, we introduce the concept of failure-driven transformational case reuse of explanation strategies, which involves transforming suboptimal solutions using relevant components from nearest neighbours in sparse case bases. To represent these explanation strategies, we use behaviour trees and demonstrate their usefulness in solving similar problems. Our approach uses failures as a starting point for generating new solutions, analysing the causes and contributing factors to the failure. From this analysis, new solutions are generated through a nearest neighbour-based transformation of previous solutions, resulting in solutions that address the failure. We compare different approaches for reusing solutions of the nearest neighbours and empirically evaluate whether the transformed solutions meet the required explanation intents. Our proposed approach has the potential to significantly improve problem-solving efficiency in sparse case bases with complex case solutions.

Keywords: case-based reasoning · case reuse · explainable AI · behaviour trees

1 Introduction

iSee project uses case-based reasoning (CBR) to systematically capture, retrieve, reuse, revise, and retain user explanation experiences for the benefit of other users. The primary objective is to establish a comprehensive repository of best practices, which can subsequently pave the way to compliance in explainable AI (XAI). An explanatory experience, in its most fundamental form, comprises two key components: the explanation requirement (a detailed description of the case problem) and the suggested explanation approach (a thorough depiction of the case solution).

The problem description should primarily capture the enquiries for which end-users are expected to seek answers through an explanation. However, the

This research is funded by the iSee project. iSee is an EU CHIST-ERA project which received funding for the UK from EPSRC under grant number EP/V061755/1.

S. Massie and S. Chakraborti (Eds.): ICCBR 2023, LNAI 14141, pp. 279–293, 2023.
https://doi.org/10.1007/978-3-031-40177-0_18

problem description encompasses more than just these queries. It must also incorporate the context, considering factors such as the application domain, the black-box model, the data utilised in model creation, and crucially, the end-users' knowledge levels. By addressing these aspects, an explanation experience within the iSee project guarantees that the recommended strategies cover all facets of XAI. The solution description captures the explanation strategy, which unlike a single explanation captures alternative ways in which end-users' explanation needs can evolve. Recent work suggests that multiple explanations (such as factual, semi-factual, and counterfactual) using alternative explanation techniques are necessary to achieve user satisfaction and engagement with XAI [11,12]. In iSee, an explanation strategy is captured as a behaviour tree [14] in order to manage transitions between alternative explanation styles in an interactive manner (e.g., conversational interaction using a chatbot).

Given the complex structure (as opposed to a class label) and inherent sparseness of the collection of explanation experience cases, it is unlikely that a solution derived from a single neighbouring case would be sufficient to satisfy the end-user's explanation needs. This circumstance necessitates the implementation of efficient reuse operations to ensure that the CBR system can combine explanation strategies from multiple cases. In particular, we examine the impact of failures in aligning with end-user questions on suboptimal explanation strategies, and alternatively, identify neighbouring cases wherein entire or partial explanation strategies can be amalgamated based on varying degrees of correspondence. Specifically, we study the impact of failures in matching end-user questions which lead to suboptimal explanation strategies and instead identify neighbouring cases wherein entire or partial explanation strategies can be combined based on levels of match. Since the underlying CBR engine used with iSee is CloodCBR [9], it becomes important to implement reuse operators that are compatible with the microservices architecture upon which CloodCBR is built. Accordingly, the key contributions of this paper are as follows.

- Formalise a novel reuse operator as a transformational adaptation method for CloodCBR aligned with the modular and scalable design requirements of its microservices architecture.
- Evaluate the effectiveness of the reuse operator and provide insights into its operation.

The remainder of this paper is structured as follows. Section 2 provides a brief overview of previous work on adaptation techniques for case reuse. Section 3 introduces our failure-driven reuse technique and the updates to CloodCBR to support the reuse operation. Section 4 measures the extent to which the reuse operation satisfies the intent of the query and discusses our findings. Section 5 concludes the paper with considerations for future work.

2   Related Work

There are two main approaches to learning adaptation knowledge for case reuse: weighted majority voting and case difference heuristic (CDH) [15]. Weighted majority voting is a method used in k-NN retrieval to determine the solution of a query by calculating the weighted majority of the solutions of the k-nearest neighbours [6,13]. To determine the optimal value of k, several techniques in this method employ a leave-one-out test that computes a set of n closest neighbours for each query case, where n ranges from 1 to the size of the case base. Weighted majority voting is applied to each set of neighbours to calculate the solution of the query, which is then compared to the actual solution. The value of n that results in the best overall quality of the CBR system is used as the value of k in the future. The CDH approach, first proposed by Hanney and Keane [3], involves pairing cases from the case base and using each pair to learn a rule for adapting one case to another [4,5,7,16]. Liao, Liu, and Chao [5] proposed a CDH adaptation method for regression tasks that employs a case difference heuristic approach and a neural network to learn the difference characterisation. Their approach involves training a network to map problem differences to differences in output values, eliminating the need for pre-defined generalisation strategies. Additionally, Jalali, Leake, and Forouzandehmehr [4] used the CDH approach for classification by using a statistical method to generate case adaptation rules while Ye, Xiaomeng, et al. [16] introduced an approach that uses neural networks to learn adaptation knowledge from pairs of cases. Unlike the case solutions in this paper, these adaptation techniques work with simple structures such as class labels in classification tasks and numbers in regression tasks.

3   Failure-Driven Reuse

Organising multiple end-user enquiries into distinct intents can streamline their management and improve efficiency. This approach involves systematically categorising questions based on their underlying purpose or intent, resulting in more coherent and targeted responses to each group of enquiries. Additionally, this organisation facilitates the evaluation of failure for Reuse by identifying the extent to which questions have been matched during the retrieval process and the degree to which intents have been addressed.

3.1   Case Representation

In iSee, a case c consists of attributes which include a user intent and a set of questions that express that intent as shown in Fig. 1. The explanation strategy for the intent-related questions forms the case solution. Other attributes in the case description are used to express the context of the explanation strategy such as the attributes of the AI Model (e.g., AI task and dataset type), the explanation criteria (e.g., explanation scope) and the user/user group (e.g., knowledge level). The attributes that form the representation of the case are formalised by iSeeOnto[1].

---

[1] iSee ontologies that form part of the iSee project https://w3id.org/iSeeOnto/ explanationexperience.

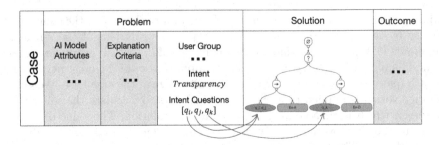

Fig. 1. Explanation Experience Case structure.

As depicted in Fig. 1, the focus of this paper is the explanation intent that is expressed as questions and how the solution aligns with the questions to satisfy the intent. For example, a user can express their explanation need, i.e. intent for transparency of the AI model or the decisions of the AI model by using one or more questions. A complete case should consist of a solution that addresses each question to the user's satisfaction.

Case solution is an explanation strategy modelled using Behaviour Trees (BT). A BT is a conceptual model that formalises the behaviours and navigation of an entity in an environment [1]. We adapt BTs for designing explanation strategies by introducing behaviours such as detecting an intent or a question and executing an explainer. Table 1 presents the nodes and functionalities used in the Explanation Strategy BT design.

Table 1. Explanation Strategy Behaviour Tree Nodes.

Type	Node	Description
Composite	Sequence	Has one or more children nodes and the children nodes are executed from left to right until one fails
	Priority	Has one or more children nodes and the children nodes are executed from left to right until one succeeds
Condition	Intent	Given user intent, checks if it matches the node intent
	Question	Given user question, checks if it matches the node question
Action	Explainer	Given context of an explanation requirement including data instance and AI model decision, execute the explanation technique to generate an explanation

A sub-tree that consists of a Sequence Node with a Question Node and an Explainer Node as children is considered a self-contained sub-tree that is not affected by (or influences) other parts of the tree. Accordingly, an explanation strategy can be seen as a collection of such sub-trees that essentially guides the user to receive explanations as they raise questions. Figure 2 presents an example explanation strategy which can be interpreted as follows. If the intent is transparency and the user expressed this intent by posing *Q-A* question, the Integrated Gradients explainer is executed to provide an explanation. If the user has a follow-on question *Q-B*, the Nearest Neighbour explainer is executed. Similarly, if the user asked a Q-C question in relation to the performance intent, the AI Model Performance explainer is executed. Note that questions A, B and C can be pre-set questions which an AI system designer have considered to be relevant to end-users who might be seeking explanations. For instance, in a loan applicant assessment system aimed at determining eligibility for a loan, the question "how can I get a different outcome" represents an anticipated inquiry from applicants and falls under the category of actionability intent. Figure 3 presents examples of questions classified by their corresponding intents, as used in this work. The case solution BT is also formalised by iSeeOnto.

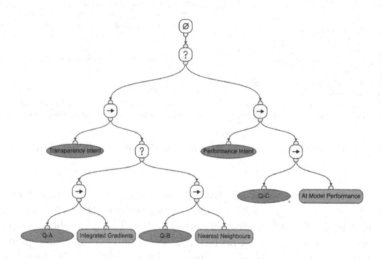

Fig. 2. A case solution modelled as a Behaviour Tree.

3.2 Reuse Failure and Transformation Using Gale-Shapley Algorithm

Due to the complex structure of BT case solutions and the sparse collection of explanation strategies, a single neighbouring case may not provide sufficient explanation for the end-user needs. Thus, we propose a reuse operation to combine explanation strategies from multiple cases. Specifically, we align end-user questions with case questions using the Gale-Shapley algorithm [2] to amalgamate entire or partial explanation strategies from neighbouring cases.

The Gale-Shapley algorithm, also known as the deferred acceptance algorithm, is a mechanism for solving the stable marriage problem. The problem involves finding a stable matching between two sets of equal size, such as men and women, doctors and hospitals, or students and schools. The algorithm works

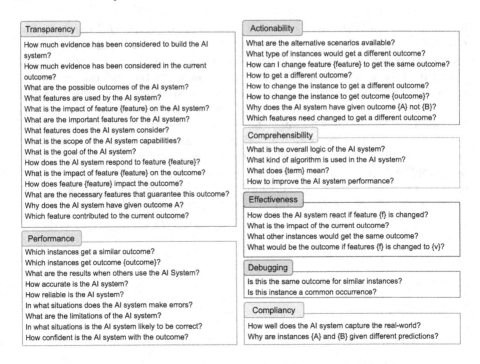

Fig. 3. Examples of question templates for different explanation intents.

by having each member of one set, say the men, propose to their most preferred member of the other set, say the women. Each woman then reviews her proposals and rejects all but her most preferred suitor. The men who were rejected then propose to their next most preferred woman, and the process repeats until every woman is engaged. The algorithm guarantees that a stable matching will be reached, meaning that there are no two pairs who would both prefer to be with each other instead of their current partners. In addition, the matching is "men-optimal", which means that every man is matched with his most preferred woman among all possible stable matchings, and "women-pessimal", which means that every woman is matched with her least preferred man among all possible stable matchings.

Given a query, we perform a retrieval of K nearest cases using an appropriate retrieval strategy. Starting with the closest case to the query, we match the query questions with the case questions using the Gale-Shapley algorithm. The preference order of a question in one set is determined by the similarity of that question with every question in the other set. We use Sentence-BERT (SBERT), a variant of the pretrained BERT network that utilises siamese and triplet network architectures to derive semantically meaningful sentence embeddings [10]. When applied to the question texts, the resulting embeddings are then compared using cosine similarity. After a stable matching is found, we determine the average similarity of the returned question pairs using SBERT and check if the score is up to an acceptance threshold, α. If the average similarity score reaches the threshold, we stop and reuse the explanation strategies that are associated with the matched case questions. Otherwise, we increase the case neighbourhood by 1 and apply the Gale-Shapley algorithm again. This process of increasing the neighbours continues until either the average score of the question pairs reaches α or we have considered all K cases.

The matching process is as shown in the recursion in Eq. 1. NN_i is the set of questions in the ith nearest case retrieved and K is the maximum number of cases that are retrieved for the reuse operation. We initialise α to a real value in the interval $[0, 1]$, $i = 1$ and $L_q = NN_i$.

$$MATCH(c_q, L_q) = \begin{cases} \text{pairs, score } = match(c_q, L_q), & \text{if score } \geq \alpha \text{ or } i = K \\ MATCH(c_q, L_q + NN_{i+1}), & \text{otherwise} \end{cases}$$

(1)

The function $match(c_q, L)$ in Eq. 1 implements the Gale-Shapley algorithm and is executed whenever we call $MATCH(c_q, L_q)$. Operation $L_q + NN_{i+1}$ increases i by 1 and also increases the neighbourhood for consideration of reuse by 1. In our experiments, we observed that α values in the range of 0.6 to 0.9 yielded positive results. $match(c_q, L)$ matches unequal sets (that is, query questions and questions of retrieved cases) as follows.

1. Let c_q be the set of query-associated questions and L_q be the set of questions from k nearest cases that are retrieved for the query
2. For each $x \in c_q$, create a preference list $pref(x, L_q)$ that orders the elements of L_q by similarity (decreasing) to x. Create similar preference lists for each $y \in L_q$ for the elements of c_q
3. Initialize all $x \in c_q$ and $y \in L_q$ to be without partners (unpaired)
4. While there exists at least one x without a partners and $y \in L_q$ which x has not attempted to pair with:
   (a) Choose x
   (b) Let y be the highest-ranked L_q in $pref(x, L_q)$ to whom x has not yet attempted to pair with
   (c) If y is free (i.e. not already paired), then pair x and y
   (d) Otherwise, if y is currently paired to another $\bar{x} \in c_q$, then compare x and $\bar{x}$ using y's preference list $(pref(y, c_q))$:
      i. If y prefers x over $\bar{x}$, then break the pairing between y and $\bar{x}$ and pair x and y
      ii. Otherwise, x remains unpaired and continues the attempt to pair with the remaining $\bar{y} \in L_q$
5. The algorithm terminates when every free c_q has attempted to pair with every member of L_q.

When the matching method is terminated, we return *pairs* (pairs of matched query and case questions) and *score* (average similarity of *pairs*). The solution that is being constructed from *pairs* is considered to have failed whenever *score* is less than α.

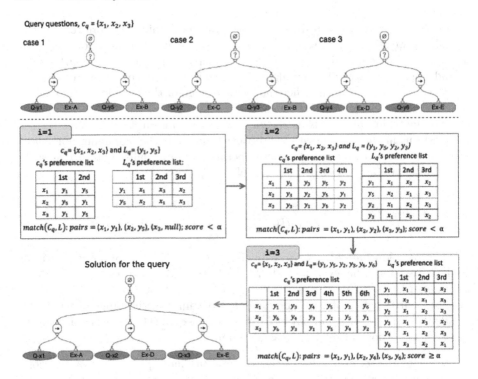

Fig. 4. Example showing how the solution of a query case is transformed using the nearest case.

We demonstrate how $MATCH(c_q, L_q)$ works using the example in Fig. 4. The example shows the query case c_q with three questions and the solution parts of three closest cases that have been retrieved from the case base. In the first matching attempt (that is, $i = 1$) and L_q containing *case 1* only, the Gale-Shapley algorithm ($match(c_q, L_q)$) is used to determine a stable matching between c_q and L_q based on their preference lists. The list of preferences for c_q shows that x_1 prefers y_1 over y_2 because $sim(x_1, y_1) > sim(x_1, y_2)$. The similarity function $sim(x, y)$ determines the similarity of x and y and in our case, we used the cosine similarity of vector representations from SBERT. Using the similarity function, the preference list for y_1 shows that $sim(y_1, x_1) > sim(y_1, x_3) > sim(y_1, x_2)$. With the preference lists, x_1 matches y_1 to form the first pair of $match(c_q, L_q)$ and x_2 matches y_5 as the second pair. When we attempt to match x_3, we find that its first preference y_1 is already paired with x_1. We consult the list of preferences of y_1 which shows that y_1 prefers x_1 over x_3. Consequently, the pair (x_1, y_1) remains unchanged. Continuing the attempt to pair x_3, we check the next entry in its preference list, which is y_5. As y_5 is already paired with x_2 and y_5 prefers x_2 over x_3, x_3 remains unpaired in this round. At this point, we determine *score* of the pairs as:

$$score = \frac{sim(x_1, y_1) + sim(x_2, y_5)}{|c_q| = 3}.$$

Assuming *score* is below the acceptance threshold α, we increase i which expands L_q to include the next closest neighbour. $match(c_q, L_q)$ is repeated which can undo previously matched pairs. For example, at $i = 2$ in Fig. 4, y_2 was found to be a better match for x_2 than its previous pairing. This results in an update of the pair from (x_2, y_5) to (x_2, y_2). When the algorithm ends (that is, when $score \geq \alpha$ or all retrieved cases have been considered), we construct the BT solution (explanation strategy) with the final pairs using the relevant parts of the matched cases.

3.3   Solution Construction and execution

A constructively adapted explanation strategy is executed as part of a conversational interaction, which is also modelled as a BT. While the complete interaction model is not within the scope of this paper, Fig. 5 shows how an explanation strategy is incorporated into the interaction model. The interaction model is designed to be generalisable to any explanation strategy. Accordingly, at runtime, the explanation strategy dynamically replaces the Explanation Strategy placeholder Node. The immediate parent sub-tree is a "Repeat-until-success" node that iteratively interacts with the user to get their intent question (Get explanation need Node) and executes the respective sub-tree in the explanation strategy. This is repeated until a failure occurs. There are two cases which we consider as failures to exit the iteration: when the user indicates that they have no other questions, or when the explanation strategy is not able to answer user questions. The latter is recorded as feedback for future improvements to the explanation strategy.

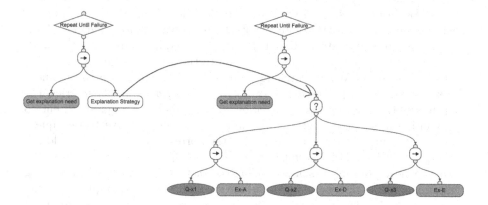

Fig. 5. Dynamic adaptation of the interaction model to execute the Explanation Strategy.

3.4   CloodCBR Enhancements For the Reuse Operation

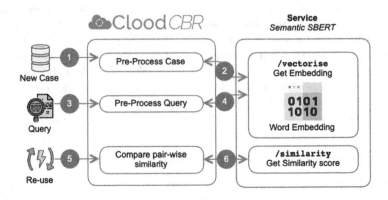

Fig. 6. CloodCBR Changes to Support Sentence Transformers.

As CloodCBR is the CBR framework for iSee, we briefly discuss the changes to CloodCBR to support the reuse operation. CloodCBR's microservices architecture and extensibility facilitates the seamless integration of new similarity metrics. To incorporate state-of-the-art text embedding models (such as SBERT [10]), we first developed an independent *semantic-sim* service with API endpoints */vectorise* and */similarity*. The *vectorise* endpoint returns the text-embedding for a given string while the *similarity* endpoint vectorises and returns the cosine similarity between the embeddings of a pair of texts. The service was then integrated in CloodCBR as follows.

1. Case Creation - When a new case is added to the case base, CloodCBR undergoes a pre-processing step that can include various similarity metrics, such as ontology retrieval or text embedding. For attributes that have been configured to use Sentence-BERT for word embedding similarity, the word embeddings are generated via an API call to the semantic-sim service.

2. Query/Retrieval - When searching the case base for similar cases, the query case undergoes pre-processing according to the chosen similarity metrics. For an attribute that requires word embedding similarity, a request is sent to semantic-sim service to retrieve the word embedding. The vectorised query attribute value is then compared with the corresponding case embeddings using a cosine similarity script in the case base [8].

3. Post-retrieval/Reuse - When we need to compare texts using word embedding after case retrieval, e.g., determining the similarity of a pair of question texts in the Gale-Shapley implementation for reuse, we use a call to *similarity*.

The reuse operation is implemented as a Python function and forms part of the core service for managing the phases of the CBR cycle. We have open-sourced the integration and API service for semantic-sim on GitHub[2].

4 Evaluation

We conducted an experiment to evaluate the effectiveness of the reuse operation with CloodCBR by measuring the alignment between the intent of the constructed solution and the intent of the query.

4.1 Experiment Setup

In the experiment, we generate cases using a bank of intents with associated questions as shown in Fig. 3. We randomly assign a name and an intent to each case. Using the intent-question bank, we randomly sample questions for the selected intent based a Poisson distribution (lambda = 2). As shown in Fig. 7, there are instances where no questions are sampled because the Poisson value is 0. In such situation, we repeatedly generate a new Poisson value until it is greater than 0. We ensure that every case in the case base is unique and that there is one intent per case for simplicity.

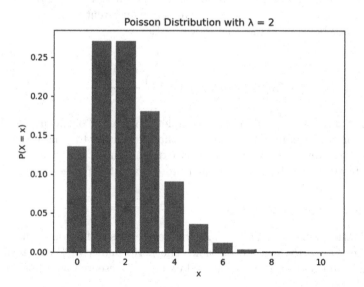

Fig. 7. Poisson distribution for sampling intent questions for the generation of cases and queries.

---

[2] https://github.com/RGU-Computing/clood/tree/master/other-services/semantic-sim.

Using the CloodCBR framework, we create and configure a CBR application with the case-base structure as described in Sect. 3.1. We investigate the reuse of cases for different case base sizes (20, 30, 40, 60, 80, and 100) and acceptance thresholds (0.5 to 0.9) using the introduced Gale-Shapley matching technique (GSA). We analyse the impact of deferred acceptance between iterations of $MATCH(c_q, L_q)$ (see Eq. 1) by including a variant with non-deferred acceptance (NDA). In the NDA approach, any question-pair similarity that reaches α is not unpaired when L_q is increased in subsequent iterations. Reuse of closest-neighbour best match (BM) forms the baseline approach. Both GSA and NDA approaches can be viewed as transformations of BM by reusing solutions from multiple cases.

The queries are generated in a manner similar to the cases but have no solutions. We used a set of 50 queries for the experiments and retrieved the five nearest neighbours for each query ($K = 5$). The case solutions are the explanation strategies that are associated with the questions.

In the evaluation, we estimate the level of satisfaction with the intent of the query by assessing how well the intent of the constructed solution aligns with the intent of the query. Specifically, we analyse the extent to which the intent of the questions of the cases that were matched with the query aligns with the intent of the query. Recall that the algorithm of the GSA reuse operation returns a set of question pairs, P with each pair $< x, y >$ consisting of $x \in c_q$ and $y \in L_q$ as described in Sect. 3.2. Let I_x represent the intent of c_q and I_y represent the intent of the case to which y belongs. We define an intent satisfaction metric as a real number between 0 and 1 as shown in Eq. 2.

$$\text{Intent Satisfaction} = \frac{\sum_{i=1}^{|P|}(I_q = I_{c_i})}{|c_q|} \tag{2}$$

Intent Satisfaction $= 0$ shows a complete mismatch between the intent of the question and the intent of the cases that were used to construction a proposed explanation strategy. At the other extreme, Intent Satisfaction $= 1$ show a complete alignment between the query intent and the reused cases.

4.2 Results and Discussion

The evaluation results in Fig. 8 show the degree of satisfaction with the intent of the query after the reuse operation. The performance of BM, which always reuses the solution of the best-matched case, is represented as a line because it is not affected by α.

As expected, it was better to reuse the solutions of more cases than the best-matched case alone. GSA tends to outperform NDA at low α value (0.5). This is also expected since GSA uses the average similarity of pairings to check for failure, while NDA identifies failure per question. The impact is that NDA reuses more cases than GSA for constructing a solution. At $\alpha = 0.5$, GSA reuses 2 closest-neighbours cases, while NDA reuses 2.5 cases. GSA has the better

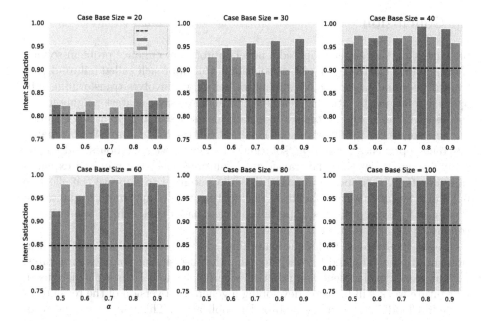

Fig. 8. Results showing the level of satisfaction with the query intent using different reuse methods for different case base sizes and acceptance thresholds (α).

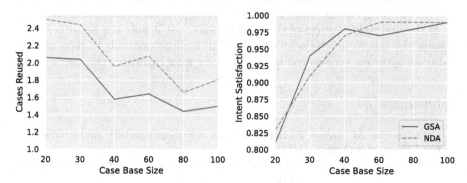

Fig. 9. Average number of nearest cases used for the reuse operation with the corresponding intent satisfaction for different case base sizes.

performance when the case base is sparse (i.e., 30 and 40) while NDA was better for case base sizes 60 and 80. When the case base is relatively large (i.e. 100) both GSA and NDA have identical intent satisfaction measures except that NDA continues to reuse more case than GSA as shown in Fig. 9. In general, the GSA approach uses fewer cases to achieve solutions with relatively high intent satisfaction compared to NDA for all case base sizes. The ability to reuse a smaller number of cases to construct a good solution is crucial in situations where the sparsity of the case base is a significant concern.

5   Conclusion

In conclusion, this paper proposed a novel approach to enhance problem-solving efficiency through the reuse of case solutions. Our approach called failure-driven transformational case reuse of explanation strategies involves transforming suboptimal solutions by utilising relevant components from nearest neighbours in sparse case bases. Our approach uses failures as a starting point for generating new solutions, resulting in solutions that address the failure. We compared different approaches for reusing solutions of the nearest neighbours and empirically evaluated whether the transformed solutions meet the required explanation intents. The proposed approach has the potential to improve the effective reuse of relevant cases and facilitate the identification of appropriate adaptation strategies for new problems, especially in case bases that exhibit sparsity and complexity in case solutions.

The proposed reuse technique is not limited to its current domain of application and can be extended to other domains that use similar complex structures, such as game development and robotics, where behaviour trees are widely used. Our future work will focus on developing a generalised version of the reuse technique in CloodCBR to enable its broader application. This will include incorporating options for different use cases, such as allowing duplicates in the second element of the matching pairs (i.e., different explanation needs are satisfied by the same explainer), to enhance its flexibility and adaptability to a wider range of scenarios. Also, the intent satisfaction index used in the experiments measures one of the desirable features of the explanations, but it may not be sufficient to measure the quality of the solutions. We will explore methods to measure the quality of solutions such as conducting a study with real cases and users.

References

1. Colledanchise, M., Ögren, P.: Behavior Trees in Robotics and AI: An Introduction. CRC Press, Boca Raton (2018)
2. Dubins, L.E., Freedman, D.A.: Machiavelli and the gale-shapley algorithm. Am. Math. Mon. **88**(7), 485–494 (1981)
3. Hanney, K., Keane, M.T.: Learning adaptation rules from a case-base. In: Smith, I., Faltings, B. (eds.) EWCBR 1996. LNCS, vol. 1168, pp. 179–192. Springer, Heidelberg (1996). https://doi.org/10.1007/BFb0020610
4. Jalali, V., Leake, D., Forouzandehmehr, N.: Learning and applying case adaptation rules for classification: an ensemble approach. In: IJCAI, pp. 4874–4878 (2017)
5. Liao, C.K., Liu, A., Chao, Y.S.: A machine learning approach to case adaptation. In: 2018 IEEE First International Conference on Artificial Intelligence and Knowledge Engineering (AIKE), pp. 106–109. IEEE (2018)
6. Lowe, D.G.: Similarity metric learning for a variable-kernel classifier. Neural Comput. **7**(1), 72–85 (1995)
7. McSherry, D.: An adaptation heuristic for case-based estimation. In: Smyth, B., Cunningham, P. (eds.) EWCBR 1998. LNCS, vol. 1488, pp. 184–195. Springer, Heidelberg (1998). https://doi.org/10.1007/BFb0056332

8. Nkisi-Orji, I., Palihawadana, C., Wiratunga, N., Corsar, D., Wijekoon, A.: Adapting semantic similarity methods for case-based reasoning in the cloud. In: Keane, M.T., Wiratunga, N. (eds.) Case-Based Reasoning Research and Development. ICCBR 2022. LNCS, vol. 13405, pp. 125–139. Springer, Cham (2022). https://doi.org/10.1007/978-3-031-14923-8_9

9. Nkisi-Orji, I., Wiratunga, N., Palihawadana, C., Recio-García, J.A., Corsar, D.: CLOOD CBR: towards microservices oriented case-based reasoning. In: Watson, I., Weber, R. (eds.) ICCBR 2020. LNCS (LNAI), vol. 12311, pp. 129–143. Springer, Cham (2020). https://doi.org/10.1007/978-3-030-58342-2_9

10. Reimers, N., Gurevych, I.: Sentence-bert: sentence embeddings using siamese bert-networks. arXiv preprint arXiv:1908.10084 (2019)

11. Schoonderwoerd, T.A., Jorritsma, W., Neerincx, M.A., Van Den Bosch, K.: Human-centered XAI: developing design patterns for explanations of clinical decision support systems. Int. J. Hum. Comput. Stud. **154**, 102684 (2021)

12. Sokol, K., Flach, P.: One explanation does not fit all: the promise of interactive explanations for machine learning transparency. KI-Künstliche Intelligenz **34**(2), 235–250 (2020)

13. Wettschereck, D., Aha, D.W.: Weighting features. In: Veloso, M., Aamodt, A. (eds.) ICCBR 1995. LNCS, vol. 1010, pp. 347–358. Springer, Heidelberg (1995). https://doi.org/10.1007/3-540-60598-3_31

14. Wijekoon, A., Corsar, D., Wiratunga, N.: Behaviour trees for conversational explanation experiences. arXiv preprint arXiv:2211.06402 (2022)

15. Wilke, W., Vollrath, I., Althoff, K.D., Bergmann, R.: A framework for learning adaptation knowledge based on knowledge light approaches. In: Proceedings of the Fifth German Workshop on Case-Based Reasoning, pp. 235–242 (1997)

16. Ye, X., Leake, D., Jalali, V., Crandall, D.J.: Learning adaptations for case-based classification: a neural network approach. In: Sánchez-Ruiz, A.A., Floyd, M.W. (eds.) ICCBR 2021. LNCS (LNAI), vol. 12877, pp. 279–293. Springer, Cham (2021). https://doi.org/10.1007/978-3-030-86957-1_19

A Case-Based Approach for Workflow Flexibility by Deviation

Lisa Grumbach[1(✉)] and Ralph Bergmann[1,2]

[1] German Research Center for Artificial Intelligence (DFKI),
Branch University of Trier, Behringstraße 21, 54296 Trier, Germany
{lisa.grumbach,ralph.bergmann}@dfki.de
[2] Business Information Systems II, University of Trier, 54296 Trier, Germany
bergmann@uni-trier.de
http://www.wi2.uni-trier.de

Abstract. This paper presents a case-based approach for workflow flexibility by deviation. In previous work, a constraint-based workflow model and engine have been developed that allow for flexible deviations from predefined workflow models during run-time. When encountering deviations, domain-independent strategies can be applied for a resolution in order to regain support for the process participant. To improve this deviation handling, a case-based approach is presented that integrates experiential knowledge by exploiting previously terminated workflows as cases. Similar cases are retrieved through a time-series based similarity measure and reused through null adaptation. The experimental evaluation showed an improvement of the defined utility value concerning the computed work items, when comparing the constraint-based workflow engine and the case-based deviation management.

Keywords: Workflow Flexibility · Case-Based Reasoning · Knowledge Management

1 Introduction

Flexible workflows have been researched for more than a decade [14], as customer-orientation is becoming more and more important and therefore adapting to specific needs is substantial. In traditional workflow systems, models are specified at design-time and describe the ideal order of tasks. During run-time these models are instantiated and strictly prescribe the order of task execution, whereas deviations are only possible when circumventing the system. Thus, all possible execution variants have to be modelled at design-time, which requires a great effort and is barely possible, as not all situations can be foreseen. A solution would be to model the standard procedure with few but frequent workflow variants and allow controlled deviations at run-time. To this end, an approach is necessary that handles deviations from predefined models in an automated manner and offers flexibility through continuous support to the process participant about how to successfully terminate the workflow.

S. Massie and S. Chakraborti (Eds.): ICCBR 2023, LNAI 14141, pp. 294–308, 2023.
https://doi.org/10.1007/978-3-031-40177-0_19

On the one hand, we proposed a constraint-based workflow approach, that is able to retract violated constraints at run-time and subsequently utilize remaining constraints for workflow control. On the other hand, domain-specific knowledge can be used to suggest tasks for workflow progression. For this purpose, we aim at exploiting experiential knowledge.

Flexible workflows are beneficial in several domains, such as production planning [9] or situation management [11]. We investigate this approach in the context of the exemplary domain of deficiency management in construction. This workflow is essential in the construction sector, as all projects require a final approval for which all defects have to be eliminated. For this process, flexibility is crucial, as not all types of defects and their handling can be known in advance.

In Sect. 2 relevant foundations for the approach are presented including workflow flexibility, semantic workflows and our constraint-based workflow engine. In Sect. 3, the concept of the envisioned case-based deviation management is introduced, which aims at enhancing deviation handling capabilities of the constraint-based workflow engine. The focus is laid on the retrieve and reuse phase. The approach is evaluated based on an experiment in the chosen domain of deficiency management in construction that simulates the usage of the flexible workflow system in Sect. 4. The paper concludes with reflecting the findings and giving an outlook on future research in Sect. 5.

2 Foundations

In this section a basic classification of workflow flexibility and a specification of the underlying terminology will be given. This includes the used semantic workflows and our previously presented constraint-based workflow engine.

2.1 Workflow Flexibility

Workflow flexibility can be categorized into four types [15]. *Flexibility by Design* requires to incorporate all execution alternatives into the model at design-time. *Flexibility by Underspecification* allows instantiating partial models that require integrating placeholders during design-time, either blank ones or several alternatives, specified during run-time. *Flexibility by Change* allows interventions during run-time and a re-modeling of parts of the workflow. All of these flexibility variants require either knowledge about all possible alternatives at design-time, which is impossible, or an adaptation at run-time, which requires expert knowledge concerning workflow modeling. The fourth variant, *Flexibility by Deviation* tries to counteract these disadvantages by enabling deviations at run-time, without necessary modeling effort, but still supporting the process participant with suggestions about the next activities. Thus, single instances may not fit to the workflow model. Therefore we explicitly distinguish between modeled, denoted as *de jure*, and executed workflow, called *de facto* [1]. The de facto workflow is not an instantiated de jure workflow, but represents the actually enacted tasks traced sequentially. Based on this definition we developed a workflow engine facilitating flexibility by deviation. Only few research exists concerning this approach, which still requires a manual intervention of the process participant [2].

2.2 Constraint-Based Workflow Engine

During previous projects we developed a flexible workflow engine based on constraints. We presented an approach [5,6] that allows flexible deviations from prescribed workflows, but still maintains control and recommends valid work items to a limited extent. The proposed method is applied to imperatively modeled block-oriented workflows. Those workflows are constructed through a single root block element, which in turn consists of a single task node, a sequence of two block elements or a control-flow block. Start and end of control-flow blocks are clearly defined through control-flow nodes. An example is shown in Fig. 1.

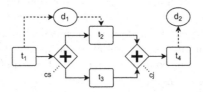

Fig. 1. Example Block-Oriented Workflow.

The exemplary workflow consists of four task nodes (rectangles), two data nodes (ovals) and two control-flow nodes (rhombuses), which represent a parallel control-flow block ("+"). Additionally, the edges denote either control-flow (solid lines) or data-flow (dashed lines, input or output relation).

In our approach we transform these imperative workflow models into declarative constraints, which indicate sequential dependencies, to be able to determine task activations and thus possible executions in a specific unterminated state of the workflow. A constraint satisfaction problem (CSP) is constructed on the basis of these generated constraints and logged task enactments. A solution of the CSP is searched for, which tries to calculate a valid sequential enactment of all already executed and possible future executions of tasks. Thus, with a solution we are able to recommend valid task enactments. Consider the example of Fig. 1, the constraint set as logical formula is constructed as follows: $t_1 < t_2 \land t_1 < t_3 \land t_2 < t_4 \land t_3 < t_4$. If task t_1 is executed, a value is assigned, in this case $t_1 = 1$, and added to the constraint set. Task recommendations are calculated by regarding possible task assignments of the next sequential value, in this case 2. Considering the constraint set either with $t_2 = 2$ or with $t_3 = 2$ a solution is found. Thus, t_2 and t_3 are added as work items to the work list.

An advantage of using a CSP is that it is easy and fast to retract violated constraints at run-time for restoring consistency in case of a deviation. Still, by regarding the remaining constraints valid solutions can be computed. In our work [5], we described a method which detects deviations and retracts violated constraints to restore consistency and re-enable the workflow engine to recommend work items. Different domain-independent strategies can be applied that assume a deviation category and transform the constraint net to adapt to the deviating situation. However, to apply these strategies, a choice must be made that requires knowledge about the deviation and the impact of the strategy. To further automate the deviation handling and to offer more sophisticated decision support based on experiential knowledge, we proposed a case-based approach.

2.3 Semantic Workflows

In the proposed case-based deviation management, semantic workflows are used as case representation, as they allow for an enrichment of semantic descriptions for tasks and data nodes and the workflow as such. Since the similarity assessment is additionally based on these semantic annotations, it is more sophisticated. The utilized specification of semantic workflows is denoted as *NEST-Graph* [3], and specified as quadruple $W = (N, E, S, T)$ where

- N is a set of nodes and
- $E \subseteq N \times N$ is a set of edges.
- $S : N \cup E \to \Sigma$ associates to each node and each edge a *semantic description* from a semantic metadata language Σ.
- $T : N \cup E \to \Omega$ associates to each node and each edge a type from Ω.
- Ω contains the following types of nodes: workflow, task, data, control-flow and types of edges: part-of, data-flow, control-flow and constraint.

Figure 2 shows an excerpt of a workflow instance from the domain of deficiency management in construction. This workflow consists of six task nodes, five data nodes and one workflow node. The edges denote either control-flow, data-flow

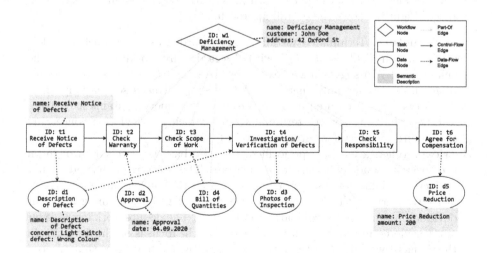

Fig. 2. Exemplary Block-Oriented Semantic Workflow Graph.

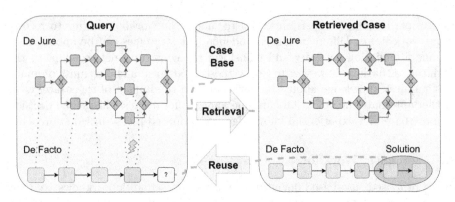

Fig. 3. Case-Based Deviation Management [5]. (Color figure online)

(input/output relation) or part-of edges. Furthermore, each node is associated with a semantic description, which contains additional information. In Fig. 2, some exemplary semantic descriptions are shown. The workflow node relates to some general information that concerns the whole workflow. The tasks' semantic descriptions only contain the name. The additional information of data nodes differ concerning the attributes. For instance in data node $d1$ further details are provided about the *description of defect* such as *concern* and *defect*.

The developed case-based approach [5,13] is presented in the next section.

3   Concept for a Case-Based Deviation Management

The case-based deviation management includes previously terminated workflows in the decision process of how to continue with the workflow after a deviation occurred. Figure 3 shows the overall approach.

Case Structure. Terminated workflows are regarded as cases. Each workflow case is a pair $WC = (J_C, F_C)$ with J_C as de jure workflow, which is the default model for suggesting an execution order, and F_C as de facto workflow, representing the actually enacted tasks, which are traced sequentially. Both workflows are represented as *NESTGraphs*. The query contains a de facto workflow that has not yet terminated and is facing a deviation concerning the de jure workflow (see orange node in Fig. 3).

Retrieve. When a query is performed, the case base is searched through on the basis of an adequate similarity measure. The objective is to find similar de facto workflows whose subsequences match the current instance (see de facto workflows with blue and orange nodes in Fig. 3), containing a similar deviation (orange node) compared to the query. The de jure workflow is so far not considered in the similarity assessment, as the focus is on the deviation in the de facto workflow. In the retrieved cases, the subsequences that succeed the deviation (see green-coloured nodes in Fig. 3) should not be considered when assessing the similarity, as this part is not existent in the query, but is rather a solution candidate.

Reuse. This most similar case or even several similar cases are then used to recommend tasks. The simplest reuse option, denoted as null adaptation, is to propose those tasks of the case that followed the subsequence ending with the deviation (see green-coloured nodes in Fig. 3).

Revise. As tasks are only recommended, the process participant is still able to execute a task that was not part of the solution resulting from the reuse step. Thus, by continuing the query workflow, the solution can be revised. Still, an evaluation of the terminated workflow is pending. This assessment decides whether the revised case can be retained as successful or failed case.

Retain. When the query workflow has terminated, its de facto workflow, containing the actual execution, can be integrated in the case base. Ideally, some kind of validation, positive or negative, is stored with the case in order to draw the correct conclusions in subsequent reuse steps. Before integrating single cases, it needs to be evaluated whether the informativeness can be increased or whether this additional knowledge is already covered by adaptation methods. Nevertheless, the case base can be enhanced continuously, which ultimately leads to a learning system.

This paper focusses on retrieval and reuse. On account of this, two variants of a similarity measure and one adaptation method are presented. The revise and retain phase are part of future work and were therefore only presented as abstract idea.

3.1 Retrieval with a Time-Series Based Similarity Measure

The retrieval phase bases on a similarity measure that is able to compare time series, presented in our previous work [13]. This measure is applied on the sequential de facto workflows and searches for a mapping of tasks considering edit distance by applying either the Smith-Waterman-Algorithm (SWA) [16] or warping of elements through the use of dynamic time warping (DTW) [4,12]. Besides, analogously to the vector similarity of Gundersen [7], local mappings are weighted according to their distance to the currently regarded task based on the assumption that tasks which are more far in the past have less influence on the deviation and subsequent tasks. Furthermore, data-flow similarity is included in the local similarity values of tasks considering their input and output data objects. The local similarity sim_T for tasks t^Q and t^C is used during alignment:

$$sim_T(t^Q, t^C) =$$
$$\frac{l_t * sim_N(t^Q, t^C) + l_i * sim_D(N_{t^Q}^{D_{in}}, N_{t^C}^{D_{in}}) + l_o * sim_D(N_{t^Q}^{D_{out}}, N_{t^C}^{D_{out}})}{l_t + l_i + l_o}$$
$$(1)$$

Each task node similarity is calculated by comparing the semantic descriptions of task nodes sim_N, finding a mapping of ingoing ($N^{D_{in}}$) and outgoing ($N^{D_{out}}$)

data nodes sim_D. Both variants of the similarity measure are based on computing a scoring matrix, integrating the temporal weighting factor. For more details we refer to our previous work [13]. The main difference of both methods is visible in the computation of the scoring matrix. Whereas DTW weights the similarity value according to warp or mapping of elements, SWA includes a penalty, which can be a constant value or a function, when the mapping origins out of an insertion or deletion and only considers the similarity when matching elements. The maximum value in the last row of the matrix represents the non-normalized global similarity score, which is further normalized to a value $sim \in [0, 1]$. More details were presented in our previous work [5, 13].

3.2   Reuse Through Null Adaptation

With the previously presented similarity measure, the most similar terminated workflow or a set of workflows can be retrieved from the case base. This can include several distinct cases with the same similarity score. Let $retrieved_Q$ be the set of retrieved cases with the highest similarity values. From these case workflows, work items can be derived.

Let $WC_i \in retrieved_Q$ be one of the similar cases. Then, one work item can be derived from the alignment in the scoring matrix. The position in the de facto workflow of the case that was aligned with the deviating task of the query needs to be determined (cf. orange-coloured node in Fig. 3). Let $align = \{(0,0), \ldots, (n, k)\}$ denote the alignment path. Then, the task $t_{last}^C \in N_{F_C}^T$ with position $pos(t_{last}^C) = k$ is the task of the case workflow that was the last to be aligned with an element of the query workflow. All tasks that are subsequent to t_{last}^C were not aligned to tasks of the query. The next one of these tasks can be recommended to the process participant as the next task, thus at $pos(t_{next}) = k + 1$ (cf. green-coloured nodes in Fig. 3).

$$workItems = \{t_{next} | t_{next} \in N_C^T \wedge pos(t_{next}) = pos(t_{last}^C) + 1 \wedge \\ WC_i = ((N_C^T, E, S, T), F_C) \in retrieved_Q\} \quad (2)$$

This adaptation method is efficient, as it simply bases on the mapping that origins from the retrieval phase without requiring additional handling.

4   Evaluation

The actual usefulness of the proposed approach considering the exemplary domain can only be evaluated in an empirical study with real experts in the construction industry. However, the necessary effort is too high. Instead, we conducted a study with simulated users under the assumption that the simulation at least roughly reflects the behaviour of real process participants [5].

4.1 Utility Criteria for Defined Process Participant Types

The essential criteria which is investigated is the *utility*. It is interpreted in this domain of flexible workflows as the degree to which the workflow can be terminated successfully. The overall utility can be determined through measuring the utility of work items during execution. To assess this property, various types of process participants are regarded in order to investigate and evaluate different behaviour of process participants and the corresponding reaction of the system.

Experienced. The experienced process participant constitutes an expert and knows how to handle any situation during process execution. This not only includes the ideal way of completing a workflow, but also recovering after deviations in case the workflow system is in an exceptional state without proper task suggestions. Her/his expectations of a flexible workflow system concern the support of those workflow instances that s/he would produce. The workflow engine is useful for this expert if the proposed work items correspond to the task executions s/he has in mind. Hence, utility of the workflow engine is measured as amount of support in contrast to misguidance. This is assessed by comparing the pursued task execution with the proposed work items of the workflow engine. If the task, which the experienced process participant would execute, is not among the list of proposed work items, the workflow engine would lead to a miscontrol, which is not useful. The utility can then be assessed on the basis of the ratio of the number of miscontrols ($nrOfMiscontrols$) and the number of task executions ($nrOfTasks$) in a workflow as degree of support:

$$utility_{experienced} = 1 - \frac{nrOfMiscontrols}{nrOfTasks} \tag{3}$$

Inexperienced. The inexperienced process participant, who can be regarded as a novice, relies on the support of the workflow engine, as s/he is not aware of the correct workflow execution and does not know how to continue after deviations. Each workflow instance executed by him/her is strictly adhering the suggested work items. Consequently, the success of an inexperienced process participant completely depends on the appropriateness of the work items proposed by the workflow engine. Hence, the workflow instances that can result from the execution of proposed work items are the basis to assess the degree of utility. Therefore, these resulting workflow instances can be compared to valid workflow instances. The minimum edit distance [8] gives information about the amount of conformance. Relating this edit distance ($editDistance$) to the total number of executed tasks ($nrOfTasks$) in the workflow instance indicates the utility:

$$utility_{inexperienced} = 1 - \frac{editDistance}{nrOfTasks} \tag{4}$$

Non-conforming. The non-conforming process participant executes his/her workflows in a non-conforming way, which includes executing tasks that are not part of the proposed work items, thus causing deviations from the de jure workflow with unknown consequences. The expectation of using a flexible workflow system is that, when encountering one of those undesired deviations again, the guidance leads to a better outcome than before. Successfully supporting a non-conforming process participant is interpreted as putting him/her back on the right track. The workflow engine should provide work items in order to recover from an undesired deviation. Taking a workflow instance with more than one deviation as starting point and letting the process participant complete the workflow instance, always following the work items proposed by the workflow engine after the first deviation, an adapted workflow instance emerges. In this case utility is defined as the improvement with respect to the workflow instance the user would create without support of the workflow engine, indicated by the reduction of necessary edit steps. Therefore, the minimum edit distance to a valid workflow of both the workflow instances that emerge with and without support of the workflow engine can be compared.

$$utility_{non-conforming} = 1 - \frac{\left(\frac{editDistanceNew}{nrOfTasksNew}\right)}{\left(\frac{editDistanceOriginal}{nrOfTasksOriginal}\right)} \tag{5}$$

4.2 Hypothesis

In the experimental evaluation the following hypotheses are investigated, which refer to the defined utility criteria and a comparison of the constraint-based workflow engine and the case-based null adaptation for determining work items.

H1 (*Experienced Process Participant*): When replaying a valid workflow, the executed tasks are mostly those proposed by the workflow engine. Consequently, the workflow engine achieves a high utility for the experienced process participant.

H2 (*Inexperienced Process Participant*): After a deviation from the workflow model, workflows can be terminated similarly to valid ones based on the suggestions of the workflow engine. Thus, the edit distance of proposed workflow instances compared to the most similar case of valid previous executions is small, indicating a high utility for the inexperienced process participant.

H3 (*Non-Conforming Process Participant*): The workflow engine can improve the outcome of workflow instances that have been terminated previously leading to an invalid workflow. Workflow instances that are terminated according to the proposed work items by the workflow engine after the first deviation have a smaller edit distance to the most similar valid workflow than the original workflow instance. Consequently, the utility for the non-conforming process participant is high.

H4 (*Comparing the Utility resulting from the Constraint-Based Workflow Engine and Null Adaptation*): The utility for each type of process participant is significantly higher when using the case-based null adaptation compared to using the constraint-based workflow engine.

4.3   Experimental Setup

Figure 4 shows the overall setting of the experimental evaluation.[1] As exemplary use case the domain of deficiency management in construction was regarded. Therefore two different workflow models were defined in consultation with an architect as expert. On the one hand, a model that specifies all standard cases is used as input for the workflow engine, as the situation would be when using a traditional system (see *simple model* in Fig. 4). On the other hand, this simple model was extended with various alternative execution paths, mapping the real-world handling of deficiencies (see *extended model* in Fig. 4). Generating this model means a lot of effort, which is to be avoided in practice. This extended model served for generating all possible de facto workflows that form the total list of valid cases in order to evaluate the approach. Based on these de facto workflows, workflow executions are simulated.

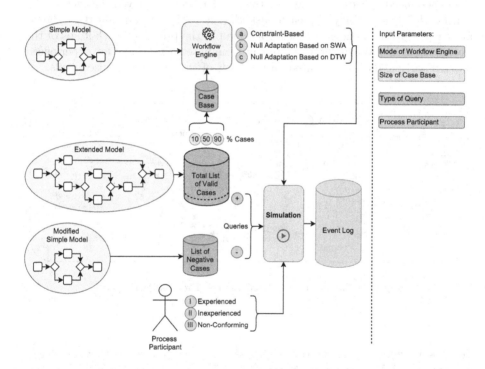

Fig. 4. Experimental Setup.

The experiment is done as a ten-fold cross validation, such that for each single validation run 10% of the cases of the total list of cases form the test set, which are used as queries. The total list of valid cases contains 2.184 positively rated

---

[1] The experiments were made on a laptop with (QuadCore) Intel(R) Core(TM) i7-10510U CPU @ 1.80 GHz 2.30 GHz, 16 GB RAM, 64 bit system, Windows 10.

traces. Each query is simulated as a trace replay several times with different parameters. The simulation produces an event log that is analysed concerning the assumed hypotheses. The parameters include:

- mode of workflow engine (ⓐ–ⓒ), which determines how work items are computed after each task
- size of case base (10/50/90%)
- type of query (⊕/⊖), *positively* rated queries are simulated for the *experienced* and *inexperienced* process participants, whereas *negatively* rated queries are simulated for the *non-conforming* process participant.
- type of process participant ((I)/(II)/(III))

Experienced. To evaluate the utility for the experienced process participant, a replay of the cases in the test set is simulated as presented in Fig. 5. For the experienced process participant, the exact trace is replayed for each query. During this trace replay, for each task that is replayed and added to the de facto workflow, it is checked if it is contained in the proposed work items of the workflow engine. When the trace replay terminates, the utility for experienced process participants is computed on the basis of the number of miscontrols.

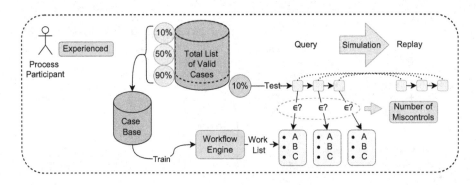

Fig. 5. Simulation of the Experienced Process Participant.

Inexperienced. The simulation of the inexperienced process participant is visualized in Fig. 6. In a first step, the query workflows are re-enacted as trace replay. For this purpose, the constraint-based workflow engine is used as ideal workflow execution reference using the simple model as input. The point of investigation concerning utility starts when a deviation occurs, in terms of a task in the replay that is not part of the work items proposed on the basis of the simple model. Then, the deviation handling modes of the workflow engine are activated and the replay is completed following the suggestions of the worklist (see blue-coloured nodes of *Replay* in Fig. 6). Work items are picked randomly. When the worklist is empty, the workflow instance concludes. This emerging workflow instance can

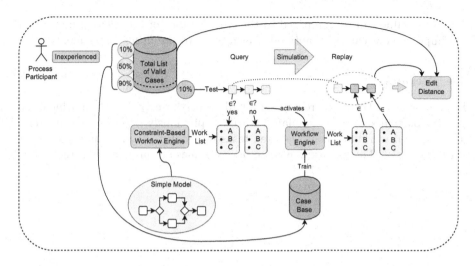

Fig. 6. Simulation of the Inexperienced Process Participant. (Color figure online)

be rated considering its similarity based on the edit distance compared to the total list of valid cases resulting in a utility value.

Non-conforming. The non-conforming process participant executes workflow instances with unknown deviations. Thus, the simulation is not based on the test set of the total list of valid cases that resulted from the extended workflow model, but the regarded query workflows are negative cases that were generated on the basis of a manipulated simple workflow model (see Fig. 7). The simulation itself is done in the same way as for the inexperienced user. Here, the resulting

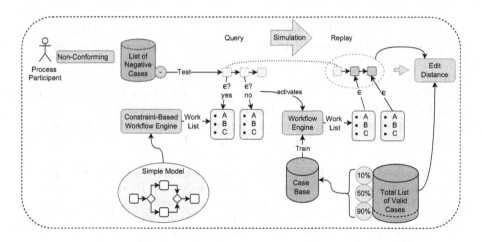

Fig. 7. Simulation of the Non-Conforming Process Participant.

similarity value can be compared to the edit distance of the original query and the improvement can be quantified, which leads to the utility assessment.

4.4 Results

In summary, 31416 trace replays resulted from the experiment in which the process participants were simulated with the previously described parameters. The replayed workflows contained ten tasks on average, at maximum 26 and at least two tasks. The resulting average utility values are presented in Fig. 8.

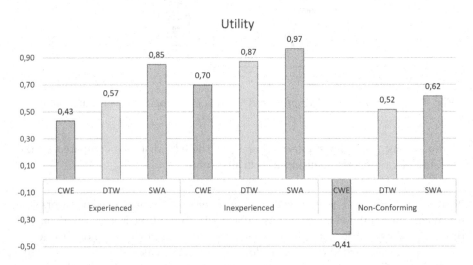

Fig. 8. Average Utility Values for the Different Types of Process Participant and for Different Modes of the Workflow Engine (CWE = Constraint-Based Workflow Engine).

Considering the resulting traces of the experienced process participant, the number of miscontrols ranges from 0 to 11, with an average of four miscontrols. Referring to the derived utility values, the null adaptation based on a retrieval with the SWA shows the most conformance with the traces with an average value of 85% of tasks that were proposed by the workflow engine, whereas this holds for only 43% on average when computing the worklist on the basis of the constraint-based workflow engine.[2] The utility value for the null adaptation with DTW lies in between. Hence, hypothesis **H1** is confirmed for both null

---

[2] The poor performance of the constraint-based workflow engine can be explained due to the differing inputs of the methods. The only input for the constraint-based approach is the simplified workflow model with a reduced set of tasks compared to the extended model. Consequently, work items are only derived from this reduced set, while all additional tasks are not part of the build CSP and therefore cannot be part of the solution. In contrast, both null adaptations rely on the experiential knowledge in form of workflow traces, which includes all tasks of the extended model.

adaptation variants, as the workflow traces are largely compliant (>50%) with the proposed work items, which verifies a great support for the experienced process participants.

Considering the results for the inexperienced process participant, the performance is similar. With an average value of 0,87 and 0,97 for both null adaptation variants, the utility is high and consequently, hypothesis **H2** is confirmed for those two methods. In contrast, the constraint-based workflow engine performs not as good with an average value of 0,7.

For the non-conforming process participants the results differ significantly, foremost of the constraint-based workflow engine. Both null adaptation variants with either the SWA or DTW yield overall high utility values around 0,5 and higher. The constraint-based workflow engine mostly leads to a negative utility value, which means it is tending to increase the edit distance slightly, resulting in an impairment of the support for the non-conforming process participant, as the original trace is more similar to the most similar valid workflow. Consequently, hypothesis **H3** can be confirmed for both null adaptation methods, but is denied for the constraint-based workflow engine.

The case-based modes of the workflow engine outperform the constraint-based one for each type of process participant, confirming hypothesis **H4**.

5   Conclusion

We presented an approach for workflow flexibility that allows for supporting alternatives when facing deviations during workflow execution. On the one hand the workflow can be controlled through a constraint-based workflow engine that uses several domain-independent strategies for conflict resolution, on the other hand the case-based deviation management on the basis of a time-series similarity measure and two null adaptation variants integrated experiential knowledge for the determination of work items. The experimental evaluation showed promising results and an improvement of utility when applying the null adaptation methods in the exemplary domain and simulated environment.

In future work, the null adaptation variants could be enhanced through considering the edit steps similar to trace-based reasoning [10]. Moreover, we developed an approach based on generative adaptation that includes the constraint net in the reuse phase in order to improve flexibility through a transfer of relational task dependencies instead of fixed task positions [5]. However, the proposed approach did not perform well and needs a further elaboration and revision. Furthermore, the evaluation needs to be extended to other domains and real-world scenarios to show the general applicability.

Acknowledgements. This work is funded by the Federal Ministry for Economic Affairs and Climate Action (BMWK) under grant no. 22973.

References

1. van der Aalst, W.M.P.: Business process management: a comprehensive survey. ISRN Software Engineering, pp. 1–37 (2012)
2. van der Aalst, W.M.P., Weske, M., Grünbauer, D.: Case handling: a new paradigm for business process support. Data Knowl. Eng. **53**(2), 129–162 (2005)
3. Bergmann, R., Gil, Y.: Similarity assessment and efficient retrieval of semantic workflows. Inf. Syst. **40**, 115–127 (2014)
4. Berndt, D.J., Clifford, J.: Using dynamic time warping to find patterns in time series. In: Fayyad, U.M., Uthurusamy, R. (eds.) Knowledge Discovery in Databases: Papers from the 1994 AAAI Workshop, Seattle, Washington, USA, July 1994. Technical Report WS-94-03, pp. 359–370. AAAI Press (1994)
5. Grumbach, L.: Flexible workflows - a constraint- and case-based approach. Ph.D. thesis, University of Trier, Germany (2023)
6. Grumbach, L., Bergmann, R.: SEMAFLEX: a novel approach for implementing workflow flexibility by deviation based on constraint satisfaction problem solving. Expert Syst. J. Knowl. Eng. **38**(7) (2021)
7. Gundersen, O.E.: Toward measuring the similarity of complex event sequences in real-time. In: Agudo, B.D., Watson, I. (eds.) ICCBR 2012. LNCS (LNAI), vol. 7466, pp. 107–121. Springer, Heidelberg (2012). https://doi.org/10.1007/978-3-642-32986-9_10
8. Levenshtein, V.: Binary codes capable of correcting deletions, insertions, and reversals. In: Soviet Physics. Doklady, vol. 10, pp. 707–710 (1965)
9. Malburg, L., Brand, F., Bergmann, R.: Adaptive management of cyber-physical workflows by means of case-based reasoning and automated planning. In: Sales, T.P., Proper, H.A., Guizzardi, G., Montali, M., Maggi, F.M., Fonseca, C.M. (eds.) EDOC 2022. LNBIP, vol. 466, pp. 79–95. Springer, Cham (2023). https://doi.org/10.1007/978-3-031-26886-1_5
10. Mille, A.: From case-based reasoning to traces-based reasoning. Annu. Rev. Control **30**(2), 223–232 (2006)
11. Rietzke, E., Maletzki, C., Bergmann, R., Kuhn, N.: Execution of knowledge-intensive processes by utilizing ontology-based reasoning. J. Data Semant. **10**(1–2), 3–18 (2021)
12. Sakoe, H., Chiba, S.: Dynamic programming algorithm optimization for spoken word recognition. IEEE Trans. Acoust. Speech Signal Process. **26**(1), 43–49 (1978)
13. Schake, E., Grumbach, L., Bergmann, R.: A time-series similarity measure for case-based deviation management to support flexible workflow execution. In: Watson, I., Weber, R. (eds.) ICCBR 2020. LNCS (LNAI), vol. 12311, pp. 33–48. Springer, Cham (2020). https://doi.org/10.1007/978-3-030-58342-2_3
14. Schonenberg, H., Mans, R., Russell, N., Mulyar, N., van der Aalst, W.: Process flexibility: a survey of contemporary approaches. In: Dietz, J.L.G., Albani, A., Barjis, J. (eds.) CIAO!/EOMAS 2008. LNBIP, vol. 10, pp. 16–30. Springer, Heidelberg (2008). https://doi.org/10.1007/978-3-540-68644-6_2
15. Schonenberg, H., Mans, R., Russell, N., Mulyar, N., van der Aalst, W.M.P.: Towards a taxonomy of process flexibility. In: Proceedings of the Forum at the CAiSE 2008 Conference, Montpellier, France, 18–20 June 2008, pp. 81–84 (2008)
16. Smith, T.F., Waterman, M.S.: Identification of common molecular subsequences. J. Mol. Biol. **147**(1), 195–197 (1981)

Lazy Adaptation Knowledge Learning Based on Frequent Closed Itemsets

Emmanuel Nauer[(✉)], Jean Lieber, and Mathieu d'Aquin

Université de Lorraine, CNRS, Inria, LORIA, 54000 Nancy, France
`nauer@loria.fr`

Abstract. This paper focuses on lazy adaptation knowledge learning (LAKL) using frequent closed itemset extraction. This approach differs from eager adaptation knowledge learning (EAKL) by the number of cases used in the learning process and by the moment at which the process is triggered. Where EAKL aims to compute adaptation knowledge once on the whole case base with the idea of solving every future target problem, LAKL computes adaptation knowledge on a subset of cases close to the target problem when a new problem has to be solved. The paper presents experiments on generated datasets from Boolean functions and on a real-world dataset, studying especially how the size of the case base used impacts performance. The results show that LAKL outperforms EAKL in precision and correct answer rate and that it is therefore better not to use the whole case base for adaptation knowledge learning.

Keywords: adaptation knowledge learning · lazy learning · closed itemset extraction · case-based reasoning

1 Introduction

Case-based reasoning (CBR [15]) aims at reusing past experience, represented by cases, and case adaptation plays an important part in many CBR applications. Adaptation often relies on the use of adaptation knowledge (AK), hence the usefulness of an AK learning (AKL) process. For example, AKL has been shown useful to improve the results of Taaable, a cooking system that adapts cooking recipes [3]. AK can take many forms. In this paper, it is assumed to be given by a set of adaptation rules.

If adaptation rules can be extracted in a general context (that is, by exploiting the cases of the whole case base), it appears that the rules extracted from a focused set of cases provide better results. In Taaable, preliminary work showed this interest in proposing an AKL suited to a given recipe (e.g., an apple tart recipe) by computing adaptation rules from recipes of the same type (e.g., fruit tart recipes) [7]. However, this approach, which focuses on a subset of recipes, computes adaptation rules a priori without considering the target problem. This

S. Massie and S. Chakraborti (Eds.): ICCBR 2023, LNAI 14141, pp. 309–324, 2023.
https://doi.org/10.1007/978-3-031-40177-0_20

paper addresses adaptation knowledge discovery and its application for adaptation with respect to the target problem, by considering the cases close to the target problem as input data for learning of adaptation rules. This work follows the idea of [2] in which knowledge acquisition is triggered opportunistically at the time of problem solving. However, if such an approach has already been used, a comparative evaluation between exploiting the whole case base or a focused subset of it has, to the best of our knowledge, never been studied. This paper addresses this issue, in the context of a Boolean representation of cases, with the AKL process being based on the extraction of frequent closed itemset (FCI) variations between pairs of cases to compute adaptation rules, as in [9,14] using only positive cases.

These two ways of using learning, either as an offline process or as a process done at problem solving time, are respectively called *eager* and *lazy* learning [1]. It can be noted that the whole CBR process can be likened to lazy learning. Indeed, one can consider that retrieving k cases nearest to the target problem and learning a solution from them matches closely the case-based problem-solving process. Now, what is studied in this paper, is lazy learning for adaptation, not for the whole CBR process and the supervised learning performed here is not on cases but on variations between cases. The objective of this paper is to study lazy adaptation learning and compare it with the performance of eager adaptation learning. This study shows that, on the tested datasets, lazy learning outperforms eager learning in an AKL process.

Section 2 recalls some general notions about CBR, AKL and the technique for extracting FCIs. Section 3 presents the approach used for AKL in a classical (i.e. eager AKL, or EAKL) way: this reuses some previous work with a little–yet significant–improvement. Section 4 presents lazy AKL (LAKL): from a general viewpoint and the way it is applied using FCI extraction. EAKL and LAKL are evaluated and compared in Sect. 5. Section 6 concludes and points out some future work.

2   Preliminaries

This section first introduces the main notions and notations related to CBR. Then it describes the principles of adaptation knowledge learning (AKL). Finally, it presents the notions related to the extraction of frequent closed itemsets (FCIs).

2.1   Case-Based Reasoning: Notions, Notations, and Assumptions

Let $\mathcal{P}$ and $\mathcal{S}$ be two sets. A *problem* (resp., a *solution*) is an element of $\mathcal{P}$ (resp., of $\mathcal{S}$). The existence of a binary relation with the semantics "has for solution" is assumed, although it is not completely known to the CBR system. Moreover, in this article it is assumed that this relation is functional (every problem has exactly one correct solution). Let $\mathbf{f}$ be the function from $\mathcal{P}$ to $\mathcal{S}$ such that $\mathbf{y} = \mathbf{f}(\mathbf{x})$ if $\mathbf{y}$ is the solution of $\mathbf{x}$. A *case* is a pair $(\mathbf{x}, \mathbf{y}) \in \mathcal{P} \times \mathcal{S}$ where $\mathbf{y} = \mathbf{f}(\mathbf{x})$.

A CBR system on $(\mathcal{P}, \mathcal{S}, \mathbf{f})$ is built with a knowledge base KB $=$ (CB, DK, RK, AK) where CB, the case base, is a finite set of cases, DK is the domain knowledge, RK is the retrieval knowledge (in this work, RK $=$ dist, a distance function on $\mathcal{P}$), and AK is the adaptation knowledge often represented by a set of adaptation rules.

A CBR system in $(\mathcal{P}, \mathcal{S}, \mathbf{f})$ aims to associate to a query problem x^{tgt} a $y^{tgt} \in \mathcal{S}$, denoted by $y^{tgt} = \mathbf{f}_{CBR}(x^{tgt})$. The function $\mathbf{f}_{CBR}$ is intended to be an approximation of $\mathbf{f}$. It is built using the following functions:

- The retrieval function, with the profile $\mathtt{retrieval} : x^{tgt} \mapsto (x^s, y^s) \in$ CB;
- The adaptation function, with the profile $\mathtt{adaptation} : ((x^s, y^s), x^{tgt}) \mapsto y^{tgt} \in \mathcal{S}$; it is usually based on DK and AK. $((x^s, y^s), x^{tgt})$ is an *adaptation problem*.

Thus, $\mathbf{f}_{CBR}(x^{tgt}) = \mathtt{adaptation}(\mathtt{retrieval}(x^{tgt}), x^{tgt})$.

Adaptation Principle Using Adaptation Rules. Generally speaking, an adaptation rule $\mathtt{ar}$ is a function that maps an adaptation problem $((x^s, y^s), x^{tgt}) \in$ CB $\times \mathcal{P}$ into a $y^{tgt} \in \mathcal{S} \cup \{\mathtt{failure}\}$. If $y^{tgt} \neq \mathtt{failure}$ then it is proposed as a solution to x^{tgt}, by adaptation of (x^s, y^s) according to $\mathtt{ar}$. The adaptation consists in selecting a set $\mathtt{ApplicableAR}$ of applicable adaptation rules, i.e. for each $\mathtt{ar} \in \mathtt{ApplicableAR}$, $\mathtt{ar}((x^s, y^s), x^{tgt}) \neq \mathtt{failure}$ (the number of selected adaptation rules and the way they are selected depends on the approach and is presented further in the article). Then, the multiset of solutions proposed by the $\mathtt{ar} \in \mathtt{ApplicableAR}$ is combined (e.g. by a majority vote) in order to propose a solution y^{tgt} to x^{tgt}.

One way to represent an adaptation rule is by an ordered pair $(\Delta x, \Delta y)$ where Δx is a *problem variation* and Δy is a *solution variation*. Intuitively, a problem variation is the representation of changes in a problem knowing that this notion depends on the way the problems are represented (and this is similar for solutions): this idea is clarified in Sect. 3.

Given an adaptation rule $\mathtt{ar} = (\Delta x, \Delta y)$ and an adaptation problem $((x^s, y^s), x^{tgt})$, $\mathtt{ar}((x^s, y^s), x^{tgt})$ is computed according to the following principle:

- The variation $\Delta x^{s,tgt}$ from x^s to x^{tgt} is computed.
- If $\Delta x^{s,tgt}$ does not match exactly Δx then the value $\mathtt{failure}$ is returned (the adaptation rule is not applicable to this adaptation problem).
- Else, from y^s and Δy, a solution y^{tgt} is computed, such that the variation $\Delta x^{s,tgt}$ from y^s to y^{tgt} matches Δy, and, if such a y^{tgt} exists, it is returned (else the process returns $\mathtt{failure}$).

2.2 Adaptation Knowledge Learning

Adaptation based on adaptation rules requires the acquisition of rules that can be done thanks to a learning process. In [10], an approach to adaptation knowledge learning (AKL) is presented that is based on the case base. The intuition is that, given $(x^i, y^i), (x^j, y^j) \in$ CB, one can consider $((x^i, y^i), x^j)$ as an adaptation problem—(x^i, y^i) is the case to be adapted and x^j is the target problem—and y^j is a solution to this adaptation problem. Therefore, each pair of distinct source cases can be used as an example for a supervised learning process. This idea has been successfully applied to CBR in many studies (e.g. [4,5,11]).

More precisely, the idea is to consider, for a pair of distinct source cases $((x^i, y^i), (x^j, y^j))$, the problem variation Δx^{ij} from x^i to x^j and the solution variation Δy^{ij} from y^i to y^j. Then, the supervised learning system provides a model that maps a problem variation Δx into a solution variation Δy. This model may be of different natures, for example, it can be a neural network (see e.g. [6]). In this article, the learning technique used is frequent closed itemset extraction, in the continuation of previous studies (see e.g. [14]).

2.3   Frequent Closed Itemset Extraction

Itemset extraction is a collection of data mining methods to extract regularities from data, by aggregating object items that appear together. Like formal concept analysis, itemset extraction algorithms start from a *formal context* $\mathcal{K}$, defined by $\mathcal{K} = (\mathcal{G}, \mathcal{M}, \mathcal{I})$, where $\mathcal{G}$ is a set of objects, $\mathcal{M}$ is a set of items, and $\mathcal{I}$ is the relation on $\mathcal{G} \times \mathcal{M}$ stating that an object is described by an item [8].

An *itemset* I is a set of items, and the *support* of I, $\mathrm{supp}(I)$, is the number of objects of the formal context that have all the items of I. I is frequent, with respect to a threshold τ_{supp}, whenever $\mathrm{supp}(I) \geq \tau_{\mathrm{supp}}$. I is closed if there does not exist a proper superset J of I ($I \subsetneq J$) with the same support.

Given an itemset $I \subseteq \mathcal{M}$ with at least two items, an association rule R generated from I is any pair (U, V) of nonempty itemsets such that $I = U \cup V$ and $U \cap V = \emptyset$. Such a rule is denoted by $U \to V$. The support of R is the support of I and the confidence of R is $\mathrm{conf}(R) = \frac{\mathrm{supp}(U \cup V)}{\mathrm{supp}(U)}$. The confidence of R can also be defined as the conditional probability of an object having the items of V knowing that it has the items of U (given a uniform probability distribution on G).

3   EAKL Based on FCI Extraction

In previous studies, AKL based on FCI extraction has already been studied as an offline process, that is, as an eager AKL [9,14]. This section recalls the principles of this approach with an improvement in the way the set of adaptation rules is selected at adaptation time.

This (eager) learning process, as mentioned in Sect. 2.2, uses the following training set:

$$\mathrm{TS} = \left\{ \left(\Delta x^{ij}, \Delta y^{ij} \right) \mid (x^i, y^i), (x^j, y^j) \in \mathrm{CB}, (x^i, y^i) \neq (x^j, y^j) \right\} \qquad (1)$$

This involves the issue of the representation of problem and solution variations. It is assumed that a problem can either be represented by a set of attribute-value pairs with Boolean values or that it can be translated into such a formalism,[1] which is consistent with the choice of FCI as a learning technique. The attribute-value pair $(a, 1)$ is simply written a and the attribute-value pair $(a, 0)$ is simply written $\bar{a}$. It is also assumed that problems are fully described: for a problem x and for each attribute a in $\mathcal{V_P}$, either $a \in$ x or $\bar{a} \in$ x.

Now, let us consider the following examples of problems:

$$x^i = \{a, \bar{b}, \bar{c}, d\}$$
$$x^j = \{a, \bar{b}, c, \bar{d}\}$$

The variation Δx^{ij} is represented by a set of expressions of the form a^v where $a \in \mathcal{V_P}$ and v is a *variation symbol*. The variation symbols considered here are $=0$, $=1$, $+$, and $-$, meaning respectively "staying false", "staying true", "changing from false to true", and "changing from true to false". Therefore,

$$\Delta x^{ij} = \{a^{=1}, b^{=0}, c^+, d^-\}$$

Solution variations are represented similarly, on the set of attributes $\mathcal{V_S}$ (and it is assumed that $\mathcal{V_P} \cap \mathcal{V_S} = \emptyset$).

Then, the EAKL process builds a formal context $\mathcal{K} = (\mathcal{G}, \mathcal{M}, \mathcal{I})$ from TS as follows:

- $\mathcal{G}$ is the set of elements of TS, indexed by the pairs (i, j), thus $|\mathcal{G}| = |\text{CB}| \times (|\text{CB}| - 1)$;
- $\mathcal{M}$ is the set of a^v for $a \in \mathcal{V_P} \cup \mathcal{V_S}$ and $v \in \{=0, =1, +, -\}$ thus $|\mathcal{M}| = 4 |\mathcal{V_P} \cup \mathcal{V_S}|$;
- $\mathcal{I}$ is defined by the fact that the object indexed by (i, j) is described by the item a^v meaning that $a^v \in \Delta x^{ij} \cup \Delta y^{ij}$.

After this, FCI extraction is run on $\mathcal{K}$ and the results is filtered in order to keep only the itemsets I having at least one item a^v where $a \in \mathcal{V_P}$ and one item A^w where $A \in \mathcal{V_S}$ (with v and w, two variation symbols). Each FCI I is then translated into an adaptation rule. For example, $I = \{a^{=1}, c^+, A^-\}$ is translated into ar $= (\Delta x, \Delta y)$ with $\Delta x = \{a^{=1}, c^+\}$ and $\Delta y = \{A^-\}$.

In this way, a set AK of NER adaptation rules is built and can be used at adaptation time, where NER is a parameter that sets the number of rules to be extracted, selecting the ones with greater support. The value for NER has to be chosen carefully, since an insufficient number of rules can cause the adaptation process to fail, while a large number of rules would make the process too time-consuming. Given an adaptation problem $((x^s, y^s), x^{tgt})$, $\Delta x^{s, tgt}$ is computed and, for each adaptation rule $(\Delta x, \Delta y)$ the application process follows the principle given in Sect. 2.1 knowing that

- $\Delta x^{s, tgt}$ matches Δx if $\Delta x \subseteq \Delta x^{s, tgt}$ (and the same definition of matching holds for solutions);

---

[1] This translation may involve some loss of information. For example, a numerical feature is typically translated into several Boolean attributes, each of them consisting in the membership to an interval.

- Δy is said to be *applicable* to y^s if there exists a $y \in S$ such that the variation from y^s to y matches Δy (for example, $\{A^+\}$ is applicable on $\{\overline{A}, B\}$ but not on $\{A, B\}$);
- If Δy is not applicable to y^s, then the application of the rule fails, else, for each $A \in \mathcal{V}_S$:
  - If no A^w occurs in Δy then the value of attribute A in y^s is reused for y^{tgt} (if $A \in y^s$ then $A \in y^{tgt}$ else $\overline{A} \in y^{tgt}$);
  - Else, the value of attribute A in y^{tgt} is computed according to its value in y^s and the variation w (e.g. if $y^s = \{A\}$ and $w = -$ then $y^{tgt} = \{\overline{A}\}$).

For the purpose of selecting adaptation rules among AK, it is useful to assign them a score used to rank adaptation rules in order of preference: the higher the score, the more preferred the adaptation rule. In the previous work, this score was simply the support of the itemset on which the adaptation rule is built. In this work, the notion of confidence of an adaptation rule has been used and has led to better results. We therefore switched to the use of confidence in our experiments. This confidence is defined as follows. First, four new variation symbols $1\bullet$, $\bullet 1$, $0\bullet$ and $\bullet 0$ are introduced: $1\bullet$ (resp. $\bullet 1$) corresponds to a variation from a true value to any value (resp. from any value to a true value), and similarly for the two other variations. Therefore, $\{A^{=1}\}$ can be rewritten as $\{A^{1\bullet}, A^{\bullet 1}\}$, $\{A^+\}$ can be rewritten as $\{A^{0\bullet}, A^{\bullet 1}\}$, etc. This decomposition is useful to separate the information on y^s (in the premise of the rule) from the information on y^{tgt} (in its conclusion). Let $(\Delta x, \Delta y)$ be an adaptation rule built from an itemset I, where the A^w for $A \in \mathcal{V}_S$ are replaced with A^{w_1} and A^{w_2}, $w_1 \in \{1\bullet, 0\bullet\}$ and $w_2 \in \{\bullet 1, \bullet 0\}$. Then, the confidence of the adaptation rule $(\Delta x, \Delta y)$ is the confidence of the association rule $U \to V$ where V is the subset of I with variation symbols $\bullet 1$ and $\bullet 0$, and $U = I \setminus V$. For example, if $\Delta x = \{a^{=1}, b^-, c^{=0}\}$ and $\Delta y = \{A^-\}$ then $U = \{a^{=1}, b^-, c^{=0}, A^{1\bullet}\}$ and $V = \{A^{\bullet 0}\}$.

4   LAKL Based on FCI Extraction

LAKL consists in learning AK at adaptation time, that is, when an adaptation problem $((x^s, y^s), x^{tgt})$ is known. Therefore, unlike EAKL, LAKL can rely on knowledge of the retrieved case (x^s, y^s) and the target problem x^{tgt}. The general principle of LAKL is presented in Sect. 4.1 and its application using FCI extraction, in Sect. 4.2. In Sect. 4.3, it is explained that an approach to CBR developed in previous studies can be considered as a particular approach to LAKL.

4.1   Main Principles

The main idea of LAKL is to restrict the training set TS defined by (1) by taking into account the adaptation problem: given two distinct source cases (x^i, y^i) and (x^j, y^j), the pair $(\Delta x^{ij}, \Delta y^{ij})$ is filtered out from the training set if these source cases do not satisfy conditions related to (x^s, y^s) and x^{tgt}. Generally speaking, three types of conditions are considered below in an informal way.

($\mathbf{x}^i, \mathbf{x}^j \simeq \mathbf{x}^{tgt}$) The problems $\mathbf{x}^i$ and $\mathbf{x}^j$ are "around" $\mathbf{x}^{tgt}$: the way adaptation works for the target problem is assumed to be better represented in its neighborhood then elsewhere in the problem space;

($\Delta\mathbf{x}^{ij} \simeq \Delta\mathbf{x}^{s,tgt}$) The variation between the two source problems $\mathbf{x}^i$ and $\mathbf{x}^j$ are similar to the variation between the problem $\mathbf{x}^s$ of the retrieved case and the target problem.

($\mathbf{y}^i \simeq \mathbf{y}^{tgt}$) The variation $\Delta\mathbf{y}^{ij}$ from $\mathbf{y}^i$ to $\mathbf{y}^j$ has to be "compatible" with the value of the solution of the retrieved problem so that rules that are not applicable to $\mathbf{y}^s$ are avoided; this condition adds a constraint on the "left part" of $\Delta\mathbf{y}^{ij}$, that is, $\mathbf{y}^i$.

Our approach to applying LAKL, as described in the following, consists in specifying and implementing these conditions.

4.2 Lazy Adaptation Knowledge Learning Based on FCI Extraction

The principles of LAKL have been implemented for an AKL based on FCI extraction.

Condition $\mathbf{x}^i, \mathbf{x}^j \simeq \mathbf{x}^{tgt}$ is implemented simply by choosing the k nearest cases to the target problem that are different from the case $(\mathbf{x}^s, \mathbf{y}^s)$. This can be done at retrieval time: $k+1$ nearest cases are retrieved, the nearest one being the retrieved case, and the k other ones being selected for building the training set. Different values of k can be considered. In our experiments, those values have been chosen to correspond to different percentages of the size of the case base, starting with 10% |CB|.

One effect of applying this condition $\mathbf{x}^i, \mathbf{x}^j \simeq \mathbf{x}^{tgt}$ on the training set is to reduce the number of objects in the formal context $\mathcal{K} = (\mathcal{G}, \mathcal{M}, \mathcal{I})$, which goes from $|CB| (|CB| - 1)$ to $k(k-1)$, hence a reduction of about $(|CB|/k)^2$ of its size. For example, if $k = 10\%\,|CB|$, this leads to a reduction by a factor 100.

In this version, the condition $\Delta\mathbf{x}^{ij} \simeq \Delta\mathbf{x}^{s,tgt}$ has not been implemented for practical reasons and this is left for future work.

Finally, the condition $\mathbf{y}^i \simeq \mathbf{y}^{tgt}$ is implemented in this work considering that $\mathbf{y}^i$ and $\mathbf{y}^{tgt}$ must be equal. This can be justified as follows, in the situation where there is only one solution attribute A (as in the experiments). Considering an $(\mathbf{x}^i, \mathbf{y}^i)$ such that $\mathbf{y}^i \neq \mathbf{y}^s$ would lead to the extraction of FCIs that are interpreted as inapplicable rules. For example, $\mathbf{y}^i = \{\overline{A}\}$ would lead to extract adaptation rules containing either A^+ or $A^{=0}$. Therefore, if $\mathbf{y}^i \neq \mathbf{y}^s$ then $\mathbf{y}^s = \{A\}$ and no such adaptation rule can be applied on $\mathbf{y}^s$, hence not contributing to the learning effort. This condition further reduces the number of objects in the formal context. Moreover, the set of items $\mathcal{M}$ is also reduced since items not related to any object are not included in the formal context: in the example above, the items A^+ and $A^{=0}$ are excluded from $\mathcal{M}$ (and this reduces the computing time).

4.3 Analogical Extrapolation Seen as a LAKL Process

In [13], the analogical extrapolation approach to CBR is described. It is based on analogical proportions, i.e. quaternary relations denoted by $a{:}b{:}c{:}d$ ("a is to b as

c is to d") where a, b, c, and d are four objects of the same space. The analogical proportion on Booleans used in this article is defined by $a{:}b{:}{:}c{:}d$ if $a = b$ and $c = d$, or $a = c$ and $b = d$, and on tuples of Booleans by $a{:}b{:}{:}c{:}d$ if $a_p{:}b_p{:}{:}c_p{:}d_p$ for each component p. Analogical extrapolation, at adaptation time, consists in the following steps:

- Selection of all pairs $((\mathbf{x}^a, \mathbf{y}^a), (,\mathbf{y}^b)) \in \mathrm{CB}^2$ such that $\mathbf{x}^a{:}{:}{:}\mathbf{x}^s{:}\mathbf{x}^{\mathrm{tgt}}$;
- For each of these pairs, solve the analogical equation $\mathbf{y}^a{:}\mathbf{y}^b{:}\mathbf{y}^c{:}y$ in y and, if it has at least one solution, add this solution to a multiset Y of candidate solutions (initially, Y is empty);
- The solution $\mathbf{y}^{\mathrm{tgt}}$ is based on a vote on Y (this vote is weighted in [12] using the notions of support and confidence of a case pair, that are similar to the notions of support and confidence of an FCI).

This analogical extrapolation adaptation process can be reformulated as an adaptation following a LAKL process with the training set corresponding to some implementation choices for the conditions introduced in 4.1. More precisely, conditions $\mathbf{x}^i, \mathbf{x}^j \simeq \mathbf{x}^{\mathrm{tgt}}$ and $\mathbf{y}^i \simeq \mathbf{y}^{\mathrm{tgt}}$ are not considered and condition $\Delta \mathbf{x}^{ij} \simeq \Delta \mathbf{x}^{s,\mathrm{tgt}}$ is defined as follows:

- The set of variation symbols is reduced to $\{-, +\}$ (i.e. items of the forms $a^{=1}$ and $a^{=0}$ are discarded[2]);
- The matching between the two problem variations is implemented as an equality: $\Delta \mathbf{x}^{ij} = \Delta \mathbf{x}^{s,\mathrm{tgt}}$.

5   Evaluation

The objective of the evaluation is to study the behavior of LAKL compared to EAKL, in representative types of Boolean functions as well as on a "real life" dataset, in order to determine which approach achieves greater performance and under which circumstances. The experimental results are presented and discussed.

5.1   Experiment Setting

In the experiment, problems have 16 Boolean features and $\mathcal{S}$, 1. The function $\mathbf{f} : \mathcal{P} \to \mathcal{S}$ is generated randomly using the following generators that are based on two normal forms, with the purpose of generating a wide variety of functions:

DNF $\mathbf{f}$ is generated in a disjunctive normal form, i.e., $\mathbf{f}(\mathbf{x})$ is a disjunction of n_{conj} conjunctions of literals, for example $\mathbf{f}(\mathbf{x}) = (\mathbf{x}_1 \wedge \neg \mathbf{x}_7) \vee (\neg \mathbf{x}_3 \wedge \mathbf{x}_7 \vee \mathbf{x}_8) \vee \mathbf{x}_4$. The value of n_{conj} is randomly chosen uniformly in $\{3, 4, 5\}$. Each conjunction is generated on the basis of two parameters, $p^+ > 0$ and $p^- > 0$, with $p^+ + p^- < 1$: each variable $\mathbf{x}_i$ occurs in the disjunct in a positive (resp. negative) literal with a probability p^+ (resp., p^-). In the experiment, the values $p^+ = p^- = 0.1$ were chosen.

---

[2] This is related to the following result. Let $\delta \mathbf{x}^{ij} = \{a^v \in \Delta \mathbf{x}^{ij} \mid v \in \{-, +\}\}$. Then, it can be shown that $\mathbf{x}^a{:}{:}{:}\mathbf{x}^s{:}\mathbf{x}^{\mathrm{tgt}}$ iff $\delta \mathbf{x}^{ab} = \delta \mathbf{x}^{s\ \mathrm{tgt}}$.

Pol is the same as DNF, except that the disjunctions ($\vee$) are replaced with exclusive or's ($\oplus$), thus giving a polynomial normal form. The only different parameter is $p^- = 0$ (only positive literals occur in polynomial normal form).

A case base CB of a given size ($|\text{CB}| \in \{128, 256, 512\}$) is generated randomly in the following way: each source case (x, y) is generated by randomly choosing x in $\mathcal{P}$ with a uniform distribution and $y = f(x)$.

Let ntp be the number of target problems posed to the system, na be the number of (correct or incorrect) answers (ntp − na is the number of target problems for which the system fails to propose a solution), and nca be the number of correct answers (i.e., number of problems for which the predicted answer is the correct answer). For each method, the following scores are computed:

The precision prec is the average of the ratios $\dfrac{\text{nca}}{\text{na}}$.

The answer rate arate is the average of the ratios $\dfrac{\text{na}}{\text{ntp}}$.

The correct answer rate car is the average of the ratios $\dfrac{\text{nca}}{\text{ntp}}$.

The average is calculated by solving 100 problems for each of 20 generated functions, for each function generator. For the sake of reproducibility, the code for this experiment is available at https://tinyurl.com/EAKLvsLAKLTests with the detailed results of this paper (generated functions and details of the evaluation).

5.2   Results

Comparing EAKL and LAKL requires a lot of attention because some parameters involved in the evaluation may have an impact on the interpretation of the results. For example, one of the parameters is the number of rules to be learned using FCI extraction, and it is not fair to use the same number of rules for EAKL, in which rules are extracted once to solve all coming target problems, as for LAKL, in which a focused rule extraction is done for each target problem. The number of extracted rules has a direct and important impact on the answer rate for EAKL, since it is less likely to find applicable rules for a given target problem if that number is too small. The impact of the number of rules is lower for LAKL, and the same number of rules will more likely lead to a higher answer rate in LAKL than in EAKL. Table 1 illustrates this with precision and answer rate scores for EAKL with a number of rules extracted ranging from 100 to 2,400. It can be seen that an answer rate of 100% is almost always achieved if a sufficient number of rules is used. This sufficient number of rules depends on the size of the case base, sometimes requiring more than 1,000 rules. However, a (close to perfect) score of 99% is reached in all cases from 400 rules.

The precision also increases with the number of rules until a plateau is reached. Therefore, using more rules (e.g. 2,000 for DNF functions with a size of case base of 256) improves precision and, thanks to an almost perfect answer rate, the correct answer rate. It appears that precision could have a higher score

Table 1. Precision, standard deviation, answer rate, and correct answer rate (in %) for EAKL (100% of CB) with various numbers of extracted rules (NER) to solve the target problems.

	NER	100	200	300	400	500	600	700	800	1000	1200	1400	1600	1800	2000	2200	2400
							DNF										
128	prec	84	83	83	84	85	85	85	85	85	85	**86**	**86**	**86**	**86**	**86**	**86**
	σ	8	8	8	**7**	**7**	**7**	**7**	**7**	**7**	**7**	8	8	8	8	8	8
	arate	94	99	99	99	99	100	100	100	100	100	100	100	100	100	100	100
	car	79	82	83	84	84	85	85	85	85	85	**86**	**86**	**86**	**86**	**86**	**86**
256	prec	87	87	87	88	88	89	89	89	89	89	89	89	89	90	90	90
	σ	9	9	9	8	8	7	8	7	7	7	7	7	**6**	**6**	**6**	**6**
	arate	95	99	99	99	99	99	99	99	99	100	100	100	100	100	100	100
	car	83	86	87	88	88	89	89	89	89	89	89	89	89	90	90	90
512	prec	**95**	94	93	93	93	93	93	93	93	93	93	93	93	93	93	93
	σ	4	4	4	4	4	4	4	**3**	4	4	4	4	4	4	4	4
	arate	91	96	98	99	99	99	99	99	100	100	100	100	100	100	100	100
	car	87	90	91	92	**93**	**93**	**93**	**93**	**93**	**93**	**93**	**93**	**93**	**93**	**93**	**93**
							POL										
128	prec	74	**75**	**75**	**75**	74	74	74	74	74	74	74	74	74	74	74	74
	σ	15	**14**	15	15	15	16	16	16	16	16	17	17	17	17	17	17
	arate	96	**99**	**99**	**99**	**99**	**99**	**99**	**99**	**99**	**99**	**99**	**99**	**99**	**99**	**99**	**99**
	car	71	**74**	**74**	**74**	**74**	**74**	**74**	**74**	**74**	**74**	**74**	**74**	**74**	**74**	**74**	**74**
256	prec	74	75	76	77	77	78	78	78	**79**	**79**	**79**	**79**	**79**	**79**	**79**	**79**
	σ	18	16	17	16	15	15	15	15	**14**	15	**14**	**14**	**14**	**14**	**14**	**14**
	arate	99	99	100	100	100	100	100	100	100	100	100	100	100	100	100	100
	car	73	75	76	77	77	78	78	78	**79**	**79**	**79**	**79**	**79**	**79**	**79**	**79**
512	prec	79	79	80	81	81	81	81	82	82	82	82	82	**83**	**83**	**83**	**83**
	σ	20	18	17	16	16	16	16	15	**14**	**14**	**14**	**14**	**14**	**14**	**14**	**14**
	arate	91	98	99	99	99	99	99	100	100	100	100	100	100	100	100	100
	car	72	78	80	80	80	81	81	82	82	82	82	82	**83**	**83**	**83**	83

with fewer rules (e.g., 100 rules for DNF functions using 512 cases), but in this case, at the cost of a lower answer rate.

The standard deviation is also stable with lower values when the number of rules is high. Based on these observations, the tests for comparing EAKL and LAKL (presented in the next section) have been performed with the extraction and use at most 2,400 rules for EAKL and 1,000 for LAKL, with the idea of having the best possible results for EAKL (best answer rate, best precision and therefore best correct answer rate) and of studying how LAKL performs in comparison.

EAKL vs. LAKL Results. Table 2 shows the precision, standard deviation, answer rate, and correct answer rate obtained with the nearest neighbor adap-

Table 2. Precision, standard deviation, answer rate, and correct answer rate (in %) for all approaches.

		NN	EAKL	LAKL with x% of |CB|									
				10	20	30	40	50	60	70	80	90	100
				DNF									
128	prec	76	[83; 86]	86	88	88	89	89	89	89	89	**90**	85
	σ	5	[7; 8]	6	6	**5**	6	6	7	7	7	7	7
	arate	100	[94; 100]	**100**	**100**	**100**	**100**	**100**	**100**	**100**	**100**	99	**100**
	car	76	[79; 86]	86	88	88	89	89	89	89	89	**90**	85
256	prec	79	[87; 90]	91	**92**	**92**	**92**	**92**	**92**	**92**	**92**	**92**	89
	σ	6	[6; 9]	5	**4**	5	5	5	6	6	6	6	7
	arate	100	[95; 100]	**100**	**100**	**100**	99	99	99	99	99	99	99
	car	79	[83; 90]	91	**92**	**92**	**92**	**92**	**92**	**92**	**92**	**92**	89
512	prec	83	[93; 95]	96	96	**97**	**97**	**97**	96	96	96	96	93
	σ	5	[3; 4]	**2**	3	**2**	3	3	3	3	3	4	4
	arate	100	[91; 100]	**100**	99	99	99	99	99	99	99	99	**100**
	car	83	[87; 93]	96	96	**97**	**97**	**97**	96	96	95	95	93
				POL									
128	prec	65	[74; 75]	69	72	75	76	77	**78**	**78**	**78**	**78**	74
	σ	13	[14; 17]	20	19	17	17	**16**	**16**	**16**	**16**	18	**16**
	arate	100	[96; 99]	**100**	**100**	**100**	**100**	**100**	**100**	**100**	**100**	99	99
	car	65	[71; 74]	69	72	75	76	77	**78**	**78**	**78**	**78**	74
256	prec	64	[74; 79]	73	79	81	**82**	81	80	79	79	78	79
	σ	17	[14; 18]	19	15	**13**	14	14	15	16	16	17	14
	arate	100	[99; 100]	**100**	**100**	**100**	**100**	**100**	**100**	**100**	**100**	99	**100**
	car	64	[73; 79]	73	79	81	**82**	81	80	79	79	78	79
512	prec	69	[79; 83]	85	**89**	88	87	85	84	83	84	84	82
	σ	15	[14; 20]	14	**11**	12	14	16	17	17	17	16	14
	arate	100	[91; 100]	**100**	**100**	99	99	99	99	99	99	99	**100**
	car	69	[72; 83]	85	**89**	88	87	85	84	83	83	83	82

tation (NN, i.e., simply reusing the solution of the most similar problem) used as baseline, EAKL, and LAKL. The left part of the table presents the results for NN and EAKL while the right part presents the LAKL results with various sizes of subparts of the case base used for learning. For EAKL, all measures vary according to the number of rules used in the adaptation process; the detailed EAKL results of Table 1 are presented through an interval in the column titled EAKL. The interval is defined by the minimum and maximum scores, using between 100 and 2,400 rules. For example, in the first line, for \|CB\| = 128, the precision of the eager approach varies between 83% and 86% depending on the number of rules used in the adaptation process.

The first remark is that EAKL always outperforms the NN approach. This is not a surprise since previous studies (e.g. [9]) already showed this. Also unsur-

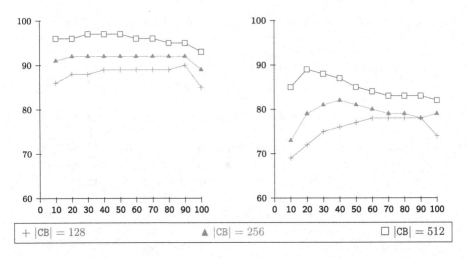

Fig. 1. Correct answer rate (y-axis) given a percentage (x-axis) of CB used for 1000 rules extraction (DNF at the left, Pol at the right).

prisingly, the larger the case base size, the better the results of EAKL in precision and correct answer rate (up to +4% and +6% for both measures, respectively, for DNF and Pol functions when |CB| = 512).

The comparison of EAKL and LAKL shows that LAKL performs better with some variations in the DNF and Pol functions. For DNF, it can be observed that LAKL always provides better scores for all measures regardless of the percentage of cases used for learning, except for the limits (10% and 100% of CB). At best, the correct answer rate has been improved respectively by +4%, +2% and +4% for |CB| of 128, 256 and 512. For the Pol functions, the results are slightly different. The same observations can be made (i.e. improvement of all measures) but in different conditions. The best correct answer rate scores are, respectively, +4%, +3% and +6% for |CB| of 128, 256 and 512, and depend more on the percentage of CB used for learning: concentrated between 50% and 90% with |CB| = 128, between 30% and 50% with |CB| = 256, and between 20% and 30% with |CB| = 256. Moreover, except for Pol with |CB| = 128, a lower standard deviation is also achieved with LAKL.

The best precision, as well as the best correct answer rate (because the answer rate is at its maximum), is obtained with a size of the subpart of the case base between 20% and 50% of CB. Figure 1 shows the correct answer rate according to the percentage of CB used. This measure is relatively stable, except for the extreme percentage: 10% and 100% for which the adaptation rules are of lower quality. Thus, an unexpected result is that it is better not to use the whole case base to learn adaptation rules.

Computation Aspects. The experiments use CORON, a software platform that implements efficient algorithms for symbolic data mining and, especially, FCI computation [16].

LAKL provides an important advantage for large case bases. Indeed, computing frequent closed itemset is a process with a high level of complexity, especially with the use of case variations. For 1024 cases, the formal context is of $1,024 \times 1,023$ pairs of cases, so over one million objects. Extracting up to $2,500$ rules requires to compute closed itemsets with a low support (around 1% of the number of objects). Our experiment has shown that this computation is not possible on a computer without at least 32Gb of memory available for this process with CORON. Therefore, computing the adaptation rules on a smaller formal context (e.g. with $|CB| = 1024$, taking 10% produces a formal context of around $10,000$ objects, instead of $1,000,000$) is an interesting option for a large case base. This remark holds also for the execution time, for which the smaller the set of cases used to compute adaptation rules, the shorter the computational time. For example, for the DNF functions, with $|CB| = 512$ and $2,500$ rules extracted for EAKL, the mean computation time is 41.78 seconds. This can be compared to the time increases from 8.66 seconds using 20% of CB to 11.6 for 50%, up to 31.2 seconds for 90%, when getting $1,000$ rules with LAKL.

Table 3. Precision, standard deviation, answer rate, and correct answer rate for NN, EAKL and LAKL for various percentages of CB used for adaptation rules learning, for the student dataset.

		NN	EAKL	LAKL with x% of $|CB|$									
				10	20	30	40	50	60	70	80	90	100
128	prec	58	56	59	**62**	60	59	57	57	56	56	55	56
	σ	5.95	6.55	3.10	**0.45**	3.50	1.85	1.15	0.85	1.00	1.40	4.20	6.55
	arate	**100**	**100**	95	98	99	99	99	99	99	99	99	**100**
	car	58	56	56	**60**	**60**	58	57	56	56	55	55	56
256	prec	58	53	**60**	59	57	56	56	54	53	53	52	53
	σ	4.00	2.25	**0.05**	5.25	6.70	6.00	7.10	5.50	3.40	2.90	1.80	2.25
	arate	**100**	98	98	98	98	98	99	99	99	99	99	98
	car	58	52	**59**	58	56	55	55	54	53	52	52	52

However, even if LAKL is more scalable, FCI extraction being done at adaptation time, and therefore for every target problem, its computational time cannot be claimed to be advantageous.

5.3 Experiment on a Real-World Dataset

To further validate the benefits of LAKL, we conducted an experiment on a real-world dataset. This dataset, taken from the UCI Machine Learning Repository, describes students and their results in a final exam.[3] In fact, there are 2 datasets, but we only use the one with the final result of the math exam. The raw attributes that are binary, multivalued, or even numeric have been transformed to fit our Boolean representation formalism. The details of the transformation are described at https://tinyurl.com/EAKLvsLAKLTests.

In this experiment, problems have 29 Boolean features and $\mathcal{S}$, 1. The dataset contains 395 records, which produces 391 cases after removing duplicates. The distribution of the solutions of these 391 cases is 207 (resp. 184) results over (resp. lower or equal to) the class's mean result (10.42). One run consists of a random selection in CB and the evaluation of 100 random target problems that are not in CB, using 1,000 rules for EAKL as well as for LAKL, as this leads to high answer rates. 20 runs were performed for $|CB| = 128$ and $|CB| = 256$. Table 3 presents the results for NN, EAKL and LAKL depending on various percentages of CB used for adaptation rule learning. EAKL and LAKL with 100% give the same results because they both use the same number of rules and the same number of cases. The analysis of the results is similar to the experiment on Boolean functions: LAKL outperforms EAKL. In this particular experiment, when at most 60% of CB is used. The results are especially good for low percentages. For $|CB| = 128$ (resp. 256), the better result is when using 20% (resp. 10%) of CB, with an improvement of the correct answer rate of +4% (resp. +7%) compared to EAKL. Moreover, in this experiment, EAKL leads to results that are less satisfactory than those of NN, which is not the case with LAKL.

6   Conclusion

This paper addresses FCI-based adaptation rule learning using a lazy approach. The AKL is triggered at problem-solving time to compute adaptation rules using cases close to the target problem, rather than a priori and on the entire case base, with the idea of solving every target problem. The lazy approach has many advantages. Experiments on Boolean functions and on a real-world dataset show that the lazy approach (LAKL) outperforms the eager approach (EAKL) in precision and correct answer rate. Moreover, computing adaptation rules in a lazy process is demonstrably more scalable as it requires a fewer number of objects to be involved in the most complex step, namely FCI extraction.

A first direction of work is the study of various ways of implementing the conditions $x^i, x^j \simeq x^{tgt}$, $\Delta x^{ij} \simeq \Delta x^{s,tgt}$, and $y^i \simeq y^{tgt}$ that restricts the training set for LAKL. Two implementations have already been considered: the one studied in this article and the one corresponding to analogical extrapolation as a LAKL (cf. Section 4.3).

Another direction of work consists in studying LAKL with other assumptions on case representation. First, in some domains, cases cannot adequately be translated into sets of Boolean properties. This motivates the study of LAKL with other learning techniques, suited to other case representations (e.g. texts, logical formulas or complex objects). Second, the assumption of an a priori separation

---

[3] https://archive.ics.uci.edu/ml/datasets/student+performance.

between the problem and solution parts in a case is not always acceptable: for instance, in Taaable, an apple pie recipe can be seen as a solution of many problems (e.g. "Recipe of dessert with apples?" or "Recipe of pie with fruits?"). On the contrary, the knowledge at problem-solving time of the query/target problem makes it possible to make this distinction. Therefore, LAKL can benefit from this knowledge whereas EAKL cannot: studying this in detail is a future work. For example, the confidence of an adaptation rule relies on this problem-solution distinction, and using this confidence is beneficial for AKL.

References

1. Aha, D.W.: Lazy Learning. Springer, Heidelberg (2013)
2. Badra, F., Cordier, A., Lieber, J.: Opportunistic adaptation knowledge discovery. In: McGinty, L., Wilson, D.C. (eds.) ICCBR 2009. LNCS (LNAI), vol. 5650, pp. 60–74. Springer, Heidelberg (2009). https://doi.org/10.1007/978-3-642-02998-1_6
3. Cordier, A., et al.: TAAABLE: a case-based system for personalized cooking. In: Montani, S., Jain, L. (eds.) Successful Case-based Reasoning Applications-2. Studies in Computational Intelligence, vol. 494, pp. 121–162. Springer, Heidelberg (2014). https://doi.org/10.1007/978-3-642-38736-4_7
4. Craw, S., Wiratunga, N., Rowe, R.C.: Learning adaptation knowledge to improve case-based reasoning. Artif. Intell. **170**(16–17), 1175–1192 (2006)
5. d'Aquin, M., Badra, F., Lafrogne, S., Lieber, J., Napoli, A., Szathmary, L.: Case base mining for adaptation knowledge acquisition. In: Veloso, M.M. (ed.) IJCAI 2007, Proceedings of the 20th International Joint Conference on Artificial Intelligence, Hyderabad, 6–12 January 2007, pp. 750–755 (2007)
6. d'Aquin, M., Nauer, E., Lieber, J.: A factorial study of neural network learning from differences for regression. In: Keane, M.T., Wiratunga, N. (eds.) ICCBR 2022. LNCS, vol. 13405, pp. 289–303. Springer, Cham (2022). https://doi.org/10.1007/978-3-031-14923-8_19
7. Gaillard, E., Lieber, J., Nauer, E.: Adaptation knowledge discovery for cooking using closed itemset extraction. In: The Eighth International Conference on Concept Lattices and their Applications - CLA 2011, Nancy, France (2011)
8. Ganter, B., Wille, R.: Formal Concept Analysis: Mathematical Foundations. Springer, Cham (1999). https://doi.org/10.1007/978-3-642-59830-2
9. Gillard, T., Lieber, J., Nauer, E.: Improving adaptation knowledge discovery by exploiting negative cases: first experiment in a boolean setting. In: Proceedings of ICCBR 2018–26th International Conference on Case-Based Reasoning, Stockholm, Sweden (2018)
10. Hanney, K., Keane, M.T.: Learning adaptation rules from a case-base. In: Smith, I., Faltings, B. (eds.) EWCBR 1996. LNCS, vol. 1168, pp. 179–192. Springer, Heidelberg (1996). https://doi.org/10.1007/BFb0020610
11. Jalali, V., Leake, D., Forouzandehmehr, N.: Learning and applying adaptation rules for categorical features: an ensemble approach. AI Commun. **30**(3–4), 193–205 (2017)
12. Lieber, J., Nauer, E., Prade, H.: Improving analogical extrapolation using case pair competence. In: Bach, K., Marling, C. (eds.) ICCBR 2019. LNCS (LNAI), vol. 11680, pp. 251–265. Springer, Cham (2019). https://doi.org/10.1007/978-3-030-29249-2_17

13. Lieber, J., Nauer, E., Prade, H., Richard, G.: Making the best of cases by approxi-
    mation, interpolation and extrapolation. In: Cox, M.T., Funk, P., Begum, S. (eds.)
    ICCBR 2018. LNCS (LNAI), vol. 11156, pp. 580–596. Springer, Cham (2018).
    https://doi.org/10.1007/978-3-030-01081-2_38
14. Lieber, J., Nauer, E.: Adaptation knowledge discovery using positive and negative
    cases. In: Sánchez-Ruiz, A.A., Floyd, M.W. (eds.) ICCBR 2021. LNCS (LNAI),
    vol. 12877, pp. 140–155. Springer, Cham (2021). https://doi.org/10.1007/978-3-
    030-86957-1_10
15. Riesbeck, C.K., Schank, R.C.: Inside Case-Based Reasoning. Lawrence Erlbaum
    Associates Inc., Hillsdale (1989)
16. Szathmary, L., Napoli, A.: CORON: a framework for levelwise itemset mining
    algorithms. In: Supplementary Proceedings of The Third International Conference
    on Formal Concept Analysis (ICFCA 2005), Lens, France, pp. 110–113 (2005)

Case-Based Applications

An Overview and Comparison of Case-Based Reasoning Frameworks

Alexander Schultheis[1]([✉])(iD), Christian Zeyen[1](iD), and Ralph Bergmann[1,2](iD)

[1] German Research Center for Artificial Intelligence (DFKI) Branch, University of Trier, Behringstraße 21, 54296 Trier, Germany
{alexander.schultheis,christian.zeyen,ralph.bergmann}@dfki.de
[2] Business Information Systems II, University of Trier, 54286 Trier, Germany
http://www.wi2.uni-trier.de

Abstract. *Case-Based Reasoning* (CBR) is a methodology with many applications in industrial and scientific domains. Over the past decades, various frameworks have been developed to facilitate the development of CBR applications. For practitioners and researchers, it is challenging to overview the landscape of existing frameworks with their specific scope and features. This makes it difficult to choose the most suitable framework for specific requirements. To address this issue, this work provides an overview and comparison of CBR frameworks, focusing on five recent, open-source CBR frameworks: CloodCBR, eXiT*CBR, jColibri, myCBR, and ProCAKE. They are compared by supported CBR types, knowledge containers, CBR phases, interfaces, and special features.

Keywords: Case-Based Reasoning · CBR Framework · CBR Applications · CloodCBR · eXiT*CBR · jColibri · myCBR · ProCAKE

1 Introduction

Case-Based Reasoning (CBR) applications have been developed for over 30 years. The first systems implementing parts of the CBR methodology date back to the 80s [26,28,60]. Up to now, numerous CBR frameworks have been developed to ease the creation of CBR systems. In this work, a framework is regarded as a generic, domain-independent, and extensible software component that enables the implementation of specific applications. In particular, some non-commercial frameworks that are publicly available under an open-source license became widely used within the CBR research community. In the past, some publications addressed the comparison of CBR frameworks [3,16,18,57,60]. However, no publication covers a broad range of the most recent frameworks.

This work aims to overview all open-source CBR frameworks still under active development or used for current research, to help find suitable frameworks for developing specific CBR applications. This paper mainly describes and compares five recent open-source CBR frameworks: CloodCBR, eXiT*CBR, jColibri, myCBR, and ProCAKE. In particular, the supported CBR types and case representations, the framework's capabilities for implementing the four knowledge

S. Massie and S. Chakraborti (Eds.): ICCBR 2023, LNAI 14141, pp. 327–343, 2023.
https://doi.org/10.1007/978-3-031-40177-0_21

containers [48], the supported CBR phases [1], interfaces, and special features will be considered.

The remainder of this paper is organized as follows: Sect. 2 gives some background on the results of previous CBR framework overviews. Then, Sect. 3 provides a general overview of CBR frameworks found in the literature, including commercial frameworks. A more in-depth description of the five selected frameworks is presented in Sect. 4. On this basis, a comparison is made in Sect. 5. Finally, Sect. 6 summarizes the main findings of this work.

2   Background

In 1994, Watson and Marier [60] present and compare the three CBR frameworks Isoft ReCALL, Cognitive Systems Inc. ReMind, and AcknoSoft KATE, among other CBR systems, including applications of these. They show the early evolution of CBR although they do not explicitly use the term framework.

Atanassov and Antonov [3] describe the two non-commercial frameworks, jColibri and myCBR. The authors highlight the GUI and modification of weights in myCBR and the supported database interfaces of both frameworks.

ElKafrawy and Mohamed [16] compare a selection of CBR frameworks (CBR-Shell, FreeCBR, jColibri, myCBR, and eXiT*CBR) based on several criteria. They introduce and compare the frameworks regarding case selection strategies, retrieval, revision, storage, speed, and handling of missing or noisy data. In addition, they compare the retrieval phase in their evaluation. As a result, they find that freeCBR and eXiT*CBR are easy to use, especially because of their GUI. In contrast, myCBR and jColibri are suitable for more complex applications, whereby the interface as well as the set of functions of myCBR is rated higher in a direct comparison.

Thakur et al. [57] investigate the context in which CBR systems should be created and the tools that can be used for this purpose. Therefore, the frameworks AIAI CBR Shell, myCBR, and jColibri are presented and compared in the context of comparative analysis. Factors such as case structures, CBR phases, GUIs, and handling of uncertain data are considered.

In 2016, He and Wang [18] present a review of CBR shells and frameworks. They define a shell as an application generator to build specific applications quickly using a GUI. A CBR framework is defined as software designed for extensibility. The authors do not explain whether the shells can also be used as frameworks. He and Wang consider Caspian CBR Shell, CBR-Express, Cognitive Systems Inc. ReMind, CBRWorks, AIAI CBR Shell as shells and jColibri, myCBR, IUCBRF, Empolis Orenge, and freeCBR as frameworks and provide an overview of these.

Peixoto, Martinazzo, and Weber [42] survey cyberinfrastructure requirements for researchers as a target audience to reduce the entry barriers for using such infrastructures. The CBR community is used as an example, where an external inventory of CBR tools is conducted. CAKE, AIAI CBR Shell, CBR Works, Colibri Studio, eXiT*CBR, freeCBR, and myCBR are comparatively described as examples based on operating systems, required programming experience, ease of use, tutorials, and free availability.

Several publications addressed an overview and comparison of CBR frameworks in the past. However, there is no recent and complete survey of the latest frameworks. This work tries to close this gap and focuses on providing decision support for practitioners and researchers to find suitable frameworks for developing CBR applications.

3   General Overview of CBR Frameworks

To identify CBR frameworks, an extensive literature search was conducted on the following citation databases and search engines: Google Scholar, Semantic Scholar, BASE (Bielefeld Academic Search Engine), IEEE Xplore, DBLP (Digital Bibliography & Library Project), and CiteSeerX. We used full-text searches except for DBLP, which only supports a search of title and abstract.

We collected and reviewed publications that address CBR frameworks, systems, applications, and the comparison. We examined the literature and associated online resources to distinguish frameworks for developing arbitrary CBR applications from specific CBR applications. Systems and specific applications such as CasePoint [60], CBR-Express [60], CLAVIER [20,35], Compaq SMART [7,38], Eclipse – The Easy-Reasoner [60], ESTEEM—Case-Based Reasoning Shell [60] and CasePower [60] are not further considered for that reason. As a result, eleven open-source frameworks and five closed-source/commercial frameworks are selected. Table 1 shows the numbers of related publications for the respective framework, the period of the publications, and the year the source code was updated the last time. Due to many irrelevant results, we do not show the number of publications on CiteSeerX.

Some open-source frameworks are no longer under development and are thus not further considered in this paper: AIAI CBR Shell[1], CASPIAN CBR Shell[2], CAT-CBR [2], freeCBR[3], INRIA CBR*Tools[4] [24,25], and IUCBRF[5] [11,12]. However, the source code is still available (publicly or upon request) for some of the frameworks.

Over the years, several commercial frameworks have been developed, some of which have emerged from the research. However, these frameworks are not further considered in this overview due to the proprietary code: Brightware ART*Enterprise [60], AcknoSoft KATE [59], CBR Works [53] (emerged from research at the University of Kaiserslautern and parts of it have been adopted in the open-source framework myCBR [55]), Empolis Orenge [54] (emerged from CBR Works [53] and is now part of Empolis Information Access Suite [18]), Cognitive Systems ReMind [59,60], and Isoft ReCALL [60].

Regarding the identified frameworks' actuality, popularity, and source code availability, we selected the following open-source frameworks to be further considered in this work: CloodCBR, eXiT*CBR, jColibri, myCBR, and ProCAKE.

---

[1] http://www.aiai.ed.ac.uk/project/cbr/CBRDistrib/.
[2] https://www.aber.ac.uk/~dcswww/Research/mbsg/cbrprojects/getting_caspian.shtml.
[3] http://freecbr.sourceforge.net/.
[4] http://www-sop.inria.fr/aid/software.html.
[5] https://homes.luddy.indiana.edu/leake/iucbrf/.

Table 1. Search Results on Publications Related to the Respective CBR Frameworks, Ordered by Code Accessibility and Search Results (requested on 04/18/2023).

CBR Framework	Google Scholar	Semantic Scholar	BASE	IEEE Xplore	DBLP	Publication Period	Last Code Update
jColibri	1,030	89	63	21	11	Since 2004	Jan. 2019
myCBR	626	49	42	7	10	Since 2007	Dec. 2022/ May 2019[a]
eXiT*CBR	105	4	35	0	7	Since 2008	Jan. 2017
IUCBRF	101	4	0	0	1	2001–2005	Dec. 2013
freeCBR	78	6	4	1	0	2005–2018	Mar. 2013
CAT-CBR	68	8	1	0	0	Since 2002	–
ProCAKE	41	4	16	0	1	Since 2005[b]	Apr. 2023
AIAI CBR Shell	17	16	0	0	0	1990–2019	Sep. 2010
Caspian CBR Shell	6	3	0	0	0	1990–2019	Jan. 1997
INRIA CBR*Tools	2	1	1	0	0	Since 1991	Sep. 2001
CloodCBR	6	0	0	0	0	Since 2020	Mar. 2023
Brightware ART*Enterprise (Closed Source)	306	1	0	0	0	Since 1997	–
AcknoSoft KATE (Closed Source)	177	122	1	0	0	1993–2021	–
CBR Works (Closed Source)	168[c]	22	10	0	1	1998–2017	–
Cognitive Systems ReMind (Closed Source)	124	1	1	0	0	Since 1997	–
Isoft ReCALL (Closed Source)	104	103	0	0	0	1994–2020	–
Empolis Orenge/ Empolis Information Access Suite (Closed Source)	42/31	2/1	1/0	0/0	1/2	2002–2017	–

[a] Two different branches of myCBR exist that are being developed separately.
[b] Search results for the CAKE framework led to several false positive results. However, the start of publications can be dated to 2005. In 2019, CAKE was renamed ProCAKE.
[c] Due to several false results (807 for "CBR Works"), "CBR Works" Shell was queried.

4 Presentation of Selected CBR Frameworks

This section presents the five selected open-source frameworks in more detail. The authors collected the information from the literature, which was checked and completed by the framework's developers. We checked the information on the framework's profiles based on the available source code.

4.1 CloodCBR

CloodCBR supports textual and structural CBR ("Clood" is a Scottish word for cloud). A focus is put on support for distributed and highly scalable generic CBR systems based on a microservices architecture.

General Information

Developer	AI and Reasoning (AIR) Group, Robert Gordon University Aberdeen, United Kingdom
Homepage	http://cloodcbr.com/
CBR Types	Textual, structural
Applications based on the Framework	Talent management [23] Explainable Artificial Intelligence (via tool iSee) [62]
Documentation about the Framework	**Publications**: [39–41] **Guide and Documentation**: https://github.com/rgu-computing/clood
Source Code	**URL:** https://github.com/RGU-Computing/clood **Last Update:** Version 2.0 (March 2023) **Programming Language:** Python

Knowledge Containers

Vocabulary	**Case Representation**: Text, attribute-value, object **General Knowledge Representation**: Ontologies, taxonomies (table-based)
Case Base	**Structure**: Flat **Persistence**: NoSQL Search Engine (OpenSearch), CSV, JSON
Similarity Measures	**Local Measures (18)**: 1 generic measure (equals), 6 string measures (e. g., BM25 measure, word embedding vector-based), 5 numeric measures (e. g., interval, nearest number), 2 categorical measures (distance, table), 1 date measure (nearest date), 1 location measure (nearest location), 2 ontology measures (path-based, feature-based) **Global Measures (1)**: 1 aggregation measure (weighted sum) Supports integration of custom similarity measures via scripts Full list available at https://github.com/RGU-Computing/clood#available-similarity-metrics
Adaptation Knowledge	Not supported

CBR Phases

Retrieve	Parallel linear retriever, supporting strategies best match or minimum for each attribute
Reuse	Null adaptation, supports custom adaptation via scripts
Revise	Supports manual adjustment of values via GUI
Retain	Maintenance tasks like forgetting cases or recomputing of similarities

Interfaces

GUI	AngularJS-based client dashboard "Clood CBR Dashboard", visualizing complete CBR cycle Parallel plots visualization
API	Generic REST API, Docker interface

Additional Information

Distributed CBR	Supports building distributed, highly scalable, and generic CBR systems based on a microservices architecture
Special Features	API token management, cloud native implementation (serverless framework), multiple programming languages supported (e. g., Java, Python, JavaScript), scalable
Planned Features	Support graph data structures for case representation, include case adaptation methods, incorporate common case base maintenance techniques, improve access management for multi-tenancy by enhancing the user management module

4.2 eXiT*CBR

eXiT*CBR supports structural CBR and follows a modular approach. The framework is specifically developed for use in medical systems but is also applied in other domains. eXiT*CBR has an executable version with a comprehensive GUI.

General Information	
Developer	Control Engineering and Intelligent Systems (eXiT) Research Group, University of Girona, Spain
Homepage	http://exitcbr.udg.edu/
CBR Types	Structural
Applications based on the Framework	Medicine and Healthcare: Cancer prognosis [33], premature baby monitoring [29], insulin dose recommendation [32,58] Industry: Fault detection, plastic injection molding process Full list available at: exitcbr.udg.edu/publications.html
Documentation about the Framework	**Publications**: [30,31,43] **User Tutorial**: http://exit.udg.edu/files/eXiTCBR-4.0/exitCBRUserTutorial.pdf
Source Code	Source code is not publicly available, but sharable upon request. **URL:** http://exitcbr.udg.edu/downloads.html (Executable Version) **Last Update:** Version 4.1 (January 2017) **Programming Language:** Java

Knowledge Containers	
Vocabulary	**Case Representation**: Attribute-value **General Knowledge Representation**: Not supported
Case Base	**Structure**: Flat **Persistence**: CSV
Similarity Measures	**Local Measures (9)**: 1 measure for unknown attributes, 1 string measure (Hamming distance), 2 numeric measures (Hamming and Euclidean distance), 1 boolean measure (equals), 1 date measure (distance-based), 3 sequence-measures (e. g., distance-based) **Global Measures (6)**: 6 aggregation measures (e. g., Euclidean, mean)
Adaptation Knowledge	Not supported

CBR Phases	
Retrieve	Linear retriever
Reuse	Copy, 2 probabilistic methods for binary cases, 3 majority methods, 2 probabilistic multi-class methods
Revise	Not supported
Retain	Methods for deleting or adding cases are provided

Interfaces	
GUI	GUI application for configuration, retrieval, visualization of results, and data export
API	Not supported

Additional Information	
Distributed CBR	Supported since version 2.0 as a multi-agent-based system (partially supported with the executable version for experimental purposes, but not for deployment in a real distributed environment.)
Special Features	Provides plugin capabilities for special purpose: genetic algorithms (for feature learning), family risk calculator to manage GEDCOM data.
Planned Features	Adding existing methods for CBR phases reuse and retain from special-purpose development branches

4.3 jColibri

jColibri [46] supports textual, structural and conversational CBR [14]. The framework has a model to describe domain-specific knowledge. jColibri is a further development of the Colibri architecture [46]. It provides a library of problem-solving methods for knowledge-intensive CBR based on its own ontology. According to the developers, no further updates are currently planned, but the framework continues to be used in research like *Explainable Case-Based Reasoning* [50].

General Information	
Developer	Group for Artificial Intelligence Applications (GAIA), Universidad Complutense de Madrid, Spain
Homepage	https://gaia.fdi.ucm.es/research/colibri/jcolibri/
CBR Types	Textual, structural, conversational
Applications based on the Framework	Medicine: Pain therapy [45], cancer [36], decision support [13] Industry: Energy optimization [19], knowledge management [36] Full list available at: https://gaia.fdi.ucm.es/research/colibri/index.php#users
Documentation about the Framework	**Publications**: [8,14,44,46] **Examples**: https://gaia.fdi.ucm.es/research/colibri/jcolibri/index.php#examples **API Documentation**: https://gaia.fdi.ucm.es/research/colibri/jcolibri/doc/apidocs/index.html
Source Code	**URL:** https://sourceforge.net/projects/jcolibri-cbr/ **Last Update:** Version 3.0 (Jan. 2019) **Programming Language:** Java

Knowledge Containers	
Vocabulary	**Case Representation**: Text, attribute-value Case divided into description, solution, justification of solution and result **General Knowledge Representation**: Ontology that includes cases
Case Base	**Structure**: Flat, index-based (KD tree), ontology-index **Persistence**: databases, plain text, XML, CSV, ontology
Similarity Measures	**Local Measures**: 1 generic measure (equals), 2 string measures (case-independent equals, maximum common substring), 4 numeric measures (e. g., interval, threshold), 2 categorical (e. g., enumeration distance), 4 ontology measures (e. g., cosine, path-based) **Global Measures (1)**: 1 aggregation measure (average)
Adaptation Knowledge	Not supported

CBR Phases	
Retrieve	Linear retriever, index-based retriever, filter-based retriever, MAC/FAC retriever, ontology retriever
Reuse	Null adaptation, numeric proportion
Revise	Generic constructs given, no methods implemented
Retain	Generic constructs given, methods for deleting or adding cases are provided, noise removal methods available (case base maintenance)

Interfaces	
GUI	Tool "Colibri Studio" enables no-code usage of the framework (https://gaia.fdi.ucm.es/research/colibri/colibristudio/) Case base visualization tools
API	Java interface

Additional Information

Distributed CBR	Not supported
Special Features	Includes metrics for evaluating the case base (including visualization), ReColibry (https://gaia.fdi.ucm.es/research/colibri/recolibry/index.php): extension for the construction of case-based recommender systems, xColibri(https://gaia.fdi.ucm.es/research/colibri/xcolibri/): evolution of the Colibri platform, for the explanation of intelligent Systems with CBR
Planned Features	**Short Term**: Inclusion of case-based explanation methods **Long Term**: Deployment of PyColibri, a python port of jColibri

4.4 myCBR

myCBR is designed for structural CBR. A focus is put on knowledge-intensive measures and the retrieval phase. In myCBR, elements of the CBR Works framework (see Sect. 3) have been adopted. The last release of myCBR3 documented on the project website is from May 2015. However, the framework is being further developed in two different branches. In the following profile, features that are only available in one branch are marked with either *UH* or *NTNU*.

General Information

Developer	Competence Center Case-Based Reasoning (CCCBR), DFKI, Germany School of Computing and Technology, University of West London, UK University of Hildesheim (UH), Germany Norwegian University of Science and Technology (NTNU), Norway
Homepage	http://mycbr-project.org/ NTNU: https://github.com/ntnu-ai-lab/mycbr-sdk
CBR Types	Textual, structural
Applications based on the Framework	Cooking domain (CookIIS), planning in games, config. of racing cars [61] UH: Recruiting processes [51], architectural floor plans [15,49], aircraft maintenance [47] NTNU: selfBACK (https://www.selfback.eu/), SupportPrim https://www.ntnu.no/supportprim
Documentation about the Framework	**Publications**: [4,6,22,55], UH: [56], NTNU: [5] Tutorial: http://mycbr-project.org/tutorials.html
Source Code	**URL:** http://mycbr-project.org/download.html Version 3 (May 2015) UH: https://github.com/jmschoenborn/myCBR-SDK (Dec. 2022) NTNU: https://github.com/ntnu-ai-lab/mycbr-sdk (May 2019) **Programming Language:** Java

Knowledge Containers	
Vocabulary	**Case Representation**: Text, attribute-value, object **General Knowledge Representation**: Taxonomies
Case Base	**Structure**: Flat **Persistence**: CSV, databases
Similarity Measures	**Local Measures (8)**: 4 string measures (e. g., equals, word-based, character-based, taxonomy-based), 2 numeric measures (default and user-defined distance), 2 categorical measures (order-based, table-based) **Global Measures (4)**: 4 aggregation measures (weighted sum, Euclidean, minimum, maximum) Supports the integration of custom similarity measures written in Jython
Adaptation Knowledge	Manual acquisition of adaptation rules

CBR Phases	
Retrieve	Linear retriever, index-based retriever
Reuse	Null adaptation, adaptation rules
Revise	Not supported
Retain	Generic constructs given, no methods implemented

Interfaces	
GUI	Tool "myCBR Workbench", provides modeling similarity measures and case base view
API	Java SDK (UH), REST-API (NTNU)

Additional Information	
Distributed CBR	Not supported
Planned Features (UH)	**Short Term**: Adding Jaro-Winkler distance for string comparison, integration of explainability via explanation patterns, counterfactuals, and visualization, integration of maintenance methods (work in progress) **Long Term**: Extension of explanation capabilities with additional approaches, integration of the case factory maintenance approach with domain-specific language, explanation capabilities for maintenance actions, integration of adaptation step for rule-based adaptations, knowledge modeling and visualization with a virtual reality component

4.5 ProCAKE

ProCAKE (*Process-oriented Case-based Knowledge Engine*) is a domain-independent CBR framework that focuses on structural and process-oriented CBR [10]. ProCAKE has evolved from CAKE (*Collaborative Agile Knowledge Engine*) [9]. It provides a generic data type model for custom case representations, various syntactic and semantic similarity measures, and several retrieval algorithms [10].

General Information	
Developer	Department of Business Information Systems II, University of Trier, Germany Experience-Based Learning Systems, DFKI Trier Branch, Germany
Homepage	https://procake.uni-trier.de
CBR Types	Textual, structural, process-oriented

Applications based on the Framework	Cooking domain: CookingCAKE (https://cookingcake.wi2.uni-trier.de/) IoT/Smart factory data: Adaptive production, cyber-physical systems [34] Business and scientific workflows: Modeling, adaptation [63], flexible execution [17] Full list available at: https://procake.uni-trier.de/publications
Documentation about the Framework	**Publications**: [10] **Demo Project**: https://gitlab.rlp.net/procake/procake-demos/ **Wiki**: https://procake.pages.gitlab.rlp.net/procake-wiki/
Source Code	**URL**: https://gitlab.rlp.net/procake/procake-framework **Last Update**: Version 4 (Apr. 2023) **Programming Language**: Java

Knowledge Containers

Vocabulary	**Case Representation**: Text, attribute-value, object, (semantic) graphs, collections (list, set), custom data classes (XML, Java) **General Knowledge Representation**: Ontologies, taxonomies
Case Base	**Structure**: Flat **Persistence**: JSON, XML, CSV
Similarity Measures	**Local Measures (41)**: 2 generic measures (table-based, equals), 12 string measures (e. g., Levenshtein, taxonomy-based), 5 numeric and date measures (e. g., distance, Sigmoid), 6 sequence measures (e. g., DTW, SWA), 1 interval measure (distance-based), 8 ontology measures (e. g., path-based, equivalence), 7 graph/process measures (e. g., DTW, SWA, Levenshtein, A*-based mapping) **Global Measures (7)**: 7 aggregation measures (e. g., average, maximum, minimum, Minkowski) Possibility to write own similarity measures (Java) Full list available at https://procake.pages.gitlab.rlp.net/procake-wiki/
Adaptation Knowledge	Domain-independent adaptation manager

CBR Phases

Retrieve	Linear retriever, parallel linear retriever, MAC/FAC retriever A*-parallel retriever (for graphs)
Reuse	Null adaptation, integration of custom adaptation methods supported
Revise	Not supported
Retain	Methods for deleting or adding cases are provided

Interfaces

GUI	Object editor for all system and custom data classes (https://gitlab.rlp.net/procake/procake-gui)
API	Java interface, generic REST API (https://gitlab.rlp.net/procake/procake-rest-api)

Additional Information

Distributed CBR	Not supported
Special Features	Embedding-based similarity measures and retrieval methods for structural and process-oriented cases (https://gitlab.rlp.net/procake-embedding)[21] Consideration of inter-case dependencies [27] Evaluation methods for retrievers
Planned Features	**Short Term (Work in progress):** integration of existing adaption algorithms (e.g., generalization/specialization, rule-based), integration of existing learning methods (e.g., embedding approaches) **Long Term**: Support for distributed CBR, cluster-based retrieval [37], conversational CBR [64], additional interfaces (GUI, docker, command line), explanation by visualization of similarities [52]

5   Comparison of Selected CBR Frameworks

In this section, the five presented frameworks are compared regarding the categories of the fact sheets[6]. Table 2 shows the supported case representations.

Table 2. Supported Case Representations per Framework.

CBR Framework	Text	Attribute-Value	Object	Graph
CloodCBR	X	X	X	
eXiT*CBR		X		
jColibri	X	X		
myCBR	X	X	X	
ProCAKE	X	X	X	X

In general, all frameworks support structural CBR. Except for eXiT*CBR, all frameworks also support textual CBR, storing texts as individual cases and providing corresponding similarity measures. jColibri is the only framework with a conversational component, while ProCAKE is the only one that can handle graphs or processes as cases. Some frameworks have been applied in the same application domains. For example, eXiT*CBR and jColibri are used in the medical domain, while myCBR and ProCAKE are used in the cooking domain. All frameworks are written in Java, except for CloodCBR, which is implemented in Python. The published source code of CloodCBR and ProCAKE is currently the most up-to-date. However, eXiT*CBR and myCBR are both still under active development. Only for jColibri, no further updates are currently planned.

ProCAKE is the only one that explicitly supports defining user-specific data classes. For general knowledge representations, CloodCBR, myCBR, and Pro-CAKE support taxonomies, and CloodCBR, jColibri, and ProCAKE support ontologies. While all frameworks provide a flat case base structure, jColibri follows an index- and an ontology-based approach, enabling more efficient storage. The case bases can be imported in different formats. It stands out that jColibri can connect to ontologies and databases and that CloodCBR connects to NoSQL databases. The built-in similarity measures differ greatly by the framework. Pro-CAKE has most of the similarity measures, both at the local and global level. For semantic measures, myCBR and ProCAKE support taxonomy-based measures, and CloodCBR, jColibri, and ProCAKE support ontology-based measures. CloodCBR incorporates neural language measures. For incorporating adaptation knowledge, myCBR provides manual acquisition of adaptation rules.

Regarding the CBR phases, it can be seen that the focus of all frameworks is on the retrieval and reuse phases. CloodCBR and eXiT*CBR each provide a single linear retriever. The retrieval is parallelized in CloodCBR by default.

---

[6] A complete overview table is available at: https://git.opendfki.de/easy/overview-and-comparison-of-cbr-frameworks/-/blob/main/Overview-Table.pdf.

ProCAKE has several retrievers built in. MAC/FAC retrievers are implemented in jColibri and ProCAKE. myCBR and jColibri also have index-based retrievers. jColibri has an ontology-based retriever, while ProCAKE has a special graph retriever. In the reuse phase, all frameworks support null adaptation. eXiT*CBR provides several probabilistic and majority methods, jColibri provides numeric proportion. myCBR supports adaptation rules. CloodCBR enables the integration of custom adaptation methods via scripts. ProCAKE does this similarly via its adaptation manager. The frameworks do not provide specific support for the revise phase. CloodCBR offers a manual adaptation of values in the interface, jColibri has generic methods built in. CloodCBR has maintenance tasks for the retain phase, such as forgetting or re-computing similarity values. jColibri provides methods for noise removal. myCBR and jColibri provide a generic framework for retainment. Basic maintenance tasks can be performed in any framework. In general, it can be seen that the retrieve and reuse phases are well-supported, whereas support for revise and retain can be enhanced in the frameworks.

Regarding the interfaces, the frameworks differ in the provided GUIs and APIs. CloodCBR, eXiT*CBR, and jColibri can be configured via GUI without programming. Hence, they are recommended for no-code development. myCBR and ProCAKE only provide partial GUIs for specific tasks. Java and REST interfaces are available for CloodCBR, myCBR, and ProCAKE. CloodCBR also provides a Docker interface.

Each framework provides some special features listed in the respective fact sheets. With the ever-growing amounts of data, it is assumed that Distributed CBR will become more relevant. jColibri, myCBR, and ProCAKE do not support distributed approaches yet. eXiT*CBR allows for the development of a multi-agent system for experimental purposes. CloodCBR also offers Distributed CBR through its microservices architecture and is the most advanced system in this respect. However, it can be stated that building applications for larger real environments needs further development of all frameworks.

To conclude, no framework is the most feature-rich or best in all categories. They all have different strengths or unique features. For specific application requirements, more suitable frameworks can be identified. For instance, eXiT*CBR or CloodCBR is suitable for Distributed CBR, jColibri supports dialog-oriented applications, and graph or process-oriented applications can be implemented with ProCAKE. It is desirable to provide interfaces between the different frameworks to combine the strengths of the different frameworks. For example, frameworks could integrate similarity measures or adaptation methods of other frameworks or case bases, and general knowledge could be exchanged more easily.

6   Conclusion

This paper aims to overview and compare the CBR frameworks developed to facilitate the development of CBR applications. As the most recent open-source frameworks, CloodCBR, eXiT*CBR, jColibri, myCBR, and ProCAKE have been identified and presented based on various criteria. Similarities and differences between the frameworks are examined, whereby it becomes apparent that each framework has its strengths and that certain frameworks are more suitable for different application areas. Some features, such as the support for Distributed CBR, are built in the frameworks with varying extent and maturity, so further investigation is needed to select the most suitable framework as a basis for developing specific applications. This work aims to provide decision support for this purpose.

The developers of the frameworks have various plans for further development of existing and for adding new features, from which trends for future research can be derived. A common goal of myCBR, jColibri, and ProCAKE is integrating explanation methods, which aligns with the recognized need for explainable Artificial Intelligence. myCBR and ProCAKE plan to extend the visualization components. CloodCBR, eXiT*CBR, and myCBR plan to integrate maintenance methods and approaches. The implementation of reuse methods (eXiT*CBR) or the inclusion of adaptation methods (CloodCBR and ProCAKE), as well as the extension of adaptation (myCBR), are other common goals. Certain features already provided in some frameworks will also become available in other frameworks according to the development plans. For example, support for graphs is planned for CloodCBR, ProCAKE plans to support distributed and conversational CBR, and jColibri plans to port the framework to Python. As a novel planned feature, a virtual reality component for knowledge modeling and visualization is mentioned for myCBR.

We thank all developers for their efforts and for making the frameworks available to the public.

Acknowledgments. We would like to thank the following people for contributing to the compilation of the CBR framework fact sheets: Ikechukwu Nkisi-Orji and Chamath Palihawadana (CloodCBR), Beatriz López, Oscar Raya, and Jonah Fernández (eXiT*CBR), Juan Antonio Recio García (jColibri), and Pascal Reuss (myCBR). This work is funded by the Federal Ministry for Economic Affairs and Climate Action under grant No. 01MD22002C *EASY*.

References

1. Aamodt, A., Plaza, E.: Case-based reasoning: foundational issues, methodological variations, and system approaches. AI Commun. **7**(1), 39–59 (1994)
2. Abásolo, C., Plaza, E., Arcos, J.-L.: Components for case-based reasoning systems. In: Escrig, M.T., Toledo, F., Golobardes, E. (eds.) CCIA 2002. LNCS (LNAI), vol. 2504, pp. 1–16. Springer, Heidelberg (2002). https://doi.org/10.1007/3-540-36079-4_1
3. Atanassov, A., Antonov, L.: Comparative analysis of case based reasoning software frameworks jColibri and myCBR. J. Chem. Technol. Metall. **47**(1), 83–90 (2012)
4. Bach, K., Althoff, K.-D.: Developing case-based reasoning applications using myCBR 3. In: Agudo, B.D., Watson, I. (eds.) ICCBR 2012. LNCS (LNAI), vol.

7466, pp. 17–31. Springer, Heidelberg (2012). https://doi.org/10.1007/978-3-642-32986-9_4

5. Bach, K., Mathisen, B.M., Jaiswal, A.: Demonstrating the myCBR rest API. In: 27th ICCBR Workshop Proceedings. CEUR Workshop Proceedings, vol. 2567, pp. 144–155. CEUR-WS.org (2019)

6. Bach, K., Sauer, C.S., Althoff, K., Roth-Berghofer, T.: Knowledge modeling with the open source tool myCBR. In: 21st ECAI Workshop Proceedings. CEUR Workshop Proceedings, vol. 1289. CEUR-WS.org (2014)

7. Begum, S., Ahmed, M.U., Funk, P., Xiong, N., Folke, M.: Case-based reasoning systems in the health sciences: a survey of recent trends and developments. IEEE Trans. Syst. Man Cybern. Part C **41**(4), 421–434 (2011)

8. Bello-Tomás, J.J., González-Calero, P.A., Díaz-Agudo, B.: JColibri: an object-oriented framework for building CBR systems. In: Funk, P., González Calero, P.A. (eds.) ECCBR 2004. LNCS (LNAI), vol. 3155, pp. 32–46. Springer, Heidelberg (2004). https://doi.org/10.1007/978-3-540-28631-8_4

9. Bergmann, R., Gil, Y.: Similarity assessment and efficient retrieval of semantic workflows. Inf. Syst. **40**, 115–127 (2014)

10. Bergmann, R., Grumbach, L., Malburg, L., Zeyen, C.: ProCAKE: a process-oriented case-based reasoning framework. In: 27th ICCBR Workshop Proceedings (2019)

11. Bogaerts, S., Leake, D.: Technical report 617 IUCBRF: a framework for rapid and modular case-based reasoning system development report version 1.0. IU Bloomington (2005)

12. Bogaerts, S., Leake, D.B.: Increasing AI project effectiveness with reusable code frameworks: a case study using IUCBRF. In: 18th FLAIRS. FloridaOJ, pp. 2–7. AAAI Press (2005)

13. Bruland, T., Aamodt, A., Langseth, H.: Architectures integrating case-based reasoning and Bayesian networks for clinical decision support. In: Shi, Z., Vadera, S., Aamodt, A., Leake, D. (eds.) IIP 2010. IAICT, vol. 340, pp. 82–91. Springer, Heidelberg (2010). https://doi.org/10.1007/978-3-642-16327-2_13

14. Díaz-Agudo, B., González-Calero, P.A., Recio-García, J.A., Sánchez-Ruiz-Granados, A.A.: Building CBR systems with jColibri. SCP **69**(1–3), 68–75 (2007)

15. Eisenstadt, V., Langenhan, C., Althoff, K.D.: Generation of floor plan variations with convolutional neural networks and case-based reasoning - an approach for unsupervised adaptation of room configurations within a framework for support of early conceptual design. In: eCAADe SIGraDi Conference, Porto (2019)

16. ElKafrawy, P., Mohamed, R.A.: Comparative study of case-based reasoning software. IJSRM **1**(6), 224–233 (2015)

17. Grumbach, L., Bergmann, R.: Towards case-based deviation management for flexible workflows. In: Jäschke, R., Weidlich, M. (eds.) LWDA 2019. CEUR Workshop Proceedings, vol. 2454, pp. 241–252. CEUR-WS.org (2019)

18. He, W., Wang, F.: Integrating a case-based reasoning shell and web 2.0: design recommendations and insights. World Wide Web **19**(6), 1231–1249 (2016). https://doi.org/10.1007/s11280-015-0380-y

19. Heilala, J., et al.: Ambient intelligence based monitoring and energy efficiency optimization system. In: ISAM 2011, pp. 1–6. IEEE (2011)

20. Hinkle, D., Toomey, C.: Applying case-based reasoning to manufacturing. AI Mag. **16**(1), 65–65 (1995)

21. Hoffmann, M., Bergmann, R.: Using graph embedding techniques in process-oriented case-based reasoning. Algorithms **15**(2), 27 (2022)

22. Hundt, A., Reuss, P., Sauer, C.S., Roth-Berghofer, T.: Knowledge modelling and maintenance in myCBR3. In: 16th LWA Workshop Proceedings. CEUR Workshop Proceedings, vol. 1226, pp. 264–275. CEUR-WS.org (2014)
23. Husni, H.S., Ramadhan, A., Abdurachman, E., Trisetyarso, A.: Indonesia digital government auditing model using rule based and cloud case-based reasoning. Int. J. Sci. Technol. Res. 1(2), 60–63 (2022)
24. Jaczynski, M.: A framework for the management of past experiences with time-extended situations. In: 6th CIKM Proceedings, pp. 32–39. ACM (1997)
25. Jaczynski, M., Trousse, B.: An object-oriented framework for the design and the implementation of case-based reasoners. In: CBR Workshop Proceedings (1998)
26. Kolodner, J.L.: Reconstructive memory: a computer model. Cogn. Sci. 7(4), 281–328 (1983)
27. Kumar, R., Schultheis, A., Malburg, L., Hoffmann, M., Bergmann, R.: Considering inter-case dependencies during similarity-based retrieval in process-oriented case-based reasoning. In: 35th FLAIRS. FloridaOJ (2022)
28. Lebowitz, M.: Memory-based parsing. AI 21(4), 363–404 (1983)
29. López, B., et al.: Intelligent system for premature babies healthcare at home based on case-based reasoning. In: 2nd IWBBIO, pp. 1278–1289. Copicentro Editorial (2014)
30. López, B., Pous, C.: eXiT*CBR: a tool supporting RRI. In: 21st CCIA. Frontiers in Artificial Intelligence and Applications, vol. 308, pp. 176–179. IOS Press (2018)
31. López, B., Pous, C., Gay, P., Pla, A., Sanz, J., Brunet, J.: eXiT*CBR: a framework for case-based medical diagnosis development and experimentation. Artif. Intell. Med. 51(2), 81–91 (2011)
32. López, B., et al.: APPRAISE-RS: automated, updated, participatory, and personalized treatment recommender systems based on grade methodology. Heliyon 9(2), e13074 (2023)
33. López, B., Pous, C., Plá, A., Gay, P., Brunet, J.: Breast cancer prognosis through CBR. In: 27th ICCBR Workshop Proceedings, pp. 105–110 (2012)
34. Malburg, L., Brand, F., Bergmann, R.: Adaptive management of cyber-physical workflows by means of case-based reasoning and automated planning. In: Sales, T.P., Proper, H.A., Guizzardi, G., Montali, M., Maggi, F.M., Fonseca, C.M. (eds.) EDOC 2022. LNBIP, vol. 466, pp. 79–95. Springer, Cham (2022). https://doi.org/10.1007/978-3-031-26886-1_5
35. Mark, W.S.: Case-based reasoning for autoclave management. In: CBR Workshop Proceedings, pp. 176–180. DARPA - Information Science (1989)
36. Martín, A., León, C.: Expert knowledge management based on ontology in a digital library. In: 12th ICEIS Proceedings, pp. 291–298. SciTePress (2010)
37. Müller, G., Bergmann, R.: A cluster-based approach to improve similarity-based retrieval for process-oriented case-based reasoning. In: 21st ECAI, vol. 263, pp. 639–644. IOS Press (2014)
38. Nguyen, T., Czerwinski, M., Lee, D.: Compaq QuickSource: providing the consumer with the power of artificial intelligence. In: IAAIC Proceedings, pp. 142–151 (1993)
39. Nkisi-Orji, I., Palihawadana, C., Wiratunga, N., Corsar, D., Wijekoon, A.: Adapting semantic similarity methods for case-based reasoning in the cloud. In: Keane, M.T., Wiratunga, N. (eds.) ICCBR 2022. LNAI, vol. 13405, pp. 125–139. Springer, Cham (2022). https://doi.org/10.1007/978-3-031-14923-8_9
40. Nkisi-Orji, I., Wiratunga, N., Palihawadana, C., Recio-García, J.A., Corsar, D.: CLOOD CBR: towards microservices oriented case-based reasoning. In: Watson, I., Weber, R. (eds.) ICCBR 2020. LNCS (LNAI), vol. 12311, pp. 129–143. Springer, Cham (2020). https://doi.org/10.1007/978-3-030-58342-2_9

41. Palihawadana, C., Nkisi-Orji, I., Wiratunga, N., Corsar, D., Wijekoon, A.: Introducing Clood CBR: a cloud based CBR framework. In: 30th ICCBR Workshop Proceedings. CEUR Workshop Proceedings, vol. 3389, pp. 233–234. CEUR-WS.org (2022)

42. Peixoto, T.F., Martinazzo, L.A., Weber, R.O.: Cyberinfrastructure requirements for research communities. In: 7th CIKI, vol. 1 (2017)

43. Pla, A., López, B., Gay, P., Pous, C.: eXiT*CBRv.2: distributed case-based reasoning tool for medical prognosis. Decis. Support Syst. **54**(3), 1499–1510 (2013)

44. Recio, J.A., Sánchez, A., Díaz-Agudo, B., González-Calero, P.: jColibri 1.0 in a nutshell. A software tool for designing CBR systems. In: 10th UKCBR Workshop Proceedings, pp. 1–11 (2005)

45. Recio-Garcia, J.A., Díaz-Agudo, B., Jorro-Aragoneses, J.L., Kazemi, A.: Intelligent control system for back pain therapy. In: Aha, D.W., Lieber, J. (eds.) ICCBR 2017. LNCS (LNAI), vol. 10339, pp. 287–301. Springer, Cham (2017). https://doi.org/10.1007/978-3-319-61030-6_20

46. Recio-García, J.A., González-Calero, P.A., Díaz-Agudo, B.: jColibri2: a framework for building case-based reasoning systems. SCP **79**, 126–145 (2014)

47. Reuss, P., Stram, R., Althoff, K.-D., Henkel, W., Henning, F.: Knowledge engineering for decision support on diagnosis and maintenance in the aircraft domain. In: Nalepa, G.J., Baumeister, J. (eds.) Synergies Between Knowledge Engineering and Software Engineering. AISC, vol. 626, pp. 173–196. Springer, Cham (2018). https://doi.org/10.1007/978-3-319-64161-4_9

48. Richter, M.M.: Knowledge containers. In: Readings in CBR. MKP (2003)

49. Sabri, Q.U., Bayer, J., Ayzenshtadt, V., Bukhari, S.S., Althoff, K.D., Dengel, A.: Semantic pattern-based retrieval of architectural floor plans with case-based and graph-based searching techniques and their evaluation and visualization. In: ICPRAM, pp. 50–60 (2017)

50. Schoenborn, J.M., Weber, R.O., Aha, D.W., Cassens, J., Althoff, K.D.: Explainable case-based reasoning: a survey. In: AAAI-2021 Workshop Proceedings (2021)

51. Schoenborn, J.M., Reuss, P., Wenzel, C., Althoff, K.: Towards a case-based decision support system for recruiting processes using T-shapes. In: Modellierung-C 2020. CEUR Workshop Proceedings, vol. 2542, pp. 165–171. CEUR-WS.org (2020)

52. Schultheis, A., Hoffmann, M., Malburg, L., Bergmann, R.: Explanation of similarities in process-oriented case-based reasoning by visualization. In: Massie, S., Chakraborti, S. (eds.) ICCBR 2023. LNAI, vol. 14141, pp. 53–68. Springer, Cham (2023)

53. Schulz, S.: CBR-works - a state-of-the-art shell for case-based application building. In: 7th GWCBR Proceedings, vol. 99, pp. 3–12. Citeseer (1999)

54. Schumacher, J.: Empolis Orenge - an open platform for knowledge management applications. In: 1st German Workshop on Experience Mgmt, pp. 61–62. GI (2002)

55. Stahl, A., Roth-Berghofer, T.R.: Rapid prototyping of CBR applications with the open source tool myCBR. In: Althoff, K.-D., Bergmann, R., Minor, M., Hanft, A. (eds.) ECCBR 2008. LNCS (LNAI), vol. 5239, pp. 615–629. Springer, Heidelberg (2008). https://doi.org/10.1007/978-3-540-85502-6_42

56. Stram, R., Reuss, P., Althoff, K.-D.: Dynamic case bases and the asymmetrical weighted one-mode projection. In: Cox, M.T., Funk, P., Begum, S. (eds.) ICCBR 2018. LNCS (LNAI), vol. 11156, pp. 385–398. Springer, Cham (2018). https://doi.org/10.1007/978-3-030-01081-2_26

57. Thakur, N., Chhabra, T., Verma, D., Kumar, D., Dayal, M.: Case based reasoning: a comparative analysis of CBR tools. IJIRCST **4**, 11190–11196 (2016)

58. Unsworth, R., et al.: Safety and efficacy of an adaptive bolus calculator for type 1 diabetes: a randomized controlled crossover study. Dia. Technol. Ther **25**(6), 414–425 (2023)
59. Watson, I.D.: Applying Case-Based Reasoning - Techniques for the Enterprise Systems. MKP (1997)
60. Watson, I.D., Marir, F.: Case-based reasoning: a review. Knowl. Eng. Rev. **9**(4), 327–354 (1994)
61. Wenzel, C., Reuss, P., Rose, K., Althoff, K.D.: Multi-agent, case-based configuration of custom-built racing cars. In: 19th UKCBR Workshop Proceedings (2014)
62. Wijekoon, A., Wiratunga, N., Palihawadana, C., Nkisi-Orji, I., Corsar, D., Martin, K.: iSee: intelligent sharing of explanation experience by users for users. In: 28th IUI Companion Proceedings, pp. 79–82 (2023)
63. Zeyen, C., Malburg, L., Bergmann, R.: Adaptation of scientific workflows by means of process-oriented case-based reasoning. In: Bach, K., Marling, C. (eds.) ICCBR 2019. LNCS (LNAI), vol. 11680, pp. 388–403. Springer, Cham (2019). https://doi.org/10.1007/978-3-030-29249-2_26
64. Zeyen, C., Müller, G., Bergmann, R.: Conversational process-oriented case-based reasoning. In: Aha, D.W., Lieber, J. (eds.) ICCBR 2017. LNCS (LNAI), vol. 10339, pp. 403–419. Springer, Cham (2017). https://doi.org/10.1007/978-3-319-61030-6_28

Case-Based Cleaning of Text Images

Éric Astier[1], Hugo Iopeti[2], Jean Lieber[3(✉)], Hugo Mathieu Steinbach[2], and Ludovic Yvoz[2,3]

[1] Persée, École Normale Supérieure de Lyon, 69007 Lyon, France
[2] Université de Lorraine, master informatique, Nancy, France
[3] LORIA, Université de Lorraine, CNRS, Inria, 54000 Nancy, France
`jean.lieber@loria.fr`

Abstract. Old documents suffer from the passage of time: the paper is becoming more yellow, the ink is fading and the handling of these documents can still cause them to be damaged (e.g. stains may appear). The online edition of such documents can have profit of a cleaning step, the aim of which is to improve its readability. Some image filtering systems exist that require proper parameters to perform a cleaning. This article presents GEORGES, a CBR system designed to predict these parameters, for images of texts written in French, with several variants based on approximation, interpolation and extrapolation, based respectively of similarity, betweenness, and analogical proportion relations. The images are characterized by a dirtiness index, with the assumption that two images with similar dirtiness indexes would require similar sets of parameters for being cleaned. This index is based on the detection of the occurrences of a frequent French word on the pages and of averaging these occurrences. Human and automatic evaluations show that the proposed approach (with its variants) provides high-quality results.

Keywords: case-based reasoning · approximation · interpolation · extrapolation · image processing · image cleaning

1 Introduction

The notion of similarity between a source case and a target problem is well-known to play a key role in case-based reasoning (CBR [14]). This involves the question of what similar means for a given CBR application and this is linked with the problem-solving task (i.e. to the nature of the relation between a problem and a solution). Consider, for example, problems represented by grayscale images. This problem can be represented by an $m \times n$ matrix of nonnegative numbers, so a naive way to assess the similarity between two problems would be to compute a classical norm-based distance between matrices such as $(A, B) \mapsto \sum_{i=1}^{m} \sum_{j=1}^{n} |B_{ij} - A_{ij}|$.

In this article, GEORGES, an application of CBR is presented in which problems are represented by such grayscale images, but similarity would be poorly modeled using such a norm-based distance function. For this application, a problem corresponds to such an image and a solution is given by a triple of values parametrizing a filter to be applied on the image for having it cleaned. More precisely, this image is obtained by scanning a page containing some text. Two problems would be similar if their "dirtinesses" are assessed to be close, where the dirtiness of an image characterizes how it should be cleaned.

After some preliminaries (Sect. 2), related studies are presented (Sect. 3). Section 4 presents the application context and explains that one of the steps of the chain of treatments consists in choosing a parameter triple, which has been done manually so far. Several CBR approaches are proposed to generate triples of parameters (Sect. 5), thus making the semiautomatic cleaning step automatic. Section 6 evaluates and compares these approaches. Section 7 concludes, discusses the scope of this approach beyond the application, and points out some future work.

2   Preliminaries

This section presents some notions and notations in the domains of mathematics, CBR and image processing, useful for the remainder of the article.

2.1   Some Mathematical Notions and Notations

Let $\mathbb{N}$ be the set of natural integers, $\mathbb{N}^* = \mathbb{N} \backslash \{0\}$, $\mathbb{R}$ be the set of real numbers, $\mathbb{R}_+ = \{u \in \mathbb{R} \mid u \geq 0\}$, and $\mathbb{R}_+^* = \mathbb{R}_+ \backslash \{0\}$.

A *distance function* in a set $\mathcal{U}$ is a mapping $\mathtt{dist} : \mathcal{U}^2 \to \mathbb{R}_+$ such that (for $u, v, w \in \mathcal{U}$): (1) $\mathtt{dist}(u, v) = 0$ iff $u = v$, (2) $\mathtt{dist}(u, v) = \mathtt{dist}(v, u)$, and (3) $\mathtt{dist}(u, w) \leq \mathtt{dist}(u, v) + \mathtt{dist}(v, w)$. For $n \in \mathbb{N}^*$, let $\mathcal{U} \subseteq \mathbb{R}^n$ and $\mathtt{dist1}$ and $\mathtt{dist2}$ be the two distance functions defined, for $(u, v) \in \mathcal{U}^2$ by

$$\mathtt{dist1}(u, v) = \sum_{i=1}^{n} |v_i - u_i| \qquad \mathtt{dist2}(u, v) = \sqrt{\sum_{i=1}^{n} (v_i - u_i)^2}$$

For $u \in \mathcal{U}$, $\|u\|_{\mathtt{dist1}}$ denotes the value $\mathtt{dist1}(u, \mathbf{0})$, where $\mathbf{0} = (0, 0, \ldots, 0) \in \mathbb{R}^n$.

The notion of betweenness can be used to apprehend the ternary relation "a is between b and c" where a, b and c are objects of the same set $\mathcal{U}$. In [1], this kind of relations is studied in the framework of the Gärdenfors conceptual spaces [5]. In particular, some postulates for such a relation are given and one of the ways to define a betweenness relation based on a distance function on $\mathcal{U}$ is introduced.[1] It is reformulated as follows. Let $[b, c]_{\mathtt{dist}}$ be the set of $a \in \mathcal{U}$ such that $\mathtt{dist}(b, c) = \mathtt{dist}(b, a) + \mathtt{dist}(a, c)$. For example, if $\mathcal{U} = \mathbb{R}^n$, $[b, c]_{\mathtt{dist2}}$ is the

---

[1] The authors of [1] also criticize this definition by the fact that two distances on $\mathcal{U}$ defining the same topology do not necessarily correspond to the same betweenness relation. However, this is the definition considered in this paper, because it has the advantage of simplicity.

segment line $[b, c]$ in the usual sense and $[b, c]_{\text{dist1}} = [b_1, c_1] \times [b_2, c_2] \times \ldots \times [b_n, c_n]$ where $[b_i, c_i] = [b_i, c_i]_{\text{dist1}}$ is the set of $a_i \in \mathbb{R}$ such that $\min(b_i, c_i) \leq a_i \leq \max(b_i, c_i)$. Then the dist-betweenness relation is defined, for $a, b, c \in \mathcal{U}$ by a is between c and d if $a \in [b, c]_{\text{dist}}$.

An *analogical proportion* on a set $\mathcal{U}$ is a quaternary relation $\mathcal{AP}$ on $\mathcal{U}$ verifying some postulates (not detailed here: see, e.g., [13] for details). For $a, b, c, d \in \mathcal{U}$, $\mathcal{AP}(a, b, c, d)$ is usually written as $a{:}b{::}c{:}d$. In this paper, the only analogical proportion that is considered is the *arithmetic analogical proportion*, defined on a subset $\mathcal{U}$ of $\mathbb{R}^n$ (for some $n \in \mathbb{N}^*$) as follows:

$$a{:}b{::}c{:}d \text{ if for every } i \in \{1, 2, \ldots, n\}, \ b_i - a_i = d_i - c_i$$

An *analogical equation* is an expression of the form $a{:}b{::}c{:}y$ where $a, b, c \in \mathcal{U}$ and y is a symbol called the unknown. Solving this equation consists in finding all the bindings of y by values d such that $a{:}b{::}c{:}d$. For the arithmetic analogical proportion, such an equation as at most 1 solution.

If $\mathcal{U}$ is a set of $m \times n$ matrices on real numbers, the above definitions (distance functions, betweenness relations, analogical proportions) also apply, the only difference being that the indexes in the definitions are $(i, j) \in \{1, 2, \ldots, m\} \times \{1, 2, \ldots n\}$ instead of $i \in \{1, 2, \ldots, n\}$.

2.2   CBR: Notions, Notations and Assumptions

The way in which CBR is presented in this section is strongly biased by the work presented in this article. For instance, a case is given by any problem-solution pair (and this is not true for every CBR application). Therefore, it should not be used as a short introduction to CBR in general.

Let $\mathcal{P}$ and $\mathcal{S}$ be two sets. A *problem* (of the current application domain) is by definition an element of $\mathcal{P}$ and a *solution*, an element of $\mathcal{S}$. A *case* is a pair $(\mathbf{x}, \mathbf{y})$ where $\mathbf{x} \in \mathcal{P}$ and $\mathbf{y} \in \mathcal{S}$. The case $(\mathbf{x}, \mathbf{y})$ can be read as the statement "$\mathbf{y}$ is a solution of $\mathbf{x}$." However, given two cases $(\mathbf{x}, \mathbf{y}^1)$ and $(\mathbf{x}, \mathbf{y}^2)$ sharing the same problem, the two solutions $\mathbf{y}^1$ and $\mathbf{y}^2$ are not equal: it is assumed that there exists an expert assessment of the quality of a solution $\mathbf{y}$ to a problem $\mathbf{x}$ (from the worst solution to the best one), where the expert is a human who can solve problems of this domain. This assessment is not known by the CBR system, except for the case base, which is a finite set CB of cases $(\mathbf{x}^s, \mathbf{y}^s)$ such that the expert assesses that $\mathbf{y}^s$ is a good solution to $\mathbf{x}^s$. A *source case* is an element of CB.

Let $\mathbf{x}^{\text{tgt}} \in \mathcal{P}$ be a problem to be solved, called the *target problem*. The CBR solving session of $\mathbf{x}^{\text{tgt}}$ consists of two steps. *Retrieval* aims at selecting $k \geq 1$ source cases based on some criteria relative to $\mathbf{x}^{\text{tgt}}$ (e.g. similarity to $\mathbf{x}^{\text{tgt}}$, but this is not the only possibility). *Adaptation* uses these retrieved cases in order to propose a solution $\mathbf{y}^{\text{tgt}}$ to $\mathbf{x}^{\text{tgt}}$.

2.3   About Image Processing

The pixels of the images considered in this article are associated with gray levels. A *grayscale value* is modeled by a real number in the $[0, 1]$ interval.[2] The gray level 0 (resp. 1) corresponds to a black pixel (resp. to a white pixel). An image x is modeled by an $m \times n$ matrix of grayscale values: a pixel of x is a pair $(i, j) \in \{1, 2, \ldots, m\} \times \{1, 2, \ldots, n\}$ and the grayscale value associated with a pixel (i, j) is x_{ij}.

The treatment of an image considered in this paper is parametrized by a triple $(b\ell, w\ell, \gamma) \in [0, 1] \times [0, 1] \times \mathbb{R}_+^*$ and is the composition of 3 treatments, as described below.

Let $b\ell \in [0, 1]$. Applying the "black level" transformation on a grayscale image x consists of substituting darker pixels according to the threshold $b\ell$ by a black pixel:

$$\texttt{applyBlackLevel}(b\ell, \mathbf{x}) = \mathbf{x}' \text{ with } x'_{ij} = \begin{cases} x_{ij} & \text{if } x_{ij} > b\ell \\ 0 & \text{else} \end{cases}$$

The "white level transformation" is described similarly (for $w\ell \in [0, 1]$):

$$\texttt{applyWhiteLevel}(w\ell, \mathbf{x}) = \mathbf{x}' \text{ with } x'_{ij} = \begin{cases} x_{ij} & \text{if } x_{ij} < w\ell \\ 1 & \text{else} \end{cases}$$

The "Gamma transformation" is defined below, for $\gamma \in \mathbb{R}_+^*$:

$$\texttt{applyGamma}(\gamma, \mathbf{x}) = \mathbf{x}' \text{ with } x'_{ij} = x_{ij}^{\gamma}$$

The effect of this transformation is essentially applied on the darker pixels: if $\gamma < 1$ these pixels get lighter, if $\gamma > 1$, they become darker.

Finally, given a triple $\mathbf{y} = (b\ell, w\ell, \gamma)$, the clean treatment consists of applying in sequence these 3 transformations:

$$\texttt{clean}(\mathbf{y}, \mathbf{x}) = \texttt{applyGamma}(\gamma, \texttt{applyWhiteLevel}(w\ell, \texttt{applyBlackLevel}(b\ell, \mathbf{x})))$$

In practice, a triple $(b\ell, w\ell, \gamma)$ should satisfy $b\ell \leq w\ell$, otherwise, the "cleaned" image would be fully white.

A *binarization* task on a grayscale image x consists in turning all pixels black or white. One way to do this consists of choosing a value $b\ell$ and computing $\texttt{clean}((b\ell, w\ell, \gamma), \mathbf{x})$ with $w\ell = b\ell$ (and γ chosen arbitrarily). It should be noted that the goal of the clean treatment in our application is *not* to make a binarization. Indeed, its objective is to improve the readability of the page by human readers, and intermediate gray levels are useful for this purpose. However, the related work that is, to the best of our knowledge, the closest to our work is a binarization, as the next section presents.

---

[2] In practice, grayscale values are integers ranging from 0 to 255, but, it has been chosen to normalize them in $[0, 1]$: from a $g \in [0, 1]$, the corresponding integer value is $\lfloor 255x + 0.5 \rfloor$.

3   Related Works

The area of image processing is broader than the one presented below. In particular, image interpretation aims at finding high level descriptions of images and some CBR approaches have been successfully applied to this task (see e.g. [11,12]). CBR can also be used to help experts in image processing, by helping them to build a relevant sequence of tasks to be applied on an image [4].

In this article, the goal is to find transformations on images so that they are more readable for human beings and we have not found CBR approaches for this purpose. By contrast, there are many research on the binarization of images (see [2,10,17] for surveys).

The   binarization   approach   of   Ergina   Kavallieratou   and Hera Antonopoulou [7] appears to be close to the objective of our work and this, for two reasons. First, they have worked on text images of old documents (in their work, handwritten or typed documents in Greek, which differs from the typed documents in French). Second, the main step of their process transforms grayscale images into grayscale images giving a cleaned image that is not black and white (the binarization takes place after this main step). The algorithm of this main step describes a cleaning procedure that is described briefly as follows, given an input image x. First, a histogram of the grayscale values that are below the average value of the pixels is computed (this histogram is a function associating to $g \in [0,1]$ the number of (i,j) such that $x_{ij} = g$). Then, this histogram is rescaled, so that minimum values get to 0 and maximum values get to 1 (the darkest pixels become black, the lightest pixels become white) and the image is changed accordingly. This process is repeated until the difference between two successive images gets lower than a given threshold.

A qualitative comparison of the result of the process presented in [7] and the result of the process presented in this article is given in Sect. 6.4.

4   Application Context

Persée is a support and research unit of *ENS de Lyon* and CNRS assisting research by ensuring enriched digitization, quality processing, open dissemination and long-term preservation of scientific documentary heritage written in French. The missions of Persée are structured around 3 axis:

- Enhancing the value of collections of scientific publications through the Persée portal (https://www.persee.fr);
- Design, production and dissemination of research corpora (https://info.persee.fr/section/perseides);
- Making data available in a triplestore (https://data.persee.fr).

Given a document to be edited (a book, a journal, proceedings of a conference, etc.), its digital publication by Persée follows a workflow of tasks that are described below in a partial and simplified way:

(T1) The document is digitized (either by Persée or by the client) and put in an appropriate image format, i.e. a sequence of bitmap images in grayscale.

(T2) An OCR is run on all images, which extracts its words and there respective positions on the image.

(T3) The image is cleaned in a semi-automatic way:

 (T3.1) A page of the document is chosen (typically not one of the first or last pages with the cover, the table of contents, etc.).

 (T3.2) The expert chooses a triple $\mathbf{y} = (b\ell, w\ell, \gamma)$ for the image $\mathbf{x}$ of this page, visualizes the result $\texttt{clean}(\mathbf{y}, \mathbf{x})$ and makes changes to the triple if the result is not adequate.

 (T3.3) The filter $\texttt{clean}$ is applied to all images in the document with the same triple $\mathbf{y}$ (assuming that the degradation of the images over time is the same on all pages of the document).

(T4) The next steps are not described here. It is sufficient to know for this article that some further verifications are made that may lead to go back to step (T3) (which is relevant, in particular, when a page of the document has been degraded significantly more than the other pages).

5   CBR Approaches to Case-Based Text Image Cleaning

This section presents several approaches for automatizing the cleaning step (step number (T3)) presented in the previous section and gathered in the CBR system GEORGES. Section 5.1 describes the representation of the cases and the constitution of the case base (Sect. 5.1). Then, the question of comparing images from the cleaning task viewpoint is addressed (Sect. 5.2): the images are characterized by a "dirtiness index" and the comparisons between the source images and the target image are based on this index. Section 5.3 describes the application of several CBR approaches to this problem. These approaches have been introduced in [8] and the current article also provides an opportunity to study them within a concrete application domain.

5.1   Representation of Cases and Constitution of the Case Base

The task GEORGES has to solve is to associate to an image $\mathbf{x}^{\text{tgt}}$ a triple of parameters $\mathbf{y}^{\text{tgt}}$, such that $\texttt{clean}(\mathbf{y}^{\text{tgt}}, \mathbf{x}^{\text{tgt}})$ is a cleaned version of $\mathbf{x}^{\text{tgt}}$. Therefore, in this application, a problem $\mathbf{x}$ is a grayscale image, a solution $\mathbf{y}$ is a triple of parameters $(b\ell, w\ell, \gamma)$, and a case is an image-triple pair $(\mathbf{x}, \mathbf{y})$.

The step (T3) has been semi-automatic during several years, the experts associating to an image $\mathbf{x}$ a triple $\mathbf{y}$. Since the pairs $(\mathbf{x}, \mathbf{y})$ have been retained, they constitute cases, thus the case base is constituted by such cases: only a part of them have been kept for the case base (this is detailed in Sect. 6.1).

5.2   Representing Image Dirtiness

The images considered in this work are images of French texts (and potential illustrations), so the notion of cleanness (and, dually, the notion of dirtiness) is

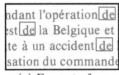

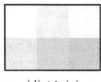

(a) Excerpt of an image x, with 3 framed "de".

(b) Average "de" on x.

(c) idx(x) (variant 1 × 1).

(d) idx(x) (variant 2 × 3).

Fig. 1. The dirtiness indexing of an image of French text.

related to the readability of this text: the more a text image requires efforts to a reader, the more dirty it is.

It is noticeable that the goal here is not to assess a dirtiness level: two images could be qualified equally dirty, but could be dirty in different ways (e.g. one being too dark and the other one too light). It should also be noted that this representation of image dirtiness is related to the whole image, since the treatment at this step is global, but taking, e.g. the average grayscale of the page is a bad idea: it is easy to imagine two images having the same average of grayscale, one being rather clean and full of text, the other one being very dark, with a gray background, and having only a few lines of text.

So, the idea has emerged to qualify the dirtiness of an image using samples of the image that can be found (with various levels of dirtiness) in most images. Since these are images of French texts, a first idea was to use the occurrences of "e", the most frequent letter in French. In order to have a slightly larger number of pixels, the most frequent French word was chosen instead: the word "de".[3] Therefore, given an image x, the index of dirtiness of x, denoted by idx(x), is characterized by the average "de" in x. More precisely, the indexing process is illustrated in Fig. 1 and it can be described by the following process (in practice, these steps are combined, but are easier to explain this way):

1. From the OCR treatment of the image x, the set of bounding boxes of occurrences of "de" in x is collected (which necessitates some recalibration) and then, these bounding boxes are normalized by scaling, so that each occurrence of "de" corresponds to an $m \times n$ matrix of grayscale values.
2. Then, the average "de" is computed by a arithmetic mean of these normalized bounding boxes, giving MGV, a matrix of grayscale values.
3. The last step has two variants:

---

[3] This word corresponds approximately to "of". Its average number of occurrences by page in the studied corpus is 16.2, with a standard deviation of 11.5. For one of the rare pages in the corpus containing no "de", the backup solution is to use the solution of another page of the same document. Documents in French that contain no "de" are very rare, though one of them is famous: it is *La disparition*, a novel of Georges Perec which is about 300 pages lipogram in "e" and thus, contains no "de". This is a paradoxical explanation of the choice of GEORGES, as the name of our system.

(1×1) In the first variant, $\mathtt{idx(x)}$ is simply the average of grayscale values of MGV, i.e. $\dfrac{1}{mn} \displaystyle\sum_{1 \leq i \leq m} \sum_{1 \leq j \leq n} MGV_{ij}$.

(2×3) In the second variant, the matrix MGV is split in 6 parts by splitting the ranges of the line number i into 2 parts and the ranges of the line number j into 3 parts and taking the average of the grayscale values in each of the 6 parts. In other terms, $\mathtt{idx(x)}$ is a 2×3 matrix defined by:

$$\mathtt{idx(x)}_{Pq} = \frac{6}{mn} \sum_{\lfloor \frac{(p-1)m}{2} \rfloor + 1 \leq i \leq \lfloor \frac{pm}{2} \rfloor} \sum_{\lfloor \frac{(q-1)n}{3} \rfloor + 1 \leq j \leq \lfloor \frac{qn}{3} \rfloor} MGV_{ij}$$

for $p \in \{1, 2\}$ and $q \in \{1, 2, 3\}$, with $\lfloor r \rfloor$ the floor of r.[4]

In the approaches presented in the following, the only information used in the images $\mathbf{x}$ is given by $\mathtt{idx(x)}$. For a target problem $\mathbf{x^{tgt}}$, computing $\mathtt{idx(x^{tgt})}$ is a pretreatment of the processes. For $\mathbf{x}^s$ such that $(\mathbf{x}^s, \mathbf{y}^s) \in CB$, $\mathtt{idx(x}^s)$ is computed offline and stored in a database. For any source case $(\mathbf{x}^s, \mathbf{y}^s)$, $\mathtt{idx(x}^s)$ is denoted by $\mathbf{i}^S$; $\mathtt{idx(x^{tgt})}$ is denoted by $\mathbf{i^{tgt}}$.

5.3   Proposed Approaches

The approaches presented in this section are based on the retrieval of k source cases, respectively with $k = 1$, $k = 2$ and $k = 3$, and the adaptation of these cases to solve $\mathbf{x^{tgt}}$. These approaches correspond to the following reasoning scheme. It is assumed that $\mathcal{R}_{pb}$ (resp. $\mathcal{R}_{sol}$) is a $(k + 1)$-ary relation on $\mathcal{P}$ (resp. on $\mathcal{S}$). Then, the inference is based on the following *plausible* inference rule:

$$\frac{\mathcal{R}_{pb}(\mathbf{x}^1, \mathbf{x}^2, \ldots, \mathbf{x}^{k+1})}{\mathcal{R}_{sol}(\mathbf{y}^1, \mathbf{y}^2, \ldots, \mathbf{y}^{k+1})} \qquad \text{(with } \mathbf{y}^i \text{ a solution of } \mathbf{x}^i \text{ for } i \in \{1, 2, \ldots, k+1\})$$

The search aims to find k source cases $(\mathbf{x}^1, \mathbf{y}^1)$, $(\mathbf{x}^2, \mathbf{y}^2)$, ..., $(\mathbf{x}^k, \mathbf{y}^k)$ such that $\mathcal{R}_{pb}(\mathbf{x}^1, \mathbf{x}^2, \ldots, \mathbf{x}^k, \mathbf{x^{tgt}})$ and adaptation consists of solving the constraint $\mathcal{R}_{sol}(\mathbf{y}^1, \mathbf{y}^2, \ldots, \mathbf{y}^k, \mathbf{y})$ with unknown $\mathbf{y}$: a solution of this constraint is a proposed solution $\mathbf{y^{tgt}}$ of $\mathbf{x^{tgt}}$.

This inference rule can be reinterpreted when $\mathcal{R}_{pb}$ becomes a fuzzy (or gradual) relation, i.e. $\mathcal{R}_{pb}(\mathbf{x}^1, \mathbf{x}^2, \ldots, \mathbf{x}^{k+1})$ may be neither false nor true, but may take intermediate truth values. Then, the inference rule is read as follows:

The more $\mathcal{R}_{pb}(\mathbf{x}^1, \mathbf{x}^2, \ldots, \mathbf{x}^{k+1})$ is, the more plausible $\mathcal{R}_{sol}(\mathbf{y}^1, \mathbf{y}^2, \ldots, \mathbf{y}^{k+1})$ is.

The implemented approaches are based on this "fuzzy interpretation" of the inference rules.

---

[4] Other variants $p \times q$ could have been considered but the differences between the variants 1×1 and 2×3 in the first experiments have not pushed us towards this direction.

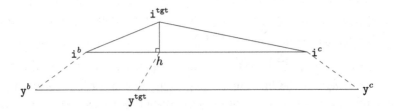

Fig. 2. Some Euclidian geometry for interpolation.

Approximation corresponds to $k = 1$, and $\mathcal{R}_{pb}$ and $\mathcal{R}_{sol}$ chosen as "similarity relations". This means that if x^s is similar to x^{tgt} then y^s is similar to the searched solution y^{tgt}.

One way to implement this approach is based on the interpretation of the similarity relation as a fuzzy relation, i.e. in selecting the source case (x^s, y^s) that is the most similar to x^{tgt} and taking y^s as a solution to x^{tgt} (i.e. $y^{tgt} = y^s$). For this purpose, the similarity between the problems is computed thanks to the distance `dist1` between the indexes $i^S = \text{idx}(x^s)$ and $i^{tgt} = \text{idx}(x^{tgt})$: the most the dirtiness index of the images are similar, the most plausible it is that the solution triple of the first image is good for the second one. The approaches implemented are denoted by `approx1x1` and `approx2x3` (approximation approaches with 1×1 and 2×3 dirtiness indexes).

Interpolation corresponds to $k = 2$ and to betweenness relations, following the ideas of interpolative reasoning as presented in [15]. Depending on the choice of the distance functions between dirtiness indexes and between solutions, and on the choice between crisp and fuzzy interpretations of the inference rules, there are several interpolation approaches.

One way to consider it corresponds to the crisp interpretation of the inference rule, the `dist1` distance function between 1×1 dirtiness indexes and the `dist1` distance function between solutions. This means that retrieval selects two source cases (x^b, y^b) and (x^c, y^c) such that $i^{tgt} \in [i^B, i^C]$ (if no such pair of cases exist, the interpolation fails). To have the most accurate framing of $\text{idx}(x^{tgt})$, the pair of retrieved source cases are chosen according to these criteria:

$$i^b = \max\{i^s \mid (x^s, y^s) \in CB \text{ and } i^s \leq i^{tgt}\}$$
$$i^c = \min\{i^s \mid (x^s, y^s) \in CB \text{ and } i^s \geq i^{tgt}\}$$

Then, the plausible inference leads to a range $[y^b, y^c]_{dist1}$ for y^{tgt}, that is,

$$b\ell^{tgt} \in [b\ell^b, b\ell^c] \qquad w\ell^{tgt} \in [w\ell^b, w\ell^c] \qquad \gamma^{tgt} \in [\gamma^b, \gamma^c]$$

where $y^{tgt} = (b\ell^{tgt}, w\ell^{tgt}, \gamma^{tgt})$, $y^b = (b\ell^b, w\ell^b, \gamma^b)$ and $y^c = (b\ell^c, w\ell^c, \gamma^c)$. This has not been implemented but is considered as future work (see Sect. 7).

Another way to consider interpolation corresponds to the fuzzy interpretation of the inference rule, the `dist2` distance function between dirtiness indexes, and the dist2 distance function between solutions. The Euclidian distance dist2 allows us to use the notion of orthogonal projection of a point on a line. Let (x^b, y^b) and (x^c, y^c) be two source cases and let h be the orthogonal projection of i^{tgt} on the line $(i^b i^c)$ (see Fig. 2, for illustration). If h does not belong to the segment $[i^b, i^c]_{dist2}$ or is equal to one of its extremities then this pair of source cases is not a candidate for retrieval. So, in the following, it is assumed that $h \in [i^b, i^c]_{dist2} \setminus \{i^b, i^c\}$. Let $D^{bc} = \text{dist2}(i^{tgt}, h)$, the distance between i^{tgt} and the segment $[i^b, i^c]_{dist2}$. i^{tgt} is between i^b and i^c iff $D^{bc} = 0$. The betweenness relation is fuzzified according to the following principle: the lower D^{bc} is, the more i^{tgt} is between i^b and i^c. Therefore, the retrieval aims to find a pair of source cases (x^b, y^b) and (x^c, y^c) to minimize D^{bc}. The interpolation principle entails that the proposed solution belongs to $[y^b, y^c]_{dist2}$. However, this interpolation approach proposes a precise value for y^{tgt} by applying the following principle: the closer h is to x^b, the closer the solution y^{tgt} proposed for x^{tgt} is to y^b. In other words, if h is the barycenter of (i^b, α) and (i^c, β) (where $\alpha, \beta \in \mathbb{R}_+^*$) then the proposed y^{tgt} is the barycenter of (y^b, α) and (y^c, β), as illustrated in Fig. 2.[5] This has been implemented for the two variants of the dirtiness index, with the implementation names interp1x1 and interp2x3.

Extrapolation corresponds to $k = 3$ and to analogical proportions on dirtiness indexes and on solutions. Retrieval aims at finding 3 source cases (x^a, y^a), (x^b, y^b) and (x^c, y^c) such that $i^a{:}i^b{::}i^c{:}i^{tgt}$ (the analogical proportion is computed on image dirtiness indexes). Adaptation consists of solving the analogical equation $y^a{:}y^b{::}y^c{:}y$ and giving the solution y as a proposed solution y^{tgt} to x^{tgt}.

In order to put this principle into practice, a few remarks can be made.

First, the situations where $i^a{:}i^b{::}i^c{:}i^{tgt}$, i.e. $i^b - i^a = i^{tgt} - i^c$, appear to be rare, so a gradual approach is used by finding the triple of cases for which this relation is best approximated. For this purpose, the measure used consists in computing $\mathcal{AD}(a, b, c, \text{tgt}) = \left\| (i^b - i^a) - (i^{tgt} - i^c) \right\|_{dist1}$: the lower $\mathcal{AD}(a, b, c, \text{tgt})$ is, the best the approximation is supposed to be (the exact analogy holds iff $\mathcal{AD}(a, b, c, \text{tgt}) = 0$). This is inspired by the idea of analogical dissimilarity [9].

---

[5] The implementation of this approach requires some classical (and tedious) Euclidian geometry recalled in this note. First, the fact that h belongs or not to the segment $[i^b, i^c]_{dist2}$ can be tested by computing the scalar products of $(i^c - i^b)$ by $(i^{tgt} - i^b)$ and $(i^{tgt} - i^c)$: both products are positive iff h belongs to the segment and is different from the extremities of this segment. Second, D^{bc} is computed as follows. The area A of the triangle $i^b i^{tgt} i^c$ can be computed using the Heron formula: $A = \sqrt{p(p - \ell)(p - m)(p - n)}$ where $\ell = \text{dist2}(i^b, i^c)$, $m = \text{dist2}(i^c, i^{tgt})$, $n = \text{dist2}(i^b, i^{tgt})$, and $p = (\ell + m + n)/2$. Then, the length D^{bc} of the segment $[i^{tgt}, h]_{dist2}$ can be computed by $\text{dist2}(i^{tgt}, h) = 2A/\ell$. Then, $\text{dist2}(i^b, h)$ can be computed thanks to the Pythagorean theorem: $\text{dist2}(i^b, h) = \sqrt{\text{dist2}(i^b, i^{tgt})^2 - (D^{bc})^2}$. This provides the value of y^{tgt} as a barycenter of y^b, y^c with proper weights: $y^{tgt} = y^b + \frac{\text{dist2}(i^b, h)}{\text{dist2}(i^b, i^c)} (y^c - y^b)$.

Second, with this approach, it may occur that the inferred solution $y^{tgt} = (b\ell^{tgt}, w\ell^{tgt}, \gamma^{tgt})$ does not respect the ranges, i.e. $b\ell^{tgt} \notin [0,1]$, $w\ell^{tgt} \notin [0,1]$, $b\ell^{tgt} > w\ell^{tgt}$, or $\gamma^{tgt} < 0$. If such situations occur, the extrapolation fails with these retrieved cases and another triple of cases has to be retrieved and adapted.

A naive implementation of this idea would consist in making 3 nested loops ranging on the case base 3 times, which would lead to a complexity in $\mathcal{O}(|CB|^3)$. A more efficient algorithm has been implemented. It consists first in an offline treatment building a database that stores, for each ordered pair of source cases $((x^a, y^a), (x^b, y^b))$, the value $i^b - i^a$. This offline treatment is in $\mathcal{O}(|CB|^2)$ but this complexity can be reduced when dealing with larger case bases, by considering, for example, only pairs of similar source cases. Then, given x^{tgt}, for each $(x^c, y^c) \in CB$, the difference $i^{tgt} - i^c$ is computed and the database is searched for the nearest $i^b - i^a$ (the one minimizing $\mathcal{AD}(a, b, c, tgt)$) by a binary search, hence giving the best pair of source cases $((x^a, y^a), (x^b, y^b))$, given (x^c, y^c). So, after this loop on $(x^c, y^c) \in CB$, the best triple of source cases is retrieved and can be adapted. This implementation is in $\mathcal{O}(|CB| \log |CB|)$.

The two implementations are named `extrap1x1` and `extrap2x3`.

6   Evaluations

The approaches presented in the previous section have been evaluated with a case base and two test sets (Sect. 6.1). It is composed of an evaluation by experts (Sect. 6.2), of an automatic evaluation (Sect. 6.3), and of a qualitative evaluation comparing GEORGES's output with the output of a selected related work (Sect. 6.4). The section ends with a discussion on the results of the evaluation (Section 6.5).

6.1   The Case Base and the Test Sets

Persée has edited a very large number of documents following the editing process presented in Sect. 4 and, for each page x of these documents, the triple $y = (b\ell, w\ell, \gamma)$ has been stored. The first experiment has shown that with a rather limited case base, the results were good (as the more comprehensive evaluation presented below confirms), so the case base used in the experiments was chosen with a reasonable size of $|CB| = 11\,166$ and this is the case base used in the three following subsections. Another set of 19 cases has been selected for evaluation by a human expert (see Sect. 6.2).

Now, as explained before, the triple y associated to an image x has been chosen by experts on an image of the same document as x, not necessarily on x itself: the result is considered good (since it is validated by further editing steps) but may be less good than the one the expert would have chosen on x, and the information about which page of each document was used by the expert has not been retained. For the automatic evaluation (see Sect. 6.3) a set of 39 cases have been defined by the expert as gold standards: they constitute pairs (x, y) where y was determined on the image x itself. Such cases are called "ideal cases" in the following: they are based directly on the expert's assessment.

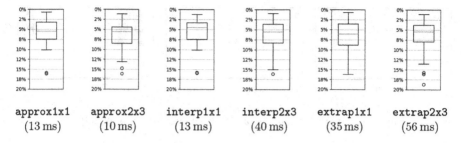

approx1x1   approx2x3   interp1x1   interp2x3   extrap1x1   extrap2x3
(13 ms)   (10 ms)   (13 ms)   (40 ms)   (35 ms)   (56 ms)

Fig. 3. Results of the automatic evaluation, with computing times per target problem (computed on a simple laptop).

6.2 An Evaluation by a Human Expert

Let TS be the set of 19 cases selected for this evaluation (TS is disjoint from CB). An interface has been implemented for this evaluation that consists, for each $(x, y) \in$ TS, in presenting to the expert the original image x and 7 cleaned images presented in a random order: the image cleaned by the edited process of Persée (i.e. clean(y, x), thus a good solution, but in general not an ideal solution) and the 6 images clean(y^g, x) for the 6 approaches implemented in GEORGES. The expert had the possibility to compare images by pairs, with a possibility of zoom to see the details, and associate to each 7 cleaned images a mark in the scale $\{1 = \text{very bad}, 2 = \text{bad}, 3 = \text{good}, 4 = \text{very good}\}$.

The results are as follows, where $a \pm \sigma, b$ means that the average value is a with a standard deviation of σ and b images of this approach were the best ones in the series:

Persée	approx1x1	approx2x3	interp1x1	interp2x3	extrap1x1	extrap2x3
$2.63 \pm 1.07, 3$	$2.88 \pm 0.99, 3$	$2.84 \pm 1.01, 3$	$2.95 \pm 0.85, 2$	$3.21 \pm 0.98, 5$	$2.58 \pm 0.96, 1$	$2.42 \pm 1.12, 2$

6.3 An Automatic Evaluation

The automatic evaluation aims at comparing the different implemented approaches, using the 39 ideal cases as test sets. For each ideal case (x, y), the target problem is set to x ($x^{tgt} = x$) and for each approach, the predicted solution y^{tgt} is compared to the solution y. Now, this comparison cannot be done only on triples, since two different triples may clean in the same way a given image. Therefore, this comparison is done by comparing directly the resulting images, i.e. by computing dist1(clean(y^{tgt}, x^{tgt}), clean(y, x^{tgt})) and normalize it on a $[0\%, 100\%]$ scale (0% stands for identical images).

Figure 3 presents the result of this evaluation using box plots, as well as indicative computing times per target problem. It seems that interp1x1 is the best one, but the differences from the other approaches is not very significant.

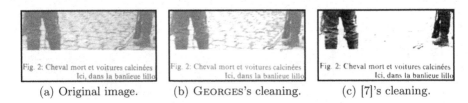

(a) Original image.   (b) GEORGES's cleaning.   (c) [7]'s cleaning.

Fig. 4. Comparing cleanings of GEORGES and [7] on an example.

6.4   A Qualitative Comparison with the Work of [7]

As presented in Sect. 3, a system close to GEORGES, in terms of expected output, is the one described in [7]. One advantage of this previous work, compared to GEORGES, is that it is language independent and could be used successfully for documents written for any language, whereas GEORGES requires a case base of text for the same language and an OCR analysis for situating a frequent word (or letter) of this language in text images.

Now, we suspected that the approach presented in this previous work would be harmful for non-textual elements of a page, such as illustrations. To test this hypothesis, this algorithm has been (re-)implemented and compared to GEORGES on several documents containing texts and illustrations and this hypothesis was confirmed. Figure 4 illustrates this (using the approach `interp1x1`).

Other comparisons of GEORGES with cleaning and binarization tools have been carried out and have led to the same conclusion: GEORGES outperforms these generic tools especially on pages combining texts and illustrations. Indeed, GEORGES has benefited from the specific context of images of French texts with potential illustrations. The idea of separating the treatments of texts and illustrations has been rejected because of the inexact segmentation of illustrations and because of the discontinuity of treatment within the same page.

6.5   Discussion

Human evaluation has shown that GEORGES behaves nicely and proposes solutions that are in the average better than what is proposed in the case base CB. This is quite surprising, but it can be explained by the fact that although the cases of CB are good (in the sense that they are the values accepted by experts after the execution of the entire editing process), they are not ideal cases in general. For example, if the approximation approach is used, given a case (x, y) used in the test set, the closest case $(x^s, y^s) \in$ CB may be taken from an image of a different document. Therefore, the benefits of the automatic CBR approach for cleaning text images are (1) a gain in expert working time, as expected (a few hours per month) and (2) an improvement of the quality of the cleaning process, which has been a surprise.

Automatic evaluation needed a comparison with a gold standard test set, with only ideal cases. Its aim was to compare the different approaches of GEORGES.

Now, the result has not shown a clear winner. This is consistent with the human evaluation, where the best approach was not always the same one. This suggests that a combination of these approaches could be profitable and this is practically feasible, since the approaches take reasonable computing time.

7 Conclusion

This article has presented an application of CBR to the cleaning of images of French texts, using the approximation, interpolation, and extrapolation approaches to CBR and an indexing of images by a dirtiness index. From an application point of view, this work has two main benefits. First, it has transformed a semi-automatic task into an automatic task saving this way several hours per month. Second, it has improved the quality of the result. Indeed, the semi-automatic approach was applied for one page by document (using the same parameters for cleaning its other pages), whereas the automatic approach has made it possible to treat every individual pages, which has resulted in better solutions as the evaluation has shown.

Beyond this application, this work can be used for other applications where a semi-automatic work is based on the choice of parameters by a human expert: this choice could be suggested by a CBR system similar to GEORGES to lighten the workload of the expert. The remaining difficulty to apply GEORGES's principle is to build a relevant index on the problems.

A first direction of future work is on the definition of a new dirtiness index: currently, it is based on averages of grayscale values of the occurrences of "de" on the image. It would be interesting to examine how taking into account the standard deviation of "de" occurrences in the image can be used.

Another direction for future work for the development of GEORGES (and similar CBR applications) is the design of a combination of the different proposed approaches. An obvious approach to do so is to take the average of the solutions proposed by the different approaches.

A less obvious way to do so is to use non-fuzzy approaches for approximation and interpolation. For the latter, the idea has already been presented in Sect. 5.3: it leads to plausibly inferring that the solution y^{tgt} belongs to a range $[y^b, y^c]_{dist1}$. A similar idea for approximation can be to considered: if x^s and x^{tgt} are similar then this gives for the solution y^{tgt} a solution range by the set of $y \in S$ whose similarity to y^s is constrained by the distance between x^s and x^{tgt}: this idea has been presented in [3] and further developed in [6]. In both approaches, a range is plausibly inferred for y^{tgt} and this range could be used in order to improve the combination of the current approaches. An first idea to be explored is to use these ranges as constraints, by keeping only the solutions that are consistent with these ranges.

Finally, the automatic experiment of Sect. 6.3 has been rerun with a case base of 1 000 cases, chosen randomly in the case base of 11 166 cases, without significant decrease in result. This suggests that a case base maintenance (see e.g. [16]) lowering the number of cases while maintaining the quality of the results should be beneficial.

References

1. Aisbett, J., Gibbon, G.: A general formulation of conceptual spaces as a meso level representation. Artif. Intell. **133**(1–2), 189–232 (2001)
2. Chaki, N., Shaikh, S.H., Saeed, K.: A comprehensive survey on image binarization techniques. In: Exploring Image Binarization Techniques. SCI, vol. 560, pp. 5–15. Springer, New Delhi (2014). https://doi.org/10.1007/978-81-322-1907-1_2
3. Dubois, D., Hüllermeier, E., Prade, H.: Flexible control of case-based prediction in the framework of possibility theory. In: Blanzieri, E., Portinale, L. (eds.) EWCBR 2000. LNCS, vol. 1898, pp. 61–73. Springer, Heidelberg (2000). https://doi.org/10.1007/3-540-44527-7_7
4. Ficet-Cauchard, V., Porquet, C., Revenu, M.: CBR for the reuse of image processing knowledge: a recursive retrieval/adaptation strategy. In: Althoff, K.-D., Bergmann, R., Branting, L.K. (eds.) ICCBR 1999. LNCS, vol. 1650, pp. 438–452. Springer, Heidelberg (1999). https://doi.org/10.1007/3-540-48508-2_32
5. Gärdenfors, P.: Conceptual Spaces: The Feometry of Thought. Cambridge (2000)
6. Hüllermeier, E.: Credible case-based inference using similarity profiles. IEEE Trans. Knowl. Data Eng. **19**(6), 847–858 (2007)
7. Kavallieratou, E., Antonopoulou, H.: Cleaning and enhancing historical document images. In: Blanc-Talon, J., Philips, W., Popescu, D., Scheunders, P. (eds.) ACIVS 2005. LNCS, vol. 3708, pp. 681–688. Springer, Heidelberg (2005). https://doi.org/10.1007/11558484_86
8. Lieber, J., Nauer, E., Prade, H., Richard, G.: Making the best of cases by approximation, interpolation and extrapolation. In: Cox, M.T., Funk, P., Begum, S. (eds.) ICCBR 2018. LNCS (LNAI), vol. 11156, pp. 580–596. Springer, Cham (2018). https://doi.org/10.1007/978-3-030-01081-2_38
9. Miclet, L., Bayoudh, S., Delhay, A.: Analogical dissimilarity: definition, algorithms and two experiments in machine learning. J. Artif. Intell. Res. **32**, 793–824 (2008)
10. Nandy, M., Saha, S.: An analytical study of different document image binarization methods. arXiv preprint arXiv:1501.07862 (2015)
11. Perner, P.: Why case-based reasoning is attractive for image interpretation. In: Aha, D.W., Watson, I. (eds.) ICCBR 2001. LNCS (LNAI), vol. 2080, pp. 27–43. Springer, Heidelberg (2001). https://doi.org/10.1007/3-540-44593-5_3
12. Perner, P., Holt, A., Richter, M.: Image processing in case-based reasoning. Knowl. Eng. Rev. **20**(3), 311–314 (2005)
13. Prade, H., Richard, G.: From analogical proportion to logical proportions. Log. Univers. **7**(4), 441–505 (2013)
14. Riesbeck, C.K., Schank, R.C.: Inside Case-Based Reasoning. Lawrence Erlbaum Associates Inc, Hillsdale, New Jersey (1989) Available on line
15. Schockaert, S., Prade, H.: Interpolative and extrapolative reasoning in propositional theories using qualitative knowledge about conceptual spaces. Artif. Intell. **202**, 86–131 (2013)
16. Smyth, B., Keane, M.T.: Remembering to forget. In: Proceedings of the 14th International Joint Conference on Artificial Intelligence (IJCAI 1995), Montréal (1995)
17. Tensmeyer, C., Martinez, T.: Historical document image binarization: a review. SN Comput. Sci. **1**(3), 173–198 (2020)

A Multi-agent Case-Based Reasoning Intrusion Detection System Prototype

Jakob Michael Schoenborn[1,2]([⊠]) [ID] and Klaus-Dieter Althoff[1,2]

[1] University of Hildesheim, Universitaetsplatz 1, 31141 Hildesheim, Germany
schoenb@uni-hildesheim.de
[2] German Research Center for Artificial Intelligence (DFKI), Trippstadter Str. 122, 67663 Kaiserslautern, Germany

Abstract. The number of actors, costs, and incidents in terms of internet criminality is rising each year as many devices in our daily routines become increasingly connected to the internet. 'Security by design' is gaining increased awareness in software engineering, but it is not to be expected to catch all security issues as the range of potential security issues and the creativity of the attackers are both seemingly endless. Thus, we propose a multi-agent case-based reasoning system to detect malicious traffic in a computer network. We mainly rely on the commonly used UNSW_NB15 data set including 82332 training cases with mostly numeric attributes, but the application design is open to operate with other data sources, such as NSL-KDD and CICIDS-2017 as well.

Purpose. The aim of the proposed system is to detect malicious network traffic and alert the security engineer of a company to take further actions such as blocking the source IP address of the potential attacker.

Findings. We were able to successfully detect seven out of ten attacks with an average true-positive rate of 82,56% and leave the remaining attacks (Analysis, Backdoor, Worms) for further investigation and improvements.

Implications and value. The results are close to other research results with room for improvement. Due to the nature of a multi-agent framework, this application could be integrated into other existing intrusion detection systems and serve as an add-on.

Keywords: Case-based Reasoning · SEASALT · Intrusion Detection System · Multi-Agent System

1 Introduction

Supply chains and production processes become increasingly more digital and connected with online services through industry 4.0 and a higher rate of globalization. Additionally, the pandemic forced organizations further into digitisation by communicating to their employees located in their newly established home offices. Through the increasing necessary network connections, the dependence on a faultless and uninterrupted network is also increasing as well. The recent

S. Massie and S. Chakraborti (Eds.): ICCBR 2023, LNAI 14141, pp. 359–374, 2023.
https://doi.org/10.1007/978-3-031-40177-0_23

world events showed the negative influence for multiple countries as soon as the production and shipping of goods is interrupted. This can be seen as an analogy for computer network traffic: if important computers are not reachable in the network, if important services cannot be reached, the production rate of a company decreases - in the worst case, the company has to shut down its production entirely. It is not only the loss of income through the not produced goods, which negatively affects the company, but also further indirect consequences such as damage of reputation and legal consequences by not fulfilling service level agreements (SLA)[1] [18] or, in case of a data leak, general data protection regulation (GDPR) or California privacy rights act (CPRA). For Europe, the European Union Agency for Cybersecurity publishes annually the NIS[2] Investments report. According to this report, the top components of direct incident costs are *incident response costs* (33%), *costs related to data recovery and business continuity management* (22%) and *loss of productivity* (19%) [7].

Worldwide, the investment in cyber threat intelligence is annually increasing by 16% [7] with the top three investments by solution type are *cloud access security brokers* (33%), *vulnerability assessment* (25%) and *web application firewalls* (25%) [6], which matches the needs in a stable network environment as mentioned above and where our approach can be supportive. Nevertheless, medium-sized companies and startups are financially not able to invest in security or do not have a dedicated ransomware defense program, e.g., 44% of the companies in the health sector [7]. The lack of security professionals and the lack of established certified processes, e.g. ISO27001, enables potential attackers to enter and attack the computer network of a company. It is not uncommon for companies to have multiple thousands of known vulnerability issues - even for larger IT companies. Thus, a network intrusion detection system to detect potential attacks can be helpful in the mitigation of an attack and consequently to reduce the effective costs.

For the support on intrusion detection for any interested individual or company, we develop a case-based reasoning (CBR) intrusion detection system (IDS). CBR is a methodology cycling through four steps: retrieve, reuse, revise, retain. Generally, CBR follows the paradigm "Similar problems have similar solutions", thus retrieving experience from old situations (cases) to solve a new occurring problem. For any given data package, we *retrieve* the most similar data package (case) and might *reuse* its solution (label) to flag an incoming data package as potential attack. If certain attributes are missing or the usage is not immediately possible, we might *revise* the case and query the system again. Based on the results, a knowledge engineer might decide to *retain* the new case into the case base. Another possible consequence of the *retain* step might also only be to adjust the similarity measures, which is one of the knowledge containers for the knowledge representation, along the casebase, adaptation knowledge, and vocabulary according to Richter [11]. As there are different kinds of attacks and

---

[1] Def. SLA: *An explicit statement of expectations and obligations that exist in a business relationship between two organizations: the service provider and customer.* [4].

[2] Network and Information Systems Directive.

different kinds of (training-) data sets, we propose a multi-agent system according to the SEASALT architecture [2] to ensure the scalability of the system. Using this way of modularization allows us to initialize and query CBR agents whenever they are needed and adjust resources accordingly to the amount of incoming data packages (potential attacks). Using only a single classifier was not feasible due to limited computational resources triggered by a large casebase[3].

In the following sections, we begin to take a closer look at related work and similar approaches in the literature. This will provide us insight in which data sets are most commonly used and how other approaches fare in terms of detecting malicious traffic. Section 3 describes the concept of our application, including the reasoning behind the knowledge modeling and case representation. Consequently, we provide a brief overview on the application itself in Sect. 4 and continue with an evaluation of our approach in contrast to other approaches in Sect. 5. The paper closes with a conclusion and an outlook into future work.

2   Literature Review

The aim of the literature review is to identify categories of AI methods and to find common data sets, which are used to measure the detection rate of malicious traffic. As database, we chose IEEExplore[4], arXiv[5], and Google Scholar[6]. We filtered for articles, which have been published in conferences using peer reviews as review criteria[7]. The time frame ranges from 2015 to 2022; from 2014 backwards, the number of relevant literature rapidly decreases. After additional filtering, we identified 206 relevant articles.

2.1   Data Sets

In terms of data sets, we could identify the following usage:

Four 'main' data sets can be identified: KDD-CUP-99, NSL-KDD, UNSW-NB15 and CIC-IDS-2017. The former both were predominantly existent in the early literature, also before 2015, with both data sets releasing in 1999. NSL-KDD has been steadily updated and seems to be the most used data set up until today, while KDD-CUP-99 lost its popularity. 2018 was a year where multiple new datasets have been created[8], but seemingly have not been used furthermore. Instead, the latter two, UNSW-NB15 and CIC-IDS-2017 are newer data sets, rising in popularity and are becoming possible alternatives. Figure 1 presents an overview of the popularity of the mentioned data sets in the relevant literature since 2015.

---

[3] It has to be tested, whether approaches to optimize the retrieval on large casebases will ease this limitation; see also Sect. 5.1: Limitations.

[4] https://ieeexplore.ieee.org/Xplore/home.jsp.

[5] https://arxiv.org/.

[6] https://scholar.google.com/.

[7] Assumed to exist, if not explicitly mentioned.

[8] But their share was 10% or lower, thus, not depicted in this graphic.

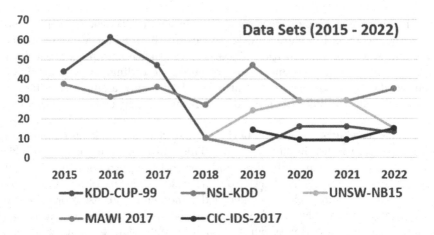

Fig. 1. Used datasets and their share in the relevant literature since 2015. x-axis: year of publication; y-axis: number of publications using the corresponding data set.

2.2 Classifiers

In terms of classifiers, we could identify the following usage (Fig. 2):

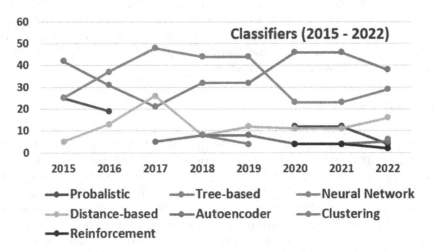

Fig. 2. Used classifiers and their share in the relevant literature since 2015. x-axis: year of publication; y-axis: number of publications using the corresponding classifier.

Unsurprisingly, as the most approaches are based on machine learning algorithms, neural networks (mostly with feature-selection techniques) and tree-based classifiers (mostly random forests to prevent overfitting) are the most dominant classifiers since 2015 up until today. Distance-based models (mostly support vector machines) also achieved reasonable results, but overall worse than its contenders.

2.3 Related Work

In this section, we briefly present related work, which is using the data set UNSW_NB15[9]. To our best knowledge, our approach is the first in the CBR domain, thus, referring to related approaches using the same dataset.

Ullah and Mahmoud focus on identifying malicious traffic in IoT networks. The authors propose a two-level hybrid anomalous activity system [15]. The first level distinguishes traffic between 'normal' and 'anomalous' using flow-based features extracted from the CICIDS2017 and UNSW-NB15 dataset. If an anomaly activity is detected, the flow is forwarded to the level-2 model to find the category of the anomaly, using recursive feature elimination, synthetic minority over-sampling technique, edited nearest neighbours for cleaning the aforementioned datasets and random forest classifier for the level-2 model [15]. Their results propose a 97% F1 score with both respectively 97% precision and recall across all attacks. A validation using a real-world scenario to validate the model is promised, but seemingly never published[10].

Anwer et al. present 'A Framework for Efficient Network Anomaly Intrusion Detection with Features Selection', applying different strategies by using filter and wrapper feature selection methodologies [1]. For classification, J48 and Naïve Bayes algorithms are used. By trying to find the lowest required number of attributes, the authors achieve an accuracy of 80% across all attacks using 18 features. Future work suggests using support vector machines, artificial neural networks and a majority voting scheme between all classifiers to increase the accuracy.

Wu and Guo propose 'LuNet: A Deep Neural Network for Network Intrusion Detection' [19]. The authors focus on decreasing the false-positive rate of the system, motivated by the efficiency of the system overall, which often is not accounted for in publications with high detection rates, according to the authors. LuNet is highly focused on convolutional and recurrent neural networks - these learn input traffic data in sync with a gradually increasing granularity such that both spatial and temporal features of the data can be effectively extracted [19]. The results are separated in eight different algorithms, reaching at best an accuracy of 82.78% with a FPR of 4.72%.

3 Concept

3.1 Dataset

The concept of the prototype relies to some extend on the chosen dataset. While we propose a multi-agent approach, each agent needs to establish its casebase and cases. For the agents that will be evaluated in Sect. 5, we chose the UNSW-NB15 dataset based on the recommendations by Divekar et al. (2018): "In summary

---

[9] See Sect. 3 for the reasoning of this choice.

[10] The authors continued their work in IDS in IoT, but generated new (flow-based) data set.

the results strongly indicate that UNSW-NB15 can satisfactorily substitute the archaic KDD CUP 99 dataset and even NSL-KDD when used to train machine learning anomaly-based NIDSs." [5] and by Ring et al. (2019): *"Further, we'd like to give a general recommendation for the use of the [...] CICIDS 2017 and UNSW-NB15 data sets. [...] CICIDS 2017 and UNSW-NB15 contain a wide range of attack scenarios."* [12]. Both authors published an extensive literature review on the current datasets; their recommendation seems to confirm the trend shown in Fig. 1. As KDD-CUP-99 and NSL-KDD both are based on 42 attributes, we are optimistic for our approach to work similar with those data sets - but the confirmation remains open for future work.

UNSW_NB15 has been created by N. Moustafa and J. Slay and spans over 47 different attributes, which can be sub-categorized into basic features, connection features, content features, time features, additional generated features, and labeled features. The attack categories are labeled as 1, while normal traffic is labeled as 0 [9]. Table 1 provides a brief description of the attack categories, so that the interested reader is able to gain a picture of the attacks we are trying to prevent from happening.

The dataset is split into training data (82332 packages, thus, in sum 82332 cases) and testing data (175341 packages). For a detailed description of the 47 features, we refer to the original publication by Moustafa and Slay [9].

Table 1. Description of the attack categories by Moustafa and Slay [9]

Analysis	a type of variety intrusions that penetrate the web applications via ports, emails, and web scripts
Backdoor	a technique of bypassing a stealthy normal authentication, securing unauthorized remote access to a device.
DoS	intrusion which disrupts the computer resources, to be extremely busy in order to prevent the authorized requests from accessing a device.
Exploit	a sequence of instructions that takes advantage of a vulnerability to be caused by an unintentional behavior on a host or network.
Fuzzers	attacker attempts to discover security loopholes in a network by feeding it with massive inputting of random data to make it crash.
Generic	technique that establishes against every block-cipher to collision without respect to the configuration of the block-cipher.
Reconnaissance	can be defined as a probe; an attack that gathers information about a computer network to evade its security controls.
Shellcode	an attack in which the attacker penetrates a slight piece of code starting from a shell to control the compromised machine.
Worms	an attack whereby the attacker replicates itself in order to spread on other computers. Often, it uses a computer network to spread itself

3.2   Case-Based Reasoning Agents

In terms of efficiency and scalability, we suggest a multi-agent system with at least one agent per attack category and one agent for normal data traffic.

We begin with two agents on top (the first layer): A BurpAgent and WiresharkAgent. Those agents are trained and fed with data of their respective commonly used programs "Burp" and "Wireshark". Both tools are commonly used in the domain: the former, for intercepting and manually manipulating traffic but also capturing traffic in general, the latter mainly for capturing and filtering traffic. Wireshark is known for creating "packet capture"-files (.pcap), which are the foundation of the training- and test datasets of all discussed data sets. Those .pcap file are usually translated into .csv files. These files can be imported by the WiresharkAgent, which then can flag each packet with "normal" or "suspicious" traffic. Suspicious traffic can be forwarded to the next layer to further identify the incoming packet. This leaves us for the UNSW-NB15 data set with ten agents - which can be multi-threaded, if the amount of incoming traffic makes it necessary. The agents can easily be incorporated into multi-agent frameworks such as the SEASALT architecture [2]. The structure is also depicted in Fig. 4 in Sect. 4.

We[11] use case-based reasoning agents, each containing four knowledge containers according to Richter [11]: *vocabulary, similarity measure, adaptation knowledge, casebase.*

In terms of *vocabulary* structure, we use an attribute-value representation, as the measurable data contains 35 attributes in addition to twelve derived attributes. No set of attributes contains unknown values; thus only complete situations are evaluated. Correlations between certain attributes could not be detected, yet. Certainly, attributes contain correlation to attack categories, which will be covered next in the *similarity measure* container.

Following the weighted Hamming similarity measure

$$sim(q,p) = \sum(g_i \times sim_i(q_i, p_i) \mid 1 \leq i \leq n) \qquad (1)$$

as Richter and others suggested, we utilize the local-global principle [3,11,16]. For local measures sim_i, we inspect the attributes A_i based on their minimum and maximum values and calibrate a symmetrical polynomial function with heavily decreasing similarity for differing attributes based on the variability of an attribute. The narrower the data points of an attribute, the stronger decreasing the similarity function. For the amalgamation function, we set values for the non-negative real weight vector coefficients $g = (g_1, ..., g_n)$, normalized to $\sum g_i = 1$ [11].

For the values of g, we calculate the average value of each attribute ranging over the whole data set and also the average value filtered by each attack category. This enables us to identify attributes which seem to hint at a certain attack

---

[11] The remainder of this section is mostly similar to Schoenborn et al. [13]. The overall structure described below has not drastically changed since. However, we slightly changed the used similarity metrics and weights for our agents, leaving us with a different implementation and overall better results.

for given values. For example, *spkts* (='*source packets*') depicts the source-to-destination packet count with the following calculated average values for each attack category, reading: "For an exploit attack, 37,7 packets have been sent on average from the source to the destination":

AVG	Analysis	Backd	DoS	Exploit	Fuzzer	Generic	Normal	Recon	Shellc	Worm
18,67	3,12	4,39	*28,9*	**37,7**	11,8	2,8	6,97	6,97	6,07	*16,78*

While the average on the whole data set is at 18,67 and has lower values for other attacks, Exploit points out with an average value of 37,7 packets from source to destination. This confirms the intuitive expectation of an exploit attack: *to exploit* means in the IT-security context to systematically abuse known security issues of a given system. However, it needs to be tested, which security issues the target might have - resulting into multiple requests and consequently an increased amount of packets running from source-to-destination. Therefore, *spkts* receives a higher weight than other attributes for the exploit agent. The more distinct an attribute-value, the higher the weight. Figure 3 further illustrates the construction.

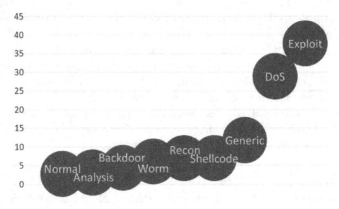

Fig. 3. Example for weight selection for the attribute *spkts*. *y*-axis depicts the average values calculated for the attribute *spkts*. Exploits and DoS attacks can mostly be easily classified, e.g., if the value is >35, it is most likely an exploit. Thus, exploit- and DoS agents receive a higher weight for the attribute *spkts*. If the value is inside the interval [23, 32], it is most likely a DoS attack. Most other values <15 cannot easily be assigned to an attack category, thus, *spkts* receiving a lower weight for the respective agents.

On a similar notion, this situation also holds true for the denial of service (DoS) attack: with a value of 28,9, it is also distinct enough from other attack categories, which range on average between 2,8 and 16,78. Therefore, we are also able to identify attribute values, which are not the maximum, but still unique to a certain attack category - and use this information to increase the weight of the given attribute for the corresponding agent (see Fig. 3). We repeat this process for each agent and each attribute.

Each agent is trained to detect its respective attack, i.e., a DoS agent only contains cases labeled with denial of service attacks. Thus, the *case base* contains the experiences based on the training data set. We store each line of the data set as a case, resulting in 82332 cases overall. However, there is still room left for improvement regarding the two conflicting goals: having the case base as large as possible for increased competence knowledge, while having the case base as small as possible for better efficiency, relative to the available resources.

For each package in the testing data set, each agent votes by submitting its n most similar cases to a coordination agent. For now, it will be left open for discussion in Sect. 5 whether n should be 1 to submit only the most similar case or to calculate the average similarity of $n > 1$ cases to reduce the risk of outliers. For our experiments, we choose $n = 10$ to remove outliers and gain insight whether the similarity of other similar cases is decreasing correctly, as to be expected. The votes with the highest similarities will be reported to the (human) user. After receiving the results, the user may decide which agent is ultimately correct - leaving the responsibility and legal liability to the human user - and might choose to start further actions to stop the attack, such as blocking the source IP address of the potential attacker.

4   Implementation

We implemented the system described in Sect. 3 by using myCBR 3.4 and the programming language JAVA. MyCBR is an open-source similarity-based retrieval tool and software development kit (SDK)[12] and has been further developed by students of the University of Hildesheim and by the authors, hence the increased version number. MyCBR 3.4 and the prototype presented in this contribution are available for free under the LGPL licence at Github[13].

Figure 1 provides a brief overview of the multi-agent system. We would like to emphasize that each agent underlies the SEASALT architecture by Bach [2]. First, the user will be provided with a simple graphical web interface, asking to import either a Burp-Export file, a Wireshark .csv Export, or the UNSW-NB15 training- or test data set. In either cases, the Coordination Agent will forward the data to the corresponding agents. However, in the first three cases, the agent will print average statistics on the data visibly to the IDE console or log file. This is especially important for the knowledge engineer to view and control the training data.

In case of importing training data, each agent will be initialized with the given training data, corresponding to its agent type. Each topic agent extents the abstract class *Agent*, which forces each agent to implement methods relevant for any CBR functionality, such as initializing a myCBR project file (.prj) and initializing the four knowledge containers.

For String (text) values, such as protocol, service, and state, we use either the Levenshtein similarity function, or check for equality - depending on the

---

[12] see http://mycbr-project.org/index.html.

[13] see https://github.com/jmschoenborn.

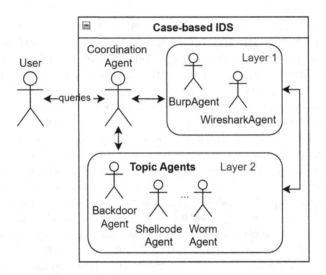

Fig. 4. Overview of the implementation, including ten topic agents.

attribute. For example, for protocol, we check whether the same protocol has been used, as a lexicographical distance is not applicable here (in contrast to the IP source address, as it might be interesting whether the attack is originating from the same subnetwork). For the most numeric attributes, a symmetrical polynomial function has been established. Exception here is the attribute "Port": Port numbers are assigned in various ways, based on three ranges: System Ports (0-1023), User Ports (1024-49151), and the Dynamic and/or Private Ports (49152-65535); the different uses of these ranges are described in RFC6335[14]. We treat the similarity of ports to the three groups accordingly. After all knowledge containers are initialized with given values of the knowledge engineer and the training data, the myCBR files are stored to the local disk and the initialization process of the agent is finalized. Using the stored files allows us to load agents for the testing data set on the fly. The agents can easily be adjusted to fit for other training data sets, such as mentioned in Sect. 2.1, as well.

In case of importing the testing data set, already established agents are activated by the coordination agent. Additionally, the user provides a positive number a for the minimum number of different attack categories that should be displayed in the result and a positive number $c \geq a$ for the number of cases that should be presented. This allows the user to receive a broader picture of the similarity distribution between multiple attack categories to prevent missing out on ambiguous results.

Before going through the test dataset, we filter the test dataset by attacks and confront the pool of all agents with a certain attack for training purposes.

---

[14] see   https://www.iana.org/assignments/service-names-port-numbers/service-names-port-numbers.xhtml.

For example, consider we filter the dataset by the attack 'Shellcode'. The goal is to identify, whether the corresponding agent can identify its attack, i.e., wins the majority votum. Figure 5 shows (left) one exemplary end result after one voting iteration. The first three values (above the horizontal line) are **not** the overall three best cases, but instead the best cases of three distinct attacks[15]. For the test case labeled as Shellcode, the ShellcodeAgent provides the best case with 99,99% similarity (ID 6530). However, 7 votes of the GenericAgent made it into the best 10 cases (below the horizontal line). Thus, in terms of a majority vote, the attack has been incorrectly identified (False-Positive). Figure 5 shows (right) the end result of the Shellcode Agent. The result reads as follows: Out of 1000 iterations, the attack 'Shellcode' has been voted for by 0,1,2,....,10 times by the Shellcode Agent. 6 or more votes are treated as 'success' ($\rightarrow$ the sum of all results below the horizontal line). The more votes, the better the detection rate of an attack.

```
ID: 6530 (0.9999999999999997): Shellcode   Endresult for 1000 iterations,
ID: 64098 (0.9722871133156012): Generic    searching for 'Shellcode':
ID: 5765 (0.966183923137073): Fuzzers      0: 14
----                                       1: 163
ID: 6530 (0.9999999999999997): Shellcode   2: 82
ID: 64098 (0.9722871133156012): Generic    3: 86
ID: 15808 (0.9719427049207273): Generic    4: 78
ID: 51936 (0.9700155694032748): Generic    5: 122
ID: 54057 (0.9684539454236284): Generic    ------
ID: 60882 (0.9680125282344887): Generic    6: 83
ID: 63977 (0.9680114449916848): Generic    7: 68
ID: 12705 (0.9671897332233353): Generic    8: 71
ID: 5765 (0.966183923137073): Fuzzers      9: 95
ID: 9851 (0.9648157773748365): Shellcode   10: 138
```

Fig. 5. (left) Example result after one voting iteration; (right) End result of the ShellcodeAgent. Both are used to analyze the performance of the classifiers for the domain expert to validate the systems output and performance, e.g., validating the similarity assessment.

Table 2 presents the results for all ten agents for the described test phase. The agents Analysis, Backdoor, DoS, Shellcode, Worm are not able to identify their attacks, whereas Normal and Generic agents achieve good results. Exploit, Fuzzer, and Reconnaissance agents achieve acceptable, but improvable results. We explicitly listed the counter for false-positives: for example, in 575 of 1000 cases where Analysis was the labelled attack, the Exploit agent won the majority vote instead. Further investigating the amount of false-positives, the DoS, Exploit and Reconnaissance agents cause a high amount of disturbance.

---

[15] As mentioned before, this is done to identify how close different attacks are to each other. This can be helpful to adjust similarities regarding false-positive results.

Table 2. Training scenario: 1000 cases per agent are presented. The table depicts how well agents are able to detect test cases with their respective label. The top half of the table presents the results of the majority votum, reading: 'Out of 1000 cases, the attack *column name* has been voted for by x agents for n times.'

Vote x	Analys	Backdo	DoS	Exploi	Fuzzer	Generi	Normal	Recon	Shell	Worm
0	908	823	481	192	162	14	124	131	325	119
1	38	53	112	23	95	5	50	102	267	10
2	33	67	147	20	65	7	33	45	155	1
3	9	12	35	27	61	12	10	24	98	0
4	8	43	59	40	70	9	15	21	53	0
5	4	2	48	23	72	18	23	5	51	0
6	0	0	46	61	73	14	9	15	25	0
7	0	0	14	186	72	20	15	13	12	0
8	0	0	33	58	88	20	13	11	13	0
9	0	0	8	87	116	141	33	90	0	0
10	0	0	17	283	126	740	675	603	1	0
False-Pos.	Analys	Backdo	DoS	Exploi	Fuzzer	Generi	Normal	Recon	Shell	Worm
Analysis	–	0	0	0	0	0	0	0	0	0
Backdoor	0	–	0	0	0	0	0	0	0	0
DoS	104	183	–	98	48	8	10	50	77	1
Exploits	575	451	502	–	200	16	127	221	259	87
Fuzzers	15	14	16	15	–	10	32	3	12	0
Generic	0	2	0	2	1	–	0	0	0	12
Normal	17	0	1	0	9	0	–	0	2	0
Recon	67	94	109	71	47	1	24	–	254	12
Shellcode	0	3	1	0	1	0	0	0	–	0
Worms	0	0	0	0	0	0	0	0	0	–
TPR	0	0	11.80	67.50	47.50	93.50	74.50	67.20	05.10	0
FPR	77,80	74,70	62.90	18.60	30.60	03.50	19.30	27.40	60.04	11.20
Precision	0	0	15.80	78.40	60.82	96.39	79.42	71.04	7.83	0
Recall	0	0	11.80	67.50	47.50	93.50	74.50	67.20	5.10	0
F1	0	0	13.51	72.54	53.34	94.92	76.88	69.06	6.17	0

5   Evaluation

5.1   Limitations

During the first test runs we encountered a few challenges with the data set, which resulted into limitations to this prototype version.

1. *Redundancy*
   As to be expected, the training data set contained multiple redundant cases, containing the same attribute-value pairs. If these cases turn out to be the most similar case for a given testing data input query case, the majority

vote will easily be flooded by the redundant cases. A relatively quick fix to this challenge would be to simply remove redundant cases and remain with one pivotal case. The occurrence of a large amount of redundant cases might contain context information, which should not easily be discarded. However, a more elegant and efficient way would be a proper introduction of case base maintenance under the aspect of pivotal cases, and coverage and reachability of cases in a casebase as introduced by Smyth & Keane [14].

2. *Same case, different attack category*
   We identified multiple cases with exactly the same attribute-value pairs, but different attack category labels (249-Analysis, 710-DoS, 1413-Reconnaissance, 1416-Exploits, 3421-Fuzzers). During the training phase, and tests within the training data set, this resulted into a 100% similarity for a given case for multiple different attack categories, which can easily lead to an increased rate of false-positives.

5.2   Results

Table 3 presents our results of querying the topic agents with the test data set. We confronted the agents with 50 000 cases randomly selected out of the test data set[16]. Each activated topic agent voted with their $n = 10$ most similar cases. Out of this pool of best cases (100 with 10 active agents), the 10 most similar cases overall have been chosen. Each correct vote will be counted: if there are at

Table 3. Results of quering the MAS using the test dataset. Additionally, direct comparison to other approaches using the same data set.

	Analys	Backdo	DoS	Exploits	Fuzzers	Generic	Normal	Recon	Shell	Worm
Count	869	739	4567	12916	7366	6653	12591	3806	439	53
TPR	0,00	0,00	70,73	94,59	86,97	98,15	99,42	97,32	30,77	0,00
FPR	0,00	0,00	74,48	84,28	72,03	59,34	32,86	64,80	26,32	0,00
TNR	100,00	100,00	25,52	15,72	27,97	40,66	67,14	35,20	73,68	0,00
FNR	100,00	100,00	29,27	5,41	13,03	1,85	0,58	2,68	69,23	0,00
Precision	0,00	0,00	26,22	59,11	70,39	98,30	98,37	54,38	28,57	0,00
Recall	0,00	0,00	70,73	94,59	86,96	98,14	99,41	97,32	30,76	0,00
*F*1	0,00	0,00	38,26	72,76	77,81	98,23	98,89	69,78	29,63	0,00

Results of other approaches (no CBR) using the same dataset	
Wheelus et al. [17]	ranging from 69% to 83% TPR for all attacks
Pratomo et al. [10]	69,21% TPR on average for all attacks
Mebawondu et al. [8]	76,96% TPR for all attacks
Ullah and Mahmoud [15]	97% F1 score with 97% precision and recall
Anwer et al. [1]	accuracy of 80% using 18 features
Wu and Guo [19]	accuracy of 82.78% at best, FPR of 4.72%
Our proposed approach	82,56% TPR (excluding Analysis, Backdoor, Worms)

---

[16] The complete test data set contains 175341 entries.

least six correct votes, the query is considered as classified[17]. All correct votes will be summarized and we provide all necessary variables to calculate Precision $\left(\dfrac{TPR}{TPR+FPR}\right)$, Recall $\left(\dfrac{TPR}{TPR+FNR}\right)$, F1 $\left(2\dfrac{precision*recall}{precision+recall}\right)$.

As the results in Table 3 show and as the preliminary results of Table 2 suggested, we receive very good results for Normal and Generic agent and acceptable results for Exploits, Fuzzers and Reconnaissance agents. As described earlier, DoS, Exploits and Reconnaissance agents are disturbing with too many false-positive results. This is very likely the result of an improper similarity modeling of those agents and will be further investigated in future work. Excluding Analysis, Backdoor, and Worm Agents - as these attacks cannot be detected by the proposed system, yet - leaves us with 82,56% TPR which is competitive with similar approaches. The exclusion of the mentioned agents is easily done by having the multi-agent structure.

To receive better results, we plan to integrate SHAP (SHapley Additive exPlanations) as a technique for explaining the output by assigning importance values to the input features. The SHAP value of a feature represents the contribution of that feature to the difference between the actual prediction and the average prediction for all possible combinations of features. This will allow us to further sharpen the similarity measures, more precisely, the weights of the attributes. Furthermore, it can aid in model debugging, interpretation, and communication of results. Nevertheless, the results indicate a possibility of using CBR in an important domain - the IT security - with promsing results.

6   Conclusion

We present a transparent multi-agent based CBR system for supporting intrusion detection in a network using the UNSW_NB15 data set for training and testing. Each topic agent of the multi-agent system contains its own casebase, similarity measure, vocabulary, and adaptation knowledge. The modeling, e.g., the assessment of similarity measures and weights, has mostly been done based on our expertise of the domain and based on the identification of distinct attribute-value pairs, characterizing given attack categories described in Sect. 3.

Despite the limitations described in Sect. 5.1, we were able to detect normal and generic traffic - competitive with other (non-CBR) approaches. Four agents need further adjustments to achieve better results, while four agents need to be remodeled. Especially the Worm agent seems to suffer from a low casebase (44 cases in the training set). Nevertheless, Worms contain by far the most distinct and characteristic values, which leaves us optimistic to receive better results after further fine-tuning of the local similarity measures.

For further adjustments and future work, we are looking to integrate the KDD-CUP-99 data set and the NSL-KDD data set. As the results of Anwer et al. [1] suggests, it seems possible to achieve reasonable results with a relative low number of attributes. Thus, it could be helpful to find overlapping attributes in

---

[17] Either true-positive or false-negative.

the three different data sets and include these in the casebase of the corresponding agents. This way, we can further emphasize on the usefulness of a multi-agent system by using different sources to enrich our agents.

Furthermore, the modeling can possibly be supported by introducing SHAP values, as we are already planning to integrate explainability to the system a next milestone. Explainability further increases the transparency of the system and should help both, the knowledge engineer, and the user of the system, to understand its decision making process.

References

1. Anwer, H.M., Farouk, M., Abdel-Hamid, A.: A framework for efficient network anomaly intrusion detection with features selection. In: 9th International Conference on Information and Communication Systems (ICICS), Irbid, Jordan, pp. 157–162 (2018)
2. Bach, K.: Knowledge acquisition for case-based reasoning systems. Ph. D. thesis, University of Hildesheim (2013). http://www.dr.hut-verlag.de/978-3-8439-1357-7.html
3. Bergmann, R. (ed.): Experience Management: Foundations, Development Methodology, and Internet-Based Applications. LNCS, vol. 2432. Springer, Heidelberg (2002). https://doi.org/10.1007/3-540-45759-3
4. Verma, D.: Supporting service level agreements on IP networks. In: Proceedings of IEEE/IFIP Network Operations and Management Symposium, NY, USA, vol. 92, no. 9, pp. 1382–1388 (2004)
5. Divekar, A., Parekh, M., Savla, V., Mishra, R., Shirole, M.: Benchmarking datasets for anomaly-based network intrusion detection: KDD CUP 99 alternatives. In: IEEE 3rd International Conference on Computing, Communication and Security (ICCCS), Kathmandu, Nepal, pp. 1–8 (2018)
6. Enisa - European Union Agency for Cybersecurity, p. 15 (2021). NIS Investments 2021. https://www.enisa.europa.eu/publications/nis-investments-2021. Accessed 04 Nov 2023
7. Enisa - European Union Agency for Cybersecurity, pp. 10,44,72 (2022). NIS Investments 2022. https://www.enisa.europa.eu/publications/nis-investments-2022. Accessed 04 Nov 2023
8. Mebawondu, J.O., Alowolodu, O.D., Mebawondu, J.O., Adetunmbi, A.O.: Network intrusion detection system using supervised learning paradigm. Sci. Afr. **9**, e00497 (2020)
9. Moustafa, N., Slay, J.: UNSW-NB15: a comprehensive data set for network intrusion detection systems (UNSW-NB15 network data set). In: Military Communications and Information Systems Conference (MilCIS), pp. 1–6 (2015)
10. Pratomo, B.A., Burnap, P., Theodorakopoulos, G.: Unsupervised approach for detecting low rate attacks on network traffic with autoencoder. In: International Conference on Cyber Security and Protection of Digital Services (Cyber Security), pp. 1–8 (2018)
11. Richter, M.M.: The knowledge contained in similarity measures. In: Invited Talk at the First International Conference on Case-Based Reasoning, ICCBR-95, Sesimbra, Portugal (1995)
12. Ring, M., Wunderlich, S., Scheuring, D., Landes, D., Hotho, A.: A survey of network-based intrusion detection data sets. Comput. Secur. **86**, 147–167 (2019)

13. Schoenborn, J.M., Althoff, K.D.: Multi-agent case-based reasoning: a network intrusion detection system. In: LWDA 2022, Lernen, Wissen, Daten, Analysen, Hildesheim, pp. 258–269 (2022)
14. Smyth, B., Keane, M.T.: Remembering to forget: a competence-preserving case deletion policy for case-based reasoning systems. In: Proceedings of the Fourteenth International Joint Conference on Artificial Intelligence, IJCAI 1995, Montréal Québec, Canada, 20–25 August 1995, vol. 2, pp. 377–383. Morgan Kaufmann (1995)
15. Ullah, I., Mahmoud, Q.H.: A two-level hybrid model for anomalous activity detection in IoT networks. In: 16th IEEE Annual Consumer Communications & Networking Conference (CCNC), Las Vegas, NV, USA, pp. 1–6 (2019)
16. Wess, S.: Fallbasiertes Problemlösen in wissensbasierten Systemen zur Entscheidungsunterstützung und Diagnostik: Grundlagen, Systeme und Anwendungen (translated: Case-based problem solving in knowledge-based systems for decision support and diagnostic: basics, systems and applications). Ph.D. thesis, University of Kaiserslautern, Infix-Verlag (1995)
17. Wheelus, C., Bou-Harb, E., Zhu, X.: Tackling class imbalance in cyber security datasets. In: IEEE International Conference on Information Reuse and Integration (IRI), pp. 229–232 (2018)
18. Wu, L., Garg, S.K., Buyya, R.: Service level agreement (SLA) based SaaS cloud management system. In: ICPADS 2015, pp. 440–447 (2015)
19. Wu, P., Guo, H.: LuNet: a deep neural network for network intrusion detection. In: IEEE Symposium Series on Computational Intelligence (SSCI), Xiamen, China, pp. 617–624 (2019)

A Case-Based Reasoning Approach to Company Sector Classification Using a Novel Time-Series Case Representation

Rian Dolphin[1][✉], Barry Smyth[1,2], and Ruihai Dong[1,2]

[1] School of Computer Science, University College Dublin, Dublin, Ireland
rian.dolphin@ucdconnect.ie, {barry.smyth,ruihai.dong}@ucd.ie
[2] Insight Centre for Data Analytics, University College Dublin, Dublin, Ireland

Abstract. The financial domain has proven to be a fertile source of challenging machine learning problems across a variety of tasks including prediction, clustering, and classification. Researchers can access an abundance of time-series data and even modest performance improvements can be translated into significant additional value. In this work, we consider the use of case-based reasoning for an important task in this domain, by using historical stock returns time-series data for industry sector classification. We discuss why time-series data can present some significant representational challenges for conventional case-based reasoning approaches, and in response, we propose a novel representation based on the factorization of a similarity count matrix, which can be readily calculated from raw stock returns data. We argue that this representation is well suited to case-based reasoning and evaluate our approach using a large-scale public dataset for the industry sector classification task, demonstrating substantial performance improvements over several baselines using more conventional representations.

Keywords: Case-Based Reasoning · Time-Series · Finance · Representation Learning

1 Introduction

Case-based reasoning (CBR) approaches have been applied in financial domains, and for a variety of tasks, from the early days of the field; see for example the work of [23] on the use of CBR for financial decision-making. In the years since, there have been many efforts made to apply CBR ideas to a diverse range of financial decision-making and prediction tasks [1,6,13,25]. Nevertheless, the use of CBR in such domains is not without its challenges, not the least of which concerns the very nature of many financial datasets and their relationship to the similarity assumption that underpins CBR. The central dogma of CBR is that similar problems have similar solutions, yet financial regulators are always at pains to point out that "past performance is not a guarantee of future results" suggesting that this principle may not be so reliable in financial domains, at least

S. Massie and S. Chakraborti (Eds.): ICCBR 2023, LNAI 14141, pp. 375–390, 2023.
https://doi.org/10.1007/978-3-031-40177-0_24

when it comes to predicting the future. As society changes and economies ebb and flow, companies that were once the stock market darlings fall out of favour, while new winners seem to emerge, with some regularity, albeit unpredictably and often with little or no warning. Two companies that were similar in the past may no longer be considered similar in the present, while the trajectories of companies with divergent histories might suddenly converge if future circumstances conspire in their favour. All of this greatly complicates the central role of similarity in case retrieval.

In addition, the feature-based (attribute-value) representations that are commonplace in CBR systems may not provide such a good fit with the type of sequential time-series data (e.g. daily, weekly, and monthly stock prices/returns) that are the norm in financial domains. This is not to say that case-based methods cannot be used with time-series data. Certainly, there is a wealth of literature on representing time-series data for use with case-based methods in a range of application domains from agricultural science [3] to sports science [7]. Usually, the approach taken is to use various feature extraction techniques to identify landmark features from the raw time-series data; to effectively transform a raw time-series into a more conventional feature-based representation that can be used with standard similarity metrics. Similar approaches have been applied in the financial domain [12] but, as mentioned above, the stochastic nature of financial markets makes it difficult to effectively isolate useful case representations from market noise, which further complicates the similarity assessment even given a suitable fixed representation.

Thus, in this work, our main technical contribution is to propose and evaluate a novel approach to learning case representations for financial assets (companies/stocks) using raw time-series data made up of historical daily returns. We describe how to transform raw, time-series data into an embedding-style representation of each stock/company; see for example [16,17] for examples of embedding representations. We argue that this facilitates the capture of more meaningful patterns and sub-patterns over extended periods of time, while facilitating the type of temporal alignment that is necessary during case comparison and similarity assessment. We argue that this approach is well-suited to the use of case-based and nearest-neighbour approaches in financial domains, because it can be used with a variety of standard similarity metrics, as well as more domain/task specific metrics. We demonstrate its performance benefits in a comparative evaluation of the industry sector classification task, an important and practical benchmark problem in many financial applications [18].

The remainder of this paper is organised as follows. In the next section, we review the use of CBR in the financial domain and with time-series data more broadly, highlighting several common tasks and the approaches taken thus far, as well as the important challenges that remain with respect to representation and similarity assessment. Then, in Sect. 3 we discuss the details of our proposed approach, by describing how raw time-series data, such as financial returns, can be transformed into an embedding-based representation that is well suited to case-based approaches. In Sect. 4 we evaluate our proposed approach by using it to classify companies into their market sectors based on their historical returns data. We present the results of a comprehensive quantitative evaluation, which compares our proposed representation to a variety of baseline and naive approaches. We demonstrate how our embeddings-based representations can offer significant classification improvements, relative to more conventional representations of the raw time-series data, as well as state-of-the-art neural models [4,20]. In addition, before concluding with a summary of our findings and a discussion of limitations and opportunities for further work, we present further qualitative evidence in support of the proposed approach, by using our representations to visualise the industry sectors that emerge from the clustering of our cases and some examples of nearest-neighbours in the resulting representation space.

2 Background

CBR continues to offer many benefits even in a world of big data and deep learning. Its so-called *lazy* approach to problem-solving, which retains the raw cases, offers several benefits when it comes to transparency, interpretability, and explainability [14]. And, the central role similarity plays – using similar cases to solve future problems – helps to lift the computational veil that all too often obscures the processes that drive more recent machine learning approaches [26]. That being said, the success of CBR is contingent upon the quality of the available cases and the suitability of the case representations and metrics used to evaluate case similarity and drive inference. CBR approaches have been particularly effective in domains where cases are plentiful and where feature-based representations are readily available. For example, in loan/credit approval tasks [24], past decisions provide a plentiful supply of relevant cases, and each case can be represented by salient features such as the value of the requested loan, the debt-load of the applicant, the current earnings of the applicant, the purpose of the loan etc.

However, in other financial domains the situation is more complex, especially when the available data is sequential/temporal in nature, as is often the case. When it comes to representation, several approaches have been proposed to capture the salient features of financial time-series data, such as asset prices of stock returns. They can be broadly categorised into three groups: (i) traditional feature-based summaries, (ii) raw time-series, and (iii) machine learning-based representations.

Feature-based representations of financial time-series tend to derive summary features from statistical moments and technical indicators [8]. For example, time-series data can be represented by extracting key statistical features (e.g. max/min values, mean and standard deviations etc.) over fixed time periods. In addition, the financial domain has the advantage of the availability of several widely-accepted technical indicators, which correspond to common patterns observed in historical trading data such as *on-balance volume*, the *accumulation/distribution line*, the *average directional index*, or the *Aroon indicator* [8].

These exotic-sounding indicators are among the tools of the trade for technical analysts and day traders and can be readily extracted from financial time series data to provide a valuable source of domain-specific features.

In contrast to feature-based representations, some researchers have explored the use of raw time-series data in CBR applications. Here, instead of computing domain-specific features, the choice of similarity metric accounts for the temporal nature of the data. One popular time series similarity technique used in CBR is Dynamic Time Warping (DTW) [19], which measures the similarity between two time-series by allowing for temporal shifts in alignment in order to optimise the correspondence between the two time-series. While DTW has been successfully applied in CBR systems across various domains [3], it is not directly applicable to financial returns data, at least according to the type of tasks that are of interest in this work, because allowing significant temporal shifts in alignment can distort the relationships that exist between two stocks/assets; two stocks having similar returns only constitutes a meaningful relationship if those returns are aligned over the same period of time (in phase). More specifically, in the financial domain, authors in [1] propose a geometrically inspired similarity metric for financial time series, while [6] proposes a metric combining cumulative returns with an adjusted correlation. However, as we show in Sect. 4, applying a similarity metric to raw time-series data may not capture all of the relational information needed leading to poorer performance in some tasks.

More recently, so-called *distributed representations* [16] and the use of *embeddings* have become important in the machine learning literature, especially in natural language domains. Embeddings provide a way to translate a high-dimensional representation (such as text) into a low-dimensional representation, which can make it more straightforward to use machine learning techniques when compared with high-dimensional, sparse vectors such as a one-hot encoded vocabulary. Embeddings have been shown to do a good job of capturing some of the latent semantics of the input by locating semantically similar examples close to each other in the embedding space [16]. Indeed they have recently helped to transform many approaches to natural language processing. Similar ideas have been recently explored with financial time series data [4,5,20] and serve as state-of-the-art baselines. In what follows, we show how to learn case representations, by using the financial returns data of individual companies, and by mapping this high-dimensional raw time-series data into a low-dimensional embedding space. We do this by constructing a similarity-based representation of companies across several time periods and using matrix factorization techniques to compute a low-dimensional representation of these similarity patterns, which can then be used as the basis for our case representation.

3   An Embeddings-Based Case Representation

In this section, we describe the technical details of our approach to transforming raw time-series data into an embeddings-based representation. We will do this using a dataset of stock market *returns* data (see below) for $N = 611$ stocks spanning 2000–2018 [5]. Equivalently, we could use data for other types of financial assets, or more generally a variety of alternative time-series data from other domains. In our evaluation, we use daily, weekly, and monthly returns but the approach described is, in principle, agnostic to granularity.

3.1   From Raw Cases to Sub-Cases

We can consider each complete time-series as a *raw case* so that, for example, $c(a_i)$ corresponds to the full time-series for company/asset a_i as in Eq. 1. Note that in this work the time-series provides so-called *returns* data rather than actual *pricing* data. The former refers to the relative movement in stock price over a given time period; for example, a return of 0.02 indicates that a price increased by 2% over a given time period whereas a return of -0.005 indicates that a stock price fell by 0.5% over a given time period. From this daily returns dataset, we can also aggregate to weekly or monthly returns in a straightforward manner by accumulating returns across longer periods.

$$c(a_i) = \{r_1^{a_i}, r_2^{a_i}, ..., r_T^{a_i}\} \tag{1}$$

The first step in our approach transforms these raw cases into a set of *sub-cases* such that $c(a_i, t, n)$ denotes the sub-sequence of n (the *look-back*) returns ending at time t, as shown in Eq. 2. For example, later we consider a representation that is based on daily returns with a look-back of five (trading) days (one trading week), which is based on sub-cases with five returns ($n = 5$).

$$c(a_i, t, n) = \{r_{t-n+1}^{a_i}, r_{t-n+2}^{a_i}, ..., r_t^{a_i}\} \tag{2}$$

These sub-cases serve as useful and manageable sub-sequences of returns data for the purpose of similarity comparison during the next step.

3.2   Generating the Count Matrix

Thus, each company/asset can be transformed into a set of sub-cases and for each asset, look-back duration, and point in time there is a unique sub-case. Next, given a suitable similarity metric, we can produce a $N \times N$ matrix, $\mathcal{S}^{[t,n]}$ of pairwise similarities for any time t and look-back n, such that each element is given by $\mathcal{S}_{i,j}^{[t,n]} = sim(c(a_i, t, n), c(a_j, t, n))$. Taking stock a_i as an example, we can then use $\mathcal{S}^{[t,n]}$ to identify the stock a_j which is most similar to a_i at time t by finding the column with the maximum value in row i of $\mathcal{S}^{[t,n]}$.

By repeating this procedure for every a_i and t we can count the number of times that every stock a_j appears as the most similar stock to a given a_i, across all time points. The result is a so-called *count matrix* $\mathcal{C}$ such that $\mathcal{C}_{i,j}$ denotes the number of time periods where stock a_j appeared as the most similar stock to a_i; see Eq. 3.

$$\mathcal{C}_{i,j} = \sum_{\forall t} \delta \left(j, \; \arg\max_{j \neq i} sim \left(c_{a_i, t}, c_{a_j, t} \right) \right) \tag{3}$$

where $\delta(i,j)$ is the Kronecker delta function as defined in Eq. 4.

$$\delta(i,j) = \begin{cases} 0 & \text{if } i \neq j, \\ 1 & \text{if } i = j. \end{cases} \tag{4}$$

This approach to computing $\mathcal{C}$ can be viewed as a special case of a more general approach to computing $\mathcal{C}^{[k]}$. Since $\mathcal{C}$ is based on counts that come from the *single* most similar stocks, we can view it as $\mathcal{C}^{[k]}$ where $k = 1$. More generally then, $\mathcal{C}^{[k]}_{i,j}$ denotes the number of times where stock a_j appeared among the k most similar stocks to stock a_i. In other words, rather than limiting the count matrix to the single most similar stocks we can include a hyper-parameter k to accommodate a more *generous* counting function in order to encode information about a greater number of pairwise similarities. In fact, this is an important practical distinction as our preliminary studies found that representations based on higher values of k performed better during our evaluation. As such for the remainder of this work we will implicitly assume $k = 50$, which is the setting used during the evaluation in the next section; we will continue to refer to $\mathcal{C}^{[k]}$ as $\mathcal{C}$, without loss of generality.

In this way, $\mathcal{C}$ tells us about the most similar comparison stocks for a given stock over time. As the time-series data fluctuates to reflect complex, noisy, and unpredictable market changes, different stocks will appear among the *top-k* most similar stocks at different points in time and for different periods of time. We note that every value in $\mathcal{C}$ must be less than or equal to T, the number of time points in our raw data, and that cases are not compared to themselves, so the diagonal entries in $\mathcal{C}$ are fixed as 0.

As an aside, the count matrix may initially seem superfluous, with the temptation to aggregate similarity scores directly over time instead of using this more discrete approach. However, we found that direct aggregation yielded inferior representations evidenced by poorer downstream performance on financial classification tasks. We hypothesise that the benefit of the proposed approach stems from filtering out some of the noise inherent in market data that make for spurious raw similarities.

3.3   Generating Embedding Representations

We can use the count matrix to generate our final case representation by generating an embedding matrix $\mathcal{E} \in \mathbb{R}^{N \times d}$ (randomly initialised) where d is a hyperparameter to determine the dimensionality of the embedding, and N is the number of companies as before. If $\mathcal{E}_i \in \mathbb{R}^d$ denotes the ith row of $\mathcal{E}$, which represents the embedding for stock a_i, then we can learn the $N \times d$ embedding matrix, $\mathcal{E}$, using matrix factorization techniques by minimising the loss function shown in Eq. 5 with respect to $\mathcal{E}$. This is related to the problem of learning user and item embedding matrices (U and V respectively) from a rating matrix R, in recommender systems, by optimising for $R = UV^T$ [11], except that here we are producing a case embedding matrix ($\mathcal{E}$) based on $\mathcal{C} = \mathcal{E}\mathcal{E}^T$. However, since we are only optimising a single matrix we must adjust the approach to exclude the diagonal entries of C from the optimisation.

$$\mathcal{L} = \sum_{i \in \{1,...,N\}} \sum_{j \neq i} \left(\mathcal{C}_{i,j} - \mathcal{E}_i^T \mathcal{E}_j \right)^2 \tag{5}$$

To complete the process of learning case embeddings there are a number of routine adjustments that need to be made in order to deal with the type of overfitting and scaling problems that may occur due to the presence of outliers and skew within the distribution of values in the count matrix. First, to prevent the learned embeddings from overfitting to outliers, we define an upper bound for values in C as the 99.9^{th} percentile of off-diagonal elements in C, clipping any values in C above this boundary to the boundary; this produces a clipped matrix which we refer to as $\tilde{C}$. Second, to reduce skew in $\tilde{C}$ we apply a standard log transformation in Eq. 6. Finally, we apply min-max scaling to the resulting clipped and transformed count matrix, and regularization to the embedding vectors, which gives the final loss function as shown in Eq. 7. In this final loss function. $\mu(\cdot)$ represents the min-max scaling of a matrix over all elements, $f(\cdot)$ represents the log transformation in Eq. 6 and λ is the regularization rate, which takes a value of 0.1 in our later experiments.

$$f(\mathbf{x}) = \left(\frac{1}{2} \log(1 + \mathbf{x}) \right)^2 \tag{6}$$

$$\mathcal{L} = \sum_{i \in \{1,...,N\}} \sum_{j \neq i} \left[\mu \left(f(\tilde{\mathcal{C}}_{i,j}) \right) - \mathcal{E}_i^T \mathcal{E}_j \right]^2 + \lambda \cdot \left(||\mathcal{E}_i||^2 + ||\mathcal{E}_j||^2 \right) \tag{7}$$

3.4   Discussion

In summary then, the above procedure transforms a raw, $(N \times T)$ times series dataset into a more compact $(N \times d$, where $d << T)$ matrix of embeddings vectors. Each company case corresponds to a single d-dimensional embedding vector; that is, a row of $\mathcal{E}$ with its d feature values. This has the advantage of greatly reducing the dimensionality of our cases $(d << T)$ but, in addition, we also hypothesise that the manner in which these embeddings have been produced means that they will capture more useful information than the raw returns data alone, or than more traditional summary features, by surfacing important temporal similarity information about the relationship between stocks.

It is worth noting too that this approach serves as a framework for generating case representations with different levels of granularity, context windows/look-back durations, and different similarity metrics. For example, it may be useful to focus on daily returns over a 5-day look-back period (sub-cases that correspond to single trading weeks) for one task and weekly returns over a 12-week look-back period for a different task. Or it may be useful to consider ways in which the resulting embedding representations can be combined to provide even richer representations. For example, the Orthogonal Procrustes Problem [22] offers a robust solution for aligning embeddings produced by different models. Given two embedding spaces A and B, the objective is to find an orthogonal transformation matrix Ω, most closely mapping A to B. Mathematically, this can be expressed as the minimization problem $\arg\min_\Omega \|\Omega A - B\|_F$ subject to Ω^T. In principle, such an approach may facilitate combining case representations produced from different sub-cases but we leave this as a matter for future work.

4   Evaluation

So far, this paper has presented a novel approach for learning embedding-based case representations from financial time-series data, specifically the daily, weekly, and monthly returns data from stocks. We argue that this approach allows us to encode important temporal relationships between financial assets, which are otherwise difficult to capture in more traditional case representations (such as summary, raw feature-based or fixed, attribute-value style representations). In this section, we demonstrate the value of this new approach by evaluating the efficacy of these representations using several qualitative and quantitative techniques. In particular, we provide the results of a comparative evaluation of our embeddings-based representations versus more conventional CBR approaches, as well as recently proposed domain-specific methods [4, 20], in a common financial domain classification task.

4.1   Dataset and Methodology

In this evaluation, we evaluate the performance of several approaches to industry sector classification using a real-world, publicly available dataset. This is a challenging classification task in its own right, which is instrumental to a multitude of downstream tasks in the financial domain [18].

Evaluation Dataset. As mentioned previously, the dataset used in this work is a publicly available dataset of *returns* data for 611 individual company stocks, spanning the years 2000–2018 [4]. Each stock is associated with a time-series of stock returns (relative changes in price) over daily, weekly, or monthly time periods. The dataset also contains additional (meta) data about each company stock, including industry sector classification data, which will be used in this evaluation. It is important to note that the industry sector labels in the dataset are not orthogonal (companies can operate across a number of sectors), and that they are assigned subjectively by analysts at the Global Industry Classification Scheme (GICS). As a result, in the classification task to come, perfect agreement with ground-truth labels is not a realistic goal, but high agreement serves as a strong indication that the representations are capturing useful information.

Industry Sector Classification Task. For this evaluation we will perform *industry sector classification*, which involves predicting a company's primary industry sector, based on their returns time-series data. This is a vital task for many types of financial and economic analyses—identifying peers and competitors, quantifying market share and benchmarking company performance—none of which would be possible without sector classification schemes [18]; notably approximately 30% of publications in the top-three finance journals make use of industry classification schemes [27]. In this work, our primary focus is to use a CBR approach to classify stocks, using different representations (see below) to produce different case-base configurations. In each configuration, the problem description of a case corresponds to its returns data (whether using a raw, summary, or embeddings representation) and the solution part of a case corresponds to the stock's sector classification. Then, for a target/query stock a_q we identify its 5 nearest-neighbours, using a straightforward Euclidean or correlation metric (as given in Table 1), with simple *majority voting* to identify the predicted industry sector for a_q.

Algorithmic Configurations. In this evaluation we will test a number of different approaches, each distinguished according to the representation used for cases and the granularity of the returns data (daily, weekly, monthly) used. Arguably the simplest approach is to generate a feature-based representation based on summary features extracted from the raw returns data. These summary features include standard statistical features such as *mean, min, max, volatility, 25th percentile, median, 75th percentile* calculated over the daily, weekly and monthly returns data. These (×3) configurations are referred to as *Summary* in what follows; see the first 3 rows in Table 1. We also implement two versions using the raw returns data as case representations (*Raw*) one set (×3) uses a Euclidean distance metric (referred to as E in Table 1) when computing the k nearest-neighbours, and another (×3) uses Pearson's correlation to identify the k nearest-neighbours (referred to as P in Table 1); the latter being a more common similarity metric to use in financial domains. Finally, we test several (×18) varieties of our newly proposed embeddings-based representation (*Embedding*), with varying look-back durations for the daily, weekly, and monthly returns; the final three sections of Table 1. In particular, we vary the similarity metric used when *computing the count matrix* to look at the effect of using Euclidean distance (E) versus Pearson's correlation (P) versus the more recent hybrid metric (H), which combines Euclidean distance with a modified correlation component [6]. We note that for all of these embedding representations, the dimensionality is chosen as $d = 15$ and the standard Euclidean distance metric is used during the subsequent kNN classification (with the exception of raw with correlation) to enable a like-for-like comparison with the other baselines. In addition, we evaluate the proposed approach against non-CBR baselines including more general time series classification approaches [9,15,21], as well as domain-specific neural methods [4,20].

Evaluation Metrics. For each of these different variations, we use a standard 5-fold cross-validation to generate and test the classifications produced. For each variation, we produce a standard *classification report*[1] which provides *precision* (the ratio of true positives to the sum of true and false positives), *recall* (ratio of true positives to the sum of true positives and false negatives), and F1 (the harmonic mean of precision and recall). The reported values are the weighted average for each class weighted by the number of samples in each class. There are 11 sector classes in the dataset: Basic Industries, Capital Goods, Consumer Durables, Consumer Non-Durables, Consumer Services, Energy, Finance, Health Care, Public Utilities, Technology, Transportation.

4.2   Results

The results are presented in Table 1. Each row corresponds to a specific algorithmic configuration and shows the representation used (*Summary, Raw,* and *Embeddings*), the granularity of the returns data (*Daily, Weekly, Monthly*) and the similarity metric used for the final *k*NN classification task (*Euclidean or Correlation*). In addition, for the *Embedding* representations, we also include settings for the relevant look-back periods. Finally, each configuration is associated with an overall weighted precision, recall, and F1 score as mentioned previously. Additionally, non-CBR baselines are reported in the lower section of the table with the same evaluation metrics.

A number of performance patterns are evident in these results. The poorest performances are associated with the *Summary* representations (F1≤ 0.15). This is not surprising given that these representations abstract away a lot of the detail that exists in the returns data. While it may be possible to improve upon these representations, for example by including more domain-specific technical features, they provide a useful naive baseline against which to evaluate the improvements of more sophisticated approaches. The more reasonable *Raw* representations perform considerably better, with F1 values as high as 0.43 found among the variations that use a correlation-based similarity metric, arguably the most popular metric in the financial literature. In general, these *Raw* variations using correlation (*Raw+P*) out-perform the corresponding representations using Euclidean distance (*Raw+E*); the former report with $0.33 \leq F1 \leq 0.36$ compared to $0.41 \leq F1 \leq 0.43$ for the latter. Thus, the *Raw+P* variations serve as a useful baseline against which to evaluate the efficacy of the new embeddings-based representations.

Most of the embeddings-based representations outperform these *Raw+P* baselines, regardless of granularity or look-back duration. And, we note too that shorter look-back periods are associated with better performance than longer look-back periods. As further evidence that correlation-based similarity is more appropriate for financial returns data than Euclidean metrics, we note that the embeddings-based representations that are learned using correlation-based similarity (*Embedding + P* with $0.41 \leq F1 \leq 0.64$) out-perform the corresponding

---

[1] In this work all code is written in Python and uses the standard SciKit Learn implementation of *k*NN, cross-validation, and classification reporting. Non-CBR baselines were implemented in sktime where available, and PyTorch in other cases.

Table 1. Results for the case-based industry sector classification task for each of the 27 variations under consideration.

Representation	kNN Metric	Granularity	Lookback	Precision	Recall	F1
Summary	E	Daily	–	0.11	0.15	0.12
Summary	E	Weekly	–	0.13	0.15	0.13
Summary	E	Monthly	–	0.15	0.18	0.15
Raw	E	Daily	–	0.46	0.39	0.33
Raw	E	Weekly	–	0.45	0.43	0.36
Raw	E	Monthly	–	0.39	0.40	0.33
Raw	P	Daily	–	0.56	0.48	0.41
Raw	P	Weekly	–	0.50	0.49	0.42
Raw	P	Monthly	–	0.54	0.49	0.43
Embedding + E	E	Daily	5	0.67	0.62	0.63
Embedding + E	E	Daily	22	0.59	0.55	0.55
Embedding + E	E	Weekly	4	0.60	0.56	0.57
Embedding + E	E	Weekly	52	0.44	0.36	0.38
Embedding + E	E	Monthly	12	0.38	0.31	0.32
Embedding + E	E	Monthly	24	0.35	0.29	0.31
Embedding + P	E	Daily	5	0.68	0.62	0.64
Embedding + P	E	Daily	22	0.67	0.64	0.64
Embedding + P	E	Weekly	4	0.66	0.60	0.61
Embedding + P	E	Weekly	52	0.46	0.39	0.41
Embedding + P	E	Monthly	12	0.51	0.46	0.47
Embedding + P	E	Monthly	24	0.50	0.42	0.44
Embedding + H	E	Daily	5	**0.69**	**0.65**	**0.66**
Embedding + H	E	Daily	22	0.65	0.62	0.62
Embedding + H	E	Weekly	4	0.66	0.60	0.61
Embedding + H	E	Weekly	52	0.50	0.44	0.46
Embedding + H	E	Monthly	12	0.56	0.50	0.51
Embedding + H	E	Monthly	24	0.49	0.43	0.44
Non-CBR Methods			Granularity	Precision	Recall	F1
Shapelet Transform [9]			Daily	0.39	0.46	0.40
WEASEL [21]			Daily	0.50	0.47	0.47
Canonical Interval Forest [15]			Daily	0.57	0.56	0.52
Financial Time Series Embeddings [4]			Daily	0.62	0.60	0.60
Financial Correlation Graph Embeddings [20]			Daily	0.64	0.60	0.61

representations that were based on Euclidean distance (*Embedding + E* with $0.31 \leq F1 \leq 0.63$). Furthermore, the hybrid metric introduced by [6], which combines elements of Euclidean distance and correlation, tends to perform as well as, and usually better than, the embeddings-based representations using correlation alone (*Embeddings + H* with $0.44 \leq F1 \leq 0.66$). Indeed, the embed-

Table 2. Examples of top-3 nearest neighbours for given query stocks

Query Stock Sector - Industry	3 Nearest Neighbours - Sector - Industry	Similarity
JP Morgan Chase	Bank of America Corp - Finance - Major Bank	0.98
Finance	State Street Corp - Finance - Major Bank	0.98
Major Bank	Wells Fargo & Company - Finance - Major Bank	0.97
Microsoft	IBM - Technology - Computer Manufacturing	0.95
Technology	HP - Technology - Computer Manufacturing	0.93
Software	Adobe - Technology - Software	0.92
Walmart	Costco - Consumer Services - Dept Store	0.89
Consumer Services	Kroger - Consumer Services - Food Chains	0.82
Department Store	McDonalds - Consumer Services - Food Chains	0.78

dings produced with this hybrid metric always outperform the $Raw + P$ baseline regardless of granularity and look-back.

The domain agnostic non-CBR methods proposed in [15, 21] outperform the raw and summary baselines, while the recent task-specific approaches [4, 20] are stronger again ($0.60 \leq F1 \leq 0.61$). However, the proposed approach remains the strongest performer.

4.3   Discussion

These results support the hypothesis that the proposed embeddings-based representations are capable of capturing more useful information from the time-series returns data than more conventional representations. The best proposed representation is associated with an F1 score of 0.66 compared to just 0.43 for the best CBR baseline representation and 0.60/0.61 for the task specific baselines. Moreover, the proposed representation is well-suited for use in a CBR setting which, due to the retrieval of existing labelled cases, offers further advantages when it comes to interpretability.

By way of further explanation, Table 2 shows some examples of the nearest neighbours that are identified for 3 different query companies (JP Morgan Chase, Microsoft and Walmart) using an embeddings-based representation. For each query company, we summarise the top-3 nearest neighbours, the sector class (e.g. Finance), a finer-grained industry label (e.g. Major Bank), and their corresponding similarities to the query stock. The results align with our intuitions and in each case, the nearest neighbours match the query's industry sector (Finance, Technology, and Consumer Services, respectively).

As another example, Fig. 1 shows a 2D visualisation of the clusters of companies that emerge when using the embeddings-based representations. Each node corresponds to an individual stock and an edge is created between two stocks if their similarity exceeds some minimum threshold (0.75 in this example). Then, a force-directed graph drawing algorithm [10] is used to position the nodes in such a way as to optimise their placement in the resulting similarity space. The nodes have been colour-coded based on their ground-truth industry sectors and

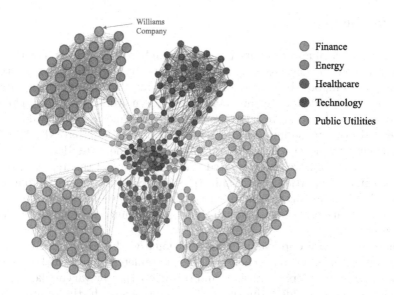

Fig. 1. Visualization of embedding clustering. A subset of sectors is used for visual clarity.

we can see clearly how nodes from the same industry sector tend to be clustered together, indicating that the embeddings-based representations are doing a good job of capturing this relationship; as an aside it is worth noting that the embedding representations also exhibited clear clustering using visualisation approaches such as PCA and t-SNE.

We also observe some interesting patterns in the graph that are not immediately obvious from the sector labels. For example, a node from the Public Utilities sector (indicated in orange) appears as an outlier in the Energy cluster (green). This node, highlighted in Fig. 1, is an energy supply company called Williams Company, whose primary business is natural gas processing and transportation. Thus, although it has Public Utilities classification in our dataset, the case representation facilitates recognising its similarity with the Energy business and it is positioned accordingly.

Visualisations such as this are powerful tools for technical analysts to better understand the evolving structure of modern markets, but to be useful they must rely on representations that are capable of reasonably accurately capturing meaningful relationships between different stocks and companies. The case representation proposed here should help to improve the utility of such tools because it does a better job at recognising the relationships that exist between companies but that may be obscured by the raw time-series data and not captured by traditional subjective industry classification schemes.

5   Conclusion

Using CBR with time-series data presents a number of challenges, not the least of which is how to generate case representations that are capable of capturing the complex temporal behaviour of the underlying data. Time-series data are becoming more and more common in the modern world with the increasing ability to capture and store large amounts of real-time, real-world data. This is especially true in the financial domain and this work, we have described the development of a novel representation of financial time-series data that is well suited to CBR. We have demonstrated the effectiveness of this representational approach on the important task of industry sector classification, in comparison to several CBR baselines as well as recent task-specific neural methods. The results indicate that the proposed approach offers performance benefits compared to these alternatives.

There are several opportunities for additional work arising from this initial study. For example, no comprehensive hyper-parameter tuning has been carried out for the proposed representations and it is likely that by varying key parameters, such as the embedding dimensionality (d), k, and λ, further improvements could be found; the fact that significant improvements were obtained for the "default" settings used here speaks to this. And, although the focus of this work has been on the use of the proposed representation in a CBR context, the representation should be equally applicable as a training data representation for other machine learning models. In fact, preliminary results, not provided here for reasons of space and clarity, suggest further performance gains if the embeddings are applied within a non-CBR classifier.

Within the financial domain, there are many other tasks that can be explored as targets for this type of representation. For example, risk management and portfolio optimisation [4] are obvious candidates in this regard. Moreover, given the proliferation of time-series data across many domains (clinical health [2], exercise and fitness [7] etc.) it will be interesting to assess whether this type of representation can add value across different task types.

Acknowledgements. This publication has emanated from research conducted with the financial support of Science Foundation Ireland under Grant number 18/CRT/6183.

References

1. Chun, S.H., Ko, Y.W.: Geometric case based reasoning for stock market prediction. Sustainability (Switzerland) **12** (2020). https://doi.org/10.3390/su12177124
2. Delaney, E., Greene, D., Keane, M.T.: Instance-based counterfactual explanations for time series classification. In: Sánchez-Ruiz, A.A., Floyd, M.W. (eds.) ICCBR 2021. LNCS (LNAI), vol. 12877, pp. 32–47. Springer, Cham (2021). https://doi.org/10.1007/978-3-030-86957-1_3
3. Delaney, E., Greene, D., Shalloo, L., Lynch, M., Keane, M.T.: Forecasting for sustainable dairy produce: enhanced long-term, milk-supply forecasting using k-NN for data augmentation, with prefactual explanations for XAI. In: Keane, M.T.,

Wiratunga, N. (eds.) ICCBR 2022. LNCS, vol. 13405, pp. 365–379. Springer, Cham (2022). https://doi.org/10.1007/978-3-031-14923-8_24

4. Dolphin, R., Smyth, B., Dong, R.: Stock embeddings: learning distributed representations for financial assets. arXiv preprint arXiv:2202.08968 (2022)

5. Dolphin, R., Smyth, B., Dong, R.: A machine learning approach to industry classification in financial markets. In: Longo, L., O'Reilly, R. (eds.) AICS 2022. CCIS, vol. 1662, pp. 81–94. Springer, Cham (2023). https://doi.org/10.1007/978-3-031-26438-2_7

6. Dolphin, R., Smyth, B., Xu, Y., Dong, R.: Measuring financial time series similarity with a view to identifying profitable stock market opportunities. In: Sánchez-Ruiz, A.A., Floyd, M.W. (eds.) ICCBR 2021. LNCS (LNAI), vol. 12877, pp. 64–78. Springer, Cham (2021). https://doi.org/10.1007/978-3-030-86957-1_5

7. Feely, C., Caulfield, B., Lawlor, A., Smyth, B.: Using case-based reasoning to predict marathon performance and recommend tailored training plans. In: Watson, I., Weber, R. (eds.) ICCBR 2020. LNCS (LNAI), vol. 12311, pp. 67–81. Springer, Cham (2020). https://doi.org/10.1007/978-3-030-58342-2_5

8. Gold, S.: The viability of six popular technical analysis trading rules in determining effective buy and sell signals: MACD, AROON, RSI, SO, OBV, and ADL. J. Appl. Financ. Res. 2 (2015)

9. Hills, J., Lines, J., Baranauskas, E., Mapp, J., Bagnall, A.: Classification of time series by shapelet transformation. Data Min. Knowl. Disc. 28, 851–881 (2014)

10. Jacomy, M., Venturini, T., Heymann, S., Bastian, M.: ForceAtlas2, a continuous graph layout algorithm for handy network visualization designed for the Gephi software. PLoS ONE 9(6), e98679 (2014)

11. Koren, Y., Bell, R., Volinsky, C.: Matrix factorization techniques for recommender systems. Computer 42(8), 30–37 (2009)

12. Kumar, G., Jain, S., Singh, U.P.: Stock market forecasting using computational intelligence: a survey. Arch. Comput. Methods Eng. 28(3), 1069–1101 (2020). https://doi.org/10.1007/s11831-020-09413-5

13. Li, S.T., Ho, H.F.: Predicting financial activity with evolutionary fuzzy case-based reasoning. Expert Syst. Appl. 36(1), 411–422 (2009)

14. McSherry, D.: A lazy learning approach to explaining case-based reasoning solutions. In: Agudo, B.D., Watson, I. (eds.) ICCBR 2012. LNCS (LNAI), vol. 7466, pp. 241–254. Springer, Heidelberg (2012). https://doi.org/10.1007/978-3-642-32986-9_19

15. Middlehurst, M., Large, J., Bagnall, A.: The canonical interval forest (CIF) classifier for time series classification. In: 2020 IEEE International Conference on Big Data (Big Data), pp. 188–195. IEEE (2020)

16. Mikolov, T., Chen, K., Corrado, G., Dean, J.: Efficient estimation of word representations in vector space. arXiv preprint arXiv:1301.3781 (2013)

17. Nalmpantis, C., Vrakas, D.: Signal2Vec: time series embedding representation. In: Macintyre, J., Iliadis, L., Maglogiannis, I., Jayne, C. (eds.) EANN 2019. CCIS, vol. 1000, pp. 80–90. Springer, Cham (2019). https://doi.org/10.1007/978-3-030-20257-6_7

18. Phillips, R.L., Ormsby, R.: Industry classification schemes: an analysis and review. J. Bus. Financ. Librarianship 21(1), 1–25 (2016)

19. Sakoe, H., Chiba, S.: Dynamic programming algorithm optimization for spoken word recognition. IEEE Trans. Acoust. Speech Signal Process. 26(1), 43–49 (1978)

20. Sarmah, B., Nair, N., Mehta, D., Pasquali, S.: Learning embedded representation of the stock correlation matrix using graph machine learning. arXiv preprint arXiv:2207.07183 (2022)

21. Schäfer, P., Leser, U.: Fast and accurate time series classification with weasel. In: Proceedings of the 2017 ACM on Conference on Information and Knowledge Management, pp. 637–646 (2017)
22. Schönemann, P.H.: A generalized solution of the orthogonal procrustes problem. Psychometrika **31**(1), 1–10 (1966)
23. Slade, S.: Case-based reasoning for financial decision making. In: Proceedings of the First International Conference on Artificial Intelligence Applications on Wall Street. IEEE Computer Society, New York (1991)
24. Smyth, B., Cunningham, P.: A comparison of incremental case-based reasoning and inductive learning. In: Haton, J.-P., Keane, M., Manago, M. (eds.) EWCBR 1994. LNCS, vol. 984, pp. 151–164. Springer, Heidelberg (1995). https://doi.org/10.1007/3-540-60364-6_34
25. Wang, Y., Wang, Y.: A case-based reasoning-decision tree hybrid system for stock selection. Int. J. Comput. Inf. Eng. **10**(6), 1223–1229 (2016)
26. Warren, G., Smyth, B., Keane, M.T.: "Better" counterfactuals, ones people can understand: psychologically-plausible case-based counterfactuals using categorical features for explainable AI (XAI). In: Keane, M.T., Wiratunga, N. (eds.) ICCBR 2022. LNCS, vol. 13405, pp. 63–78. Springer, Cham (2022). https://doi.org/10.1007/978-3-031-14923-8_5
27. Weiner, C.: The impact of industry classification schemes on financial research. Available at SSRN 871173 (2005)

An Integrated Approach to Predicting the Influence of Reputation Mechanisms on Q&A Communities

Yi Yang[1,2,3] (iD), Xinjun Mao[1,3](✉), and Menghan Wu[1,3]

[1] College of Computer, National University of Defense Technology, Changsha, China
xjmao@nudt.edu.cn
[2] College of Information Science and Engineering, Hunan Women's University, Changsha, China
[3] Key Laboratory of Complex Systems Software Engineering of Hunan, Changsha, China

Abstract. The reputation mechanism is a commonly used incentive mechanism to motivate users to participate in Q&A communities, which needs to be carefully reviewed before application. Predicting the impact of reputation mechanisms can help community managers to choose an appropriate mechanism. However, existing methods are difficult to establish the connection between users and reputation mechanisms and their influence in Q&A communities, which may lead to misleading results. Hence, we propose a MASC method combining multi-agent and case-based reasoning systems. We model incentive rules as norms in a multi-agent system composed of heterogeneous agents. We describe the impact of incentive mechanisms from three aspects: user attributes, behaviour, and content structure. Based on past user behaviour data, we present how to predict future behaviour and interaction based on similar user contribution patterns. In addition, we use the developed simulator to reproduce the impact of reputation mechanisms on Q&A communities. We use a new reputation mechanism of the Stack Overflow community to evaluate the performance of MASC. Except for questioning preference, the prediction accuracy for the influence exceeds 65%.

Keywords: Case-Based Reasoning · Multi-Agent System · Reputation Mechanism · Influence Prediction · Q&A Community

1 Introduction

The reputation mechanism is one of the most widely used incentives in Q&A communities [1]. It encourages users by giving them virtual points and corresponding status and privileges to achieve community goals, such as encouraging users to answer [2]. These incentives must be carefully deliberated and revised before implementation in real communities to avoid potential harm to their communities.

Predicting the impact of incentives can help select appropriate incentives to ensure that they promote the development of their communities. The existing methods predict the influence of reputation mechanisms by equation-based modelling (EBM) [3–5].

© The Author(s), under exclusive license to Springer Nature Switzerland AG 2023
S. Massie and S. Chakraborti (Eds.): ICCBR 2023, LNAI 14141, pp. 391–407, 2023.
https://doi.org/10.1007/978-3-031-40177-0_25

These methods apply a set of statistical or mathematical equations to construct the connections between incentives and their influence, such as user questioning preference. Their results indicate what macro impact reputation mechanisms have on actual communities. For instance, Zhang et al. [6] designed a new reputation mechanism to inhibit "free riding" and evaluated its effect using the game-theoretic model.

However, existing EBM methods face the challenge of building the connection between users at the micro level and reputation mechanisms and their influence at the macro level. Q&A community is a type of complex socio-technical system [7]. The users in these communities are heterogeneous worldwide, with varying reputations, preferences, and behaviour patterns. Massive non-linear interactions and relationships exist in these communities, e.g., the non-linear relationship between questioners and answerers. These interactions result in a specific phenomenon emergence [8], which cannot be deduced from the sum of individual behaviour. The equations become too complicated to analyse when modelling these non-linear interactions and their resulting emergence. While using a simplified model may lead to misleading results [9].

An alternative to EBM is the Multi-Agent System (MAS) simulation [10]. Agents in a MAS can autonomously interact with others or their environment. To achieve goals, a MAS uses norms to regulate agents' behaviour. These features of a MAS closely match that of Q&A communities that employ incentives to motivate autonomous users to contribute. More importantly, a MAS can simulate the generation of emergence.

However, predicting the impact of incentive mechanisms based on MAS requires anticipating user behaviour or interactions resulting in community emergence. A feasible method to solve this challenge is the case-based reasoning (CBR) system [11]. In Q&A communities, users participate in the questioning and answering process based on their experience. A CBR can retrieve similar problems and their solutions in its case base when encountering new problems by comparing the context differences between new and old problems to reuse and revise the old case solutions to solve new problems. Accordingly, we can abstract user behaviour generation as a problem and leverage the CBR and historical user behaviour data to infer their future behaviour.

Based on the above analysis, we propose a MASC integration method that combines a MAS and a CBR system. We use the Stack Overflow (SO) community as the context and model its reputation rules as norms in the MAS composed of heterogeneous agents. We describe the impact of the reputation mechanism on the community from three aspects: user attributes, behaviour, and content structure. According to the five-month behaviour history of users from June 1, 2019, to November 12, 2019, we establish a CBR system to estimate a user's behaviour based on his/her current attributes and the experience of users with similar attributes. In addition, we develop a simulator to reproduce the impact of a new reputation mechanism on the community. Given the difficulty and limited research in predicting the impact, our study, even if modest success, may help community managers to compare and make decisions on incentive mechanisms more effectively and accurately. Our contributions include the following:

1. **Design of an integrated method combining MAS and CBR**. The method can naturally represent users, contents, reputation rules and their influence on Q&A communities. More importantly, our method can simulate the process of reputation mechanisms affecting user interactions at the micro level and these interactions achieving emergence at the macro level.
2. **Design of a user behaviour CBR system**. We designed a user behaviour case base according to user experience and proposed a metric to evaluate the similarity between current and past individuals. Hence, the system can deduce the generation of user behaviour under reputation mechanisms.
3. **Development of a reputation mechanism simulator.** We developed a simulation system that can simulate the non-linear interactions between users and reproduce the emergence of Q&A communities under reputation mechanisms.

2   Related Works

Much literature has studied Q&A community emergence using the MAS-Based approach [9, 12, 13]. These studies mainly focused on user behaviour patterns, such as question selection [14], knowledge cooperation behaviour [15], and answer patterns [16]. These studies analyzed the influence of user characteristics (such as activity and preference) and community content on their behaviour, providing insights for developing our method.

Our work is strongly related to using CBR for reasoning individual behaviour or action. Malek et al. [17] developed a CBR approach for predicting website user requests. Zehraoui et al. [18] present a hybrid neuro-symbolic system combining CBR and artificial neural networks to cluster and classify users' behaviour. Herrero-Reder [19] proposed a CBR-based learning method to build a set of nested behaviours. Lee [20] proposed a novel recommender system based on users' behavioural model, which recommended optimal virtual communities for an active user by CBR using behavioural factors.

Various efforts have recently been proposed incorporating a CBR architecture with MAS. Ajjouri [21] presented a novel architecture based on MAS/CBR for intrusion detection. To anticipate the risks of surgery, Perez et al. [22] employed an integrated strategy that included case-based reasoning with agent-based modelization. Pinto et al. [23] proposed an innovative CBR/MAS-based recommender system for intelligent energy management in buildings.

Different from the above studies, our study considered the reputation mechanism factor. Aiming to predict the influence of reputation mechanisms on their communities, we integrated CBR and MAS to simulate the generation of user behaviour under reputation mechanisms and the process of generating community emergence resulting from massive user behaviour and interaction.

3 Motivating Scenario

To facilitate the discussion in this paper, we place our study in the context of Stack Overflow, a community with tens of millions of users who ask and answer questions. Peers' votes, in the form of upvotes and downvotes, provide positive or negative feedback on these questions and answers.

Table 1 represents the regulation of the SO reputation mechanism on users' contribution behaviour. For example, according to rule 1, a user is rewarded with five points when others upvote his/her question. Conversely, rule 2 states that a user may incur a two-point deduction for a downvoted question. The rise and fall of a user's reputation can influence his/her motivation to participate and contribute to the community.

Table 1. Reputation rules in Stack Overflow (before November 13, 2019).

Rule	User behaviour	Reputation change
1	Upvoting a question	+5 to the owner
2	Downvoting a question	−2 to the owner
3	Upvoting an answer	+10 to the owner
4	Downvoting an answer	−2 to the owner, −1 to the voter

On November 13, 2019, Stack Overflow announced a change in its reputation rules, setting reputation points for upvoted questions the same as answers[1]. This change sparked significant discussion, with some users expressing disagreement and even stating that they would reduce their participation or abandon the community. To mitigate the potential adverse effects of this change, the community needs a decision-support method to predict the influence of reputation mechanisms on the community and estimate the risks associated with changes in reputation rules.

4 Architecture of the MASC Method

The architecture of the MASC method, as illustrated in Fig. 1, primarily consists of MAS and CBR. We conceptualize the SO community as a MAS, wherein agents represent users within the community, and a norm set embodies its reputation mechanism. Questions and answers in the community are represented as a class of passive entities that agents can create and utilize. Norms at the macro level govern agents' interactions with each other, leading to emergent behaviour at the macro level. As such, our method naturally captures the influence process of reputation mechanisms on the community and its effects.

In the architecture, we employ CBR to reason about user behaviour based on historical user behaviour data under past reputation mechanisms. As depicted in Fig. 1, when an individual needs to make a behaviour choice, it retrieves relevant experiences

---

[1] http://meta.stackoverflow.com/questions/391250/upvotes-on-questions-will-now-be-worth-the-same-as-upvotes-on-answers.

stored in the case base. It employs them to reason about their behaviour under the current circumstances. If similar cases are found in the case base, these cases are reused to guide the individual's behaviour. If user behaviour patterns evolve in the community, we can revise the suggested parameter values in the case base. Subsequently, after review, appropriate cases are retained in the case base for future reference.

Sections 4.1 and 4.2 introduce the MAS model of Q&A communities and the generation of user behaviours based on CBR, respectively.

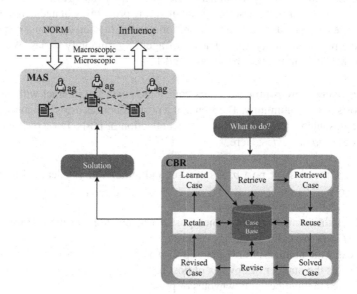

Fig. 1. Overall architecture of the MASC method.

4.1 MAS Model for Q&A Communities

We described the community as a three-tuple $NMAS = <AG, POST, NORM>$. AG is a set of agents representing community users. $POST$ represents users' environment, a collection of posts they generate. In addition, $NORM$ represents a set of reputation rules.

Modelling Users. For users in the community, we mainly considered their attributes related to the community's core assets (questions and answers). For $ag \in AG$, we defined $ag = <r, pa, va, qr, ur, qp, up>$. Here,

- r indicates the reputation of agent ag. According to the reputation rules in SO, a user's reputation must be greater than or equal to 1, i.e., $r \geq 1$.
- pa indicates agent ag's posting-activeness, reflecting a user's posting frequency. We used the average daily posts of the user to measure it.
- va indicates the voting-activeness of agent ag, reflecting the voting frequency of a user. We used the average daily votes of the user to measure it.

- **qr** represents agent *ag*'s questioning preference, reflecting how much a user's reputation influences his/her preference to ask questions. It can be measured by the total number of questions from the user as a percentage of his/her total posts, including questions and answers. Accordingly, 1-*qr* indicates the user's answer preference.
- **ur** represents agent *ag*'s upvoting preference, reflecting how much a user's reputation influences his/her preference to upvote. It can be measured by the total number of upvotes from the user as a percentage of his/her total votes, including upvotes and downvotes. Accordingly, 1-*ur* indicates the user's downvote preference.
- **qp** and **up** are the current questioning and upvoting probability of agent *ag*, representing the intensity of a user's current desire for questioning and upvoting, respectively. As in the real community, the intensity of agent *ag* randomly varies. We simulate them using random numbers between 0 and 1.

Modelling Users' Environment. Users contribute posts and interact with each other through posts in the community. The status of a post influences users' behaviour. Therefore, we represented users' environment as a collection of posts. For a post p in *POST*, $p = <c, ag, t, na, nu, nd>$. Here,

- **c** indicates the class of post p. A question and an answer are denoted by 0 and 1, respectively.
- **ag** indicates the creator of post p.
- **t** indicates the number of days since post p was created. On the day the post p is created, $t = 0$. We call t as the age of post p.
- **na** indicates the number of answers of post p. If post p is an answer, $na = -1$.
- **nu** indicates the number of upvotes of post p.
- **nd** indicates the number of downvotes of post p.

Representing Users' Behaviour. Like the description of attributes of users, we focused on user behaviours related to posts.

- **C(ag, p)** represents agent *ag* creates post p.
- **U(ag, p)** represents agent *ag* upvotes post p.
- **D(ag, p)** represents agent *ag* downvotes post p.

Representing Reputation Mechanisms. We used Eq. 1 and Eq. 2 to represent the incentive of reputation mechanisms to users under the "upvote" and "downvote" scenarios. Here, R(*ag*, *pt*) is an incentive function representing the reward of *pt* reputation points to agent *ag*.

$$\forall ag1, ag2 \in AG \; \exists p \in POST$$
$$U(ag1, p) \land C(ag2, p) \rightarrow R(ag1, pt1) \land R(ag2, pt2). \quad (1)$$

Equation 1 describes rules 1 and 3 in Table 1. When agent ag_1 upvotes post p created by agent ag_2, the agents are rewarded pt_1 and pt_2 points, respectively.

$$\forall ag1, ag2 \in AG \; \exists p \in POST$$

$$D(ag1, p) \wedge C(ag2, p) \rightarrow R(ag1, pt3) \wedge R(ag2, pt4). \quad (2)$$

Equation 2 describes rules 2 and 4 in Table 1. When agent ag_1 downvotes post p created by agent ag_2, the agents are penalized pt_3 and pt_4 points, respectively.

Representing the Influence on Q&A Communities. We investigated the impact of reputation mechanisms on Q&A communities from three aspects: user attribute, user behaviour, and community content structure, as shown in Table 2. The first reflects the attribute distribution of users with different reputations. The second describes the influence of reputation mechanisms on user behaviour patterns. The last reflects the distribution of community posts under the reputation mechanism.

Table 2. Emergence related to the influence of reputation mechanisms.

Type	Emergence	Description
attribute	posting-activeness	Relationship between reputation and posting activeness
	voting-activeness	Relationship between reputation and voting activeness
	question-rate	Relationship between reputation and question preference
	upvote-rate	Relationship between reputation and upvote preference
behaviour	questioning	Influence of reputation on user questioning
	answering	Influence of reputation on user answering
	upvoting	Influence of reputation on user upvoting
	downvoting	Influence of reputation on user downvoting
structure	fast-answers	Answers to different questions ages
	questions	Questions of different answer numbers

4.2 CBR for User Behaviour Generation

The following paragraphs briefly describe five steps in which case-based reasoning generates user behaviour.

Case Representation. In Q&A communities, the generation of user behaviour is related to their attributes (e.g. reputation and preference) and current behaviour probability being affected by their environment. We assume that users ask questions when their current questioning probability qp is less than their questioning preference qr. If not, they answer a question. Similarly, users randomly vote on others' posts. They upvote posts when their current upvoting probability up is less than their upvoting preference ur. Otherwise, they downvote on posts.

Based on the above analysis, we represented the case of user behaviour in the community as a five-tuple $cb = <r, pr, pc, op, b>$. A detailed description of the tuple is shown in Table 3. The first four items describe the problem to be solved: how an agent chooses its behaviour in the current state. The latter describes the solution to the problem, that is, the corresponding behaviour.

Case Retrieve. We constructed a user behaviour case base according to their historical behaviour data. Using the case base, we, at the retrieval step, identified the source case that most closely resembles the target case (the case that needs to be retrieved). In our context, we compared the similarity of user attributes between a target case and a source case according to their Mean Relative Error (MRE) [24]. The calculation formula is shown in Eq. 3.

Table 3. Characteristics of each case.

Variable	Description
r	The logarithm of users' reputation. $r \in [0, 14]$
pr	Users' behaviour preference degree. $pr \in [0, 1]$
pc	Users' behaviour preference type. $pc \in \{1, 2, 3, 4\}$. 1 to 4 represent questioning, answering, upvoting, and downvoting preferences
op	Logical relationships. $op \in \{1, 2\}$. 1 and 2 represent greater-than-equal and less-than relations between a user's behaviour probability and preference
b	Users' behaviour type. $b \in \{1, 2, 3, 4\}$. 1 to 4 represent questioning, answering, upvoting, and downvoting

$$\text{sim}(A, B) = 1\text{-MRE}(A, B) = 1 - \frac{1}{N} \sum_{i=1}^{N} \left| \frac{A_i - B_i}{A_i} \right|. \tag{3}$$

Here, A and B are the target and source case, respectively. A_i and B_i represent their elements. Moreover, $N = 4$ indicates the item number of the problem to be solved.

Case Reuse. We took the source case with the most significant similarity as the solved case and recommended it to the MAS to simulate user behaviour.

Case Revision and Retain. We can revise the suggested parameter values based on the community's evolution in user behaviour while recommending user behaviour. The system retains the revised cases in the case base for future use.

5   A Simulator for Influence Prediction

As shown in Fig. 2, the simulator built from the NetLogo platform [25] consists of four areas: input area, control area, interaction area, and result area.

- **Input area** sets the simulator initialization parameters, including the initial parameters of agents, the maximum run times (ticks), and reputation rules.

- **Control area** includes the setup button and go button. The former performs model initialization, while the latter controls the running of the simulator.
- **Interaction area** shows the information on the interactions between agents. The small monitor window shows agents and their environment. The white humanoid turtles are agents representing users who can create and vote on posts. Blue and red squares are patches representing questions and answers, respectively. These patches generated and updated by turtles (agents) have no behaviour.
- **Result area** collects the information of agents and their environment to capture emergence for predicting the influence of reputation mechanisms.

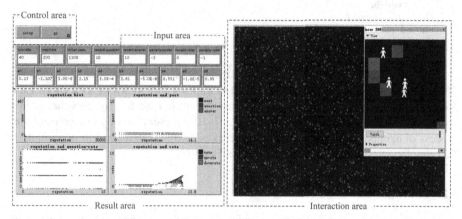

Fig. 2. Global vision of the developed simulator.

5.1 Overall Algorithm of the Simulator

As shown in Algorithm 1, the inputs of the simulator are agents' initial parameter set *PA*, including initial agent number and attribute parameters, the reputation rule parameter set *PN*, agents' growth rate *joinRate*, and the maximum simulation times *maxTicks*, describing the working days of the community.

Algorithm 1 : Reputation mechanism simulator

Input: $PA, PT, joinRate, maxTicks$
Output: $AG, POST$
 1: $tick \leftarrow 0$
 2: $POST \leftarrow \emptyset$
 3: $AG \leftarrow$ genSimulationData(PA)
 4: $CB \leftarrow$ genCaseBase()
 5: **while** $tick < maxTicks$ **do**
 6:     $AG \leftarrow AG \cup$ newAgent($joinRate$)
 7:     **for** $ag \in AG$ **do**
 8:         $solvedCase \leftarrow$ selectCase(ag, CB)
 9:         $POST \leftarrow$ do($ag, solvedCase, POST, PT$)
10:     **end for**
11:     $tick \leftarrow tick + 1$
12: **end while**
13: return $AG, POST$

The first two lines clear the simulation tick and the agent interaction environment. The third line generates the simulation data to improve the prediction efficiency. Line 4 creates the case base stored as the List data structure. Line 6 represents that agents are continually added to the simulator. Lines 7–10 represent the ongoing contribution process of agents. The action selection process of agents is described in Algorithm 2. The simulation number is controlled by lines 5 and 11.

5.2 The Algorithm of SelectCase

The behaviour generation of agents is shown in Algorithm 2. The inputs are contributor ag and the case base CB. Lines 1–2 initialize the parameters $maxSim$ and $solvedCase$, representing the maximum similarity and solved case, respectively. Lines 3–9 describe the solved case selection procedure of ag. Here, the function calSimilarity evaluates the similarity between ag and each case. The algorithm selects the case with the greatest similarity as the solved case to simulate the users' behaviour.

Algorithm 2 : selectCase

Input: ag, CB
Output: $solvedCase$
 1: $maxSim \leftarrow 0$
 2: $solvedCase \leftarrow \emptyset$
 3: **for** $case \in CB$ **do**
 4:     $sim \leftarrow calSimilarity(ag, case)$
 5:     **if** $sim > maxSim$ **then**
 6:         $sim \leftarrow maxSim$
 7:         $solvedCase \leftarrow case$
 8:     **end if**
 9: **end for**
10: return $solvedCase$

---

6 Experiment Evaluation

In this section, we evaluate the MASC using the case in Sect. 3 as an example.

6.1 Research Questions

RQ1: Can MASC Predict How the Incentives Impact the Q&A Community? One of our fundamental but essential requirements for the method is that the predicted effects should be consistent with those observed in actual communities. The goal of RQ1 is to test whether our predictions are consistent with the observations from the community.

RQ2: Does MASC'S Predictive Performance Show Consistency Across Different Data Sets? Our predictions are executed across various language communities. These communities would exhibit variances in prediction performance due to disparities in data sets. We expect a high degree of consistency in the predictive performance employing data from multiple communities. RQ2 aims to assess the consistency of our method's predictive performance across different datasets.

6.2 Evaluation Methodology

Dataset. We examined the impact of the newly revised rules on November 13, 2019, on the top five SO language communities. The data set covers users who contributed between June 1, 2019, and May 31, 2020, and ignores users who have been dormant in the community for a long time. The datasets are from the Stack Exchange data dump website[2]. The number of users and their posts are shown in Table 4. Users1 and posts1 are the numbers of users and posts created in the five top language communities between June 1 and November 12, 2019. Similarly, users2 and posts2 are the numbers of users and posts on the communities between November 13, 2019, and May 31, 2020. To improve the prediction efficiency, we used one per cent of the users in real language communities as the simulation data. The reputation distribution of both users is similar to ensure that the simulation data has sufficient ability to represent real data.

Table 4. An overview of the five top language communities in SO (2019.06.01–2020.05.31)

Language	User1	Post1	User2	Post2
Python	110,842	112,960	136,816	175,901
JavaScript	101,876	95,046	115,548	136,500
Java	70,947	63,108	81,083	85,994
C#	49,932	47,654	54,661	59,761
PHP	38,310	33,842	42,092	43,206

---

[2] https://archive.org/details/stackexchange.

Experimental Setup. We first constructed a user behaviour case base using user behaviour data collected between June 1, 2019, and November 12, 2019. Subsequently, we generated simulation data for real communities. Following that, we ran the simulator with the newly revised reputation rules on the simulation data to simulate the process of user interactions within the community. Finally, we captured the simulator's emergence to predict the new rules' impact on the community.

Evaluation Metrics. We evaluated the prediction accuracy of our method from the trend and deviation. For the former, we used Pearson correlation coefficient (*pcc*) [26] to calculate the consistency between the emergence of the simulator and that of the community, as described in Eq. 4. For the latter, we used average value approximation (*ava*) for the deviation between the two types of emergence, as described in Eq. 5. In addition, we used the harmonic value of the two indices to evaluate our predictive performance (Eq. 6).

$$pcc(S, M) = \frac{\sum_{i=1}^{n} (S_i - \bar{S})(M_i - \bar{M})}{\sqrt{(S_i - \bar{S})^2}\sqrt{(M_i - \bar{M})^2}}. \tag{4}$$

$$ava(S, M) = 1 - \frac{1}{n}\sum_{i=1}^{n} \frac{|S_i - M_i|}{\max(S)}. \tag{5}$$

$$acc(S, M) = \frac{pcc(S, M) + ava(S, M)}{2}. \tag{6}$$

S and M represent the emergence of Stack Overflow and MASC, respectively. Accordingly, S_i and M_i are their ith elements, respectively.

6.3   Result

RQ1. To evaluate the prediction accuracy of the method, we took the Python language community as an example. We compared the emergence of the prediction with the real community emergence between November 13, 2019, and May 31, 2020. The adopted evaluation metrics are from Eqs. 4–6.

As shown in Fig. 3(a) and Fig. 3(b), users' posting-activeness and voting-activeness increase as their reputation increases. Our method accurately predicted the influence of reputation mechanisms on them with accuracies of 0.848 and 0.867, respectively.

The prediction of user preferences presents different performances. Figure 3(c) shows no significant correlation between user question-rate and reputation, and our prediction accuracy is only 0.333. In contrast, users' upvote-rate tends to decrease with the increase in reputation, which is predicted with an accuracy of 0.908 in Fig. 3(d).

Users generate their behaviour with a certain degree of randomness, leading to some deviation between our method and the real community regarding the quantity of user behaviour. In contrast, our method performs better in user behaviour trend prediction. SO user behaviour increases significantly as their reputation grows (see Fig. 4). Our method predicted the effect of reputation on user behaviour with an accuracy above 0.69. The prediction accuracy of questioning and answering is 0.69 and 0.872, respectively, and that of upvoting and downvoting is 0.77 and 0.805, respectively.

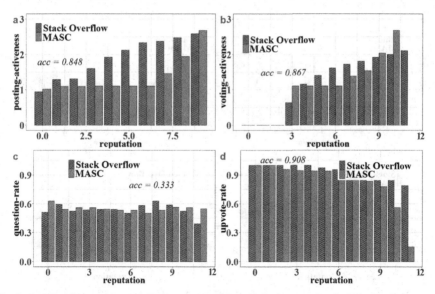

Fig. 3. Attribute emergence prediction on the Python language community. The horizontal axis represents the logarithmic values of user reputation.

Moreover, we investigated the influence of reputation mechanisms on community content structure. Affected by the reputation rules, SO users tend to provide answers fast to earn a great reputation [27]. As shown in Fig. 5, most users answer questions on the same or the next day. Our method predicted the influence with an accuracy of 0.97. Similarly, SO users are reluctant to answer questions with more than two answers because it is hard to earn a reputation for getting peers' upvotes. The prediction accuracy of our method is 0.935.

The result confirms that the proposed approach can predict the influence of the new reputation rules on the Python language community with adequate accuracy.

RQ2. To test the stability of the predictive performance of the proposed method, we ran the developed simulator to reproduce the influence of the reputation mechanism on the five top language communities. As shown in Table 5, most prediction accuracies on different language communities, except the emergence of question-rate, are greater than 0.65, and the deviation is less than 0.05. The low predictive performance of the question-rate emergence confirms that reputation mechanisms do not significantly affect users' question preferences.

The result in Table 5 provides evidence that the MASC has consistent prediction capability across various language communities.

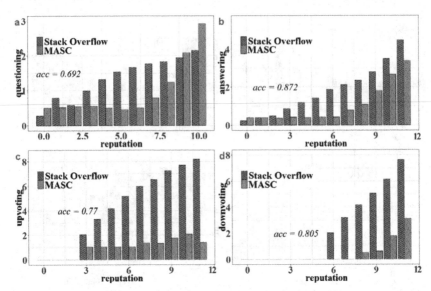

Fig. 4. Behaviour emergence prediction on the Python language community. The horizontal axis represents the logarithmic values of user reputation.

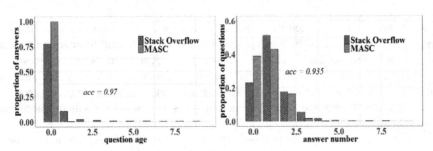

Fig. 5. Structure emergence prediction on the Python language community.

Table 5. The prediction performance of five top SO language communities

Type	Emergence	Mean	Max	Min	St. Dev
attribute	posting-activeness	0.849	0.868	0.807	0.024
	voting-activeness	0.868	0.883	0.863	0.008
	question-rate	0.543	0.883	0.333	0.207
	upvote-rate	0.865	0.908	0.842	0.026
behaviour	questioning	0.659	0.706	0.596	0.043
	answering	0.870	0.892	0.845	0.018
	upvoting	0.771	0.777	0.765	0.005
	downvoting	0.771	0.805	0.745	0.024
structure	fast-answers	0.926	0.949	0.894	0.020
	questions	0.879	0.888	0.866	0.010

7 Conclusion

Aiming to predict the effects of reputation mechanisms on Q&A communities, we presented a combination strategy based on MAS and CBR. Our method incorporates a formal representation model based on MAS, a case-based reasoning system for agent behaviour, and a simulator for predicting the impact of reputation systems. To demonstrate the accuracy of our approach in predicting the effects of reputation mechanisms on actual communities, we conducted an empirical study using the Stack Overflow reputation rules. Our approach inspires academics to investigate the emergence of complex socio-technical systems, such as Q&A communities and gives community administrators guidelines for anticipating the impact of incentives.

Our strategy, however, has two drawbacks. First, we did not take into account how reputation rules can affect the quality of community content. Expertise is not a factor in constructing agent attributes in our method. Hence it cannot explain how reputation mechanisms control the quality of user contributions. Further refinement of our approach is necessary to investigate how reputation systems affect the quality of community content.

Second, there is no evidence to suggest that reputation mechanisms are the only factors affecting user contributions. It is important to carefully test the practicality of our method under the combined action of various incentive measures, such as badges and privileges, in real communities.

Future research will focus on improving our method by considering community content quality and the role of various incentives. We will test the applicability of our prediction method in other online communities. Moreover, our approach will aid the incentive design for Q&A communities.

Acknowledgements. This work was supported by the National Science Foundation of China (Granted No: 62172426).

References

1. Goes, P.B., Guo, C., Lin, M.: Do incentive hierarchies induce user effort? Evidence from an online knowledge exchange. Inf. Syst. Res. **27**(3), 497–516 (2016)
2. Lu, Y., et al.: Motivation under gamification: an empirical study of developers' motivations and contributions in stack overflow. IEEE Trans. Softw. Eng. **48**(12), 4947–4963 (2022)
3. Srba, I., Bielikova, M.: Why is stack overflow failing? Preserving sustainability in community question answering. IEEE Softw. **33**(4), 80–89 (2016)
4. Gao, Y., Chen, Y., Liu, K.J.R.: Understanding sequential user behavior in social computing: to answer or to vote? IEEE Trans. Netw. Sci. Eng. **2**(3), 112–126 (2015)
5. Mogavi, R.H., Gujar, S., Ma, X., Hui, P.: HRCR: hidden Markov-based reinforcement to reduce churn in question answering forums. In: Nayak, A.C., Sharma, A. (eds.) PRICAI 2019. LNCS (LNAI), vol. 11670, pp. 364–376. Springer, Cham (2019). https://doi.org/10.1007/978-3-030-29908-8_29
6. Zhang, Y., Schaar, M.V.D.: Robust reputation protocol design for online communities: a stochastic stability analysis. IEEE J. Sel. Top. Signal Process. **7**(5), 907–920 (2013)
7. Jiao, Z., Chen, J., Kim, E.: Modeling the use of online knowledge community: a perspective of needs-affordances-features. Comput. Intell. Neurosci. **2021**, 3496807–3496818 (2021)
8. Mnif, M., Muller-Schloer, C.: Quantitative emergence. In: 2006 IEEE Mountain Workshop on Adaptive and Learning Systems, pp. 78–84. IEEE, Logan (2006)
9. Gilbert, N., Terna, P.: How to build and use agent-based models in social science. Mind Soc. **1**(1), 57–72 (2000)
10. Dastani, M., Dix, J., Verhagen, H., Villata, S.: Normative multi-agent systems. Dagstuhl Rep. **8**(4), 72–103 (2018)
11. Mustapha, S.S.: Case-based reasoning for identifying knowledge leader within online community. Expert Syst. Appl. **97**, 244–252 (2018)
12. Xu, J., Yilmaz, L., Zhang, J.: Agent simulation of collaborative knowledge processing in Wikipedia. In: The 2008 Spring Simulation Multiconference (SpringSim 2008), pp. 19–25. ACM, Ottawa (2008)
13. Yang, Y., Mao, X., Xu, Z., Lu, Y.: Exploring CQA user contributions and their influence on answer distribution. In: The 32nd International Conference on Software Engineering and Knowledge Engineering, pp. 1–6. KSIR Virtual Conference Center, Pittsburgh (2020)
14. Yu, F., Janssen, M.A.: How behavior of users impacts the success of online Q&A communities. Adv. Complex Syst. **23**(06), 2050016–2050038 (2021)
15. Aumayr, E., Hayes, C.: Modelling user behaviour in online Q&A communities for customer support. E-Commer. Web Technol. **88**, 179–191 (2014)
16. Jiang, G., Feng, X., Liu, W., Liu, X.: Clicking position and user posting behavior in online review systems: a data-driven agent-based modeling approach. Inf. Sci. **512**, 161–174 (2020)
17. Aha, D.W., Watson, I.: COBRA: a CBR-based approach for predicting users actions in a web site. In: Aha, D.W., Watson, I. (eds.) ICCBR 2001. LNCS, vol. 2080, pp. 336–346. Springer, Heidelberg (2001). https://doi.org/10.1007/3-540-44593-5_24
18. Zehraoui, F., Kanawati, R., Salotti, S.: Hybrid neural network and case based reasoning system for web user behavior clustering and classification. Int. J. Hybrid Intell. Syst. **7**(3), 171–186 (2010)
19. Herrero-Reder, I., Urdiales, C., Peula, J.M., Sandoval, F.: CBR based reactive behavior learning for the memory-prediction framework. Neurocomputing **250**, 18–27 (2017)
20. Lee, H., Ahn, H., Han, I.: VCR: Virtual community recommender using the technology acceptance model and the user's needs type. Expert Syst. Appl. **33**(4), 984–995 (2007)
21. Ajjouri, M. E., Benhadou, S., Medromi, H.: Use of O-MaSE methodology for designing efficient intrusion detection based on MAS to learn new attacks. In: 24th International Conference on Cloud Technologies & Applications, pp. 1–7. IEEE, Marrakech (2015)

22. Perez, B., Lang, C., Henriet, J., Philippe, L., Auber, F.: Risk prediction in surgery using case-based reasoning and agent-based modelization. Comput. Biol. Med. **128**(104040), 1–11 (2021)
23. Pinto, T., Faia, R., Navarro-Caceres, M., Santos, G., Corchado, J.M., Vale, Z.: Multi-agent-based CBR recommender system for intelligent energy management in buildings. IEEE Syst. J. **13**(1), 1084–1095 (2019)
24. Landeis, K., Pews, G., Minor, M.: Particle swarm optimization in small case bases for software effort estimation. In: Keane, M.T., Wiratunga, N. (eds.) ICCBR 2022. LNCS, vol. 13405, pp. 209–224. Springer, Cham (2022). https://doi.org/10.1007/978-3-031-14923-8_14
25. Tisue, S., Wilensky, U.: NetLogo: Design and implementation of a multi-agent modeling environment. In: Proceedings of the Agent 2004 Conference on Social Dynamics: Interaction, Reflexivity and Emergence, pp. 1–10. Springer, Chicago (2004). https://digital.library.unt.edu/ark:/67531/metadc901709/m2/1/high_res_d/939907.pdf
26. Emerson, R.W.: Causation and Pearson's correlation coefficient. J. Vis. Impairment Blindness **109**(3), 242–244 (2015)
27. Lu, Y., Mao, X., Zhou, M., Zhang, Y., Wang, T., Li, Z.: Haste makes waste: an empirical study of fast answers in Stack Overflow. In: 36th IEEE International Conference on Software Maintenance and Evolution, pp. 23–34. IEEE, Adelaide (2020)

Retrieval of Similar Cases to Improve the Diagnosis of Diabetic Retinopathy

Álvaro Sanz-Ramos[1], Luis Ariza-López[1], Cristina Montón-Giménez[2], and Antonio A. Sánchez-Ruiz[1(✉)] (iD)

[1] Departamento de Ingeniería del Software e Inteligencia Artificial, Instituto de Tecnología del Conocimiento, Universidad Complutense de Madrid, Madrid, Spain
{alsanz16,luiariza,antsanch}@ucm.es
[2] Hospital Universitario Severo Ochoa, Madrid, Spain

Abstract. Diabetic retinopathy is the leading cause of new cases of blindness in adults and its early detection is fundamental. In this work we propose a technique to retrieve similar fundus images of already diagnosed eyes to support the physicians when they must diagnose a new patient. The similarity between images is computed using standard distances on image embeddings extracted from the last layers of a neural network. Our preliminary experiments seem to confirm that embeddings encode important medical information, the similarity between embeddings aligns with the specialist's concept of similarity, and the similar images retrieved are almost always relevant for the diagnosis.

Keywords: Case-based Reasoning · Deep Learning · Image embeddings · Diabetic retinopathy

1 Introduction

Diabetes is one of the most widespread and difficult to control diseases today. It is estimated that 783 million people will be living with diabetes by 2045, and the cost of treating the disease has tripled in the last 15 years[1]. Diabetic Retinopathy (DR) is a common complication of diabetes (affecting 40–45% of diabetic patients) caused by vascular damage from persistently elevated blood sugar. In fact, DR is already the leading cause of new cases of blindness in adults and costs more than $500 million in the United States alone.

Early detection is key in this disease, as the most obvious signs appear when the disease is already too advanced to be effectively treated. The most common detection technique is *ophthalmoscopy*, which consists of dilating the pupil to photograph the retinal *fundus* (which includes the central and peripheral retina, the optic disc and the macula) using a specialized camera. The diagnosis of the disease is then made by a physician, who carefully examines the photographs

---

[1] Diabetes Atlas https://diabetesatlas.org/.

S. Massie and S. Chakraborti (Eds.): ICCBR 2023, LNAI 14141, pp. 408–423, 2023.
https://doi.org/10.1007/978-3-031-40177-0_26

to determine whether the patient has the disease and its degree of development (mild, moderate, severe or proliferative).

Diagnosis of the disease is not without difficulties. The equipment needed to take the photographs is expensive and the training of specialists capable of interpreting the images requires years of study. Some signs of the disease, such as microaneurysm or narrowing of the blood vessels, are difficult to detect even by trained professionals. In fact, studies have found that different physicians agree on the exact classification of DR in one eye in only 69% of cases [5]. For all these reasons, research has been underway for years on the development of automated methods to effectively detect DR to diagnose the disease earlier and thus treat the disease more effectively.

Based on previous research in other medical settings and the availability of labeled datasets, we believe that Case-based Reasoning (CBR) strategies could play an interesting role providing support during the diagnosis of DR. CBR is based on the idea that similar problems tend to require similar solutions, and it is usually easier to build those solutions by adapting solutions applied to previous similar problems than to build them from scratch from general domain knowledge. This problem-solving strategy is more intuitive and transparent than other approaches based on black-box models, being especially interesting in some domains such as, for example, medicine. For example, when a specialist must diagnose a new patient, we can provide similar cases already diagnosed that can be of support.

The retrieving of similar cases, however, is challenging when working with non-symbolic representations of information such as medical images. In this work, we propose the use of image *embeddings*, generated by a deep neural network architecture, and standard distances to retrieve similar cases. Embeddings are a compact, low-dimensional representation that tends to group images with similar characteristics. Moreover, training deep learning models can be a time-consuming and computationally expensive process. To speed up training, we preprocess the images and use an efficient network architecture pretrained on ImageNet. Transfer learning has proven to be a very effective technique even among domains as different as object recognition and medical image diagnosis. Finally, our preliminary experiments have yielded promising results: similarity between embeddings seems aligned with the specialist's concept of similarity when analyzing the images, and the images retrieved are almost always relevant.

In summary, the main contributions of our work are:

- Using a efficient network architecture pretrained on ImageNet to train a competitive DR classifier with low computational resources.
- Carefully selecting an embedding-based representation that allows a kNN classifier to obtain network-like performance.
- A preliminary evaluation with a specialist that seems to confirm that similarity between embeddings is aligned with similarity from a medical point of view.

The rest of the paper is organized as follows. Next section describes the related work. Section 3 describes in more detail the disease and its diagnosis. Section 4 describes the dataset used and the preprocessing of the images. Section 5 describes the neural network architecture used to diagnose DR from images of the retina. Section 6 explains how to perform a semantic search to retrieve similar images using embeddings extracted from the last layers of the network. Section 7 describes the experiments we have conducted with the help of an ophthalmologist to validate our proposal. Finally, the paper ends with some conclusions and lines of future work.

2   Related Work

Case-based reasoning (CBR) has been successfully applied in the medical field for clinical decision-making applied to therapy and diagnosis [19]. Respect to cancer treatment, researchers used clinical data to select classified breast cancer tissue and then reduced the cases by searching for similar DNA methylation patterns [2]. Other researchers performed adaptation of the adjustment of parameters before segmentation on an existing CBR system to segment renal parenchyma [15].

CBR has also been used in conjunction with deep learning techniques. Retrieval is an important aspect in which neural networks can play an important role. We find examples in the literature were Class-to-Class Siamese Networks [24] or Siamese Graph Neural Networks [8] have been used for this purpose. Other works study the capabilities and limitations of neural networks to learn adaptation knowledge in CBR systems [23,25].

Regarding the use of embeddings, it is known that the layer from with the embeddings are extracted may vary their quality [12]. In the medical field, there are several works that use embeddings. For example, to perform medical image report generation where a visual attention branch captures image embeddings [22]; to label medical images to introduce as much novelty as possible to an existing dataset [3]; or for abnormalities detection on chest radiographs [6].

Medical Image similarity has been subject of study due to the interest in accurately relating information in the different images for diagnosis and treatment. For example, color and texture histograms help to identify similar images from an endoscopy and reduce the entire volume of frames, so it will be easier for a diagnosing physician [9].

3   Diabetic Retinopathy

Diabetic retinopathy (DR) is a common complication of diabetes, caused by high blood sugar levels damaging the blood vessels and nerve tissue of the retina. The earliest anatomical changes linked to the disease are the narrowing of the retinal arteries and the dysfunction of neurons of the inner retina. As the disease progresses, damage may reach the outer retina, provoking subtle visual dysfunction, and weaken the blood-retinal barrier, that protects the retina from many substances present in blood, as immune cells or toxins.

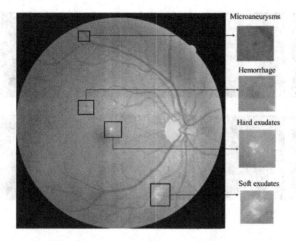

Fig. 1. Example of lesions associated to diabetic retinopathy [1].

In the later stages of the disease, the basement membrane of the retinal blood vessels thickens and the capillaries degenerate. This leads to a progressive ischemia of the tissues, which leads to degeneration of the neurons and glial cells of the retina. Narrower capillaries are prone to the appearance of micro-aneurysms, which may cause swelling or leak of them. DR is comorbid with macular edema, caused by the deposition of fluid and protein under the macula of the eye, causing it to thicken and swell.

According to the International Clinical Diabetic Retinopathy Disease Severity Scale [21], the severity of DR can be graded into five stages (0–4): no retinopathy (0), mild non-proliferative DR (NPDR) (1), moderate NPDR (2), severe NPDR (3), and proliferative DR (4). The grading depends on the number and size of different related lesions and complications.

Figure 1 shows some examples of lesions indicating the presence of DR. It is important to note that lesion detection is a challenge even for medical specialists after several years of training, especially in the early stages of the disease. Besides, the quality of the image is usually not this good and depends on several factors over with the physician has little control, including the age of the equipment and the patient cooperation.

4   Dataset and Preprocessing

For training our model, we have chosen the EyePacs Dataset [4]. This dataset was offered for the Diabetic Retinopathy Detection Kaggle competition[2] and it can be freely used for research after accepting the conditions of the competition. The dataset has a total of 88,704 labeled images, divided into two sets: a training set consisting of 35,126 images and a test with 53,578 files.

---

[2] https://kaggle.com/competitions/diabetic-retinopathy-detection.

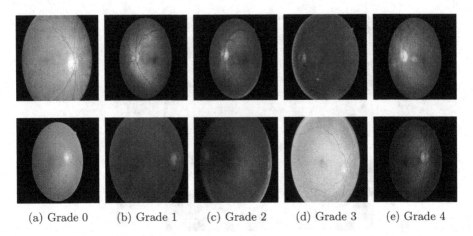

(a) Grade 0   (b) Grade 1   (c) Grade 2   (d) Grade 3   (e) Grade 4

Fig. 2. Example of images of different classes. Notice the different color, brightness and scale of each image.

The images come from a variety of cameras and may have different colors, resolutions and capture different part of the eyes. Also, different images may have different orientations, depending on the type of equipment used to take the photograph.

Both train and test images have been graded for DR by a professional ophthalmologist: the rating is a number between 0 and 4 representing no DR, mild, moderate, severe DR, or proliferative DR. Concerning class distribution, the dataset is heavily unbalanced, as no DR images account for 73.48% of the training set, while the Mild, Moderate, Severe and Proliferative DR have a representation of 15.06%, 6.95%, 2.49% and 2.02% respectively. Figure 2 shows examples of different fundus images of the dataset according to the degree of diabetic retinopathy diagnosed. The last nuance about the dataset is the strong correlation between the left and right eye grading (Pearson correlation coefficient $\rho = 0.85$), which made us explore *binocular* methods, that consider information coming from both eyes for grading.

The first step of the preprocessing is to crop the background as it does not give any information, however, this is not immediate, as the color varies in the images, although it is dark in all cases. After several approximations, we used a scheme inspired by the one carried by the winner of the Kaggle competition, Ben Graham[3], consisting in 3 steps: scaling down the image, so the radius has a fixed length by finding the diameter of the eye, then we overlap Gaussian noise over the image by convolving it with a kernel created by extracting values from a $Normal(\eta = 0, \sigma = 10)$ distribution and lastly, we homogenize the background and crop the image with radius equal to 0.9 times the radius of the eye and then set all the pixels outside the circle to gray.

---

[3] https://www.kaggle.com/competitions/diabetic-retinopathy-detection/discussion/15801.

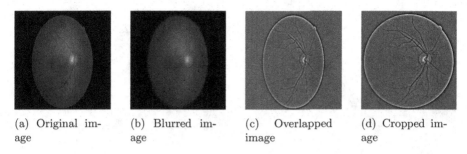

(a) Original image

(b) Blurred image

(c) Overlapped image

(d) Cropped image

Fig. 3. Process of preprocessing an image. The original image is rectangular, so it appears stretched when scaled to a squared image.

Figure 3 shows the entire preprocessing process for an image, except for changes in scale. The application of Gaussian noise successfully highlights the blood vessels and the main anatomical structures, as the optic nerve. It also removes some undesirable effects, as the changes in brightness. While this method sacrifices most color information, we have found that color is mostly dependent on the brightness conditions and does not contain diagnostic information by itself. Since we have limited data, it is convenient to use data augmentation techniques to create small variations of images. We apply the following transformations (from the Albumentations[4] library) to each image with probability 0.5: scaling the image by a random factor, rotating it by a random angle, flipping it vertically, horizontally or both. Also, normalization is applied after data augmentation and immediately before feeding the image to the model. The normalized image I' is calculated from the augmented image I as:

$$I' = \frac{I - \mu}{\sigma}$$

where μ is the mean and σ is the standard deviation, calculated separately for each channel over the whole training set.

5   Network Architecture and Training

To generate the embeddings we use an EfficientNetv2-B3 network [20], a medium-sized convolutional neural network which strikes a good compromise between accuracy and complexity. The output of the convolutional network is pooled using *global average pooling* and fed to a classifier, designed as a stack of four dense layers with decreasing width (Fig. 4).

Using a multilayer classifier increases the risk of overfitting and usually does not improve performance, but serves as a gentle way to perform dimensionality reduction on the features extracted by the convolutional network.

---

[4] https://albumentations.ai.

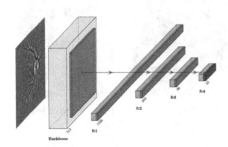

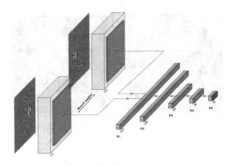

Fig. 4. Architecture for embeddings extraction.

Fig. 5. Architecture for predictions. The classifier *blends* the information from both images

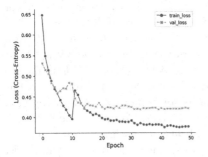

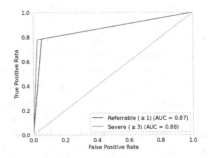

Fig. 6. Loss evolution during training.

Fig. 7. The ROC curve shows promising results with an area under the curve of 0.87 for referrable cases (some sign of diabetic retinopathy) and 0.88 for severe cases (at least grade 3).

The EfficientNet implementation, from the open source library *Pytorch Image Models*[5], has been pretrained on ImageNet21K, a large dataset for general purpose image classification problems. This technique has been proved to improve performance and reduce training time in several types of datasets (including medical ones [10]) even if they are quite different to the pretraining one, as the network can reuse most of the features originally learned [16].

The model was trained on the preprocessed images from the EyePACS training dataset to grade diabetic retinopathy, using cross-entropy as the loss function. We found the best results using AdamW [11,14] as an optimization method, combined with L^2 weight decay and *label smoothing* [18] to prevent overfitting. We performed data augmentation to increase the effective size of the dataset, by randomly applying the following operations: a rescale by a random factor between 0.9 and 1.1, a rotation by a random amount of degrees and a vertical,

---

[5] https://github.com/rwightman/pytorch-image-models.

horizontal or mirror flip, each with probability 0.5. After the augmentation, the images were resized to a 512×512 resolution, normalized and fed to the model.

Figure 6 shows the evolution of train and validation loss during training: the peak on iteration 10 is caused by the inclusion of late dropout [7,13] to the first two layers of the classifier in order to address overfitting. The model was trained for 50 iterations (around 10 hours) on a single Nvidia GeForce GTX 1070 GPU.

To evaluate the performance of the model, we designed a variation of the classifier with twice as wide layers as the original (Fig. 5). The classifier is simultaneously fed the left and right eyes pooled features, so it can combine the information for both eyes, and will output a vector of *logits* containing the unnormalized probability of each grade of the disease for each eye. This classifier was trained independently using AdamW as the optimization method, freezing the weights of the convolutional network.

This classifier was fed five copies of each pair of images in the test dataset, each rotated independently by a random amount of degrees and normalized. We obtained the final prediction by computing $\sum_{i=0}^{4} i \operatorname{softmax}(y^{(k)})_i$ for each of the $y^{(1)}, \ldots, y^{(k)}$ vector of logits and averaging the results, exploiting the fact that the grades of the disease are ordered. Instead of rounding up the result to the closest integer, we used the set of thresholds that maximized Cohen's κ over the validation set (0.57, 1.37, 2.30, 3.12).

The final accuracy of the model is 83.31% and the obtained Cohen's kappa score is $\kappa = 0.8491$. The ROC curve (Fig. 7) shows promising result, with solid detection of the disease from the early stages. We found that our model compares favourably to much larger architectures reported in the literature, requiring a fraction of the computational resources both for training and inference. To provide some context, these results would set us second in the *Diabetic Retinopathy Detection* Kaggle competition, with a difference of just 0.0005 from the first solution, which uses an ensemble of three neural networks, each one significantly larger than ours. While ensembles are a reliable way to improve performance, they are inconvenient since they increase training costs and, what is more important, multiply the time and resources needed for inference. Our approach shows the viability of using pretrained smaller models to obtain excellent results in a computationally efficient way.

6 Semantic Search Based on Embeddings

To generate embeddings for each image, we use the neural network from the previous section (Fig. 4) as a feature extractor by feeding each image of the dataset rotated by a random number of degrees and normalized. A differently sized representation is extracted by intercepting the activation of the different layers of the classifier. This process generates multiple embeddings for each image, of dimensions 1536, 384, 96 and 32.

Interestingly, we found that applying classical dimensionality reduction techniques (as UMAP, t-SNE or PCA) to the output of the convolutional neural

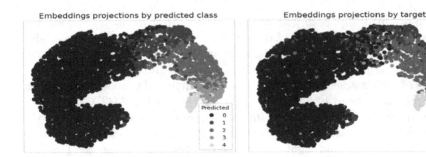

Fig. 8. Projections of the embeddings of a sample (N = 5,000) from the training dataset, labelled by predicted DR grade and target (real grade)

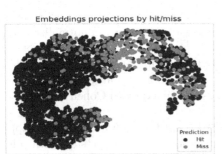

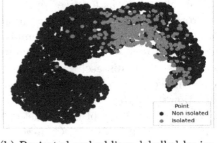

(a) Projected embeddings labelled by hit/miss on the original image (grade predicted correctly)

(b) Projected embeddings labelled by isolation (distance to the closest point is over two standard deviations of the average distance)

Fig. 9. Projections of the embeddings of a sample (N = 5,000) from the training dataset, labelled by hit/miss and isolation

network creates very low-quality embeddings. In contrast, the multilayer classifier works as a non-linear context-aware technique for dimensionality reduction that produces much better results.

The generated embeddings have a different nature than the ones created by an *autoencoder* architecture, as the latter encodes the input data (the graphical structure of the image itself) while the former encodes the diagnostic information of the image, ideally disregarding extraneous information, as varying brightness or contrast conditions.

Since the output layer of the classifier is purely linear, the last layers of the classifier should represent images of different classes in (approximately) linearly separable regions. Therefore, we should expect that some diagnostic factors (at least the grading of the image itself) are encoded in the spatial structure of the embeddings. Figure 8 puts this hypothesis to test: it shows a visualization of the 32-dimensional embeddings for a sample of 3.000 points, projected to the plane using UMAP [17] and labelled both by predicted and target class. The

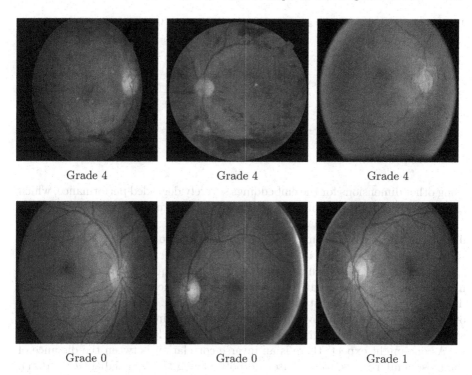

Fig. 10. Two instances (one per row) of retrieval of the two most similar images to a given one (leftmost image), measuring similarity as the distance between 96-dimensional embeddings using cosine distance.

image leads us to two relevant assertions: (1) the network successfully creates a representation of the input image that spatially encodes diagnostic information of the disease and (2) the spatial structure is robust enough to persist after severe dimensionality reduction.

Figure 9a explores the distribution of embeddings of wrongly predicted images. These images concentrate over some small regions of the space of the embeddings, which can be used to classify "high risk" areas, where the performance of the model may be suboptimal. Interestingly, these zones mostly coincide with the areas of distribution of isolated points (Fig. 9b), characterized as those points which distance to the closest point is over two standard deviations the average one.

In order to further test our assertions, we implemented a k-NN classifier using the 96-dimensional embeddings and different metrics. The class is obtained as the weighted average of the neighbors, weighted by the inverse of the distance.

The results, shown in Table 1, are impressively solid, achieving even a higher accuracy than the neural network for some choices of k and a reasonable value for Cohen's κ. The results are robust between metrics and choices of k but

Table 1. Results obtained by a k-NN classifier ($k = 11$) on 96-dimensional embeddings.

	k = 3		k = 11		k = 15	
	Accuracy	κ	Accuracy	κ	Accuracy	κ
Manhattan	0.8322	0.7810	0.8437	0.7945	0.8439	0.6078
Euclidean	0.8324	0.7825	0.8439	0.7951	0.8440	0.6084
Cosine	0.8336	0.7840	0.8431	0.7958	0.8425	0.6059

using other dimensions for the embeddings severely degraded performance, which reinforces the importance of using adequately sized embeddings for each task.

We can use the fact that the spatial structure of the embeddings contains diagnostic information to model *semantic search*, the retrieval of images with similar diagnostic signs to a given one, as a *nearest neighbor search* problem.

Figure 10 shows the result of applying this technique to find the two images in the train set most similar to a base image from the test set, by using cosine distance to measure the distance between embeddings. We found that in 80.49% of the cases, the image recovered as the closest one using cosine distance has the same grading than the original one and is within one level in 93% of the cases.

As one might expect, there is an inverse correlation between the distance of the most similar image to the base and both having the same label ($\rho = -0.21$). In fact, an increase of the cosine distance between both images of 0.01, reduces the probability of both having the same grade by 50.39% on average.

Surprisingly, given the robustness of k-NN to the choice of metrics, we found that different distance functions retrieved generally different images and the measured similarity of a given image can significantly vary between metrics. For example, we found that the closest image according to the cosine distance only was between the top 5 closest images according to the Euclidean distance in 38.53% of cases.

7   Experiments and Results

Two preliminary experiments have been conducted with the collaboration of an ophthalmologist with experience in the treatment of retinal diseases.

The purpose of the first experiment is to check whether the similarity computed from the image embeddings is consistent with the specialist's intuition of similarity when analyzing the same images. To this end, we show the specialist 1 unlabeled base image from the test set and 5 labeled images from the training set. The 5 images from the training set were selected according to their similarity to the test image so that the most similar image and one in the first 4 quintiles appear. The specialist is then asked to sort the images from the training set in order of similarity to the base image. The specialist can view all the images as many times as she wants with no time limit. This process was repeated 10 times with 10 different images from the test set.

Table 2. Summary of the results of experiment 1. The first column contains the ids of the base images. The second column shows the specialist's order (no order is assumed within each set). The last column shows the order according to the cosine similarity and the embeddings.

Base	Specialist order	Embeddings order
1935l	{18311 46571 129001 277821} {282271}	18311 277821 129001 46571 282271
208831	{246561} {162231 21921r 32104r 351321}	246561 351321 21921r 32104r 162231
30476r	{11219r} {13843r 204641 25222r 323581}	11219r 25222r 13843r 323581 204641
314661	{24711r 29906r 334691} {309191} {10047r}	29906r 24711r 334691 309191 10047r
36651r	{27153r} {13714r 133121 3395r}	27153r 133121 13714r 67881 3395r
37151r	{33251r} {3291 6569r 29141r}	33251r 29141r 6569r 3291 314281
38582r	{74871} {263811 279731} {282271} {172211}	74871 279731 263811 172211 282271

At the beginning of the experiment, the specialist asked what was exactly meant by "similarity between images". There are many different criteria that can be taken into consideration: same eye (right or left), similar age of the patient, same type of lesions, same degree of DR development, images made by the same type of imaging device, ... As our neural network calculates the embeddings in the context of a system to diagnose the degree of DR, we instructed the specialist to only take into consideration lesions related to the diagnosis of that disease. Once the similarity criterion was set, the specialist made us realize that she could not sort the images corresponding to healthy eyes, as none of them had lesions. After analyzing the situation, we asked the specialist to group the images according to their similarity to the test image, but without having to order the images in the same group.

Of the 10 test images analyzed, 3 were discarded because they did not have adequate quality for diagnosis. The results of the other 7 images are shown in Table 2. In most cases, the specialist grouped the images into 2 or 3 sets using the type and number of lesions present in each image as the main criterion (her diagnosis of the degree of RD did not always match the image label). These sets should be considered as equivalence classes with no internal order but linearly ordered with respect to its similarity with the base image.

To measure the agreement between the expert's similarity ranking

$$\{d_1^{(1)}, \dots, d_{n_1}^{(1)}\}, \dots, \{d_1^{(m)} \dots, d_{n_m}^{(m)}\}$$

with the order retrieved from the embeddings $\mathcal{O} = d_{j_1}^{i_1} < d_{j_2}^{i_2} < \dots < d_{j_l}^{i_l}$, we define the cost of a transposition as $c(d_{j_1}^{(i_1)}, d_{j_2}^{(i_2)}) = \|i_1 - i_2\|$ and calculate the sequence of transpositions of minimum cost transforming the order $d_1^{(1)} < d_2^{(1)} < \dots < d_{n_1}^{(1)} < d_1^{(2)} < \dots < d_{n_m}^{(m)}$ into $\mathcal{O}$.

We found this distance to be 0 in all but one case. Notably, the image retrieved as the most similar one using the embeddings is classified by the expert in the group of the most similar images in all cases, which sustains the claim that our strategy retrieves diagnostically similar images.

Table 3. Summary of the results of experiment 2. The first 2 columns contain the id of the base image to be diagnosed and its initial diagnosis. Columns 3 and 4 show the ids and labels of the 2 most similar images retrieved. The last 3 columns show, respectively, whether the specialist considered the retrieved images to be similar to the original one, whether seeing those images was useful and if, after viewing the images, she wanted to modify her initial diagnosis.

Base	Diagnosis	Retr. images	Retr. tags	Similar?	Useful?	Modify diagnosis?
1935r	0	18311 16115r	0 0	yes	yes	no
208831	2	246561 236051	3 2	yes	yes	no
30476r	3	11219r 41551	3 3	yes	yes	no
314661	0	29906r 12448r	0 0	yes	yes	no
36651r	2	27153r 175221	3 2	no	no	no
37151r	1	33251r 235411	2 1	yes	yes	no
38582r	0	74871 25632r	0 0	yes	yes	no

The purpose of the second experiment is to make a preliminary study of the usefulness and quality of the retrieved images to help the specialist in her diagnosis. To do this, we again showed the specialist the same 7 base images from the previous experiment and for each of them we followed the following protocol: (1) ask for an initial diagnosis of the image, (2) show the two most similar labeled images from the training set, (3) ask the specialist if she thought they were similar to the base image, (4) ask the specialist if it was useful to be able to see those images, and (5) ask if, in view of those images, she wanted to modify her initial diagnosis.

The results of the experiment are collected in the Table 3. The initial diagnosis of the specialist always corresponds to the label of one of the images retrieved using the embedding-based similarity and never differs by more than one degree from the other. Furthermore, in none of the cases are images of diseased eyes retrieved from healthy eyes or vice versa. All retrieved images were considered similar to the originals, except in the case of image 36651 in which the specialist indicated that the retrieved images had different types of lesions. In all other cases, the specialist considered that being able to view those similar images could be helpful for diagnostic support. In no case did the specialist modify her initial diagnosis.

Asked about the possibility of modifying the diagnosis if the system retrieved images with very different labels, the specialist said that she would continue to rely on her judgment unless the system could provide a really convincing explanation. Finally, asked about her overall impressions, she told us that she had been surprised by the system's ability to find similar images and that this feature could be useful for residents.

8 Conclusions

In this work we propose a technique to retrieve fundus images of already diagnosed eyes similar to undiagnosed ones, with the aim of providing relevant cases to a specialist who must diagnose whether a patient suffers from diabetic retinopathy (DR). The search for similar images is based on the use of embeddings extracted from the last layers of a neural network trained to diagnose DR. To speed up the network training, we preprocess the images, use an efficient network architecture (with a good trade-off between performance and size) and start from a pre-trained model on ImageNet. In addition, to improve the quality of the predictions we use images from both eyes of the patient.

The embeddings produced by the network encode information relevant for the diagnosis and group images corresponding to the same degree of the disease in contiguous areas of the latent space. Applying standard distances on the embeddings, we can perform semantic searches and retrieve images with similar medical characteristics. The choice of the distance function significantly influence the images retrieved but we have not found convincing evidence on which function better reflects diagnostic similarity.

Preliminary experiments performed with the collaboration of an ophthalmologist have produced promising results that encourage us to continue this line of research. The similarity between embeddings (measured by the cosine distance) seems aligned with the specialist's concept of similarity when analyzing the images, and the similar images retrieved are almost always relevant.

During the experiments we have learned that the concept of inter-image distance for a specialist is not so simple to define and can be based on a multitude of factors. Moreover, it is much easier for the specialist to define a partial ordering relationship between images than to order them by similarity. In general, the retrieval of diagnosed images is useful to reinforce the specialist's opinion, but it is not sufficient to change the specialist's mind.

However, there is the risk of leading the expert to confusion, by presenting images that the specialist does not consider related. Our conjecture, supported by our experiments, is that the mismatch between embedding distance and semantic similarity is more likely to happen for embeddings in certain "high risk" areas of the latent space. These regions share defining characteristics: they are formed by relatively isolated points, they contain points from different classes and are much more likely to contain misclassified points. The identification of these areas can be used to detect the cases where retrieval based in semantic embeddings may offer suboptimal results.

Acknowledgements. This work has been partially supported by the Spanish Committee of Science and Innovation (PID2020-114596RB-C21, PID2021-123368OB-I00) and the UCM (Group 921330). We would also like to thank everyone involved in the creation and publication of the EyePacs Dataset.

References

1. Alyoubi, W.L., Abulkhair, M.F., Shalash, W.M.: Diabetic retinopathy fundus image classification and lesions localization system using deep learning. Sensors **21**(11), 3704 (2021). https://doi.org/10.3390/s21113704
2. Bartlett, C.L., Liu, G., Bichindaritz, I.: Classifying breast cancer tissue through DNA methylation and clinical covariate based retrieval. In: Watson, I., Weber, R. (eds.) ICCBR 2020. LNCS (LNAI), vol. 12311, pp. 82–96. Springer, Cham (2020). https://doi.org/10.1007/978-3-030-58342-2_6
3. Chinn, E., Arora, R., Arnaout, R., Arnaout, R.: Enrich: exploiting image similarity to maximize efficient machine learning in medical imaging. medRxiv (2021)
4. Cuadros, J., Bresnick, G.: EyePACS: an adaptable telemedicine system for diabetic retinopathy screening. J. Diabetes Sci. Technol. **3**(3), 509–516 (2009). https://doi.org/10.1177/193229680900300315
5. Gangaputra, S.S., et al.: Comparison of standardized clinical classification with fundus photograph grading for the assessment of diabetic retinopathy and diabetic macular edema severity. Retina **33**, 1393–1399 (2013)
6. Gozzi, N., et al.: Image embeddings extracted from CNNs outperform other transfer learning approaches in classification of chest radiographs. Diagnostics **12**(9) (2022). https://www.mdpi.com/2075-4418/12/9/2084
7. Hinton, G.E., Srivastava, N., Krizhevsky, A., Sutskever, I., Salakhutdinov, R.: Improving neural networks by preventing co-adaptation of feature detectors. CoRR abs/1207.0580 (2012). http://arxiv.org/abs/1207.0580
8. Hoffmann, M., Malburg, L., Klein, P., Bergmann, R.: Using Siamese graph neural networks for similarity-based retrieval in process-oriented case-based reasoning. In: Watson, I., Weber, R. (eds.) ICCBR 2020. LNCS (LNAI), vol. 12311, pp. 229–244. Springer, Cham (2020). https://doi.org/10.1007/978-3-030-58342-2_15
9. Ionescu, M., Glodeanu, A., Marinescu, I., Ionescu, A., Vere, C.: Similarity analysis for medical images using color and texture histograms. Curr. Health Sci. J. **48**(2), 196–202 (2022)
10. Kim, H.E., Cosa-Linan, A., Santhanam, N., Jannesari, M., Maros, M.E., Ganslandt, T.: Transfer learning for medical image classification: a literature review. BMC Med. Imaging **22**(1), 69 (2022). https://doi.org/10.1186/s12880-022-00793-7
11. Kingma, D.P., Ba, J.: Adam: a method for stochastic optimization. In: Bengio, Y., LeCun, Y. (eds.) 3rd International Conference on Learning Representations, ICLR 2015, San Diego, CA, USA, 7–9 May 2015, Conference Track Proceedings (2015). http://arxiv.org/abs/1412.6980
12. Leake, D., Wilkerson, Z., Crandall, D.: Extracting case indices from convolutional neural networks: a comparative study. In: Keane, M.T., Wiratunga, N. (eds.) ICCBR 2022. LNCS, vol. 13405, pp. 81–95. Springer, Cham (2022). https://doi.org/10.1007/978-3-031-14923-8_6
13. Liu, Z., Xu, Z., Jin, J., Shen, Z., Darrell, T.: Dropout reduces underfitting. CoRR abs/2303.01500 (2023). https://doi.org/10.48550/arXiv.2303.01500
14. Loshchilov, I., Hutter, F.: Decoupled weight decay regularization. In: 7th International Conference on Learning Representations, ICLR 2019, New Orleans, LA, USA, 6–9 May 2019. OpenReview.net (2019)
15. Marie, F., Henriet, J., Lapayre, J.-C.: A new adaptation phase for thresholds in a CBR system associated to a region growing algorithm to segment tumoral kidneys. In: Watson, I., Weber, R. (eds.) ICCBR 2020. LNCS (LNAI), vol. 12311, pp. 97–111. Springer, Cham (2020). https://doi.org/10.1007/978-3-030-58342-2_7

16. Matsoukas, C., Haslum, J.F., Sorkhei, M., Söderberg, M., Smith, K.: What makes transfer learning work for medical images: feature reuse & other factors. CoRR abs/2203.01825 (2022). https://doi.org/10.48550/arXiv.2203.01825

17. McInnes, L., Healy, J., Saul, N., Großberger, L.: UMAP: uniform manifold approximation and projection. J. Open Source Softw. 3(29), 861 (2018)

18. Müller, R., Kornblith, S., Hinton, G.E.: When does label smoothing help? In: Wallach, H.M., Larochelle, H., Beygelzimer, A., d'Alché-Buc, F., Fox, E.B., Garnett, R. (eds.) Advances in Neural Information Processing Systems 32, NeurIPS, pp. 4696–4705 (2019). https://proceedings.neurips.cc/paper/2019/hash/f1748d6b0fd9d439f71450117eba2725-Abstract.html

19. Noll, R., Schaaf, J., Storf, H.: The use of computer-assisted case-based reasoning to support clinical decision-making - a scoping review. In: Keane, M.T., Wiratunga, N. (eds.) ICCBR 2022. LNCS, vol. 13405, pp. 395–409. Springer, Cham (2022). https://doi.org/10.1007/978-3-031-14923-8_26

20. Tan, M., Le, Q.V.: EfficientNetv2: smaller models and faster training. In: Meila, M., Zhang, T. (eds.) Proceedings of the 38th International Conference on Machine Learning, ICML. Proceedings of Machine Learning Research, vol. 139, pp. 10096–10106. PMLR (2021). http://proceedings.mlr.press/v139/tan21a.html

21. Wilkinson, C.P., et al.: Proposed international clinical diabetic retinopathy and diabetic macular edema disease severity scales. Ophthalmology 110(9), 1677–1682 (2003)

22. Yang, Y., Yu, J., Zhang, J., Han, W., Jiang, H., Huang, Q.: Joint embedding of deep visual and semantic features for medical image report generation. IEEE Trans. Multimed. 25, 167–178 (2023). https://doi.org/10.1109/TMM.2021.3122542

23. Ye, X., Leake, D., Crandall, D.: Case adaptation with neural networks: capabilities and limitations. In: Keane, M.T., Wiratunga, N. (eds.) ICCBR 2022. LNCS, vol. 13405, pp. 143–158. Springer, Cham (2022). https://doi.org/10.1007/978-3-031-14923-8_10

24. Ye, X., Leake, D., Huibregtse, W., Dalkilic, M.: Applying class-to-class Siamese networks to explain classifications with supportive and contrastive cases. In: Watson, I., Weber, R. (eds.) ICCBR 2020. LNCS (LNAI), vol. 12311, pp. 245–260. Springer, Cham (2020). https://doi.org/10.1007/978-3-030-58342-2_16

25. Ye, X., Leake, D., Jalali, V., Crandall, D.J.: Learning adaptations for case-based classification: a neural network approach. In: Sánchez-Ruiz, A.A., Floyd, M.W. (eds.) ICCBR 2021. LNCS (LNAI), vol. 12877, pp. 279–293. Springer, Cham (2021). https://doi.org/10.1007/978-3-030-86957-1_19

Author Index

S. Massie and S. Chakraborti (Eds.): ICCBR 2023, LNAI 14141, pp. 425–426, 2023.
https://doi.org/10.1007/978-3-031-40177-0

Printed in the United States
by Baker & Taylor Publisher Services